Office 2011 for Macintosh

the missing manual®

The book that should have been in the box®

Office 2011 for Macintosh: The Missing Manual
by Chris Grover

Printed in the Unites States of America.

Published by O'Reilly Media, Inc., 1005 Gravenstein Highway North, Sebastopol, CA 95472.

O'Reilly Media books may be purchased for educational, business, or sales promotional use. Online editions are also available for most titles: *http://my.safaribooksonline.com*. For more information, contact our corporate/institutional sales department: 800-998-9938 or *corporate@oreilly.com*.

Printing History:

December 2010:   First Edition.

ISBN: 978-1-449-39335-9

[LSI]   [2011-06-10]

Office 2011 for Macintosh

the missing manual®
The book that should have been in the box®

Chris Grover

O'REILLY®

Beijing | Cambridge | Farnham | Köln | Sebastopol | Tokyo

Table of Contents

Part Four: PowerPoint

Part Five: Office As a Whole

Part Six: Appendixes

The Missing Credits

About the Author

 Chris Grover is a veteran of the San Francisco Bay Area advertising and design community, having worked for over 25 years in print, video, and electronic media. He began using Word and Excel on his trusty Mac Plus, and as Rick from Casablanca says, it was the beginning of a beautiful friendship. In addition to using Office on Macs and PCs, Chris has provided training, support and custom programming for Office users at home and work. Chris is the owner of Bolinas Road Creative (*www.BolinasRoad.com*), an agency that helps small businesses promote their products and services. He's also the author of *Premiere Elements 8: The Missing Manual, Google SketchUp: The Missing Manual, Flash CS5: The Missing Manual,* and *Word 2007: The Missing Manual.*

About the Creative Team

Nan Barber (editor) has worked with the Missing Manual series since its inception—long enough to remember booting up her computer from a floppy disk. Email: *nanbarber@oreilly.com*.

Nellie McKesson (production editor) spends her spare time doing DIY home renovation projects and pursuing her love of layout and template design in InDesign Website: *www.dessindesigns.com*.

Stacie Arellano (proofreader) is a freelance proofreader and copy editor from Wisconsin with a background in marketing and web development. When she isn't editing, she's working on a fantasy adventure graphic novel at TributeWaters.com. Email: *stacie@staciearellano.com.*

Julie Hawks (indexer) is an indexer for the Missing Manual series. Her other life includes testing software, tinkering with databases, reading Vedanta texts, and enjoying nature. Email: *juliehawks@gmail.com.*

Tina Spargo (technical reviewer), her husband (and professional musician) Ed, their preschooler Max, their two silly Spaniels, Parker (Clumber), and Piper (Sussex), all share time and space in their suburban Boston home. Tina juggles being an at-home mom with promoting and marketing Ed's musical projects and freelancing as a virtual assistant. Tina has over 20 years' experience supporting top-level executives in a variety of industries. Website: *http://www.tinaspargo.com.*

Acknowledgements

First of all, I'd like to tip my hat to all the authors who wrote previous Office for Mac Missing Manuals. That club includes Jim Elferdink who wrote the previous book and Nan Barber who wrote the first. Nan is also the excellent editor of this book and most of my others. Thanks to Nellie McKesson for putting all the pieces together to create this book. My gratitude also goes out to Stacie Arellano for cleaning up my errors and Julie Hawks for creating an index to help you zero in on the answers to your questions. A big thanks to the technical reviewers who asked all the right questions while I was writing. As always, thanks and love to my wife Joyce, my proofreader, partner and fellow adventurer in life.

—*Chris Grover*

The Missing Manual Series

Missing Manuals are witty, superbly written guides to computer products that don't come with printed manuals (which is just about all of them). Each book features a handcrafted index; cross-references to specific pages (not just chapters); and RepKover, a detached-spine binding that lets the book lie perfectly flat without the assistance of weights or cinder blocks.

Recent and upcoming titles include:

Access 2007: The Missing Manual by Matthew MacDonald

Access 2010: The Missing Manual by Matthew MacDonald

Buying a Home: The Missing Manual by Nancy Conner

CSS: The Missing Manual, Second Edition, by David Sawyer McFarland

Creating a Web Site: The Missing Manual, Second Edition, by Matthew MacDonald

David Pogue's Digital Photography: The Missing Manual by David Pogue

Dreamweaver CS4: The Missing Manual by David Sawyer McFarland

Dreamweaver CS5: The Missing Manual by David Sawyer McFarland

Droid X: The Missing Manual by Preston Gralla

Droid 2: The Missing Manual by Preston Gralla

Excel 2007: The Missing Manual by Matthew MacDonald

Excel 2010: The Missing Manual by Matthew MacDonald

Facebook: The Missing Manual, Second Edition, by E.A. Vander Veer

FileMaker Pro 10: The Missing Manual by Susan Prosser and Geoff Coffey

FileMaker Pro 11: The Missing Manual by Susan Prosser and Stuart Gripman

Flash CS4: The Missing Manual by Chris Grover with E.A. Vander Veer

Flash CS5: The Missing Manual by Chris Grover

Google Apps: The Missing Manual by Nancy Conner

Google SketchUp: The Missing Manual by Chris Grover

The Internet: The Missing Manual by David Pogue and J.D. Biersdorfer

iMovie '08 & iDVD: The Missing Manual by David Pogue

iMovie '09 & iDVD: The Missing Manual by David Pogue and Aaron Miller

iPad: The Missing Manual by J.D. Biersdorfer and David Pogue

iPhone: The Missing Manual, Second Edition, by David Pogue

iPhone App Development: The Missing Manual by Craig Hockenberry

iPhoto '08: The Missing Manual by David Pogue

iPhoto '09: The Missing Manual by David Pogue and J.D. Biersdorfer

iPod: The Missing Manual, Eighth Edition, by J.D. Biersdorfer and David Pogue

JavaScript: The Missing Manual by David Sawyer McFarland

Living Green: The Missing Manual by Nancy Conner

Mac OS X: The Missing Manual, Leopard Edition by David Pogue

Mac OS X Snow Leopard: The Missing Manual by David Pogue

Microsoft Project 2007: The Missing Manual by Bonnie Biafore

Microsoft Project 2010: The Missing Manual by Bonnie Biafore

Netbooks: The Missing Manual by J.D. Biersdorfer

Office 2007: The Missing Manual by Chris Grover, Matthew MacDonald, and E.A. Vander Veer

Office 2008 for Macintosh: The Missing Manual by Jim Elferdink

Office 2010: The Missing Manual by Nancy Connor, Chris Grover, and Matthew MacDonald

Palm Pre: The Missing Manual by Ed Baig

PCs: The Missing Manual by Andy Rathbone

Personal Investing: The Missing Manual by Bonnie Biafore

Photoshop CS4: The Missing Manual by Lesa Snider

Photoshop CS5: The Missing Manual by Lesa Snider

Photoshop Elements 8 for Mac: The Missing Manual by Barbara Brundage

Photoshop Elements 8 for Windows: The Missing Manual by Barbara Brundage

Photoshop Elements 9: The Missing Manual by Barbara Brundage

PowerPoint 2007: The Missing Manual by E.A. Vander Veer

Premiere Elements 8: The Missing Manual by Chris Grover

QuickBase: The Missing Manual by Nancy Conner

QuickBooks 2010: The Missing Manual by Bonnie Biafore

QuickBooks 2011: The Missing Manual by Bonnie Biafore

Quicken 2009: The Missing Manual by Bonnie Biafore

Switching to the Mac: The Missing Manual, Leopard Edition by David Pogue

Switching to the Mac: The Missing Manual, Snow Leopard Edition by David Pogue

Wikipedia: The Missing Manual by John Broughton

Windows XP Home Edition: The Missing Manual, Second Edition, by David Pogue

Windows XP Pro: The Missing Manual, Second Edition, by David Pogue, Craig Zacker, and Linda Zacker

Windows Vista: The Missing Manual by David Pogue

Windows 7: The Missing Manual by David Pogue

Word 2007: The Missing Manual by Chris Grover

Your Body: The Missing Manual by Matthew MacDonald

Your Brain: The Missing Manual by Matthew MacDonald

Your Money: The Missing Manual by J.D. Roth

Introduction

Wherever you go, there you are—and wherever you are you're probably not far from a computer running Microsoft Office. Installed on Macs and Windows PCs, no other program is so omnipresent at work and at home. In most corporations, anyone *not* using Word, Excel, and PowerPoint is considered an oddball. Office's familiar .docx and .xlsx file formats for Office are a common language, so even if you use iWork or some other program, chances are you save your documents in an Office file format.

Office has been on the Mac in one form or another since 1985, but it gained greater acceptance with the release of Office 2001. Then before the year 2001 was even torn off the calendar, Office X exploded onto the scene with some of the first—and best—productivity programs available for the Mac's new operating system, Mac OS X. With each new version, Microsoft has not only given Office greater speed and more new features, but has designed the programs to work better together. This continued evolution led to the subject of this book: Office 2011.

Keeping Up with the Macs

When Mac owners complained about earlier incarnations of Office, it was usually about one of three issues—One: Why doesn't Office for Mac have all the features of the Windows version? Two: Why can't Word, Excel, and PowerPoint look and feel more Mac-like? And last but not least: I'm required to use Outlook at work—why is there no Outlook for the Mac?

Microsoft has stumbled more than once trying to answer these questions, but Office 2011 is a big step in the right direction. The new Office for Mac features are closer than ever to those in the Windows version. No more Entourage for email—the business version of Office includes Outlook. If you share your work with the Windows crowd, you'll find life a lot easier using the collaboration tools built into the programs. At the same time, Office 2011 makes extensive use of your Mac's native tools like Spotlight, the Mac OS X Help system, and Mac's gorgeous color pickers. Now available only for Intel Macs, you'll find Office 2011 loads faster and is more responsive than previous versions.

Microsoft continues to declutter and modernize windows, icons and other features, but don't worry, you won't confuse Office 2011 with Apple offerings like iWork. Office still has those Microsoftian characteristics that Mac fans love to hate. On the love side, you get exquisitely detailed control over just about every aspect of every element in your text files, spreadsheets, and presentations. On the hate side, this control is achieved through labyrinthine menu→submenu paths and multipaneled dialog boxes. Office 2011's commands may be better organized, but there are enough of them to fill the Oxford English Dictionary. That's why you've got this book to help you zero in on the commands and tools you need.

One of the most visible changes in Office programs is the *ribbon*—a supercharged toolbar attached to the top of document windows (Figure I-1). The ribbon thankfully replaces the floating toolbars that seemed to multiply like rabbits with each version of Office. You'll find the most common commands logically arranged on the ribbon; tabs at the top of the ribbon organize these commands into activities. Creating a Chart? All the commands are there on the Chart tab. Best of all, there's consistency between Word, Excel, and PowerPoint. Learn your chart-making skills in one program and you can use them in the others.

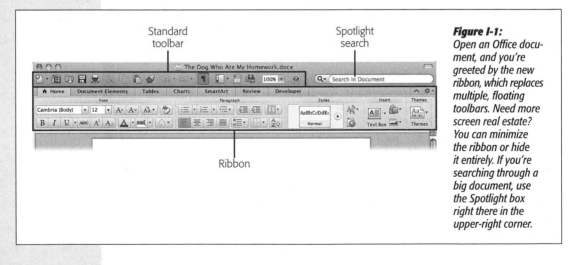

Standard toolbar

Spotlight search

Ribbon

Figure I-1:
Open an Office document, and you're greeted by the new ribbon, which replaces multiple, floating toolbars. Need more screen real estate? You can minimize the ribbon or hide it entirely. If you're searching through a big document, use the Spotlight box right there in the upper-right corner.

More Integrated Than Ever

Although Microsoft originally designed Word, Excel, and PowerPoint as individual, disparate programs, over the years it's designed the programs to look and work more alike—sharing elements and working much more like a cohesive whole. This trend continues with Office 2011, letting you work more effectively within Office *and* with other programs. For example:

- The **ribbon** brings logic and consistency to Office commands. Features like Charts, SmartArt, and Tables work the same way whether you're in Word, Excel, or PowerPoint.

- The **Media Browser** gives you easy access to the photos, movies, clip art and sound files on your computer and it works in the same way for all Office programs.

- The **Office Art graphics engine** makes the most of the Mac's Quartz graphics, providing effects like 3-D, reflections, and shadows to enhance objects and charts.

- **Excel's charting templates** let you easily create modern looking charts that can include 3-D, transparency, and shadows. You can insert charts directly in Word and PowerPoint using the Charts tab on the ribbon.

- **SmartArt graphics** offers a collection of dozens of carefully designed graphic elements that can help you visually represent lists, hierarchies, and processes in Word, PowerPoint, and Excel.

- **My Day** gives you a simplified view of your appointments and to-do items without even opening Outlook—and without the danger of getting sucked into your email.

- Word's **Publishing Layout View** is a true page-layout program, complete with dozens of professionally designed templates that make it incredibly easy to produce complex document like newsletters, brochures, or posters.

- The **Full Screen views** in Word and Excel should please your minimalist instincts. They strip the work space down to the bare essentials.

- **Excel's Formula Builder** helps even non-mathematicians create formulas quickly and accurately, search for functions, and easily learn more about any function.

- **Templates** bring preformatted layouts to Excel to perform common tasks such as checkbook registers, invoices, budgets, expense reports, and so on. These templates open with all the appropriate columns and formulas built in.

- PowerPoint gets the template treatment also with an array of **slide themes** that help you get a visually attractive presentation underway in no time.

Rather than marketing the programs individually, Microsoft pushes the Office suite for the same reason that there's one Missing Manual covering all four programs: If you use only one of the Office programs without the others, you miss out on a lot of timesaving shortcuts.

What's New in Office 2011

Microsoft gave Office 2011 significant improvements over its predecessor, Office 2008. You can't miss the new ribbon and Spotlight search box—but there's also an array of less obvious enhancements. Here's a list of the most interesting new features.

Word

- **Coauthoring features.** You can work with equal ease with colleagues whether they're of the Mac or Windows persuasion. It's now possible to edit the same document at the same time, and there are multiple ways to share over the Internet or your office network.

- **SkyDrive.** Similar to Mac's MobileMe, this service lets you save Word documents on the Internet. Once they're there, you can share and edit them with coworkers.

- **Full Screen view.** This new view makes the most of your screen real estate and lets you focus on your text rather than computer widgets. Use the Read mode when you don't want to make any changes. Use Write mode to edit in Full Screen. When you need to save, print, or format your precious prose, just mouse up to the top of your screen for quick access to a simplified set of tools.

- **3D Publishing Layout view.** Word's Publishing Layout view gives you a separate page-layout program at no extra cost. Now when you want to change the way text, pictures, and other objects overlap on the page, you can use a snazzy 3D view to see their exact position.

Outlook

- **Threads.** This feature arranges messages with the same subject in a single collapsible conversation. It helps you organize your messages and cuts down on Inbox clutter.

- **Multiple Email accounts.** If you have different email accounts for work and home, Outlook lets you manage incoming mail your way. Want to see everything in one unified inbox? No problem. Want to filter email and stash it in separate folders based on the subject or sender? You can do that too.

- **Scheduling Assistant.** When you're responsible for scheduling a meeting, inviting attendees, and keeping track of who's coming and who isn't, this tool puts you in control. Outlook makes it easy to give everyone all of the details and update them when plans change

- **Sharing Calendars and Contacts.** It's much easier to share your information with Windows workers whether your office uses Microsoft Exchange or not.

- **Spotlight search**. Find what you're looking for quickly with Spotlight—which now can search even in message attachments.

- **Enhanced junk filter**. Outlook now does an even better job filtering out junk email—and can even warn you when it detects phishing messages.

Excel

- **Sparklines.** These little graphs, also called datawords, are here to help you spot trends. They can reveal interesting trends that you'd miss on a full sized chart.

- **Conditional formatting.** Makes important data stand out. Your spreadsheet can speak to you in a clear voice when you apply conditional formatting to your data.

- **Data tables.** With this new answer to List Maker, it's easier than ever to keep track of data in Excel. The tools to sort and filter your data are in one spot and better organized.

- **Coauthoring features.** Like Word, Excel has new, improved tools for sharing and working with others. You can work with Mac or Windows folks over the Internet or on a local network.

PowerPoint

- **Broadcast presentations online.** Use Microsoft's web servers to broadcast your presentations. These are live broadcasts, so you need to gather everyone to their computer screens at the same time.

- **3D layering tools.** As in Word's Publishing Layout view, PowerPoint gives you a 3D view of the elements on a slide. You can change the way elements overlap by dragging layers to a different spot.

- **Media Browser.** Use the Media Browser to drop photos and audio visual clips into your presentation. The streamlined media browser works with all the Office programs, but it really shines in PowerPoint.

- **Coauthoring.** Often presentations are more than a solo act. If you work with others, PowerPoint makes it easy to review and comment as you build your presentation.

- **Slide templates**. PowerPoint comes packed with dozens of professionally designed slide templates with coordinated fonts, backgrounds, and effects. Assemble your presentation quickly, with elegant results.

- **Export to iPhoto.** Keep your presentations always available on your iPod—no laptop required! You can give presentations directly from a video iPod thanks to PowerPoint's ability to export presentations to iPhoto. Then transfer the resulting photo album to your iPod, which you can then connect to a video projector, for example.

- **Apple remote control enabled**. If you're giving your presentation on a MacBook, iMac, or other Mac that came with a remote control, you can control your presentation without being anywhere near your computer.

Office as a Whole

- **Office Web Apps.** Along with Office for Mac, you get SkyDrive, where you can store your documents and Web Apps that you can use to edit documents, spreadsheets and presentations from almost any computer with a browser.

- **Ribbon.** This über-toolbar adds order and consistency to Office commands. Great for beginners, the ribbon puts the most-used tools within reach. Even if you're a grizzled Office veteran, you owe it to yourself to give the ribbon a test drive.

- **Visual Basic returns.** Gone in Office 2008, Visual Basic for Application makes a comeback in 2011. You can record macros and write visual basic code for Word, Excel and PowerPoint programs.

- **Elements Gallery.** Quickly find templates, charts, tables, SmartArt graphics, and so on in the Elements Gallery—located below the toolbar in Word, Excel, and PowerPoint. No more choosing from the labyrinthian Insert menu or fumbling with the Toolbox.

- **SmartArt graphics**. Quickly create designer quality diagrams and charts using SmartArt graphics. Use these highly customizable graphic elements to illustrate processes, hierarchies, and so on.

- **Improved Help**. No hokey help icons. Office now provides better help using familiar OS X help tools.

UP TO SPEED

Which Way Did It Go?

If you've used Office on your Mac since the previous century, you've grown accustomed to the Formatting Palette, a petite panel of tools for formatting text, paragraphs, pages, tables, and just about every part of a document. Indeed, in Office 2008, the Formatting Palette was merged with the Toolbox, so you only had that one familiar little rectangle to refer to.

You can quit looking around for the Formatting Palette—it's gone. Tools for adding and formatting objects and documents are now larger and easier to get to on the toolbar and ribbon.

The Office Toolbox still exists, but it's back to its old Office 2004 minimalist structure. For example, in Word it holds Styles, Citations, the Scrapbook, Reference Tools and the compatibility report. If you like to use menus to open the toolbox, the commands are in the same place whether you're using Word, Excel, or PowerPoint. So, if you want to add an image from your scrapbook to your PowerPoint presentation, just go to View→Toolbox→Scrapbook.

The Very Basics

You'll find very little jargon or nerd terminology in this book. You will, however, encounter a few terms and concepts that you'll see frequently in your Macintosh life. They include:

- **Clicking**. This book gives you three kinds of instructions that require you to use the mouse or trackpad attached to your Mac. To *click* means to point the arrow cursor at something onscreen and then—without moving the cursor at all—to press and release the clicker button on the mouse (or trackpad). To *double-click*, of course, means to *click* twice in rapid succession, again without moving the cursor at all. And to *drag* means to move the cursor while keeping the button continuously pressed.

  When you're told to ⌘-click something, you click while pressing the ⌘ key (next to the space bar). Such related procedures as *Shift-clicking, Option-clicking,* and *Control-clicking* work the same way—just click while pressing the corresponding key in the lower corner of your keyboard.

- **Menus**. The menus are the words in the lightly shaded bar at the top of your screen. The menu titles are slightly different in each of the Office programs. You can either click one of these words to open a pull-down menu of commands (and then click again on a command), or click and *hold* the button as you drag down the menu to the desired command (and release the button to activate the command). Either method works fine.

- **Ribbon.** The ribbon (Figure I-1) puts the commands that you use most of the time front and center. Click one of the tabs at the top of the ribbon—Format, Charts, or Reviewing, for example. Home is not only where the heart is, it's the tab you'll keep visible most of the time because it has the most-used commands whether you're in Word, Excel, or PowerPoint. Select an object in your document, and special purple tabs may appear on the ribbon. These purple tabs give you specific tools to work with the object you've selected.

- **Keyboard shortcuts**. Every time you take your hand off the keyboard to move the mouse, you lose time and potentially disrupt your creative flow. That's why many experienced Mac fans use keystroke combinations instead of menu commands wherever possible. ⌘-B, for example, is a universal keyboard shortcut for boldface type throughout Office 2011 (as well as in most other Mac programs). ⌘-P opens the Print dialog box, ⌘-S saves whatever document you're currently working in, and ⌘-M minimizes the current window to the Dock.

  When you see a shortcut like ⌘-W (which closes the current window), it's telling you to hold down the ⌘ key, and, while it's down, type the letter W, and then release both keys.

- **Pop-up buttons**. The tiny arrows beside many of Office 2011's buttons are easy to overlook—but don't. Each one reveals a pop-up menu of useful commands. For instance, the arrow button next to the Undo button on the Standard toolbar lets you choose any number of actions to undo. Meanwhile, the arrow next to the New button in Outlook lets you specify what *kind* of item you want to create—an appointment for the calendar, an address book entry, and so on.

- **Choice is good**. Microsoft wouldn't be Microsoft if it didn't give you several ways to trigger a particular command. Sure enough, nearly everything you could ever wish to do in Office 2011 is accessible by a menu command *or* by clicking a toolbar or ribbon button *or* by pressing a key combination. Some people prefer the speed of keyboard shortcuts; others like the satisfaction of a visual command array available in menus or toolbars.

One thing's for sure, however: You're not expected to memorize all of these features. In fact, Microsoft's own studies indicate that most people don't even *know* about 80 percent of its programs' features, let alone use them all. And that's OK. Great novels, Pulitzer Prize–winning articles, and successful business ventures have all been launched by people who never got past Open and Save.

Tip: This book alternates between showing you menu, toolbar, ribbon, and keystroke commands, so you can try your hand at all of them. In the end, it's up to you to settle on your favorite ways of doing things in Office. Just remember, no matter what you're doing, there may be a faster and better method just a mouse click away. Experiment! Every new keystroke or ribbon widget you add to your repertoire may afford you more free time to teach ancient Greek to three-year-olds or start your own hang gliding club.

About This Book

Office 2011 comes in a shiny, attractive package adorned with application icons. What you won't find inside, however, is a printed manual. To learn this vast set of software programs, you're expected to rely on sample documents and built-in help screens.

Although Office Help is detailed and concise, you need to know what you're looking for before you can find it. You can't mark your place (you lose your trail in the Help program every time you close an Office program), you can't underline or make margin notes, and, even with a laptop, reading in bed or by firelight just isn't the same.

The purpose of this book, then, is to serve as the manual that should have accompanied Office 2011. Although you may still turn to online help for the answer to a quick question, this book provides step-by-step instructions for all major (and most minor) Office features, including those that have always lurked in Office but you've never quite understood. This printed guide provides an overview of the ways this comprehensive software package can make you act like a one-person, all-purpose office.

About the Outline

This book is divided into five parts, each containing several chapters.

- Parts 1 through 4, **Word, Outlook, Excel,** and **PowerPoint,** cover in detail each of the primary Office programs. Each part begins with an introductory chapter that covers the basics. Additional chapters delve into the more advanced and less-frequently used features.

- Part 5, **Office as a Whole,** shows how the programs work together for even more productivity and creativity. For example, it covers the graphics features that work in all Office programs, customizing Office's menus and keystrokes, and writing scripts—little programs that automate your work.

- Four appendixes await you at the end of the book: Appendix A offers guidance on installing, updating, and troubleshooting the software; Appendix B explains the Office online help system; and Appendix C, Menu by Menu, describes the function of each menu command in each of the four major programs, with cross-references to the pages where these features are discussed more completely. Finally, Appendix D gives the complete Missing Manual treatment to the Office Web Apps.

About→These→Arrows

Throughout this book, and throughout the Missing Manual series, you'll find sentences like this one: "Open the System→Libraries→ Fonts folder." That's shorthand for a much longer instruction that directs you to open three nested folders in sequence. That instruction might read: "On your hard drive, you'll find a folder called System. Open that. Inside the System folder window is a folder called Libraries. Open that. Inside *that* folder is yet another one called Fonts. Double-click to open it."

Similarly, this kind of arrow shorthand helps to simplify the business of choosing commands in menus, as shown in Figure I-2.

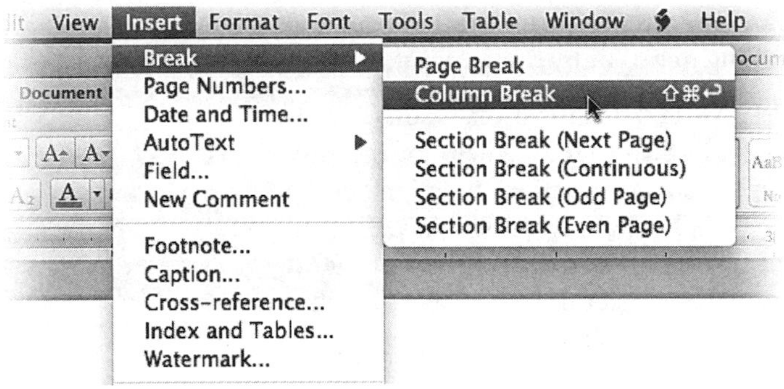

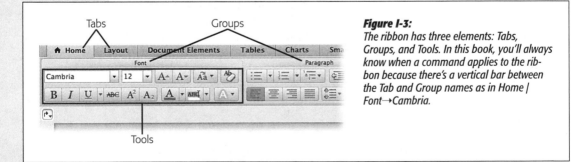

Figure I-2:
When you read "Choose Insert→Break→Column Break" in a Missing Manual, that means: "Click the Insert menu to open it; click Break in that menu; choose Column Break in the resulting submenu."

Note: If you read "Choose Edit→Preferences→Mail tab," click the tab called Mail in the Preferences box that appears.

Office document windows display a ribbon of visual, clickable commands along the top. The ribbon is made of three elements Tabs, Groups, and Tools. In this book, you'll know when it's a ribbon command because the Tab name appears first and is followed by a bar: |. After the bar, there's usually a group name and then the tool commands follow separated by arrows. For example, the instructions for setting a font in Word look like this: Home | Font→Cambria.

Tabs   Groups

Figure I-3:
The ribbon has three elements: Tabs, Groups, and Tools. In this book, you'll always know when a command applies to the ribbon because there's a vertical bar between the Tab and Group names as in Home | Font→Cambria.

Tools

Office Up-to-Date

Writing complex software is never easy—and few companies write more complex software than Microsoft. It's also no wonder that few companies issue more "Service Packs" and updates than Microsoft—with the possible exception of Apple. You'll do yourself a big favor by making sure that you have the most updated versions of both Office 2011 and Mac OS X.

To get the latest Office update, go to *www.microsoft.com/mac* and look under "Downloads" at the top of the page. When you reach the download page, follow the onscreen instructions.

Of course, you can avoid all that hassle if you wish. When you install Office 2011, it automatically installs Microsoft's AutoUpdate for Mac. After that, your Mac will periodically check Microsoft's website and prompt you to download the latest updates to your Office suite. You can determine how often you want to "Check for Updates" (daily, weekly, or monthly) by choosing Help→"Check for Updates" from any of the Office programs. Or turn on the "Manually" radio button in the AutoUpdate window. That way, AutoUpdate will run only when you choose Help→"Check for Updates".

With the help of AutoUpdate, you'll always have every update and fix that Microsoft makes to Office 2011.

About the Online Resources

As the owner of a Missing Manual, you've got more than just a book to read. Online, you'll find example files so you can dig right into some hands-on experience, tips, articles, and maybe even a video or two. You can also communicate with the Missing Manual team and tell us what you love (or hate) about the book. Surf over to *www. missingmanuals.com*, or go directly to one of the following sections.

Missing CD

This book doesn't have a CD pasted on the back cover, but you're not missing out on anything. Go to *www.missingmanuals.com/cds/office2011macmm* to download this book's online examples, exercises, and the PowerPoint feedback form mentioned in Chapter 18 (page 524). And so you don't wear down your fingers typing long web addresses, the Missing CD page also offers a list of clickable links to the websites mentioned in this book.

Registration

If you register this book on O'Reilly.com, you'll receive updates about *Office 2011 for Macintosh: The Missing Manual.* You'll also be eligible for special offers. Registering takes only a few clicks. To get started, type *http://tinyurl.com/yo82k3* into your browser to hop directly to the Registration page.

Feedback

Got questions? Need more information? Fancy yourself a book reviewer? On our Feedback page, you can get expert answers to questions that come to you while reading, share your thoughts on this Missing Manual, and find groups for folks who share your interest in Office for the Mac. To have your say, go to *www.missingmanuals.com/feedback*.

Errata

In an effort to keep the book as up-to-date and accurate as possible, each time we print more copies of this book, we'll make any confirmed corrections you've suggested. We also note such changes on the website, so you can mark important corrections into your own copy of the book, if you like. Go to *http://tinyurl.com/office2011-mm* to report an error and view existing corrections.

Newsletter

Our free monthly email newsletter keeps you up-to-date on what's happening in Missing Manual land, meet the authors and editors, see bonus video and book excerpts, and more. Go to *www.missingmanuals.com/newsletter* to sign up.

Safari® Books Online

Safari Books Online is an on-demand digital library that lets you easily search over 7,500 technology and creative reference books and videos to find the answers you need quickly.

With a subscription, you can read any page and watch any video from our library online. Read books on your cell phone and mobile devices. Access new titles before they are available for print, and get exclusive access to manuscripts in development and post feedback for the authors. Copy and paste code samples, organize your favorites, download chapters, bookmark key sections, create notes, print out pages, and benefit from tons of other time-saving features.

O'Reilly Media has uploaded this book to the Safari Books Online service. To have full digital access to this book and others on similar topics from O'Reilly and other publishers, sign up for free at *http://my.safaribooksonline.com*.

Part One: Word

1

Word Basics: Opening, Editing, Saving, Printing

Word is a powerful tool for creating all types of documents. Lawyers use it to create contracts and screenwriters use it to write scripts. You can add charts, graphs, photos, and videos to your Word docs, but most word documents are simple, created with the techniques described in this chapter.

This chapter gets you up and running fast. If you're using Word for the first time, it covers the basics, like creating new documents and saving them. If you're familiar with Word, you'll find some time-saving tips, tricks, and shortcuts.

Document Basics Covered Quickly

You launch Word like any other program on your Mac, just pick your favorite method. Use the Word icon in the Dock or launch Word from your Applications folder or Finder. If your hands are glued to the keyboard, press ⌘-space to open Spotlight and begin typing *Word*. When you see Word highlighted in the list, hit Return. The very first time you start Word, you see the Word Document Gallery. If you feel that slows you down too much, see the box on page 17.

When it comes to the basics—opening, closing, and printing documents—Word works like Mail or TextEdit and other Mac apps. Shortcut keys are the fastest way to perform operations and chances are these keys are burned in your memory because they're the same for most Mac programs. If you prefer, or don't remember the command, you can always use your trusty mouse (see Figure 1-1):

- ⌘-N (File→New Blank Document) creates a new document.

- ⌘-O (File→Open) opens a window where you find and open existing documents.

- ⌘-P (File→Print) opens the Print dialog box.

- ⌘-S (File→Save) saves the document you're editing.

- ⌘-W (File→Close) closes the document window.

- ⌘-Q (Word→Quit) closes the Word application.

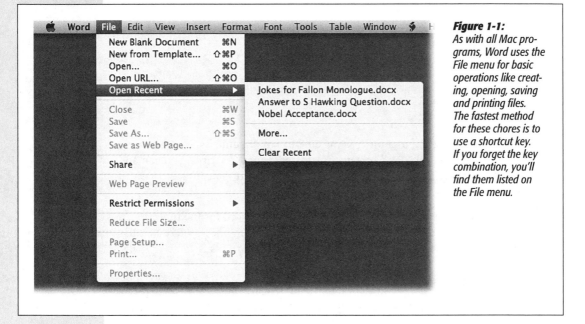

Figure 1-1:
As with all Mac programs, Word uses the File menu for basic operations like creating, opening, saving and printing files. The fastest method for these chores is to use a shortcut key. If you forget the key combination, you'll find them listed on the File menu.

There are some Word-specific nuances with each of these commands, but no real surprises if you've already spent some quality time with your Mac. For example, if you Close or Quit when you haven't saved a document, Word pops up a dialog box asking if you want to save your work. If you Save a document that hasn't been named, it's just like using the Save As command, where you choose a name and folder to hold your document.

Tip: These same basic document commands work with the other Office applications, too.

Bypass the Gallery on Startup

The first time you launch Word, you're greeted by the Word Document Gallery (Figure 1-2), which holds dozens of Microsoft-designed templates for projects like calendars, mailing labels, resumés and business proposals. So, if you want to create a slick-looking document while investing a minimum amount of design time, this is the place to start. After you create or add your own templates, they're in the gallery too. The gallery also collects your recently opened Word documents and groups them by time period, such as Today, Past Week, and Past Month.

After a while, you may find the gallery a distraction when you launch Word and you may prefer to jump into action from the Word file menu. Perhaps you want to polish up that sales report you've been working on or maybe you

want to create a brand new document from scratch. You can easily do all that from the familiar File menu. There are a couple of ways to keep the Word Document Gallery from popping up every time you launch Word. If the gallery is already open, you can turn on the "Don't show this when opening Word" box shown in Figure 1-2. Otherwise, you can go to Word→Preferences→General and turn off "Open Word Document Gallery when application opens". Now, when Word starts up, you see a blank document. To open a recent document, go to File→Open Recent and choose from the list.

You'll learn more about the gallery and templates on page 89.

Show/Hide Template Preview
and Settings Pane

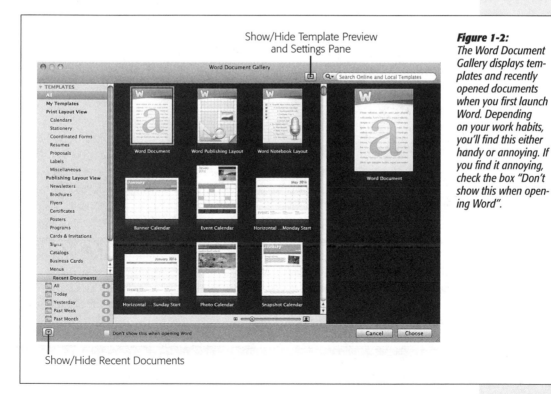

Show/Hide Recent Documents

Figure 1-2:
The Word Document Gallery displays templates and recently opened documents when you first launch Word. Depending on your work habits, you'll find this either handy or annoying. If you find it annoying, check the box "Don't show this when opening Word".

Creating New Documents

Office gives you several ways to issue a command; it's up to you to decide which is your favorite. You almost always have a choice between the File menu, shortcut keys, and buttons on the Standard toolbar, shown in Figure 1-3. If you find yourself wondering what a toolbar button does, just move your cursor over the button. After a second or two, you see a text description.

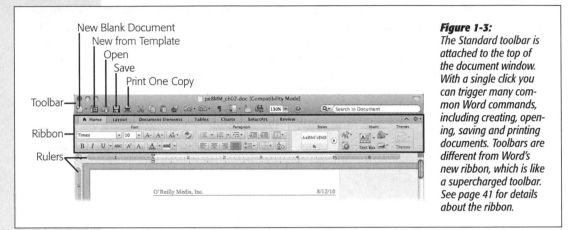

New Blank Document
New from Template
Open
Save
Print One Copy

Toolbar
Ribbon
Rulers

Figure 1-3:
The Standard toolbar is attached to the top of the document window. With a single click you can trigger many common Word commands, including creating, opening, saving and printing documents. Toolbars are different from Word's new ribbon, which is like a supercharged toolbar. See page 41 for details about the ribbon.

So, suppose you want to pound out a grocery list. Your document doesn't need any fancy formatting and it certainly doesn't need page numbers, headers, or footers. All you need is a blank page. So, you do one of the following:

- Press ⌘-N.
- Use the menu File→New Blank Document.
- On the toolbar, click the Create New Word Document.

Tip: If you click the little arrow beside the toolbar's Create New Word Document button, you'll see many of the same commands from the File menu.

In short order, a new document window appears on the screen, and you can start typing out that grocery list. Don't forget the horseradish.

Word may call this a "blank" document, but it's already loaded up with settings for fonts, margins, style sheets, and more. These settings come from a special template called the Normal template.

Tip: Initially, Word names your document something like Document1 or Document2. It's a good idea to save your masterpiece early on with a more suitable name. Press ⌘-S and a window appears where you can do the trick. For all the details, see page 28.

A Quick Tour of the Document Window

Once you've created a new document, a blank page appears on your screen—the primary source of writer's block through the ages. Around the edges of that blank page are all sorts of menus, widgets, and gadgets that in theory make your job of writing easier but at first may seem overwhelming. However, if you divide and conquer, it won't take long to figure out what these tools do. Some widgets you'll use constantly and others you may end up ignoring.

Naturally, you have your menu bar at the top of the screen. The toolbars and the ribbon appear at the top of your document window, as shown in Figure 1-3. Above the page you see a horizontal ruler, which is used to set page margins and tabs. Sometimes, a vertical ruler appears on the left side of the document window, which you use to set top and bottom page margins. It's also helpful for aligning objects and laying out your pages. You'll learn how to wrestle the ruler into submission on page 106 (margins), 128 (indents), and 130 (tabs).

To the right of the page you see a scroll bar, which works just like the one in your web browser. Below, the scroll bar there are "browse" buttons: the double-triangles and round button. They help you jump to specific points in your document; you'll learn how to use them on page 194.

As you see in Figure 1-4, the bottom of the document window holds several more handy tools. On the left, you have several buttons that change your view of the document. In the middle, you see the status bar, which provides up-to-date details about your document, like the number of pages and words. On the right, there's a slider that magnifies your view of the document. Drag right to zoom in and left to zoom out.

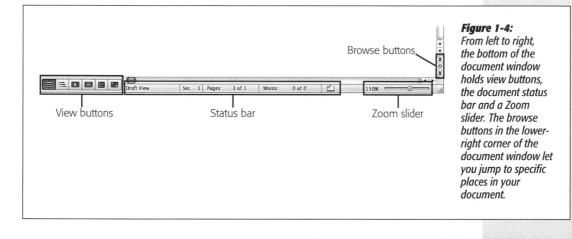

Browse buttons

View buttons   Status bar   Zoom slider

Figure 1-4:
From left to right, the bottom of the document window holds view buttons, the document status bar and a Zoom slider. The browse buttons in the lower-right corner of the document window let you jump to specific places in your document.

Tip: If you've read Mac OS X Leopard The Missing Manual, you may recall that document title bars have a few, not-so-obvious tricks, as shown later in Figure 1-13.

The Minimalist's Document Window

If you're one of those people who work best with the least clutter, you may want to hide the toolbar, ribbon, and some other widgets that bedeck your Word document window. Follow these steps to strip that window down to the basics:

1. **In the upper-right corner of the document window, click the Window mode button to hide the toolbars (Figure 1-5).**

2. **Go to View→Ruler to hide the rulers.**

3. **Click the ribbon collapse/expand button to collapse the ribbon so that only the tabs show.**

4. **Optional: To make the ribbon disappear entirely, click the gear-shaped menu and choose Ribbon Preferences. The Preferences window opens where you can deselect the "Turn on ribbon" option. (If you want to bring the ribbon back later, go to Word→Preferences→Personal Settings→Ribbon.)**

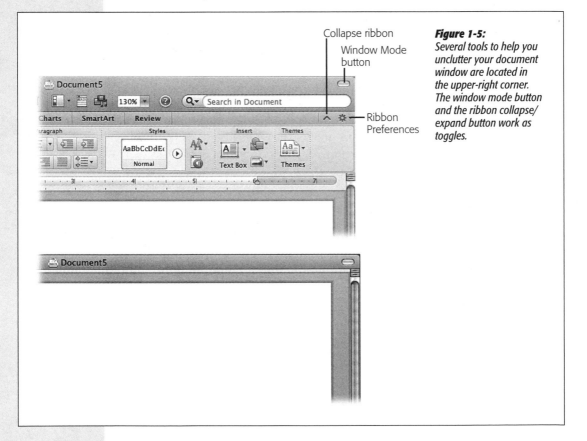

Collapse ribbon

Window Mode button

Ribbon Preferences

Figure 1-5:
Several tools to help you unclutter your document window are located in the upper-right corner. The window mode button and the ribbon collapse/ expand button work as toggles.

Tip: If you're a hard core minimalist, choose View→Full Screen. Word hides just about everything except the page. Mouse up to the top of the screen and a minimalist's toolbar appears. With the button on the left, you can choose Write mode where you can edit, or Read mode where you can't.

Creating Documents from a Template

For more complicated documents, you may not want to start from scratch. Save yourself some time and use one of the many templates that come with Word. Create a business proposal from a template and you don't have to design the page headers and footers. You don't have to worry about where the page numbers appear and how they're formatted. You won't spend valuable time choosing color combinations for headlines, charts and graphs. Instead, you spend your time actually writing the report.

To open the Gallery with all your templates, do one of the following:

- Press Shift-⌘-P.
- Use the menu File→New from Template.
- Click the New From Template toolbar button.

The Word Document Gallery (Figure 1-2) appears. Use the sidebar on the left to select a category like Calendars, Labels, or Resumes. The center pane displays thumbnail versions of the documents so you can choose the design that works best for you. In the right pane, you may have a chance to tweak the template a bit before you use it by choosing color and font sets (see Figure 1-6). In some cases, such as labels, the Gallery leads to a *wizard* that helps you create the document. For example, the wizard for labels helps you zero in on the specific brand and size. Got a box full of Avery 2160 address labels?

Double click the template thumbnail to open it or you can select it and then hit the Open button. Either way, a document based on that template opens in a document window. Keep in mind, the changes you make to this document don't change the original template. It's still stored with the other templates, so you can use it again.

When a template-based document opens, you may find that Word has filled in some text and used placeholder text in other spots. For example, a report template may include your actual company name and address, but the title consists of fake Latin… the ubiquitous Lorem Ipsum. Word gets your name and address from the User Information in Word→Preferences→Personal Settings, but since it doesn't know the subject of your report, it uses filler text. Some templates include pictures, charts, and other graphics. You can customize these to suit your purpose or you can click them and hit the Delete key. Some of the graphics are easily, customizable SmartArt, which is explained on page 609.

Note: Want to turn the memo you're working on into a template? Make sure you've saved your work first. Then go to File→Save As and choose Word template as the format. For the complete details, see page 91.

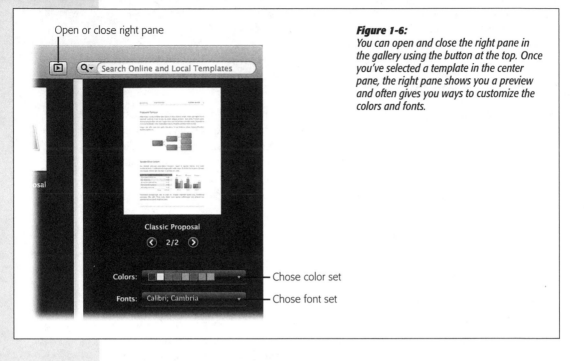

Open or close right pane

Figure 1-6:
You can open and close the right pane in the gallery using the button at the top. Once you've selected a template in the center pane, the right pane shows you a preview and often gives you ways to customize the colors and fonts.

Chose color set

Chose font set

Opening Documents

Opening an existing document is a cinch, provided you know where that document lives. Fortunately, Word and your Mac's Spotlight feature gives you some help. As usual, there are a few ways to initiate the command:

- Press ⌘-O.
- Use the menu File→Open.
- Click the Open toolbar button. It looks like a folder.

The "Open: Microsoft Word" window appears and as you can see in Figure 1-7, it looks a lot like the Open windows used for other standard Mac programs like Preview or TextEdit. There are only a couple Word-specific features at the bottom of the window. To open a Word document, double-click the icon or select it and click the Open button.

Tip: You can bypass the Open window by going to File→Open Recent and choosing your recently opened document from the submenu.

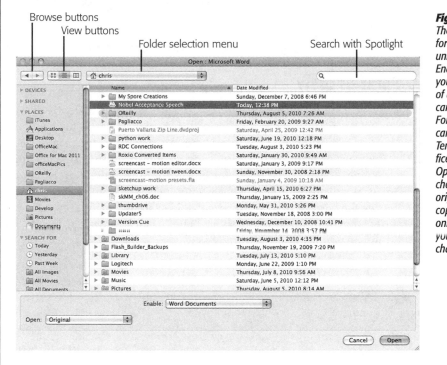

Browse buttons
View buttons
Folder selection menu
Search with Spotlight

Figure 1-7:
The Open window for Word has two unique features. The Enable menu lets you choose the type of documents you can select and open. For example, you can choose Word Templates or All Office Documents. The Open menu lets you choose to open the original document, a copy or a "read-only" version, where you can't make any changes.

If you're an experienced Mac user, you'll feel right at home. If this is new ground, here's a quick tour. On the left, the sidebar lists locations where your file may lurk. The locations are divided into a few major categories: such as Device (your hard drives, iDisk, Time Machine disks), Shared (other computers or storage devices on your network), Places (favorite folders on your computer's hard drive), Search for (items organized by time and type), and Media (music, photos and movies). You click objects in the list to display their contents. You may want to keep your documents in the Documents folder or in named subfolders within Documents. Word remembers where you opened your last document and initially shows you that folder. You can navigate to any other folder you want, using the location list on the left, or at the top, you have the forward and back browse buttons and the folder selection menu. The menu displays all the folders in the path to the current folder and also shows folders you've recently used.

If you can't remember where you saved a document, use the Search box in the window's upper-right corner. If you've done any searching on your Mac, the process will seem familiar because Word uses Spotlight to keep track of all your valuable files. Just start typing, and the Open window immediately begins to list files that match. It not only matches file and folder names, it searches inside your documents, too.

Note: You can tell Word where you'd like to stash your documents through the preference settings. Go to Word→Preferences→Personal Settings→File Locations. Choose Documents and then click Modify, where you can select a specific folder. You can still save your documents in any folder you want, but Word suggests this folder first.

Your Point of View

Ever notice how a scene looks entirely different when you view it from a different angle? Nothing has really changed; it's all a matter of perspective. Word's has several views that work just like that. For example, you can view your document in Draft view, Outline view, or Print Layout view. Each view displays the same document without changing a comma inside, but the appearance on your screen is dramatically different. What's the value in looking at your document with different views? It helps stimulate the creative process. Some views, like Outline, are great when you're in the initial planning stages. Other views are better when you're reviewing the final document and imagining it the way your boss will see it.

There are other views that actually change the way your document is organized and stored. Those include Web Layout view, Publishing Layout view and the Notebook Layout view. You can think of these as separate document creation tools used for very specific chores.

- **Draft view** is a minimalist view for writing. You won't see headers, footers, or page numbers, so you can focus on your priceless prose.

- **Web Layout view** is a tool for viewing and creating web pages, which are formatted in HTML (hypertext markup language). Word isn't the best tool to view or create web pages, but you can use it in a pinch.

- **Outline view** turns your document into an outline organized by the headers and their various levels. Outline view is great for brainstorming before you write or those moments when you want to focus on one tree or branch in the forest of your document. For more on outlines, see page 173.

- **Print Layout view** displays your document as it'll look on the printed page. Some people like to work in Print Layout view most of the time.

- **Publishing Layout view** turns Word into a page layout program. This view actually changes your underlying document, but you're given a warning in advance. For more on using Word for desktop publishing, see page 225.

- **Notebook Layout view** turns Word into a note-taking application and it's another view that changes the underlying document. Notebook keeps track of your random thoughts, snapshots and scribbles and organizes them in sections so you can find them later. It's fun to play with during boring lectures. For more on using Word's notebook features, see page 183.

- **Full Screen** is a macro view with a minimum of clutter. Your page fills the screen with just a few Word widgets at the top. If you want to read without making changes, there's a special mode for that.

Changing from one view to another is easy. You can use the View menu or you can use the View buttons in the lower-right corner of the document window, shown in Figure 1-4. If you're not sure what a view button does, just point to it with the mouse. In a second or two a text description appears.

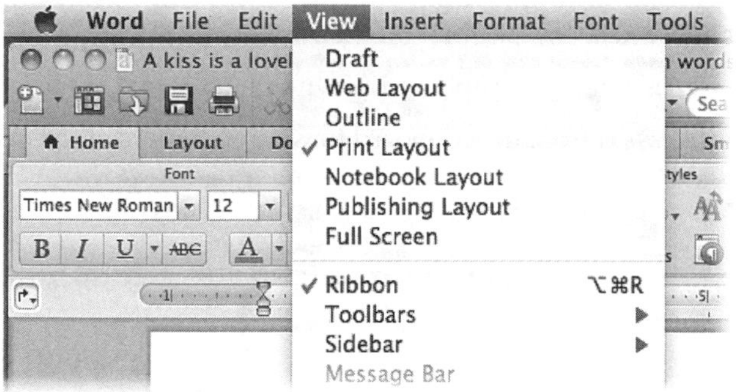

Figure 1-8:
You can reach all the View options from the menu as shown here. The view buttons in the bottom right corner of the document window (not shown) give you a quick way to change to the most popular views.

Basic Editing in Word

Unless you're coming to Word from an ancient typewriter, you probably know how to add words to your document. Press the keys and letters appear at the little blinking insertion point. Press the Delete key to remove the letters you just typed. Those are the kind of basics you know from using Mail or your iPhone. If you're new to word processing, here are some tips that'll save you time and aggravation:

- **Don't hit return at the end of a line**. Word automatically wraps text to the next line.
- **Don't add hyphens to split words between two lines**. Word hyphenates automatically.
- **Don't hit Return twice to separate paragraphs**. Word's paragraph styles set the spacing (page 119).
- **Don't use tabs at the beginning of each paragraph**. Word styles also set first line indents for paragraphs.
- **Don't use Return to force page breaks**. Instead, use Insert→Break→Page Break.
- **Don't put two spaces after punctuation, like periods and colons**. You guessed it, Words adjusts spaces automatically.

As you can see, the recurring theme is to let Word work the way it wants to. You'll find it easier to re-educate yourself than to fight with Word. The reward is that you'll spend less time fiddling with your document's formatting.

Natural (and Un-Natural) Selection

Even among the best writers, a first draft needs editing before it's ready for the public. Most editing is a two-step process. You select text, pictures or graphics and then you issue a command via menu, toolbar, or ribbon. The hammer, saw, and drill for writers are the cut, copy, and paste commands.

- Edit→Cut (⌘-X) removes text and places it on the clipboard.
- Edit→Copy (⌘-C) copies text to the clipboard, leaving the original in place.
- Edit→Paste (⌘-V) pastes text from the clipboard to your document at the insertion point.

Note: For details about advanced cut, copy, and paste techniques like linking and embedding objects or using Word's Scrapbook, see page 626.

Before you perform these operations you have to select some text. That's most often done by clicking a starting point and dragging your mouse across the selection. But that's certainly not the only way to select text. Add a couple of tricks to your selection repertoire and you can cut valuable time off your editing chores. For example, out of the box, Word likes to select entire words—especially when selecting multiple words. That's helpful most of the time, but maddening, if you're trying to remove the "ing" from a gerund. The solution is to hold down the Option key down. Then, Word grabs exactly the text you selected.

Here are some more selection tips:

- **Select a word.** Double-click the word.
- **Select a sentence.** ⌘-click the sentence.
- **Select a line.** Move the cursor into the left margin. The cursor changes to an arrow. Click next to the line you want to select.
- **Select a paragraph.** Move the cursor into the left margin. When the cursor changes to an arrow, double-click. Want to add a second paragraph? Keep your finger on the mouse button and drag to highlight another paragraph.
- **Select a block of text.** Click to place the insertion point at the beginning of the block you want to select. (No need to keep pressing the mouse button.) Press the Shift key and then click at the other end of the selection.
- **Select disconnected bits of text.** Want to grab a word from here and a sentence from there? Press ⌘ while you select the bits and pieces from different spots.
- **Select an entire document.** Move the cursor into the left margin, and triple-click.

Selecting Text with the Keyboard

Speed typists resist moving their hands away from the keyboard to grab the mouse, so Word offers keyboard selection techniques, too. It's good to remember that the Shift key comes into play for most of the keyboard selection techniques. You can usually select forward or backward, but the original insertion point always anchors the beginning or end of the selection.

- **Select individual characters**. While pressing Shift, use any of the arrow keys. You can continue to add or remove text from the selection as long as you're pressing the Shift key.

- **Select a Word**. Use Shift-Option and the Arrow keys. You can continue to select multiple words using this technique.

- **Select to beginning or end of line**. Press ⌘-Shift while using any of the arrow keys.

- **Select a "screenful" of text**. Hold Shift key while using Page Up or Page Down keys.

- **Select to the beginning or end of a document**. Use ⌘-Shift Home or ⌘-Shift End.

You can use the keyboard techniques in combination. For example, you can use Shift-Page Down to select big chunks of text and then, while still holding the Shift key, fine-tune the selection with the Arrow keys.

Tip: Word has a nifty Extend selection mode that keeps on selecting as long as the mode is toggled on. Some beginners find this mode bewildering. These days, the problem with the Extend mode is that it uses the F8 key, which conflicts with Mac's Spaces feature. If the extend mode is important to your work, you can turn off the keyboard shortcut for Spaces. Go to Apple→System Preference→Keyboard-Expose and Spaces. Deselect the checkbox next to Activate Spaces.

Undo, Redo and Repeat

The undo command is everyone's friend. Press ⌘-Z (Edit→Undo) to undo the last bit you typed or to replace the stuff you accidentally deleted. Best of all, Undo remembers everything from edits to formatting and it has a long memory. You can keep pressing ⌘-Z to step back through your last actions or you can use the Undo button and menu, as shown in Figure 1-9.

If you end up undoing more than you should, you can use the companion Redo command: ⌘-Y (Edit→Redo). It works like Undo but in reverse, stepping back through the commands you've undone.

Tip: If you haven't undone anything recently, ⌘-Y morphs into the Repeat command (Edit→Repeat). Use this command to repeat what you last typed or to repeatedly apply the same formatting. Get used to using the Repeat command and you'll save a lot of time and keystrokes.

Figure 1-9:
You can step back through your past few mistakes by pressing ⌘-Z repeatedly, or you can click the little menu next to the Undo button on the toolbar.

Save Me

Here's the most important rule in word processing: "Save early and save often." All you have to do is press ⌘-S. Word saves your document under its current name, overwriting the previous version. The first time you save a document, Word prompts you to give it a name. Otherwise, there are no dialog boxes or questions to answer. So, press ⌘-S when you pause to think, when you reach for your beverage of choice, when you pet the dog, and when the phone rings. Be sure to save before you perform some major, potentially Word-choking operation such as adding a movie clip or generating a table of contents. (For help when you forget this rule, see the box on page 31.)

Wondering about the differences between the Save and Save As commands? Here's some guidance:

- Use **File→Save (⌘-S)** to quickly save a document that's already named. If you haven't named your document, you see the Save box where you can provide a name and choose a folder. It's essentially the same as the Save As command, described next.

- Use **File→Save As** to save your open document under a new name or in a new folder. The original document remains in its last-saved form. The newly named document is open in Word and ready for any changes you want to make.

While saving early and often is the most important thing to know about saving, it's not the only thing. You don't get off that easy. Word saves documents in a gazillion ways. You can save documents as web pages (HTML), Acrobat files (PDF), and in a variety of Word flavors with or without macros. To get a sense of the variety, see Figure 1-10.

Out of the box, Word wants to save your documents in the .docx format. If you're working with other people who use older versions of Word, save your files in one of the .doc formats.

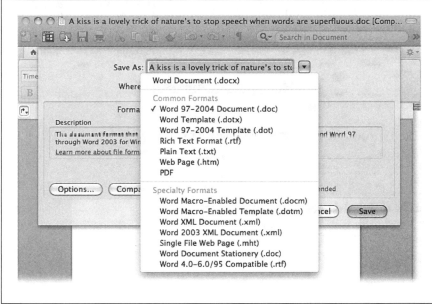

Figure 1-10:
Press File→Save As and when the Save box appears, click the Format menu. You see all the different file formats you can use to save your Word document.

More Saving Graces

Another critical aspect of the initial Save or Save As process is to save your document where you can find it later. The tools to name your file and select a folder are similar to those used in other programs. Word starts you off with a simple box and the last location where you saved a file. If you need to search for a different folder, you can expand the Save box as shown in Figure 1-11.

You can customize Word's Save settings, so you don't have to make the same changes every time you save a document. These changes are made in Word Preferences (Figure 1-12) which you reach through menus (Word→Preferences→Output and Sharing→Save) or by clicking the Option button in the Save box. So, if you want to always save your Word documents as PDF files, you can make that change in Preferences.

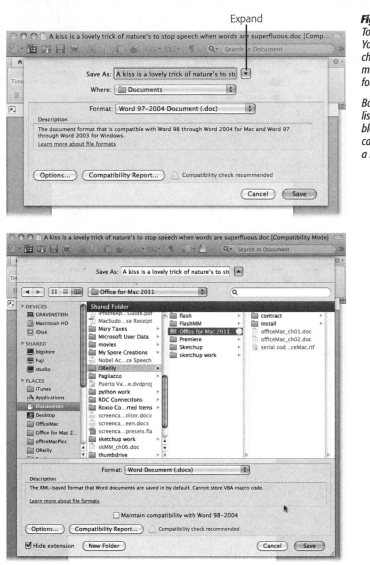

Expand

Figure 1-11:
Top: This is the simple save box. You can use it to name your file and choose a file format. Click the Where menu to choose a recent or favorite folder.

Bottom: If the folder you want isn't listed, click the expand button for full-blown, Finder-style assistance. You can even hit the New Folder to create a new folder.

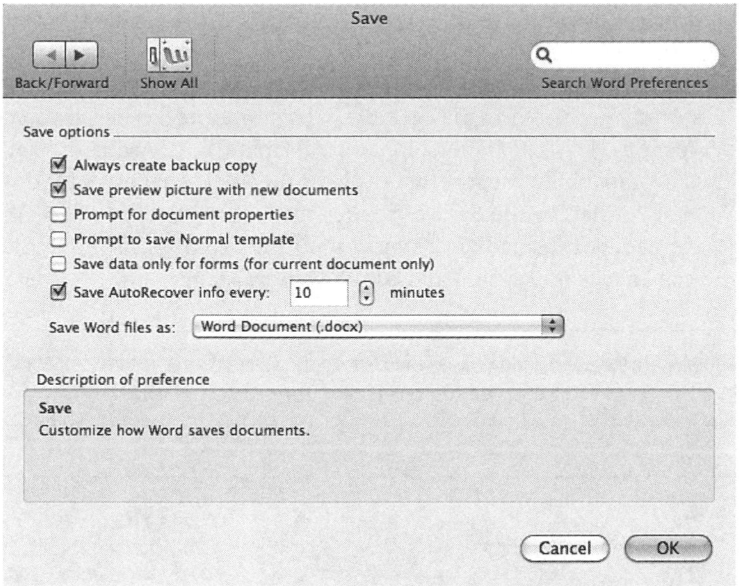

Figure 1-12:
Use the Save preferences to customize the way Word saves your documents. If you can't figure out what one of the options does, point to it and a good description appears in the bottom box.

AutoRecovery and Backup Save You from Yourself

For those lapses when you don't follow "save early and often" rule, Word provides some safety nets.

AutoRecovery. Behind the scenes, Word saves your file in a special folder: Documents→Microsoft User Data→Office 2011 AutoRecovery. So, if Word freezes or your MacBook battery fails or the dog trips over the power cord, you've got a fairly recent, saved file. The next time you fire up Word, it displays the AutoRecovery file and gives you an opportunity to use it in place of the last file you manually saved. If you want to open the file manually, you can go to the folder and open it. It will have a name like "AutoRecovery save of [filename]." However, the file will be there only if Word crashes. If you successfully save and close a document, Word erases the AutoRecovery files because they're not needed.

Initially, Word writes the AutoRecovery file every 10 minutes, but you can make changes by going to Word→

Preference→Output and Sharing→Save. Just type a new number in the "Save AutoRecover info every" box. If you want to save your files in a different folder, you can do that in your preferences, too. Under Personal Settings, click File Locations, and then, in the list, select AutoRecover files. Click the Modify button. At that point, you can browse your way to any folder on your Mac or create a new one.

Backup. There's safety in numbers. You can have Word save an extra copy of your file with the words "Backup of" in front of the filename. That way, you'll always have a second copy if disaster strikes the main one. Go to Word→ Preferences→Output and Sharing→Save and turn on the "Always create backup copy" checkbox. Word creates or updates the backup with every Save or Save As command. The backup lives in the same folder as the original.

Word has been around since the days of the first Macintosh computers. There have been lots of changes in the way Word stores documents in a file, so there are a bunch of Word file formats. So you have do a little extra thinking about how you want to save a document. For example, if you create a file in the latest greatest version of Word and want to share it with someone who uses Office 98 (or Office 97 on Windows), some nifty new features may get lost in translation. Likewise, if you convert your document to HTML, PDF or some other format. To help with translation, Word provides a Compatibility Report that explains precisely what works and what doesn't in the new format. In the Save box, click the Compatibility button. Word automatically runs a report using the last version setting and displays the results. If necessary, you can change the version and run the report again.

Tip: In its expanded form, the Save window has a "Hide extension" checkbox. That means your Mac won't display the .docx or one of the other identifying extension at the end of the filename.

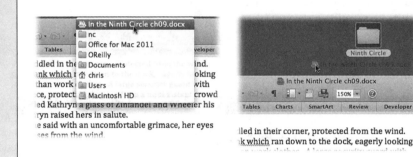

Figure 1-13:
Left: When you ⌘-click the document name, you can choose and open any folder or disk in the list.

Right: After holding for a second, you can drag the tiny document item anywhere on your desktop. If the icon is dimmed, save your document before dragging.

Reducing File Size

In Chapter 2, you'll learn how to add pictures to your documents. Adding pictures can make your Word files big, sometimes too big to email or send over the Internet gracefully. The solution is to change the resolution of the pictures to match the job. You don't need print-quality pics if someone's only viewing the document on a computer screen. Word has an easy command for right-sizing your pictures. Go to File→Reduce File Size to open the box shown in Figure 1-14.

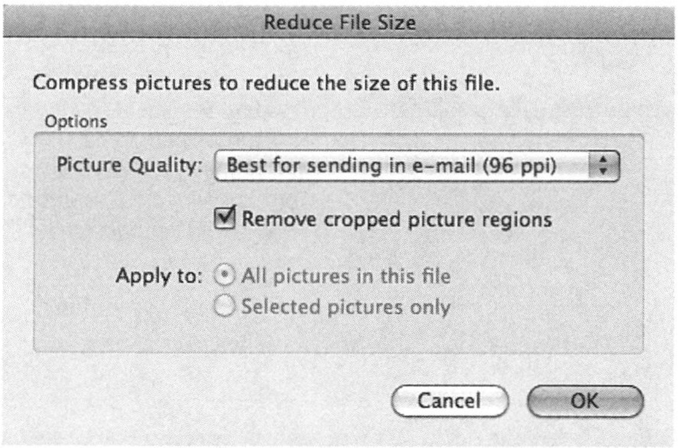

Figure 1-14:
The Reduce File Size box gives you options to resize photos for printing, viewing onscreen, or emailing. If you cropped the pictures in Word as explained on page 78, use the checkbox to shrink your file even more. For more details about working with pictures, see page 77.

Document Password Protection

It's easy to open Word documents—sometimes too easy. Using passwords, you can make it hard for an unauthorized person to open or make changes to your precious words. While your document is open:

1. **Go to Word→Preferences→Personal Setting→Security.**

   A window like Figure 1-15 appears with the Security preferences. At the top you see a section that says "Security options for" and the name of your document.

2. **Change the settings as needed.**

   There are three options to protect your document:

   - Require password to open. Type a password in the "Password to open" box.
   - Require password to edit. Type a password in the "Password to modify" box.
   - Suggest read-only mode. Turn on the "Suggest read-only" box.

3. **Press OK and re-enter your password in the Confirm Password box.**

   Word double-checks passwords to avoid mistakes.

Word's password-protection system works well, but it's not Fort Knox. If a determined hacker has your file, they can probably read the text through nefarious methods combined with other file-snooping programs. Word documents aren't encrypted even when they're password-protected.

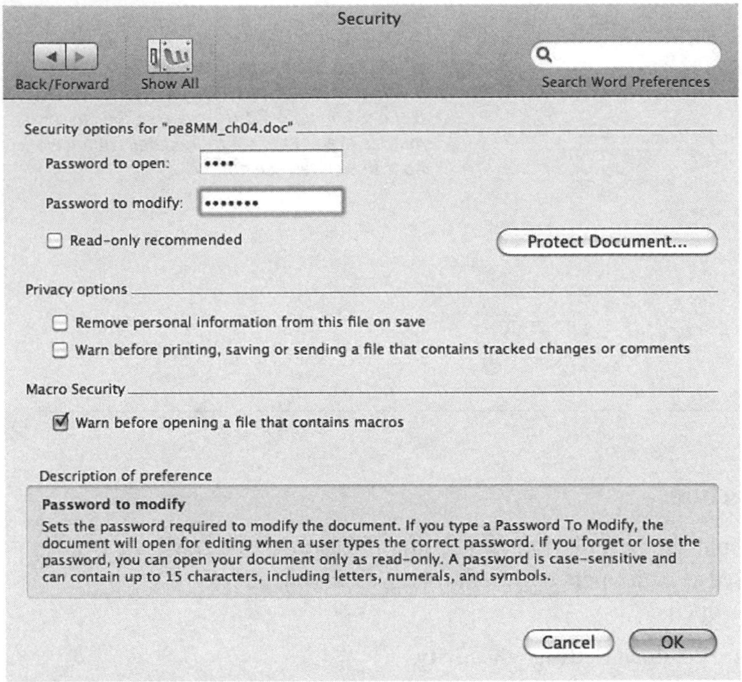

Figure 1-15:
Use the security preferences (Word→Preferences→Personal Setting→Security) to limit the way others can view and change your Word docs. You can require passwords to open or edit your document.

Tip: There's one gotcha with this protection system—you *must* remember your password. Microsoft won't help you if you forget it. So write it down somewhere and come up with a system for remembering where you wrote it.

Save to Web Page

Word isn't the world's best tool in the world for creating web pages. If you're serious about the Web, get a tool like Dreamweaver. If you're new to web design or just dabbling, give iWeb a try. If you're in a pinch, you can turn your Word document into a web page by choosing File→Save as Web Page. Your document is saved in HTML format used for web pages, after which it can be viewed in any browser. Click the Web Options button to fine-tune the web page settings. For example, there's no paper size for a web page, but you can choose the computer screen size for your document.

Share Word Documents via Email

You have a few ways to share your Word docs using email:

- **File→Share→Email (as Attachment).** Use this option when you want the person getting the email to open the Document in their copy of Word. When they get your email, they can save the attached Word file on their computer.

- **File→Share→Email (as HTML).** Embeds your document into the body of the email. The person on the receiving end will see your formatted headers and embedded graphics as long as their email is set up to view HTML. If they've got their email set to view only plain text, they'll see your words but not the fancy formatting and pics.

- **File→Share→Email (as Link).** This option works when you're collaborating with someone over a network. By sending them a link to your file, they can find it on the network.

WORKING WITH WINDOWS

Sharing Words with Windows Folks

If you're the kind of person who associates with Windows PC users, you don't have to do anything special to share Word documents. It's really no different from sharing your work with Mac users. The main issue that's likely to come up is their version of Word. If they've got the latest, greatest version of Word, they'll be able to open and use any document you send. If they've got an older version of Word, you need to follow the tips on page 29 to make sure you save the file in a format they can read.

If you regularly work with the Windows PC crowd (and who doesn't?), look for these Working with Windows boxes throughout this book. You'll find some especially useful tips for Mac and Windows cooperation.

Printing from Word

You probably work in one of those modern paperless offices, so you don't really need to read this section. No? Well, read on to learn how to move your words from screen to page. In the best of worlds, when everything is set up just right, all you have to do to print is press ⌘-P or click the printer icon on the toolbar. After a second or two, your printer starts pumping out pages. What could possibly go wrong? Well, what if you have more than one printer and need to choose? What if you want to print on both sides of the page, but you don't have one of those fancy duplex printers. What if you want to print to a PDF file? That's where Word's special print settings and options come in to play. This section gives you the printing basics. For more details, and special operations such as printing envelopes and labels, see Chapter 4.

Pressing ⌘-P or clicking the printer icon on the toolbar sends your document to what's known as the default printer. No fuss, no questions, and no dialog boxes. The *default* printer is the one your Mac always uses unless you specifically tell it otherwise. If you work in an office with several printers, some may have special features such as color, duplex printing, or blazing speed. When you want to choose a printer other than the default, or if you need to make other technical tweaks before printing, go to File→Print to open the Print window, shown in Figure 1-16.

The Print window has two modes: a simple mode and an expanded mode with more options. In the simple mode, you can:

- **Choose a printer from your computer or network**. Use the Printer menu; you'll see printers connected to your computer and available network printers

- **Choose a printing preset that defines specific print options**. Initially, Word uses the Standard presets but the menu also offers a Last Used Settings option. If your needs are more complex, you can create your own presets. Make your changes to the printing options then choose Save As from the Presets menu. Then, the next time you print you can choose your newly created preset.

- **Print to a PDF.** (Portable Document File, sometimes called an Acrobat file). There are several options on the PDF menu. Most of the time, you'll want to use the first option, Save as PDF. Use Mail PDF if you want to email the document using your Mac's Mail program. Use Fax PDF if you want to send a FAX using your Fax/Modem.

- **Preview your document**. Click Preview to examine your document using your Mac's standard Preview app.

Click the expand button, next to the Printer menu, and the window grows, showing additional options where you can:

- **Print multiple copies**. Type a number in the Copies box.

- **Collate pages when printing multiple copies**. Check the Collated box next to Copies.

- **Print specific pages and ranges of pages**. You can choose All, Current page or specify a ranges of pages in the From and to boxes. If your needs are highly complex you can enter combinations in the Page Range box like *2,5, 7-12, 15*.

- **See a thumbnail size preview of your pages**. Select the Show Quick Preview box to see a mini version of your page. You can use the navigation buttons below the preview to jump to specific pages.

- **Change the Page Setup**. Want to tweak things like margins before you commit to paper? Click the Page Setup button. For more details on page setup see page 87.

- **Jump to Apple's web page where you can order printer supplies**. There's nothing like a little sheer commercialism right there in your software. Order from Apple if you find it handy, but remember you can probably find the same supplies for less elsewhere.

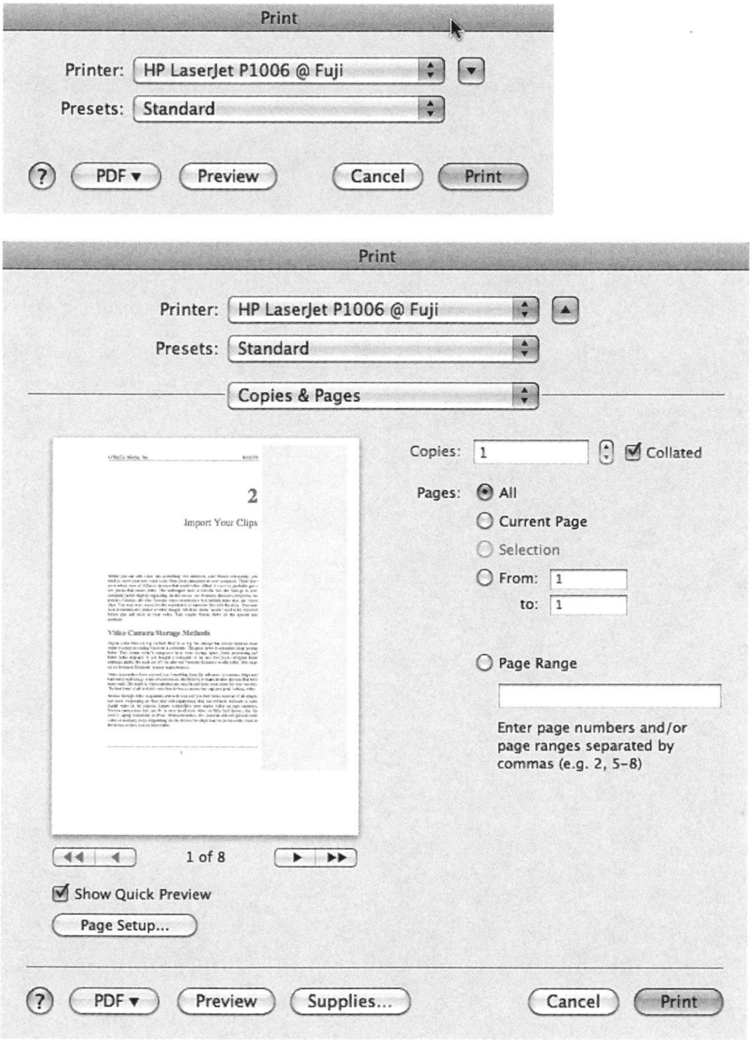

Figure 1-16:
The Print dialog box shown at the top comes in handy when you want to make changes before you print. For example, you can choose a different printer or you can choose to print only a few pages in the document. Click the expand button to see more print options, as shown at the bottom.

Tip: If you want to inspect your pages before you print, you can switch to the Print Layout view (View→Print Layout). For an even more exact representation of your finished pages go to File→Print and then in the Print dialog box, click the Preview button. This option lets you view your soon-to-be-printed page in Mac's Preview app.

These are the settings that you use most of the time. If you have more complex printing needs, Chapter 4 covers all the details.

CHAPTER 2.

Advanced Editing in Word

When your document grows longer than a grocery list, you'll begin to need Word's advanced editing tools. In this chapter, you'll learn where to find your tools and how to use 'em. Word helps you save time with tools for searching through your prose, checking your spelling and grammar, and correcting your errors on the fly. But Word goes way beyond words: You can add tables, pictures, even video. Finally, you'll even learn how to make Word do your work for you.

Toolbars and the Ribbon

Chapter 1 introduced the Standard toolbar with the buttons like Open, Save and Print. Instead of burrowing deep into menus, toolbars let you issue commands by simply clicking buttons that graphically represent the operation. These picture-button toolbars are popular because they're easy to understand, save time, and conserve screen space. Developers who customize Word love toolbars, too, because they make it easy to add new commands while hiding others that are seldom used. Responding to toolbar popularity, Microsoft added and refined toolbar features with each version of Word.

There's a major drawback to the proliferation of toolbars and custom toolbars. It's easy to get confused if a toolbar is hidden, or if it's floating instead of docked. Making the problem worse, specific buttons may be added, removed, or moved to a different spot. Microsoft has tackled these issues with this version of Office and the introduction of the *ribbon*.

If you're used to an earlier version of Office, here are some of the changes:

- The Standard and Formatting toolbars start off locked in place at the top of the document window. The less-frequently used Data toolbar starts off as a floating palette.

- The ribbon replaces the dozens of task-specific toolbars that appeared in recent versions of Word.

- The position of the ribbon and the position of the buttons in each tab are fixed in place, making it easier to find them no matter what kind of document you're working on.

For those of you who like to customize Word as if it were a hot rod, you can still:

- Add, move, and remove commands on Word menus.

- Create custom toolbars. Custom toolbars are always floaters.

- Add, move and remove buttons on any toolbar.

- Create custom commands using Visual Basic and attach them to toolbars or menus.

- Show, hide and move tabs on the ribbon.

There's more about customizing Word and the other Office programs on page 631. In this section, you'll learn how to show and hide toolbars and how to use the ribbon—the new, souped-up variation of the toolbar.

Word 2011 comes with three predesigned toolbars: Standard, Formatting, and Database. When you first use Word, the Standard toolbar is displayed and the other two are hidden. To show or hide a toolbar, go to View→Toolbars and choose from the submenu.

The Standard Toolbar

The Standard toolbar is fixed in place at the top of your document window. It crams the commands you're most likely to use into a very small piece of real estate. Chapter 1 covered the basic file and editing commands. Figure 2-1 shows you what all the buttons do. Here's a description of the remaining toolbar buttons, identified by the often verbose tooltip that appears when you point at them:

- **Show/hide ¶**. Visually identifying paragraph marks and spaces can help you troubleshoot paragraphs that don't look quite right. Paragraph marks are one of the invisible characters that you may not notice as you write. In Word, they look like ¶ and they sit at the end of every paragraph. They play an important formatting role in Word because they hold a information about things like spacing, tabs, and indents. You won't see paragraph marks unless you click this button. When you reveal invisible characters, you see spaces (represented by small dots), line breaks, and other document features.

- **Sidebar (show/hide).** The Sidebar opens on the left side of the document window, and it's actually four tools in one: the Document Map Pane, the Thumbnail Pane, the Reviewing Pane, and the Search Pane. These tools are particularly helpful when you work with long documents, a topic covered in Chapter 6.

- **Toolbox (show/hide).** Like the Sidebar, the Toolbox, which appears in a floating palette, holds several different tools. They include: Styles (page 119), Citations (page 221), Scrapbook (page 625), Reference Tools (page 270), and the Compatibility Report (page 32).

- **Media Browser (show/hide).** You use the media browser to add photos, graphics, and audiovisual media to your documents. The process is covered later in this chapter on page 76.

- **Zoom.** You can reduce or enlarge the display of the document by typing a percentage here or choosing from the drop-down menu. Make your page look bigger or smaller on the screen, without really changing the size on the printed page.

- **Help**. Opens the Word help files that the Office installer places on your hard drive. If you need more help, you'll see links to more extensive and more up-to-date help that's available on the Internet.

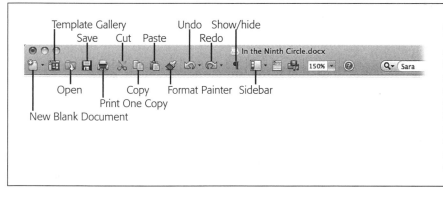

Figure 2-1:
These buttons appear on Word's Standard toolbar (provided you haven't customized it, as explained on page 633). From left to right, commands are grouped into file commands, editing commands, view commands, and help.

Introducing the Ribbon

If you've used previous versions of Word, you may be wondering where some of the specialty toolbars went. Well, they've been replaced by the ribbon (Figure 2-2). If you've used toolbars a lot, you won't have any trouble transferring that button-clicking expertise to the ribbon. About three times the thickness of your average toolbar, the ribbon is organized by tabs. Each tab holds commands related to typical Word tasks:

- **Home** is not only where your heart is, it's the tab you're most likely keep displayed while you work. On the home tab you can make all the usual changes to fonts, paragraphs and styles. Buttons on the Home tab make it easy to insert graphics and choose Themes.

- **Layout** gives you tools to set up your page. You can choose portrait or landscape orientation and set your margins. If you want multiple columns, borders, watermarks or grids, this is where you get them.

- **Document Elements** gathers the commands for things like headers, footers and page numbers. Want to add a table of contents, bibliography, or citations? Those are document elements, too.

- **Tables** are great when you want to arrange blocks of text and graphics on a page. Word puts the tools for designing tables on this one tab.

- **Charts** give you column, line, pie, bar, and some other styles of charts. It's almost enough to make Excel jealous. Speaking of which, if you want to embed and work with Excel data, this tab can help.

- **SmartArt** collects Microsoft's newly developed, easy-to-customize graphics in one spot. Graphics are often a real time-sink, but SmartArt, as you'll see on page 609, can cut design time down to size.

- **Review** is the tab to use when you're tracking changes in a document and working collaboratively with others.

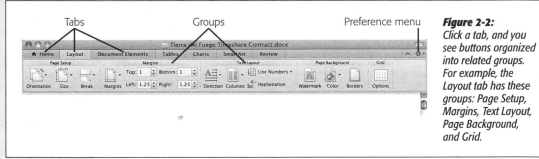

Figure 2-2:
Click a tab, and you see buttons organized into related groups. For example, the Layout tab has these groups: Page Setup, Margins, Text Layout, Page Background, and Grid.

The buttons and widgets on the ribbon aren't uniformly sized. Each is designed to be large enough to do its job. For example, you may see two rows of little buttons to help you select a font, size, and color, but a scrolling panel to help you visualize and pick a style. Icons make it pretty easy to figure out what the tools do, but if you're in doubt just move the mouse arrow over the tool. After a second or two, a tooltip appears with an explanation. Triangular arrows indicate there's a menu, window, or scrolling pane that shows more options—hence the name *option button*. Click deep enough in the ribbon, and you may find yourself back at some of those same old-fashioned dialog boxes that Word is famous for.

Space-saving Ribbon Tricks

The ribbon takes up a bit of screen space. When you launch Word after installation, it starts out showing you the ribbon. If you need to recover some of that real estate or if you want minimize clutter, here are ways to do it:

- **Temporarily hide ribbon buttons**. Click the tab to show and hide buttons on the ribbon. Working this way, you can click a tab, and then click a button. Click the tab when you're done, and the buttons hide.

- **Start documents with the buttons hidden**. Click the gear-shaped menu in the upper-right corner of the ribbon and choose Ribbon preferences (Figure 2-3). Then, in the preferences, turn off the "Expand ribbon when document opens" checkbox.

- **Hide the group names**. After you get used to the ribbon, you may not need the group names to guide you to the right button. Click the gear-shaped menu to open Ribbon preferences, and then select "Hide group titles".

Note: You may want to keep the group names displayed while you're working with this book because the group names are included in the commands.

- **Hide the ribbon entirely**. In ribbon preferences, deselect "Turn on ribbon". This option makes the ribbon unavailable, so you'll have to come back to preferences to turn it on.

You'll learn more ways to customize the ribbon and other aspects of Word in Chapter 22.

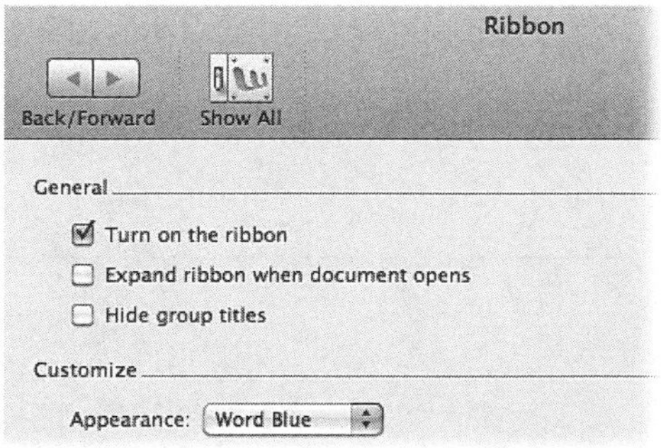

Figure 2-3:
You can open Ribbon preferences from the ribbon or by using the command Word→Preferences→Personal Settings→Ribbon. Use the checkboxes at the top to fine-tune the appearance and behavior of ribbon.

Tip: For the most part, ribbon buttons and menus stay put; however, if you reduce the width of your document menu, the ribbon adjusts to the space available. For example, the scrolling view of paragraph styles may display fewer choices or turn into a drop-down menu. If you can't find a widget you knew was there yesterday, try stretching the document window a bit.

Lists: Bulleted and Numbered

In the classic play *A Thousand Clowns*, Murray Burns is disappointed when he fears his nephew and protégé has turned into a "list maker." However, in real life, there are times when a list is the right tool for the job. Word gives you bulleted and numbered lists with enough options in each group to please the most dedicated list maker. Best of all, Word easily handles chores such as indenting paragraphs, adding bullets and updating the numbers for you. As you see in Figure 2-4, the ribbon clearly shows the different styles, so about all you have to do to make your list is click a button. You don't have to waste time numbering and formatting.

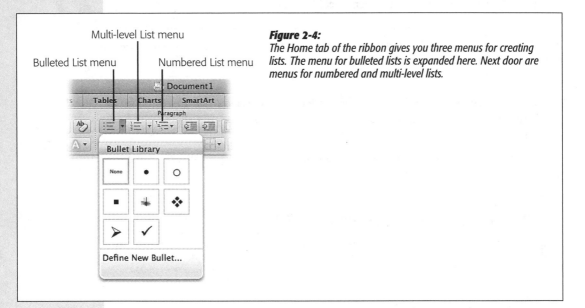

Figure 2-4:
The Home tab of the ribbon gives you three menus for creating lists. The menu for bulleted lists is expanded here. Next door are menus for numbered and multi-level lists.

Making Lists with Bullets

Bulleted lists are great for setting a group of items off from the rest of your text. The term *bullet* refers to the symbol that precedes the text. The name probably comes from the circular, bullet-hole shape that's often used. Perhaps you want to create a list of future writing projects—here are the steps for making your bulleted list:

1. Type *Projects to tackle with Word for Mac:*, press **Return**.

   You have a new line on which to begin your list.

2. **Using the ribbon, go to Home | Paragraph→Bulleted List and click the down arrow.**

   When you click the down arrow you see a menu with several styles of bullets. If you click the button, instead of the menu arrow, Word automatically selects the bullet style you last used.

3. **Click one of the bullet shapes.**

   The menu closes and Word automatically formats the text with an indentation and a bullet.

4. **Enter some text for the bulleted line, like:** *Letter to my congresswoman.*

   Word automatically applies space between the bullet and your text.

5. **Press Return.**

   Word gives you a second bulleted line.

6. **Add a long line of text like:** *Doctoral Thesis – Migratory patterns of Tierra del Fuego Amphibians.*

   If your line is long enough, you see that Word wraps the text to the next line and keeps the left side aligned with the list text. See Figure 2-5.

You can keep adding to your list, and Word continues to supply the bullets. When you're ready to go back to regular text, hit Return to add a new line and then click the Bulleted List button to toggle the formatting off.

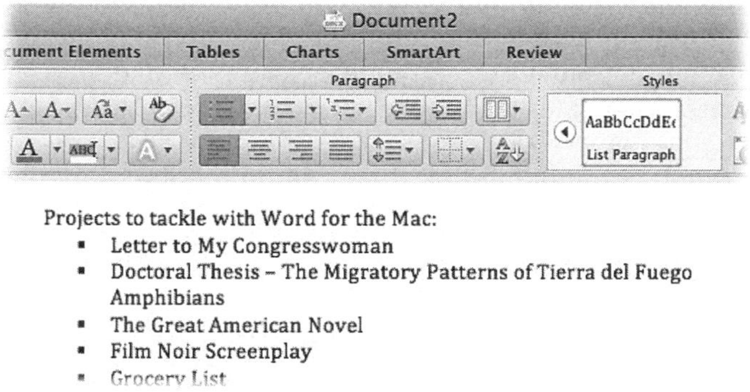

Figure 2-5:
When the insertion point is in a bulleted list, the Bulleted List button in the ribbon is highlighted. If you click the button, you can toggle the list formatting on and off.

It's even easier to turn text that you've already typed into a bulleted list. Just select the text and then click the bulleted list button. You can use this same method to change the style of the bullets.

Making Numbered and Multi-level Lists

You may stumble upon Word's numbered lists accidentally, if you start to create a numbered list manually. If you type *1.* at the beginning of a line, when you hit Return at the end of the line, Word automatically indents and gives you a new, already-numbered line to continue your list. Pretty handy if you are, in fact, making a list. If you aren't, press ⌘-Z, and you're back to a regular paragraph.

You can choose different number styles and create multi-level lists, using the ribbon menus shown in Figure 2-4. Instead of a choice of bullet styles, you can choose number styles including: Arabic, roman numeral, and alphabetic "numbering" in lower and upper case.

Restart numbering at 1

Word keeps track of the numbering automatically, which is great. That means if you insert a new item in the middle of your list, you don't have renumber every other item. Sooner or later though, Word will pop in a number that you don't want. Perhaps you're creating and new list and you want the numbers to start back at 1. Not a problem. Just right-click (Control-click) and choose Restart Numbering from the shortcut menu. If the reverse situation occurs, and Word starts a new list when you wanted to continue the old, simply choose Continue Numbering from the shortcut menu.

Managing Multi-level lists

Multi-level lists work like outlines. They use different number styles for different, indented levels in the list. Word even offers styles that use legalese numbering like "Article 1" or "Section 1.01." Once you've selected your multi-level list style, you can stop worrying about the numbering because Word handles it for you. All you have to do is use the Increase Indent and Decrease Indent buttons (Figure 2-6) to organize your list items.

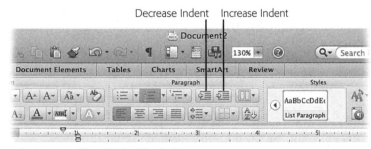

Figure 2-6:
Use the Increase Indent and Decrease Indent buttons to set the hierarchy for items in your list. Word automatically applies the numbering.

Customizing Word's Automatic Lists

Even though Word offers lots of choices when it comes to lists, that may not be enough to please you. Maybe you want to use your company logo as a bullet. Or perhaps your office uses its own unique numbering scheme. The last item on each of the list menus has an option like "Define New Bullet" or "Define New Number Format". Click that and you see a dialog box like the one in Figure 2-7.

The box for bullets lets you define new bullets from fonts and symbols on your computer. The Pictures button leads to additional bullets provided by Microsoft or you can use your own graphics or photos. Use the Bullet position and Text position settings to adjust the spacing between margins, bullets and text.

The numbered and multi-level lists have similar boxes that let you customize their number systems and appearance.

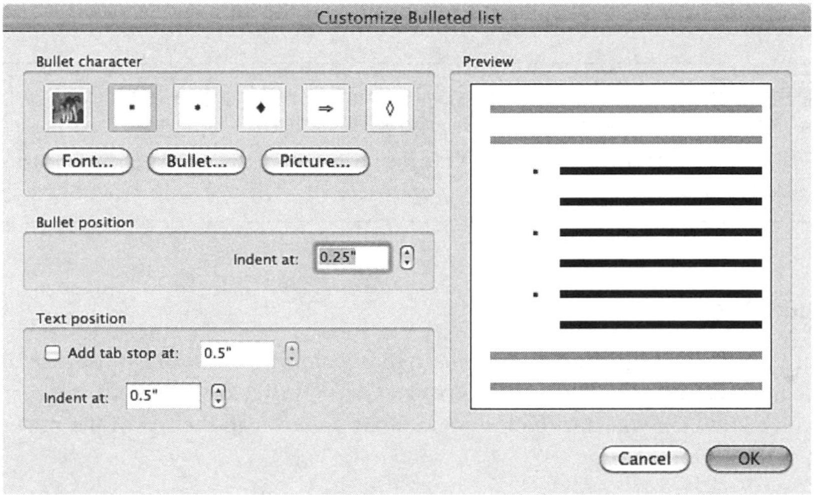

Figure 2-7:
Word has more variety in bullets than you find displayed in the menu. Use the Customize Bulleted List box to define new bullets and adjust the spacing of your list. To use your own artwork or a photo as a bullet, click the Picture button.

Line, Page, and Column Breaks

Word automatically flows text from line to line and page to page. Nice, huh? However, an important part of document design is placing text right where you want it, breaking it up, and generally controlling the flow. A *break* is an invisible barrier that stops your text in its tracks, and then starts it again on a new line, column, or page.

Paragraph Break

In Word, pressing Return (or Enter) creates a paragraph break. Although you may not have been aware of the term, Word creates them every time you end a paragraph. Unless you've chosen a different *following paragraph* style (see page 123), the new paragraph assumes the same formatting as the previous.

Line Break

Pressing Shift-Return inserts a *line break*. It's similar to a paragraph break except that the text on the new line remains part of the original paragraph, and retains its style and paragraph formatting. No matter how you edit the surrounding text, the line break remains where you inserted it—until you remove it, of course.

Page Break

Choose Insert→Break→Page Break (or press Shift-*Enter*—using the keypad) to force a *hard* page break. No matter how much text you add above the break, the text *after* the break will always appear at the top of a new page.

Use a page break when your want to start a new topic at the top of the next page. If you're writing a manual for your babysitters, for example, inserting a hard page break at the end of the *How to operate the home theater system* section causes *The care and feeding of Alice the cat* to begin at the top of the following page.

Tip: In Page Layout view, page breaks are generally invisible. The text just ends in the middle of a page and won't go any further, which can be disconcerting if you've forgotten about the page break you added.

To view the dotted lines that represent a page break, choose View→Draft, or click the Show ¶ button on the Standard toolbar.

Column Break

To jump text to the top of a new *column* (in multicolumn layouts like those described in the next section), choose Insert→Break→Column Break. Word ends the current column and, when you start typing again, hops you over to the top of the next column at the top of the page.

If you choose this option when you're not using multiple columns, it behaves like a hard page break. (On the other hand, if you later switch to a two- or three-column format, the column break behaves like a normal column break. If you plan to make two different versions of your document—one with columns and one without—you may therefore want to use column breaks instead of page breaks.) *Keyboard shortcut:* Shift-⌘-Return.

Section Break

A *section* is like a chapter—a part of a document that can have formatting independent of the other parts. For example, each section can possess unique margins, page numbering, pagination, headers and footers, even printing paper size.

To begin a new section, insert a section break by choosing Insert→Break and choosing the specific type of section break that you want. See page 196 for all the details on sections.

Find and Replace

Whenever possible, make your computer handle time-consuming drudgework. Finding and replacing text is the perfect example. Your Mac is faster than you at finding the text "Tierra del Fuego timeshare" in your 57-page contract. If you need to repeatedly replace that with "Barrow, Alaska timeshare," Word can do that in a snap. There are three different tools you can use to find and replace text, from the simplest to the most powerful:

- Use the **Search Box** in the upper-right corner of the Standard toolbar for simple searches.

- Use the **Find and Replace Sidebar** when you want to replace text or have special searching needs. Perhaps you want to search for entire words or just the ending of words.

- Use the **Find and Replace Window** when you need a high-octane search machine. Suppose you want to find every instance of "Tierra del Fuego Condominiums" and format it to appear in 16-point, bold type.

Using the Search Box

The Search box appears in the upper-right corner of the Standard toolbar. If the Standard toolbar is hidden, you can turn it on by choosing View→Toolbars→Standard. The quick way to start a search as you're typing is to press ⌘-F and then type your search text. (If you're a menu person, you can go to Edit→Find→Find.) Use either one of these commands when the Standard toolbar is hidden and you're taken to the Find and Replace sidebar, covered next.

Your text appears in the search box in the upper-right corner of the document window and it will feel familiar if you've used Spotlight on your Mac. Word highlights matching text in your document and you can use the browse buttons (shown in Figure 2-8) to jump to each instance of matching text.

Here are some tips to make the Search box work harder:

- **To find and select the next instance** that matches your search text, press ⌘-G.

- **To find and select the previous instance**, press Shift-⌘-G.

- **Use the special wildcard character ^? that matches any character**. So, if you type ^?ill, word highlights "will", "kill," "bill," "dill," and so forth.

- **To clear the search text and remove highlights,** click the Clear button in the Search box.

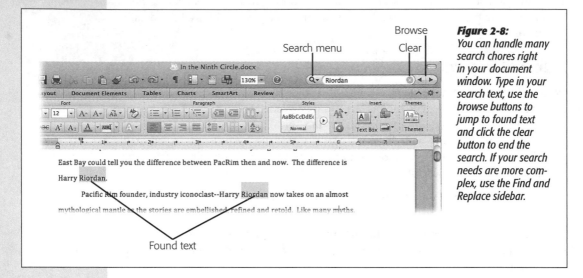

Found text

Figure 2-8:
You can handle many search chores right in your document window. Type in your search text, use the browse buttons to jump to found text and click the clear button to end the search. If your search needs are more complex, use the Find and Replace sidebar.

The Find and Replace Sidebar

For more options and for search and replace operations, use the Find and Replace sidebar. Press Shift-⌘-H, or if you find that difficult to remember, you can choose Replace from the Search options menu shown in Figure 2-8. When the sidebar opens, you see boxes for the text you want to find, and the replacement text, as shown in Figure 2-9. Click Find, and Word adds a yellow highlight to all the matching instances in your text. Look carefully, and you'll notice that one instance is a little darker and includes a blue highlight at the bottom. Word begins searching from the insertion point and the text with the blue highlight is the currently selected instance. Hit Find again, and Word moves to the next instance. When it reaches the end of your document, it circles back to the beginning and continues the search. The sidebar also displays found instances of the search text in context. Click an instance to jump to that point in your document.

If you're replacing text, hit the Replace button. Word replaces the text and moves to the next match.

Warning: Be cautious using the Replace All button. The good news is it's fast. It quickly replaces every instance of the search text. The not so good news is that it sometimes surprises you. Suppose you're replacing "Sara" with "Sarah." If Word comes across Saratoga, you may be changing the city name to Sarahtoga.

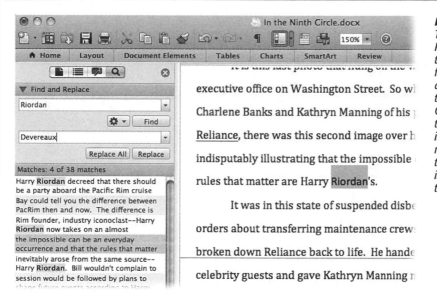

Figure 2-9:
To use the Find and Replace sidebar, type the text you want to find in the top box and the replacement text in the bottom. Click Replace All to change every instance in your document, or click Replace to change the current instance and move on to the next one.

Sometimes you want to search and replace things like paragraph marks or a page break. Since it's hard to type those into the little text boxes, Word gives you a menu for entering such things (Figure 2-10). This menu also leads to other find and replace tricks, such as wildcards that match any character or digit or search for you text at the beginning or end of a word.

On the sidebar, next to the Find button there's one of those gear-shaped menu buttons. Use it to fine-tune your search criteria with these options:

- **Whole Words** finds your search text only if it's a complete word. For example, a search for "man" with this option turned on will skip "manners" and "management."

- **Ignore Case** makes the capitalization of your search term irrelevant. "Tierra del Fuego", "Tierra Del Fuego" and "tierra del fuego" are all hits.

- **Sounds Like** finds words that sound like your entry. (Consider this help for the spelling-impaired.) If, say, you type *inglund*, then Word finds "England."

- **All Word Forms** is extremely well versed in grammar. Type *is*, and Word finds "was," "were," and "being."

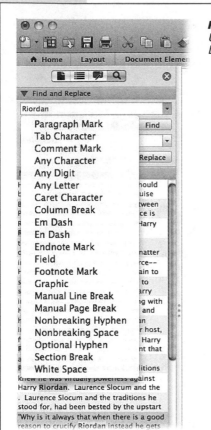

Figure 2-10:
Use the menu to enter special characters into the Find and Replace text boxes.

The Advanced Find and Replace Window

Word has one more Find and Replace tool, and it provides the most complete set of features. You may remember this window from past versions of Word, and it's just the thing for more complicated searches. Choose Edit→Find→Advanced Find and Replace. To see this tool in all its glory (as shown in Figure 2-11), click the triangular expand button. Use the buttons at the top to switch between the Find, Replace, and Go To views.

In the Find view, you can have word highlight all the instances that match your search or use Find Next to browse through each instance. If you're using the "highlight all" method, you can have Word search either your entire document or just a portion that you've previously selected.

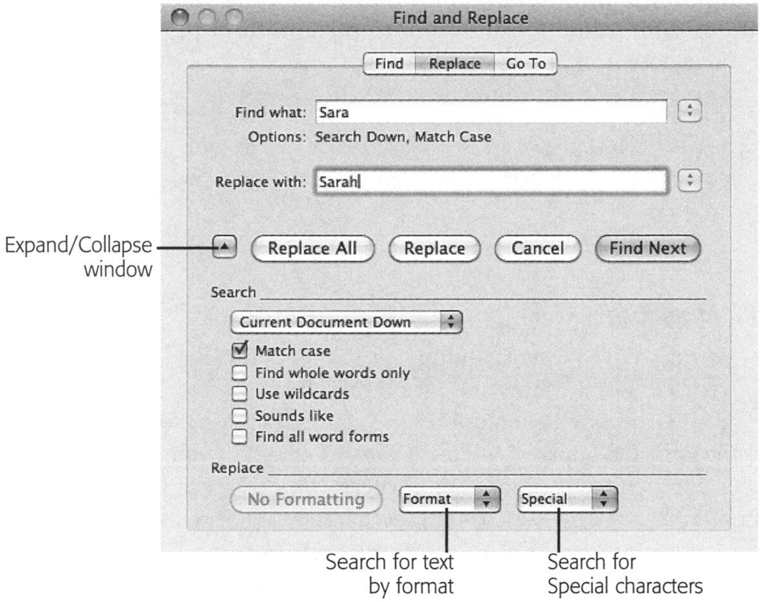

Figure 2-11:
The Advanced Find and Replace window has three different views: Find, Replace, and Go To. The Replace window is shown here. Use the buttons at the top to select the one you need. Click the expand/collapse button to see more or less of the window and its options.

Expand/Collapse window

Search for text by format

Search for Special characters

Here's how to use the "highlight all" method:

1. **Select the text you want to search. If you're searching the entire document, skip this step.**

2. **Type your search phrase in the box.**

3. **Turn on "Highlight all items found in".**

4. **Use the menu to choose either Main Document or Current Selection.**

5. **Click Find All.**

Word highlights matching instances of your search text based on the criteria you provide. In the bottom half of the Find view, you'll notice some of the same options available in the Find and Replace sidebar, like Match Case and Sounds Like. The one additional option provided here is "Use wildcards". Wild cards are special symbols which Word uses to match any character or multiple characters. The question mark *?* matches any single character. So if your search text is *?ill*, Word matches "bill," "will" and "dill." The asterisk * matches any multiple characters. So if your search text is **ill*, Word not only matches "bill" and "will," it also matches "thrill" and "duckbill."

It's the tools at the bottom of the Find and Replace window that make it so powerful. Using them, you can search for Special Characters or, the biggie, search for specific formatting.

Search and replace special characters

When you're entering text in either the "Find what" or "Replace with" boxes, you can add special "invisible" characters such as paragraph marks or page breaks. Just click the menu and choose from the lengthy list of options.

Note: The Go To view is stowed away in the same window as Find and Replace, but it does a different job. It helps you jump to specific objects and places in your document , such as bookmarks, footnotes, sections, or specific pages.

Find specific formatting

One of the less used but powerful options in the Find and Replace window is the ability to search for specific fonts and formatting. Want to find "Tierra del Fuego" but only when it is displayed in bold, 17-point, Cambria font? Word will oblige you. Make sure the Find and Replace window is expanded as shown in Figure 2-11. Then click the Format menu and choose Font, where you can select the font specs you want to find. You may also search for Tab characters (Format→Tabs) or specific styles such as Heading 2 or TOC 3 (Format→Style). You can limit your search to page headers or footers. You can search for frames that hold pictures or graphics. And you can search text that you've designated as being in a specific language. If you're group-editing a document, you may find it handy to search for highlighted text. All these options are available in the Format menu at the bottom of the Find and Replace window.

FREQUENTLY ASKED QUESTION

Converting Quotes from Curly to Straight, or Vice Versa

How do I convert all Word's automatic, typographically correct "curly quotes" into Internet-friendly "straight quotes" before posting my work on a web page or sending it by email?

Word converts quotes automatically as you type, curling open and close quotes around words and phrases. To turn this feature off, go to Tools→AutoCorrect→AutoFormat as You Type and then turn off the checkbox for replacing "Straight quotation marks" with "smart quotation marks."

If you want to leave "smart quotes" on, you can manually change curly quotes to straight quotes by pressing ⌘-Z immediately after typing the quote.

To make changes after you've finished your 1,000 page opus, you need the power of Find and Replace. It's a two-part operation. First, as explained above, turn off the "Straight quotation marks" with "smart quotation marks" option. Then in Find and Replace, type " in both boxes. When Word makes the replacement, it inserts straight quotes. Repeat the process for ' the single quote.

You can reverse this operation, changing a doc from straight to curly quotes by turning the AutoFormat option *on* before you do a Find and Replace.

AutoText: Abbreviation Expanders

If you have big chunks of text that you type over and over, you'll love AutoText. In short, it's an abbreviation expander. Figure 2-12 shows AutoText in action, in its AutoComplete mode. You can also pop any AutoText entry into your document by using the menu. Go to Insert→AutoText and then choose an entry from the submenu and the complete text appears at the insertion.

Figure 2-12:
You're typing along. Suddenly you see a floating yellow screen tip just above the insertion point. That's Word's AutoText feature in action. It's proposing a replacement for what you just typed. If you want to accept the suggestion, press Return; if not, just keep on typing.

AutoText keeps a list of pieces of text that it offers to fill in for you. Microsoft primed the pump by adding things like names of months, days, of the week, and common greetings and closings. If you provided your name and company name when you installed Word, those are in the AutoText list too.

It's easy to add your own items to the list, and don't worry about it being too much. AutoText takes whatever you throw at it: entire paragraphs, pictures, charts. Just select the content that you want to convert to AutoText and then go to Insert→AutoText→New. Figure 2-13 shows the Create New AutoText box that appears with an explanation and a suggested name for the entry. The name is important because those are the letters that trigger the AutoText prompt. You can type in a different abbreviation for the name if you prefer. So, for the example shown in Figure 2-13, you may decide to use the initials "tfcoa" for "Tierra del Fuego Condominium Owners Association" entry. After all, they're less likely to come up in your daily typing and inadvertently trigger AutoText. When you're happy with the name, click OK and it's added to the list.

To view and manage your AutoText list, choose Insert→AutoText→AutoText and the big AutoCorrect dialog box appears showing the AutoText panel (Figure 2-14). Use the checkboxes at the top to turn on and off features. For example, turn off the first option, "Show AutoComplete tip for AutoText and dates", if you don't want to see the yellow screen tips prompting you to use AutoText. In the middle of the panel, you can click a name on the left and preview the complete AutoText on the right. Use the buttons at the bottom to add and delete entries. The Insert button pops the selected entry into your text.

Note: AutoText, Macros and some other Word tools are stored in templates. If an entry that you created doesn't seem to be available, it may be stored in a different template. You'll learn more about templates on page 89.

Figure 2-13:
It doesn't take long to create your own AutoText entries. Select the text you want to use and go to Insert→AutoText→New and this simple box appears where you provide a name. It's a great tool if you're constantly typing the same company name, address or long-winded explanations.

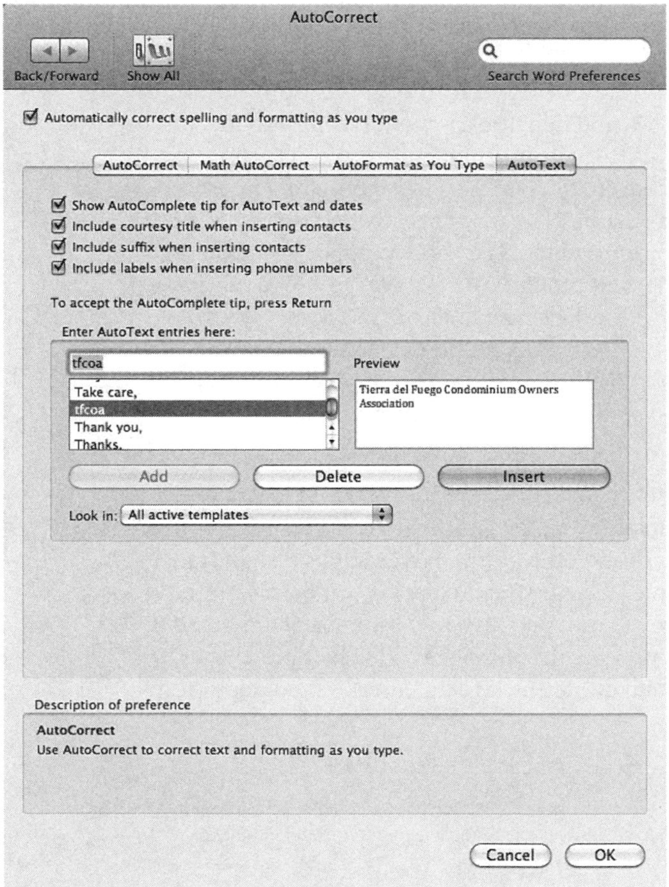

Figure 2-14:
Use the AutoCorrect settings to fine-tune the way your abbreviation expander works. You can turn on and off some of the predesigned AutoText entries and add new ones of your own.

Spelling and Grammar

Whatever your document—term paper, resumé, or letter to the milkman—typos can hinder its effectiveness and sully your credibility. When you let mistakes remain in your document, your reader may doubt that you put any time or care into it at all. Word helps you achieve the perfect result by pointing out possible errors, leaving the final call up to you.

Tip: A spelling-related feature may have been benefiting you without you even noticing. When you make a typo that even a Sominex-drugged reader would notice, such as "wodnerful" or "thier", Word makes the correction automatically, instantly, and quietly. Press ⌘-Z or F1 immediately afterward if you actually intended the misspelled version. (Technically, Word is using its spelling dictionaries as fodder for its Auto-Correct feature, as described on page 67.)

As a bonus, the spell checker is smart enough to recognize run-together words (such as intothe and giveme) and propose the split-apart versions as corrected spellings.

The next two sections describe the two basic modes for Word's spelling and grammar features.

Check Spelling as You Type

Word's factory setting is to check spelling and grammar continuously, immediately flagging any error it detects as soon as you finish typing it. Each spelling error gets a red, squiggly underline; each grammatical error gets a green one. These squiggly underlines (which also appear in the other Office programs) are among the most noticeable hallmarks of Office documents, as shown in Figure 2-15.

If you can spot the problem right away—an obvious spelling error, for example—simply edit it. The squiggly underline disappears as soon as your insertion point leaves the vicinity. It's often more fun, however, to right-click (or Control-click) each error (see Figure 2-15, top), which opens a shortcut menu to help you handle the correction process. Here are the commands you'll find in this shortcut menu:

- The top segment of the shortcut menu lists spelling suggestions from Word's dictionary. It says "(No Spelling Suggestions)" if Word has none. If one of these suggestions is the word you were trying to spell, click it. Word instantly replaces the error in your document, thus evaporating the squiggly line.

- If you click **Ignore**, Word moves on to the next spelling error. If the same misspelled word appears later in your document, Word points it out.

- Choosing **Ignore All** from the shortcut menu tells Word to butt out—that this word is spelled exactly the way you want it. Once you've chosen this command, the underlines disappear from all occurrences of that term in this document. (If you use the same spelling in a new document, however, Word flags it as an error again. To teach Word the word forever, add it to the custom dictionary, as described next.)

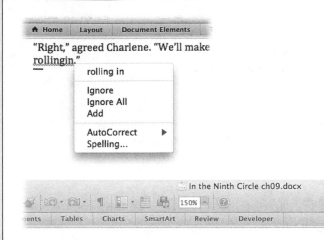

Figure 2-15:
Top: When Word is set to check spelling and grammar as you type, it underlines errors as you go. Right-clicking (or Control-clicking) each error opens a shortcut menu that lists suggested spellings and commands to help you choose or ignore the suggestion.

Bottom: Right-click (Control-click) a green underline and choose Grammar from the pop-up menu to display the Grammar window, where Word explains what it thinks is the matter with your prose. Press Return if you don't agree and want to move on to the next grammar error.

- As you've probably figured out by now, Word underlines a word not necessarily because it's spelled incorrectly, but because it's not on Word's list of correctly spelled words. Occasionally, you have to "teach" Word a new word. The **Add** command does exactly that.

  Word maintains word lists called custom dictionaries. When Word checks a word's spelling as you type it, the Add command on the shortcut menu instantly adds that word to the current custom dictionary. (If the Add command is gray, you haven't yet created a custom dictionary. See page 65 to create a dictionary, and bring the Add button to life.) You can also edit a custom dictionary directly, as described on page 66.

- The **AutoCorrect** pop-up menu provides access to matching choices from Word's AutoCorrect list (see page 67). Often, but not always, these choices are the same as the alternate spellings from the custom dictionary.

- **Spelling** opens the Spelling dialog box and performs a spelling and grammar check on whatever you selected and clicked.

Checking Spelling and Grammar All at Once

If it annoys you when Word flags incorrect or unusual spellings as you type, there's something you can do about it. Turn that feature off, as described in Figure 2-17, and check spelling when you want to—once at the very end, for instance. If that's the way you like it, choose Tools→"Spelling and Grammar" (or press F7, or Option-⌘-L) to open the "Spelling and Grammar" dialog box (Figure 2-16).

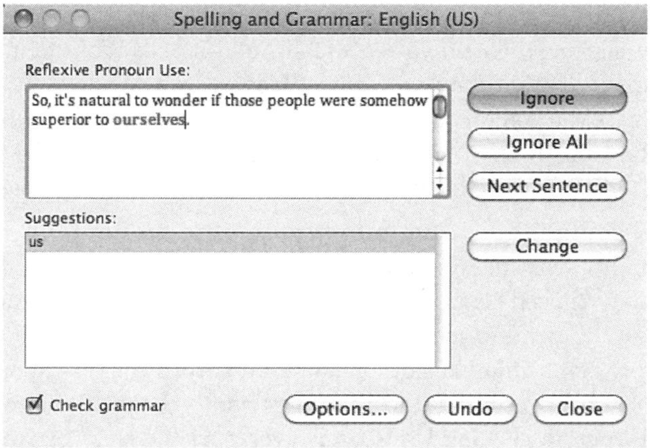

Figure 2-16:
If you want Word to check spelling only and keep its grammatical comments to itself, turn off the "Check grammar" box in the lower-left corner.

Word scans your document, starting at the insertion point, and displays errors one by one in the "Not in dictionary" box, as shown at the bottom of Figure 2-15. As a courtesy, Word shows you the "error" in context, placing the whole sentence in the text box with the specific spelling error shown in red. Your options are as follows:

- Click **Ignore** (⌘-I) to skip over the error without doing anything. If you don't want Word to flag this particular error again (in this document), click Ignore All (⌘-G).

- As described under "Check spelling as you type," clicking **Add** (⌘-A) adds the highlighted word to the custom dictionary. From here on out, in every document, Word understands this spelling to be a correct one.

- In the lower **Suggestions** list box, Word shows you some similarly spelled words from your main and custom dictionaries. Using the mouse or the up/down arrow keys, highlight one of them and click Change to accept that spelling just this once, or Change All (⌘-L) to swap all occurrences of the highlighted word—in this document only—with the selected suggestion.

  If you agree that something is misspelled, but you don't see the correct spelling in the Suggestions list, you can make the correction directly in the top text area, using any of Word's editing tools. (This is a handy trick when Word discovers a typo like ";lkjijjjjjjj"—a sure sign that you'd fallen asleep on the keys. Just drag across the mess—right there in the dialog box—and press the Delete key to fix the error.)

  Then click **Change** or **Change All**, to apply your change to the document itself. You can also click **Undo Edit** (⌘-U) if you change your mind. (The **Ignore** button changes into Undo Edit as soon as you start typing in the window.)

- Whether you make a choice from the Suggestions window or make a change in the editing window, clicking the **AutoCorrect** (⌘-R) button tells Word to make the change from now on, using the AutoCorrect feature (see page 67). When you do so, Word enters your typo/correction pair to its AutoCorrect list, which you can view by choosing Tools→AutoCorrect and scrolling through the list. (See page 69 for more information on working with the AutoCorrect dialog box.)

- The **Undo** (⌘-U) button is a lifesaver for the indecisive. Once you've made a correction, after you've clicked Change, and even if you've created a new Auto-Correct pair, you can click Undo and take back your last change. Better still, the Undo command works even after you click Change, and Word has moved on to the next error. In that case, Word backtracks to the previous change and undoes it. In fact, you can keep on clicking Undo and reverse all the changes you've made since the beginning of your document.

  The Undo button is particularly valuable when you're spell checking rapidly and realize that you've just accepted one of Word's suggestions a bit too hastily.

- The **Options** (⌘-O) button opens the "Spelling and Grammar" panel of the Preferences dialog box, shown in Figure 2-17.

- **Close** (Esc) calls a halt to the spelling and grammar check and dismisses the dialog box.

Over the years, Word's grammar checker has grown smarter and less likely to underline perfectly correct sentences or make incorrect suggestions. Sometimes, however, you still need to rely on your own knowledge of grammar (and a healthy dose of common sense) in order to decide when to accept Word's suggested grammar changes—and when to click Ignore.

Spelling and Grammar Options

To tell Word how much (or little) help you need with your spelling and grammar, choose Word→Preferences; in the Preferences dialog box, click the "Spelling and Grammar" button. You'll find these options:

- **Check spelling as you type** turns on and off the red, wavy underlines that mark spelling errors in all Word documents.

- **Hide spelling errors in this document** turns off "Check spelling as you type" in the current document only.

- **Always suggest corrections** prompts Word to show you alternative spellings during spelling checks using the Spelling dialog box. Without this option, Word will flag errors without proposing suggestions.

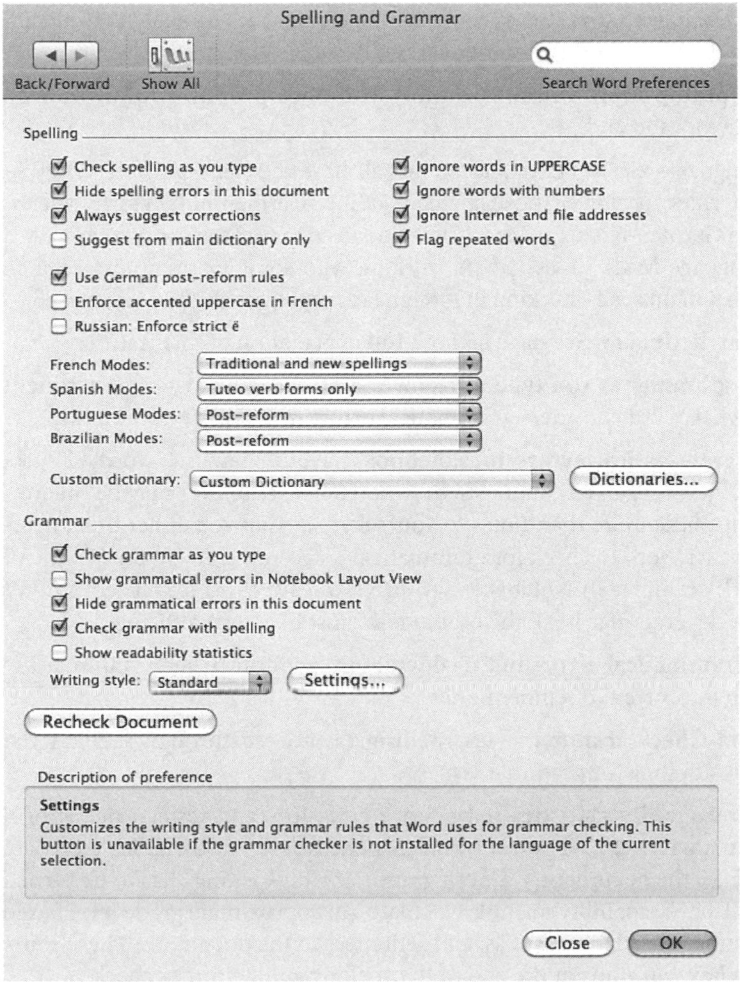

Figure 2-17:
The Word→Preferences→ "Spelling and Grammar" panel is command central for making Word's spelling and grammar features work for you. When you click "Check spelling as you type" or "Check grammar as you type," Word automatically turns off the "hide" choices. You can still turn on "Hide spelling errors" or "Hide grammatical errors" to temporarily remove Word's squiggly underlines on a document-by-document basis.

Note: Right-clicking (Control-clicking) a squiggly-underlined word produces spelling suggestions regardless of the "Always suggest corrections" setting.

- **Suggest from main dictionary only** instructs Word to use only the list of words that came installed with it, ignoring your custom dictionaries. (See page 65 for more detail on custom dictionaries.)

- Turn on **Ignore words in UPPERCASE** if you frequently use acronyms or stock symbols (such as WFMI or ADM). Otherwise, Word interprets them as misspelled words.

- Turn on **Ignore words with numbers** if you'd like Word to leave words like 3Com and R2D2 alone.

- **Ignore Internet and file addresses** governs whether or not Word interprets URLs (*www.missingmanuals.com*) and file paths (*Macintosh HD:Users:[user name]:Documents:Tests*) as spelling errors. Because it's unlikely that most Web addresses are in Word's dictionaries, you'll usually want this option turned on.

- **Flag repeated words** finds those spots where you paused to think, then typed "the the" or "and and."

- The language-related boxes and menus all have the same purpose. They select spelling rules specific to those languages. Since German post-reform rules work only on German-language Macs, there's no need to turn this option on with English-language Macs, unless you're working with some German text. (For more information on spell-checking in foreign languages, see the box on page 63.)

- **Custom dictionary.** See page 65 for a full explanation of this feature.

- **Check grammar as you type** turns on and off the green, wavy underlines that mark what Word considers grammatical errors in all Word documents.

- **Show grammatical errors in Notebook Layout view.** In Word's Notebook Layout view (page 183), many of your notebook ramblings may be incomplete thoughts, little more than notes to yourself, stuff that you either don't need (or don't want) Word to check for grammatical correctness. If you don't want Word to check grammar in Notebook Layout view leave this box turned off. (Word still checks grammar in all the other views, just like normal.)

- **Hide grammatical errors in this document** turns off "Check grammar as you type" in the current document only.

- Turn off **Check grammar with spelling** to proceed through spelling checks without stopping for grammar issues.

- **Show readability statistics** may please educators and testers, but is of little value to anyone else. If you turn on this checkbox, Word applies a readability formula to the document. ("Check grammar with spelling" has to be turned on as well.) The readability formula calculates an approximate grade level based on the number of syllables, words, and sentences in the document. These statistics are displayed in a box at the end of the spelling and grammar check.

Word uses one of two formulas to interpret the results. The Flesch Reading Ease score uses a scale of 0 to 100, with 100 being the easiest. A score of 60 or 70 indicates text that most adults could comfortably read and understand. The FleschKincaid Grade Level Score, on the other hand, calculates grade level according to U.S. averages. A score of 8, for example, means that the document is on the eighth-grade reading level. For a general audience, that's a good level to shoot for.

Either way, remember that this is a software program analyzing words written by a human being for specific audiences. By no means, for example, should you base somebody's entrance to a school on these scores—they're only crude approximations of approximations.

GEM IN THE ROUGH

Checking Foreign Language Text

The spell checkers in ordinary word processors choke on foreign terms. But not Word—it actually comes with different spelling dictionaries for dozens of languages. The program can actually check the English parts of your document against the English dictionary, the French portions against the French dictionary, and so on—all in a single pass.

This amazing intelligence works only if you've taken two preliminary steps. First, you must install the foreign-language dictionaries you intend to use (they're not part of the standard installation), using the technique described in Appendix A.

Second, you must tell Word which language each passage is in. To flag a certain word, passage, or document as Danish, for example, first highlight it. Then choose Tools→Language; in the resulting dialog box, select the language and click OK.

You've just applied what Microsoft calls language formatting—that is, you've flagged the highlighted text just as though you'd made it blue or bold. From now on, your spell checks will switch, on the fly, to the corresponding spelling dictionary for each patch of foreign language text in your document.

Writing Styles

Grammar can be very subjective. Contractions, for example, aren't incorrect; they're just appropriate in some situations and not in others. In an academic or medical paper, long sentences and the passive voice are the norm; in a glossy magazine article, they're taboo. On the other hand, other kinds of errors, such as writing the contraction "it's" when you mean the possessive "its," are things you always want to avoid. And when writing poetry or a play in dialect, the usual rules of grammar simply don't apply.

In other words, there are different writing styles for different kinds of documents. Word not only recognizes that fact, it lets you choose which one you want to use in a given situation. Better still, it lets you decide which specific grammatical issues you want flagged.

To select a writing style from Word's preconfigured list, choose Word→Preferences→ "Spelling and Grammar". In the resulting dialog box, choose a writing style from the pop-up menu near the bottom of the box under Grammar.

To customize writing styles to your own needs, thus becoming your own grammar czar or czarina, click Settings. The Grammar Settings dialog box opens, as shown in Figure 2-18. (If the Grammar settings are dimmed in the dialog box, it's because the Grammar module isn't installed. See Appendix A for installation instructions.)

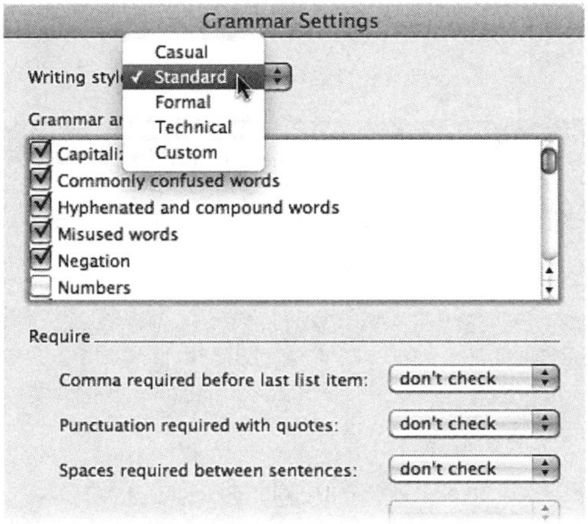

Figure 2-18:
You can modify existing writing styles (Standard, Casual, Formal, or Technical), or create your own combination of grammar standards (Custom), by turning options in the list on or off. Clicking Reset All returns the currently selected style to its original condition. (To restore all writing styles to their original settings, you have to reset them one by one.)

The choices you make from the pop-up menus, under Require, apply to all writing styles. Each menu gives you a chance to customize points of style that are more a matter of individual choice than grammar. Word doesn't automatically check for any of the three Require items listed here: whether you put a comma after the second-to-last item in a list (as in: *planes, trains, and automobiles*), whether punctuation goes inside or outside of quotation marks, or the number of spaces between sentences.

If you learned how to write in England, you probably put periods and commas after the quotation marks at the end of a quote. In the United States, punctuation is expected to go before the quotes. Choose "inside" or "outside" from the second pop-up menu to have Word check if you're doing it consistently, one way or the other.

If you're sending your text to an editor or layout person for desktop publishing, you'll probably be asked to put just one space between sentences. You can choose 1 or 2 from the bottom menu to instruct Word to check the spacing for you.

You can create your own unique style by choosing Custom from the pop-up menu at the top of the box and turning on any combination of options. When you click OK, the custom style applies to your document; you can't name the style or create more than one custom style at a time.

Custom Dictionaries and Preferred Spellings

As noted earlier, Word maintains a list of thousands of words that it "knows" how to spell. When it checks your spelling, Word simply compares the words in your document to the words in the list.

To teach Word the words that you use frequently, you have two options: You can add them to a custom dictionary, or, if you have large batches of words that you only use for specific situations, you can create multiple custom dictionaries. Then choose which dictionary you wish to apply to the document you're currently working on.

You can't add words directly to Word's main (built-in) dictionary, which is permanently hard-wired—specially encoded for speed. In fact, you aren't even allowed to see the main dictionary. However, when you add words to a custom dictionary, Word uses them seamlessly along with the main dictionary (as long as you haven't turned on the "Use main dictionary only" box in the Word→Preferences→"Spelling and Grammar" panel).

Editing the custom dictionary

To add words to a custom dictionary, choose Word→Preferences, and then click the "Spelling and Grammar" panel (Figure 2-17). Now click the Dictionaries button. In the Custom Dictionaries dialog box that opens (Figure 2-19), one custom dictionary is listed and checkmarked, meaning that it's currently in use. Any words that you've ever added to Word's dictionary during a spell check appear in this custom dictionary.

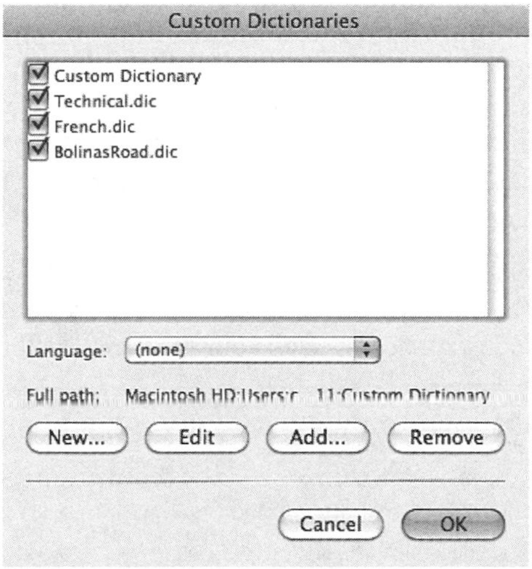

Figure 2-19:
The checked boxes show the custom dictionaries currently in effect. Uncheck one if you would like Word to stop using it in spell checks. For example, if you turn off the French Dictionary, Word will interpret French words as spelling errors.

To review the list of words, click Edit. (If a message appears to warn you that Word will now stop checking your spelling, click Continue.) Suddenly, all your added words appear listed in a new Word document, which you're now free to edit. You can add, delete, and edit words using any of Word's editing tools; just remember to use the Return key to ensure each word is on a separate line.

Creating a new custom dictionary

In some cases, you may want to create a new custom dictionary for specific projects. For instance, suppose that you're writing something in a foreign language or a paper filled with technical terms. If you add these foreign or technical terms to the same custom dictionary that you use for everyday correspondence, they'll show up in spell checks and sometimes even create false errors.

To create a new custom dictionary, click New in the Custom Dictionaries dialog box (Figure 2-19). Type a name for the new dictionary, and then click Save. Word saves the new custom dictionary in your Home folder's Library→Preferences→Microsoft folder.

Now you can add words to the custom dictionary in one of two ways:

- To add new words occasionally, in the course of your everyday writing career, click the name of the desired dictionary in the Custom Dictionaries dialog box. (Turn off any other dictionaries that may be listed in the box. Otherwise, Word will add newly learned terms to the default custom dictionary, for example, instead of your own foreign/technical one.) Then just go to work in your document. Whenever you check spelling, choose Add to place the unfamiliar term in your new custom dictionary.

- You can also add words all at once, by selecting the custom dictionary in the Custom Dictionaries dialog box and clicking Edit as described above. If there's a list of vocabulary words or technical terms in front of you, simply type or paste them into the text document that is the custom dictionary. Just make sure that each word is on a separate line before you click Save.

You can also copy and paste words from one custom dictionary into another. Thus, you can always copy the contents of the original custom dictionary into your specialized dictionary, so that you'll have constant access to all your preferred spellings.

Tip: When editing custom dictionaries, you can access them easily by going directly to the Library→Preferences→Microsoft→Office 2011 folder in your Home folder (although you could create and store a custom dictionary anywhere). You can open them easily in a program like TextEdit and edit away.

You can also rename these files. For example, if you've created new custom dictionaries, you may want to rename the default custom dictionary "original," "default," or "old."

Adding and removing custom dictionaries

After creating a new custom dictionary, you may decide to exclude it from certain documents. To do so, turn off its box in the Custom Dictionaries dialog box as described in Figure 2-19.

If you select a dictionary and click Remove, it disappears from this list and no longer appears in the pop-up menu in the Preferences→"Spelling and Grammar" panel. This is the way to go if you never again want this custom dictionary as an option and don't want anyone else to see it in Preferences. However, a removed custom dictionary doesn't go away forever. It remains in the Library→Preferences→Microsoft→ Office 2011 folder (in your Home folder), or wherever you stored it on your Mac's hard drive. To return it to the Custom Dictionaries dialog box, click Add and choose it in the Add Dictionary dialog box.

Foreign language dictionaries

If your new dictionary is in a foreign language, there's an extra step. After creating the new custom dictionary, as described above, select the new foreign dictionary in the Custom Dictionaries dialog box. Then choose the appropriate language from the Language pop-up menu. Now Word will know to apply the correct spelling rules for that language.

Choosing custom dictionaries before spell checking

From now on, before you check spelling, you can specify which custom dictionaries you want Word to consider as it pores over your document. To do so, choose Word→Preferences→"Spelling and Grammar" panel, and then choose a custom dictionary from the pop-up menu.

AutoCorrect

Like the Spelling and Grammar tools, AutoCorrect is one of those tools that saves you from the embarrassment of sending an imperfect document to your boss, your professor or your loved one. If you type *teh*, Word changes it to "the" before you even have a chance to hit Delete. You start to type the name of the month, and all of a sudden today's date pops up on the screen—and you didn't even know what day it was.

You're witnessing Word's AutoCorrect feature at work—two of the least understood and most useful tools in Word's arsenal. They can be frustrating if you don't understand them, and a writer's best friends if you do.

Like AutoText, AutoCorrect is a *substitution* feature. All it does is replace something you're typing (the typo) with a replacement that word has memorized and stored (the correct spelling). Unlike AutoText, though, the correction takes place as soon as you type a space or punctuation mark after the incorrect word—no further action is required from you. And it happens so fast, sometime you may not even notice the telltale blue line under the corrected word. Mouse over the word and you see a lightning bolt and menu arrow. Click and a shortcut menu like the one in Figure 2-20 appears, which gives you options like:

- **Change back to** (the word you actually typed).

- **Stop automatically correcting** (the word you typed).

- **Control AutoCorrect Options**—where you can fine-tune AutoCorrect's editorial behavior.

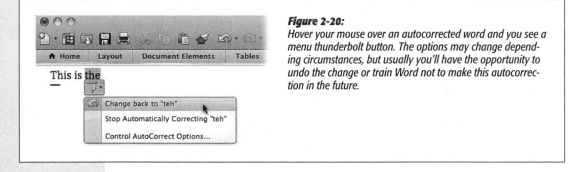

Figure 2-20:
Hover your mouse over an autocorrected word and you see a menu thunderbolt button. The options may change depending circumstances, but usually you'll have the opportunity to undo the change or train Word not to make this autocorrection in the future.

How does this work? Word maintains a file of common misspellings and their corrections. Many of these have to do with keyboard layout and finger trips. Word makes certain corrections and not others: Not all possible error/corrections combinations that you need come installed on the list. To see this list, choose Tools→AutoCorrect and click the AutoCorrect tab (Figure 2-21). (Here you'll also find the most important checkbox in the world of AutoCorrect: the master on/off switch, called "Replace text as you type".)

The first three checkboxes cover capitalization errors; they save you from the errant ways of your pinky fingers on the Shift keys. When the first two boxes are turned on (see Figure 2-21), Word makes sure that you get a capital letter at the beginning of every sentence, whether you hold the Shift key down too long ("Correct TWo INitial CApitals") or not long enough ("Capitalize first letter of sentences").

Tip: Efficiency-addicted Word fans eventually stop capitalizing the first letters of sentences altogether. Word does it automatically, so why twist your pinkies unnecessarily?

If you turn on "Capitalize first letter of Sentences," bear in mind that Word assumes every period is the end of a sentence. So why doesn't it auto-cap the first word after you type U.N. or Jan.? Because it's smart enough not to auto-cap after all-cap abbreviations (U.N.), and because it maintains a list of lowercase abbreviations that shouldn't be followed by caps. (To see the list, choose Tools→AutoCorrect, click Exceptions, then click the First Letter tab; you can add your abbreviations to this list, too.)

If you turn on "Automatically use suggestions form the spelling checker," AutoCorrect will go above and beyond the list of substitution pairs in this dialog box. It will use Word's main dictionary as a guide to proper spelling and automatically change words that almost but not quite match ones in the dictionary. (When Word can't decide on a match, it simply squiggly-underlines the misspelled word in the document.)

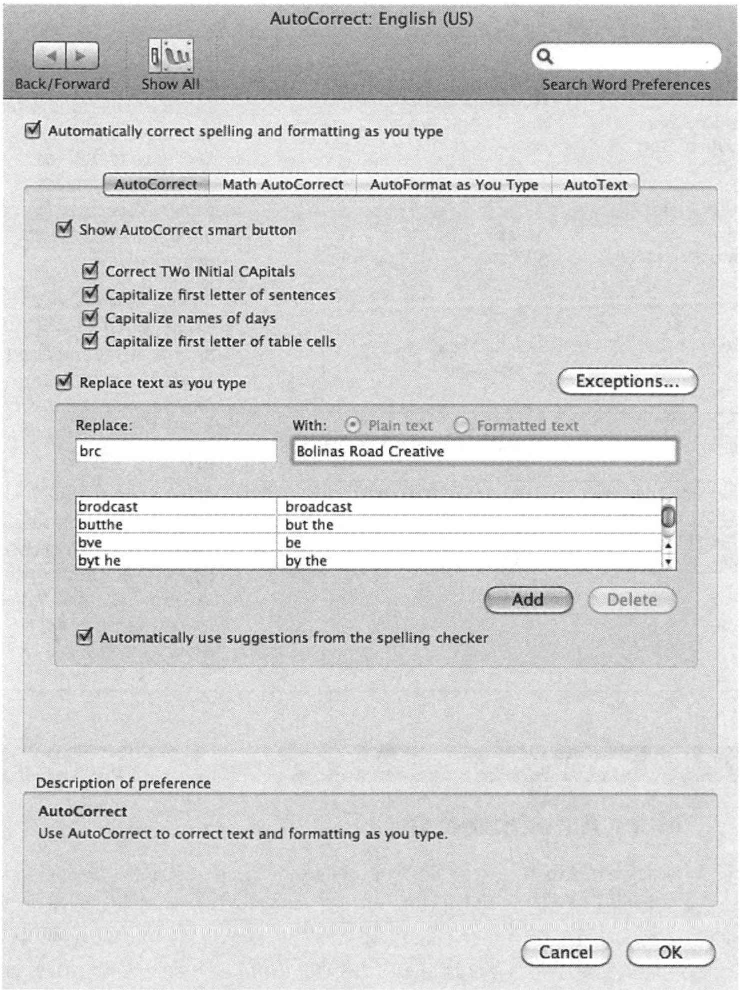

Figure 2-21:
You can open this dialog box by choosing Tools→AutoCorrect or clicking Control AutoCorrect Options whenever you see the menu shown in Figure 2-20. Feel free to add your own word combinations here, too. Put the type in the Replace box and the replacement in the With box, then click Add. Think beyond typos, too—remember you can make Word expand anything into anything. Make it replace "int" with "Internet," your initials with your full name and so on.

Adding and Formatting Tables

Words don't always flow in linear paragraphs. In some cases, like resumés, agendas or multiple choice tests, you want to organize your words into blocks of text that are aligned horizontally. You can try to do this using the Tab key, but that way lies frustration and madness, as explained in Figure 2-22. Using Word's table feature is light-years easier and more flexible, because each row expands to accommodate whatever you put in it, while everything else stays aligned. Use the ribbon to add tables to your document, and you can take advantage of automatic formatting. If you need to make changes to your tables, you'll find it easy to change column widths and to add and remove columns and rows.

Song	Album	Artist
Down to the River to Pray	A Wish	Wonderland Jazz Ensamble
Nuclear War	A Fireside Chat	Sun Ra Arkestra
Romance	The Myth of Red	Sasha Lazard
Super Life	Funk This	Chaka Kahn

Song	Album	Artist	
Down to the River to Pray/Lullaby of Forrealville Jazz Ensamble		A Wish	Wonderland
Nuclear War Arkestra	A Fireside Chat With Lucifer		Sun Ra
Romance	The Myth of Red	Sasha Lazard	
Super Life	Funk This	Chaka Kahn	

Song	Album	Artist
Down to the River to Pray/ Lullaby of Forrealville	A Wish	Wonderland Jazz Ensamble
Nuclear War	A Fireside Chat With Lucifer	Sun Ra Arkestra
Romance	The Myth of Red	Sasha Lazard
Super Life	Funk This	Chaka Kahn

Figure 2-22:

Top: If you use tabs to set up a table, things may look good at first—as long as every line fits within its space and you never plan to insert any additional text.

Middle: Here's what's wrong with the tab approach: When you insert words into the columns, they push the text too far to the right, causing an ugly ripple effect.

Bottom: If you use a table, you never have this kind of problem. Just type as much text as you like in a "cell," and that row of the table simply expands to fit it.

WORDAROUND WORKSHOP

Telling AutoCorrect to Chill

Sometimes Word is more diligent in correcting errors that you'd like. What if you're trying to type a letter to a Mr. Porvide, and Word constantly changes it to Provide. Or maybe you work for a company called Intelligence, and you're tired of changing the "e" to an "a" every time Word helpfully "corrects" it.

You don't want to turn AutoCorrect off, because you want Word to catch all your other typos. You could press ⌘-Z after Word makes each change, but there's a better way.

Click the Exceptions button in the AutoCorrect tab (see Figure 2-21). Then click the Other Corrections tab. Type your

preferred spelling into the "Don't Correct" box and click Add. If you have many preferred spellings that you'll need to re-educate Word about, turn on the "Automatically add words to list" checkbox. Now, each time Word makes an incorrect correction, press ⌘-Z (Edit→Undo) and Word will remember that Intelligence is an acceptable word.

But you're not quite done yet, since the substitution pairs in the AutoCorrect dialog box (Figure 2-21) may override the list in the Exceptions box. To be perfectly safe, delete the "porvide" to "provide" correction in the AutoCorrect list.

Creating Tables

If you never created a table in a Word document before, don't worry—it's easy and even fun, especially if you use the drawing-with-the-mouse method.

There are three methods for creating tables:

- **Ribbon Mini-map method.** Click Tables | Table Options→New and then use the grid to set the number of rows and columns.

- **Dialog box method.** Choose Table→Insert→Table. When the Insert Table dialog box appears type in the number of rows and columns you need.

- **Drawing method.** You can draw your table on the page with your mouse, which gives you complete control over size and shape. Click the Tables tab and in the Draw Borders group, click Draw. Your cursor will change into a table drawing tool.

Creating a Table from the Ribbon

The ribbon approach to adding tables is quick, easy and visual. Click the Tables tab and you see all the tools you need to insert, format, and edit your tables. As you see in Figure 2-23, you use a menu to visually define the number of cells in your table.

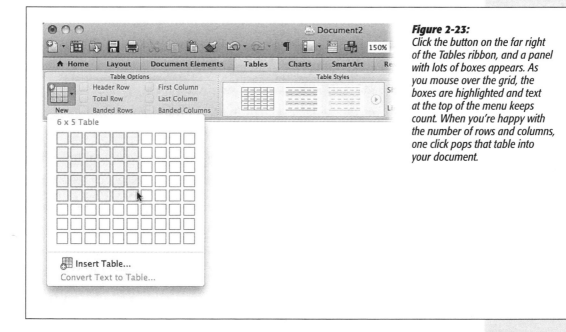

Figure 2-23:
Click the button on the far right of the Tables ribbon, and a panel with lots of boxes appears. As you mouse over the grid, the boxes are highlighted and text at the top of the menu keeps count. When you're happy with the number of rows and columns, one click pops that table into your document.

Using the Insert Table Box

The insert table box is the more traditional—and boring—way to create a table. You can open the box from the menus (Table→Insert→Table) or from the ribbon Tables→New→Insert Table. The box is a simple affair. Just type numbers in the text boxes at the top for columns and rows. This dialog box also lets you choose the AutoFit behavior, as explained below:

- **Initial column width.** Use this option if you want to start off with columns at a specific width. You can enter a number or if you choose Auto, Word creates a table that fits into your current margins, with the number of columns you specified set to equal widths.

- **AutoFit to contents.** With this option, the column width adjusts automatically to accommodate the amount of text you type in the cells. Use this option if you're not sure how much space your text will take up until you type it.

- **AutoFit to window.** This option is more suited to web pages than printed documents. It makes the table expand and contract to fit a browser window. Web pages are designed to work on all different computers, smart phones, and TV sets. AutoFit tables like these help web designers create pages that work on screens with dramatically different capabilities.

Drawing a Table

The least mechanical and most creative way to insert a table is to draw your own. It's a great technique if you need an irregularly shaped table. With Word's table tools you can draw tables, and divide them into columns and rows in just about any configuration imaginable. You can do just about anything except make a curve.

1. **On the ribbon, choose Tables | Draw Borders→Draw.**

   Your mouse cursor changes into a pencil, inviting you to start drawing.

2. **On an empty place on the page, drag diagonally to draw your first rectangle.**

   The rectangle that appears on your page marks the borders for your table. Soon you'll divvy it up, creating columns and rows inside. Word adds paragraph breaks, adjusts margins, and generally does whatever's necessary to place your table exactly where you draw it.

3. **Next, drag to draw a vertical line to divide your table in half.**

   Your line separates the table into two cells. You can draw lines wherever you want to divide your table into cells of just about any shape. When you drag diagonally, you create rectangles instead of lines. Rectangles turn into cells or if they're far enough from the original table, they're new tables.

4. **Draw a horizontal line on the left half of your table.**

   When you draw the horizontal line, you divide one of the cells into two cells, creating a row. You can draw the line to the vertical divider or you can continue onto the right side of the table. This horizontal line creates two rows in your table.

   You can continue to divvy up your table into additional cells.

5. **When you're done, click the Draw button on the right side of the ribbon (Tables | Draw Borders→Draw).**

   This toggles the Draw mode off and your cursor changes from the pencil to the usual I-beam, or an arrow if it's over the table.

If you make a mistake while you're drawing your table, you can click the Erase button (next to Draw on the Ribbon) and erase some of the lines in your table. The eraser is also a good way to merge two cells into one large cell.

Editing Your Table

To add text to your table, just click in one of the cells and start typing. If you get wordy, the table expands, wrapping your text to a new line and making the cell taller. If you want to force Word to add another line to the cell, press Option-Return. You can move from cell to cell using the arrow keys or Tab (to move forward) and Shift-Tab (to move backward).

- **To add columns or rows to your table** use the menu Table→Insert and choose either Columns to the Left or Columns to the Right. There's a similar command for adding rows.

- **To delete columns or rows**, make sure your insertion point is in the table and then choose Table→Delete→Columns. You can delete multiple columns by selecting them before using the command. The operation for deleting rows is similar.

- **To merge two or more cells to create a single large cell**, select the cells you want merge and then right-click the cells. A shortcut menu appears where you can choose the command Merge Cells.

- **To split a cell in two**, put your cursor in the cell and then right-click (Control-click). Choose Split Cells from the shortcut menu, and then a box appears. Type the number of rows and columns you want to place in the cell and click OK.

Deleting cells is sort of like pulling a brick from the middle of a wall. Other bricks have to move to take its place. But it doesn't happen at random: Word lets you choose how you want cells to fill in the space. When you give the command to delete a cell or a group of cells (right-click→Delete Cells), Word shows a dialog box asking if you want to pull cells up or bring them over to the left (Figure 2-24).

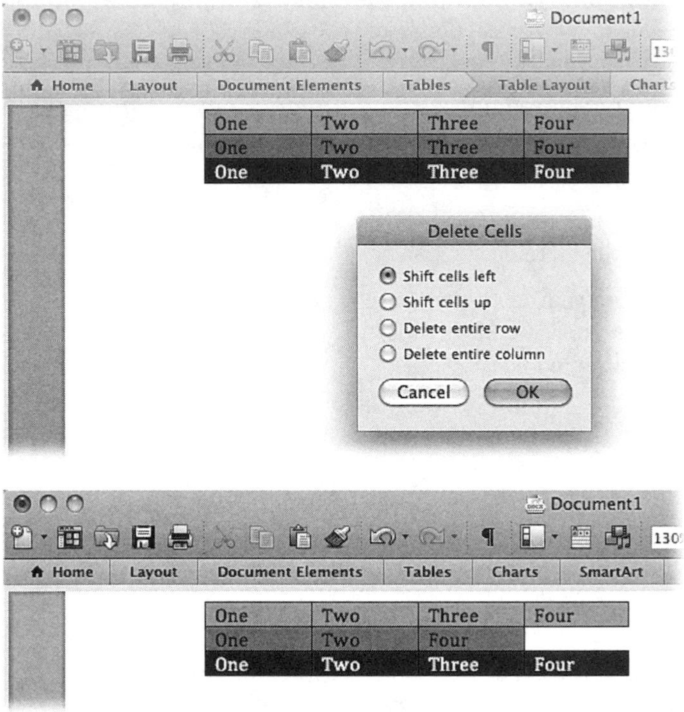

Figure 2-24:
Top: The second cell from the left and the second from the top is selected for deletion. After invoking the Delete Cells command, Word asks for advice on how to shift the rest of the cells.

Bottom: With the "Shift cells left" button selected, the cells in the second row shift over from the right.

Formatting Tables

The easiest way to format a table is to use one of the predesigned styles from the ribbon. Make sure the insertion point is in the table you want to format, then click the Tables tab. The Table styles are displayed in the center. Click the right-pointing arrow to scroll through the styles available. If you want to see more styles at one time, click the down-pointing arrow and a window opens as shown in Figure 2-25. When you see a style that fits the bill, click it. Instantly, your table is formatted with the cell shading and border styles of your selection. If the applied style doesn't live up to your dreams, you can undo it (⌘-Z) or choose another style.

The Table Options group is pretty nifty. As you make choices and check off options, the styles displayed in the Table Styles group changes per your specs. Here are your options:

- **Header Row** puts an emphasis on the top row, either with a color or a strong border. This option works best when your top row contains headings.

- **Total Row** puts an emphasis on the bottom row. As the name implies, this style is ideal for emphasizing the totals at the bottom of columns when your table is a spreadsheet.

- **Banded Rows** uses alternating colors to help readers track text and numbers horizontally. It's useful for wide spreadsheets, but you can also use it for design effect.

- **First Column** puts an emphasis on the first column, like when your left column holds a list of categories.

- **Last Column** puts an emphasis on the last or right-hand column. It's particularly useful when you sum up rows of numbers in the right column.

- **Banded Columns**, like banded rows, help guide your reader's eye, but you can also use them strictly for design purposes.

Open large table styles window

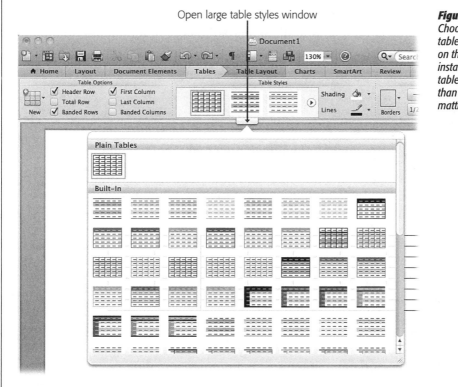

Figure 2-25:
Choose one of the table styles displayed on the ribbon to instantly format your table. It's a lot faster than manually formatting your table.

Inserting Photos and Media

In spite of the name, Word isn't all about words these days. For that matter, neither are we, the communicating public. More than ever, we capture photos or video on our phone and shoot them to our friends almost immediately. Keeping in step with the multimedia revolution, Word makes it ridiculously easy to pop photos, sound, and movies into your document. The main reason you don't see more people using Word this way is that it makes your document files really big.

In Word, the portal to your media is the media browser. As usual, you can approach it several different ways:

- Press Shift-⌘-M (think "media").

- On the Standard toolbar, click the Show or Hide Media Browser button.

- Use any of the "Insert" commands like Insert→Photo or Insert→Audio.

- On the Home tab of the ribbon, in the Insert group, click Photo browser.

Use any of these commands and the Media browser appears. As you can see in Figure 2-26, the media browser divides the collection up by:

- Pictures in your iPhoto albums and Photo Booth.

- Audio from your iTunes collection and other folders.

- Video found in your iMovie and Movies folders.

- ClipArt installed with Office.

- Symbols installed with Office.

- Shapes installed with Office.

Figure 2-26:
The media browser gives you one-stop shopping for pictures, audio, video, clip art, symbols and shapes. Just click one of the buttons at the top, then use the menu to zero in on the media you need. Adding the media to your document is as simple as dragging it from browser to page.

The quick and easy way to use any item from the media browser is to drag it from the browser to your page. After you've popped a picture or other media object into your text, the next step is to format it. Does it need to be resized or cropped? Do you want to add a border or drop-shadow? Do you want to wrap text around the media or should it stand alone?

Inserting a Photo

Most Word documents are more likely to receive a photo, clip art or some other graphic image as opposed to an audio or video file. Here are the steps for dropping a photo into your document and then formatting it so that it looks good. Keep in mind; you can use these same techniques to place an audio or video file in your document. The big difference is how much they swell the file size.

1. **Click the Media browser button in the Standard toolbar (or use any of the methods on page 76).**

   The media browser opens.

2. **Click the Photos button and then use the menu to find a photo you want to insert.**

   The menu lists iPhoto locations and other places where you may have stashed your photos.

3. **Drag the photo from the media browser preview window to a place in your document as shown in Figure 2-27.**

   The photo snaps into line with the text, as if it's just another character. Usually, your photo will be so big that it commands an entire line to itself. That's a situation you can fix with a little formatting.

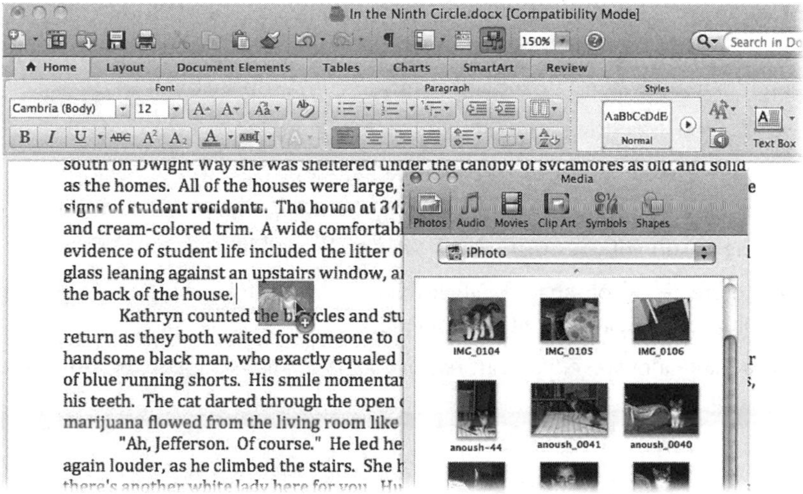

Figure 2-27:
Placing a picture or any other media object into your Word document is a drag-and-drop affair. In most cases, you'll also want to do some formatting after the fact.

4. **Click the red Close button on the media browser and click on your picture.**

   You don't need the media browser anymore: what you need are tools to format your picture and those automatically appear on the ribbon when you click the photo.

5. **Drag the handles around your picture to resize it.**

   When you drag a corner you can adjust the height and width proportionally. Drag one of the edge handles to adjust height or width individually.

6. **On the ribbon in the Arrange group, open the Wrap Text menu and choose an option.**

   For a photo, you'll often want to choose Square or Tight as shown in Figure 2-28. Here's a description of each option:

   - **Inline** treats the inserted media as an inline text character. This often looks odd for photos, but works well with symbols or small images.
   - **Square** wraps text around the image in a square shape.
   - **Tight** conforms text closely to the wrap boundary.
   - **Behind Text** makes text visible as if the text is printed on top of the media.
   - **Front of Text** conceals text behind the image. If you want the text to show through, you can use the transparency slider on the Format Picture ribbon.
   - **Top and Bottom** places the media so that there's text above and below, but none to the sides.
   - **Through** conforms the wrapping text to an object with an irregular shape.
   - **Edit Wrap Boundary** give you the opportunity to reshape the boundary that controls text wrapping. Drag the handles to change the boundary shape.

7. **Make any other necessary adjustments to make your photo look good.**

   You can continue to tweak the photo until you're happy. That's why adding graphics to your Word document seems to gobble up so much time!

   - To reposition the photo, drag it to a new spot.
   - To resize the photo, drag one of the handles.
   - To crop your picture, click the Crop button and then drag a rectangle over the portion of your picture you want to be visible.
   - To create a drop-shadow, click the Shadow button and then set the angle, blur and transparency for the shadow.

   If you make a mistake, you can remove all your picture formatting by clicking the Reset button.

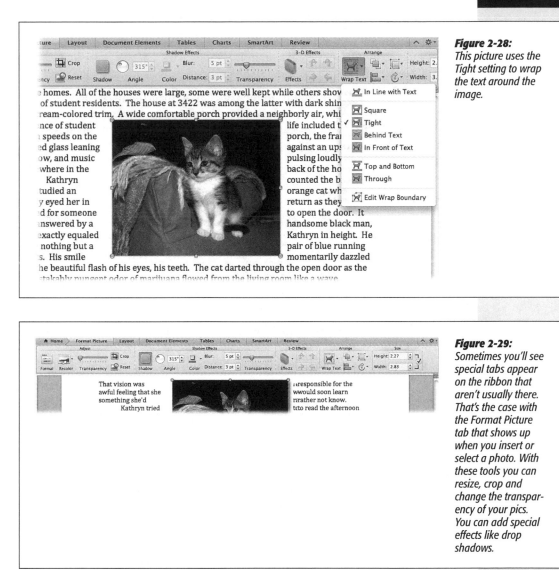

Figure 2-28:
*This picture uses the
Tight setting to wrap
the text around the
image.*

Figure 2-29:
*Sometimes you'll see
special tabs appear
on the ribbon that
aren't usually there.
That's the case with
the Format Picture
tab that shows up
when you insert or
select a photo. With
these tools you can
resize, crop and
change the transpar-
ency of your pics.
You can add special
effects like drop
shadows.*

Dropping other media into your Word document follows pretty much the same
steps described on page 77. You drag the object from the media browser (Shift-⌘-M)
and drop it on the page. Then you format it using the tools on the ribbon. ClipArt
uses the same Format Picture tab that you use with photos, while the Format tabs for
shapes is slightly different. Symbols are treated like characters, so there's no special
formatting tab. Audio and video media are simple to use, but require a couple special
techniques.

Playing Audio and Video in your Word Documents

You're probably going to want to preview a video or audio clip before you drop it into your Word document. That's easy to do from the media browser, just double-click the likely candidate.

Use the familiar drag-and-drop technique to copy your media from the browser to your document page. Video clips display a picture from the movie, while audio clips display a speaker icon. You can resize either of these images in your document using the same techniques you'd use to format a picture. To play audio or video clips, right-click (Control-click) the object and then choose Play from the shortcut menu.

Recording and Running Macros

A macro is like a script: a step-by-step series of commands that Word performs, rapid-fire, each time the macro is run. Although they definitely qualify as a power-user feature, you should consider this feature any time you find yourself facing a repetitive, tedious editing task. For example:

- Changing three different character names in one pass (which is required for each chapter of the novel you just finished).
- Drawing a table with the months of the year automatically listed down the first column and the names of all salespeople across the top. (All you have to do to complete the daily sales report is fill in the figures.)
- Saving the table document above as a Word document in your Sales folder and saving an additional copy as a web page (which you can now upload to the company intranet).

Office's macros are actually tiny programs written in a programming language called Visual Basic for Applications (VBA). People with programming skills and a lot of time on their hands can make VBA do astounding tricks; fortunately, you don't need to learn the language. You can generally get away with using Word's macro recorder, a "watch me" mode where Word writes the macro for you as you traverse the various steps once yourself. Once you've recorded the macro in this way, Word is ready to execute those actions automatically, like a software robot that's wired on caffeine.

Tip: A macro is saved into a document or a template. Thereafter, it works only when you've opened that same document (or a document based on that template). Macros in global templates are loaded whenever the template is loaded

To make a macro available in all Word documents, move it into the Normal template, as described under "Organizing Your Templates" on page 85. Fortunately, macros you create by recording are stored in the Normal template, so they're always available.

Creating a Macro

Even without knowing Visual Basic, you can create a macro for almost anything you know how to do in Word. Think of the macro recorder as a tape recorder that "listens" to what you do, and then replays it on command.

Note: The macro-recording feature in Word can't record mouse movements (other than menu selections and button clicks); so if your macro involves selecting text or moving the insertion point on the page, do it using keyboard shortcuts.

In this example, the company you work for has been sold, and you'd like to create a macro that goes through a document and replaces the old company name with the new one. Because you'll have to do this on dozens or hundreds of existing documents, you decide to store it as a macro that you can trigger at will.

1. **Open a document that needs your Find/Replace surgery. Choose Tools→ Macro→Record New Macro.**

   The Record Macro dialog box opens, as shown at bottom in Figure 2-30.

2. **Type a name for the new macro.**

   If you find it a bit nerdy that you have to name the macro before you've even created it, just wait—Word's nerdiness is only warming up. For example, you're not allowed to use commas, periods, or even spaces in the name of your macro. In Figure 2-30, the macro has been named ReplaceCo.

Note: If you assign a macro the same name as an existing macro, Word replaces the original one without so much as a by-your-leave. If you give your macro the same name as a macro that already exists, Word gives you a warning.

Type a description, too, so that later you'll remember what this macro was designed to do.

Again, before you've even created the macro, you must now tell Word how you intend to trigger this macro in the future. To do so, either press a key combination of your choice or click a button on a toolbar. (You can always change your mind, or choose both methods, later.)

3. **To create a button on one of your toolbars for this macro, click Toolbars.**

   The Customize dialog box appears, with a mutant version of your macro's name (such as Normal.NewMacros.ReplaceCo) displayed on the right. Drag the macro's name from the Customize dialog box to the Standard toolbar or any open toolbar. (More on dragging to toolbars in Chapter 22.)

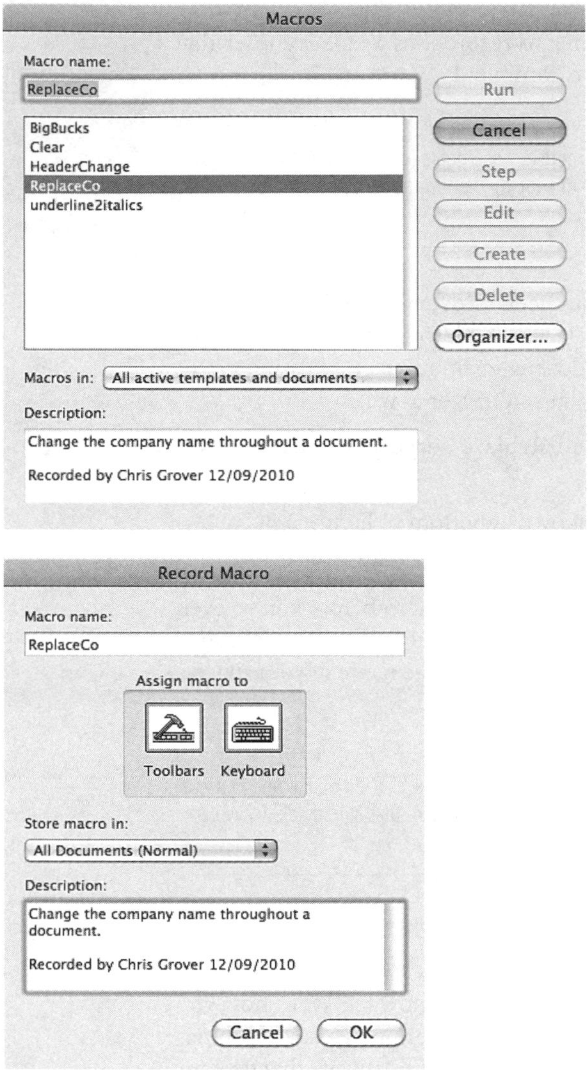

Figure 2-30:
Top: The Macros dialog box, listing all macros you've created. Here's your opportunity to delete one or edit it, line by line. You can't rename one, however, except by entering the Visual Basic Editor described at the end of this chapter.

Bottom: All currently open documents appear in the "Store macro in" pop-up menu. If you store it in the Normal template, it will be available to you in all Word documents. You can click Pause while recording the macro if you need to leave the Mac for any reason.

4. **If you want this macro to be available in only one document (as opposed to all Word documents), choose the name of the current document from the "Store macro in" pop-up menu.**

   Initially, Word assumes that you want the macro available to any Word document, so it stores the macro in your Normal template.

5. **To assign a keyboard shortcut to the new macro, click Keyboard.**

   The Customize Keyboard dialog box opens, with the cursor blinking in the "Press new shortcut key" box. Press a key combination on your keyboard (⌘-R, say) that will be easy for you to remember.

   The combination must include Control, ⌘, Control-⌘, or Shift-Control plus one or two other keys, such as letters and numbers. If the combination you press is already in use, you'll see the name of the conflicting command under "Currently assigned to"; see page 643 for more on changing Word keystrokes.

   Click Assign, and then click OK.

6. **Click OK to begin recording the macro.**

   Finally, you return to your document. Everything appears to be as it was. This is your opportunity to actually perform the steps that you want Word to reproduce later. In this example, you'll record a search-and-replace operation, thusly:

7. **Choose Edit→Replace. Type the old company name in the "Find what" box, press Tab, and then type the new name in the "Replace with" box. Click Replace All.**

   Word makes the replacement everywhere in the document.

8. **Close the Replace box, and then Tools→Macro→Stop Recording.**

   That's it—you've just recorded a macro. If you'd like to test it on the document that's still open before you, choose Edit→Undo Replace All (to undo the effects of your manual search-and-replace), and then trigger the macro as described below.

Tip: The macro doesn't become immortalized in your Normal template until you quit Word. If your Mac has a tendency to crash or freeze every now and then, you'd be wise to quit Word shortly after recording any important macros. Otherwise, you'll launch Word after a freeze or crash only to find that the macro has disappeared.

Running a Macro

As with so much else in Office, there are several ways to run a macro that you (or other people) have recorded. Here's a list:

- Press the keystroke that you assigned to the macro when you created it.
- Choose the macro in the Tools→Macro→Macros dialog box (Figure 2-30, top) and then click Run.
- Click the toolbar button that you assigned to the macro when you created it.

- Set up a macro to run automatically. To do this, give the macro one of these special names: AutoExec (runs when Word first launches), AutoExit (when you quit Word), AutoOpen (when you open an existing document), AutoNew (when you start a new document—very useful), or AutoClose (close a document).

You can also add your macro to any of the Word menus, as described on page 740. If you save a document that has macros, you need to choose the .docm file format. For the reasons why, see the explanation on page 445.

Tip: If you plan to record and tweak a lot of macros, it's worthwhile adding the Developer tab to your ribbon (see Figure 2-31). It gives you a quick and easy way to record, pause and stop the macro recorder. To add the Developer tab, click the ribbon preferences button in the lower-right corner of the ribbon. Scroll the "Show or hide tabs…" list until you see the Developer checkbox. Select it and click OK.

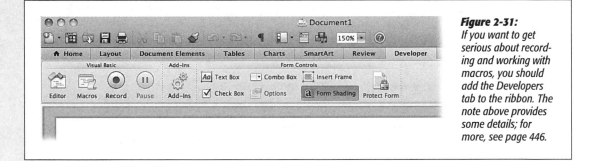

Figure 2-31:
If you want to get serious about recording and working with macros, you should add the Developers tab to the ribbon. The note above provides some details; for more, see page 446.

The Macro Organizer

As with styles, AutoText, and toolbars, you can copy macros between documents or templates using Word's Organizer (see page 85 for complete instructions). Only these two subtleties make macro copying different:

- In the steps on page 85, click the Macro Projects tab instead of the Templates tab.
- You can't copy individual macros—only macro bundles called macro projects. (All of the macros you create wind up in a single macro project called NewMacros.)

Learning about Visual Basic

When you record a macro, Word automatically translates it into the Visual Basic programming language. To see how it looks, click a macro in the Macros dialog box (choose Tools→Macro→Macros) and click Edit. A supplementary program called Visual Basic Editor opens, displaying all the code for that macro. If you know anything about programming, you can learn quite a bit about Visual Basic just by examining the code.

Sometimes even the novice can make some sense of this code. For example, if you've recorded a macro that blows up your document window to 150 percent, you'll see a line of code that says ActiveWindow.ActivePane.View.Zoom.Percentage = 150. You don't have to be a rocket scientist to realize that you can edit the 150 if it turns out to be too much magnification. You could replace that number with 125 and then choose File→Close and Return to Microsoft Word, having successfully edited your macro. (The same trick works very well for modifying search-and-replace macros; it's very easy to change the phrases Word searches for and replaces with.)

Word also has help screens that describe the Visual Basic objects (commands) that you assemble to create a macro. Some commands are difficult or impossible to record in a macro. If you create lots of macros, or feel inclined to debug existing macros, the time may come when you need to delve into Visual Basic.

Note: There are more details about recording macros and tweaking Visual Basic code in Excel on page 441. You can apply the techniques you learn there to your Word macros.

Organizing Your Templates

Every Word document is based on at least one document template. If you don't choose a specific template from the Document Gallery, Word uses the Normal template to specify things like font and paragraph styles. If you want to change the settings in the Normal template, you can open and edit it like any other template or document. You'll find Normal.dotm at Home→Library→Application Support→ Microsoft→Office→User Templates. When you open Normal.dotm, you see a blank document, but behind the scenes are the settings for fonts, margins, and paragraph styles. So, for example, if you want to change the font used in the Normal template, simply choose a new font, size, and style from the font menu and then save (⌘-S) and close (⌘-W) the template. Now when you choose File→New Blank Document, the new document uses your newly chosen font.

The Styles, AutoText, Toolbars, and Macros stored in Normal.dotm are available to your new blank documents, but what if you want to copy a new item, say a paragraph style from one template to another (see Figure 2-32)? That's a job for the Organizer. First, open the documents that have the styles you want to copy. If you want to copy styles from more than one template, go ahead and open them in different windows. To open the Organizer, go to Tools→Templates and Add-ins and then click the Organizer button in the lower-right corner. The Organizer window opens, displaying two boxes. You load a template into the Organizer using the menus below the boxes, and then use the buttons in the middle to copy, delete, or rename the items. The Organizer works the same whether you are managing styles, AutoText, Toolbars, or Macro Projects. You aren't limited to working with the Normal template; you can copy items to and from any template that's displayed in the Organizer.

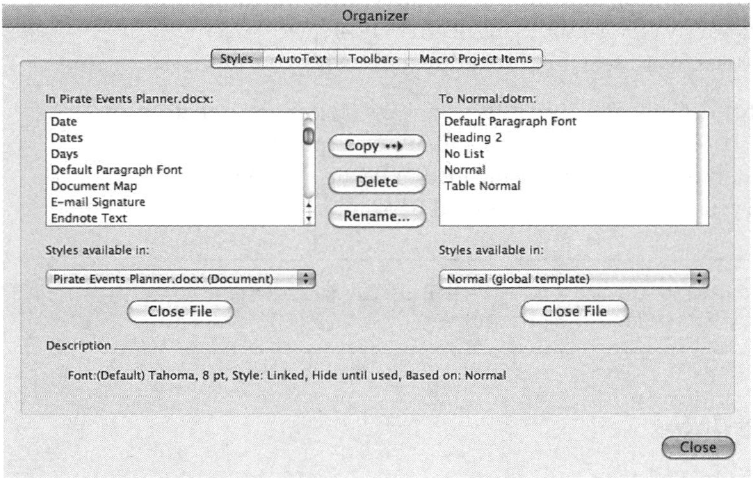

Figure 2-32:
Say you've created a paragraph style in a document (Pirate Events Planner.docx, in this example), and you'd like to be able to use it in every new, blank document you start. Click the style in the left box (Date, for example), and then click the Copy button. Word adds the Date style to the Normal template, so you can apply it to text in any document you create in Word.

Setting Up Documents and Pages

Your document makes a first impression before anyone reads a word. The paper size, color, and borders give the reader an overall sense of the document's theme and quality. Margins, the text layout, and perhaps a watermark send further visual clues. When your reader looks closer, the typeface, its size and style also communicate a message. Your choices about your document help to determine whether your readers are receptive to your message, or not.

This chapter shows you how to format all the elements of your document from the macro view (the document) to the micro view (individual characters). This chapter is divided into two parts. Word gives you lots of tools to format your document—some might complain that there are so many it's hard to know which to use. This book divides those tools into two camps. The first half of this chapter, "Let Word Format Your Document Automatically," focuses on the tools that are the easiest to use. You'll learn how to use Templates, Themes and Styles. Then if you want to learn more, you can roll up your sleeves and dig into the details about manually formatting your document, pages, paragraphs and fonts.

Let Word Format Your Document Automatically

Not everyone has the skill, desire or luxury of time to be a page layout artist. You may be a college student cranking out a term paper, a concerned citizen sending a letter to the Board of Supervisors or a business exec working on a quarterly report. You want your work to look good, but you know you'll be judged on the content and that's where you want to spend your time. Word can help. You can use templates, themes, and Quick Styles that were predesigned by graphic artists to make your work look professional. When you go this route, you don't have to spend time setting each margins, choosing matching fonts or deciding the point size for individual headers. Your brainpower can focus on your message.

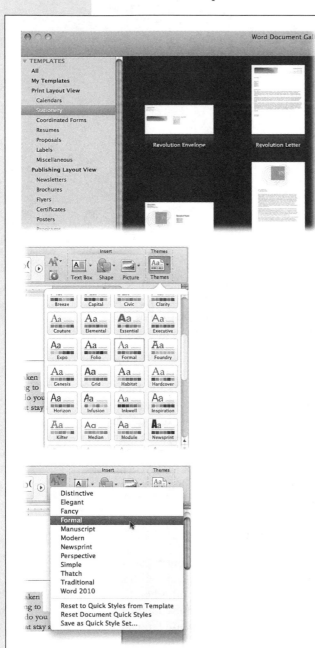

Figure 3-1:
For the quickest route to a well-formatted document, use one or more of these tools. At the top, you have templates—prebuilt documents where you fill in the blanks. In the middle you have themes—coordinated fonts, colors, and effects at the click of a button. And at the bottom you have Quick Styles—choose one to automatically format all the paragraphs in your document.

All the formatting needed for your document can be handled with a few mouse clicks when you learn how to do three simple tasks:

- **Choose a template** when you're first creating your document. Templates contain both content and design elements. Go to File→New from Template (Shift-⌘-P) to open the Word Document Gallery and pick a Template that matches your project. Templates are available for letters, proposals, resumés, and term papers.

- **Choose a theme** to change the appearance of your document. Themes are collections of matching colors, fonts, and effects. You can apply a theme when you start your document or you can change the theme midstream. All it takes is a click of your mouse.

- **Choose a Quick Style** to format a specific element on the page. Quick Styles are used to format paragraphs and they work hand in hand with templates and themes. When you use a Quick Style, word applies attractive, matching formats to the headings and body of your document. Like themes, you can choose a Quick Style when you begin or you can easily change to a different quick style at any time.

Choose a Template

When you use a template, you're taking advantage of the work and wisdom of those who have gone before you. As the saying goes, "Why reinvent the wheel?" Microsoft must adhere to this philosophy because, in Word, they keep adding templates with each new version of Word. Just look at the Gallery (press Shift-⌘-P or click the Template Gallery button). You'll find Microsoft's supplied templates in three major categories that correspond to the Word view used to work with them:

- **Print Layout view**. These are probably the templates that you'll use most of the time, they include documents like proposals, resumés, labels and forms.

- **Publishing Layout view**. Use these templates for more design-intensive projects like brochures, newsletters, catalogs, and business cards. As the name indicates, you use Word's publishing tools in Publishing Layout view.

- **Notebook Layout view**. The templates in this category work with Word's Notebook Layout view. They're designed to help you organize notes and random thoughts during lectures or when you're brainstorming.

Note: If you create your own templates as explained on page 92, Word stores them in the My Templates category.

Don't see the template you want in those groups? Don't worry. As they say in the infomercials: Wait. There's more! Scroll down to the bottom of the list and click Online Templates. The gallery connects to the Microsoft website and dozens of new categories appear in the alphabetized list. Here's a random sampling to give you an idea of what you'll find:

- Templates beginning with the letter B: brochures, budgets, business cards.
- Templates beginning with the letter F: faxes, flyers, forms.
- Templates beginning with the letter I: inventories, invitations, invoices.
- Templates beginning with the letter R: receipts, reports, and resumés/CVs.

You get the idea. However, if that's not enough, with typical Microsoftian overkill there's even a category called More Templates, where, believe it or not, you find hundreds of uncategorized templates. Now you know why there's a search box in the upper-right corner of the Gallery.

When you use a template, you're not opening a template file, you're opening a copy of it, sort of like pulling the top sheet off a pad of forms. The original template file remains untouched. Here are some of the goodies you'll find in a new document you've opened from a template:

- **Graphics**. Templates for brochures, business cards, greeting cards, and newsletters almost always include drawing, clip art, lines, and borders. Frequently, you'll find templates that include photos (Figure 3-2).
- **Formatting.** Setting up the page formats, indents, and line spacing, and positioning every single bit of text on the page can be a big job. For projects like forms, purchase orders, and invoices, you may end up tearing your hair out. Fortunately, using a template is a lot easier on your scalp.
- **Boilerplate text.** Often in templates the text is just there for position. You replace the text with your own words. However, some templates include boilerplate text that you want to leave in place. Contracts, fax cover pages, forms, and even resumés may include body text or headings that you want to keep.
- **AutoText entries.** Sophisticated templates sometimes add automated features like AutoText entries (page 55). A template designed to handle a common complaint may include a lengthy AutoText entry that begins, "We are so very sorry that the widget didn't live up to your expectations." To insert the diatribe, all you have to do is type *sorry*, and then go to Insert→AutoText and choose from the list.
- **Content controls.** Some templates include widgets, like text boxes and drop-down menus, that let you create electronic forms in Word, just like the forms you fill out on websites.

Figure 3-2:
When you use a template, you get a professionally designed preformatted document. Many templates include impressive graphics and high quality photos. All you need to do is fill in your message. More complex templates like this one for a daycare flyer use the page layout tools provided by Word's Publishing Layout view (page 225).

Using Templates

Whether it's installed on your computer or stored online at Microsoft, it's easy to start using a template. After you open the Gallery (Shift-⌘-P), click one of the template thumbnails and you see a preview in the gallery's right panel. (If you don't see a preview, click the expand button shown in Figure 3-3.) If you're happy with the template, click the Choose button to open it in Word, or you can double-click a template thumbnail. At that point you can start typing your text and headlines. As for pictures and other graphics, you may be able to use those that come with the template, or you may have some of your own that are better suited.

Make sure you replace all that fake Latin text, or you're likely to get some chuckles from your readers. Better yet, have someone else look over your document. Surprisingly, the body text almost always gets swapped just fine, it's the odd heading, caption or even address block that slips everyone's notice.

Note: Many of the Online Templates were designed and uploaded by "the Microsoft Community." When you first open one of these templates, you see a warning from Microsoft mentioning that point and absolving the company from any virus or hacker-type problems that may arise. It's unlikely that you'll run into a problem, but if you stay awake at night worrying about such things, stick to the installed templates and avoid the ones online.

Modifying, Saving, and Installing Templates

Templates bring consistency to your work, which means you can use them as a tool to promote your company image or brand. Suppose you run an office and you want all your letters, memos and reports to present the same image. Choose some templates that have the look you want. In some cases you may want to add your own boilerplate text. If you make changes to the original template, you can always save the new improved version as a template:

1. **Choose File→Save As.**

   The Save File panel opens.

2. **Set the Format menu to "Word Template (.dotx)" and click Save.**

   Word automatically saves the template on your computer in a special folder for templates. So the next time you need the template, it appears in the gallery's My Templates category. Templates that include macros must be saved in the .dotm file format. For the details see the explanation on page 445.

If you're a Word power user, you may be in charge of designing templates for your office and making sure they're available to everyone. You've followed the steps above to tweak a template for use in your office and now you need to share them in an office that includes both Macs and PCs. See the box on page 93 for details on Word's template folders.

Choose a Theme

When you're on deadline putting together, say, a business proposal, you don't want to waste precious minutes worrying about fonts, heading colors, and the design of tables, charts, and graphs. Instead, simply choose a theme with a click of your mouse, and you've got a professional-looking document, with coordinated colors, fonts, and effects. Unlike templates, themes don't mess around with page layout issues like margins or the positioning of a photograph. That means you can apply a theme to document that you've finished and it won't change the content or layout; it just changes its look.

Where Oh Where Are My Template Files?

The folder where Word stores your templates is easy for Word to find, but a little harder for humans. User templates are buried several folders deep in your Mac Library folder. If you're sharing templates with the others in your office, you'll want to make note of the location, so you can put it in the same spot on your coworkers' computers.

For Macs the Office template folder is usually: *[User]→ Library→Application Support→Microsoft→Office→User Templates→My Templates.*

If you're sharing templates with Windows users, the folder is usually: *Users→[User Name]→AppData→Roaming→ Microsoft→Templates.*

There's always a chance that someone changed the folder where Office templates are stashed. If you want to double check the template folder location, Go to Word→Preferences→Personal Settings→File Locations and look for User templates. If you can't get a complete view of the path in the click the Modify button to open a Finder window.

Thumbnails · Expand/collapse Preview panel · Preview

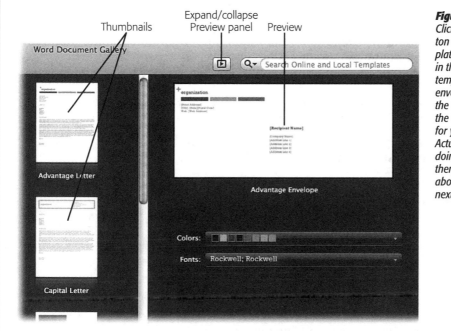

Figure 3-3:
Click the Expand button to open the template preview pane in the Gallery. Some templates, like this envelope, give you the option to change the colors and fonts for your document. Actually, what you're doing is choosing a theme. You'll learn about themes in the next section.

Themes are made up of three parts:

- **Colors.** Each theme contains twelve colors, each of which is assigned to a specific document part. One color (usually black) is used for body text. Another color (dark blue, say) is used for Heading 1 paragraphs. Lesser headings—like Heading 2 and Heading 3—may use a lighter shade of the same color. Other complementary colors are used for accent and hyperlinks (links to the Internet).

- **Fonts.** Each theme specifies one or two fonts—one for the body text and one for headings. Also known as typefaces, fonts define the actual shape of the letters on the screen and on the page. They have a subtle but significant effect on the appearance and feeling of a document. Some typefaces don't always play well with others, but fortunately, you don't have to worry about that when you choose themes, since their typeface combinations are always compatible.

- **Effects.** Each theme uses one of Word's built-in graphic effects. These effects include design touches like shadows, line styles, 3-D, and so on. Most of these effects have more of an impact in PowerPoint presentations than in Word documents, but they come with the theme's package.

Tip: It you regularly make presentations in PowerPoint, it's good to know that Word and PowerPoint share the same themes. That means after you've wowed them at the projector you can leave matching takeaway pieces printed in Word.

When you choose a theme, you're applying color, font, and effect formatting to the elements in your document (Figure 3-4).

Here are examples of the parts of your document that take their formatting cues from the selected theme:

- **Body text.** Font, size, style, and color.
- **Headings.** Font, size, style, and color.
- **Tables.** Font specs (same as above), border and line styles, and colors.
- **Charts.** Font specs, borders, lines, chart graphic styles, and colors.
- **Picture.** Border colors.
- **SmartArt.** Font specs and graphic colors.
- **Clip art.** Major outline and border colors.
- **Drop caps.** Font specs and color.
- **WordArt.** Font colors change, but the actual type style remains the same.

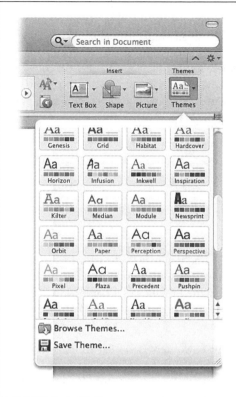

Figure 3-4:
Word's themes are prepackaged collections of colors, fonts and effects that work together to create attractive pages. To apply a theme, go to Home | Themes→Theme and click on one of the themes in the menu shown here. Not what you wanted? No problem; just click on another or press ⌘-Z to undo the theme.

FREQUENTLY ASKED QUESTION

Apply Themes from the Ribbon

On the ribbon, sometimes I see a single menu for themes and other times I see menus for fonts and colors, too. What gives?

The Theme options on the ribbon change depending on Word's view setting. If you're in Draft, Outline or Page Layout view, you see the menu shown in Figure 3-4, where a single theme applies both the fonts and colors. If you're in Publishing Layout view, you also see separate menus for fonts and colors. The Notebook Layout view doesn't make use of themes—instead you choose fonts, colors and effects manually.

If you use Themes a lot, you may want to add Themes to the Layout ribbon. To do that, go to Word→Preferences→ Personal Settings→Ribbon. Then, in the scrolling list under Layout, select the Themes checkbox.

Finding More Themes

Word comes with more than 50 built-in themes, but you may still find yourself look-ing for more. Perhaps you work in an office on a computer that was set up by your employer, and someone has created official company themes that you need to use. If that's the case, then you need to know where to look for those themes on your com-puter, especially if you (or someone you love) has inadvertently moved them. You can also look beyond your computer: Creative types are constantly coming up with new, exciting themes and sharing them on the Web.

Tip: It's not hard to create your own custom themes, especially if you start with an existing theme and make modifications.

Saving and Sharing Custom Themes

Open the Themes menu (Home→Themes), and you may find custom themes at the top of the list. Custom themes are ones that you or someone else created. In the mid-dle of the themes menu you see the predesigned themes that come with Word. At the very bottom, there are two options for the I-wanna-do-it-myself crowd: Browse Themes and Save Theme.

The process for sharing a theme with your coworkers is similar to the process for sharing templates, you need to find and copy the theme from your computer and to theirs. To open the folder where your custom themes are stored, go to Home→ Themes→Browse Themes. A Finder window opens displaying the folder and any custom themes you may have already created. It may also contain folders for sepa-rate Theme Fonts, Theme Colors, and Theme Effects.

If themes are stored (or moved) somewhere else on your computer, then they won't show up on the Themes menu, but you can search for them. To search for themes stored anywhere on your computer, type *thmx* in the Spotlight and click This Mac button, as shown in Figure 3-5.

Choose a Quick Style

You use styles to apply formatting to specific paragraphs. You want the title and headings to stand out from the text that makes up the body of your document. A paragraph style does just that by specifying the font, its size, color, and style (regular, bold, or italic). Styles also set spacing before and after a paragraph, indents from the margins, tabs and other special text-handling issues.

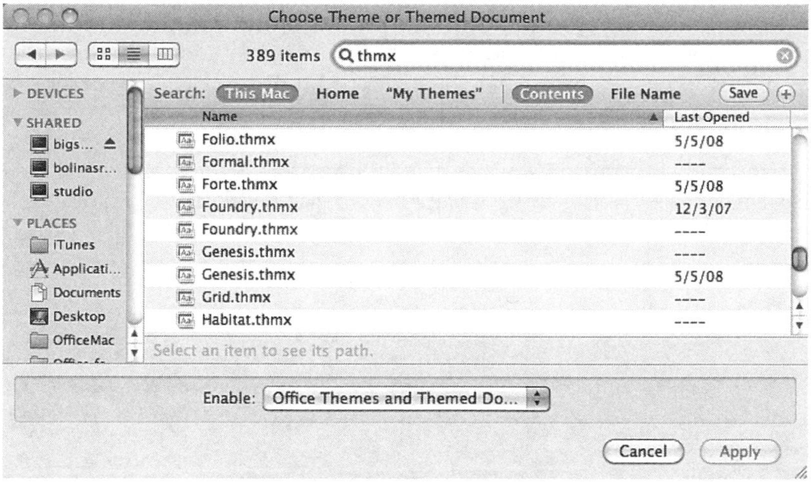

Figure 3-5:
After you type thmx
in the search box, you
can choose to search
your entire computer
(This Mac), your user
folder (Home) or in
your themes folder
(My Themes).

Writing with Style

Suppose you're creating a guide for business travelers. First you type the title for you document: *Business Travel to Pirate's Cove*. Because this is the title for the document, you want it bigger and bolder than anything else on the page. You could manually format the paragraph, but why go to all that trouble when Word has a Title style that's perfectly suited for the job? You can use the ribbon to apply that style. First make sure the insertion point is still in the title paragraph. Then, go to Home | Styles and in the scrolling list of styles, choose Title. Immediately, your title takes on a new big, bold look. Appropriately, the Title is at the top of your document, and may even be centered. When you press Return, Word gives you a new paragraph and automatically it uses the Normal style—the perfect format for body of your document. You can now add your introductory text for traveling to Pirate's Cove.

Getting into the meat of the subject, you add a major heading: "What to Wear." Again, instead of formatting the text manually, you use Word's Heading 1 style. This is a major topic, but it's not quite as important as the title, so by using the Heading 1 style, Word formats it smaller and less boldly than the title. A little more body text, and you're ready for a not-so-major heading: "Day Wear", which you style with Heading 2. You go on to describe appropriate clothing for a trip to Pirate's Cove. When you're finished, your document may look like Figure 3-6. Without having to sweat the details, you've created a good-looking document. You didn't have to delve into layer after layer of dialog boxes to make sure the spacing before a major heading is greater than the spacing before a minor heading.

As you can tell from the above experiment, a single style performs several formatting feats at once. Each paragraph style defines all the font and paragraph settings. When you apply a style you don't have to manually choose a font size or color. You don't have to dig into the dialog boxes where you set indents, tabs, and the distance between lines and paragraphs. After you've applied style names to the paragraphs in your document, you can use Quick Styles to try out different looks.

Tip: You can quickly apply heading styles as you type by using shortcut keys. Use ⌘-Option and the heading level you want to apply. For example, ⌘-Option-3 applies Heading 3 to the current paragraph.

Styles scrolling menu   Quick Styles menu

Figure 3-6:
It's easy to use the ribbon to apply styles as you type. In general, Word applies the Normal style as you work. When you need to format a heading, just click on the style in the ribbon.

Business Travel to Pirate's Cove

Are business trips all the same? No they're not. Just ask anyone whose travels have taken him or her to Pirate's Cove. When your boss asks you to risk life and limb by traveling to this most dangerous place on the planet, do you say, "You've got to be kidding!" or do you say, "Give me 10 minutes to pack." Well, if you follow the tips here, you can turn that stay a Pirate's Cove into a profitable venture for you and the home office.

What to Wear

By mixing and matching different accessories, you can carry less but have a new look for lunch, dinner and the occasional tar and feathering get-togethers. Finish your outfit with our Black Beard Boots, great for those moments when you must wade from ship to shore.

Day Wear

During the day, it's best to go for that Edward Teach look if you want to fit in with the buccaneer's of Pirates Cove and the neighboring communities. So we offer a brown pants, puffy-sleeved shirts and leather cloth vests, died in a variety of colors. This outfit lightweight, flexible and provides a certain amount

Get a New Look with Quick Styles

Want to change the look of your document with a single mouse click? You can do that from the Quick Styles menu. Go to Home | Styles and then choose Elegant from the Quick Styles menu. Suddenly, your document has a hanging title, new margins, and new font specifications all around. As you can see in Figure 3-7, when you choose a Quick Style, you change the settings for several paragraph styles all at once. The Title, Normal, Heading 1, and Heading 2 styles are quite different from the example in Figure 3-6. Go ahead and try out some of the different Quick Styles. You know you want to.

Later in this chapter, you'll learn how to manually modify a single style (page 120).

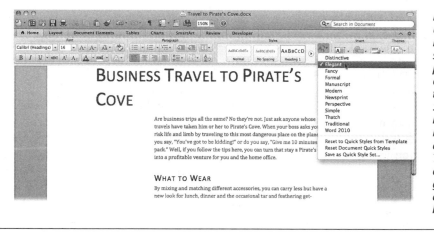

Figure 3-7:
Use the Quick Styles menu to change the settings for several paragraph styles at once. In this example, the Elegant Quick Style changed the look of the Title, Normal, Heading, 1 and Heading 2 styles. The hanging title and wide left margin give the document a dramatically different look.

UP TO SPEED

Applying Styles: Select All or Nothing At All

Sometimes it takes a while to get a handle on applying paragraph styles. If you apply styles as you're typing, Word applies the style to the entire paragraph with the blinking insertion point. If you're going back and applying styles to a paragraph, the rule of thumb is to select all (the entire paragraph) or nothing at all (just put the insertion point back in the paragraph).

Almost always, you want to apply the paragraph style to the entire paragraph. You can do this by selecting the entire paragraph, including the paragraph mark at the end of it, which is normally hidden. However the easiest way to apply a style to a paragraph is to click once to put the insertion point in the paragraph, without selecting anything, not even a single character. Then, when you choose a style from the ribbon (Home | Styles), it formats the entire paragraph. It's the same as if you selected the entire paragraph and applied the style.

If you select only a few characters in the paragraph, Word assumes you want to apply the formatting to the selected characters only, and the results might not be what you expected.

When styles aren't working the way you expect, remember that the formatting is stored with the invisible paragraph mark. (To see the paragraph marks, click the ¶ button in the Standard toolbar.) For example, if you're combining two paragraphs by deleting the break after the first paragraph, the new paragraph takes on the formatting of the second paragraph because its paragraph mark takes over the formatting chores.

Manually Formatting Your Document

It's easiest to let Word format your document automatically, using templates, themes, and Quick Styles described in the first part of this chapter. With these tools, you can dress up your documents with surprising variety. If you can't find anything that suits you, the rest of this chapter explains how to manually format all the elements in your document. Perhaps you want to tweak a single element in one of the built-in styles or maybe you have plans for an entirely new look you want to develop from scratch.

When it comes to formatting, Word attaches formatting details to three separate elements. Working from the outside toward the center, as if your document is an onion, the elements are:

- **Section formatting** determines the page size, orientation, color, and graphics (like watermarks). Many documents are a single section, so you might think of these settings as document formatting. That's not how Word sees it. These formatting options are applied to sections, so you can use different formatting for different chapters or individual pages or paragraphs in your document. Perhaps you want a couple of pages that show charts to use landscape orientation. Or maybe although most of your document uses a single column, there's one topic that lends itself to a two-column format.

- **Paragraph formatting** is handled by Word's styles. For example, you use different styles to format headings, body text or photo captions. The power of styles and Word's Quick Styles were seen earlier in this chapter. In this section, you learn how to customize paragraph settings and create your own styles.

- **Character formatting** changes the font, size and style of individual characters within a paragraph. Perhaps you want to emphasize a single word, so you apply italics or boldface to the type.

This section gives you all the details you need to manually format your document and, like the onion, it starts at the outer layer.

Choosing Paper Size and Layout

When you edit a document in Word, what you see on your computer looks almost exactly like the final printed page. To get that preview, Word needs to know some details about the paper you're using, like the page size and orientation. As usual, Word gives you more than one way to change these settings. The most visual method is to use the Layout tab ribbon (Figure 3-8). If you like the old-fashioned way, your mouse may already remember File→Page Setup leads to the Page Setup dialog box (Figure 3-9).

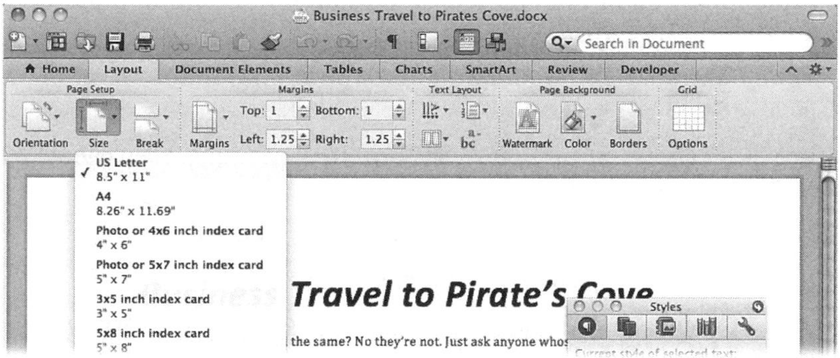

Figure 3-8:
Use the ribbon's Layout tab to choose page size, orientation and color. Here the page size menu is open, showing the variety of page options.

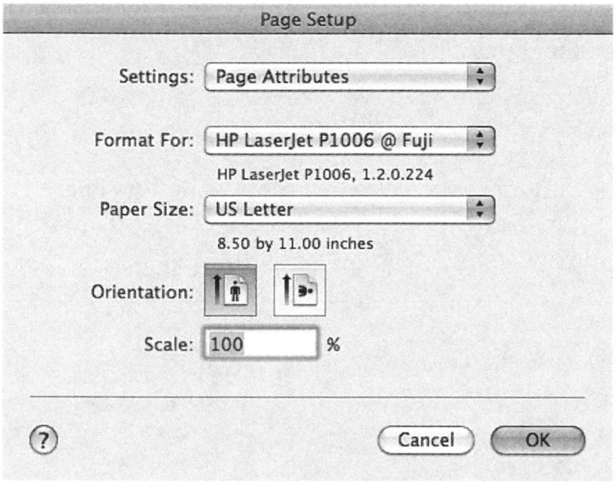

Figure 3-9:
The Page Setup box provides the same options as the ribbon, it's just not as flashy. Use the menu at the top to toggle between Page Attributes and the Microsoft Word panels.

Changing Paper Size

If you want to quickly change the page size to a standard paper size like letter, legal, or tabloid, then Layout→Page Setup→Size is the way to go (Figure 3-8). With one quick click, you change your document's size. If there's text in your document, Word reshapes it to fit the page. Say you change a 10-page document from letter size to the longer legal-size page. Word spreads out your text over the extra space, and you'll have fewer pages overall.

Suppose your company offers a gift card, and the size doesn't match any of the ones in Word's list. You can define a custom page size, but you'll need to use the Page Setup dialog box to do it.

1. **Go to File→Page Setup.**

   The Page Setup box opens.

2. **Click the Paper Size menu and scroll down to the bottom. Then choose Manage Custom sizes.**

   The Custom Paper Sizes box opens as shown in Figure 3-10.

3. **Click the + button to add a new custom size.**

   A new custom paper size item appears in the box on the left with the name "untitled." Numbers appear in the dimensions and margins, which you change in the next few steps.

4. **Type a new name for your custom paper size, such as *Gift Card*.**

   In the future, you'll use this name to choose this custom paper size.

5. **Set the width, height and margins.**

   You can use decimals, such as 6.5 inches in your sizes.

6. **Click OK.**

   From now on, your new custom paper size appears at the bottom of the Paper Size menu in the Page Setup dialog box. It doesn't appear in the ribbon's paper size list.

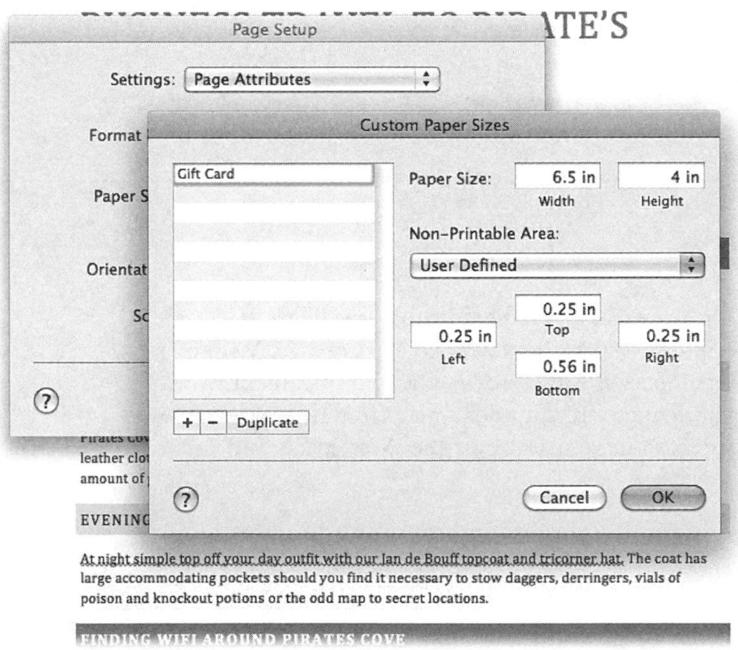

Figure 3-10:
There's a slim chance you need a paper size that's not already on Word's list. If that's the case, go to File→Page Setup and using the Paper Size menu, open the Custom Paper Sizes box shown here.

Setting Paper Orientation

Most business documents, school papers, and letters use a portrait page orientation, meaning the page is taller than it is wide. But sometimes you want a short, wide page—landscape page orientation—to accommodate a table, chart, or photo, or just for artistic effect. Whatever the reason, using the Orientation menu (Layout→Page Setup→Orientation) is the easiest way to make the change (Figure 3-11). Just click one of the two options: Portrait or Landscape.

Figure 3-11:
Click portrait or landscape to change the page orientation for your document. If you want to change the orientation for just a couple pages in the middle of a document, you need to divide your document into sections as described on page 196.

If you've already got the Page Setup box open (File→Page Setup), you'll find the Orientation options on the Page Attributes panel.

Setting Margins

Page margins are more than just empty space. The correct page margins make your document more readable. Generous page margins make text look inviting and give reviewers room for notes and comments. With narrower margins, you can squeeze more words on the page; however, having too many words per line makes your document difficult to read. With really long lines it's a challenge for readers to track from the end of one line back to the beginning of the next. Margins become even more important for complex documents, such as books or magazines with facing pages. With Word's margins and page setup tools, you can tackle a whole range of projects.

Selecting Preset Margins

Your first stop for margins should be the Preset margin menu on the ribbon Layout | Margins menu, where Word provides some standard, socially acceptable settings. The preset margins are a mixed bag of settings from a half inch to one and a quarter inches. For most documents, you can choose one of these preset margins and never look back (Figure 3-12). To select one of the preset margins, go to Layout | Margins, and then click one of the options.

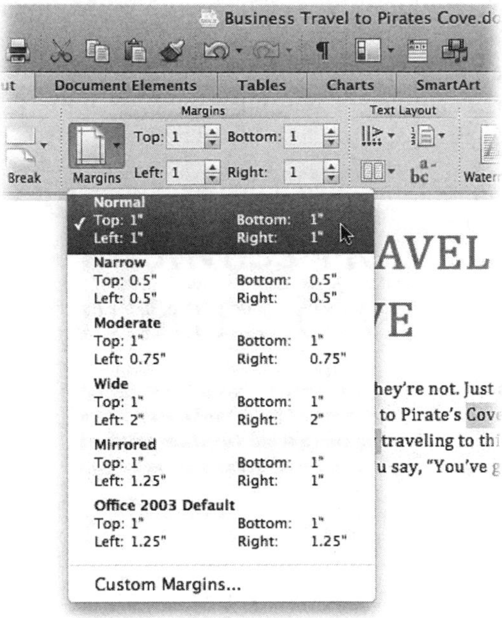

Figure 3-12:
The Margins menu provides some standard settings such as the ever popular one inch all the way around. Word calls this favorite of businesses and schools the Normal margin. If you've customized your margins, your most recent settings appear at the top of the menu.

For each of the preset margin options, you see dimensions and an icon that hints at the look of the page.

- **Normal** gives you one inch on all sides of the page.

- **Narrow** margins work well with multicolumn documents, giving you a little more room for each column.

- **Moderate** margins with three-quarter inches left and right let you squeeze a few more words in each line.

- The **Wide** preset gives you more room for marginal notes when you're proofing a manuscript.

- Use **Mirrored** margins when you're binding a document and want the outside page margins to be different from the inner margins at the binding.

- The **Office 2003 Default** margins match the standard margins for an earlier version of the Word. Use this if you want your new docs to be consistent with ghosts of Word docs past.

Note: Word measures margins from the edge of the page to the edge of the body text. Any headers and footers that you add (page 114) appear in the margin areas.

Setting Custom Margins

What if none of the preset margins on the menu suits your needs? Say your company's style guide insists on one-and-a-half-inch margins for all press releases. You need to change the Margins in the Document dialog box (Figure 3-13). Here are two ways to get there:

- On the ribbon, go to Layout | Margins→Custom Margins to open the Document box to the Margins tab.

- Using menus, go to File→Page Setup and then in the box, choose Microsoft Word→Margins.

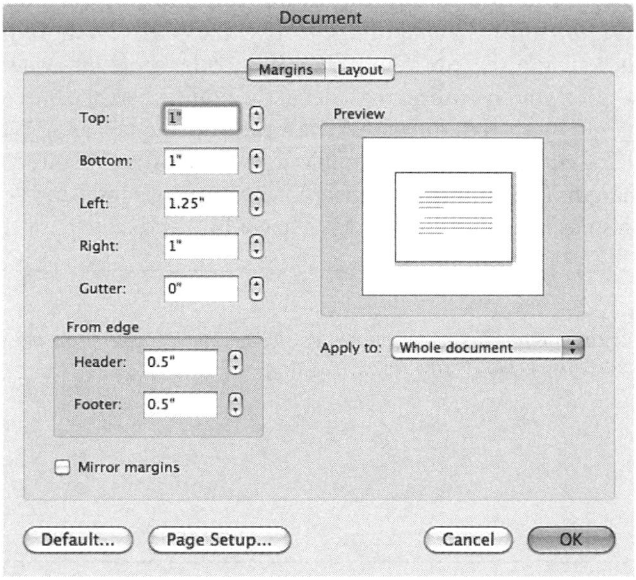

Figure 3-13:
Enter your custom margins in the boxes labeled, top, bottom, left and right. If you're binding your document, click the Mirror margins box and you can set different inside and outside margins. Margins can be applied to an entire document or, if you divide your document into sections, you can use different margins in each section.

The boxes in the Margins section already contain your document's current settings. To change the Top margin to one and a half inches, select the current setting, and then type 1.5, or you can click the arrows on the right side of the box to change the margin number. Make the same change in the Bottom, Left, and Right margin text boxes.

Tip: If inches isn't your preferred unit of measure you can use something different in most of the measurement boxes. Just type unit of measure after the number. For example, if you're a graphic artist you may prefer points, so you type *12 pt*. If you're of the metric persuasion, you can type *20 mm*.

Use the Gutter setting to account for the edge of your page that is hidden by a binding. As you change this setting, notice the cross hatch in the preview window that represents the gutter.

While you're here in the Page Setup box, double-check the page Orientation setting. Margins and page orientation have a combined effect. In other words, if you want a quarter-inch top margin, make sure the orientation is set correctly depending on whether you want the "top" of the page to be on the long side or the short side of the paper.

Using the Ruler to Set Margins

For a quick and easy way to change your margins, use the ruler. To permanently display the rulers, go to View→Ruler. To temporarily display the ruler, just move your mouse a bit beyond the left or top edge of your page and the ruler slides into view. To change the margin, position your mouse on the ruler at the point where the blue area that represents the margin meets the white area that represents the text area. When you hit the sweet spot, the cursor changes to a double arrow as shown in Figure 3-14. Drag to change the margin. This technique works on both the horizontal and vertical margins. You can also use the ruler to set indents (page 134) and tabs (page 106).

Figure 3-14:
When your cursor is over the margin on the ruler, it turns into a double arrow, as shown here. Click and drag to change the margin.

Setting Margins for Booklets

These days, you're not limited to printing on a single page and holding everything together with a staple. Many fancy printers and copy machines can print both sides of a page and there are all sorts of ways to bind your documents like a pro. If your office doesn't have the tools, there's a copy shop not far away that will do it for a price. Word has some special settings to make booklets and bound documents look sharp.

When you have a document with facing pages, click the Mirror margins box shown in Figure 3-13. The preview changes to show facing pages and the Left and Right margin boxes are renamed Inside and Outside. Notice that the gutter representation in the preview window moves to the inside of the two displayed pages.

Adding Color, Borders, and Watermarks

Every document has a paper size, orientation and margins, you're probably less likely to want to change the page color, add a border or a watermark. However, if the need arises, you can use these tools to get fancy.

Choosing Page Color

The Page Color option applies more to web pages than to printed pages, and as mentioned before, Word isn't your best option for creating web pages. When you're working with paper, you'll usually print on a different colored paper rather than printing a colored background on white paper. However, with heavy stock, you can use this feature on occasion to create postcards, colored covers, and so on.

Using the ribbon go to Layout | Page Background→Color to open the Page Color menu. You'll see two groups of colors: ones that are part of the documents Theme and standard colors such as red, blue, yellow, and so forth. Choosing a color is as simple as clicking on a color swatch.

If none of the options tickle your design fancy, click the More Colors option to open your Mac's standard color-choosing tools. For more details on using the Mac's color picker, see page 616.

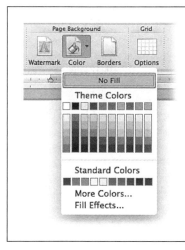

Figure 3-15:
Use this menu to change the background color for your pages. The Theme Colors for your document are shown at the top of the list, but you can click More Colors for different options or Fill Effects to create multicolor gradients.

Adding a Border

A tasteful, properly-applied border can add a certain flare to your document. However, an inappropriate border can make your document look cheesy. Enough said.

Okay, now that you've been warned, here's how to add page borders:

1. **Choose Layout | Page Background→Borders to open the Borders and Shading box (Figure 3-16).**

   The Borders and Shading box has three tabs. Make sure you're using the Page Border tab. (The first Borders tab puts borders around paragraphs, pictures, and other objects on the page.)

2. **In the left, choose a setting to define the border.**

   Start with the five settings on the left, to define the border in broad strokes ranging from no border to drop shadows. You can select only one of these settings.

3. **Choose a line style, color, and width, or choose an art border.**

   Decide whether your border will be a line or an art border—trees, hearts, pieces of cake, and so on. If you're going with a line border, choose a style from the drop-down menu. You can choose from more than two dozen lines, including solid, dotted, double, and wavy. Then use the drop-down menus to choose a line color and width.

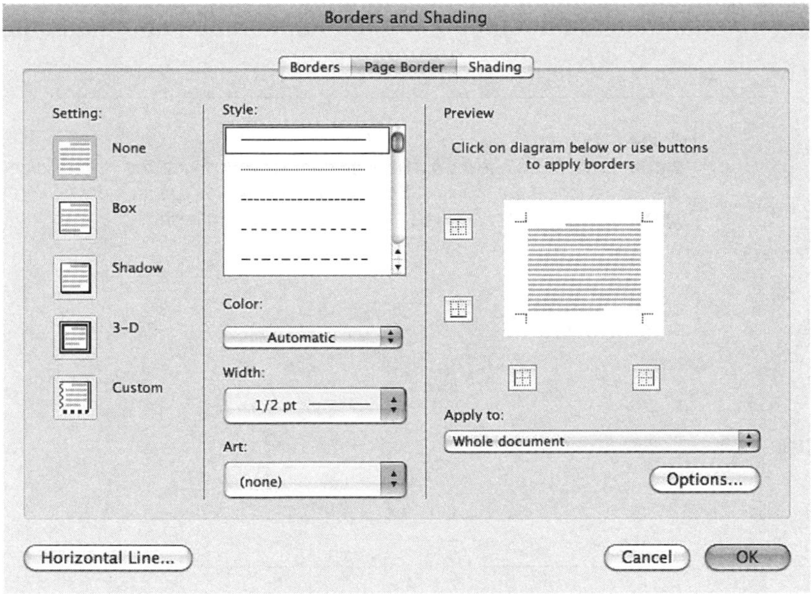

Figure 3-16:
The Borders and Shading box lets you apply borders to paragraphs, pictures, or pages. Make sure you're on the Page Border tab if you're applying page borders. You can use lines or artwork to form your borders.

If you want an art border, select your design from the menu. Note that some of the art styles use different patterns for different sides of the page and for the corner design.

Note: Whether you choose lines or art for your border, you can adjust the width. You can increase line widths to a thick 6 points and art widths to 31 points.

4. **Preview the border, and then select the sides of the page that will have borders.**

   The Preview on the right side of the Borders and Shading box shows what sides of your page will have borders. Click the borders to toggle them on or off. Using this technique, you can choose to show a border on a single side of the page or on any combination of sides.

5. **In the lower-right corner of the box, use the "Apply to" control to set the pages that will have borders.**

   Maybe you want your first page to have a different border from the rest of the document. If the first page of your document uses letterhead, you may want a first page with no border at all, so select "This section – all except first page". Or, to put a border around the cover page but no other pages, choose the "This section – first page only" setting. As with paper size and other page layout settings, Word lets you apply borders differently in different sections of your document.

6. **Click OK to accept the settings and to close the Borders and Shading box.**

Adding a Watermark

A true watermark is created in a process where a water-coated metal stamp imprints a design into the paper's surface during manufacture. The design is usually a paper company's logo. The presence of a watermark can also indicate a document's authenticity. Word can't create a real watermark, but it can replicate the effect by printing one faintly on the page, seemingly beneath the text (Figure 3-17). A watermark could be your company logo, or it could be words like CONFIDENTIAL, DRAFT, or DO NOT COPY, emblazoned diagonally across the page.

Suppose you'd like to have your company logo appear as a classy watermark on your document. Using your logo picture file as a watermark takes just a few steps:

1. **Go to Layout | Page Background→Watermark.**

   The Insert Watermark box appears. It has three main radio button options: "No watermark", Picture, and Text.

2. **Select the Picture radio button.**

   When you click one of these buttons, the appropriate fine-tuning options become available and the others fade to gray. For example, when you choose "Picture watermark," the Text watermark options are grayed out.

3. **Click the Select Picture button (shown in Figure 3-18) to open the Choose a Picture box.**

   A window opens where you can navigate to the folder with your logo's picture file.

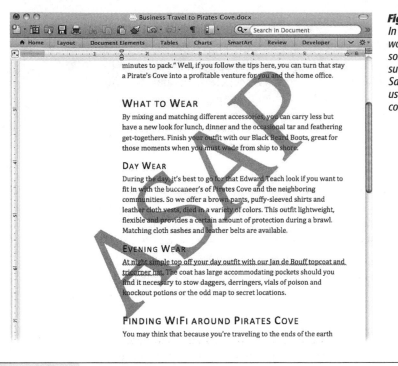

Figure 3-17:
*In Word, a watermark is a
word that tells your reader
something about the document
such as Confidential, Draft or
Sample. If you prefer, you can
use a graphic such as your
company logo.*

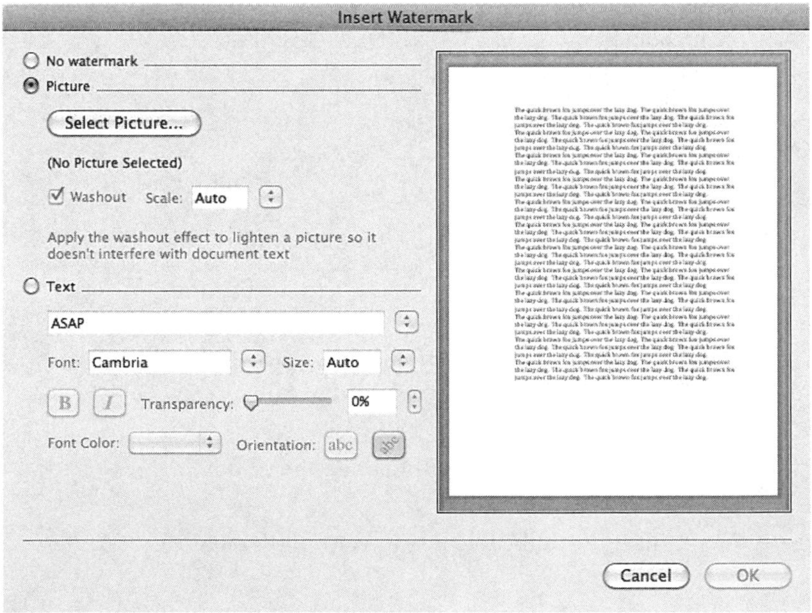

Figure 3-18:
*The Insert Watermark
box gives you three
radio buttons, "No
watermark", Picture
and Text. Click a
button to activate
the settings for that
option—the unrelated
settings are grayed
out.*

4. **Double-click the picture file to use it for your watermark, or, as an alternative, select your picture, and then click Insert.**

   The Choose a Picture box closes, and you see your picture displayed in the preview.

5. **Set the Scale and Washout options.**

   Now that you've chosen your picture file, you can use two more settings to make your watermark look spiffy. Use the Scale drop-down menu to adjust the size of your image so that it looks good on the page. You can choose from preset sizes of 50%, 100%, 150%, 200%, or 500%. Or you can choose the Auto setting, which scales your image to fit comfortably on the page. The Washout checkbox fades your image, making it easier to read text over the watermark.

6. **Click OK.**

   The Insert Watermark box closes and you see your company logo displayed behind the text in your document. Your new watermark appears on every page, but you won't see it in Draft or Outline view.

Tip: To get rid of an existing watermark, click the Watermark button and when the Insert Watermark box opens, choose "No watermark".

Adding Page Numbers, Headers, and Footers

Headers and footers are where Word puts the bits of information that appear at the top or bottom of every page (Figure 3-19). For multipage documents, they remind you of the page number, chapter title, and so on, as you read along. For business memos and reports, headers are a great place to repeat the document's subject and publication date. (If you're the author of the report and want your boss to know, consider adding your name under the title.)

Figure 3-19:
Document headers give the reader additional information that's not found in the text. This example shows the documents title and page number. A business memo might also include the date in the header.

Adding a Page Number

The most common and most helpful element that appears in headers and footers is probably the page number. So Word gives you a special tool to insert that single element. On the ribbon, go to Document Elements | Header and Footer→Page # or use the menu Insert→Page Numbers to open the box shown at the top of Figure 3-20.

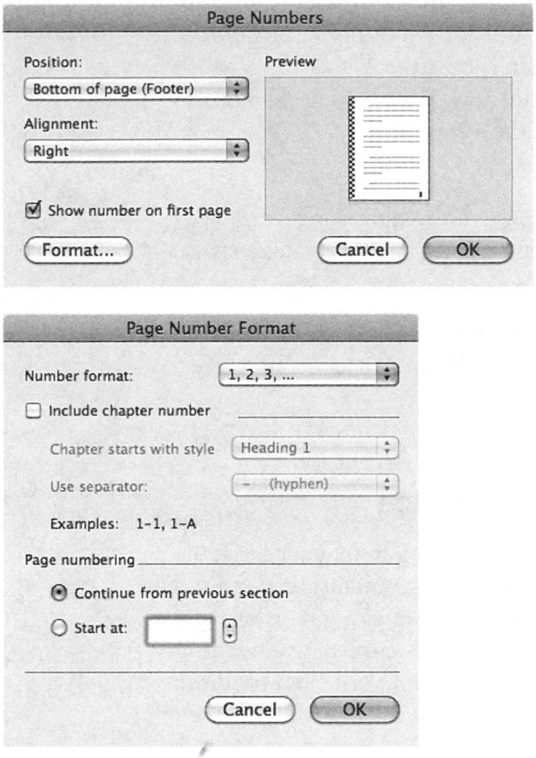

Figure 3-20:
Top: Use the Page Numbers box (View→Page Numbers) to position the numbers on the page. If you want to change the format for the number, click the Format button to open the box shown at the bottom.

Use the Position menu to select the top or bottom of your pages for the number. Then, use the Alignment to place the number left, right or center. If you're binding your document so that it has facing pages, you can choose to have page numbers on the outside or inside. Outside is the most common option for bound documents because it's easier for readers to find a page. Often documents forego a page number on the first page; however, if you want, check the "Show number on first page" box. A thumbnail size preview shows you the results of your page number settings, but for the best view, click the OK button to check out your document in Print Layout view. Naturally, Word automatically updates the numbers for each page.

You may not get your page numbers right the first time. Perhaps you need to start the page numbering for this document on a number other than 1, or maybe you just want to change the way the numbers look. To make these kinds of changes, open the Page Numbers box again, and then click the Format button to open the box shown at the bottom of Figure 3-20.

- The **Number format** menu at the top lets you choose between numerical or alphabetical numbering. Initially, Word uses 1, 2, 3, but for an introductory chapter you may prefer i, ii, iii, iv. In some cases you may want to use A, B, C.

- Click **Include chapter number** and you can display the chapter number along with the page number. Use the **Chapter starts with style** menu to let Word know what type of heading begins each chapter. Then, with the "Use separator" menu, you can choose the character (dash, period, colon) that separates the chapter number from the page number.

- The **Page numbering** section lets you start numbering pages with any number you choose. If you want to make a change, click the Start at button and type a number in the box.

Removing Page Numbers

What if you want to get rid of page numbers? Maybe you decided to go with a more complete header or footer. First make sure that you're in Print Layout view and then double-click on the header or footer area with the unneeded page numbers. When you're editing headers and footers, the rest of your document is faded out. Position the cursor over the page number, and you see a box around the number as shown in Figure 3-21. Select and delete the page number from one page and it removes the page number from all the others.

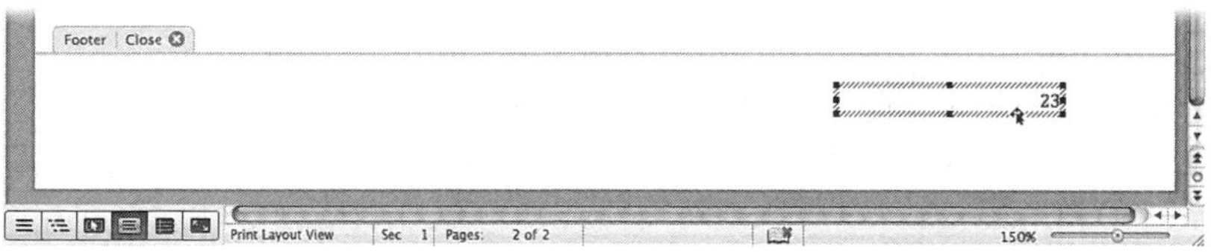

Figure 3-21:
When you see the box that holds your page number, you can click to select and then press Delete to remove the page number. To go back to your document, click the Close button or double-click the page outside the footer area.

The Easy Way to Add Headers and Footers

When you need more than a simple page number in the header or footer, it makes sense to try the easy route first. That means going to the Layout ribbon and clicking on the Header or Footer menu and checking to see if one of Microsoft's designs can do the job. As you see in Figure 3-22, some headers are simple text-only affairs, while others include lines and blocks of color. If you're lucky, you can click on one of these options and Word automatically adds the header or footer to your document. Some of the header options insert words like "[Type text]" or "[Type the document title]." Consider those subtle hints that you should replace the text with your own words. For most of the headers and footers, you won't have to worry about the page number because Word includes an automatically-updating field. For details about the fields and properties used in headers and footers see the box on page 115.

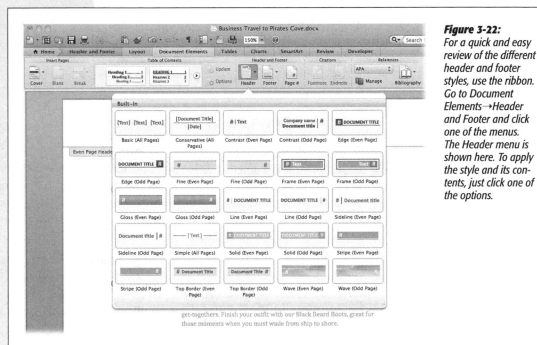

Figure 3-22:
For a quick and easy review of the different header and footer styles, use the ribbon. Go to Document Elements→Header and Footer and click one of the menus. The Header menu is shown here. To apply the style and its contents, just click one of the options.

Inspecting Your Document's Properties and Fields

When you type to replace placeholder text, something else happens behind the scenes. Every Word document has properties—defining information like author, title, and subject. You can check them out in the document properties panel: choose File →Properties→Summary. Click the General tab for technical details (similar to Get info) about the Word document file. Click the Statistics tab for the number of pages, paragraphs, words and so forth. (When you're done, click OK to close the box.) When you give the header a new title, Word takes those words and inserts them in the Title field of the Document Information Panel.

Word keeps track of the title and other document properties and uses them to fill in the placeholder "fields" you insert into your documents. As you'll see later in this chapter, you

can manually insert a field in a header, a footer, or indeed anywhere in your document by choosing Insert→Field. For example, the number of pages in a document is stored in the NumPages field (see Figure 3-23). So if you'd like to put "Page X of XX pages" in your header or footer, just replace X with the Page field and XX with the NumPages field.

To view the field codes in your document, rather than the text that they display, go to Word→Preferences→Authoring and Proofing Tools→View and then, in the Show category, check the box Field Codes. After you click OK to close the Preferences window, you'll see the codes in your document surrounded by curly brackets. For example you'll see {page} in the place of page numbers.

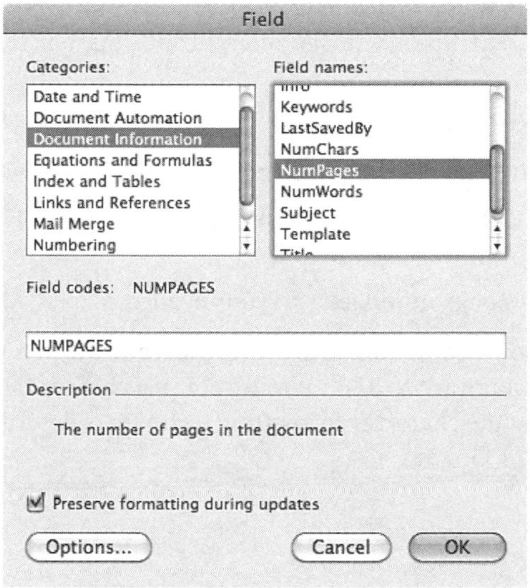

Figure 3-23:
Go to Insert→Field to display this box that's chock-full of different fields. Fields are placeholder codes that Word uses to represent changing information. For example, a page number is a field that tracks the number of pages up to that point in your document. There's also a field that keeps track of the total number of pages in your document.

Manually Adding Headers and Footers

Microsoft provides a lot of competently-designed headers and footers with Word, but you're free to create your own. Maybe you have to follow company guidelines for your documents. It's not difficult to create your own headers in Word. Here's how to create a custom header with a company name on the left and page numbers on the right:

1. **Using the menus, go to View→Header and Footer.**

   Word automatically changes to Print Layout view and moves the insertion point into the Header.

2. **Type your company name, press Return, and then type your city and country.**

   Pressing Enter puts the city and country on a new line below the company name. Text that you type directly into the footer appears on every page unless you make changes to the header and footer options.

3. **Press Tab twice to move the insertion point to the right side of the footer.**

   The first time you press Tab, the insertion point moves to the center of the page. If you enter text at that point, Word centers the text in the footer. The second time you press Tab, the insertion point moves to the right margin. Text that you enter there is aligned on the right margin.

4. **Type *Page*, and then press the space bar.**

   As you type, the insertion point remains on the right margin and your text flows to the left.

5. **Using the menus, go to Insert→Fields.**

   The Fields menu appears with two scrolling lists: Categories and Field names.

6. **Scroll down in the Categories list to select Numbering. Then in the Field names list double-click Page.**

   Word pops the field that displays page numbers into your header.

When you're done, your header should look something like Figure 3-24. You can continue to develop your header, if you want to add more text or placeholder fields. You can also format the header using the character formatting techniques described later in this chapter starting on page 135.

Dividing Your Document into Sections

All the manual formatting elements discussed up to this point are applied to sections of your document. If your document is a single section, you're likely to think
of these elements as document formatting. However, if you need to make some major changes to your document midstream, you'll appreciate sections. Consider these
situations:

- **Change page orientation**. You're working away with the standard portrait page
  orientation, but you need to insert some table, charts and graphs that will look
  better if they're in landscape orientation.

- **Change page size**. Similar to the previous situation, you realize your graphs will
  be bigger and more readable if you bump the page size up to legal.

- **Change the number of columns**. Perhaps you're inserting an extended quote
  from a newspaper or magazine article. Changing from a single column to two
  columns will emphasize the fact that this section is from a different source.

- **Change page margins**. You want to change the margins for an extended section. You could use a paragraph style with indents, but in many cases it may be
  easier to use a section break.

- **Restart automatic numbering for a new chapter**. Word uses automatic numbering for figures and other items. If you have a multichapter document, you
  may restart the numbering with each section break.

Inserting a section break is almost as easy as entering a page break, described on
page 48. In fact the commands are stashed in the same place, on the Insert menu or
the Layout tab. If you're working with the ribbon visible, that's the easiest method.

Go to Layout | Page Setup→Break and choose one of the four section break options shown in Figure 3-25. Why so many options? Word lets you choose whether or not you want to start a new page at the section break. So, if you're using section breaks to divide a long document into chapters, you probably want to start each new section on a page of it's own. If you're printing on both sides of the page and binding your document, you may have a preference about whether chapters start on the left page or the right page. Here's some guidance for choosing section break options:

- To insert a section break and start a new page, choose Next Page.

- To insert a section break without starting a new page, choose Continuous.

- To insert a section break and start text on the next page with an even page number, choose Even Page. You'll need to do your own calculations if, for example, you want to make sure that is a right hand page.

- To insert a section break and start text on the next page with an odd page number, choose Odd Page.

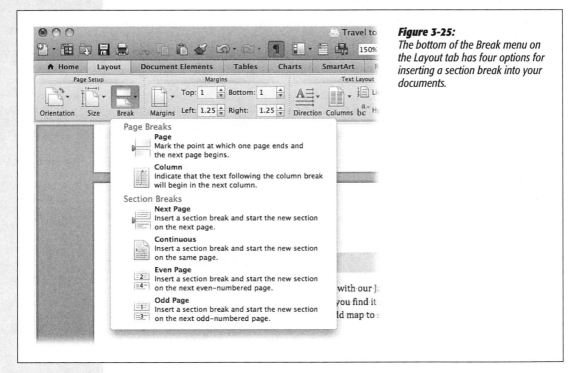

Figure 3-25:
The bottom of the Break menu on the Layout tab has four options for inserting a section break into your documents.

Insert the first section break into a document and you divide it into two pieces: Section 1 and Section 2. A glance at the status bar tells you which section you're working in, as shown in Figure 3-26. At this point any formatting changes you make, such as page orientation, apply to the current section and won't affect the other sections.

Tip: Section breaks are another one of those invisible characters like paragraph marks and page breaks. To display these non-printing markers while you work in Word, click the ¶ button in the standard toolbar.

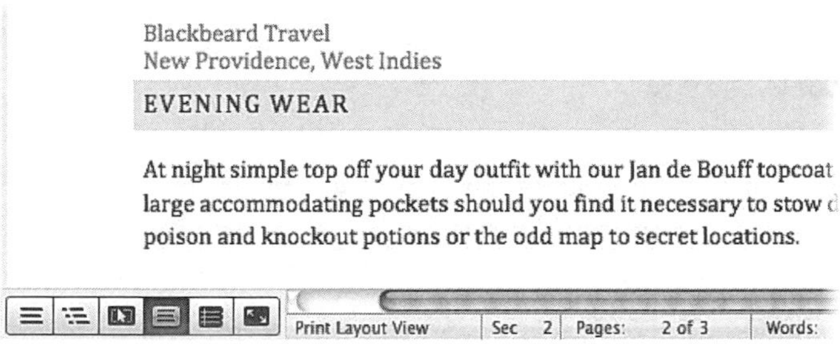

Blackbeard Travel
New Providence, West Indies

EVENING WEAR

At night simple top off your day outfit with our Jan de Bouff topcoat large accommodating pockets should you find it necessary to stow poison and knockout potions or the odd map to secret locations.

Print Layout View   Sec   2   Pages: 2 of 3   Words:

Figure 3-26:
In the status bar, the message "Sec 2" tells you that the insertion point is in section 2 of your document. Keep in mind, the page you're viewing and the page with the insertion point can be two different places.

Formatting Paragraphs with Styles

As explained on page 96, when you apply a style to a paragraph, you perform several formatting chores at once. For example, the Normal style, used for body text, selects a font, size, and color and determines the spacing between lines and paragraphs. Your document may use other styles for headings and photo captions. Each element is likely to have a different look. The Normal style may spec a serif font with a size between 10 and 12 points, while the Heading 1 Style uses a sans-serif font and a 16-point size. (This book uses a similar design.) To set photo captions off from the other elements, you may use italics and perhaps center or right paragraph alignment.

Note: Serifs are the pointy lines at the end of the strokes used in some typefaces. Serif fonts are often used for the body text because they make large blocks of small type more readable. That's one of the reasons, serif type is used for most of the text in this book. Sans-serif (used in this note and the section heading) works well for headings.

There are several advantages to developing and using styles to format your paragraphs. First of all if you've defined a style for your Normal paragraph or your major heading, you don't have to remember and apply manual settings for each paragraph. You can be sure that when you apply Heading 1 to a paragraph, it will have the same font, size and color as all the other Heading 1s. If you decide to change the look of Heading 1, you can change the style and you don't have to jump all over your document, making manual changes to every heading.

In this section, you'll learn how to:

- **Modify an existing style**, so that it changes every paragraph in the document that uses that style.

- **Override one or more of a style's format settings**. You use this method when you want to tweak one paragraph to change its appearance, without changing the other paragraphs that use the style

- **Create a new style with a new name**. Perhaps you're developing a Word template that's going to be used by everyone in your office.

Modifying an Existing Style

Your 672-page quarterly sales report looks just the way you want it, except for one thing. You've come to the conclusion that the Papyrus Condensed font used for the Normal paragraph causes eyestrain and headaches. To change all those paragraphs formatted with the pain-inducing font, you change the Normal style and Word handles the rest for you. Here are the steps:

1. **Choose Format→Style.**

   The Style dialog box opens as shown in Figure 3-27. In the upper-right corner, you see a list of styles. Use the menu below the list to filter the styles shown in the list. Your options are:

   - **Styles in Use.** Lists the styles that are defined by the template.

   - **All Styles.** Every style definition that Word can find. It's a long list.

   - **User-Defined Styles.** A list of custom styles that you or someone else has created.

2. **Scroll through the Styles list and click Normal.**

   To the right there's a preview window that shows the Normal paragraph formatting and below one that shows the Normal character formatting. At the bottom, there's a test description of the settings used for the style. For example, you'll see the font name, the size and details about the spacing and alignment.

3. **With Normal selected, click the Modify button.**

   The Modify Style box opens as shown in Figure 3-28.

4. **In the Formatting section, choose a new, easier on the eyes font, such as Cambria.**

   Cambria is one of the standard fonts that's installed with Office. It's frequently used for body text. Other fonts often chosen for the Normal style are: Georgia, Times or Times Roman.

5. **In the Modify Style box, click OK. Then, in the Style box click Apply.**

   The font change you specified is applied to every Normal-style paragraph.

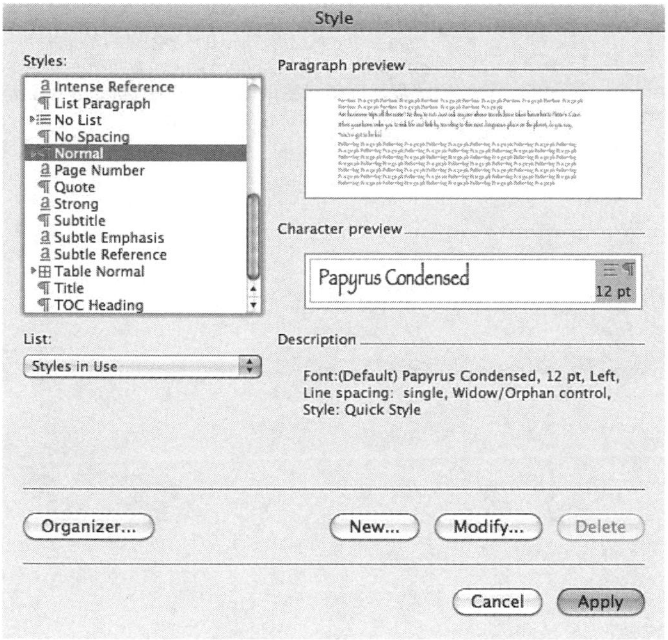

Figure 3-27:
The Style box displays a list of fonts. Select one of the fonts in the list and previews of the paragraph and character appear on the right. Buttons at the bottom of the box let you create new styles, modify existing styles, or delete styles from the list.

It's just as easy to change any other paragraph formatting element. You could change the first line indent, the space between paragraphs, the tabs, bullets and numbering or the borders, to name a few of the available options. You have all the tools to make these changes at your fingertips in the Modify Style box, so it's worth taking a little closer look.

WORKING WITH WINDOWS

Choosing Windows-Friendly Fonts

In the distant, murky, and confusing past, Macs and Windows didn't have many of the same fonts. Every time a document passed the Mac/Windows barrier, some calculated substitutions had to be made to ensure that documents looked similar on the different computer systems. (If you used Times on your Mac, Windows users had to change that to Times New Roman on a Windows computer. Helvetica translated to Arial.) These days you're more likely to find fonts that are shared by the two opposing camps. It's in Microsoft's interest to try and make things easier, so in their font list, they give you a collection of fonts that are found on Windows. To find the list, go to Font→Collections→Windows Office Compatible. If you want to make sure your document looks the same for the Windows crowd, pick one these. You can also find the same list of fonts in the Modify Style box, as shown in Figure 3-29.

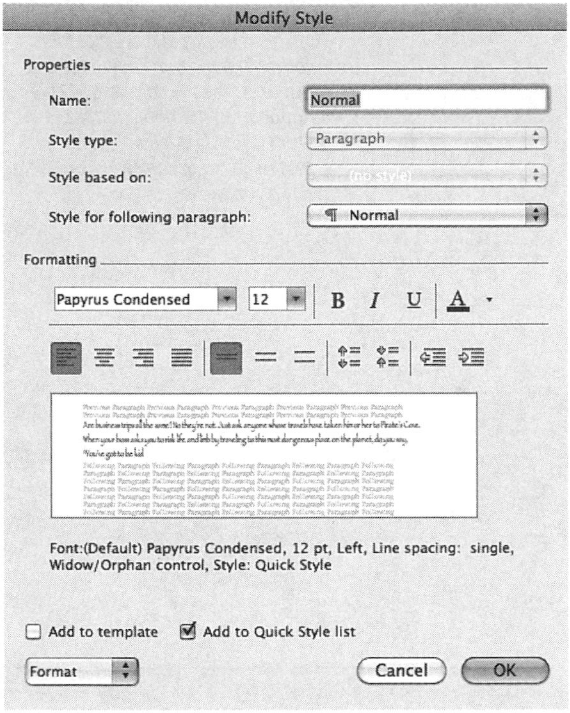

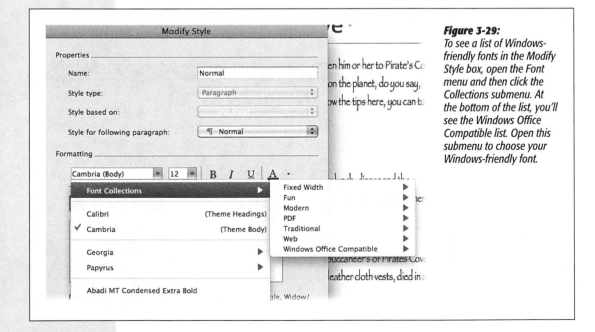

Figure 3-28:
You use the Modify Style box to make changes to an existing style. Changes you make to the Style definition will be applied to all the paragraphs in your document that use the style.

Figure 3-29:
To see a list of Windows-friendly fonts in the Modify Style box, open the Font menu and then click the Collections submenu. At the bottom of the list, you'll see the Windows Office Compatible list. Open this submenu to choose your Windows-friendly font.

Exploring the Modify Style box

The Modify Style box puts everything you need to format a paragraph in one place. Initially, it displays the settings you're most likely to tweak: fonts, alignment, and spacing options. Dig a little deeper and you find that it offers much more. Here's the complete tour of this feature-filled dialog box, starting at the top and moving to the bottom:

- **Name**. Every style has a name. Out of the box, Word comes with dozens of named styles. When you create your own styles, you get to name them.

- **Style type**. When you create your own custom styles, you can choose its type. Your choices are paragraph, character, table or list.

- **Style based on**. A style can borrow all the formatting from another style, but change just one or two format settings. For example, a Heading 2 style may be based on Heading 1, except that it specifies a smaller font size. If that's the case, the font, color, and paragraph spacing would be the same for both. The size would be the only difference. Then later, if you change the font for Heading 1 from Papyrus to Calibri, that would change Heading 2 to Calibri, but it would still use the smaller font size.

  This feature saves time when you're developing new styles and, equally important, it gives your document consistency in appearance.

- **Style for following paragraph**. Use this setting to specify the style that's used on the next paragraph after this style. An earlier example in this chapter demonstrated the most common use for this setting. When you press Return after typing a heading, Word automatically applies the Normal style to the new paragraph. The assumption being that, after a heading, you're likely to have some Normal body text. You often have more than one Normal paragraph in a row, so for the Normal style, you probably want another Normal paragraph to follow. Naturally, it's always easy to use the ribbon's Styles menu (Home | Styles) to make changes as needed.

- **Formatting**. This section shows the Formatting options you're most likely to change: fonts, size, paragraph alignment, and so on. If you don't find what you need already shown here, use the Format menu below.

- **Add to template**. If you want to add a new or modified style to the template so it's available to future documents created from this template, check this box.

- **Add to Quick Style list**. You can add a new or modified style to the list of Quick Styles that appear in the ribbon.

- **Format menu**. Use this menu to open additional formatting dialog boxes. As you see in Figure 3-30, your choices include: Font, Paragraphs, Tabs, Border, Language, Frame, Numbering, Shortcut Keys and Text Effects.

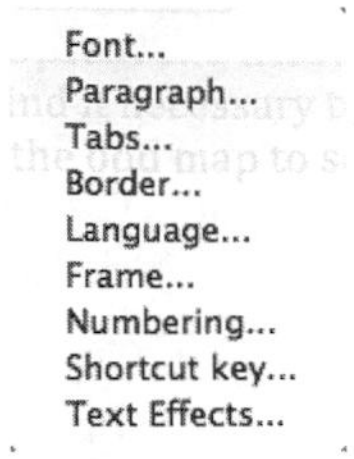

Font...
Paragraph...
Tabs...
Border...
Language...
Frame...
Numbering...
Shortcut key...
Text Effects...

Figure 3-30:
Use the format menu in the Modify Style box to dig deeper into your paragraph formatting options. Even though these options open yet another dialog box, your settings are applied to the style you're modifying.

Overriding a Style Setting

There may be times when you want to make a change to a single heading, but you don't want to change the other 95 headings that use the same style. Fortunately, it's easy to do. Simply select the paragraph by double-clicking in the margin on the left. Then, make any formatting changes you want. You can use the Font or Paragraph settings in the Home tab to do the job, or you can use Word's menus and dialog boxes to tweak the settings. The changes you make only affect the selected paragraph.

Reverting to the original style

If you've overridden style formatting here and there throughout your document, there will come the day when you need to reset one of those paragraphs to its original style definition. This is a good job for the Styles panel on the toolbox. In the standard toolbar, click the Toolbox button. The Toolbox appears as a floating palette. At the top, click the button that looks like a paragraph mark to display the Styles panel (Figure 3-31). With your cursor in the paragraph you want to revert, click the style name in the Toolbox. The paragraph changes back to the original style settings. The Styles panel in the toolbox can perform quite a few formatting chores, as described in the next few sections.

Clearing formatting

If you decide you don't like the way you changed a paragraph, you can always press ⌘-Z to undo changes immediately after the fact. But what if you come back much, much later and want to revert the paragraph back to the originally-defined style? The Clear Formatting option appears in the Toolbox Style's panel and on the ribbon (Home | Font→Clear Formatting. (The button is in the upper-right corner of the Font group.) Use this option when you want to change selected paragraphs back to the Normal style and remove any extra character formatting such as bold or italics. Just select the text you want to strip down and choose Clear Formatting in the ribbon or the Toolbox. If the results weren't what you intended, you can always Undo (⌘-Z).

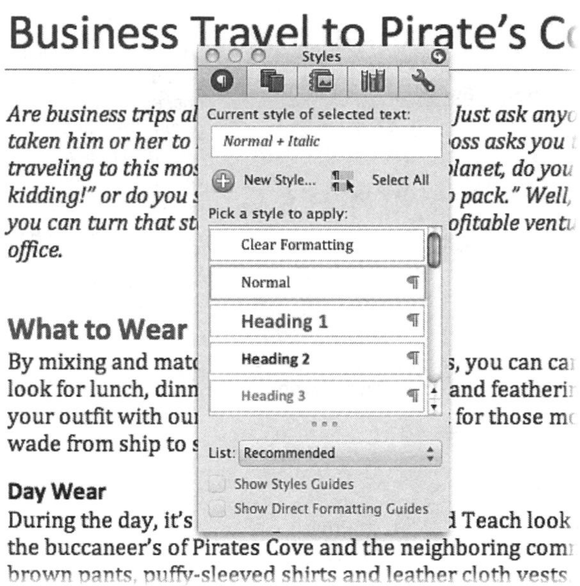

Business Travel to Pirate's C

Are business trips al ~~taken him or her to~~ *Just ask anyc traveling to this mos ~~boss asks you t~~ kidding!" or do you ~~planet, do you~~ you can turn that st ~~o pack." Well,~~ office.* ~~ofitable ventu~~

What to Wear

By mixing and matc ~~s, you can ca~~ look for lunch, dinn ~~and featheri~~ your outfit with our ~~for those mc~~ wade from ship to s

Day Wear

During the day, it's ~~d Teach look~~ the buccaneer's of Pirates Cove and the neighboring com brown pants, puffy-sleeved shirts and leather cloth vests

Styles

Current style of selected text:

Normal + Italic

New Style...   Select All

Pick a style to apply:

Clear Formatting

Normal

Heading 1

Heading 2

Heading 3

List: Recommended

Show Styles Guides

Show Direct Formatting Guides

Figure 3-31:
This handy tool puts a lot of style modifying power in a small package. To apply a style to the paragraph holding the insertion point, click the style name. From this toolbox you can also modify existing styles and create new ones.

Showing Style Guides

After you've applied several different styles to your document, it's easy to get a bit lost. If you need a visual guide to understand which paragraphs are formatted with which styles, turn to the Styles panel in the toolbox. At the bottom, click Show Styles Guides, and Word displays a multicolored border to the left of the page (see Figure 3-32). Each color and number corresponds to a paragraph style.

If you want to identify all the paragraphs using a particular style, there's another Toolbox tool that does just that. First, in the scrolling list click the style you want to find. Then above the list click Select All. In your document, Word selects all the paragraphs that use the selected style.

Manual Paragraph Formatting

The styles described in the previous section change several formatting options at one time. If you want to roll up your sleeves and tweak individual paragraph settings you'll find the options in the Paragraph dialog box (Format→Paragraph or Option-⌘-M) shown in Figure 3-33. Use the tabs at the top to switch between the Indents and Spacing panel and the Line and Page Breaks panel.

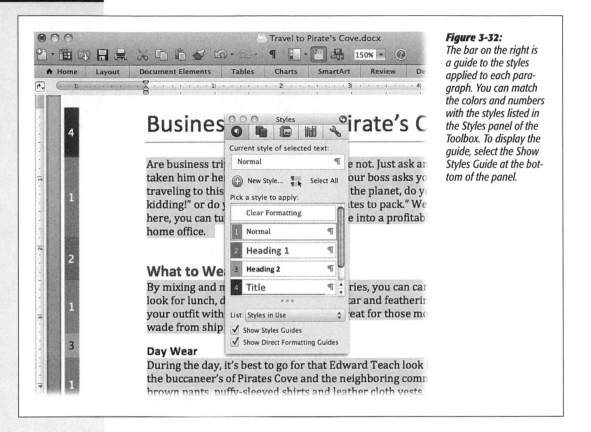

Figure 3-32:
The bar on the right is a guide to the styles applied to each paragraph. You can match the colors and numbers with the styles listed in the Styles panel of the Toolbox. To display the guide, select the Show Styles Guide at the bottom of the panel.

Paragraph Alignment

To change the alignment of text in a paragraph, make sure the insertion point is in the paragraph then choose an option from the ribbon (Home | Paragraph) or the dialog box (Format→Paragraph).

- **Left**. Aligns the lines in the paragraph flush on the left side and ragged on the right. Left alignment is standard for letters, reports, and many business documents.

- **Centered**. Centers each line in the paragraph, leaving both left and right margins ragged. This setting is appropriate for headings and short chunks of text, as in invitations and advertisements. Avoid using centered text for long paragraphs, since it's hard for readers' eyes to track from the end of one line to the beginning of the next when the left margin is uneven.

- **Right**. Aligns the lines in the paragraph flush on the right side and ragged on the left. This unusual alignment is most often used for setting captions or quotations apart from the main text.

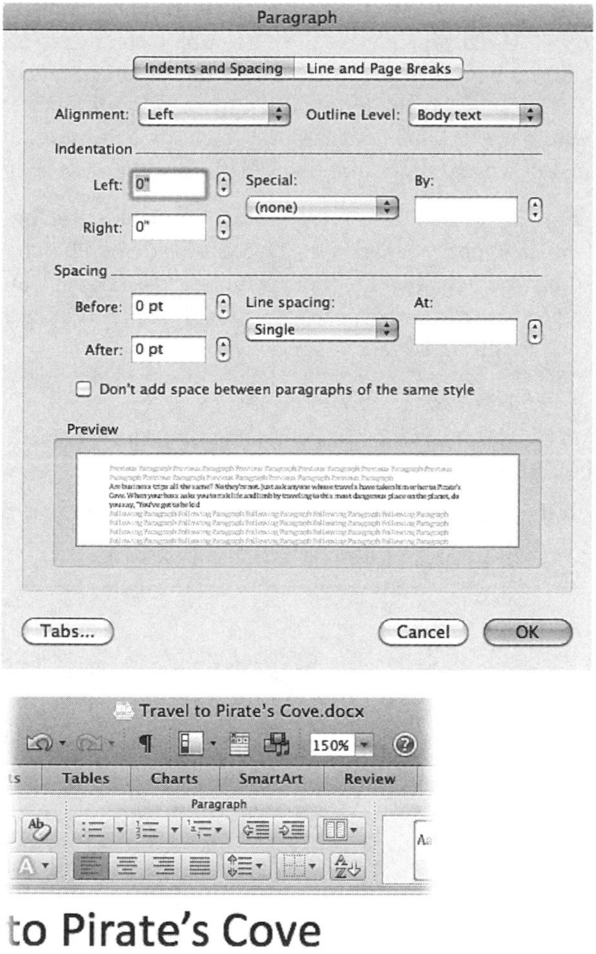

Paragraph

Indents and Spacing | Line and Page Breaks

Alignment: [Left ⬍]   Outline Level: [Body text ⬍]

Indentation

Left: [0"] ⬍   Special: By:
                   [(none) ⬍]   [   ] ⬍
Right: [0"] ⬍

Spacing

Before: [0 pt] ⬍   Line spacing: At:
                     [Single ⬍]   [   ] ⬍
After: [0 pt] ⬍

☐ Don't add space between paragraphs of the same style

Preview

[Tabs...]   [Cancel] [OK]

Travel to Pirate's Cove.docx

↶ ▾ ↷ ▾ ¶ ▯ ▾ ▤ ⬚ [150% ▾] ⓘ

...s | Tables | Charts | SmartArt | Review

Paragraph

Figure 3-33:

Top: The paragraph dialog box, with its two panels and layers of settings gives you the most complete collection of paragraph formatting options.

Bottom: The Home tab of the ribbon isn't as complete, but it does give you easy access to the most frequently used commands.

to Pirate's Cove

- **Justified**. Adds space between letters and words so that both the left and right sides of the paragraph are straight and flush with the margins. Justified margins give text a more formal look suitable for textbooks or scholarly documents. If your justified text looks odd because big gaps appear between the letters or words, try using a long line—that is, putting more characters per line. You can do this by extending the margins (Layout | Margins) or by changing the size of your font (Home | Font→Font Size).

Indenting Paragraphs

One of the most common reasons for indenting a paragraph is to set off quoted text from the rest of the document. Usually, you move the paragraph's left edge in about a half inch from the left margin. Novels, short stories, and other manuscripts often indent the first line of a paragraph instead of adding extra space between each paragraph. Hanging indents, where the first line extends past the body text into the left margin, are a less common, but work well for glossaries, bibliographies and such.

The easiest way to indent is to use the buttons on the ribbon (Home | Paragraph→Increase Indent or Home | Paragraph→Decrease Indent. The change takes place immediately and if you don't like the look, just press ⌘-Z. If you want to set indents with more precision, use the Paragraph dialog box (Format→Paragraph) and make sure you're on the Indents and Spacing panel.

- **To indent from either margin**, type a distance in the Left or Right box.

- **To indent the first line of a paragraph**, choose First line from the Special menu and then type a distance in the By box.

- **To create a hanging indent,** chose Hanging from the Special menu and then type a distance in the By box.

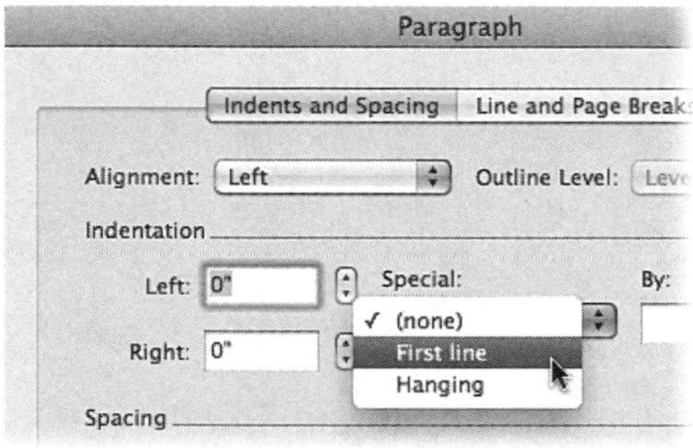

Figure 3-34:
Initially, Word expects you to use inches for the indent settings. If you prefer to specify your distance in another format just include the units of measure as in 8 pt or 5 mm.

Using the ruler to indent paragraphs

Using the ruler to adjust indentation is similar to changing margins (described on page 106). It's just a matter of clicking and dragging. Indents are a bit more complicated because you have a few more options, and that means more tools and widgets.

It can take awhile to get used to adjusting paragraph indents with the ruler (Figure 3-35). For one thing, you need a steady hand and accurate clicking to zero in on those little triangle buttons. The top triangle sets the first line indent and moves independently. The bottom triangle creates a hanging indent, and you can move it independently too, as long as you grab only that triangle. That little box below the triangle is your left indent, and if you drag it, both it and the top (first line) indent marker move together.

Figure 3-35:
To adjust paragraph indents, slide the little triangles along the ruler. The changes you make affect the paragraph with the insertion point. If you want to make changes to more than one paragraph, make a multiple selection before you start.

Spacing Between Paragraphs

For documents like business letters or reports that use block-style paragraphs, there's usually a little space between each. You can adjust this spacing between paragraphs to set off some blocks of text from the rest.

Use the Paragraph dialog box (Option-⌘-M) to adjust the distance between paragraphs. As you can see in Figure 3-36, on the left, you enter numbers to set the space before the paragraph and the space after. With body text paragraphs, it's good to set the same, relatively small distance before and after—say, three points. For headers, you may want to put a little extra space before the header to distance it from the preceding text. That space makes it clear that the header is related to the text beneath it. Generally speaking, the more significant the header, the larger the type and the greater the spacing around it.

Spacing Between Lines

In the Paragraph box, to the right of the paragraph spacing controls, you find the "Line spacing" tools. Use these controls to set the distance between lines within paragraphs. You have three presets and three custom settings:

- **Single** keeps the lines close together, with a minimum amount of space between. Single spacing is usually easy to read, and it sure saves paper.

- **1.5 lines** gives your text a little more breathing room, and still offers a nice professional look.

- **Double** is the option preferred by teachers and editors, so there's plenty of room for their helpful comments.

- **At least** is a good option if you have a mix of font sizes or include inline graphics with your text. This option ensures that everything fits.

Paragraph and Line
spacing options

- **Exactly** puts you in control. Type a number in the At box, and Word won't mess with that setting.

- **Multiple** is the oddball of the bunch. Think of Multiple as a percentage of a single line space: 1=100 percent; .8=80 percent; 1.2=120 percent; and so on.

Setting Tabs

The lowly Tab key contains more power than you may think. Sure, you can use the Tab key to scoot the insertion point across the page in half-inch increments. But Word's tab tool is capable of much loftier feats: You can use it to design a dinner menu, create a playbill, or develop a series of consistently formatted reports.

Tab stops are all about precision alignment, giving you control over the way you present text and numbers to your readers. For example, on your dinner menu you can use tab leaders (dotted lines like the ones in this book's table of contents) so that your reader's eye tracks from Wild Salmon to the exceptionally reasonable price you're asking. Once you have settings you like, you can save and reuse them. (How's that for efficiency?)

Before you start working with tabs, you need to know a few basic terms:

- **Tabs.** Technically considered tab characters, tabs are hidden formatting characters, similar to space characters. Tabs are embedded in your document's text.

- **Tab stops.** These paragraph settings define the position and characteristics of tabs in your document. Think of tab stops as definitions, describing your tabs. To define them, you use Word tools, like the Ruler or the Tabs dialog box.

- **Tab key.** The key on your computer keyboard that inserts tabs into your text.

Press the Tab key, and Word inserts a tab in the text at that point. The tab character makes the insertion point jump left to right and stop at the first tab stop it reaches. If you haven't set any new tab stops, Word uses the built-in set of tab stops—one every half inch across the width—that every new, blank document starts out with.

How tab stops work

Tab stop settings apply to paragraphs. If a paragraph has several lines, the tab stops are the same for all the lines within that paragraph. If you haven't deliberately set tab stops, Word provides built-in tab stops at half-inch intervals. These stops are left tab stops, meaning the text aligns on the left side. You can see all tab stops on the horizontal ruler—they show as small vertical tick marks in the gray area below the number scale (Figure 3-37).

Tip: If you don't see tab stops in the ruler, click within a paragraph. Remember, tab stops are paragraph settings, so your insertion point must be in a paragraph to see them.

Tab inset selection tool
Tab shown in text
Tab stop on ruler
Built-in tab stops

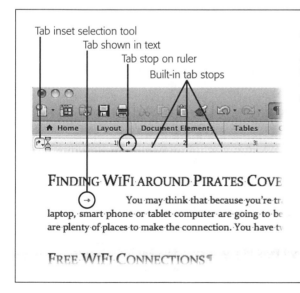

Figure 3-37:
Tabs are just white space in your text, but for Word, they're these little arrow characters that position your text on the line. You can change your Word preferences (Word→Preferences→ View→Tab characters) to show tabs on your screen.

Viewing tab marks in your text

Tabs are invisible on the printed page, like spaces or paragraph marks. Sometimes, when your document behaves unexpectedly, it helps to reveal the hidden characters so you can see if tabs are the culprit. After all, when they're hidden, all you see is white space on the page; however, spaces, tabs, and indents each behave quite differently. To view tabs within your text, click the paragraph mark (¶) on the standard toolbar.

Deleting and editing tabs

Because tabs are characters within your document, you can delete, copy, and paste them just as you would any other character or text fragment. Maybe you want to delete a tab: just click immediately after a tab character, and then press the Backspace key. If you want to copy and move a tab, click the paragraph mark (¶) on the standard toolbar, to make the non-printing characters visible while you work in Word. Then you can cut (⌘-X) and paste (⌘-V) tab marks, which show up as small arrows in your text.

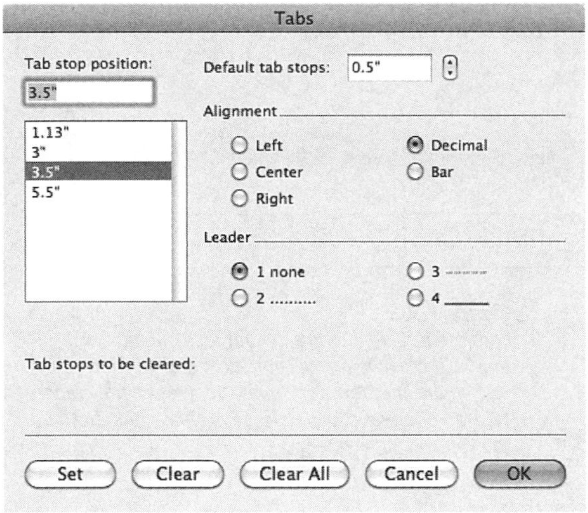

Figure 3-38:
The Tabs box puts you in complete control of all things tabular. When you select a specific tab in the upper-left box, you can customize its alignment and leader characters.

Types of Tabs

Five types of tabs are available in Word—one of which isn't a true tab but works well with the others:

- **Left tab**. The most common type of tab, it aligns text at the left side; text flows from the tab stop to the right. When you start a new, blank document, Word provides left tabs every half inch.

- **Center tab**. Keeps text centered at the tab stop. Text extends evenly left and right with the tab stop in the middle.

- **Right tab**. Aligns text to the right. Text flows backwards from the tab stop, from right to left.

- **Decimal tab**. Used to align numbers, whether or not they have decimals. Numbers align with the decimal point centered on the tab stop. Numbers without decimal points align similar to a right tab.

- **Bar tab**. The Bar tab is the oddball of the group and, no, it has nothing to do with your local watering hole. It also has nothing to do with aligning text. It inserts a vertical bar in your text as a divider. The bar appears in every line in the paragraph. This tab stop ignores tabs inserted in your text and behaves in the same manner whether or not tab characters are present.

Note: There may be a certain Microsoftian logic in grouping the bar tab with the tab feature, but Word provides other ways to place vertical lines on your pages that you may find more intuitive. You can use borders for paragraphs or tables or you can open the Media Browser from the standard Toolbar. Then, click the Shapes button and select Lines and Connectors from the menu.

Tab Leaders

Tab leaders help readers connect the dots by providing a trail from one tabbed item to the next. They're ideal for creating professional-looking menus, playbills, and more.

Here are some examples:

Hamlet, Prince of Denmark..............Sir Laurence Olivier

Ophelia, daughter to Polonius..........Julia Louis-Dreyfus

Four Leader options can be used with each type of tab stop except the bar tab:

None   No leader here

Dotted...You've seen this before

Dashed------------------------------For a different, intermittent look

Underline _____ When only a solid line will do

As visual aids, leaders are quite helpful, and they work equally well for text and numbers.

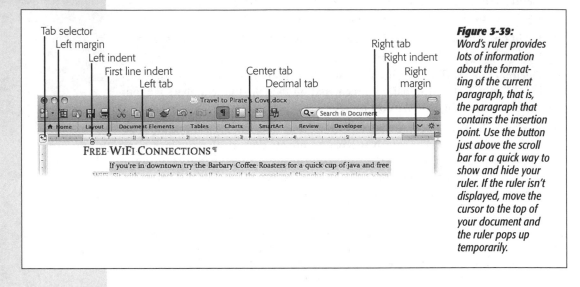

Figure 3-39:
*Word's ruler provides
lots of information
about the format-
ting of the current
paragraph, that is,
the paragraph that
contains the insertion
point. Use the button
just above the scroll
bar for a quick way to
show and hide your
ruler. If the ruler isn't
displayed, move the
cursor to the top of
your document and
the ruler pops up
temporarily.*

Managing Tab Settings with the Ruler

In Figure 3-39, the ruler measures the page in inches. The grayed areas at both ends of the ruler indicate the page margins. The numbers on the ruler mark the distance from the left margin in both directions, left and right. Note the number 1, at the left edge of the ruler in Figure 3-39.

Setting tab stops

Word's every-half-inch tab stops can work for many of your documents, but sooner or later, you may need to put a tab stop in a different place or change its style. No problem—it's easy enough to do with the ruler.

Setting a new tab stop from the ruler is a two-step process:

1. **Click the button on the left of the ruler to open the menu and choose the kind of tab you're about to apply—Left, Center, Right, Decimal, or Bar.**

2. **Click the point on the ruler where you want to place the tab stop. An icon appears on the ruler showing the position and the type of tab stop.**

Adjusting and removing tab stops with the ruler

If a tab stop isn't exactly where you want it, you don't have to delete it—just drag it to a new position on the ruler. If you wish to remove a tab stop, drag it up or down off the ruler, and it disappears. When you make these changes, your document shows the consequences. Any tabs in your text shift over to the next readily available tab stop, which can be a built-in tab stop or one that you've set.

Managing Line and Page Breaks

Some things just look wrong, such as a heading at the bottom of a page with no text beneath it. That heading should be at the top of the next page. Sure, you could force it over there with a page break, but that can cause trouble if you edit your text and things move around. You could end up with a page break in some weird spot. The solution is to adjust your Line and Page Break settings so that headings and paragraphs behave the way you want them to.

Open the Paragraph box (Option-⌘-M) and, at the top, click Line and Page Breaks (Figure 3-40). The line and page break behavior becomes part of the paragraph's formatting and travels with the text no matter where you move the text or breaks.

- **Widow/Orphan control.** Single lines abandoned at the top (widows) or bottom (orphans) of the page look out of place. Turn on this checkbox, and Word keeps the whole family, er, paragraph together.

- **Keep with next.** Certain paragraphs, like headings, need to stay attached to the paragraph that comes immediately after them. Choose the "Keep with next" option for your headings, and they always appear above the following paragraph.

- **Keep lines together.** Sometimes you have a paragraph that shouldn't be split between two pages, like a one-paragraph quote or disclaimer. Use this option to keep the paragraph as one unit.

- **Page break before.** Use this command with major headings to make sure new sections of your document start on a new page.

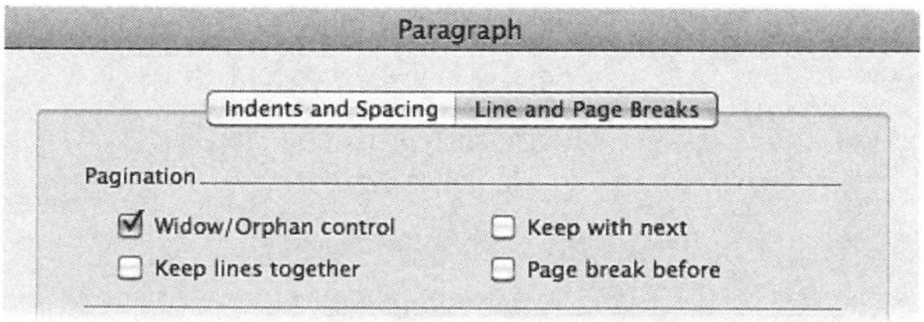

Figure 3-40:
Use the Line and Page Break settings to control the appearance of your text and to avoid awkward transitions between pages.

Formatting Individual Characters

Every character in your document is formatted. The formatting describes the typeface, the size of the character, the color, and whether or not the character is underlined, bold, or capitalized. It's easy to change the formatting, and Word gives you quite a few different ways to do it. The easiest and most visual way is with the ribbon (Home | Font). You can further fine-tune the font formatting using the Font dialog box (⌘-D).

Whichever method you use, formatting is a two-step process. First, tell Word which text you want to format by selecting it. Then format away. Or, you can set up your formatting options first, and then begin to type. Your letters and words will be beautifully formatted from the get-go.

Formatting as You Type with Shortcut Keys

One of the most common ways to apply bold or italics to words is to use shortcut keys. You're typing along and know that you want the next word to be italicized, so you hit ⌘-I before you type the word to turn italics on. You type the word and then hit ⌘-I again to toggle off the italics. This method works for bold (⌘-B), italics (⌘-I) and underline (⌘-U).

Here's a list of some more keyboard shortcuts that come in handy:

Table 3-1. Common formatting shortcut keys and their uses

Command	Keyboard Shortcut	Description
Font	⌘-D, ⌘-Shift-F	Opens Font box.
Bold	⌘-B	Toggle bold on and off.
Italic	⌘-I	Toggles italics on and off.
Underline	⌘-U	Toggles underline on and off.
Double Underline	⌘-Shift-D	Toggles double underline on and off.
Strikethrough	⌘-Shift-X	Toggles strikethrough on and off.
All Caps	⌘-Shift-A	Toggles all caps on and off.
Small Caps	⌘-Shift-K	Toggles small caps on and off.
Change Case	⌘-Option-C	Toggles between upper, lower and sentence case.
Grow Font	⌘-Shift-.	Increases font size.
Shrink Font	⌘-Shift-,	Decreases font size
Subscript	⌘-=	Toggles subscript on and off.
Superscript	⌘-Shift-=	Toggles superscript on and off.

Tip: Unless you're using a typewriter font, like Courier, you should use italics instead of underlined text.

Formatting with the Ribbon or the Font Box

Since character formatting is one of the most often used Word features, Microsoft put the most popular settings right on the Home tab. If you don't see what you're looking for there, then you must open the Font dialog box. The good thing about the dialog box is that it puts all your character formatting options in one place so you can quickly make multiple changes. It's one-stop shopping if you want to change the typeface and the size, and add that pink double-underline.

Here are the steps:

1. **Select a group of characters, as shown in Figure 3-41.**

   You can use any of the selection methods described on page 26. You can drag to select a single character. You can double-click to select a word. Or you can move the mouse cursor to the left side of a paragraph, and then double-click to select the whole paragraph.

   Of course, if you haven't typed anything yet, you can always go right to the ribbon and make your formatting choices first. Then type away.

Figure 3-41:
The Font group on the Home tab holds most of the common character formatting commands. Choices you make here apply to text you've selected (like the word "sights" in this example). If you don't see the command you need, in the lower-right corner, click the dialog box launcher to open the Font dialog box (Figure 3-42).

2. **Go to Home | Font or the Font box (⌘-D) and make your formatting choices.**

   Many of the buttons in the Font group act like toggles. So, when you select text and click the underline button, Word underlines all the characters in the selection. When you click the underline button again, the underline goes away.

   If you can't find the command you want on the ribbon, or if you want to make several character formatting changes at once, then open the Font box (Figure 3-42).

Changing Capitalization

Any letter can be uppercase or lowercase, but when you get to words and sentences, you find some variations on the theme. It's not unusual to have a heading or a company name where all the letters are capitalized. Sentences start with an initial cap on the first word only, and titles usually have the major words capped. In an effort to automate anything that can possibly be automated, Microsoft provides the Change Case menu (Home | Font→Change Case) on the ribbon (Figure 3-43).

The Change Case command defies the usual rules about selecting before you apply character formatting. If you don't select anything, Word assumes you want to apply the Change Case command to an entire word, so the program selects the word at the insertion point. If you've selected text, the command works, as you'd expect, only on the selection.

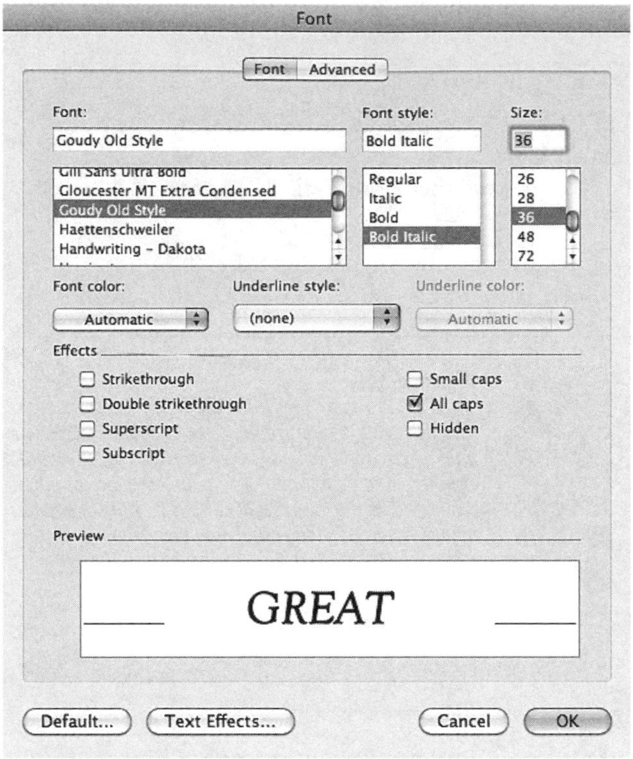

Font

Font | Advanced

Font:

Goudy Old Style

Gill Sans Ultra Bold
Gloucester MT Extra Condensed
Goudy Old Style
Haettenschweiler
Handwriting – Dakota

Font style:

Bold Italic

Regular
Italic
Bold
Bold Italic

Size:

36

26
28
36
48
72

Font color:

Automatic

Underline style:

(none)

Underline color:

Automatic

Effects

☐ Strikethrough
☐ Double strikethrough
☐ Superscript
☐ Subscript

☐ Small caps
☑ All caps
☐ Hidden

Preview

GREAT

Default... | Text Effects... | Cancel | OK

Figure 3-42:
Open the Font box (⌘-D) to change the typeface, style, size, color, and other effects. Like many dialog boxes, the Font box gives you access to more commands than you find on the ribbon.

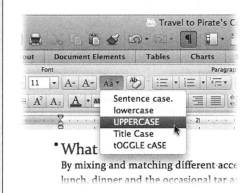

Figure 3-43:
The Change Case menu gives you five ways to change the case of a selection. To open it, click the button that looks like two letter As.

Small Caps for Headers

Small caps (Figure 3-44) are another variation on the capitalization theme. You won't find this option on the Change Case button; for small caps you have to use the Font dialog box, which you find on the right side under Effects (where underline or strike-through are). Small caps are great for headings and letterhead (especially if you're a lawyer or an accountant), but you wouldn't want to use them for body text. It's difficult to read all capitalized text for an entire paragraph.

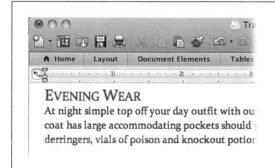

Figure 3-44:
Small caps are a great way to distinguish a heading or subheading from body text, like the words "Calm in Storm." Initial letters get full-sized capitals while the letters that would normally be lowercase get small capitals.

Advanced Font Formatting

If you really want to dig deep into typographic topics, open the Fonts box (⌘-D) and click the Advanced tab. Using the settings in this panel you can adjust character spacing and kerning. You can add ligatures to your type and choose old style number forms.

- **Character Spacing** is often called tracking by typographers. You can set the spacing to Condensed or Expanded and then enter a measurement in points in the By box. Dramatic changes make body text hard to read, but used moderately, it can make your text more attractive. Character spacing is sometimes used to give headings, logos and other design elements distinctive appeal.

- **Character Position**, otherwise known as baseline shift, sets the vertical character position. This adjustment comes in handy when writing chemical formulas or using the trademark (™) symbol. Use the up- and down-arrow button on the Position line to adjust the amount of shift while you watch the Preview panel.

- **Kerning** fine-tunes the distance between two specific characters and it's usually reserved font sizes. If you turn on the "Kerning for fonts" checkbox and set the "Points and above" box for the size of text you want to affect, Office subtly adjusts the character spacing between each pair of letters for an even appearance. For example, applying kerning to the word TAP reduces the space between the T and the A, making the letter spacing appear more consistent.

- **Ligatures** are pairs of letters that share common components when printed next to each other. Scribes writing with pen and ink in the Middle Ages originally created ligatures to save space on the parchment and increase writing speed—just like when you cross two "t's" in a word at once.

- **Number spacing** controls how much horizontal space each number takes. When set to tabular, all numbers use the same amount of space, making it easier to line up columns of numbers. When set to Proportional, the number 1 takes up less space than the number 9—just as some text characters take more horizontal space than others.

- **Number forms** makes subtle changes to the vertical position of numbers. Set to lining, the bottoms of all numbers sit on the baseline. Set to Old Style, some numbers drop below the baseline.

- **Stylistic sets** are a feature of some advanced font sets such as calligraphic style swashes and flourishes. This menu lets you choose stylistic sets when they're available.

Printing Documents, Envelopes, and Labels

The paperless office hasn't arrived yet. At some point, most Word documents head for the printer. Even when you email a document or create an Adobe Acrobat (PDF) file, your recipient may want to print it. Many people proofread a hard copy before sending off any document, believing they're more likely to catch mistakes that way.

Word puts a lot of printing power at your fingertips. The first chapter touched on the quick-and-easy way to send your document to the printer. This chapter shows you how to do things that would make Gutenberg drop his type. You'll learn how to choose and use the best printer for the job—say, your color inkjet for photos, a laser for documents, and a PDF file for good measure. And if you're sending that document via snail mail, then you'll need to print an envelope or a label. Word's got you covered there, too.

When you need to write to 650 of your closest friends with a personal message that you know will be of the utmost interest to them, it's time to dust off Word's mail merge. Sure, you could send a letter to Dear Occupant, but it's so much better to address it to Dear Edward and mention some personal details in the body of the letter. If those 650 letters are going to go out snail-mail, you'll need envelopes or at least labels to match. (Now, if only Word could lick the envelopes.) This chapter shows you how you can write one letter and reach a crowd.

Choosing a Printer

If you print a lot, no doubt you have a favorite printer that you use most of the time for Word documents. If you're lucky, you may have access to a couple of printers that are well-suited to different tasks. In general, inkjets do the best job of printing photos, while laser printers are great and more economical for printing long documents. Word is happy to work with either. In the stone-age days of computing, your printer was tethered to your computer by a cable. Today, that may be the case or you may be sharing a printer that's connected to your network. Again, this isn't an issue for Word. All you need to do to select the printer you want to use is go to File→Print. The Print box appears and at the top, next to Printer, you see a menu displaying the name of the printer Word intends to use. If that's not your choice for this print job, choose another printer from the menu as shown in Figure 4-1.

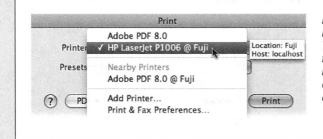

Figure 4-1:
Here's the Print box with the Printer menu open. This laptop computer can print to an Adobe PDF file or an HP LaserJet P1006. The @Fuji part of the name means the LaserJet is attached to a different computer on the local network named Fuji, like the apple.

Setting Your Default Printer

Your computer always has one printer in mind for the next print job, it's called the *default* printer. That's the printer Word uses when you press ⌘-P or click the little printer icon.

If you're always picking a different printer before you print, you may want to change the default. It's not a Word function; your default printer is part of your Mac preferences. Go to →Preferences→Print & Fax. At the bottom of the Print & Fax preferences, there are two menus. One chooses the default printer and the other chooses the default size of paper. The Default printer menu shows the printers available to your computer, which may include printers that you've used in the past but are no longer connected. Choose a printer from the list, or you may want to choose the option Last Printer Used, which sets the default to whichever printer you used most recently.

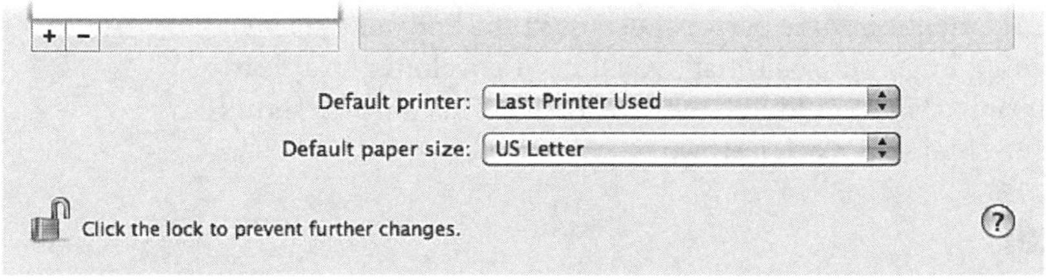

Figure 4-2:
You can choose a default printer using your Mac System Preferences. Here the default printer is set to be the last printer that was used, but it could just as easily be set to a specific printer.

Default printer: Last Printer Used

Default paper size: US Letter

Click the lock to prevent further changes.

Advanced Print Settings

The expanded Print window has some hidden panels that lead to advanced settings. Some of these settings you may never use. That's why they're tucked away. Some of the settings change depending on the selected printer.

Initially, the expanded Print window displays the Copies & Pages panel (described above), because that's the one you're most likely to use. Click the menu, as shown in Figure 4-3, and you can choose different panels.

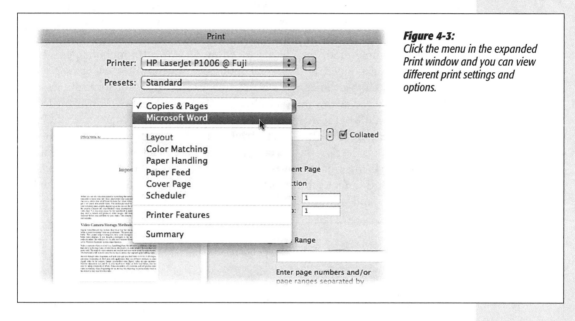

Figure 4-3:
Click the menu in the expanded Print window and you can view different print settings and options.

On the Microsoft Word panel, you can choose to print all the odd or even pages, which is handy if you want to print on both sides of a page and your printer doesn't do such things. You can print all the odd pages, then reload the pages in your printer and print all the even pages on the backside.

You can use the Microsoft Word panel to print some odd little tidbits of information, such as:

- **Document Properties.** Details about the current document
- **Styles.** Detailed technical descriptions of the styles (paragraph and text formatting rules) available to the current document. You can learn all about styles on page 96.
- **AutoText Entries.** Autotext definitions available that you can use. For more about autotext, see page 55.
- **Key Assignments.** If you've defined your own shortcut keys for Word, this is a way to print a cheat sheet.

If you're curious about any of these reports, you can view them without printing the pages. Select the report you want and then click the Preview button.

Exploring Printer-Specific Properties

Different printers have different talents. Choose from color printers and black-and-white printers, printers that can print on both sides of the paper, printers that can use huge pieces of paper, and even computer thingys that behave like printers but aren't really printers. Adobe Acrobat, covered next, falls into this category. You need some way to get at the controls for these printers and, obviously, the controls are different for each one. Your portal to your printer's features is the Print box (File→Print), which has a simple mode and an expanded mode. An extra menu appears when the Print box is expanded. It has several options. At the top you see Copies & Pages, where you can choose which parts of your document you want to print (see page 145). Initially, Word shows this panel because it's the one you're most likely to use. Listed in the middle of the menu are options like Layout, Color Matching, and Paper Handling. These are generic features, which may or may not be available to your printer. For properties specific to your printer, choose Printer Features and you see the settings the Printer manufacturer makes available through its printer driver software. Naturally, different printers have different features. Figure 4-4 shows the features for a black and white laser printer.

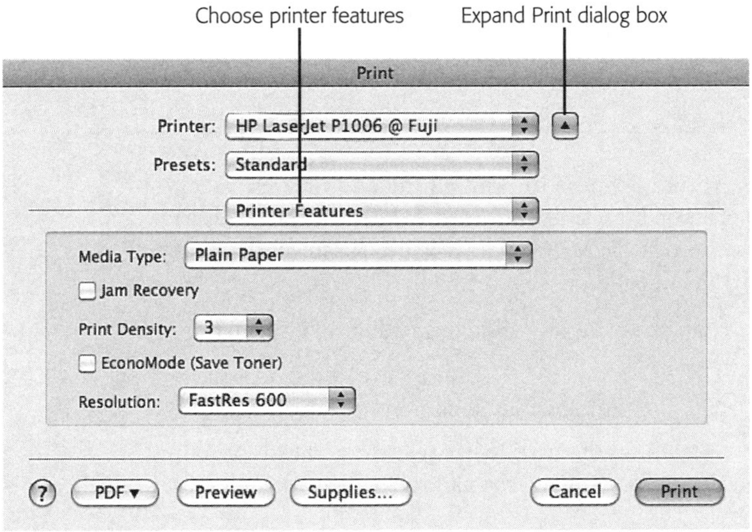

Choose printer features   Expand Print dialog box

Figure 4-4:
To see features specific to your printer, make sure the print box is in expanded mode, then choose Printer Features from the menu. This printer's features include settings for different types of paper or film, an EconoMode option that uses less toner and a resolution option that lets you choose between quality and printing speed.

Printing to an Adobe PDF File

Say you want to create an attachment that you can email or put up on a website that anyone, on any computer, can open and print. The solution, of course, is to use an Adobe PDF file. If you're not up to speed on this handy tool, see the box below.

Go to File→Save As and then in the Save As box, choose the format PDF. Give your document a name, preferably a descriptive one if you're distributing it widely. In the Save As box, you can choose to save the PDF to your desktop or a folder.

Adobe Acrobatics

The dawn of the personal computer revolution generated talk about the paperless office. Of course, that never happened. If anything, personal computers and printers brought about a quantum leap in paper consumption—just count the boxes of paper your local Staples sells every day. Still, if any computer tool came close to realizing an alternative to paper, it's Adobe Acrobat or PDF (Portable Document Format). The idea was to create a computer file format that can perfectly capture what's printed on the page—text, graphics, the whole kit and caboodle. The files need to be compact so they can be sent over the Internet. And anyone should be able to read and print these files without paying for additional software.

Adobe created Acrobat to meet all these needs, and before too long, everyone was using this new Portable Document Format to distribute reports and booklets over the Internet. Folks started calling them PDF files, because the filenames end in .pdf. Now you'll find PDFs online for just about everything. You can probably download the manual for your TV, your cell phone, and your refrigerator from the

manufacturers' websites as PDF files. The Census Bureau and many other government agencies provide the information they collect as PDFs.

When you share a PDF document, you don't have to worry much about whether the person on the other end can view it. Macs can always view a PDF file using the standard Preview app that's used to display photos. PC users probably have the Adobe Reader on their computer or they can get a free copy with minimum hassle. Success breeds imitators and Microsoft and the open source software crowd both took a run at paperless print formats, but neither reached the critical mass of acceptance of Adobe's PDFs.

Like other programs on your Mac, Office programs can create PDF files. For Word, Excel and PowerPoint, you can go to File→Save As and then choose PDF as the format. For Outlook, if you'd like to create PDFs from things like your calendars or contacts, go to File→Print and then use the PDF menu in the lower-left corner of the Print box.

Printing Part of Your Document

Sometimes you don't need to print an entire document. You may want to print only a few pages or maybe just a paragraph to take to a meeting or to proofread. Word is pretty flexible when it comes to printing bits and pieces. To handle these chores, go to the expanded Print box (File→Print) and check out the right side of the panel.

- **To print a single page**, make sure the insertion point is in the page you want to print before you open the Print box. Then, click the Current page radio button, shown in Figure 4-5, and click Print.

- **To print individual pages**, use the From-to option to print contiguous pages or use the Page range to print any assortment of pages you wish. For example, you can type *2, 5, 12-18* in the box and Word figures it out just fine.
- **To print selected text**, select the text before you open the Print box, then click the Selection radio button and hit Print.

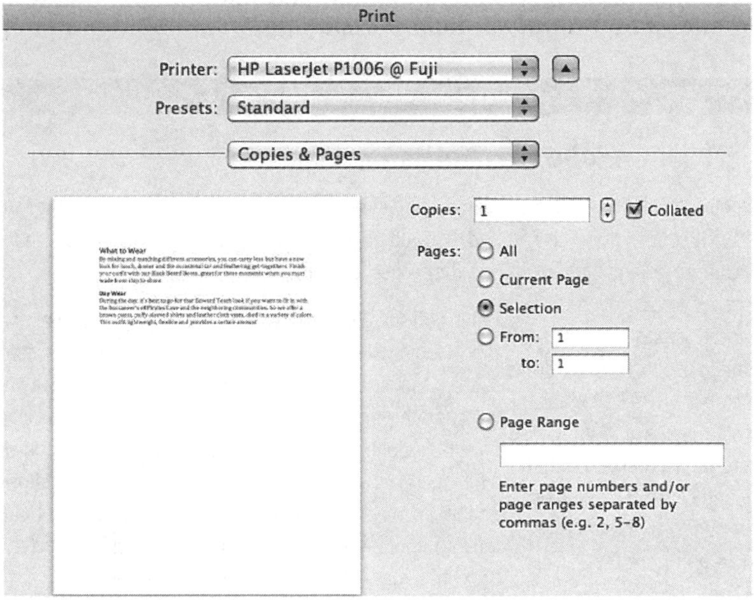

Figure 4-5:
You can choose exactly which portion of your document you print. Just select the text and graphics and then in the Print box, click the Selection button. The preview window shows the content that will be sent to the printer.

Printing Envelopes

Computers have always been great for printing documents on standard-size paper, but envelopes present a little bit more of a challenge. Envelopes are oddly shaped and kind of thick. And on some machines, the text needs to print sideways. Fortunately, Word and most modern printers have overcome the hurdles presented by printing on envelopes.

The first step for successful envelope printing is to make sure that your return address info is stored in Word. Go to Word→Preferences→Personal Settings→User Information. Word displays the name, company, address and other details about the user—that's you. If you didn't fill in these details when you installed Word, you can do it now. Click OK when you're done.

With your vital details stored in Word, you're ready to print an envelope. Here are the steps:

1. **Choose Tools→Envelope.**

   The Envelope window opens, displaying the tools you need to crank out your envelope, see Figure 4-6.

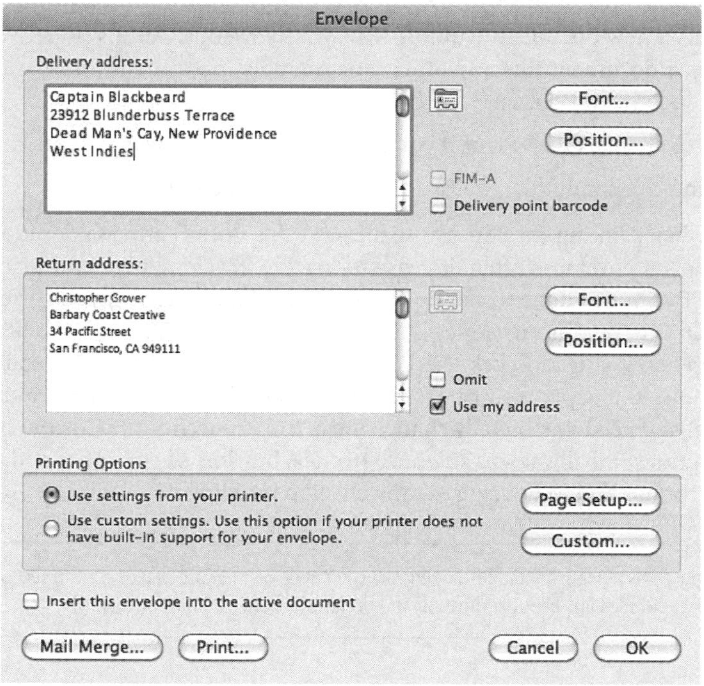

Figure 4-6:
The Envelope box provides a place to enter both a delivery and return address. To use addresses stored on Outlook Contacts (page 289) click the address card icon next to the address box.

2. **At the top of the Envelopes tab, in the "Delivery address" text box, type a name and address.**

   Just type in the information on different lines as you'd put it on an envelope. The address card icon above and to the right of the Delivery address text box opens your Outlook address book. Click it to select an existing contact. (Look, ma—no retyping!)

Tip: Even if you add a name and address from your Outlook Contacts, you can still make changes after it appears in the Delivery address box. Perhaps it would be wise to address him as Mr. Blackbeard, Esquire if you're asking for a favor.

---

3. **In the bottom text box, inspect your return address and edit if necessary.**

   If you provided an address in your Word Options, as described in the previously, that information appears in the Return address box. If you want, you can change the details now. Just delete the existing address and type the new information. (If your envelopes have a preprinted return address, turn on the Omit checkbox to prevent your stored return address from printing on the envelope.)

4. **Make sure your printer has envelopes and then click OK.**

   Word opens a new document window with your envelope. At this point, your envelope is a document like any other. For example, if you send mail to this person frequently, you can save this file and use it later.

5. **Press ⌘-P or choose File→Print if you need to choose a special printer.**

   If everything goes smoothly, you've got an envelope ready to mail.

The problem, when printing envelopes, is that everything doesn't always go smoothly. If you don't print envelopes often, it's easy to load an envelope into your printer wrong side up. Everyone's done this and wasted an envelope or two. If your printer has a special slot or tray for envelopes, look for an icon that gives you a hint. In Word's Envelope box, you can click the Page setup button to see the Orientation graphic that shows the paper feed direction. If your envelopes aren't the standard No. 10 size, or if you need to manually change the orientation, click the Custom button for more options. Finally, if you still have trouble, buy lots of envelopes and use the trial and error method to figuring out the envelope loading position.

Tip: If you're doing a mass mailing the old-fashioned way (on paper via the Post Office) see the section on mail merge, which includes tips about addressing and printing lots of envelopes at once.

Printing Labels

Word comes ready and willing to work with standard address labels. If you just want to print a single label, or if you want to print a bunch of the same label, then follow the steps in this section. (However, if you're printing labels, you're probably working on some kind of large mailing that would benefit from Word's automated mail merge feature. For details, go to page 151.)

Word is prepared to handle labels from Avery and many other manufacturers. Take note of the maker and model number of the labels you've bought, and follow the manufacturer's instructions for loading them into your printer. Then follow these steps to print one or more of the same label:

1. **Go to Tools→Labels.**

   The Labels box opens.

2. **In the Address box at top, type the address you want to put on the label.**

   If you want to print a batch of your own return address labels, click the box in the upper-right corner labeled "Use my address". Want to look up an address in Outlook? Click the address card icon.

3. **Click the Options button in the Label section.**

   The Label Options dialog box opens, as shown in Figure 4-7. Choose your label manufacturer, and then choose your label's model number. This information tells Word how many labels are on a sheet and how they're spaced. Click OK when you're done. There's also an option where you can choose your printer type: dot matrix (continuous feed) or Laser and Inkjet (sheet-fed).

   The Details button leads to additional settings if you need to fine-tune the way your printer places addresses on the page. Hopefully, you won't need to visit these settings, but if you do, you can manually enter measurements to make adjustments.

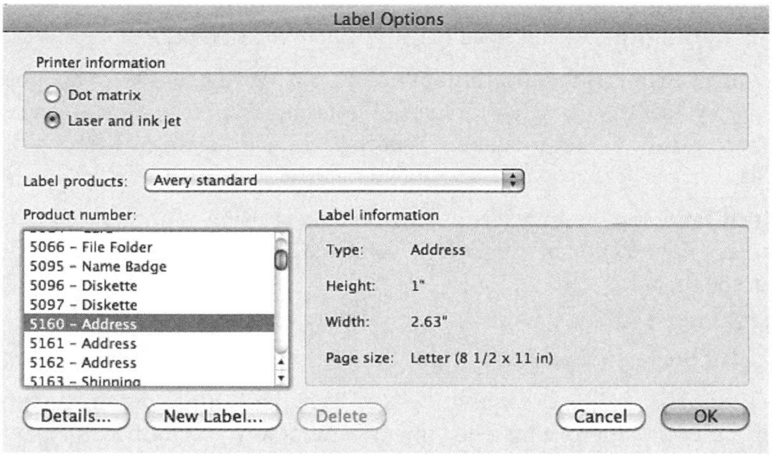

Figure 4-7:
Word's label printing tool is all set to work with a mind-boggling variety of label types. It also gives you some ways to make the most of your label resources. For example, using the Single label button, you can print one label on a sheet and save the rest for another project.

4. **Close the Label Options box by clicking OK.**

   You return to the Labels box. After you specify a label brand and model number, Word automatically sets up the page and other options.

5. **Under Number of Labels choose an option.**

   If you want to print an entire page with the same label, your return address for example, choose Full page of the same label. You can print a single label from a sheet of labels, saving the rest of the sheet for another project. Click the "Single label" radio button, and then identify the row and column for Word, so it knows which label to print on.

6. **Click Print when you're ready to go.**

   Word displays the standard Print box, where you can choose a printer or click Print.

Changing Your Print Preferences

You may never need to make changes to your print preferences, but if you do you'll find them by going go to Word→Preferences→Output and Sharing→Print.

Here's what you find:

- **Update fields.** Word fields include things like the date in a header (page 115) or a contact from your Outlook address book. It's usually a good idea to leave this box turned on because it makes sure you have the most up-to-date information before you print.

- **Update links.** Like the fields option above, this option is turned on when you install Word, and it's good to leave it that way. If you link a table or chart from an Excel spreadsheet, this option makes sure it's using the most recent info.

- **Reverse print order.** Prints from the last page to the first page.

- **Document Properties.** Turn this option on, and Word prints your document, and then prints the document properties—author, title, and so on—on a separate page at the end. (You can also inspect your document properties by going to File→Properties.)

- **Hidden Text.** You can hide text in your document using a font style command (Format→Font→Hidden). With this box turned on, that text doesn't stay hidden when you print.

- **Field Codes.** Use this option to print the actual field codes, like {PageNum} instead of the replacement text, which for this example would be a number.

- **Drawing objects.** The factory setting is to have this option turned on. Turn it off if you ever want to print a document without any graphics or floating text boxes.

- **Print data only for forms.** Use this option to fill-in the blanks on a printed form.

- **Print background colors and images.** Page color and background images work better for web pages than they do for printed documents. When you install Word, this option is turned off, but you can always toggle it back on.

- **Print PostScript over text.** Use this command to determine where a PostScript printer prints special code that's included in a PRINT field. If you don't have a PostScript printer or don't understand what this means, leave this box turned off and don't sweat it.

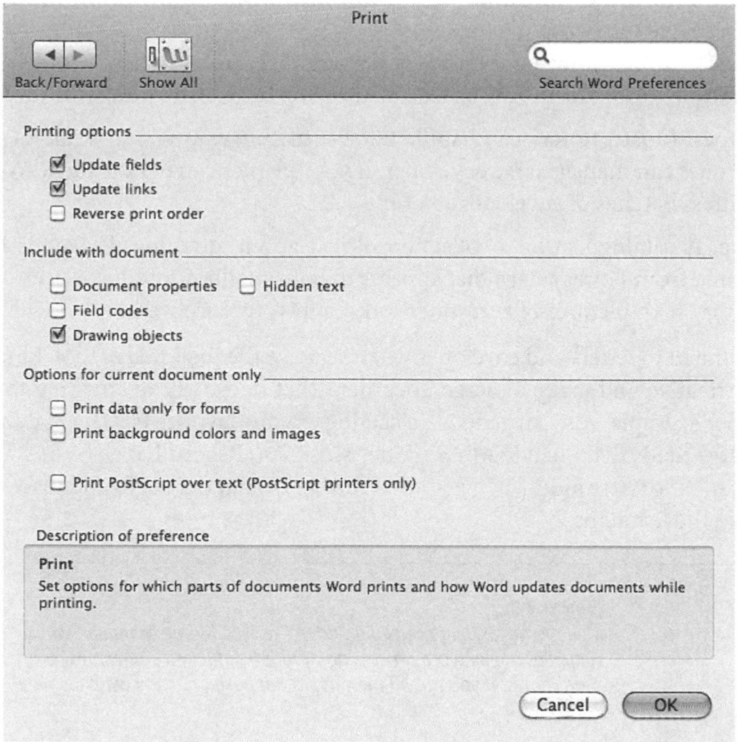

Figure 4-8:
Word's Print preferences are different from your Mac's Print & Fax preferences. You could work forever and never need to make changes in here, but if you need to fine-tune Word's printing habits, these are your options.

Understanding Mail Merge Basics

Mail merge consists of two parts: a document and a list. The document is like a form with placeholders, such as "Dear <<FirstName>>" or "We are certain that <<CompanyName>> will quadruple its annual profits by using our widget." When you initiate a merge, words from the list fill in the blanks on the form. These blanks, shown here (and in Word) by the double brackets, are called fields in mail merge lingo. So, a person's first name is a field, the Zip code is another field. When you insert a field into your letter, it gets filled in automatically from your list.

Common Types of Merge Documents

You can see the most common types of mail merge documents in the Mail Merge Manager (Figure 4-9). Go to Tools→Mail Merge Manager and click the triangle button to open the first panel. Then, click the Create New menu. You see a list that includes:

- **Form Letters.** Create form letters that begin with a real name instead of Dear Resident. For example, they can begin, "Edward Teach. You may already be a winner!"

- **Labels.** The solution for large envelopes is often labels. Mail merge reads your list of recipients and prints out sheets of labels for large envelopes or boxes.

- **Envelopes.** Most printers can handle letter-sized envelopes, and some of the fancier ones can manage large envelopes. If your printer can handle them, Word can address batches of envelopes at a time.

- **Catalog.** A catalog can be a collection of just about anything. It sounds like something from Pottery Barn that appears in your mailbox, but it could also be a directory with pictures of everyone working in your corporation.

You aren't limited to letters and envelopes when you use the mail merge tool. In fact, you can be creative and make a merge document that doesn't have anything to do with mail. For example, you can generate a catalog of your favorite CDs by making a list with merge fields that include Album Title, Musician, Record Label, Genre, Year of Release, and Short Critique. Then just use Word to design the pages and place the fields to hold the list items.

Figure 4-9:
Mail merge tasks are consolidated in the Mail Merge Manager, which simplifies one of word processing's more helpful, but sometimes puzzling chores. If you put off merging in the past, you may want to give it a try now.

Mail Merge Lists

In Word-speak, these lists are often called recipient lists, because for a form letter, envelope or label merge, a list is often the names and addresses of the recipients. The lists used in mail merge have more in common with the tables discussed in Chapter 2 than they do with your everyday shopping list. In fact, when you create a list, Word shows you an easy fill-in form but stores the content in a table (Figure 4-10). The individual bits of information (fields) in each row may include details such as First Name, City, and Zip code. So, if you do a mail merge for envelopes, Word uses the name and address in the first row to print the first envelope. The name and address in the second row go on the second envelope, and so on.

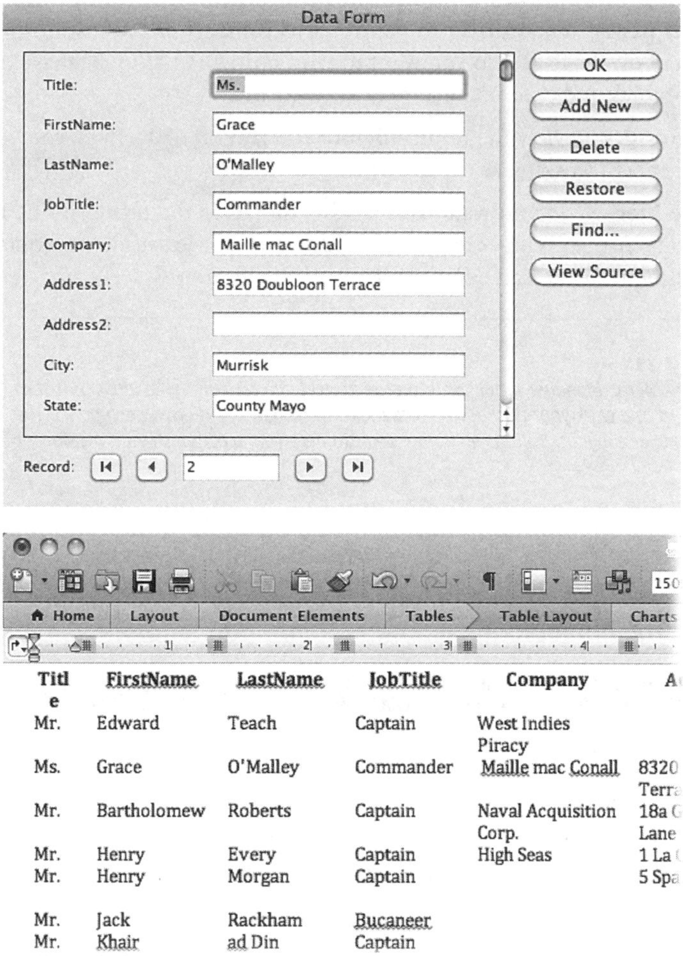

Figure 4-10:
Top: When you create a merge list inside of Word, you use a form like this. Each form is like a database record. Each box in the form is a field.

Bottom: Word saves the data in a table, similar to an Excel spreadsheet.

The Six Phases of a Mail Merge

When you open the Mail Merge Manager, it's clear that your merge project is divided into six parts (Figure 4-11). In each part, you have to answer some questions:

- **1. Select Document Type**. What type of document are you're creating? Is it a form letter? A bunch of envelopes or mailing labels? Or some other type of document?

- **2. Select Recipients List**. What list are you going to use to fill in the blanks? Does this list exist in your address book or Outlook or do you need to create it?

- **3. Insert Placeholders**. Add merge fields to your document. Where do you want to insert words from your recipient list, such as Dear <<First Name>>?

- **4. Filter Recipients**. Who exactly do you want to contact? Do you want to use every recipient on the list or do you want to trim it down? Using database type tools, you can pick and choose the targets for your mail.

- **5. Preview Results**. Review the results. Before you run off 650 letters, you want to ask: Is the merge working as expected?

- **6. Complete Merge**. Do you want to send this merge to the printer to be immortalized on paper, envelopes or labels? Or do you want to see all the letters in a Word document so you can edit each letter a little bit more?

Figure 4-11:
The Mail Merge Manager breaks your merge project into six numbered steps. Just start at the top and work your way down. Click the triangle buttons to open each panel. The panels include menus, buttons and other tools to help you accomplish your mission.

Decoding Merge-Speak

If you're familiar with databases, you may be inclined to translate Word's mail merge terminology into more familiar database language.

- **Recipient list.** Actually, just a very simple, barebones database.

- **Data source.** The computer file that holds the recipient list. When you create a list inside Word, it saves the list in a Word table. An outside data source could be an Excel file, Outlook contact list or database file.

- **Recipient.** In database terms, one recipient (that is, one page in the recipient form) is the same as a record.

- **Merge field.** For the most part, a merge field is just like a field in any database. Each box in the form represents a different field.

- **MergeRec.** The special field MergeRec is a counter that keeps track of the records that are actually used in a merge.

Running the Mail Merge Manager

If you're new to mail merges, the tabbed Mail Merge Manager is a fine way to start. You can watch how Word sets up your documents, and then later, you may want tweak the results to fit your project. The manager appears as a floating palette so it's easy to move it out of the way as you work (Figure 4-11). In many ways, it doesn't matter if your merge is creating letters for a mass mailing, printing envelopes, or cranking out multiple business proposals. If you simply start at the top of the Mail Merge Manager and work your way down the list, you'll get the job done.

Tip: If you need to change something you did in an earlier step, it's okay to backtrack. Just click the tab for the step and make your changes.

The tutorial on the following pages takes you through the steps for a typical mail merge letter.

Note: If you don't already have your own mail merge project in mind, you can download a sample form letter and recipient list *04-1_Mail_Merge.zip* from *http://missingmanuals.com/cds.html*.

---

1. Select Document Type

Word's pretty flexible when it comes to the main document for your merge. You can start with a letter that's already written or you can start with a blank document. The following exercise describes the merge mail process using files from the Missing CD (*www.missingmanuals.com/cds*). The main document is called *merge_pirate_letter.docx* and the recipient list is called *list_pirate_letter.docx*. In this scenario, the owner of a missing ship is writing to a list of known pirates. You can use your own mail merge letter if you want, it shouldn't be hard to substitute your own form letter and recipient list.

1. **Open merge_pirate_letter.docx.**

    The letter, shown in Figure 4-12, was created using one of Word's stationery templates.

2. **Go to Tools→Mail Merge Manager→Select Document Type and then click the Create New menu.**

    As shown in Figure 4-9, you have the choice of: Form Letters, Labels, Envelopes, or Catalog (as in a phonebook).

3. **Choose Form Letters.**

    The Mail Merge Manager displays information about the project as you make your choices. At this point it's determined that your merge project is a form letter and that you're using the current document. So in that step 1 panel you see:

    Main document: merge_pirate_letter.docx

    Merge type: Form Letters

    The next tab automatically opens.

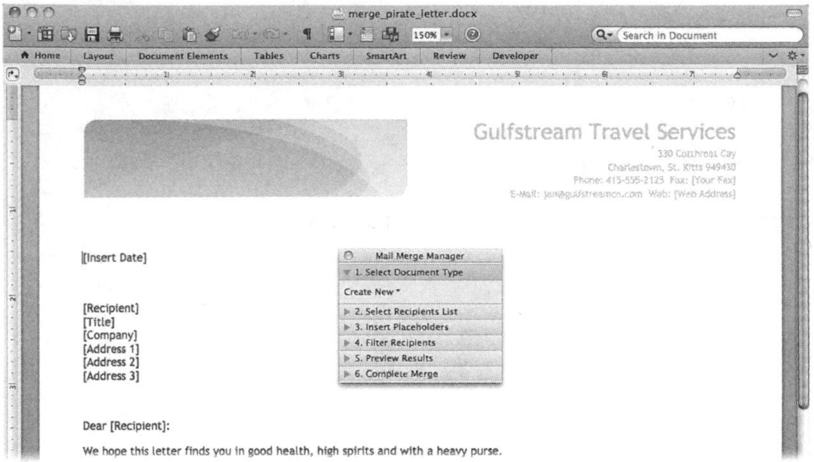

Figure 4-12:
Cleverly, the template for this letter used details from Word→Preferences→ User Information to create the letterhead and left fill-in blanks for recipient details. The Mail Merge Manager is open to the first step and eager to go.

2. Select Recipients List

You can think of the Recipient list as a table of information. Often, it's a group of people and their contact information, but it could be anything that's organized in the same manner—for example, a list of products with descriptions, dimensions, shipping weight and prices. Word is happy as long as that list is organized in database fashion where each person or product is considered a "record" and each detail in a record is considered a "field." Programs like your Mac Address Book, Outlook, Excel and FileMaker Pro are used to creating lists like this, so they're natural merge partners. If you haven't yet created your list, you can do that right inside of Word, and data is stored in a table inside of a Word document, as shown in Figure 4-10.

1. **In "2. Select Recipients List," open the Get List menu.**

   The manager displays several options for getting and attaching a recipient list to your main document.

2. **Choose list_pirate_letter.docx.**

   Mail Merge Manager connects the recipient list you choose to the current merge project. Two buttons in the Select Recipient List tab come to life. The button with the binoculars opens a dialog box where you can search the recipient list for a particular record. The button with the pencil opens your recipient list so that you can make changes. You can come back to these later if you find that your merge doesn't work exactly the way you expected.

   That's all that needs to be done for this step, so the next tab automatically opens, displaying an address card.

Tip: Word courteously opens the different panels as you work your way down the six steps on the manager, but you can open and close the panels as needed. If the manager is covering up too much or your letter, go ahead and close a couple panels.

You may have noticed the other options on the Get List menu. Here's a quick tour:

- **New Data Source.** Use New Data Source to create a new list on the fly.
- **Open Data Source.** Use Open Data Source to open a list that was previously created and saved to a file. Word can read a wide variety of files including Word documents with a single table or files exported from Excel.
- Use **Office Address Book** to open lists stored in your Outlook contacts list (page 289).
- Use **Apple Address Book** if you keep your contacts stored in your Mac's Address Book.
- Use **FileMaker Pro** to open lists stored in FileMaker Pro databases (provided you have FileMaker installed on your computer).

3. Insert Placeholders

This is the fun part of the process. The message above the address card in step 3 prompts you to drag placeholders into the document. Use the triangle buttons at the top and bottom of the address card to see the different placeholders you can use. Most of them are typical address related items except for the last one: PirateShip. As you might guess, the placeholders are defined by the recipient list.

This particular document, because it was created from a template, has some placeholder text of its own. To complete this letter, text within square brackets needs to be replaced. For example, in place of [Insert Date], you'll want to type in the date you're sending the letter. Below the date, in the address block, all those name, title and address placeholders are prime candidates for your merge placeholders.

1. **Click [Recipient] text in the address block of the form letter.**

   When you click inside the templates' placeholder, the square brackets and text disappear. If this weren't a merge project, you'd type one person's name in this spot.

2. **Drag the FirstName from the address card to the "recipient" spot in the address block.**

   Your merge placeholder appears in the document as <<FirstName>>.

3. **Press Space and then drag LastName from the address card to the recipient spot in the address block.**

   When you're done the top of the address block says <<FirstName>> <<LastName>>.

4. Continue to replace the template's address block and Dear [Recipient] place-holders with placeholders from the address card.

   When you're finished, your letter looks like Figure 4-13.

5. In the letter's third paragraph, replace the words Port Dread with the <<CountryRegion>> placeholder. Then in the second sentence, replace the words Rusty Washtub with the <<PirateShip>> placeholder.

   Everyone expects the address block to be customized; it's more impressive to add a custom touch to the body of the letter.

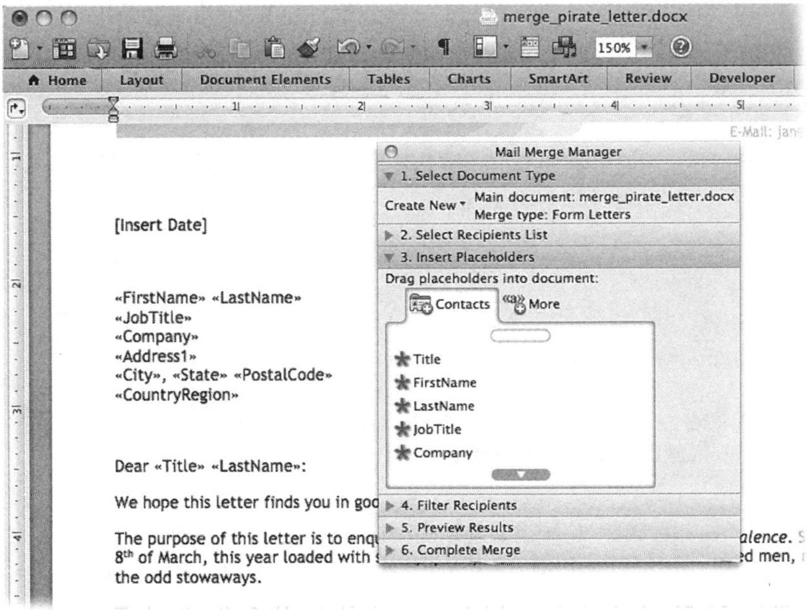

Figure 4-13:
As you drag place-holders from the Mail Merge Manager address card, your letter gets filled in with angle-bracket placeholders like the ones shown here in the address block and salutation.

4. Filter Recipients

A little preparation can make your mail merge project go better. For example, if your list is coming from your Mac's Address book, in your address book you can create a group by choosing File→New Group. Drag all your pirate contacts into the group and they're presorted for your mail merge. You can do the same thing in Outlook by going to File→New→Contact Group. If you're familiar with your favorite address book/contacts tool and find it easier to presort this way, then you can skip the Filter Recipients panel in the Mail Merge Manager. Besides, it may be helpful to have a more permanent list of pirates in the future.

If the source for your recipient list is huge, and many contact databases are, you'll find that filtering is an indispensable tool. Suppose you wanted to limit your mass mailing to pirates known to operate in a certain region; you can use the manager's tools to choose contacts from a specific region. Given the nature of your letter, it doesn't make sense to contact anyone who doesn't have a pirate ship. You can filter out the non-pirates, too.

1. **In "4. Filter Recipients", click Options.**

   The Query Options panel opens with two tabs at the top: Filter Records and Sort Records. The Filter Records tab shows drop-down menus and text boxes as shown in Figure 4-14.

2. **Open the Field menu and choose** *CountryRegion*.

   The Field menu options match placeholders in your recipient list.

3. **Use the Comparison menu to select** *Equal to* **and then in the Compare to text box, type** *West Indies*.

   With this filter in place, your mail recipient list is trimmed down to contacts in the West Indies. Notice that the next row in the Query Options box is now active and ready for your next criteria. The menu on the far left is set to "And," so you're ready to apply more conditions to the filter.

4. **Move down a row and use the Field menu to choose PirateShip. Then with the Comparison menu choose** *is not blank*.

   When you choose the "is not blank" option, there's no need to enter anything in the Compare box. Now your recipient list is limited to contacts in the West Indies that have pirate ships. Perfect!

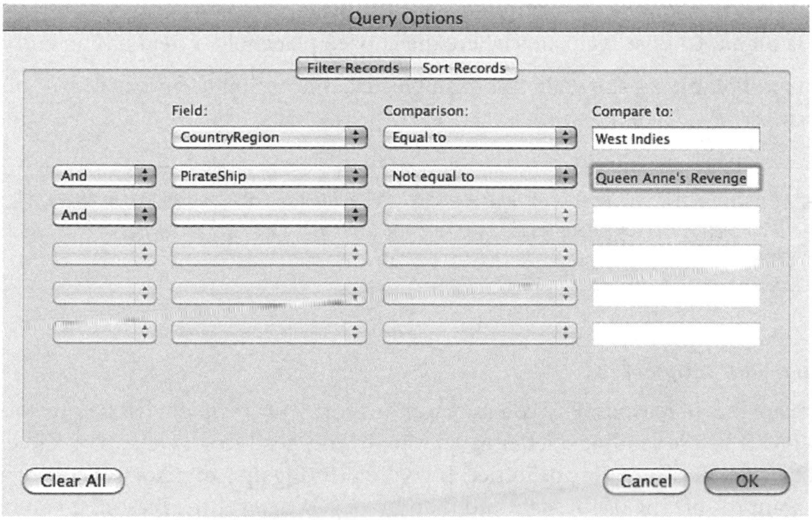

Figure 4-14:
Here the Query Options panel displays the Filter Records tab, which you use to trim down the size of an enormous contact list. You'd use the Sort records list if you wanted to alphabetize your contact list or sort the list by Zip code.

Choosing a comparison option

The widgets in the Query Options box are simple, but they give you a surprising amount of filtering power. If you've dabbled with databases, you're probably familiar with the and/or options in the menu on the far left. In the example here, you used the "and" option to filter your list on two conditions. You won't be sending letters to pirates who aren't in the West Indies and you won't be sending letters to non-pirates in the West Indies. However, if you change the "And" to "Or," your query would include every contact in the West Indies, as well as everyone with a pirate ship.

The Comparison options are powerful and their names describe their function. In most cases, the comparison options expect you to enter text or numbers in the Compare to box.

- **Equal to.** Finds a perfect match. For example, if you're working with states, "Equal to CA" finds California.

- **Not equal to.** Use "Not equal to" when you want to exclude part of your list. "Not equal to CA" removes California recipients from your list.

- **Less than.** Usually used for numbers, less than can also be used alphabetically where A is less than Z.

- **Greater than.** The opposite of "Less than," also for both letters and numbers. Greater than Smith includes, for example, Smithy and all names that come after it alphabetically.

- **Less than or equal.** This example is just like "Less than" except that it includes the number in the Compare to box.

- **Greater than or equal.** The cousin of "Less than or equal." For example, to include all recipients who have a first name, use "Greater than or equal" and type *A* in the "Compare to" box.

- **Is blank.** Choose recipients where the chosen placeholder field has no entry.

- **Is not blank.** As shown in this example, use this option to find owners of pirate ships.

Note: It's possible to filter *everyone* off your list. This can be the result of over-zealous filtering or a flaw in logic. If this happens, Word assumes it's a mistake and gives you a warning when you close the Query Options box.

Sorting your recipient list

There are lots of reasons why you may want to sort your recipient list before you do a merge. If you're sending a letter as bulk mail, you need to sort letters by Zip code to get a discount from the post office. If you're printing up a directory of clients, you may want to sort the list by state and then by city. Whatever the reason, if you need your letters to be in a specific order at the end of the merge, you need to sort your recipient list at the beginning. You can set up your sort criteria at this same point where you filter your list.

In the Query Options panel, click the Sort Records tab. Choose the field you want to sort by, such as State, and then choose whether you want the sort to ascend from A to Z or descend (Z to A). You can sort on more than one placeholder field, so you can choose to sort by State in the first row in the Query Options box and then choose to sort by cities within the states by choosing City in the second row.

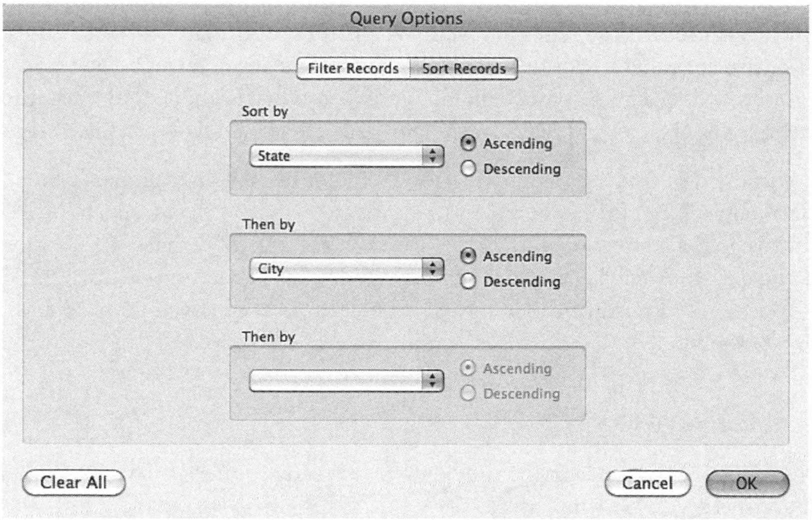

Figure 4-15:
Use the Sort Records tab on the Query Options box to determine the order for your form letters, envelopes or labels. You can sort by multiple fields. Here the sort alphabetically groups states and then cities within states.

5. Preview Results

In this step, you look over your document in the Mail Merge pane to make sure everything looks right. It's not unusual to discover a couple gotchas at this point. The key to success usually depends on the consistency of your recipient list. Like most computer programs, mail merge doesn't like special cases. So things may look off kilter if, say, one of your recipients doesn't have a street address or goes only by one name. (You do write to LeBron, Voltaire, and Pink, don't you?)

1. **In the "5. Preview Results" panel, click the <<ABC>> button.**

   This magic button turns your placeholders into real text. At the top of your letter, you see the address box filled in with a pirate's name and address. In the body of the letter you see the region and ship name are filled in.

2. **Click the navigation arrows or type a number in the text box.**

   The arrow buttons look like the ones on your DVD or iPod. You can move forward and backward or jump to the beginning or end of your recipient list. Your letter shows details for the current recipient.

3. **Click the {a} button.**

    You probably won't need to use this option often. It changes your letter to show the word "field" code. This geeky code is what makes your mail merge work. You may remember the discussion of Word fields from page 115.

Editing before the merge

Who knows what you'll find when you preview your merge, but there's one thing for sure. You don't want to waste time, paper, envelopes, labels, or that really expensive printer ink on a bad merge. It's well worth your time to find trouble spots, and you can make changes to your letter and your recipient list at the last moment. Edit your main document using any of the usual techniques. You can change the text, add new paragraphs or drag a placeholder from one spot to another. Right up to the last minute before merging you can add new placeholders and delete ones that aren't working out.

It's not unusual to find a problem with the recipient list. All your pirates have a first and last name except for Redbeard and Blackbeard. There always seems to be a contact or two that doesn't conform. If that's the case, go back to "2. Select the Recipients List" and click the pencil Edit Data Source button. Make whatever modifications you need to make Redbeard fit the merge. If it's helpful, you can even go back and add criteria to the filter.

Complete Merge

If everything looked great in the preview, you're ready to merge. The "6. Complete Merge" panel gives you some options.

-   Use **Merge to Printer** to make hard copies of your pirate letter. Word opens the standard Print window where you can choose a specific printer and make other tweaks before the deed is done.

-   Use **Merge to Document** to created a new document with a letter to each pirate on separate pages. This option is great if you need another layer of proofing before you send your letter off, or if you want to keep a computer record of each individual letter.

-   Use **Merge to Email** when you want to save money on postage. The Mail Recipient box appears where you can choose a subject for the email. Use the To menu to select the email address field for your contact. (There's no email address in this example, because pirates don't have wifi onboard.)

In addition to the major merge options, in this last step you can choose to print a portion of the merged letters using the options from the drop-down menu:

You have three options:

-   **All** prints all of the records. Make sure you have plenty of paper in your printer.

-   **Current Record** prints the record selected in the "5. Print Preview" panel.

-   **Custom** prints a range of records that you specify in the From and To boxes.

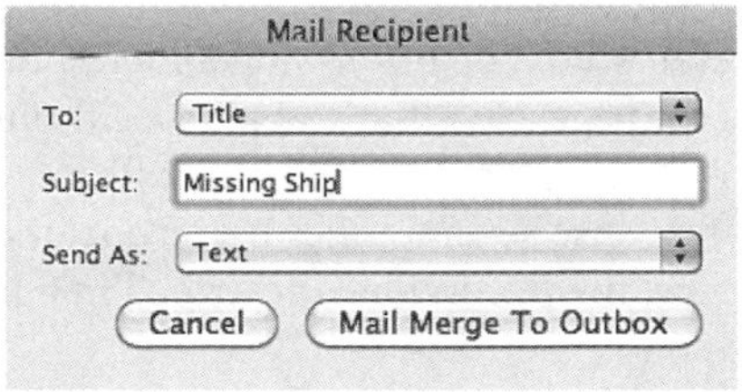

Figure 4-16:
You're not limited to snail-mail when you merge. Word's Mail Merge Manager can send your mass mailing out using email.

Advanced Merge Techniques

When you work with the mail merge tools—lists, sorting, filtering—you've entered the realm of database programming. Whether you know it or not, you're doing the same things that full-time database developers do for huge corporations every day. Why not move up to the next level—and apply some advanced fields to your merges.

The mail merge manager inserts special *merge fields* into your documents but shields you from some of the nitty-gritty programmer's details. In your document, you see simple <<FirstName>> and <<LastName>> placeholders, but the field codes behind those placeholders is a little more complex. To get a glimpse, you can display field codes in your document by going to Word→Preferences→View and then turn on Field Codes. You'll see your filed codes look something like this: {MERGEFIELD FirstName}. Fields begin and end with curly brackets and the first word in caps is basically a command. In this example the command says during mail merge put the FirstName here. There are a number of fields you can use in addition to MERGE-FIELD. To see them, choose Insert→Field and, in the Categories list, choose Mail Merge. The scrolling list on the right shows the Fields (commands) you can insert into your document when you're working on a mail merge project.

So Word's insertable fields are like mini-programs that help you set up mail merge documents that you or someone else will use in the future. So, when you don't have all the information you need when you set up the merge document, you can create a rule to help the person running the merge to correctly fill in the blanks.

For example, when you insert the "Fill in" field into a document, it makes a message pop up during the merge. This box asks a question and provides a text box where you, or whoever's running the merge, can type the answer. Word then places the typed answer into the document. In other words, the "Fill in" field acts as a reminder to fill in the blanks at the time of printing. In other cases, Word may not need input during the merge. You can set up your rule so that Word simply looks at the details in the recipient list and makes a decision on that basis. So, if a recipient's favorite baseball team is the Yankees, then you don't offer free tickets to Fenway Park.

Here's a brief rundown on some of the fields you can insert into your documents using Insert→Field→MailMerge:

- **Ask.** This field stops the merge and presents a dialog box asking for a response. Word places the response in a bookmark (page 213) that a field (specifically, a REF field) later in the document can reference. Therefore, the Ask field is the perfect tool when you want to use the response several times in the document. If you need to use the response only once, the Fill-in field, described in a moment, is a better option.

- **MergeRec.** When you merge a document to the printer or to another document, Word gives each recipient a Merge Record number. If you insert the Merge Record # field in your document, it shows that number in the text. This field may not be useful for letters, but it can come in handy when you're creating a directory of people.

- **NextIf.** Go to the next record when a condition exists. For example, the rule could be: Go to the next record if the City field equals Chicago.

- **Fill-in.** Stops the merge and presents a dialog box asking for text that's then inserted into the document. Figure 4-17 shows the dialog box you use to create a "Fill in" field.

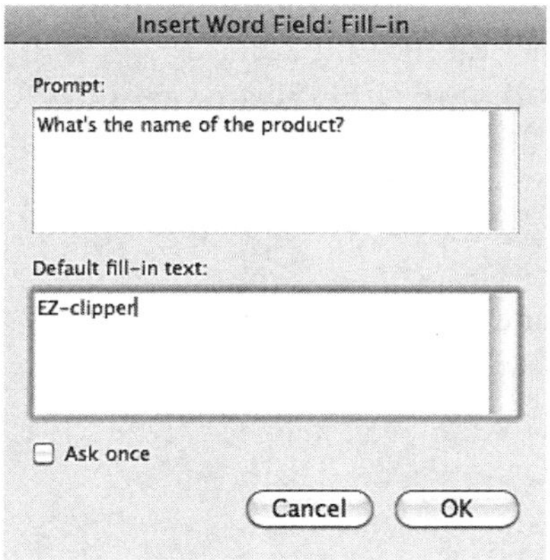

Figure 4-17:
Use this text box to set up a "Fill in" field. Type a question into the Prompt text box, and then type the most common answer to the question in the "Default fill-in text" box. The checkbox at the bottom determines whether the pop-up box appears for every recipient in the mail merge or if it just appears once at the beginning.

- **MergeSeq.** Similar to the merge record, with one significant difference. The Merge Record # takes into account all the recipients whether they're included or excluded from your merge. The Merge Sequence # is based only on those recipients that are shown in the merge.

- **Set.** Sets a bookmark in the text that you can use as a reference. For example, the rule can place a bookmark named TaxRate with a value of .0775 in a document. Other fields or macros can then use this field to calculate the tax for a sale. (You can display the bookmark's contents in your document using a REF field.)

- **If.** Makes a decision based on the contents of the recipient list. For example: If the recipient's state is California, then Word inserts the words "the Golden State" into the document, else (that is, if the recipient's state is not California), it inserts "your state."

Tip: Don't be afraid to use whole paragraphs of text with your If…Then…Else statements. If you manage a technical support department, then you can create statements that make it easy to answer the most frequently asked questions and merge them into email messages using rules.

- **Next.** Go to the next record (that is, the next row in the source list). If any other merge fields are in the document, Word fills them in using data from the next row in the recipient list. Use this option to create a directory or a page of address labels, where you want details from several recipients to appear on the same page.
- **SkipIf.** Excludes a record from the merge based on a condition.

Merging to Labels and Envelopes

Two of the most common Word mail merges are automated for you: address labels and envelopes. Either way, this is an extremely powerful feature that lets you combine the database flexibility of Outlook or your Mac Address Book with the smarts of Word. Whether you're the local soccer coach or an avid Christmas card sender, letting Word prepare your mass mailings beats addressing envelopes by hand any day.

You want to prepare for the merge in the same way you prepare for a form letter merge. As explained on page 158, you may want to create and vet your lists in advance using Outlook or Address Book groups.

Know the size of the labels or envelopes you're going to use. Have some on hand as you begin the process. (You can buy sheets of self-adhesive labels at Staples or any other office supply store; Avery is one of the best-known names and the Avery label style numbers are the gold standard of mail merging mavens everywhere. These labels come in every conceivable size and shape; the 30-per-page version—Avery 5160—is the most popular.)

Merging to Labels

Make sure that the labels you buy will fit into your printer and feed smoothly—buy inkjet or laser labels, for example, to match your printer.

To create labels, open a new blank Word document and proceed as follows:

1. **Choose Tools→Mail Merge Manager.**

   The Mail Merge Manager appears with its six steps described on page 153.

2. **In the first step Select Document Type, use the Create New menu to choose Labels.**

   The Label Options dialog box appears (see Figure 4-18, top). Unless you're that rare eccentric who uses a dot matrix (impact) printer, leave "laser and inkjet" selected.

3. **From the "Label products" pop-up menu, select the brand of labels you have.**

   Word lists every kind of label you've ever heard of, and many that you haven't.

Tip: If you've bought some oddball, no-name label brand not listed in Word's list, click New Label. Word gives you a dialog box, complete with a preview window, for specifying your own label dimensions. (But before you go to that trouble, look carefully at the fine print on the package, where it probably says something like "Equivalent to Avery 5164.")

---

4. **Inspect your label package to find out what label model number you have; select the matching product in the "Product number" list box. Click OK.**

   The main document becomes an empty sheet of labels. It's time to start dragging field names from your source document.

5. **On the Mail Merge Manager, use the Get List pop-up button to select the database or file containing your addresses.**

   For example, to use your Outlook Address Book, choose Office Address Book from this menu. If your addresses are stored in an Excel spreadsheet or a tab delimited text file, choose Open Data Source instead (then navigate to your database or data source file and open it).

   If you haven't set up your database yet, choose New Data Source and fill in the blanks on the form.

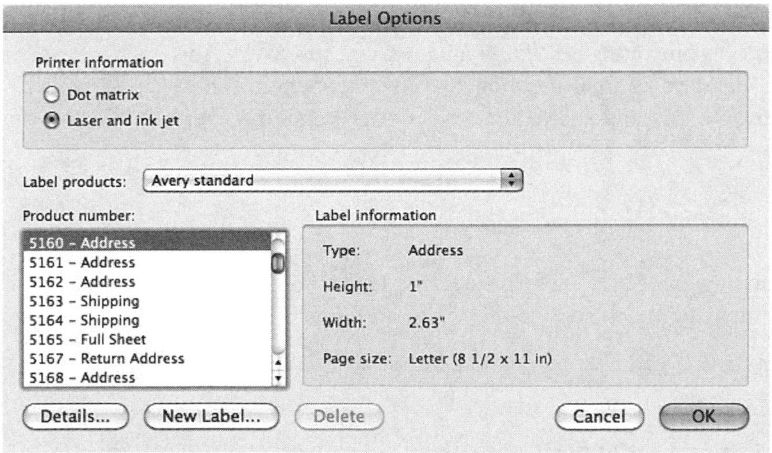

Figure 4-18:
Top: Avery 5160 is one of the most popular label products; it comes with 10 rows of three labels each. Bottom: If you're assembling a bulk mailing and therefore need to bar code your own envelopes, click Insert Postal Bar Code. Word asks you to select the name of the merge field where your Zip codes are, then prints the corresponding bar code on each envelope or label. Your mail is likely to reach its recipient faster if you use these bar codes.

6. **In the Edit Labels dialog box that appears, choose field names from the "Insert Merge Field" pop-up menu to build your address.**

   As shown at the bottom of Figure 4-18, use the space bar and Return key as you go. For example, choose FirstName, insert a space, choose LastName, then press Return to start a new line. Choose City, type a comma if you like, and then choose State; add two spaces before choosing Zip code. (If you want to change the font and other formatting at this point, use keyboard shortcuts like ⌘-B for bold or press ⌘-D to open the Font box.)

7. **Click OK.**

   You return to your main document window, where placeholders for your labels now appear. (Click the <<abc>> icon on the Mail Merge Manager's Preview Results panel to preview the actual names and addresses as they'll be printed.) If you want to further format individual labels, you can do so now. Just select the text or the field placeholders to format them. For example, if your labels are too crowded, you can select all (⌘-A) and then reduce the font size.

8. **Load a piece of plain paper in your printer and click the "Merge to Printer" button in the Mail Merge Manager's Complete Merge pane.**

   This way, you can check to see if the labels are properly aligned without wasting an expensive sheet of labels. Hold the paper printout over a label sheet and line them up in front of a window or light. Labels only have one printable side, so you might even want to mark the blank paper with a top and bottom side, to make sure you know whether you load labels face up or face down.

9. **If you need to tweak your labels' alignment, choose Create New→Labels on the Mail Merge Manager and click Details.**

   A dialog box pops up, displaying the dimensions and specifications of your currently chosen label model, along with boxes and arrows for adjusting them. Adjust the Top margin or Side margin to shift the text up, down, and side-to side in order to better fit on the labels. Then print another test sheet to be sure your changes had the intended effect.

   When everything's working properly, load the labels into your printer, and click the "Merge to Printer" button again. Click Print.

Tip: Take advantage of the Merge→Custom pop-up menu (see page 162) if you have a long mailing list. Some printers tend to jam if you try to print too many pages of labels at once.

Editing labels

You can edit a label document by opening it, just like any main document. But because of the unique problems involved in changing a sheet of labels, Word provides a couple of special tools. To make changes to an existing label document, proceed as follows:

---

1. **Open the label document.**

   Word opens the document and the Mail Merge Manager. (If not, choose Tools→Mail Merge Manager.)

2. **Click the "Add or remove placeholders on labels" button.**

   It's the third icon in the Select Recipients List section of the Mail Merge Manager palette. The Edit Labels dialog box opens.

3. **Make changes to the label format.**

4. **Add or remove merge fields or change text formatting.**

   For example, select the merge fields and use the Formatting Palette. Then click OK and proceed with the merge.

Yet another way to format labels

You can also edit labels right in the main document, which you may find easier than using the Edit Labels dialog box. The secret is in the "Fill in the items to complete your document" button on the Mail Merge Manager (the fourth icon in the Select Recipients List section of the Mail Merge Manager palette). Here's how to use this method of label editing:

1. **Open the label document; click the first label on the page.**

   Word opens the document and the Mail Merge Manager. (If the Mail Merge Manager isn't open, choose Tools→Mail Merge Manager.)

2. **Edit the label document.**

   For instance, you can drag merge fields from the Mail Merge Manager, type additional text, and format the text or field placeholders (font, color, and so on). Remember, you're doing this only in the first label.

3. **Click the "Fill in the items to complete your document" button on the Mail Merge Manager.**

   Word changes all labels on the sheet so that they match the changes you just made in the first label.

When you're satisfied with the way things look, merge and print the labels as described on the previous pages.

Merging to Envelopes

Printing envelopes on computer printers has always been an iffy proposition; in essence, you're trying to cram two or three layers of paper through a machine designed to print on sheets only one layer thick.

If your printer has guides for feeding envelopes and is envelope-friendly, so much the better. Additionally, you may find that some brands of envelopes fit your printer better than others.

When you're ready to begin, open a new blank document and follow these steps:

1. **Choose Tools→Mail Merge Manager, and then choose Create New→Envelopes.**

   The Envelope dialog box opens, as shown in Figure 4-19. If you don't care for Helvetica, Arial, or whatever, click Font to call up a Font dialog box. You can use any of Word's fonts and effects.

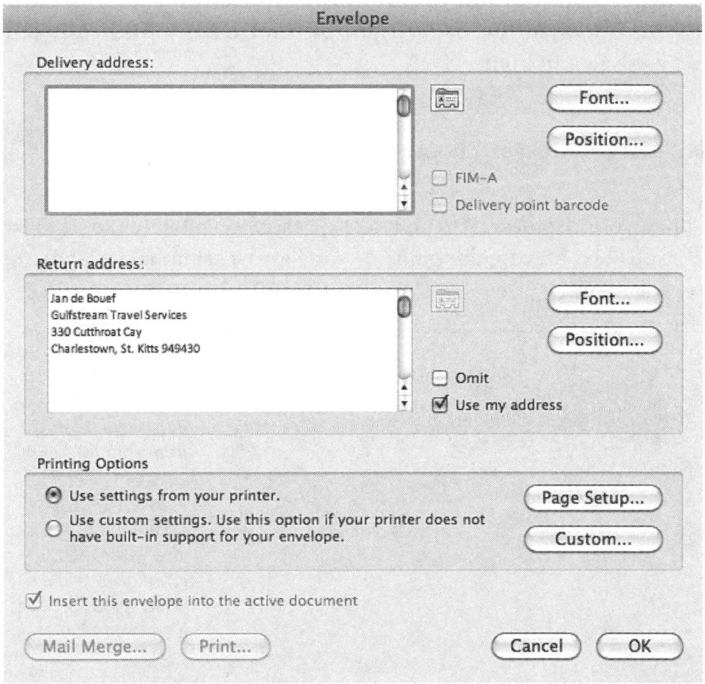

Figure 4-19:
If your return address doesn't automatically appear in the Return Address window, type in the address you want to use in the "Return address" box. Or, you can check the "Use my address" box to pull up the name and address you entered when you set up Office 2011. Turning on Omit will print the envelopes with no return address at all—so you can use preprinted envelopes or use up your supply of stick-on labels from Amnesty International.

2. **Leave the Delivery address box empty, but include a return address if you want one.**

   Type your return address, or turn on "Use my address" to import your address from Outlook, or turn on Omit to leave the return address blank.

3. **Click Position. In the Address Position window, click the arrows to move the return and delivery addresses around on the envelope, if necessary.**

   If the return address is too close to the envelope edges, for example, or the delivery address is too low, now's your chance to fix it.

4. **Click Page Setup.**

   Word opens your printer's usual Page Setup dialog box. Choose the envelope size from the pop-up menu and click OK. (If you don't see the correct size, click Cancel; under Printing Options, click the "Use custom settings" button, then click Custom. In the Custom Page Options dialog box, choose an envelope size and tell Word how you plan to feed it into the printer.)

5. **Click OK, and then OK again to dismiss the Envelope dialog box.**

   Your chosen envelope format appears in the main document; it's time to "type in" the addresses you want to print.

6. **If you want to print just one address from your Outlook Address Book, click the Address Book icon at the upper-right of the Delivery Address window, and proceed as shown in Figure 4-20.**

   If you want to run an actual mass printing of envelopes, however, do this:

7. **On the Mail Merge Manager, choose Select Recipient List→Get List→Open Data Source.**

   Select and open your database. Again, Excel spreadsheets, FileMaker databases, and tab-delimited text files are fair game. If you haven't set up your database yet, choose New Data Source (see page 152).

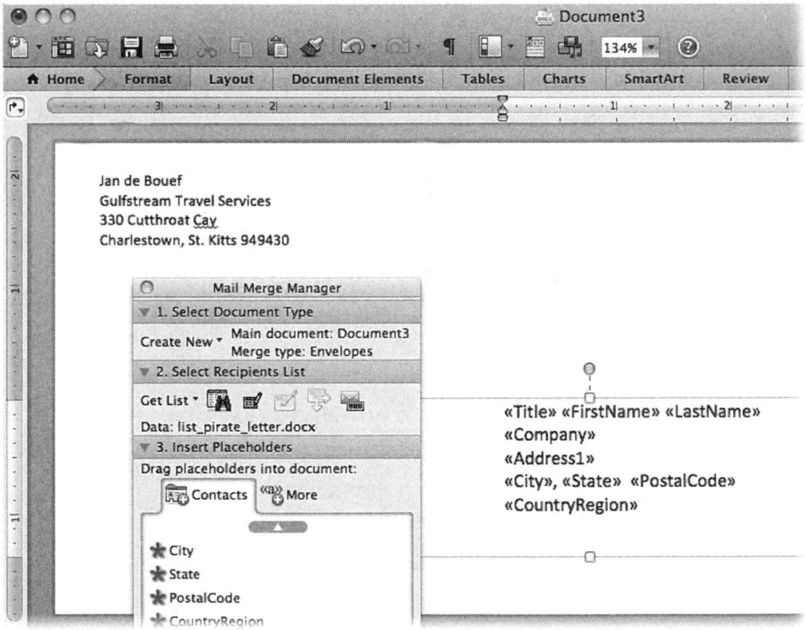

Figure 4-20:
Drag the desired name and address from your list to the envelope. Creating your envelope is similar to designing your form letter. Word gives you a pretty good idea how it's going to look.

8. **Drag field names from the Merge Field panel of the Mail Merge Manager into the address box of the envelope in the main document.**

   Add spaces and line breaks in the usual way.

9. **Prepare your printer's feed for envelopes; click Merge→"Merge to Printer". Click Print.**

   If the envelope gods are smiling, your printer now begins to print the envelopes perfectly. (If they're not, then you may discover that you'll have to rotate the envelopes in the paper slot, or worst case, remove the envelope with a pneumatic tool borrowed from your local garage). Depending on your printer model, you may have to print one envelope at a time—if so, choose Current Record from the drop-down menu at the bottom of the Mail Merge Manager.

CHAPTER 5

Working with Long Documents

Longer documents present bigger challenges to writers. The more pages there are, the more you have to plan, the more details you have to keep track of, and the tougher it is to navigate. Word can be a lot of help with your bigger projects. This chapter offers some tips on all these issues. It starts off with outlining, which is a big help when it comes to planning your project. Then it focuses on navigation, showing you how to jump quickly to different parts of your document. Voluminous documents also often require extras like tables of contents, indexes, hyperlinks, bookmarks, cross-references, footnotes, and bibliographic citations. Word has tools to make all these jobs easier and moderately less painful, and this chapter shows you how to use all of them.

Word offers a special feature—the master document—for very long documents, like books with multiple chapters. Master documents have a reputation for going bad, but this chapter shows you how to avoid problems. To wrap it all up, this chapter provides some good tips on moving around longer documents using tools like the Document Map and Thumbnails.

Switching to Outline View

If your teachers kept hammering you about how important outlining is and made you do elaborate outlines before you tackled writing assignments, forgive them. They were right. Nothing beats an outline for the planning stages of a document. When you're facing writer's block, you can start listing your main topics in a Word document, and then break your topics into smaller pieces with some subtopics underneath. Before you know it, you're filling out your ideas with some essential bits of body text. You've broken through the block.

Word's Outline view is a fabulous outlining tool. It lets you move large blocks of headings and text from one part of your document to another, and rank headings and their accompanied text higher or lower in relative importance. In Outline view, you can even show or hide different parts of your document, to focus your attention on what's important at the moment.

Best of all, Outline view is just another document view, like Normal view or Print Layout view, so you don't have to outline in a separate document. In other words, in Outline view, you're just looking at your document in outline form. When you switch into Outline view, your heading text (Heading 1, Heading 2, Heading 3, and so on) simply appears as different outline levels (Figure 5-1). Similarly, you can start a document as an outline—even do all your writing in outline form—and then switch to Print Layout view and have a perfectly normal looking document.

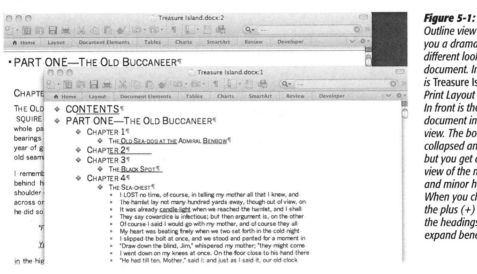

Figure 5-1:
Outline view gives you a dramatically different look at your document. In back is Treasure Island *in Print Layout view. In front is the same document in Outline view. The body text is collapsed and hidden, but you get a clear view of the major and minor headings. When you click one of the plus (+) buttons, the headings and text expand beneath.*

Tip: Jumping back and forth between Outline view and the other views can be very conducive to brainstorming. If you're working with your document in Print Layout view or Normal view and need to get a feeling for the way one topic flows into another, then pop into Outline view, collapse the body text, and examine your headings.

The easiest way to switch views is to click the buttons in the lower-left corner of the document window, but you can also use the menu as shown here:

- Use **Outline** view (View→Outline) to develop headings, establish a sequence for presenting topics, establish a hierarchy between topics, and jump from one section to another in long documents.

- Use **Normal** view (View→Normal) for writing rapidly when you don't want to worry about anything except getting ideas down on the page. In Normal view you aren't hindered by too many formatting niceties.

- Use **Print Layout** view (View→Print Layout) when you're putting the finishing touches on your document. In this view, you get a feel for the way your document looks to your readers.

Tip: You can view the same document in two different ways at once if you open a second window with the Window→New Window command. Then, for example, you could set one window to Outline view and the other to Draft view. That's exactly what's going on in Figure 5-1. Each window that you open has a number in the title bar, like the :1 and :2 shown in that figure.

When you switch to Outline view, the new Outline Tools group appears on the Home tab of the ribbon. You use the controls to move paragraphs around and change their outline levels (more on that shortly). Some of the tools, like the Formatting button and the Show menu, don't actually affect the outline—they just control the way it looks.

When it comes to outlining, Word divides your document into two distinctly different elements:

- **Headings or topics**. You can tell headings are the most important element in outlines by the big + or – button at their left. With headings, it's all about rank. Every heading has a level, from 1 to 9. More important headings have lower-level numbers and are positioned closer to the left margin. Level 1 starts at far left, Level 2 comes below it and is indented slightly to the right, followed by Level 3, 4, and so on.

  Each heading is called a subhead of the one that came before. For example, Level 2 is a subhead of Level 1, Level 3 is a subhead of Level 2, and so on.

- **Body text**. For outlining, body text takes the back seat. It just gets that little dot, and if it's in the way, you can hide it entirely, or you can view only the first line—just enough to give you a hint of what's beneath. Body text doesn't really get assigned to a level; it stays glued to the heading above it.

Promoting and Demoting Headings

Planning a document is a little bit like putting a puzzle together. You try a piece here and then over there. A topic you thought was minor suddenly looms larger in importance. When you're brainstorming and plotting, it's important to keep an open mind. Word is helpful because it's so easy to try things out, and you can ⌘+Z to undo whenever you need to.

When you promote a topic, you move it toward the left margin. At the same time, it moves up a rank in the headings hierarchy; so, a Level 3 header becomes a Level 2 header, and so forth. For most documents that means the formatting changes too.

Higher-level headers typically have larger or bolder type—something that distinguishes them from their less impressive brethren. To demote a heading is the opposite; you move a heading toward the right, usually making it a subordinate of another topic.

For you, these promotions and demotions are easy. In fact, you encounter a lot less complaining here than you'd find in promoting and demoting employees in your company. The easiest way to promote and demote is to click a header and move it to the left or to the right. When you move it a little bit, a vertical line appears, providing a marker to show you the change in rank, as shown in Figure 5-2.

Note: When you promote or demote a heading, the body text goes with it, but you have a choice whether or not the subheads move below it.

When you're brainstorming and pushing ideas around in your document, you don't want to get distracted by the mechanics. When it comes to outlines, you may be grateful that Word provides so many different ways to do the same thing. You get to choose the method that works best for you, and keep your focus on shaping your document. Word gives you three ways to manipulate the pieces of your outline:

- **Dragging.** For outlining, nothing's more intuitive and fun than clicking and dragging. You can put some words in a heading, grab them by that + or – sign, and then just drag them to another location. As you drag topics and text, Word provides great visual clues to let you know the end result (Figure 5-2).

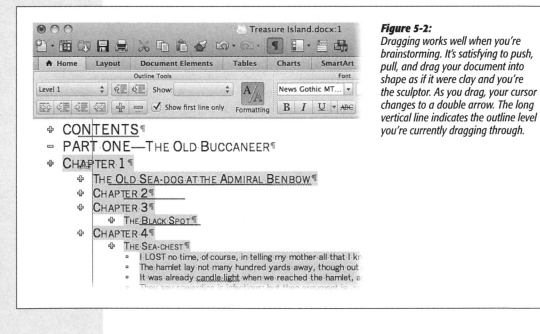

Figure 5-2:
Dragging works well when you're brainstorming. It's satisfying to push, pull, and drag your document into shape as if it were clay and you're the sculptor. As you drag, your cursor changes to a double arrow. The long vertical line indicates the outline level you're currently dragging through.

- **Ribbon.** The buttons in the Home | Outline Tools group give you quick, visual access to the commands for promoting and demoting headings and for showing and hiding all the bits and pieces of your document. It's a bit more mechanical than just clicking and dragging the pieces where you want them (Figure 5-3).

  One potentially confusing thing about the Outlining tab are those two drop-down menus showing levels. They look almost identical and both give you a choice among the nine topic levels that Outline has to offer. Here's the key: The menu on the left promotes or demotes the current item, while the menu on the right shows or hides levels.

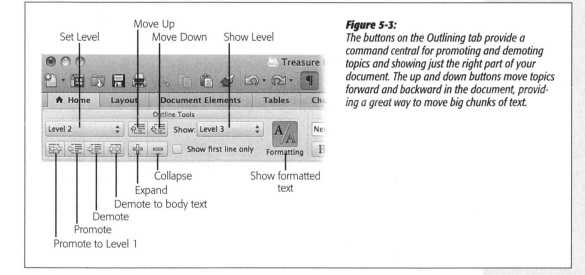

Tip: One of the handiest tools in the ribbon is the "Show the outline as formatted text" button. That one little guy conceals any fancy character formatting you've applied so you can focus on your outline. See page 181 for more details.

- **Keyboard shortcuts.** Keyboard shortcuts are ideal when your hands are already on the keys and you're typing away. During the planning stages, speed isn't as much of an issue, but if you took your teachers' advice to heart and do lots of outlining, keyboard shortcuts can really streamline your work. Just remember that most of these commands use Shift-Control plus another key, as shown in the following table.

Action	Keyboard Shortcut
Promote Heading Up a Level	Shift-Control-Left Arrow
Demote Heading Down a Level	Shift-Control-Right Arrow
Demote Heading to Body Text	Shift-⌘-N
Expand Outline Item	Shift-Control- + (+ on the keypad)
Collapse Outline Item	Shift-Control- – (– on the keypad)
Expand or Collapse Entire Outline	Shift-Control-A
Show n Level Heading	Shift-Control-n; n=number key (top row, not the number pad)
Show Only First Line of Text	Shift-Control-L

Controlling Subheads During Promotion or Demotion

When you promote or demote an outline item, any subheads and subtopics below it move with that item, but only if you collapse the items below, so that they're hidden. In other words, when you move the header above, the subheads keep their relationships even though you can't see them. When you drag topics, the subheads go along, because when you select a topic, you automatically select the subtopics, too.

Word gives you a number of ways to move the header but leave everything else where it is. Here's a step-by-step description of the ways you can promote or demote a heading all by its lonesome:

1. **Click anywhere in the text of the header.**

   Don't select the entire header; just place the insertion point somewhere in the text.

2. **Change the header level using one of the ribbon buttons or by pressing a keyboard shortcut.**

   Use the shortcut keys Shift-Control-Left arrow or Shift-Control-Right arrow to promote or demote the header. As long as the subtopics below aren't highlighted, they won't move when you do the header promoting or demoting.

   You can use any of the ribbon controls that promote and demote headers in the same way. As long as the subtopics aren't selected, they won't change (Figure 5-4). The buttons that you can use include: Promote to Heading 1, Promote, Outline Level (drop-down menu), Demote to Body Text.

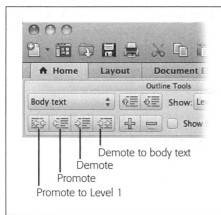

Figure 5-4:
Use the various promotion and demotion buttons and the Level drop-down menu on the Outlining tab to organize your outline. If subheads are collapsed under a topic or they're selected, they maintain their relationships when you demote or promote the header. Otherwise, if only the header is selected, it moves and the subtopics stay put.

Demote to body text
Demote
Promote
Promote to Level 1

Moving Outline Items

Part of organizing your thoughts means moving them to an earlier or later position in the document, without changing their outline level. Say you decide a section you've typed in the middle of your document would make a great introduction. You can move it to the beginning of the document, without promoting or demoting it. Moving topics and items up and down in your document is very similar to moving them left and right. (Figure 5-5). If you want to take subtopics along with an item when you move it, make sure that they're selected (or collapsed) under the item that you're moving.

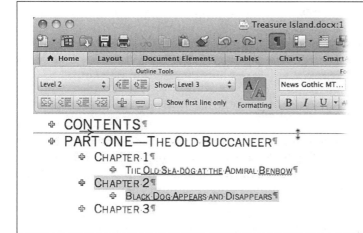

Figure 5-5:
When you drag a header up and down, you see a horizontal line that acts as a marker to show you exactly where the heading (and connected text) will appear when you let go of the mouse button.

In addition to dragging, Word gives you two other ways to move topics up and down in your outline. Select the heading you want to move, and then click the Move Up or Move Down buttons on the Outlining tab (Figure 5-6). You can also use the shortcut keys Control-Shift-up arrow or Control-Shift-down arrow.

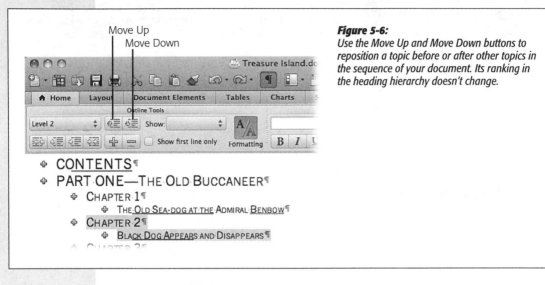

Figure 5-6:
Use the Move Up and Move Down buttons to reposition a topic before or after other topics in the sequence of your document. Its ranking in the heading hierarchy doesn't change.

Showing Parts of Your Outline

Outline view doesn't just let you see and organize the structure of your prose; it also helps you zero in on what's important while you make decisions about the shape and flow of your work. If you want, you can show your headings only so you can focus on their wording with all the other text out of the way. When you want to read inside a certain section, you can expand it while leaving everything else collapsed. (Or, if you're having trouble with a passage, you can collapse it so you don't have to look at it for a while.)

Expanding and Collapsing Levels

You know that old saying about not being able to see the forest for the trees? On the Outlining tab, the Expand and Collapse buttons help you put things in perspective (Figure 5-7). Collapse a topic, and you can read through the major headers and get a feel for the way your document flows from one topic to another.

When you need to explore the detail within a topic to make sure you've covered all the bases, expand the topic and dig in. When you're mousing around, the easiest way to expand or collapse a topic is to double-click the + sign next to the words. It works as a toggle—a double-click expands it, and another double-click closes it. The topics with a minus sign next to them have no subtopics, so you can't expand or collapse them.

If you're interested in making grander, more global kinds of changes, turn to the Outlining | Outline Tools→Show Level menu. (It's the drop-down menu on the right.) Just choose a level, and your outline expands or collapses accordingly (Figure 5-7).

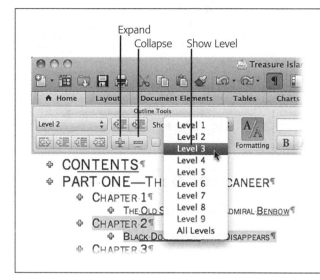

Figure 5-7:
Use the drop-down menu on the right to show and hide levels in your outline. Use the big + and – buttons in the ribbon to expand and collapse topics and the contents of lower levels.

Showing and Hiding Text

Text takes a subordinate position when it comes to outlining and planning, so it's not surprising that Word provides a couple different ways for you to hide the body text (Figure 5-8). You can double-click the headings above the body text to expand and collapse the topic, just as you would with subheads. The + and – buttons on the Outlining tab work the same way. You can also use the keyboard shortcuts Shift-Control-+ to expand and Shift-Control-- to collapse body text under a heading. Just remember that the + and – keys have to be on the keypad, not the top row.

Showing Only the First Line

Because each paragraph of body text is like a sub-subtopic, Word's outline view lets you work with them as such. Click the Show First Line Only button, and all you see is the first line of each paragraph. That should be enough to get a sense of the topic that's covered. It's just another way that Outline lets you drill down into your document while you're in a planning and plotting phase.

Showing Text Formatting

Your document's character formatting—different fonts, font colors, and sizes that may bear no relation to the Level 1, Level 2 hierarchy—can be distracting in Outline view. The easiest thing is to turn the formatting off. You can click the Show Formatting button on the Outlining ribbon (Figure 5-9) to toggle formatting on or off.

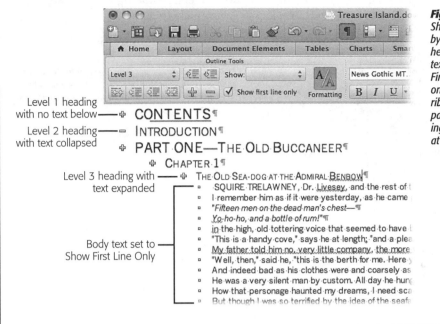

Level 1 heading with no text below ——
Level 2 heading with text collapsed ——
Level 3 heading with text expanded ——
Body text set to Show First Line Only ——

Figure 5-8:
Show and hide text by double-clicking the header just above the text. Click the Show First Line Only button on the Outlining ribbon to hide the paragraphs while leaving the first line to hint at the contents.

Show first line only
Show the outline as formatted text

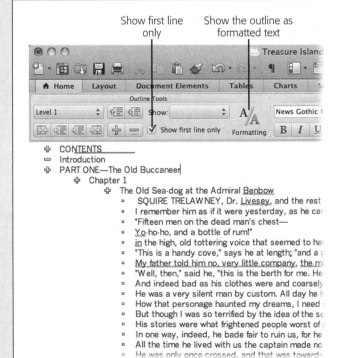

Figure 5-9:
Use the ShowText Formatting checkbox (or the / key on the number pad) to hide text formatting, as shown here. This picture also shows the result of clicking the Show First Line Only button or pressing Control-Shift-L to show and hide all the paragraph text except the first line.

Notebook: Collecting Random Thoughts

From its binder-like appearance to its ability to take "dictation," Notebook Layout view is Microsoft's attempt to let your computer work as you do. To that end, they designed something where you can take notes quickly and rearrange them as you wish.

Opening Your Notebook

To start a new notebook, click New from Template on the toolbar. Then in the Template list, scroll down to Notebook Layout View and click one of the notebook templates. When you start typing, each new block of text starts out as Note Level 1, as you can see by a quick glance at the Formatting Palette. By hitting Tab, you can indent text under a heading to indicate that it applies to, and should be grouped with, that header, as shown in Figure 5-10. This is great stuff when taking notes in class, at a meeting, or just capturing random thoughts as they pop into your head. Additionally, you can click the little button to the left of each block of text and move it wherever you want on the page.

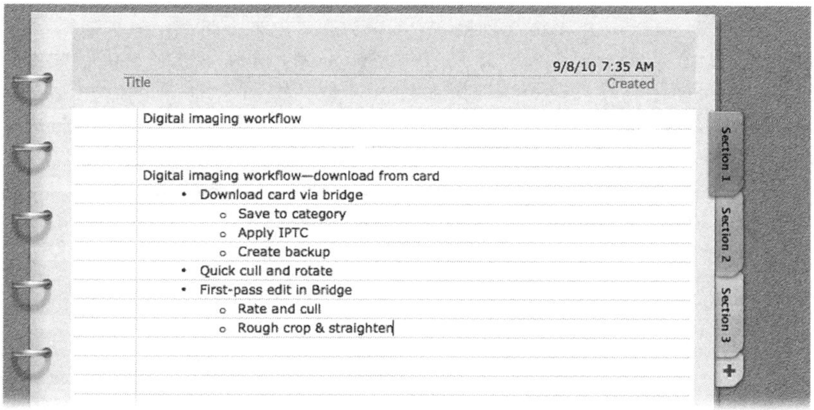

Figure 5-10:
Top: As you type into a freshly created Notebook document, text flows onto the page automatically set to Note Level 1.

Bottom: After you finish the sentence or thought, press Return, and then Tab, to indent the next section of text, shown at center. Pressing Shift-Tab moves the indent back toward the left—promoting the line to a higher level of importance.

If you already have a non-Notebook Word document in front of you, select View→Notebook Layout to open Notebook Layout view. Alternately, you can click the Notebook Layout view (it's the tiny tabbed icon) at the bottom left of your page. Or, for the keyboard- and shortcut-crazed among you, Option-⌘-B also takes you to the Notebook Layout view. However you invoke the view, the first thing you see on your Notebook Layout view journey is the pop-up message shown in Figure 5-11.

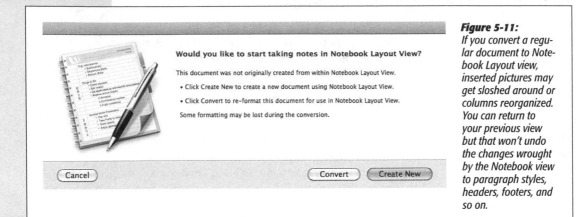

Figure 5-11:
If you convert a regular document to Notebook Layout view, inserted pictures may get sloshed around or columns reorganized. You can return to your previous view but that won't undo the changes wrought by the Notebook view to paragraph styles, headers, footers, and so on.

Within the figure:

Would you like to start taking notes in Notebook Layout View?

This document was not originally created from within Notebook Layout View.

• Click Create New to create a new document using Notebook Layout View.

• Click Convert to re-format this document for use in Notebook Layout View.

Some formatting may be lost during the conversion.

Cancel   Convert   Create New

UP TO SPEED

Where Did My Formatting Go?

Notebook Layout is a possessive view, and doesn't take kindly to other intruding views. It likes it best when you begin in Notebook Layout and stay there. When you change from other views to Notebook Layout, several things happen. Right off the bat Word asks if, in essence, you're really sure you want to do this. It opens a box asking if you wish to start a new, Notebook Layout view document, or convert the existing one (Figure 5-11). It then adds, almost in a whisper, "Some formatting may be lost in the conversion."

You don't say.

Pictures and text boxes will frequently get shoved about by the conversion. Even more important, much, if not all, of the template formatting and paragraph styles in your non-Notebook Layout view document will be lost. In other words, all those carefully crafted headers, bullet lists, and captions will morph into plain, everyday text. So, before you convert, make sure it's something you really want to do. Otherwise, it's best just to start from scratch in Notebook Layout view. That way you know what you're getting.

However you get there, once you arrive in Notebook Layout view, you see a clean new sheet (assuming you're starting with a new document) of lined notebook paper. Kinda makes you want to take a pen to your computer screen, doesn't it? But please, despite the temptation, don't scrawl "Timmy likes Sally" or "Mr. Quackenbush is a nerd," on your computer screen. Replacing computer screens gets real expensive, real quick.

Like much of Word, the Notebook Layout view is intuitive. As you type, words dance (or spew—mood depending) onto the page. You'll notice, however, that each paragraph, block of text, or picture is marked with a clear/gray bubble to its left. The bubble is similar to the little + and – symbols you see in Word's Outline view (page 175), but much easier to use. Furthermore, you can take that bubble and drag (it turns blue) your text wherever you like on the page. In fact, there's much more you can do with your text than reposition it, and most of those capabilities reside on the aptly named Notebook Layout view Standard toolbar, as shown in Figure 5-12.

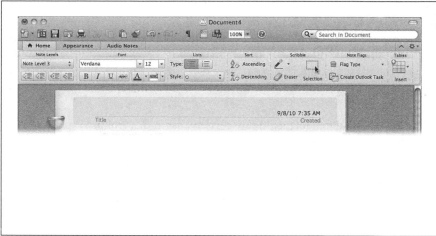

Figure 5-12:
When you enter the world of Notebook Layout view, the ribbon provides the appropriate commands. Here you can adjust the indent level, the font, bullets and numbering; sort your notes or add a background grid; and add checkboxes to your notebook items or even turn them into Outlook tasks.

The Notebook Ribbon

The Notebook Layout view significantly changes the ribbon into something that's tailored to the view at hand. Everything you need waits for your click on the ribbon and its three tabs: Home, Appearance, and Audio Notes. Compared to Word's other views, Notebook view is stripped down to the minimum, ready for quick entries with a minimum of fuss. Apparently, Microsoft wants to get all possible distractions out of your way when you're taking notes. This section gives you an overview for each of the tabs. You'll find the details in the sections that follow.

Pen to Screen

Because it's not advisable to take a Sharpie marker to your computer screen, there's a way to write into Notebook Layout view. The view supports Mac OS X's handwriting recognition program, Ink. So, if you have a Wacom or similar pen-tablet, you can pick up a stylus and "write" in Notebook view. Ink changes what you write into typed letters—though perhaps not always the letters you intended. To do so, connect your tablet to your computer and install the software. Turn on handwriting recognition in the Ink System Preferences panel, cross your fingers, and you're ready to write.

You can also draw on your notebook, by clicking on the Scribble icon on the toolbar. Choose the pen thickness and color from the pop-up menu, and commence drawing. Unfortunately, Word doesn't convert characters drawn this way into letters. They appear as AutoShapes (see the box on page 188 for the full story).

Use the Home tab for daily note taking

For most of your noting, you'll work with the Home tab displayed (Figure 5-12). The fun thing about working with notes rather than a staid, old Word doc is the formatting. The tools here help you apply distinctive formatting with a quick click.

- **Note Levels.** This group has tools that look and work like the ones in Outline view (page 175). Use the buttons to promote and demote notes, moving them left and right. If you prefer you can use the Note Level menu. Other buttons let you change the position of notes by moving them up and down. Most of the time, you'll probably use your mouse or keyboard shortcut to organize your notes.

- **Font.** The usual font formatting suspects appear in this group, so you can set the font, size, style, highlights and color.

- **Lists.** Notes are often in list form so you can apply numbers or bullets to your lists and fiddle with the styles.

- **Sort.** Numbered or not, you can sort your notes in ascending or descending order.

- **Scribble**. A pen icon represents the Scribble tool. Click here to turn your mouse into a pen with which you can draw on your document. The cursor changes to look like a pen. Press and hold the mouse button to draw and release to stop. Each masterpieces you create this way is a single scribble entity. The eraser removes an entire scribble rather than erasing part of your lines. Likewise the selection tool selects all or nothing. Scribble's convenient for drawing quick graphical marks, such as arrows, or circling important sections of your document, but it's a tad too cumbersome to write more than a word or two. The pen menu lets you set the scribble line thickness and color.

- **Note Flags**. Want to make a note jump out from the rest? You can flag them with translucent square checkboxes in different colors, arrows or punctuation marks, like this: **!?**

- **Tables.** To apply some grid-like discipline to your unruly notes, drop a table on the page and corral your thoughts within. You won't get all the bells and whistles with your notebook tables, but you can create a table, and resize and merge cells.

Changing your notebook's appearance

As you could guess the job for the Appearance tab (Figure 5-13) is to change the way your notebook and its environment look. Yes, you might call this eye candy or fluff.

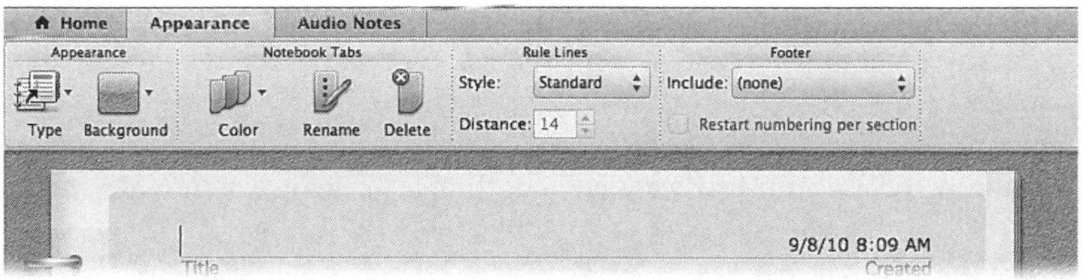

Figure 5-13:
Your notebooks are likely to have a more free-form look than the average Word document. Use the Appearance tab to change the look of the background, the book and the tabs.

- **Type.** Use this menu choose an overall style, essentially the look of the notebook rings or binding and the tabs. If you find those binder rings get in your way while you're writing (left-handed, perhaps?), select one of the Without Notebook Rings styles.

- **Background.** Your notebook rests on a surface, which can look like various species of wood, metal, or carbon fiber—for a strong, yet lightweight notebook.

- **Notebook Tabs**. Even more ways to change the look of your notebook tabs. Actually these are pretty helpful, you can color code individual notebook tabs and rename and delete them. Naturally, in Microsoftian fashion, there are alternatives for renaming (double-click) and deleting (select and Delete).

- **Rule Lines.** With these tools, you can show or hide the page lines and set the distance between lines.

- **Footer.** Show or hide page numbers in the footers.

Audio Notes tab when you don't want to write

The Audio Notes tab has several tools all dedicated to recording your words of wisdom. Use the Record and Stop buttons to capture those words and the Play and Pause buttons to hear them later. Other tools like the Input Volume and the Input Level meter help you make intelligible recordings.

Figure 5-14:
Put down that pen and exercise your pipes. The Audio Notes tab gives you easy-to-use tools to add recordings to your notebooks.

Organizing Your Notes

Notebook Layout view comes into its own when you're either taking notes on your laptop during a meeting or trying to get your arms around that huge project that you and your fellow visionaries brainstormed. It's not a view you'll often use when composing your romance novel. But that's okay; Notebook does what it does pretty darn well, by automatically and clearly applying outline levels to every thought you type.

What's That Pen Doing?

The pen actually draws a shape that you can subsequently select and drag to new locations or even resize. On the one hand that's great, giving you gobs of flexibility. On the other hand, it's not so great. Since the shape is, in essence, a hand-drawn picture, Word treats it as one. For example, if you circle a word, you may find that the word disappears because the shape is now in front of it. Of course, if you have the AutoShape's Fill properties set to "no fill," you won't have these problems. You'll be able to spot the word through your circle.

The shape you've drawn is like any Word AutoShape—it's a drawing object, and you can format it like one. To format the shape, choose Format→AutoShape. The Format dialog box (see page 613) opens, where you can choose how text will flow around the shape, whether it will reside in front of or behind the text, and all the other familiar formatting features.

The cool thing about all this leveling business is the flexibility it provides when you're viewing and organizing your Notebook document. If a heading, any heading, in the document has *subheadings* beneath it, Word tags the heading with a big blue flippy triangle, as shown in Figure 5-15. You can click this triangle to expose or hide the subheadings.

Note: Levels are kind of like golf. The lower the number, the better (more important) the level. Level 1 is the highest level, level 2 is next, and so on.

Setting text levels with the keyboard and mouse

You can set text levels with various combinations of the Tab key, as described below. You can, of course, highlight text and drag it with the mouse, just like any other text, but you may find it quicker to learn a few shortcuts and never take your hands off the keys as the ideas come gushing out.

- **Tab** or **Control-Shift-Right arrow**. These commands *demote* the text one level of importance and tuck it neatly beneath the text above it. You can also use your mouse to drag the note bubble to the right.

- **Shift-Tab** or **Control-Shift-Left arrow**. These commands *promote* the text one level, moving it back out toward the margin, where items of greater importance reside. You can also use your mouse to drag the note bubble to the left.

- **Control-Tab**. Indents the first line of text one tab without changing the level.

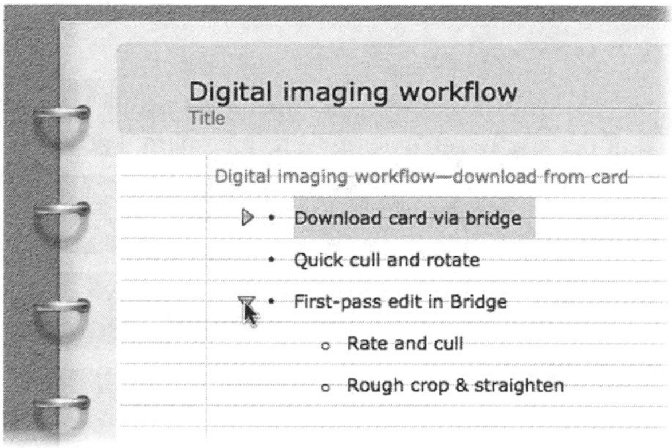

Figure 5-15:
Wherever there are subheadings, you'll see the renowned flippy triangle—though it disappears once you click it to expand the topic. Mouse over that topic again, and the triangle reappears.

- **Control-Shift-Up arrow**. Moves the selected paragraph up. Note that this keystroke physically moves the paragraph; it may change its note level as well, depending on the paragraph above it.

- **Control-Shift-Down arrow**. Moves the selected paragraph down, again without changing its note level.

- **Control-Shift-A**. Expands *all* text under *all* headings. Great if you want to see *everything* you've written.

- **Control-Shift-<number>**. Displays the selected note level. For example, Control-Shift-1 displays all the Level 1 notes.

Sorting headings

As you've probably gathered by now, there are myriad ways to sort your headings and organize and reorganize your notes. You can drag notes (and objects), promote and demote headers, and move them up and down. It's cool, it's easy, and it's fast.

What's even faster is Notebook's ability to sort your data via the sorting function that's added to the Formatting palette whenever you work in Notebook Layout view. Select the section (see page 196) you wish to sort (the sorting commands sort a section or a selection, not the entire document), open the Sorting pane by clicking Sorting in the title bar, and click either Ascending or Descending.

Note: Unless you collapse a header before sorting, Word moves the header without its subheadings.

- **Ascending** sorts from the top of the page to the bottom, 1 through 9, then A through Z. For example, it would place a heading beginning with "Aplomb" before a heading beginning with "Zealot."

- **Descending** sorts from the top of the page to the bottom, Z through A, then 9 through 1.

Placing Notes Beside Your Notes

Okay, you've organized your notes into some form of logic. Everything to do with the company party is listed under the Level 1 heading of Company Party, and all things pertaining to the boss's favorite client is tucked under the client's name. But what if you have some questions about items in both categories? Need to remind yourself to order the party food, prepare a report for that number one client, keep in mind what is what, and set priorities too? There are two ways of quickly transforming your notes into a to-do list: the Note Flags feature in Notebook Layout view, or by marshalling the forces of Outlook.

Flagging action items

The Note Flags group on the Home tab has a pop-up menu that lists checkboxes and other items for just about every flagging purpose. Place a flag in the margin next to anything in your notebook by first clicking the text (anywhere in the text line), and then selecting the flag from the list. To remove the flag, select it again.

Note: You can't apply a flag to a graphic. If you select a graphic, the Flag Type menu is grayed out.

The obvious checkboxes are great for placing beside items on your Notebook list. Once placed, you can click the box to place a check in it. So, after you've finished that step in the project, you can check it off. Instant gratification!

Important enough to track in Outlook?

Pretty icons beside your notes are all well and good, but what if you want to take your reminder out of Word and into the real world? If you use Outlook to organize your life, you could launch that program and start a new task. Fortunately, there's no need to subject yourself to that kind of strain. Just click Create Outlook Task in the Note Flags section of the Formatting Palette. Doing so opens a dialogue box where you can set the date and time when you wish to be reminded of the selected task.

This cross-program feature is a great timesaver and an ideal way to follow up on the notes that you took at yesterday's meeting. Simply click in the line of text you wish to remember, let's say "Prep sales report for Olsen by Tuesday noon," click Create Outlook Task, and set an appropriate reminder, for, say Tuesday morning.

Typing Less with Audio Notes

Hey, that's what everyone wants to do. Spend a little less time clacking on the keyboard and a little more time living a private version of the Corona commercials. Well, Notebook Layout view can't deliver a cold one to your hammock, but it can get your hands off the keyboard with the Audio Notes tab and its capabilities. For example, you're sitting in that three-hour, Monday night sociology class. Just call up Word, open a new document in Notebook Layout view, turn on Audio Notes, and let it run. Then, as you type notes, Word automatically inserts icons that link to an audio snippet of whatever it was recording when you were typing.

The beauty of this arrangement is that you don't have to worry about typing every word the professor drones. Just type main points; you can click and listen to the recording to refresh your memory later. You can also link audio notes to previously written text—something that's convenient if you wanted to connect a complex description to a point that you briefly touched on in your written notes. This feature is really designed for laptop Notebook note-takers, but works on any Mac equipped with a mic—built-in or not.

Entering an audio note

To enter an audio note, click in the text where you wish to insert the audio note, click the microphone to display the Audio Notes toolbar, click the Record button, and start speaking (or you may need to *stop* talking so that your microphone can hear the important stuff). Or, just click the microphone and type away. Word automatically creates new audio notes every few lines. Click Stop (the black square on the Audio Notes toolbar) when you wish to stop recording. When you pass the cursor over the text, the blue speaker pops into the left margin.

Note: Choose Word→Preferences→Audio Notes to adjust the recording quality for your notes. Word's standard setting of Medium quality produces monaural MP4 files at a relatively low sample rate–perfect for voice recording or lecture notes. If you require higher quality, or have attached a stereo microphone (the built-in mic in your laptop is mono), you may want to increase the quality settings. However, higher-quality means your notes take up more–perhaps much more–space on your hard drive.

Listening to an audio note

To listen to a note, click the blue speaker icon, which pops up in the left margin of the page as you mouse over notated text. Your recording fills the air, and if you wish it to fill a little more or less, you can adjust your Mac's output volume using the volume control near the right end of your menu bar. The toolbar, as shown in Figure 5-16, inserts itself beneath the standard toolbar.

Perhaps you'd like to share your captured verbal brilliance with someone who doesn't have access to your computer. No problem. Choose Tools→Audio Notes→Export Audio. Word exports *all* the audio in the notebook document as an MP4, AIFF, or WAV file (depending on your Audio Notes Preferences settings) to a location of your choosing. At that point, you can burn the file to a CD or transfer it to your iPod.

Figure 5-16:
Here are the playback tools on the Audio Notes tab. Play and Pause work as you'd expect. Use the Seek tool to jump to a particular point in a recording. The Rate slider speeds up or slows down the recording. Listen to that lecture in half the time!

Tip: Although the blue speaker pops up whenever you pass your mouse over an audio note, it's much easier to draw attention to the note with a line of text such as, "Monday meeting," or whatever. Click Show All Audio Markers in the status bar at the bottom of the window to display all the speaker icons. Now you can spot them without mousing around.

Manipulating Notebook Sections

By now you're a pro at putting words onto notebook pages. It's also important to understand how to manipulate the pages themselves, specifically how to make changes to entire sections by adding improvements such as headers, footers, or removing the characteristic lined paper look. Notebook Layout view pages, referred to as sections, are an important organizational tool.

Note: Notebook pages really aren't—pages, that is. The Notebook Layout's sections are continuous sheets of paper, kind of like a web page. In fact, you can't insert a page break into a notebook. If you convert the notebook to a different Word view, such as Draft or Print Layout, you'll see that, behind the scenes, Word delineates each tabbed section with a section break (page 196).

Labeling sections

A title resides at the top of each section. Initially—because Word can't read your mind—it's blank (the title, not your mind), but you can fill it in by clicking in the title block (as shown in Figure 5-15), and typing whatever you wish. This label doesn't, however, change the title on the tab located on the right of the notebook page. To change these tab titles, double-click the tab, type your new tab title, and press Return. Or you can right-click (Control-click) to display the tab shortcut menu shown in Figure 5-17.

Reordering the sections of your notebook is simple. Click on a section tab and drag it to its new location.

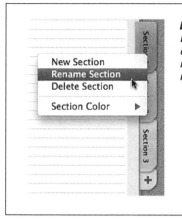

Figure 5-17:
It's a good idea to rename your sections to something useful. Dates are a good idea, as are categories. Control-click a tab to bring up this menu for adding, deleting, renaming, or color coding your section tab—or just double-click a tab and start typing to rename it.

To line or not to line

Notebook Layout view's factory settings include lined paper. It's a curious, if understandable, decision by Microsoft. Curious, because on a computer, you don't need lines to keep your writing even; understandable, because it's a notebook view, and the lines make your computer screen look like a notebook.

You can choose whether the lines appear on the page or not. Go to Appearance | Rule Lines→Style and choose Standard (lined pages) or None. Use the Distance setting to set the spacing (in points) between the ruler lines and lines of text.

Numbering Pages

Oddly enough, you can choose to number your notebook pages in a footer, even though you'll only see this page number when you print your notebook. To turn on page numbers, go to Appearance→Footer→Include and choose "page number". You can also choose to have Word begin renumbering the pages with each new tabbed section.

Navigating a Large Document

In documents of more than, say, 20 pages, that scroll bar on the right side is way too slow and inaccurate. Instead, it's faster to jump between specific points the document. You can always use the Go To box (Option-⌘-G) to jump to a specific page, but what if you don't know the exact page number? Instead, you just know which heading you're looking for. Word gives you quite a few tools to navigate large documents, like bookmarks and browse buttons. Also, a couple of special viewing and navigation tools help you find your way around long documents: the Document Map and Thumbnails (Figure 5-18).

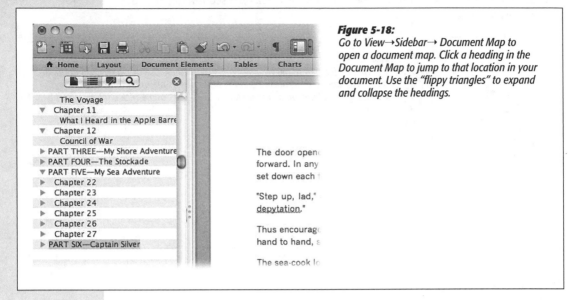

Figure 5-18:
Go to View→Sidebar→ Document Map to open a document map. Click a heading in the Document Map to jump to that location in your document. Use the "flippy triangles" to expand and collapse the headings.

- **Browse buttons.** The Browse buttons at the bottom of the scroll bar are another great tool for navigating documents of any size. By clicking the circular Select Browse Object button, you can choose to browse by headings, endnotes, comments, bookmarks, or pages. Click the double-headed arrow buttons to browse forward or backward through your document.

Tip: When you want to return to a place in your text with nothing specific (like a caption or heading) for the browse tools to look for, just attach a comment to it (page 241) like "Come back and edit this," and then you can just browse by comment. Or, use a bookmark, as described next.

- **Bookmarks.** Bookmarks are versatile tools in Word and do much more than their humble name implies. As you might guess, bookmarks are a great way to hop from place to place in your document. When you insert and name a bookmark to mark a page (or a range of pages) with the Insert→Bookmark command (Shift-⌘-F5), you can always jump to that spot using the Go To box (Option-⌘-G).

- **Navigate with the Document Map.** A document map shows you the headings and subheadings in your document. If you choose View→Sidebar→Document Map Pane, a panel opens on the left side of Word with an outline of your document (Figure 5-18). When you click a heading, Word scrolls to that part of your document.

- **Navigate with Thumbnails.** The Thumbnails panel is the document map for the visually-oriented. Instead of words, you see mini pictures of the pages in your document (Figure 5-20). You can't view the Document Map and Thumbnails at the same time. On the ribbon, if you check the box for one, the other disappears. You can use a drop-down menu in the upper-left corner of the panel to change the view from Document Map to Thumbnails.

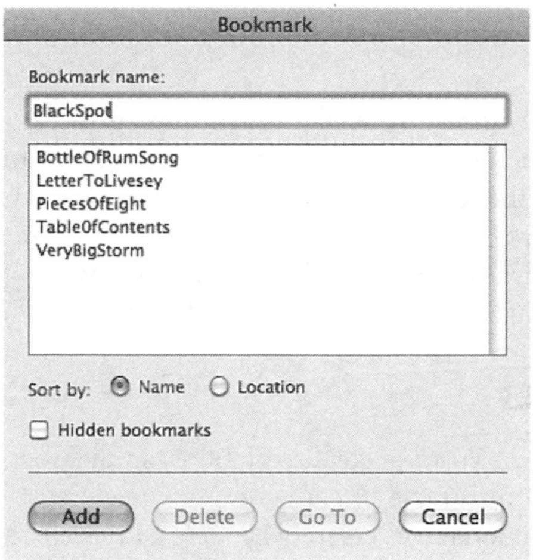

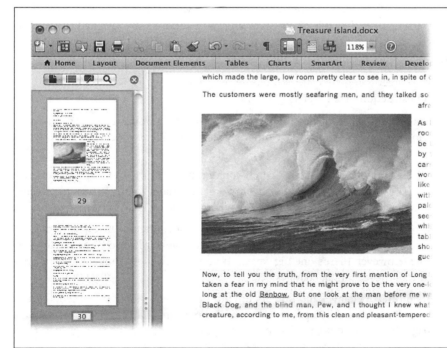

Figure 5-19:
The Bookmark dialog box is easy to use. Use the text box at the top to name your bookmarks. The list below shows all the bookmarks in your document. The two radio buttons sort the list alphabetically or by their order of appearance in your document. Use the buttons at the very bottom to create, delete and jump to your bookmarks.

Figure 5-20:
As a navigation tool, thumbnails work best for documents with graphics or pages that are visually distinctive.

Understanding Sections

The longer and more complex your document is, the more likely it is to contain different sections. Word's sections don't have anything to do with how you've divided your document with headings and subheadings. They're electronic divisions you create by adding section breaks to your document. Section breaks are a close cousin to page breaks, except that a section can contain any number of pages, or perhaps just a portion of a page. More important, each section in a Word document can have its own formatting and page setup. As explained in detail on page 48, you choose Insert→Break

Many people work with Word for years without ever really understanding Word's sections. After all, the majority of Word documents are only a single section. But sometimes Word adds section breaks behind the scenes. For example, when you add a table of contents or an index to a document, as described later in this chapter, or when you insert an envelope into the same document as a letter (page 146), Word uses a section break to separate the different page formats needed to create these features.

Creating a Table of Contents

When you create very long documents in Word—like dissertations, annual reports, or even books—you may need to provide a table of contents. Your readers will be glad you did. What's more, if you did a good job of creating headers and subheads as described on page 178, then most of the hard work is done. Word generates the table of contents automatically from your headers, looks up the page numbers for each heading, and formats the whole table for you. All you have to do is tell Word where you want to place the table of contents, and then choose a predesigned format that compliments your document—all of which you do in the Table of Contents group on the Document Elements tab, or in the Table of Contents dialog box.

Before you get going, here are some time-tested guidelines that make table of contents construction much easier.

- Use Word's standard heading styles: Heading 1, Heading 2, and so on. With some extra work, you can use other styles, but it's *soooo* much easier if you just use Word's headings.

- Create your table of contents when you're finished with your writing and editing. Because Word pulls details from your document to build the table, it only makes sense to do it at the end of the writing process.

- If possible, avoid manually editing your table of contents. Once you've created your table of contents, you can go in and edit the words or change the formatting. However, there's one big caveat: If you ever need to update the table, you lose all those manual changes.

- If you make changes to your document, update your table of contents. Word doesn't automatically update when you make changes, like, oh, adding six new pages to your document. To update the page numbers and headings, you need to manually update your table as described on page 198.

Follow these steps to insert a table of contents into your document.

Note: If you'd rather experiment with a document that's not critical to your work, you can use *06-1_ Table_of_Contents.docx* in the Missing CD at *http://missingmanuals.com/cds*.

1. **Place the insertion point where you want to put the table of contents.**

   The traditional spot for a table of contents is right after the title and before the main part of the text. It's best to put the insertion point on an empty line, so the table doesn't interfere with any other text. If you agree, click after the title, and then press Return.

2. **On the ribbon, go to Document Elements and click one of the Table of Contents options.**

   There are several different formats for Tables of Contents, so either scroll through the list or expand the group so you can see all the options as shown in Figure 5-21. Choose one of the Automatic Tables of Contents. The thumbnail for these always says Heading 1, Heading 2. The tables that say Type Here are "manual" and, as advertised, require much more manual labor.

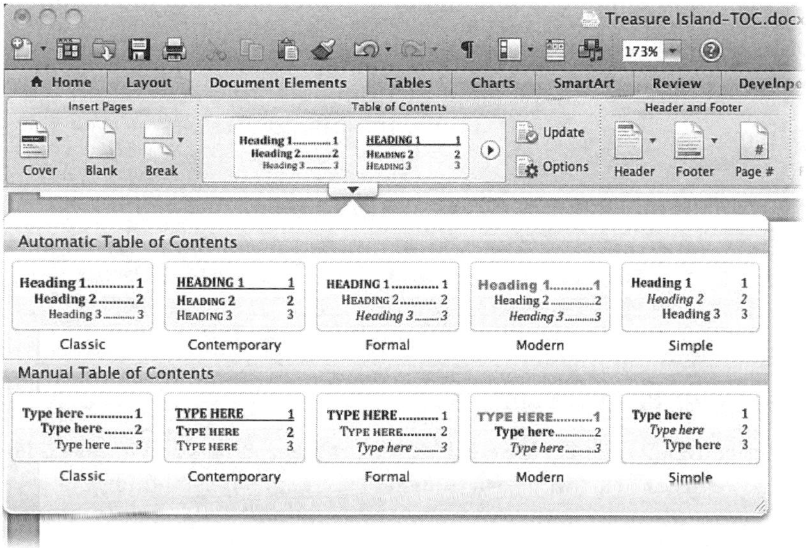

Figure 5-21:
Go to Document Elements | Table of Contents to see the different styles of tables of contents you can insert in your text. Most of the tables use the headings you created in your document.

When you click the style of your choice, Word automatically creates a table of contents like the one in Figure 5-22 and inserts the results in your document. To create the table, Word takes paragraphs you've formatted with heading styles, such as Heading 1, Heading 2, and Heading 3.

3. **Review the table of contents.**

   Don't forget to inspect the table of contents that Word created. You never know when something unexpected may happen. Maybe you forgot to format a heading with a Heading style, and it doesn't show up in the table. Or worse, some paragraph is mistakenly tagged with a heading style—oops, now it's in your table of contents.

Tip: If you'd like to reword the entries in your table of contents—shorten overly-long headings, or add some descriptive text, for example—you can edit the contents directly, like any Word text. The headings in your document aren't affected. Remember, though, that if you update the table of contents (as described in the next section), be sure to update only the page numbers, not the entire table. Otherwise, you'll lose any hand-entered changes.

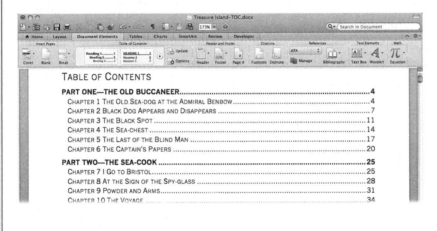

Figure 5-22:
Word makes some pretty good-looking tables of contents. They're all laid out very neatly with subheadings indented and leader characters marching off to the page numbers aligned on the right margins. Once it's in place, you can also use your table of contents to navigate. Just click one of the page numbers to jump that spot.

Updating Your Table of Contents

Back on page 163, Word's fields were described as placeholders and it was explained that Word replaces fields with text. Your table of contents is nothing but a Word field. (You can prove this to yourself by pressing Option-F9, the command that displays the field code as opposed to the replacement text.) When word sees the table of contents field in your document, it gathers up the details it needs and displays a nicely formatted table of contents in its place.

Sometimes you have to make late changes to your document. Perhaps you need to add a header, or remove or add pages. After these kinds of changes, your table of contents is invalid. Surprisingly, Word doesn't make these updates automatically—it needs a little nudge from you. So, you have to tell Word to update the table.

Here are the ways you can update your table of contents:

- Go to Document Elements | Table of Contents→Update.
- Right-click (Control-click) anywhere on the table, and then choose Update Field.
- At the top of the Table of Contents, click the menu button and choose Update Table as shown in Figure 5-23.

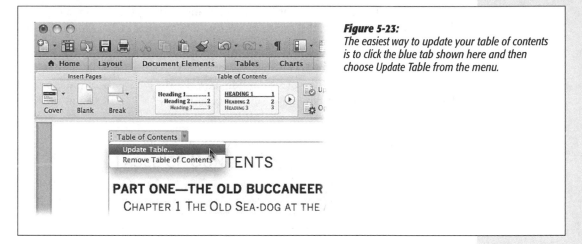

Figure 5-23:
The easiest way to update your table of contents is to click the blue tab shown here and then choose Update Table from the menu.

When you give Word the command to update the table of contents, a box appears asking you to choose exactly what you want updated (Figure 5-24):

- **Update page numbers only.** Use this option if you've edited the table and want Word to update only the page numbers in the table of contents, while leaving your customized table of contents intact. You can edit the words in your table of contents, but your changes will disappear if you use "Update entire table," as shown below.
- **Update entire table.** This option is the same as deleting the old table of contents and creating a brand new one in its place. Use it if you've made lots of changes to your document and just want to start fresh.

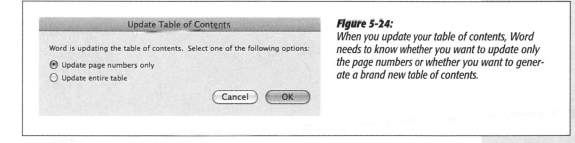

Figure 5-24:
When you update your table of contents, Word needs to know whether you want to update only the page numbers or whether you want to generate a brand new table of contents.

TOC the Harder Way: Using Other Styles

Life is easiest if you use Word's built-in heading styles (Heading 1, Heading 2…)
when preparing your manuscript—but that's not your only option. If you've arranged your document using other styles, whether built-in or ones you've created,
you can use those as the basis for your table of contents headings instead. For example, suppose every major section of your document begins with a style you've called
FancyHeadline, you can create a table of contents that lists just those headlines. To
do so, head back to the Document Elements tab and in the Table of Contents group,
click Options. Then, when the Table of Contents box appears, click Options again.

In the Table of Contents Options dialog box, you see a scrolling list of all styles in
your document (see Figure 5-25). If you scroll down, you'll see that Headings 1, 2,
and 3 have been assigned to corresponding TOC levels. Delete the numbers from
these heading styles and type new TOC level numbers (1, 2, and so on) into the
boxes next to your own styles.

Click OK and return to the Preview box to check your work.

Tip: You can even type each level number next to more than one style. For instance, if you want your
captions to be listed in the table of contents under each main topic, like your Level 3 headings, just type 3
in the box next to Caption.

In fact, you don't even have to use different levels. If you make every heading style
Level 1, every item in your Table of Contents will have equal weight—no indents or
typeface changes.

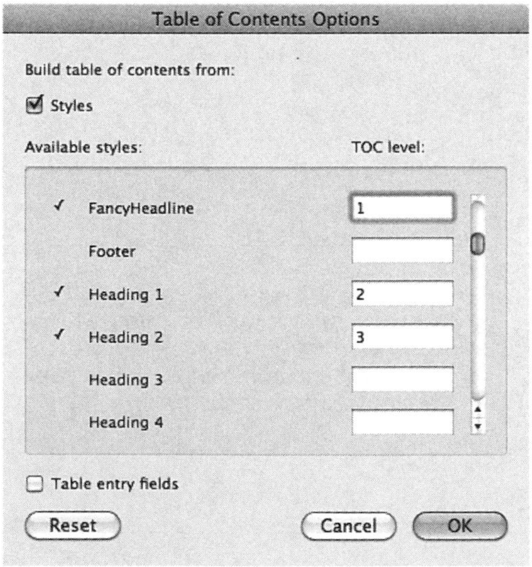

Figure 5-25:
*The Options box lets you build your table of contents
from the styles you've used in your document other than
Heading 1, Heading 2 and so on. For instance, you can add
the FancyHeadline style to the list and assign it a level as
shown here.*

Formatting Your Table of Contents

You can select text in your table of contents and format it just as you would any other text, but that's not the best way to change the look of your table. If you make changes or update your table, you'll probably lose the formatting. It's better to make changes to the table of contents styles using the Table of Contents dialog box (Document Elements→Table of Contents→Options). That way, when you add new entries or update your table, Word formats everything correctly.

Quick formatting for tables of contents

The Table of Contents box shown in Figure 5-26 lets you tweak some formatting options of the table of contents. Here are your options:

- **Formats.** Choose table of contents formatting from several different standard styles. These options change the font sizes and styles (italics, bold, and so on).

- **Show levels.** Word's standard settings create tables of contents from the first three heading styles. You can increase or decrease the number of headings used.

- **Show page numbers.** Turn off this box to remove page numbers from your table of contents. You may not want page numbers if, for example, you're doing a very short document like a newsletter or brochure, and just want an "In This Issue" list.

- **Right align page numbers.** You can make your page numbers line up against the right margin, as shown in Figure 5-26, or they can follow immediately after the entry's text.

- **Tab leader.** You can choose from any of the standard tab leaders: dots, dashes, lines, or none.

As you make changes, you see the results in the Print Preview section of the Table of Contents dialog box (Figure 5-26).

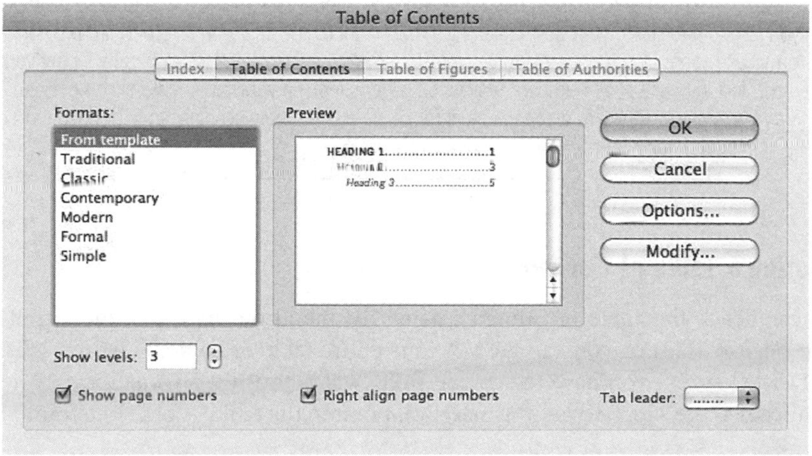

Figure 5-26:
Click one of the table of contents formats—like Classic or Modern—and you can see how it looks in the Preview window.

Detailed formatting for tables of contents

Each line in the table of contents that Word creates has a paragraph style, just like any other paragraph in your document. For the table of contents, these styles not only set the font, font size, and type style, but they also determine the indent from the left margin and the tab leader. Because these styles are ordinary, everyday Word styles, you can fiddle with them all you want. The styles are called: TOC 1 for level 1 entries, TOC 2 for level 2 entries, and so on.

Here are the steps for modifying your Table of Contents styles:

1. **On the ribbon, go to Document Elements | Table of Contents→Options.**

    The Table of Contents dialog box opens (Figure 5-26).

2. **In the lower-right corner, click the Modify button to open the Style box.**

    The Style box lists all the TOC entries 1 through 9. Click an entry, and you see a formatting description in the bottom of the box.

3. **Choose the TOC style you want to format, and then click the Style box's Modify button.**

    When you click Modify, yet another dialog box opens called Modify Style. If you've customized any paragraph styles or created your own, this box should look familiar.

4. **In the Modify Style box, choose from the Format menu at the lower-left corner to choose the formatting you want to change.**

    Your choices include Font, Paragraph, Tabs, Borders, and more. For more details on paragraph formatting, see page 125.

    You can change several different styles from the Modify Style box before closing it. Just choose a new style from the drop-down menu at the very top.

5. **Click OK to close each of the boxes and return to your document.**

Note: One of the entries in the Table of Contents menu is Manual Table of Contents. Choose this option when you just want to create your own table of contents without any help from Word. Word provides the basic format and some placeholder text to get you started. You replace the placeholders by typing your own entries, including the page numbers, which you have to look up yourself. A table of contents created in this way is just plain text. Word won't update it for you if you add new headings to your document or if the page numbers change.

Deleting a Table of Contents

You can delete the Table of Contents using the menu on the tab at the top of the table (Figure 5-23) or you can get rid your entire table of contents with a press of the Delete key, but you have to select it first. Switch to Print Layout View, if you're not already there. Click to put the insertion point in the table. A blue line frames the table of contents and there's a tab at the top labeled Table of Contents. Click the left side of the tab with the three dots. This selects the entire table so you can do things like move or delete it. Hit Delete and Word removes the entire table from your document. But don't worry, you can press ⌘-Z immediately to bring it back, or just insert a new one.

Creating an Index

An index helps readers find the material that's most important to them. In many ways, indexing is an art, because you have to decide what is likely to be important to your readers. An index that's too cluttered is almost as bad as no index at all. Word can generate and format an index, but it's no help making the important decisions about what to index. That part of the heavy lifting is up to you. On the other hand, by building the index, keeping track of page numbers, and formatting the end result, Word takes a huge burden from you.

Obviously, you don't want to create an index for your document until you're ready to print or distribute it. When you're ready, making an index with Word is a two step process. First, you mark your index entries in your document—that's the human job. Then, you generate the index—that's the computer's job.

Marking an Index Entry

The first phase of creating an index involves paging through your entire document, selecting words and phrases to index and then, by pressing a special keystroke, inserting electronic markers for the items you want listed.

As Figure 5-27 illustrates, three types of index entries are available:

- Individual words, phrases, or symbols.
- Entries that span more than one page.
- Entries that reference another index entry, such as "execution, See guillotine."

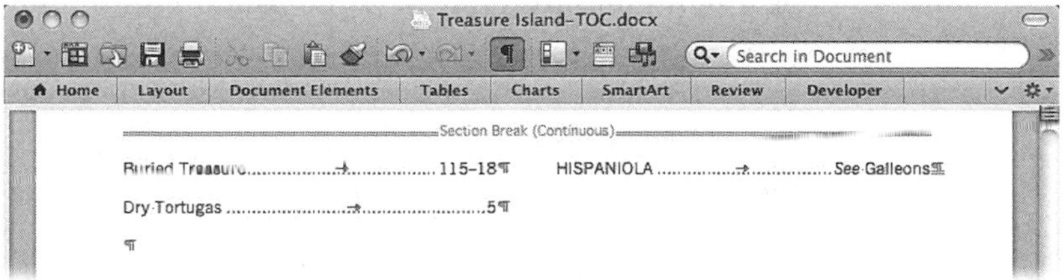

Figure 5-27:
Word automatically alphabetizes and formats your index. This example consists of two columns, with page numbers aligned to the right margin. You can format your index in a number of different ways.

What to Index

Here are some tips to keep in mind when you mark index entries:

- **Take the reader's point of view.** This tip is the most important and perhaps the hardest for an involved writer. As you mark index words, ask these questions: Why are people reading this document? What questions did I have when I first approached this subject?

- **Avoid marking too many words.** It's way easy to mark too many words, especially when you know that Word is going to spare you the job of typing out the entire index. If you want a truly helpful index, take the time to consider every marked entry carefully.

- **Consolidate entries whenever possible.** For a professional quality index, it's important to consolidate entries under the most logical index listing. Text like "Captain Teach," "Edward Teach," and "Pirate Teach" should all be consolidated under "Teach, Edward" in your index.

- **Make use of cross-references.** Cross-references help your readers find answers. For example, the entry for execution may appear: "execution, See guillotine."

- **Use page ranges to reduce clutter in the index.** The index entry for "Edward Teach" could read: "Teach, Edward...60, 70-78..." Using page ranges reduces the length and clutter of your index, which makes research easier for your readers.

Here are the steps to mark an index entry:

1. **Select the word or phrase you want to add to the index.**

   Word uses whatever text you select for the actual index listing (unless you make changes in the next step). When you select text, you're also marking its location so Word can identify the page number when it builds the index.

2. **Press Shift-Option-⌘-X.**

   (If you can't make your fingers do a four key shortcut, go to Insert→Index and Tables. In the box that opens, make sure you're on the Index tab, then click the Mark Entry button.)

   The Mark Index Entry dialog box opens (Figure 5-28). In the "Main entry" text at top, your selected text appears. You can edit or change this text. For example, you can change "Edward Teach" to read "Teach, Edward" so the index entry will be alphabetized under "Teach."

3. **In the middle of the Mark Index Entry box, choose a radio button for the index entry type.**

   As mentioned at the beginning of this section, three types of index entries are available: Select the "Cross-reference" radio button if this entry refers to another index entry. (For example, if you select the word "execution," and then type "guillotine" in the cross-reference box, the index entry looks like this: "execution, See guillotine.") For individual words, phrases, or symbols, click the "Current page" option. For entries that span more than a page, click Page Range, and then select a bookmark from the Bookmark drop-down menu.

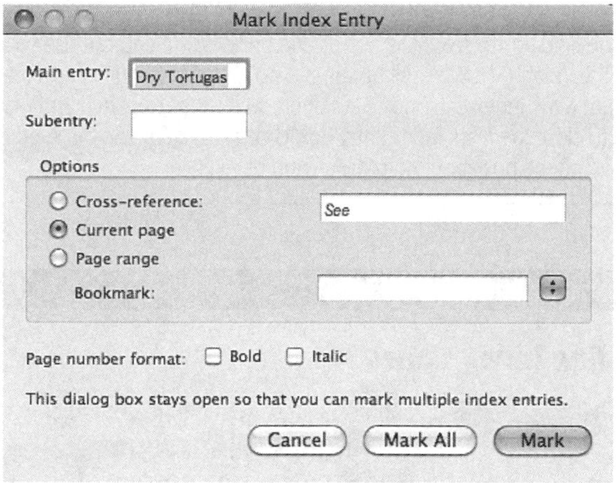

Figure 5-28:
Use the Mark Index Entry box to customize your index entry. The text in the Main entry box is used for the actual index listing. Use the three options in the middle to choose the type of index entry. With the buttons at the bottom, you can choose to mark a single entry or to mark every occurrence of the word or phrase.

Note: Before you can mark a Page Range index entry, you must create a bookmark. That's the only way Word can keep track of the page numbers. To create a bookmark, select the text, and then go to Insert→ Bookmark (Shift-⌘-F5). Detailed bookmark instructions are on page 213.

4. **Format the entry.**

    Use the checkboxes under "Page number format" to apply bold or italics formatting to the page numbers. Typically, the page that holds the most important information about an entry gets bold formatting, and page ranges get italics, but Word will do whatever you tell it. This kind of formatting is completely optional.

5. **Click Mark to create an entry for a single page, or Mark All to create entries for every instance of the selected words that Word finds in the document.**

    Word hides a special code in the text of your document to mark the entry or entries. Word reads all these hidden codes when it builds an index. (For details, read the box on page 206.)

    Say you select the word "England," and then click the Mark button. Word places a single chunk of code after the word "England" on that page. If you click Mark All, Word looks through your entire document and inserts the code everywhere the word "England" appears.

Warning: It's easy to get carried away with the Mark All button because it's so tempting just to click it, and then let Word find every occurrence of a word or a phrase. The problem is, you can end up with too many index references. Instead of using the Mark All button, consider using the Mark Index Entry box in tandem with Word's Find tool. Use the Find box to search for words and phrases, but you can use your discretion when you mark items for the index. (The Mark All button has no discretion; it just marks the occurrence of a word or a phrase.) The Mark Index Entry box stays open, so it's easy to search and mark more index entries. When you want to close the Mark Index Entry box, click Cancel. For another method to automate the mark index process, read the box about AutoMarking on page 208.

POWER USERS' CLINIC

Understanding Index Codes

Whenever you mark an index entry as described in the previous steps, Word inserts a code right within the text of the document. It's just hidden so you don't usually see it. Hidden text (page 150) doesn't show when the document is printed, but you can see it onscreen by clicking ¶ in the standard toolbar.

An index entry marking the words Edward Teach may look like this: { XE "Teach, Edward" }. The code is within the curly braces, and the XE is how Word identifies the code as an index entry.

Here are examples of the code Word inserts in your document to mark pages for different index entries:

- **Basic Index Entry.** Example: { XE "Teach, Edward" }.All the code is within the curly braces ({}), and the XE identifies the code as an index entry. Word adds the page where this code appears to the Teach, Edward index listing

- **Index Subentry.** Example: { XE "England:London" }. The colon in this code means it's a subentry. Word adds a London subentry, with the page number, under the England index listing.

- **Page Range Entry.** Example: { XE "Dover Road" \r "DoverRoad" }. The \r marks this entry as a page range entry. DoverRoad is the name of a bookmark (page 194) in the document that marks more than one page. The pages included in the DoverRoad bookmark appear as a range in the Dover Road index listing.

- **Index Cross-reference.** Example: { XE "execution" \t "See guillotine" }. The \t marks this entry as a cross-reference. Word lists "execution" in the index followed by the note "See guillotine."

To create an index, Word reads all the entries and alphabetizes them, and then removes duplicate entries. For example, if five Edward Teach entries are on page 94, Word lists the page only once.

Building an Index

Creating the actual index is a lot easier and faster than marking your index entries. You have only a couple decisions to make, and Word does all the rest. The first thing to decide is where you want to place the index.

Follow these steps to create the index:

1. **Press ⌘-End (FN-⌘-right arrow if you're on a MacBook) to move the insertion point to the end of your document, and then choose Insert→Break→Page Break to start your index on a brand new page.**

   Traditionally, an index goes at the back of a document, but Word puts it wherever you want.

2. **Type *Index* to give the section a title, and then choose Home | Styles→Heading 1.**

   Giving the title for the index a Heading 1 makes it look important and means that it shows up in the Table of Contents, to boot.

3. **Go to Insert→Index and Tables and click the Index tab to display the Index dialog box, where you make some choices about the appearance of your index (Figure 5-29).**

   The Preview box shows you how your index will look on the page. Use the other controls to change its appearance. For Type, if you select Indented, then the index lists the subentries indented under the main entry. If you choose Run-in, then subentries and page numbers immediately follow on the same line as the entry.

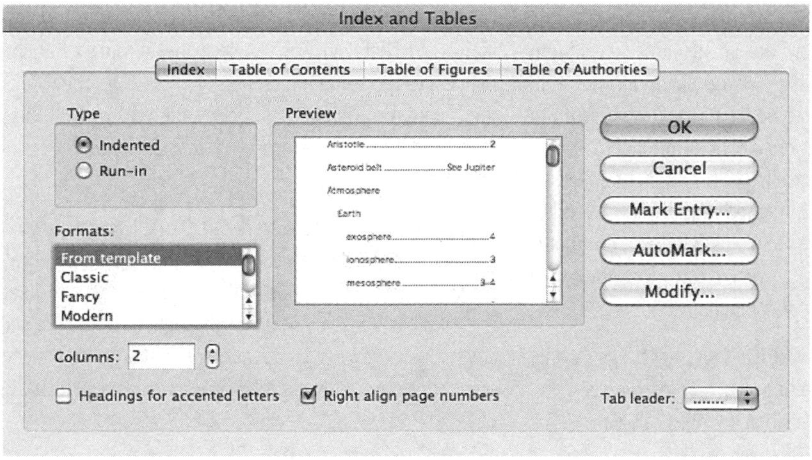

Figure 5-29:
Use the Index dialog box to create an index for your document. Make adjustments to the appearance with the Type, Columns, and other controls. The Print Preview box lets you see the results of your formatting on example text.

From the Columns menu, you can choose the number of columns per page (two or three columns usually works well). The Formats drop-down menu provides several formatting options that change the font size and style. At the bottom, you find controls to align index page numbers on the right margin and to set the leader that links the entry to the page number. If you want to customize the appearance of your index, click the Modify button, and then you can format your index using Word's standard style and text formatting tools (Chapter 3).

4. **When you're done formatting your index, click OK.**

   Word builds the index and places it in your document at the insertion point. The process may take a few moments.

Tip: The Mark Entry button closes the Index box and opens the Mark Index Entry box (Figure 5-28). Click it if you decide you're not ready to create the index and want to go back to marking entries. Clicking the AutoMark button makes Word go through your document and mark entries for you, but only if you supply a concordance file.

POWER USERS' CLINIC

AutoMarking Long Documents

If your document is very long, reviewing it can be an exercise in tedium. Although the Mark All button helps, Word's AutoMark feature can accelerate the process even further. However, this feature is only worth using on very long documents—maybe 100 pages or more—because it entails an extra step that has its own brand of tedium: creating an automark concordance file.

A concordance file is a Word document with a two-column table that you create yourself from a blank document. In the first (left) column, you type the text you want Word to look for and mark in your document. In the right column, you type the index entry itself, which may not necessarily be the same term. (Using this technique, you can index, under "printing", five pages of discussion about dot-matrix printers, laser printers, fonts, and ink cartridges; the actual word printing may never appear in the text.)

Another example: You could type egg, eggs, Egg, laying, reproduction in the left column (each in its own cell), and eggs directly across from each in the right cell. To create a subentry, use a colon. At the end of this exercise, Word will find each word in the left column and index it under the term you've specified in the right column—all of the sample terms mentioned here, for example, will be indexed under "eggs."

After logging each important term in your document this way, save and close the concordance file. You can use any name or folder you want to save the automark concordance file, just remember where you stash it. Then open the manuscript document. Click at the end of the document, and then choose Insert→"Index and Tables"→Index tab.

In the resulting dialog box, click AutoMark. Navigate to your automark concordance file and open it. Word automatically places index entry fields in the document; you can see them highlighted as you scroll through it. If you missed any major topics, just create another concordance file and repeat the process. Now build your index as explained on page 207.

Updating an Index

What if you need to update an index? Perhaps you remembered and marked some additional entries after you built your index. No problem—Word gives you a quick and easy way to add those new entries to your index. Place your insertion point inside your index, and then press Shift-Option-⌘-U. It may take a moment or two, since Word rereads all the index entries, but you end up with a new index including any new entries you've created.

If you want to change your index's formatting, place the insertion point somewhere in the index, and then go to Insert→Index and Tables and then in the box that opens, click the Index tab. Make your formatting changes, and, when you're done, click the OK button. An alert box pops up asking if you want to replace the selected index. Click OK, and the old index is gone and your all-new, improved index takes its place.

Deleting an Index

You may have a couple reasons for wanting to delete an index from your document. Perhaps you decided not to have an index, or you want to make major changes to your index, so you're going to delete the current index and insert a new one.

The index looks like a lot of words on the page, but the entire index is represented by one relatively short bit of computerese known as a field code. With one command, you reduce your entire index to a field code of just a few characters, making it much easier to delete. Press Option-F9, and your index disappears and the field code appears in its place. What you see looks something like this: { INDEX \c "2" \z "1033"}. Select this text, including both brackets, and then press Delete. Goodbye index. Press Option-F9 again to hide the field codes and see the replacement text.

Deleting an Index Entry

It may seem odd, but it's easier to delete the entire index than it is to delete individual entries from your document. For one thing, you probably don't have to search for the index—it's big and it's usually at the end of your document. The marked index entries in your document could be anywhere, and if you're deleting every vestige of Ben Gunn index entries in Treasure Island, that's a lot of deleting.

If your plan is to have a document without an index at all, you may want to delete the index as described above and not worry about deleting each and every hidden index entry code in your text. Under normal circumstances, the hidden text doesn't show when you print or view your document.

To delete an index entry, you need to find the index code in your document, and then delete it, just as you would any text. Here are the steps:

1. **Click ¶ on the standard toolbar to view the hidden text in your document.**

   You're on a search and destroy mission, so the first thing you need to do is make sure you can see your target. When you turn on hidden text, you can see the index codes (along with other hidden characters like, well, paragraph marks). The index code looks something like this: { XE "Teach, Edward" }.

   You can scroll through your document and scan for entries you want to delete, but it's faster to use the Find dialog box, as described in the next step.

2. **Press ⌘-F and type XE in the search box.**

   You can't search for the curly brackets, but you can search for some of the other text within. That way, Word searches for each index entry so you can inspect them one by one.

Tip: You can also use the special code ^*d* with the Find command, to find fields, such as Index fields, in your document. Another option is to use the browse button below the scroll bar to browse for fields. For details, see page 194.

---

3. **Select the entire code including the brackets, and then press Delete.**

   The entry is a goner. Of course, that's just a single entry on a single page. If you want to remove an item entirely from the index, you must continue to find and delete every marked entry.

Navigating with Hyperlinks

Hyperlinks are those bits of underlined text or pictures that, when you click them, take you to a new place, like another web page. Most people never think of adding links to their Word documents, because they're thinking of them as printed documents. However, if some of your readers may read your work onscreen, consider adding hyperlinks (Figure 5-30).

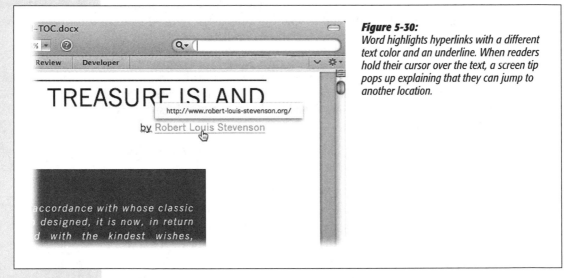

Figure 5-30:
Word highlights hyperlinks with a different text color and an underline. When readers hold their cursor over the text, a screen tip pops up explaining that they can jump to another location.

Word's hyperlinks are identical to the hyperlinks on websites. They even use the same programming language (HTML). Hyperlinks you create in Word stay intact if you save the file in a format other than Word—like a PDF file or a web page. And since other Office programs also use HTML, if you copy or cut the text and paste it in another document in a program such as Excel or PowerPoint, the hyperlink will work just fine in the new document.

Links aren't just for web pages anymore. Word lets you make hyperlinks that go all sorts of places:

- **Locations in your document.** If your document refers to another section, add a link so your readers can jump right there instead of scrolling.

- **Other documents on your computer or network.** If you're working with a group of people on an office network, hyperlinks to related shared documents can be very effective. When you click the link to a shared document, Word opens that document even if it's not on your computer, as long as you have permission to open it.

- **Documents on the Web.** Whatever topic you're writing about, you can find related web pages, photos, maps, news items, and blogs on the Internet. If you can find them, you can create hyperlinks for your readers.

- **Email forms.** You can give your readers an easy way to interact with you or your company by inserting email hyperlinks in your document. When they Control-click the link, a properly addressed email form appears. All they have to do is fill in their comments (Figure 5-31).

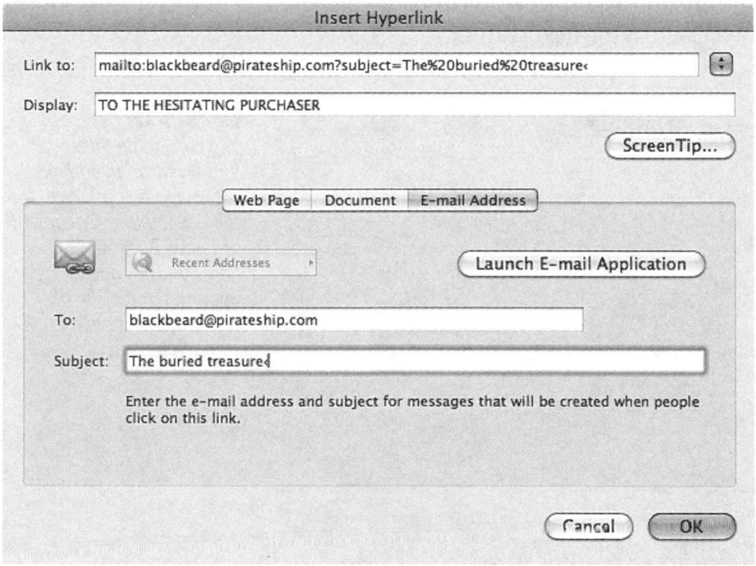

Figure 5-31:
You can use hyperlinks as a way to get feedback from your readers. An email hyperlink, like this one, opens a preaddressed email form. You provide the address when you create the hyperlink.

To create a hyperlink to any of the above places, the steps are almost the same. You select the text you want to turn into a hyperlink, and then, in the Insert Hyperlink box, you tell Word what to link it to:

1. **Select the text for the link.**

   Choose text that gives your readers a good clue to where the link goes. Two or three words is usually enough to catch your readers' attention.

2. **Go to Insert →Hyperlink (⌘-K) to open the Insert Hyperlink dialog box.**

   The Insert Hyperlink box shows different options for each of the tabs: Web Page, Document or E-mail Address.

3. **Choose the type of link you want to create.**

   You have several options as shown in Figure 5-32:

   - Choose **Web Page** to create a link to a page on the Internet. If you find the page in your Safari or another browser, you can copy the address and paste it in the Link to box. Some web pages have "anchors, " similar to bookmarks within the page. If you want to link to one of those anchors, click the Locate button. Word reads the page and displays the available anchors, if any. Select the anchor you want and click OK. Then, click OK again to close the Insert Hyperlink window.

   - Choose **Document** if you're creating a link in the current document or one that's on your computer or network. Use the Select button to choose a document other than the current one. You can skip that step if you're linking within the current document. Click the Locate button to see a list of headers and bookmarks. (If you don't have anything for Word to attach the link to, click Cancel to close the dialog box and create a bookmark, as described in the next section.)

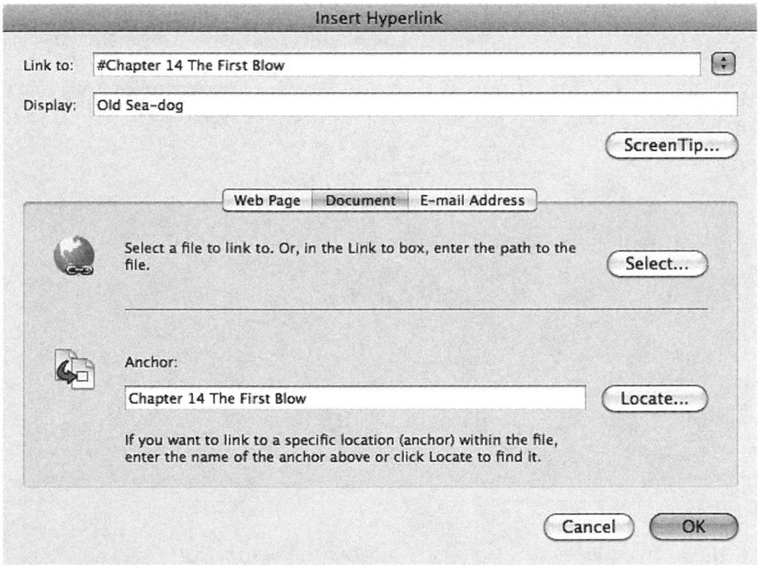

Figure 5-32:
You can create three basic kinds of hyperlinks, as shown by the options in the tabs: Web Page, Document, or E-mail Address. Each time you click one of the options, the tools in the window change to match your choice.

- **E-mail Address** creates a mailto hyperlink in your document. When you choose this option, the Edit Hyperlink box changes, as shown in Figure 5-31, so you can type the email address you want to link to. It's also helpful (but not necessary) to provide a Subject for the email. Click OK to close the box and create the link.

Tip: When you type some text in the ScreenTip box, Word displays it as a small, onscreen label whenever someone's mouse passes over the link, just like on a real live web page.

Inserting and Removing Bookmarks

Bookmarks, which mark a spot in your document, may seem like a somewhat mild-mannered Word tool, but more power is hidden under their Clark Kent exterior than you may expect. Bookmarks come in handy in long documents because so many other features depend on them:

- **Browsing by bookmark.** You give each bookmark a name when you create it, and you see those names listed in the Go To dialog box (Edit→Find→Go To). You can then use these bookmarks to hop from place to place in your document.

- **Indexing.** Because bookmarks are based on selected text, you can create a bookmark that includes several pages. In this way, you can use bookmarks to create page ranges for building indexes, as described earlier in this chapter.

- **Hyperlinks.** When you create a hyperlink (page 210) to a specific point in your document, Word needs something to anchor the link to. That can be a heading or a bookmark that you've created at any point in the text.

- **Cross-references.** When you create cross-references in your documents, you can link to headings, but what if you want to link to specific text within a topic?

  You can create a cross-reference to any part of your document, by simply creating a bookmark first, and then referencing the bookmark. (More on cross-references in the next section.)

- **Macros.** These mini-programs that automate Word tasks also frequently use bookmarks. Say you create a macro that performs a task with the text from a particular part of your document; you need to be able to identify the text. You can do that by creating a bookmark. The macro uses the bookmark's name to do its magic.

To create a bookmark, select some text, and then go to Insert→Bookmark (or press Shift-⌘-F5). Proceed as shown in Figure 5-33.

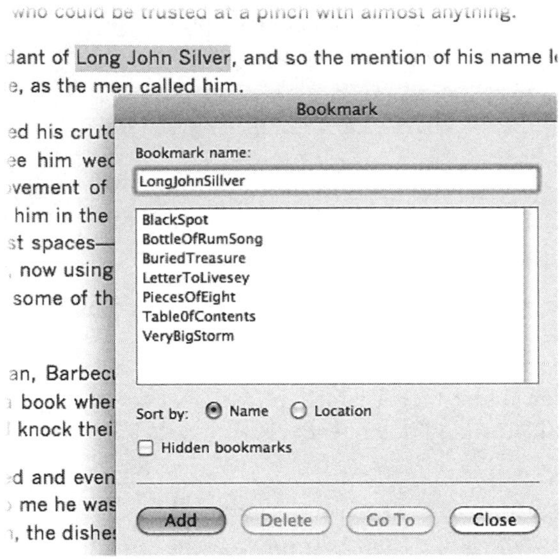

who could be trusted at a pinch with almost anything.

dant of Long John Silver, and so the mention of his name l
e, as the men called him.

ed his crutc

e him wec

ovement of

him in the

st spaces—

, now using

some of th

an, Barbecu

book wher

knock thei

d and even

me he was

, the dishes

Bookmark

Bookmark name:

LongJohnSillver

BlackSpot
BottleOfRumSong
BuriedTreasure
LetterToLivesey
PiecesOfEight
TableOfContents
VeryBigStorm

Sort by: ● Name   ○ Location

☐ Hidden bookmarks

(Add)   (Delete)   (Go To)   (Close)

Figure 5-33:
The Bookmark dialog box gives you the power to both create and destroy. To delete a bookmark, select it in the list, and then click the Delete button (or press the Delete key). To create a bookmark, you need to select text before you open this box. Type a name in the text box at the top, and then click Add.

Cross-Referencing Your Document

Schoolbooks, business reports, and a variety of other documents use cross-references to refer to photos, figures, charts, tables, and other parts of the document. When readers view your document on a computer, they can click the reference to jump to that spot. For example, clicking the words "Chart A" takes the reader right to the chart in your document. You can turn this chore over to Word with confidence that it will keep track of the reference and the page number for you, even as you add or move material.

With Word you can create cross-references to the following items:

- **Numbered item.** Numbered paragraphs in your text created with the Format→Bullets and Numbering command.

- **Heading.** A paragraph you styled with a built-in headings such as Heading 1 or Heading 2.

- **Bookmark.** Bookmarks in your text that refer to specific locations or ranges of pages. Bookmarks are inserted with the keyboard shortcut ⌘-K.

- **Footnote.** Word keeps track of your footnotes' locations and their numbers.

- **Endnote.** Endnotes are a little easier for a human to hunt down; still, Word keeps track of their locations and page numbers.

- **Equation.** For documents dealing with math, Word keeps track of all the equations created with the built-in equation editor.

- **Figure.** When you insert pictures and label them with a caption, Word keeps track of the "figure" number. For a step-by-step description of creating cross-references for figures, see page 216.

- **Table.** Tables with or without captions are tallied in Word, and you can create cross-references to them.

Here are the steps for adding a cross-reference to your document:

1. **In your document, type the text you'd like to go before the reference.**

   Usually, cross-references have some preceding introductory text, like "As shown in" or "For more details, see." You have to type this part yourself; Word adds the cross-reference (the clickable text or page number).

2. **Go to Insert→Cross-reference. When the Cross-reference dialog box opens (Figure 5-34), use the "Reference type" drop-down menu to choose the object that you're referring to.**

   Whichever type you choose, in the text box below, Word shows you a list of the specific items in your document (numbered items, bookmarks, headings, and so on) that are candidates for cross-referencing.

3. **From the "Insert reference to" menu, choose the text that describes the reference.**

   Here's where you select what appears in your document—the text that your readers can read and click. Your choices from this menu depend on what you've chosen from the "Reference type" menu. For example, if you're referring to a heading, you can choose to insert the heading text itself (Figure 5-34), or just the page number.

4. **If desired, turn on the "Insert above/below" checkbox.**

   In addition, you can insert either the word "above" or the word "below" to indicate where the item is relative to the cross-reference. For example, say you're putting the cross-reference "see Table 1," before Table 1 in your document. If you turn on this checkbox, the reference reads "see Table 1 below." If you happen to move Table 1 to before the cross-reference, Word changes it to "see Table 1 above." This way, if your readers print your document, they have a clue where to go looking for the cross-reference without the benefit of a hyperlink.

Tip: Of course, if your readers are hard-copy types, choose the page number from the "Insert reference to" menu (step 3), so they'll know exactly where to look.

---

5. **When you're done, click Insert to close the Cross-reference dialog box.**

   Back in your document, you see your newly minted cross-reference.

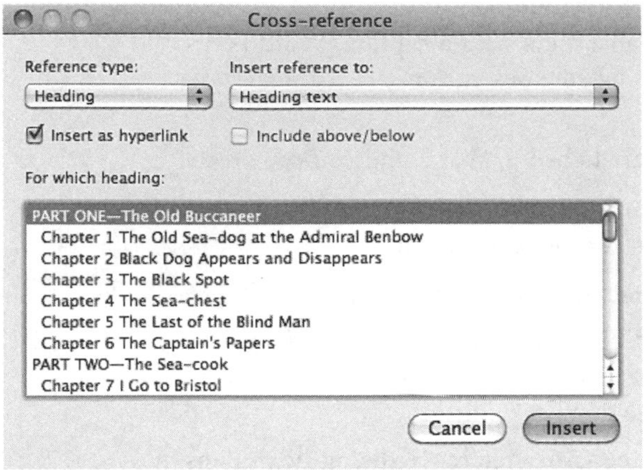

Figure 5-34:
In the Cross-reference box, use the "Reference type" drop-down menu to choose the type of item you're referring to and the "Insert reference to" menu to choose what actually appears in your text. For example, you could choose a page number, a figure number, or the text from a caption.

Deleting Cross-References

You can delete a cross-reference as you'd delete any text; just select it, and then press Delete.

Cross-Referencing Figures

Figures—those photos, drawings, and other graphics—help convey information that would be hard to describe in text. They help break up that vast sea of words as they illustrate your point. In academic papers, magazine articles, and business documents, figures usually have numbers to make it easier to refer to them.

Tip: To add a caption to a figure, right-click (Control-click) the image and then choose Insert Caption.

To create a cross-reference to a figure, you use the Cross-reference dialog box, as described in the previous section. However, since figures have a figure number and a caption as well as a location in your document, you have a few more options when creating the cross-reference, so the process is a bit more complicated.

First, of course, you need some text to introduce the figure, like "The guillotine, as shown in…". Remember to type only the words that come before the cross-reference, not the cross-reference itself, and then choose Insert→Cross-reference to open the Cross-reference dialog box. From the "Reference type" drop-down menu, choose Figure. The text box below lists the figures in your document. Select the one you want to reference, and then, from the "Insert reference to" drop-down menu, choose the text that describes the reference to the figure.

Captions have three parts: a label, (like the word "Figure"), a number, and the caption text. Your cross-reference can include any one of those items, or all three. It can also show the page number and state whether the figure is above or below the reference in the text (Figure 5-35). For example, if you turn on all of these options, you may end up with something like this: The guillotine as shown in Figure 1 on page 1 above.

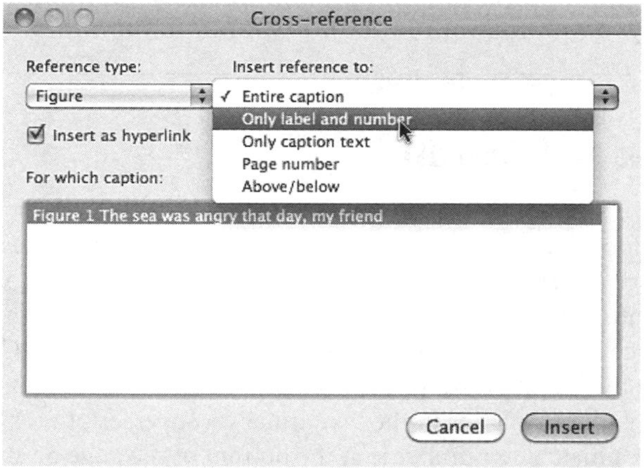

Figure 5-35:
To insert a cross-reference for a figure, choose Figure as the reference type. Use the "Insert reference to" menu to select the text that appears in the reference.

Making a Table of Figures

In addition to keeping track of figures and their captions, Word can create a table that lists the figures, shows their captions, and shows the page numbers. Inserting a table of figures is similar to inserting a table of contents. To create a table, go to Insert→Index and Tables and in the window, choose Table of Figures tab. Use the Formats list shown in Figure 5-36 to choose a style for your Table of Figures. Word can take its style cue from your template, or you can use one of several predesigned styles from the menu.

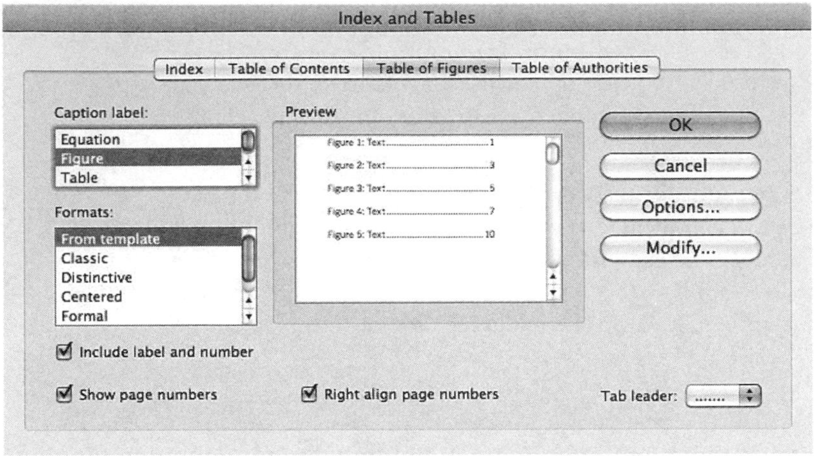

Figure 5-36:
The Table of Figures box gives you a preview of the printed table on the left. On the right you see a Web preview. Check the box below to use hyperlinks on the web page instead of page numbers. Use the other tools such as the "Show page numbers" and "Right align page numbers" box to format your table.

Creating Footnotes and Endnotes

If you've ever read—or written—a term paper, thesis, or book of a scholarly nature, you've encountered footnotes or endnotes. Typically, writers use these notes for background or explanatory information that may be of interest to some, but not all readers. Footnotes and endnotes are the exact same thing, except footnotes appear at the bottom (foot) of each page, and endnotes come all together at the end. (Citations are similar to footnotes, but in Word, you create them with a separate tool; see page 221.) A footnote or endnote marker in the text, usually a superscript number, indicates that a note with a matching number is at the bottom of the page or at the end of the document (Figure 5-37).

When you create footnotes and endnotes using Word's tools, the program keeps track of the numbering for you. If you add and remove notes, Word renumbers the rest automatically. When you print the document, Word places the footnotes and endnotes in their rightful places at the bottom of the pages or at the end of the document, just as if you'd typed them there yourself—but a whole lot easier.

Onscreen, Word provides some helpful navigation techniques. You can double-click a note to jump to its partner reference mark and vice versa. When you're working with the notes themselves, a right-click (Control-click) brings up a context menu that includes "Go to endnote" or "Go to footnote" options. Click these options to jump from the note to the reference in your text. You can also use the Browse buttons (page 194) at the bottom of the scroll bar to move between footnotes and endnotes. First, click the round Select Browse Object button and choose either footnotes or endnotes from the pop-up menu. Then you can use the double-arrow buttons to jump from note to note.

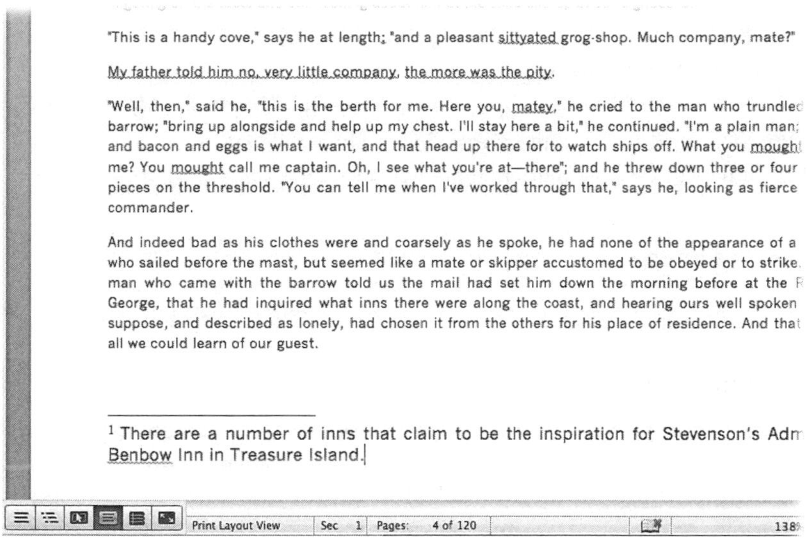

> "This is a handy cove," says he at length; "and a pleasant sittyated grog-shop. Much company, mate?"
>
> My father told him no, very little company, the more was the pity.
>
> "Well, then," said he, "this is the berth for me. Here you, matey," he cried to the man who trundled barrow; "bring up alongside and help up my chest. I'll stay here a bit," he continued. "I'm a plain man; and bacon and eggs is what I want, and that head up there for to watch ships off. What you mough me? You mought call me captain. Oh, I see what you're at—there"; and he threw down three or four pieces on the threshold. "You can tell me when I've worked through that," says he, looking as fierce commander.
>
> And indeed bad as his clothes were and coarsely as he spoke, he had none of the appearance of a who sailed before the mast, but seemed like a mate or skipper accustomed to be obeyed or to strike. man who came with the barrow told us the mail had set him down the morning before at the F George, that he had inquired what inns there were along the coast, and hearing ours well spoken suppose, and described as lonely, had chosen it from the others for his place of residence. And that all we could learn of our guest.
>
> ---
> ¹ There are a number of inns that claim to be the inspiration for Stevenson's Adm Benbow Inn in Treasure Island.

Figure 5-37:
Footnotes appear at the bottom of the page. A reference marker, usually a superscript number, appears in text that creates a link between the document and the note.

Inserting Footnotes and Endnotes

Footnotes are easier than endnotes for readers because they require less page flipping to find the note. Different types of documents have different standards, and more often than not, it's a teacher or a professor who dictates the preferred style. Back in the typewriter era, endnotes were much easier to create, because you didn't have to worry about leaving space at the bottom of the page for the notes. Fortunately, Word makes it equally easy to create footnotes and endnotes.

Just follow these steps:

1. **Click to place the insertion point in your text where you want the reference mark.**

   You may want to put the mark at the end of a sentence or paragraph. But if the note pertains to the meaning of a specific word, click-right after that word.

2. **On the ribbon go to Document Elements→Footnote (Option-⌘-F) or Document Elements→End Note (Option-⌘-E).**

   Word places the reference mark at the insertion point and takes you to the bottom of the page (where the footnote will appear) or the end of the document (where the endnote will appear). You see the note's reference mark, immediately followed by the insertion point, so you can start typing the note.

Tip: If you need fancy formatting or numbering for your footnotes go to Insert→Footnote to see your options.

3. **Type the text for the note.**

   After you type the note, right-click your footnote, and then choose Go to Footnote. Your insertion point jumps back to your original location, where you can continue work on the main body of your document.

Tip: If you want to change the text of your note later, you can edit it as you would any other text.

Formatting Footnotes and Endnotes

You can format your footnotes and endnotes just like any other text, using the methods described in Chapter 3. For example, if you want to make a word bold or italics, just select it, and then press ⌘-B or ⌘-I. However, to edit the reference marks—say, change them from superscript numbers to letters—you need to open the Footnote and Endnote dialog box Insert→Footnote.

Using the Footnote and Endnote box (Figure 5-38), you can choose where your notes appear, and you can customize the style of the reference mark. Reference numbers can be Arabic numbers, Roman numbers, lowercase Roman numbers, letters, or other symbols. The Numbering drop-down menu lets you choose whether the numbers apply to the whole document or if they start with each new section. Change the number in the "Start at" text box if you want to start at a reference other than 1 or the first symbol. For example, if your book or thesis is split between more than one document, you can make the numbering in the second document pick up where the first document left off.

Tip: If you decide (or your instructor tells you) to convert all your endnotes to footnotes or vice versa, you can do that in the Footnote and Endnote box, too. At the top of the box, click the Convert button, and then choose one of the options from the Convert Notes box.

Deleting footnote and endnotes

It's easy to delete unwanted footnotes and endnotes. Select the reference mark in your text, and then delete it by pressing Delete. Not only does the reference mark disappear, but the note does too.

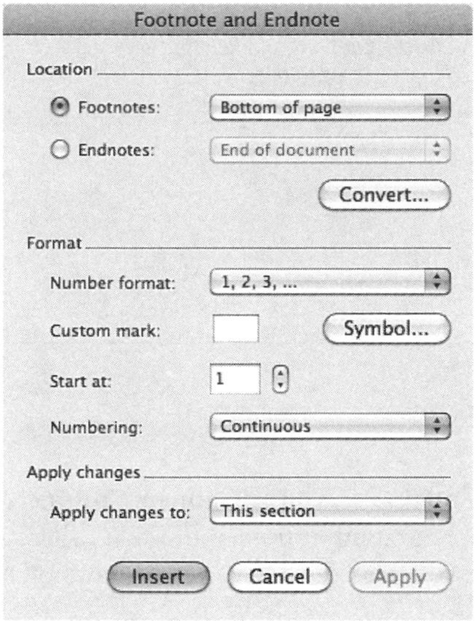

Figure 5-38:
Use the Footnote and Endnote box to format your notes. You can customize the numbers and the numbering for individual notes or for your entire document. Go to Insert→Footnote to open this box.

Inserting Citations and Creating a Bibliography

Citations are similar to endnotes in that they're listed at the end of the document, and you can click a reference link in the text to go see them. The difference is that they refer specifically to a source, such as a book, an article, or a web page. And, instead of a superscript number, a citation uses an abbreviation, like the author's last name, to refer to the source in the text.

The list of sources at the end of a document is called a bibliography, which is simply Latin for "list of books." You could create a simple bibliography by hand, by simply typing the list of books, articles, and websites you got your information from. Often, however, bibliographies must follow a specific format. For example, high schools often require students to use APA or MLA style for bibliographies. Different professional fields have their own specific styles, such as those of the American Psychological Association or the American Medical Association. All these styles have complicated rules for where the titles, authors, punctuation, and other information goes, making bibliographies incredibly tedious to produce. Fortunately, Word is familiar with all the popular style sheets, and assembles, alphabetizes, and formats the bibliography automatically from information you provide. You may just finish your term paper without that third pot of coffee.

Tip: You can create a bibliography without citing the sources in your text, but Word 2011 puts the tools for both on the Document Elements tab (Figure 5-39).

Figure 5-39:
*On the Document Elements tab, the Citations and References groups
provide the tools to give credit where credit's due.*

Developer

Search in Documen

ons   References   Text E

Chicago

Endnote   Manage   Bibliography   Text Box

ide of the captain's breakfast-table—

Adding a Citation

You need to know three things to add a citation to your document. You need to
decide on a style for your citations and bibliography. You need to know where you
want to place your citation. And, of course, you need the details, such as author, title,
and publisher.

Here are the steps for adding a citation to your document:

1. **Go to Document Elements | References and use the menu to choose a style for
   your document.**

   On the list, you see several standard styles for citations, including the Chicago
   Manual of Style; it's a style that many universities and publishing companies
   prefer. To use that one, choose Chicago from the list. When in doubt, ask your
   instructor or publisher.

2. **Place Word's insertion point where you want to place the citation.**

   Citations usually come at the end of the sentence, but you may want to place one
   mid-sentence if that's where the referenced information is.

3. **Still on the ribbon, click the Manage button.**

   The toolbox opens displaying the Citations tab as shown in Figure 5-40.

   If you've already added sources, you'll see them listed in the toolbox. Just click
   on one of the sources to use it.

   If you need to add a new source, go on to the next step.

4. **Click the + button to add a new source.**

   Word's Create New Source box opens with lots of blanks for you to fill. It looks
   like a lot of work, but it's not difficult. Just start at the top and work your way
   down. First, in the drop-down menu at the top, select the Type of Source. You
   have choices such as Book, Article in Periodical, Web site, or Report. When you

choose one that suits your source, the text boxes and the labels in the Create Source box change. Type the details providing information about the author, publisher, date, and, in the case of websites, the Internet address also known as the URL. If all you need is the bare minimum, fill in the boxes marked with an asterisk.

5. **Click the OK button to close the Create New Source box.**

   Word closes the Create New Source box closes and places a reference in your text, usually just the author's name. Word keeps track of all the other information you entered in the Create Source box to use for the bibliography. Best of all, if you want to refer to this source again, you just choose it from the ongoing list of sources on the Insert Citation menu (Figure 5-40).

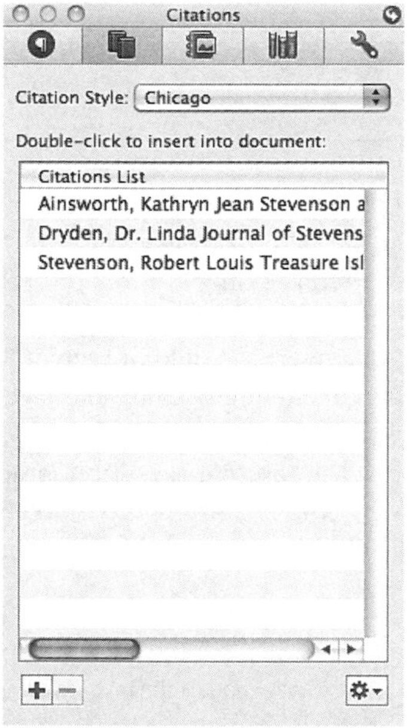

Figure 5-40:
The Citations toolbox gives you several choices. You can choose a source that you've already used, or you can add a new one. Use the menu in the lower-right corner to organize your sources. Word also lets you import sources you've used with other documents.

Adding a Bibliography

If you've already added all your sources and marked your citations, adding a bibliography to your document is a breeze. It's very similar to adding a table of contents or an index, as described earlier. Place the insertion point at the end of your document (or wherever you want your bibliography). Then go to the Document Elements | References→Bibliography, and choose the style that you want. Word inserts the bibliography into your document, completely formatted (Figure 5-41).

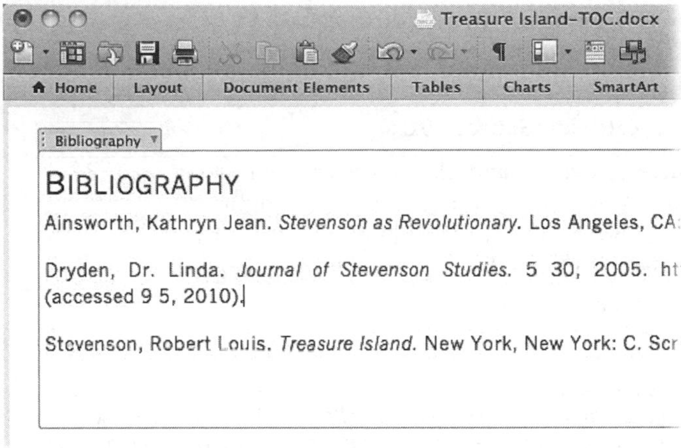

Figure 5-41:
Your bibliography appears in your document formatted in the style of your choice. You can use the menu on the blue tab to update the bibliography or to convert it to regular text.

When Word creates your bibliography, it inserts it as a Word field, just like a table of contents (page 196). It's just a chunk of computer-generated text that you can update at any time by clicking somewhere in the field, and then pressing Option-F9. When you print your document, the bibliography looks like normal text, but if you share your document as a computer file, you may want to convert the field to regular text. That way, no one using the document onscreen can accidentally cause damage by, say, deleting the field. To convert the bibliography from field to text, click any place in the bibliography, and then look for the blue tab at the top that says Bibliography. Click the menu on the right of the tab and choose "Convert bibliography to static text" from the pop-up menu. Now you can edit the bibliography just like any text in your document.

Warning: Remember, once you've converted it to text, Word can no longer update the bibliography.

CHAPTER 6

Moving Beyond Text: Publishing Layout View

I f you want to drop a picture or two into a document that's mostly text, you can go ahead and use Home | Insert→Photo. But when you have grander page layout plans with lots of pictures, multiple columns, text boxes and splashes of color, turn to the Publishing Layout view. By starting with one of dozens of professionally-designed templates, you can plug in your own text and pictures and have a polished document in a record time. You can change as much or as little about the templates as you choose to—or start with a completely blank page.

Starting with a Template: Ready-to-Use Page Designs

The best way to work with Print Layout view is to start with a new document from a template. Click New from Template on the toolbar. When the Word Document Gallery opens as shown in Figure 6-1, scroll down to the templates under Publishing Layout view. You'll find about a hundred well-designed documents for newsletters, pamphlets, posters, signs and even things like CD covers. Sure you could use Word to create your own design from scratch, but if you're in that business, you probably already have Adobe InDesign or Quark XPress on your Mac. Word's Publishing Layout view is a tool for the part-time page artist rather than the pro. It fills in the gap between Word and those full-blown publishing tools that cost as much as a new Mac.

It's best to think of Publishing Layout view as a separate program from Word, rather than just a different view. You get a hint of this if you try to switch to Publishing Layout View when you're working in a Word document. Word sends up a warning explaining that "This document was not created in Publishing Layout View." It gives you an option to Continue or Create New. If you continue, your document will be converted to a Publishing Layout View document, which means you're likely to have trouble if you ever want to convert it back to a regular old Word doc. For this reason, it's best to treat your Word docs and your Publishing Layout view documents as different creatures.

What's the big difference? It's the way elements are placed on the page. Word is designed to handle text that flows in a linear fashion from beginning to end. Publishing Layout view is designed to treat text and graphics as blocks that can be placed anywhere on the page, somewhat independent from each other.

Choosing and Using a Template

It may take you a while to pick a template for your project, because the Template Gallery (click the Template Gallery button) gives you so many options to choose from (Figure 6-1). Templates for projects like posters and certificates are single pages, but templates for brochures and newsletters are multiple pages. Make sure you use the page buttons in the preview pane to see if the back pages will do the job.

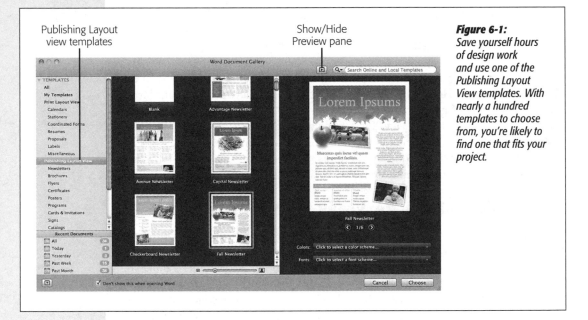

Figure 6-1:
Save yourself hours of design work and use one of the Publishing Layout View templates. With nearly a hundred templates to choose from, you're likely to find one that fits your project.

Publishing Layout view templates

Show/Hide Preview pane

Note: For all the nitty-gritty details about using and creating templates, see page 89.

Here are the steps to open and explore the Spring Newsletter template:

1. **On the toolbar, click the "New from template" button, and in the search box, type Spring Newsletter.**

   The center of the document gallery zeroes in on the Spring Newsletter template, hiding the rest.

2. **If necessary, expand the right preview pane, then click the page buttons below the preview.**

   You see the back pages for the Spring Newsletter. You won't have to use them all, but these predesigned layouts are available when you need them.

3. **Optional: Use the Colors and Fonts options to change the look of the template.**

   You can be confident that the different font and color sets on the menus will look pretty good together, but you can't go wrong using the fonts and colors in the original template either.

4. **Click Choose.**

   Your newsletter-to-be appears in Words Publishing Layout View. Unlike a standard Word doc, you'll notice the page is placed on a background as if it's sitting on a graphics table, ready for you to get at it. There are some other changes that you may not notice right away. As shown in Figure 6-2, there are new tools up there in the toolbar and the ribbon tabs are specific to your publishing project. In the lower-right corner, there are tabs named All Contents and Master Pages.

5. **In the toolbar, click the Arrow (also known as the Selection Tool). Then, one by one, click on the picture of the flower, one of the headlines and a block of body text.**

   Each time you select a page element, a box with handles appears around the object. These are the tools you use to position, resize, and rotate graphics and text boxes. (If you accidentally move one of the elements as you're selecting them, just hit ⌘-Z to pop it back into position.)

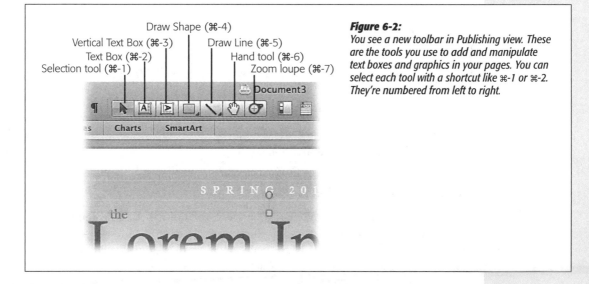

Figure 6-2:
You see a new toolbar in Publishing view. These are the tools you use to add and manipulate text boxes and graphics in your pages. You can select each tool with a shortcut like ⌘-1 or ⌘-2. They're numbered from left to right.

6. **Scroll down to view the back pages for the newsletter.**

   These are the same pages you saw in the document gallery. Notice there's a nice variety of layouts to handle all different types or articles and pictures. If you're curious about the Lorem Ipsum placeholder text, see the box on page 229.

7. **Click the Master Pages tab and scroll through the Master Pages.**

   The Master pages each have background elements but no content—no pictures, headings or blocks of text.

8. **If you're ready to create a newsletter, start making changes to the pages in the All Contents tab.**

   The rest of this chapter covers Publishing Layout View techniques in more detail, but for now, here are some tips to get you started:

   - **To swap your text for the lorem ipsum,** double click a heading or text box. Start typing or paste in your text.

   - **To swap a picture,** right-click (Control-click) on a picture and choose Change picture.

   - **To move an element,** use the Arrow (⌘-1) to drag it to a new position on the page. When you move or change a graphic, the text usually wraps around the object.

   - **To resize an element,** use the Arrow (⌘-1) to drag one of the handles. Use a corner handle if you want the element to maintain its proportion.

   - **To rotate an element,** drag the round handle sprouting from the top of the box.

Word's designers created the first page of the Spring Newsletter by using background images, text boxes, and photographs, including the flower photo, which is a transparent background. This page is composed of a collection of text boxes arranged on top of a couple of background graphics (which are actually on the Master Page, described on page 231). All three of the photos are JPEG graphics, rakishly rotated to give the newsletter an informal look. Two of the pictures display a white border or stroke (page 237), the flower has a transparent background (page 237) and overlaps one of the other photos (page 228), and they all sport drop shadows (page 237) to give the newsletter a three-dimensional feel.

Arranging the Way Objects Overlap

As far as Publishing Layout View is concerned, each of the page elements is on its own layer. To see your document as Word sees it, go to Home | Arrange→Reorder. A somewhat wild 3D view of your document takes over your display as shown in Figure 6-3. To change the stacking order of elements on the page, just drag a layer and its content to a new position.

If you find the 3D reorder view confusing, you can change the stacking position of objects on the page by using a shortcut menu. Select and then right-click (Control-click) the object you want to move. From the shortcut menu, choose Arrange. At that point you have several options, including:

- **Bring to Front.** Move this so that it appears in front of all the others on the page.
- **Send to Back.** Move this object to the bottom of the stack.
- **Bring Forward.** Move the selected graphic or text box one step forward.
- **Send Backward.** Push this object back one position in the stack.

At the bottom of the submenu are two special commands that move the selected object in relationship to text boxes. Use these when you want a graphic to appear in front of or behind text boxes.

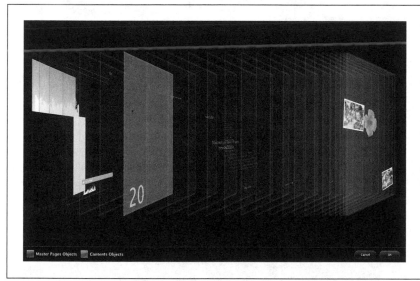

Figure 6-3:
Word gives you a 3D view of your document so that you can reorder the layers. Just click and drag to move a photo behind a headline or vice versa. Each element is on a numbered layer, sometimes called the stacking order. Word updates the number as you drag elements to a new position.

UP TO SPEED

Lorem Ipsum Dolor?

Besides the design, the first thing you'll notice about this template is that this newsletter seems to be about springtime in ancient Rome. Actually, the text used in this template—and in all Publishing Layout view templates—is *placeholder text*, intended to be replaced by whatever text you wish to place there. Typesetters call this kind of placeholder "Greek text"—even though the standard filler is derived not from a Greek text but from a 2000-year-old *Latin* treatise on ethics by Cicero, *De Finibus Bonorum et Malorum (The Extremes of Good and Evil)*.

Designers use this dummy text when creating layouts so that (non-Latin) readers aren't distracted by the content of the text—but instead pay attention to the design of the page. This practice goes back to the 1500s when lorem ipsum first appeared in a type specimen book—and it continues to this day, using that same chunk of text.

Adding, Removing and Rearranging Pages

The newsletter templates (and many others) are multipage. If you're designing a newsletter, you probably want a front page that shows the headlines and masthead, a variety of inner pages designed differently, and perhaps a back page that lets you fold and mail the newsletter without an envelope. In fact, that's the exact arrangement of the Spring Newsletter template's six pages. Open the sidebar, using the button on the toolbar and you can scroll to see all the thumbnails of the template pages (Figure 6-4).

Figure 6-4:
View thumbnails of your document in the sidebar (You can reorder pages by dragging them into a new position and remove a page by selecting it and pressing Delete or clicking the Remove button in the toolbar.

Although Microsoft's designers have provided a complete newsletter package of six pages, your newsletter can be any length at all—and you're free to remove, duplicate or reorder pages. To remove a page, select it first, then, right-click (Control-click) and choose Remove from the shortcut menu. If you like the layout of a particular page, you may want to use it more than once. Use the same technique to duplicate a page in your document, just right-click (Control-click) and choose Duplicate Page. To add a page, you guessed, it's the same drill. The difference is that the page that's added is empty. You see only the elements defined in the "master page" described next. It's up to you to add text (page 233) and graphics (page 235). To reorder pages, just drag them to a new position in the sidebar.

Managing Master Pages

Word reserves a special foundation layer for Publishing Layout view documents. The *Master Page* contains objects that appear on every page of your document, or on every page of a section if you've broken your document into sections (page 196). You'll find master pages very useful in order to do things like place a watermark, logo, or background image—usually at a very reduced opacity—on every page. Master pages are also the place to insert headers and footers in your Publishing Layout view document.

Click the Master Pages tab in the lower-right corner of the document window (Figure 6-5). Word hides all the page content that's not part of the master page and displays a tag in the upper-left corner of each page to remind you that you're working on the master page and show what type of master page you're looking at.

As you're viewing the master pages, you can make adjustments in the Master Page Options group (Layout | Master Page Options). The three checkboxes determine master page attributes:

- **Different First Page**. Choose this option if your document or section's first page is a title page or cover page and you'd like it to display different master objects than the rest of your document or section. For example, title pages usually don't have headers and footers.

- **Different Odd & Even Pages**. Turn on this checkbox if your document will be printed and bound and you want different master objects on the left and right pages.

- **Link to Previous**. If you've broken your document up into more than one section, Word makes this option available. Turn it on if you want the master objects from the previous section to continue through the current one. If you also turn on Different First Page, then the first page of the current section matches the first page of the preceding one.

You can add objects and text boxes to master pages just as you would normally. The only difference is that they'll show up on the first page, or *every* page, of that section.

To add headers or footers to a Master page, turn on the margin guides (View→Show→Margin Guides) and add text boxes outside of the margins. Choose Format→Document→Margins if you need to adjust the margins to accommodate a taller header or footer.

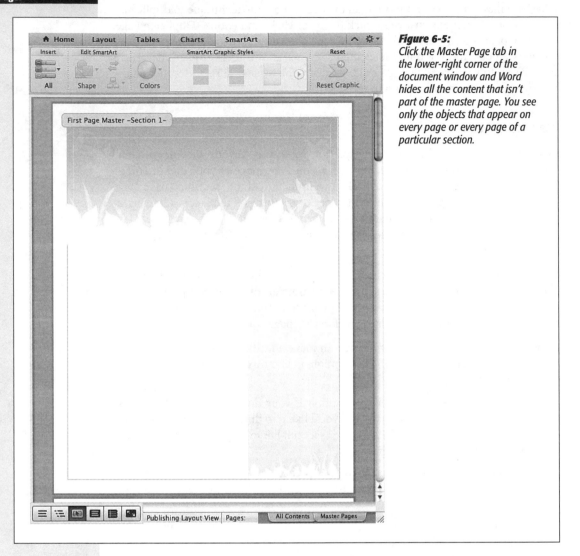

Figure 6-5:
Click the Master Page tab in the lower-right corner of the document window and Word hides all the content that isn't part of the master page. You see only the objects that appear on every page or every page of a particular section.

After making changes to your master pages, click the All Contents tab in the lower-right corner of the document window to return to the normal document view, showing the regular page elements plus the master page elements. When you're in All Contents view, you can't select any of the Master page objects. They're protected from inadvertent mouse-clicks.

Tip: You can easily transfer an object from a normal page to the master page by selecting it and choosing Edit→Copy. Then switch to the Master Pages tab and choose Edit→Paste. Word places the object in the same position on the Master page. The same technique works in reverse to move an object from the master page to a normal page.

Adding Text and Text Boxes

To replace the "lorem ipsum" with your own more intelligible words, just click on a text box and start typing. For example, if you click on the main heading in the Spring Newsletter and start typing, your text is automatically formatted like the words you're replacing. Often that's fine, but sometimes you need to make adjustments. If you're adding more text than was there originally, you may need to resize the text box, by dragging one of the handles, or you can adjust the font size. Just select the text box and then dial in a new number at Home | Font→Font Size.

It's too much work to type in text if you have it in another Word document, email or some other place where you can copy and paste it. After you've copied text, right-click a text box in your page and then choose Edit Text from the shortcut menu. You see an insertion point blinking in the text box. At this point, just paste it in (⌘-V).

When you need to create a new text box, head up to the toolbar (Figure 6-6). You have a choice of two styles. The regular, old text box (⌘-2) displays text horizontally. The Vertical Text box (⌘-3), you guessed it, displays text vertically. Good for banners, distinctive headers or individual panels on a tri-fold pamphlet.

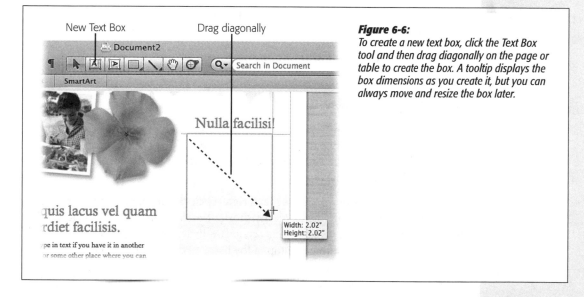

Figure 6-6:
To create a new text box, click the Text Box tool and then drag diagonally on the page or table to create the box. A tooltip displays the box dimensions as you create it, but you can always move and resize the box later.

Formatting Text

You can use all the usual tools to dress up your text. That includes choosing fonts from the Font menu and formatting from the Format→Font box (⌘-D). When you want text to wrap around graphics, right-click (Control-click) the text and choose one of the Wrap Text options on the shortcut menu (Figure 6-7).

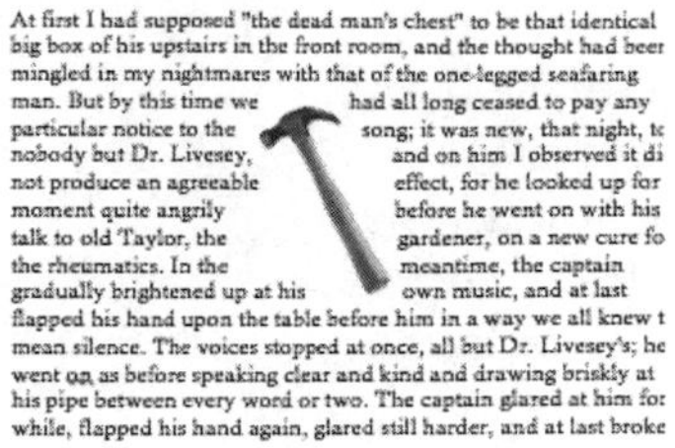

At first I had supposed "the dead man's chest" to be that identical big box of his upstairs in the front room, and the thought had beer mingled in my nightmares with that of the one-legged seafaring man. But by this time we had all long ceased to pay any particular notice to the song; it was new, that night, to nobody but Dr. Livesey, and on him I observed it di not produce an agreeable effect, for he looked up for moment quite angrily before he went on with his talk to old Taylor, the gardener, on a new cure fo the rheumatics. In the meantime, the captain gradually brightened up at his own music, and at last flapped his hand upon the table before him in a way we all knew t mean silence. The voices stopped at once, all but Dr. Livesey's; he went on as before speaking clear and kind and drawing briskly at his pipe between every word or two. The captain glared at him for while, flapped his hand again, glared still harder, and at last broke

Figure 6-7:
Use the Tight wrapping style for irregularly shaped objects with transparent backgrounds. You can further adjust the wrapping boundary for this type of object if you right-click (Control-click) and then choose Wrap Text→Edit Wrap Boundary.

In addition to Word's standard text tricks, Publishing Layout view has some special text-formatting tools that work well for headlines and special blocks of text. Right-click a text box and choose Format Text Effects. Using the tools in the Format Text Effects you can torture your text in all sorts of ways by applying shadows, beveled edges, reflections and 3D transformations. Lots of fun to play with, just keep in mind that someone's got to read this stuff!

Tip: The wood table top background is more than just a pretty face. It's a work surface, just like an art table. You can place text boxes and artwork on the table, to stash them out of the way when you're working with other page elements. Use the Customize Workspace menu to change the appearance of the table.

Add Color to Your Text Box

If you want your text box to jump out from the other elements on the page, you may want to add a splash of color. This is great for sidebars or any text that's separate from the main body text. Just make sure that there's enough contrast between the background color and the text.

To add a color background for your text, right-click on the text box and choose Format Shape from the many items on the shortcut menu. The Format Shape window has more than a dozen visual effects categories listed on the left (see page 237 for details). You want Fill, at the very top of the list. Use the Color menu to pick a color. If you use one of theme colors listed at the top, you can be sure it will mesh with your design. If you want background elements to show through the text box, adjust the transparency.

Tip: Transparent text boxes and multiple layers are fun for the graphic artist, but pros avoid designs that are so complicated they become unreadable. It's a good idea to test-print your layouts, too. Designs that look great on a computer screen may not be as crystal clear when they're transferred to the page.

Flowing Text Between Boxes

More often than not, text boxes in Publishing Layout view hold a complete block of text—there's no leftover text that's not displayed. For example, *Mad Men* advertising types usually lay out an ad, and then the copywriter writes headlines and body text to fit. Sometimes, say in the case of a newsletter, you may not work that way. You might have part of an article in one text box that continues in a different text box. Publishing Layout view can help you there.

When a text box is too small to display all the text, you see an "A…" icon at the bottom as shown in Figure 6-8. Move your cursor over the square in the lower-right corner of the text box and you see a + sign—another indication that there's excess text. Click the square and then drag diagonally to create a new text box. Automatically, the excess text flows from the first box to the second. Now, if you resize the boxes, the text adjusts automatically. You can tell text is linked, from one box to another, by the numbers that appear at the top right corner.

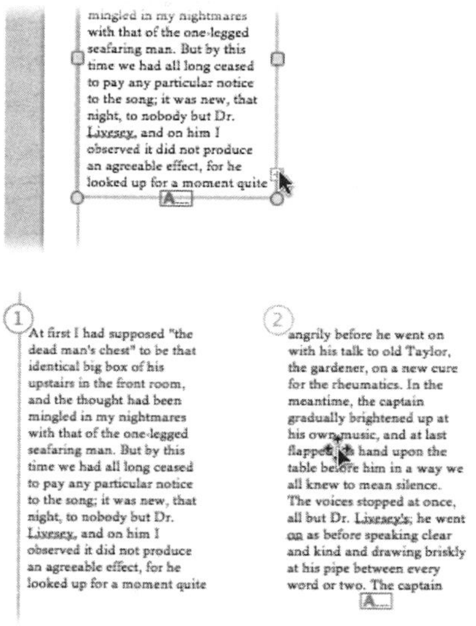

Figure 6-8:
Top: To link text between two text boxes, click the square in the lower-right corner, shown here with the Selection arrow. Then, drag out a new text box.

Bottom: When you're done, the excess text flows to the new box. Hold your cursor over a linked text box and it displays a number, indicating its order in the flow of text.

Adding Photos, Clip Art, and Other Graphics

Publishing Layout view shines when it comes to adding and formatting photos, clip art, charts, and other graphics. It's easy to do and it makes posters and newsletters sing. You can drag photos from iPhoto, a Finder window or most other sources right on to your page. If you need to find your photo you may prefer to use the Insert→Photo menu, where you can browse your way to a folder with photos. And of course, you can use any graphics you've stored in the scrapbook (View→Scrapbook) or the Media Browser (View→Media Browser).

If you need to visually describe the relationship between people, places or things, check out the options on the SmartArt tab. There are more details about SmartArt on page 609. When you're putting together your company's profit and loss statistics, you'll want to illustrate those numbers with one of the charts found on the Charts tab. These charts draw their data from Excel spreadsheets which you can learn about on page 479.

Tip: Once your artwork is on your page or on the art table in the document window, you can add it to the scrapbook for future use in other documents. Select the artwork and then click the Add button in the scrapbook. As shown in Figure 6-9, other "Add" options include: Add File and Add from Clipboard.

Figure 6-9:
The scrapbook (View→Scrapbook) is one of a few places where you can find art to add to your layout. If you're going to use the same graphic in more than one document, it's a good idea to add it to the scrapbook using the menu shown here.

Formatting Graphics

Few graphics land on the page ready to go. You usually need to resize them and add an effect or two. Select your photo or graphic and then use the handles to change its dimensions. If you have a photo or some other graphic that you don't want to distort, use the corner handles and the proportion stays fixed.

If you want to apply special effects to a photo, like the drop shadow used in the Spring Newsletter, right-click (Control-click) the photo and choose Format Picture. When the Format Picture window opens, you see more than a dozen ways you can tweak your picture. One of the options, as shown in Figure 6-10, is Shadow.

Here's a quick description of some of the other formatting options available in the Format Picture window.

Note: Many of these options also apply to text boxes, clip art or smart art. Charts from Excel use different formatting tools as explained on page 479.

- **Fill.** Fill a shape with a color, a gradient, a pattern or a texture. You can use the transparency slide to let objects below show through.

- **Line.** Fine-tune your lines by changing their color, style (dots and dashes), and weight (thickness). You can add arrowheads to your lines, too.

- **Shadow.** Shown in Figure 6-10, the shadow options let you control the look and color of the shadow. By adjusting the distance and blur, you can make objects look nearer or farther from the page.

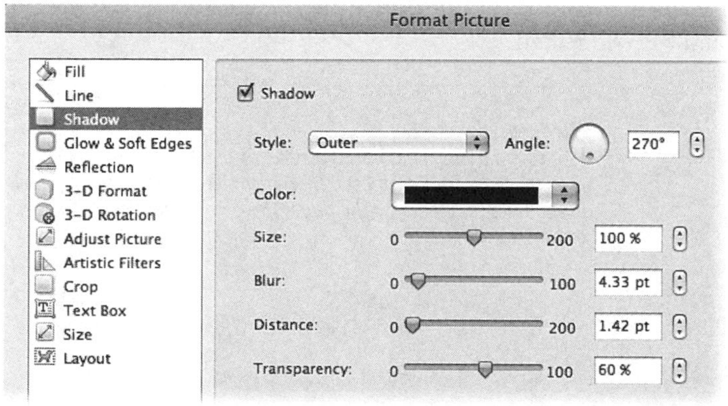

Figure 6-10:
These are the shadow settings used in the Spring Newsletter templates. The drop shadow behind the photos and the slight rotation makes them look like snapshots, casually placed on the page.

- **Glow & Soft Edges.** Similar to "glow," this tool outlines your object with a color. You can adjust the size, transparency and softness (blur) of the edge.

- **Reflection.** Want to recreate the iTunes album cover effect? Use reflection to get that cool 3-D look.

- **3-D Format.** Add bevel edges and other 3-D effects to objects on the page. These tools let you dial in different heights, widths, and angles for the effects.

- **3-D Rotation.** Spin photos or other graphics around in three dimensions.

- **Adjust Picture.** If your photos need a little last minute fine-tuning, use the brightness, contrast, and sharpen tools available here. In general, if your photos need major work, you're better off doing that in iPhoto or Photoshop.

- **Artistic Filters.** Turn a photo into a pencil sketch or a painting. Make a rectangle look like a piece of glass. Filters are easy to apply and fun. Just don't spend all your time trying out the options.

- **Crop.** Trim your photo down to the right size.

- **Text Box.** Used to format text boxes, align text, and apply margins inside of text boxes.

- **Size.** Adjust the size and rotation for any graphic element or text box. In general, it's easiest to perform these chores in your document using the Selection tool and the object's handles, but if you need numeric precision, this is the place.

- **Layout.** Choose the text-wrapping style and horizontal alignment for the selected graphic.

Aligning Objects on the Page

The Publishing Layout view offers lots of help when it comes to aligning objects. As you move graphics or text boxes around the page, temporary lines appear, when the object is in alignment with something else on the page (Figure 6-11). Just release the mouse button and you're lined up.

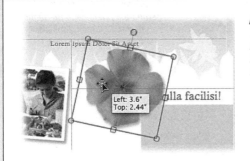

Figure 6-11:
Word's not trying to confuse you when it suddenly displays faint lines while you move objects. Those lines let you know your object is aligned with others on the page. The lines disappear if you keep moving the object.

For more deliberate aligning action, select two or more objects and then right-click (Control-click) and open the Align and Distribute submenu. The options let you align objects by top, bottom, left or right edges. If you want space objects evenly, use the distribute options.

You can display guidelines in your document. Don't worry, these lines won't appear when you print the document; they're just there to help you. First go to View→Ruler to display the rulers across the top and to the left of your page. Then click on the ruler, keep holding the mouse button down, and drag into your document. As you do, a non-printing guideline appears. To position the line, let go of the button. If the placement isn't quite right, just drag the guide to a new position. Want to get rid of a guide? Just drag it back to the ruler. With the guides in place, you'll find that objects tend to snap to the guide making it easy to position objects.

Tip: Use the Group command, when you've got objects aligned perfectly and you want them to maintain that relationship even if you move them on the page. Select the objects you want to group and then right-click (Control-click) and choose Grouping→Group. To break up a group, head back to the same spot and choose UnGroup.

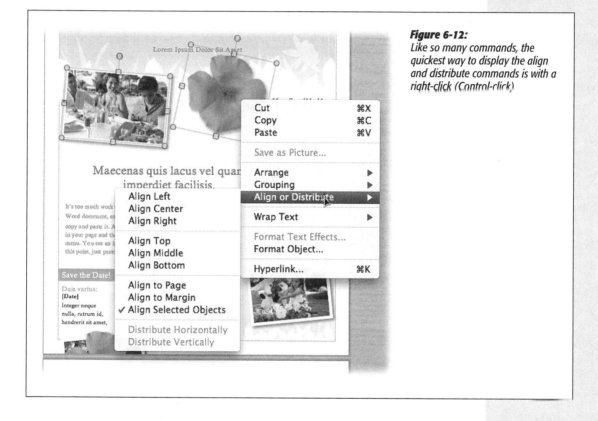

Figure 6-12:
Like so many commands, the quickest way to display the align and distribute commands is with a right-click (Control-click)

Working Collaboratively

Whether you're collaborating with a coauthor or reviewing someone else's manuscript, Word makes it easy to communicate as you edit. In precomputing days, editing a paper document resulted in a jumble of red pen marks, crossed out text, and notes scrawled in the margins. If several people reviewed a document, figuring out who said what was a nightmare. Word resolves those issues by keeping track of all changes and all reviewers. Word stores everything in the document file and, with a click of your mouse, you can show or hide the comments and edits.

This chapter looks at the reviewing process from all angles. You learn all about comments: how to insert comments into a document, how to manage reviewers comments, how to make audio comments, and how to accept or reject changes made by others. You'll even learn how to protect parts of your document, when several people are working on it at the same time. Finally, you'll learn how to combine and compare two documents so only the right parts make it to the final draft.

Adding Comments

Collaborating is all about clear communication, so Word lets you attach easy-to-read comments directly to the text you're referring to. Go to Insert→Insert New Comment. What could be clearer? It's even easier to add comments with the Review tab on the Ribbon. The "Add a comment about the selection" button is the very first item, as you can see in Figure 7-1. Even better, for documents with several reviewers, Word keeps track of who said what, when, marking comments with date, time, and a name or initials. That makes it a breeze for authors to follow up on a comment and get more details. Word lets you (and your readers) choose how you want to see these comments: as balloons or in the separate Reviewing Pane. See Figure 7-2 for details.

Note: How does Word know who's editing and commenting on a document? It uses the details stored in Word→Preferences→User Information.

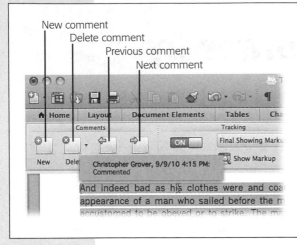

New comment
Delete comment
Previous comment
Next comment

Figure 7-1:
Hold your mouse cursor over a comment or a change in your document and a pop-up note appears, showing who added the annotation and when—even if that's you.

Choose Balloons or the Review Pane

Microsoft is seldom content giving you a single way to do anything, and this philosophy holds when it comes to reviewing comments and changes to a document. Depending on the amount of edits and your personal preferences, you can choose to display them in balloons or in the review pane:

- Balloons are like notes written in the margin. Show balloons by choosing Review→Tracking→Show Markup→Preferences→Use balloons to display changes. Comments and changes show up in the right margin preceded by the reviewer's name. A line from the balloon creates a visual link to the highlighted text. Balloons only appear when you use Print Layout View.

- The Reviewing Pane shows comments and changes in a more formal, all business panel. This view lets you read comments and simultaneously see your document. To display the Reviewing Pane, choose Review | Changes→Reviewing Pane. A vertical pane that appears on the left of your document that displays a list of comments and changes. Click a comment, and Word moves to the related point in your document and highlights the text. This makes the reviewing pane a great place to quickly work through a list of comments and edits. The Review Pane works with Normal, Outline, and Print Layout View.

When commenting, it's best to be both specific and concise, to avoid losing your readers' attention or cluttering your document with superfluous commentary. You can edit comments after you've inserted them. Say you've decided to reword your criticism to be more diplomatic. Click the text in the comment balloon or in the Reviewing Pane, and then edit just like any other text. Or select and delete text, and then type in new remarks. If you're working away without either the Reviewing Pane or the Balloons showing, you can jump to comment editing by right-clicking the highlighted text, and then choosing Edit Comment from the pop-up menu.

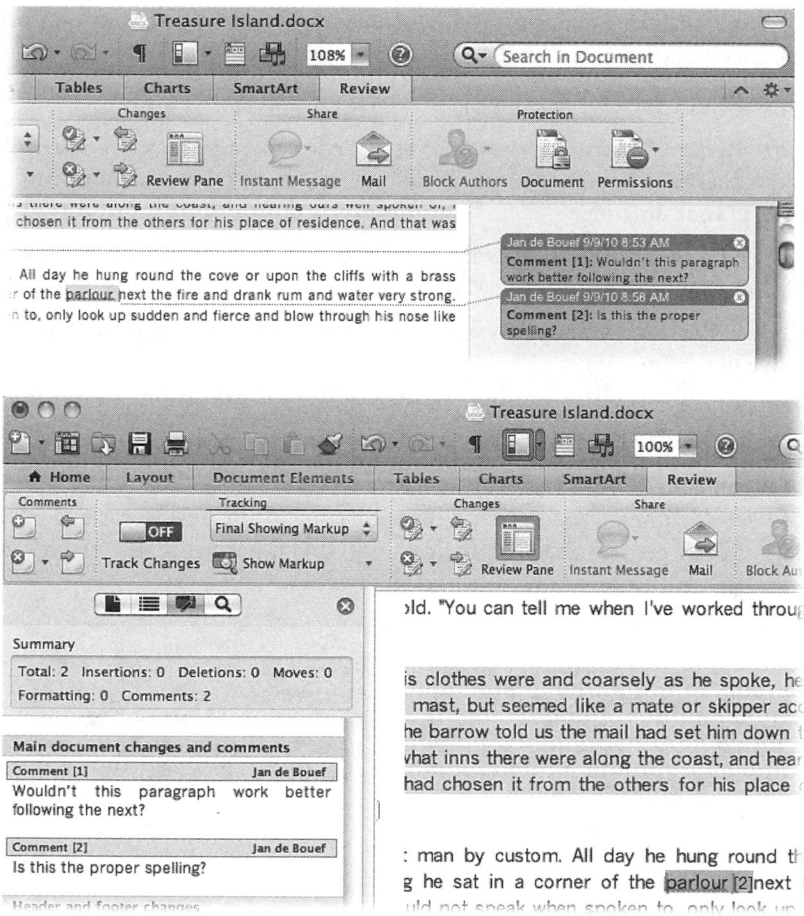

Figure 7-2:

Top: Balloon notes are like when you circle text, and then draw a line to a note in the margin.

Bottom: The Reviewing Pane opens on the left of your document. When you click the highlighted text that indicates there's a comment, the Reviewing Pane scrolls to show the related comment.

Deleting Comments

It's easy to delete a single comment. Just right-click (Control-click) the comment, and then choose Delete Comment from the shortcut menu. You can select the comment in a balloon, in the Reviewing Pane, or even the highlighted text in your document.

Notice that the Delete command on the Comments ribbon is actually a drop-down menu giving you two more handy ways to remove those helpful suggestions from your precious manuscript. You can remove all the comments in one fell swoop: Review | Comments→Delete→Delete All Comments. Or you can remove only the comments in the document that are not hidden.

This last option gives you an easy way to remove the comments from a specific reviewer while leaving comments from others in place. It's a two-step process: First, display the comments you plan to delete and hide the others. Then, choose the Delete All Comments Shown command.

Here's the step-by-step for deleting comments from a specific reviewer:

1. **Go to Review | Tracking→Show Markup→Reviewers and choose your reviewers. Put a checkmark next to a name, and you see that reviewer's comments and edits in your document.**

   The comments of reviewers without checkmarks are hidden. You can show or hide any combination of reviewers.

2. **Choose Review | Comments→Delete→Delete All Comments Shown to remove the comments.**

   The comments that were visible in your document are deleted. They're gone now, and they're no longer a part of your document.

On the other hand, the comments from any reviewers that you hid in step 1 are still part of your document. You can view them by going to Review | Tracking→Show Markup→Reviewers and checking their names. If you have second thoughts after clicking Delete All Comments, you can undo it with ⌘+Z.

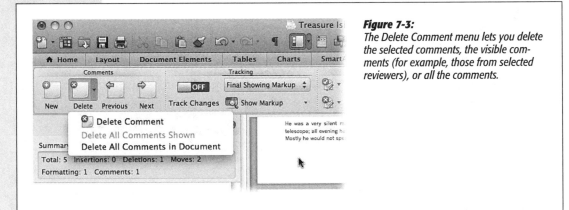

Figure 7-3:
The Delete Comment menu lets you delete the selected comments, the visible comments (for example, those from selected reviewers), or all the comments.

Highlighting Text

When you insert a comment in a document, you do two things: You select the text, and then you type the attached comment. But sometimes, all you need to do is call attention to some words in the text, just like you'd use a highlighter on a paper document. You can find Word's highlighter equivalent on the Home ribbon: Home | Font→Text Highlight Color. You can either select text and then click the command, or you can click the command and then drag your cursor over the text that you want to highlight. It works either way. If you want to get fancy, you can use different highlights colors for different issues. Word gives you a palette of 15 colors to choose from.

Tracking Changes While Editing

When you're editing a document that someone else wrote, it's only fair to let the author see your changes. In the world of paper documents, the process can be rather lengthy. You get out your red pencil and mark up the document, crossing out words you want to delete and writing in words you want to add. The document may go back and forth a few times before someone has the honor of typing up a new copy. Word gives you a way to streamline the process.

Tracking and Viewing Changes

To begin tracking changes, just turn on the feature by toggling Review | Tracking→ Track Changes. In this mode, Word remembers every change you make and shows it in the Reviewing Pane or in balloons. Depending on other settings, Word can display changes in the document, for example striking through deleted text and underlining added text. As you can imagine, your document gets pretty busy and hard to read after you've made a lot of edits. Fortunately, you can choose to show or hide the marked changes. You can also choose exactly how those changes are displayed in your document or whether the changes are displayed at all. You can even see your original document before it was sullied by other hands. Check out the four options shown in Figure 7-4:

Figure 7-4:
Choose Final Showing Markup to see only the most recent edits. Choose Original Showing Markup to see all the edits that were tracked since the document was created. Final shows the most recent version with no markup. Original shows the version before any tracked changes.

- **Final Showing Markup**. This view shows the final document with all the comments and tracked changes showing. Word displays all inserted text in a different color and packs away deleted text into balloons or the Reviewing Pane.

  When you first open a document in Word, it's set to this view to prevent you from unintentionally distributing a document with comments and edits.

- **Final**. This view shows the edited version of the document with no markup showing. You see how your document looks if you accept all the changes. The Final option is great when you want to edit your document without the markup getting in the way.

- **Original Showing Markup**. This view shows the original document along with tracked changes. It's the reverse of Final Showing Markup, as deleted text appears in your document marked with strikethrough lines. It's as if the reviewer is only suggesting the change instead of making it for you.

- **Original**. This view shows your document before all the other cooks were invited to spoil the broth. If you reject all changes, your document will look like this again.

Showing and hiding types of changes

Reviewers make a lot of different types of changes when they mark up your document. They make insertions and deletions, they change formatting, and they insert comments. When you want to focus on a specific type of change, use the Show Markup menu (Review | Tracking→Show Markup) to show and hide different types of changes (Figure 7-5). Checkmarks on the menu indicate which items are visible:

- **Comments.** Shows or hides comments in balloons and the Reviewing Pane.

- **Ink.** Shows or hides comments that were handwritten on tablets.

- **Insertions and Deletions.** Shows or hides insertions and deletions.

- **Formatting.** Shows or hides notes related to formatting changes.

- **Markup Area Highlight.** Shows or hides the background color for the balloons.

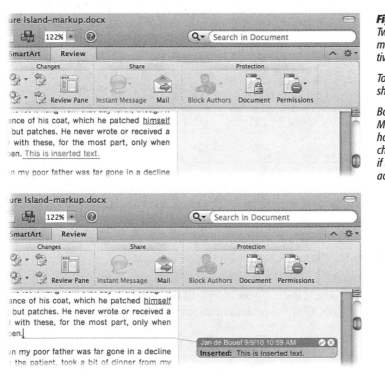

Figure 7-5:
Two views show reviewers' markup from different perspectives.

Top: Final Showing Markup shows edits in place in your text.

Bottom: Original Showing Markup shows your document how it originally appeared, with changes noted in the margins, as if they're suggestions, not a fait accompli.

Showing and hiding reviewers' markup

When several reviewers have worked in a document, you may want to filter out some of the opinions so you can concentrate on others. Use Review | Tracking→Show Markup→Reviewers to show or hide a reviewer's markup. To see edits from a reviewer, place a checkmark next to his name, as shown in Figure 7-6.

Tip: If you're ever editing a document on someone else's computer, you can change the user name so that your name appears in the markup. Go to Word→Preferences→User Information, and then enter your name and initials in the text boxes. Be kind—put the owner's name back in place when you're done.

Customizing your markup view

Word gives you lots of ways to customize the appearance of your edits and markup, but the factory settings are hard to beat:

- Deleted text shows with a line through it, and insertions are underlined, so there's no doubt which is which.

- Moved text gets a double strikethrough where it was deleted, and a double underline where it was inserted.

- A vertical line appears in the margin next to any changes. Individual reviewers' edits and comments are color-coded.

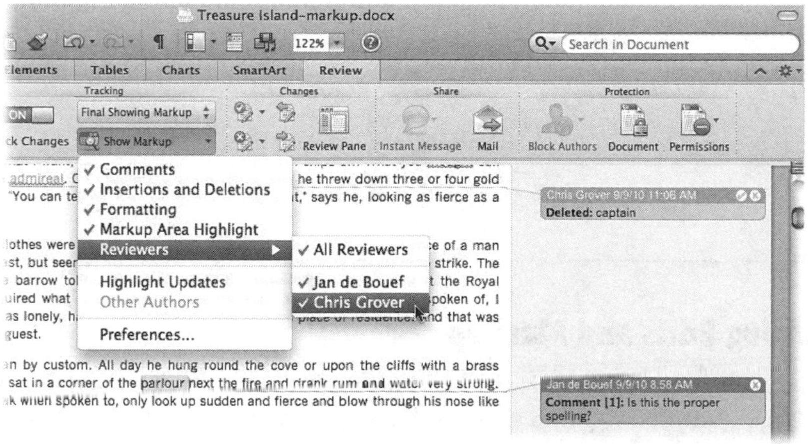

Figure 7-6:
Each comment or edit in your document bears the name or initials of the reviewer. Use the Show Markup menu to show or hide the edits and comments of different reviewers. Clicking the menu toggles a checkmark, indicating that the reviewer's edits are showing.

Word also keeps track of changes made to tables, including deleted and inserted cells. Formatting changes are listed in the Reviewing Pane and in the balloons, but they aren't marked in the text. If you're not happy with the factory settings, you can fiddle with them to your heart's content in the Track Changes box, as shown in Figure 7-7.

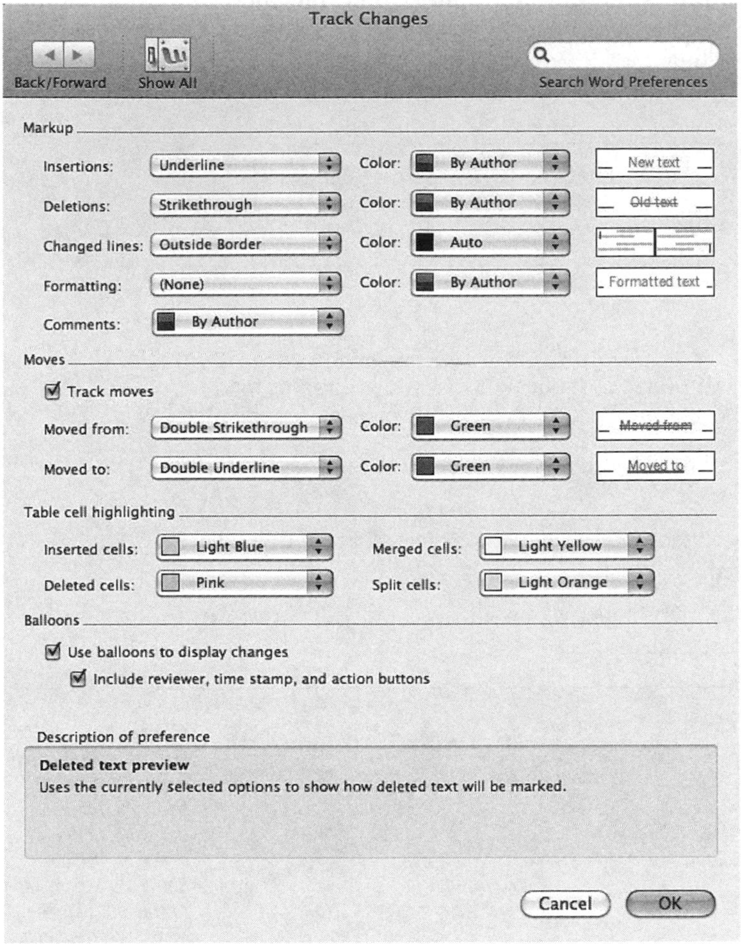

Figure 7-7:
The Track Changes Options box looks pretty intimidating at first, but most of these drop-down menus only let you choose colors for edits and comments. In the Markup section, if you leave the color and comment options set to "By author," each reviewer's comments and edits show in a different color.

Printing Edits and Markup

Sometimes you need printed pages that show that a document was edited—just ask any lawyer. The first step is to show the markup in your text, as described on page 247. Choose either Final Showing Markup or Original Showing Markup from the Review | Tracking group, then, go to Word→Print to open the Print Dialog box choose Microsoft Word, as shown in Figure 7-8. From the "Print what" menu, choose "Document showing markup," and then click Print. Your document prints slightly reduced in size to provide room to print the balloons in the right margin.

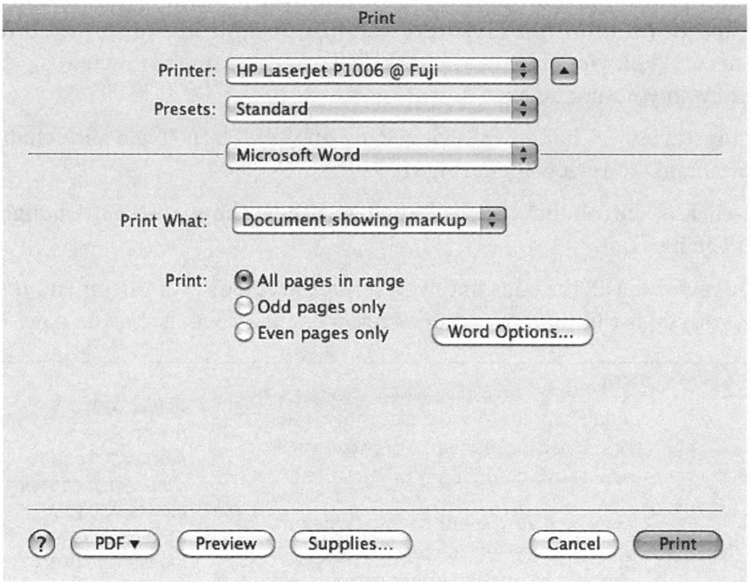

Figure 7-8:
The option to print edits and markup are tucked away in in the Microsoft Word panel in the Print dialog box. You can choose to print the document with the markup showing, or you can choose to print just a list of the edits and comments.

Accepting and Rejecting Changes

You may or may not agree with some of the changes other people make in your meticulously crafted text. In any case, you should review each edit to make sure the document is getting better, not worse. Word makes reviewing changes a quick and easy process.

Here's the step-by-step procedure for reviewing the changes and edits in your document:

1. **Move the insertion point to the beginning of your document by pressing ⌘-Home.**

   Most of the time, you want to start at the very beginning of your document to make sure you don't miss any of the changes.

2. **Choose a view, either Print Layout or Draft.**

   You need to use Print Layout view if you want to see comments and changes in balloons. The Review pane works in either view.

3. **Go to Review | Tracking and use the Menu to choose one of the options that displays markup.**

   For example, choose Final Showing Markup to see your document as if the changes have been made with notes explaining those changes, or choose Original Showing Markup to see the original document and the changes as suggestions.

4. **Go to Review | Tracking→Show Markup→Reviewers to choose the reviewers whose changes you want to see.**

   A menu appears, listing the reviewers who have commented on or edited your document. When you place checkmarks next to the names of reviewers, their edits show in your document.

5. **Click the Review→Changes→Review Pane on the ribbon. Then click changes and comments to review them (Figure 7-9).**

6. **Right-click (Control-click) each change and then choose Accept Change or Reject Change.**

   Repeat, reviewing all the edits until you reach the end of your document. If you prefer, you can use buttons to accept or reject changes. See the box on page 251.

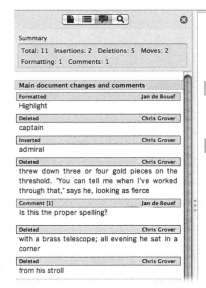

Summary

Total: 11 Insertions: 2 Deletions: 5 Moves: 2
Formatting: 1 Comments: 1

Main document changes and comments

| Formatted | Jan de Bouef |
| Highlight | |

| Deleted | Chris Grover |
| captain | |

| Inserted | Chris Grover |
| admiral | |

| Deleted | Chris Grover |
| threw down three or four gold pieces on the threshold. "You can tell me when I've worked through that," says he, looking as fierce | |

| Comment [1] | Jan de Bouef |
| Is this the proper spelling? | |

| Deleted | Chris Grover |
| with a brass telescope; all evening he sat in a corner | |

| Deleted | Chris Grover |
| from his stroll | |

what inns there were along the coast, an described as lonely, had chosen it from was all we could learn of our guest.

He was a very silent man by custom. All with a brass telescope; all evening he sa drank rum and water very strong. Mostly up sudden and fierce and blow through h who came about our house soon learned from his stroll he would ask if any seafari thought it was the want of company of h but at last we began to see he was desir at the Admiral Benbow (as now and th Bristol) he would look in at him throug parlour; and he was always sure to be as For me, at least, there was no secret abo his alarms. He had taken me aside one d first of every month if I would only keep one leg" and let him know the moment h

Figure 7-9:
After reviewers have edited and commented on your manuscript, you can quickly assess the damage they've done. Open the Review Pane (Review | Changes→Review Pane). Click on a comment or change to review it in your manuscript. Right-click (Control-click) to accept or reject changes.

Tip: You can use the Browse buttons in the lower-right corner of the document window to navigate as you check changes to your document. First, click the option you want: edit or comments. Then you can use the double-arrow buttons to move to the next or previous item.

UP TO SPEED

The Accept and Reject Buttons

When a reviewer or a collaborator makes tracked changes to your document, you're not stuck with them. You have a choice of whether to accept or reject every single one. The Review | Changes group gives you Accept and Reject buttons, which let you deal with edits either individually or in one fell swoop (Figure 7-10). Each of these buttons has two parts. Click the top part of a button to accept or reject the change and move to the next edit. Click the bottom part for some additional options:

- **Accept (or Reject) and Move to Next.** Use this option to accept or reject a change and automatically jump to the next edit. It's a great tool for quickly checking the changes that have been made. (Simply clicking the top half of the button does the same thing.)

- **Accept (or Reject) Change.** Use this option to accept or reject the change without moving to the next

edit. This way, you can inspect the command's results before you move on.

- **Accept (or Reject) All Changes Shown.** This command is a little different from the following one, in that it accepts or rejects all the changes showing– which may or may not be all the changes in the document. Use this command when you want to accept or reject only changes from a single reviewer. Use Review | Tracking→Show Markup→Reviewers to choose which reviewer's changes appear. Then, when you click Accept or Reject All Changes Shown, the other reviewers' hidden changes remain intact.

- **Accept (or Reject) All Changes in Document.** Use this command to accept or reject all the changes in a document, from all reviewers, whether they're showing or not.

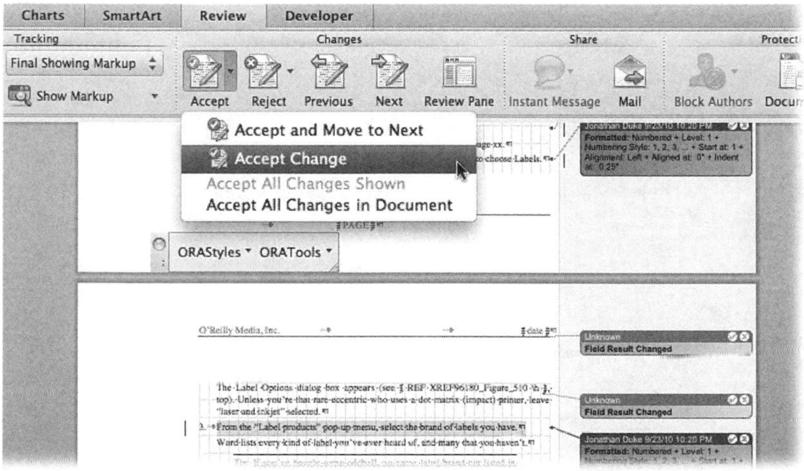

Figure 7-10:
You get to review the reviewers, when you Accept or Reject the changes that make in your document. As explained in the box above, you can accept or reject all their suggestions at once, or you can go through and examine them one by one.

Comparing and Merging Documents

You're working on a report with your colleagues, and you send a draft out for everyone to review and put in their two cents. One by one, their versions come back to you, and now you have the chore of incorporating everyone's suggestions and changes into the final draft. The quickest and easiest way to tackle the project is to merge each reviewer's comments and changes into your working copy, and then review the results.

To combine two documents and view the changes, first make sure both documents are closed. Then follow these steps:

1. **Choose Tools→Track Changes→Compare Documents.**

   When the Compare Documents dialog box opens Figure 7-11, you see two drop-down menus at the top, where you select the documents that you're merging.

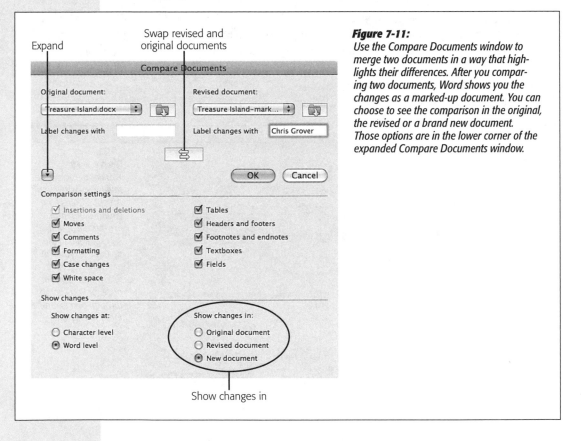

Expand

Swap revised and
original documents

Show changes in

Figure 7-11:
Use the Compare Documents window to merge two documents in a way that highlights their differences. After you comparing two documents, Word shows you the changes as a marked-up document. You can choose to see the comparison in the original, the revised or a brand new document. Those options are in the lower corner of the expanded Compare Documents window.

2. **Using the menus at the top of the Compare Documents box, choose the Original Document and the Revised Document (the one with the edits).**

   Each list shows recent documents. If you don't see the document you want, choose the Browse menu option or the folder icon next to the menu. A Finder-type window opens.

3. **To see more options, click the expand button, shown in Figure 7-11.**

   The Compare Documents box expands to provide additional options and settings. It's usually best to leave "Show changes in" set to New document. That way, the comparison is displayed in a new document, leaving both the Original and Revised document intact.

4. **If you wish, choose settings to fine-tune the way the comparisons are shown in your document.**

   At the top, you see a group of checkboxes under the heading Comparison Settings. Click to put checkmarks next to the changes you want highlighted and marked in the combined document. For example, if you don't place a checkmark next to Moves, text that was moved in the reviewer's document is shown in its new location in the combined document, but you don't see double underscores and double strikethroughs to show the move. It's as if the move has already been accepted.

5. **In the Show Changes group, choose the level of changes you want to view and where you want the combined document to appear.**

   You have two choices to make about the level of changes: Word can show changes at the character level or at the word level. It's a little easier to work at the word level. For example, if you change the word "you" to "your," Word highlights the whole word as a change rather than just showing that you inserted an "r."

6. **Click OK to combine the documents.**

   After a little hemming and hawing, Word shows you the combined documents with the differences marked as changes, just like some reviewed it with Track Changes turned on. You can use the Reviewing Pane or balloons to see the differences.

Merging Two Documents

The procedure for merging documents is almost identical to combining two documents, and the command to merge is Tools→Merge Documents. The Merge Documents box is almost identical to the Compare Documents box (Figure 7-11), since you're searching for the same types of changes in your document—moves, comments, insertions, and deletions.

What's different between the Merge and Compare commands are the results. When you merge two documents, the result incorporates the changes in both documents. When you compare two documents, the result is a marked-up document that shows differences between the two.

Quicker Document Dispatch

Word 2011 lets—nay, encourages—you to email or Instant Message (IM) your documents right from the Review tab. Granted, you could always attach a document to an email in Outlook or send a file via your Messenger chat window—but the Review tab makes these moves much easier. To email a document, click the envelope-with-arrow icon in the Review | Share tab. Doing so pops open an email message in your default email program with the document already attached (that's *so* cool). Type your message, select a recipient, and then click Send.

To send the document via IM, you (and your recipient) need a Windows Live Messenger account (available at

www.microsoft.com/mac). Click the IM icon (a word balloon), select the file recipient, and your document is now prepped for sending. Once your intended target accepts the file, it zips across the Internet. It's all part of the evil empire's desire to keep you in the Office/MSM loop for all your work and play. (Well, maybe not *all* your play.)

Of course, if you prefer instant messaging with iChat, you can use it to transfer files, too. Just drag the icon of the file you wish to transfer from the Finder right into the iChat text entry box where you usually type your message.

Protecting Your Document from Changes

Sometimes you want to show your document to people, but you don't want them to mess it up with unwanted changes. Perhaps you want them to add comments but not to fiddle with your words. Or, maybe you need them to review and edit a certain section but to leave the rest of the document alone. Using Word's Protect Document options, you're in control (Figure 7-12). You can provide specific permissions to specific reviewers, and you can even password protect the Protect Document settings.

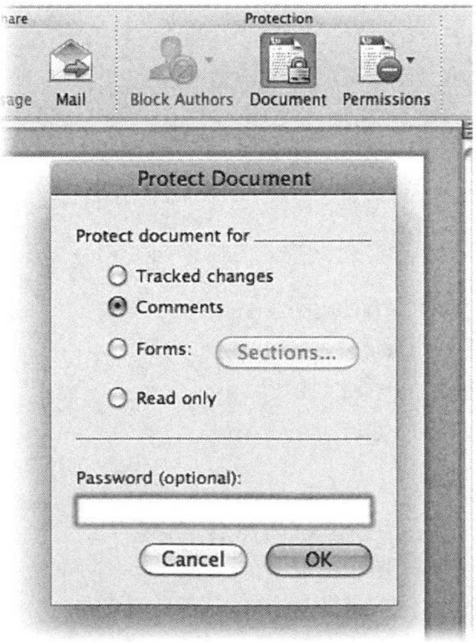

Figure 7-12:
Use the Protect Document menu on the Review tab to limit how other people can change your document. You can limit others to read only copies, to making comments or to tracked changes.

- **Tracked Changes.** Turn on this setting, and Word tracks any changes that are made by reviewers.

- **Comments.** Permits reviewers to add comments to your document but prevents them from making changes to the text.

- **Read only.** Permits reviewers to read your work but they can't change it in any way.

UP TO SPEED

Preparing to Send a Reviewed Document

If someone else will be merging the reviewed documents, there are a few things you can do when you send your edited copy to make her job easier:

- Make changes visible. Choose Tools→Track Changes→Highlight Changes before you send your document off. That way, the recipient can see immediately that it's been edited.

- Change the document's name. Add your initials to the file's name in the Finder, for example, so that it won't be confused with the original during the merging process.

Sharing Documents over SkyDrive or SharePoint

As your mother undoubtedly told you, there's no excuse for not sharing. That's certainly true with Office 2011. You can share your documents all those old passé ways—disc, thumb drive, or email. But now, there are some new options in the mix. SkyDrive is Microsoft's version of your Mac's iDisk. It's a web server out in the clouds where you can store documents. If your coworkers also use SkyDrive, they can view and edit your document according to the permissions you've given them. The other advantage of saving your document to SkyDrive is that you can access a single document from different computers, say, your office and home computers.

Note: You need a Windows Live ID and password to use the SkyDrive option. If you don't already have an account you can learn about the options at *http://explore.live.com/windows-live-skydrive.* For more details on using SkyDrive and the Windows Live Tools, see Appendix D.

---

1. **Choose File→Share→Save to SkyDrive.**

   If this is the first time you've tried to save an Office document to your SkyDrive, a window appears where you need to enter your Windows Live ID (the email address you used to sign up) and your password.

   If you've already used the SkyDrive from Office, you'll bypass the sign in process. The Save As panel opens in your Word document, as shown in Figure 7-13, where you provide a name and other details.

2. **Type a filename in the Save As box.**

   You don't have to choose a file format or give your filename any special .docx extension. Word and SkyDrive know what type of file you're creating.

3. **Click the name of the folder where you want to save your document.**

   Word saves the document in the SkyDrive folder you select.

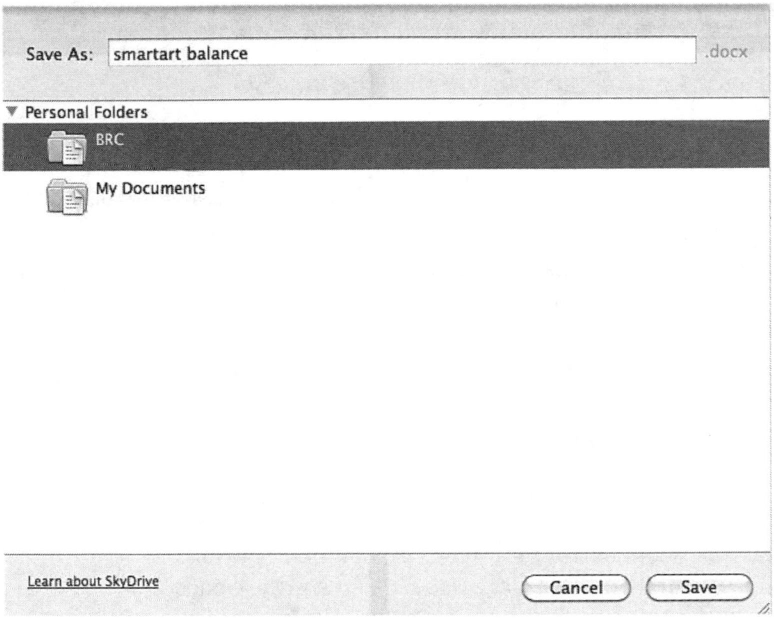

Figure 7-13:
Saving a file to your SkyDrive online folders is easier than saving it to your computer. All you have to do is provide a name and choose a folder to hold the file.

You'll probably want to double-check to make sure your file made it to SkyDrive. If you're sharing the file with others, you'll want to let them know that the file is online and available. To do that, follow these steps:

1. **In your web browser, go to** *http://explore.live.com/windows-live-skydrive*.

   The first web page has lots of promotional details regarding SkyDrive and Windows Live tools. If you don't have a Windows Live account, you can sign up from here. It doesn't cost any money, just a bit of your Apple/Mac soul.

2. **In the upper-right corner, click Sign In.**

   The Sign Up and Sign In window appears.

3. **Type the email address you used to sign up to Windows Live and click Sign In. Then, provide your password.**

   The next window looks like more Windows advertising, but you're almost on a page with tools.

4. **In the upper-left corner, click the Windows Live.**

   The next page has menus across the top with links to Microsoft online tools: Hotmail, Messenger, Office (web apps), Photos, and MSN.

5. **Click Office→Recent Documents.**

   The Office Recent Documents page shows all documents that you have access to. These may be yours or they may be documents that others have shared with you. Your documents are divided in to Personal and Shared groups. You can make folders in either category and choose who gets to peek inside those folders. Your saved document is in the folder where you saved it.

6. **Move your cursor over the document name.**

   Menus appear over the document with options to Edit in browser, Open in Word, or More.

7. **Click More→Share→Edit Permissions.**

   The menus don't work like your Mac, you need to click rather than just point to open the submenus.

   A new page appears where you can set the sharing permissions for the file. The choices at the top let you share items with friends (contacts you've added to your Windows Live account), which is fine for less specific things like vacation photos. For serious business, you'll want to use the bottom portion of the page where you can choose specific people.

8. **Type in the name or email address of the people you want to see your document.**

   If you've added email contacts to your Windows Live account, you can click "Select from your contact list" and choose from those contacts.

9. **For each colleague, choose their permission level: Can view or Can edit, then click Save.**

   A new page appears where you can send a message to your colleagues to let them know the file is available for their viewing or editing.

There's a lot more you can do with SkyDrive and the other tools that Microsoft offers on online. For the complete details see Appendix D, "Using Office Web Tools".

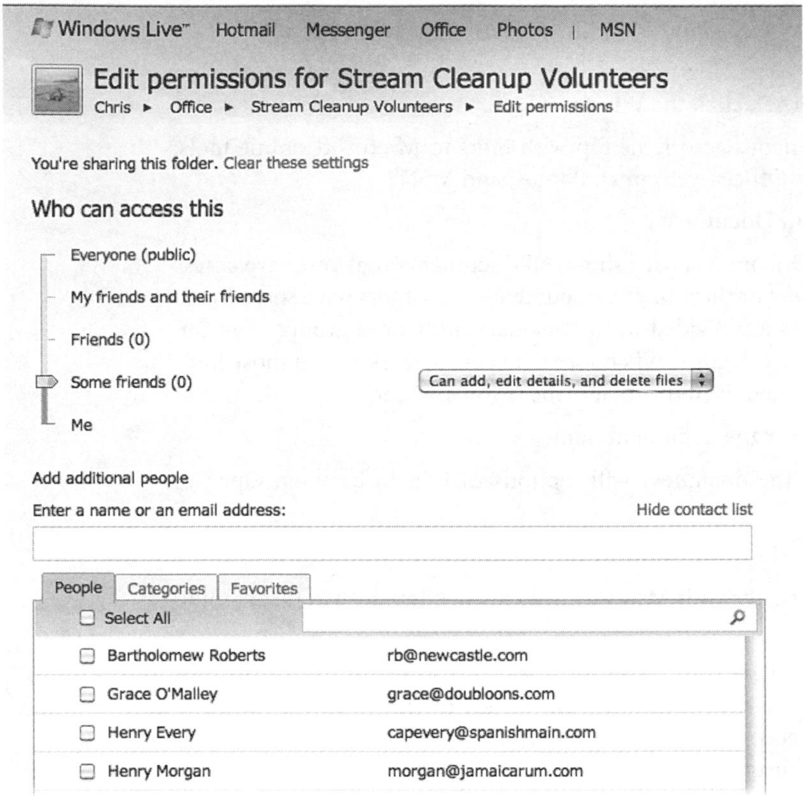

Windows Live™   Hotmail   Messenger   Office   Photos | MSN

Edit permissions for Stream Cleanup Volunteers

Chris ▶ Office ▶ Stream Cleanup Volunteers ▶ Edit permissions

You're sharing this folder. Clear these settings

Who can access this

Everyone (public)

My friends and their friends

Friends (0)

Some friends (0)   Can add, edit details, and delete files ▲▼

Me

Add additional people

Enter a name or an email address: Hide contact list

[   ]

| People | Categories | Favorites |

☐ Select All   🔍

☐ Bartholomew Roberts   rb@newcastle.com

☐ Grace O'Malley   grace@doubloons.com

☐ Henry Every   capevery@spanishmain.com

☐ Henry Morgan   morgan@jamaicarum.com

Figure 7-14:
Once your file is saved on SkyDrive, you can choose exactly who you want to view and edit the file. If you store contacts in your Windows Live account, it's simply a matter of checking the names of your colleagues.

Sharing with SharePoint

If you work in an medium to large office with a lot of Windows PC types, there's a good chance that your office uses Microsoft SharePoint server software so that you can work collaboratively on Word, Excel, PowerPoint and other Office documents. In the past, Mac users were second-class citizens when it came to Office and document sharing. With Office 2011, you're more of an equal partner.

To save your Word document to a SharePoint site, follow these steps:

1. **Choose File→Share→Save to SharePoint.**

   A panel similar to the one in Figure 7-13, appears where you can choose a location to save your file.

2. **If this is the first time you're saving to a SharePoint site, click the + button and type in the address (URL) for the site.**

   If you don't know the address, you can get it from the pocket protector types who manage your company computers.

3. **In the Save As box, give your document a name.**

4. **Choose the SharePoint library where you want to save the document.**

   You can choose the location you just added or one of the locations under Recent Locations or Shared Locations.

Once your document is saved in a SharePoint folder, you (or a colleague) can open from Word. Choose File→Open URL. In the box that appears, type the full name (URL) for the document—that's the path and the document name.

Part Two: Outlook

2

Outlook: Email and Life Management 101

I t takes careful planning and powerful computer tools to keep up with the details of modern life. That seems to be the philosophy behind Outlook. Each person you know may have a home address, a business address, a home phone, a business phone, and a cell phone. You send emails, have meetings and work on projects with deadlines. Life is full of numbers, addresses, dates, and tasks. Multiply that by a few hundred or a couple thousand and you've got a job fit for a sophisticated database. And that's exactly what Outlook is. It's a database that keeps track of your contacts, your emails, your meetings, and your to-do list. Outlook gives you a way to remember them all (Figure 8-1).

This chapter introduces Outlook by giving you a quick tour of the grounds. Then, it zeroes in on Email. You'll learn how to set up Outlook with all your email accounts. Then you'll learn how to get the most out of Outlook's state of the art email tools.

Starting Outlook the First Time

After you install Office, there's a big "O" for Outlook sitting in the dock. One click and you get a view of Outlook's somewhat busy window. The first thing Outlook encourages you to do is to set up an email account. If you had issues setting up an email account in the past, you're in for a pleasant surprise. In the new Outlook, the process is fairly simple, especially if your email is handled through one of the major providers such as MobileMe, Gmail, Yahoo, AOL, or Hotmail. In those cases, Outlook can handle most of the complicated details. You provide your email address and password, and Outlook can identify the service and automatically set up your account. If you have an email account through your company or some less famous provider, you may have a couple of extra steps.

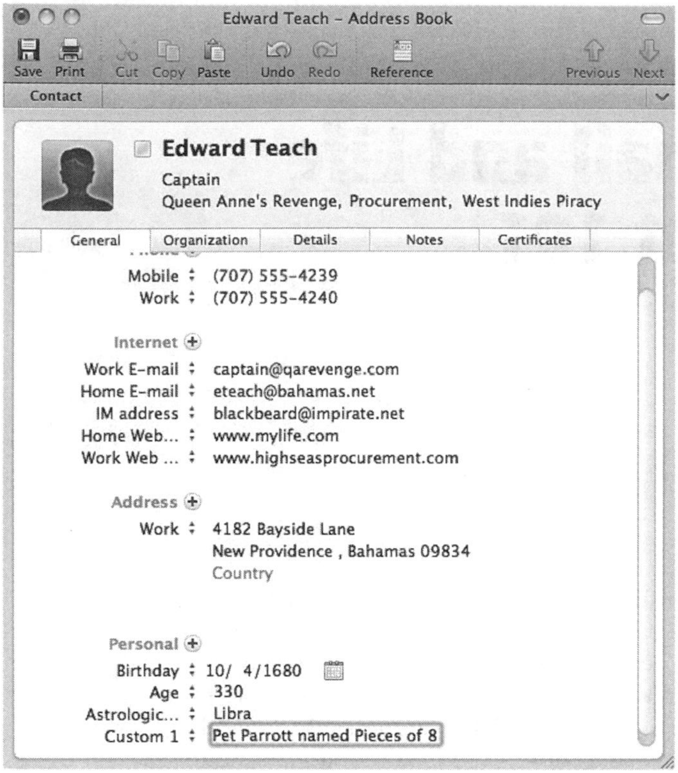

Figure 8-1:
Here's a single card from the Outlook contacts database. It takes a complex database to keep track of all your contacts, your schedule, your to-do list and your email. Outlook is designed to help with those chores.

Make sure that you're connected to the Internet, and then follow these steps to set up an email account:

1. **Launch Outlook.**

   If this is the very first time you launched Outlook, you're automatically prompted to set your email account.

2. **If this isn't your first time starting Outlook, go to Tools→Accounts to open the Accounts window. Then, click the + button in the lower-left corner and choose E-Mail.**

   When you click the + button, a menu with three options appears: Exchange (for offices that use Microsoft Exchange), E-mail (for regular old email accounts), and Directory Service (for network-based contact lists). After you choose Email, a box opens where you provide your email address and password as shown in Figure 8-2.

Note: If you ever need to delete an email account, you do it in this same window: just select the account name and click the minus (-) button.

---

3. **Provide the details about your email account as they're requested.**

   Your email address should be in the standard form that people use to email you, like *yourname@emailprovider.com*. The box disguises your password as you type it, in case someone is looking over your shoulder trying to steal your identity. If you have more than one account, you'll want to give each account an identifying name like Gmail, Me, or Acme Demolition Tools for Roadrunners.

4. **When you're done, click Add Account.**

   If everything is correct, the new email account appears in your list of accounts and Outlook displays a test message in your Inbox on the left side of the window.

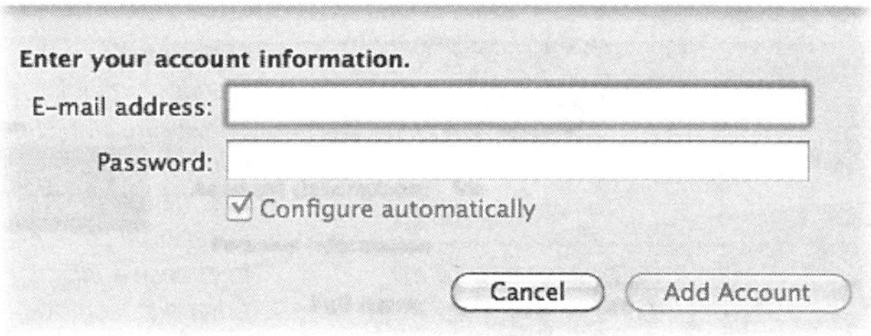

Figure 8-2:
For many email services, all you have to do to set up your account in Outlook is provide your email address, your password, and leave the Configure Automatically box checked.

Outlook Tour

If you're used to the Mac's more streamlined tools, Mail and Calendar, the first thing you'll notice about Outlook is that it feels cluttered. On the other hand, if you used Entourage from previous versions of Office, you'll find Outlook is a big improvement and more logically laid out. Figure 8-3 should give you an idea. In typical Microsoft fashion, there are lots of panes, buttons, toolbars, and tabs. Even if you have nothing scheduled for today, you feel as if you better get to work. In spite of its busy-ness, there are plenty of reasons to use Outlook. If you work with Windows-types you'll be in better shape to coordinate projects with them. Outlook works and plays well with all the other Office applications. Last, but certainly not least, beneath all those buttons, tabs, and widgets lies a lot of planning power.

When you first fire up Outlook there's a navigation pane on the left and a reading pane on the right. At the bottom of the navigation pane, there are five buttons: Mail, Calendar, Contacts, Tasks, and Notes. Click these buttons to display a different set of tools.

- **Mail** (⌘-1) organizes your email. As you send and receive emails, you can keep track of your correspondence by filing emails in different folders.

- **Calendar** (⌘-2) helps you plan for the future. If your life is a complicated web of business, family, and friend events, you can categorize each and filter your calendar to display the details.

- **Contacts** (⌘-3) is your computer address book. Unlike the one that you tend to lose in the drawer by the phone, it's easy to find Contacts and pop the important information into your email header or a Word document.

- **Tasks** (⌘-4) helps you keep track of those things you planned and promised to do. You can create reminders that pop up to keep you on track. If you have tasks that recur every month or week, you can create one reminder to pop up at the proper moment.

- **Notes** (⌘-5) is a place to jot down ideas and questions that come to mind throughout the day. Notes can be as big or small as you like. Each note is dated, and you can search through your notes to find that great screenplay idea you had three months ago.

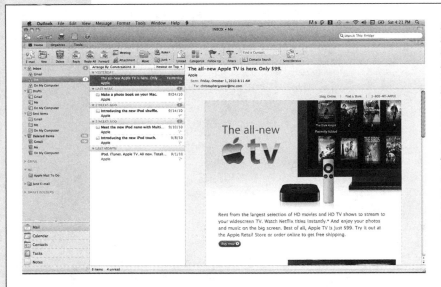

Figure 8-3:
Initially, Outlook divides the workspace into three columns. Use the tabs in the lower-right corner to choose Mail, Calendar, Contacts, Tasks, or Notes. With each view, Outlook puts tools to help you navigate and select items on the left and your work appears in the larger pane on the right.

FREQUENTLY ASKED QUESTION

Reducing Clutter in the Outlook Window

I want to use Outlook, but is there some way to reduce the clutter? It's driving me to distraction!

You can customize Outlook's view to minimize the number of panes and widgets as shown in Figure 8-4. If you remember a few of the shortcut keys you can still get full benefit of features Outlook has to offer. The key to this strategy is to use the View menu to hide the features you don't need. For starters, you can hide the Reading pane (View→Reading Pane→Hidden), Navigation pane (View→Navigation Pane) and the Toolbar (View→Toolbar). As with all Office

tools, you can show and hide the ribbon with a click on one of the tabs.

Naturally, it's just as easy to turn these features back on if and when you need them. However, you can use shortcut keys like ⌘-1 for mail and ⌘-2 for calendar. Want to create a new message, appointment, or note? Just press ⌘-N when you're in the appropriate view. Also, when you double-click an email or an appointment, they open in a new window for reading.

You can change Outlook's layout if you don't like the one that initially appears when you fire it up the first time. As explained in the box on page 266, you can show and hide the navigation and reading panes.

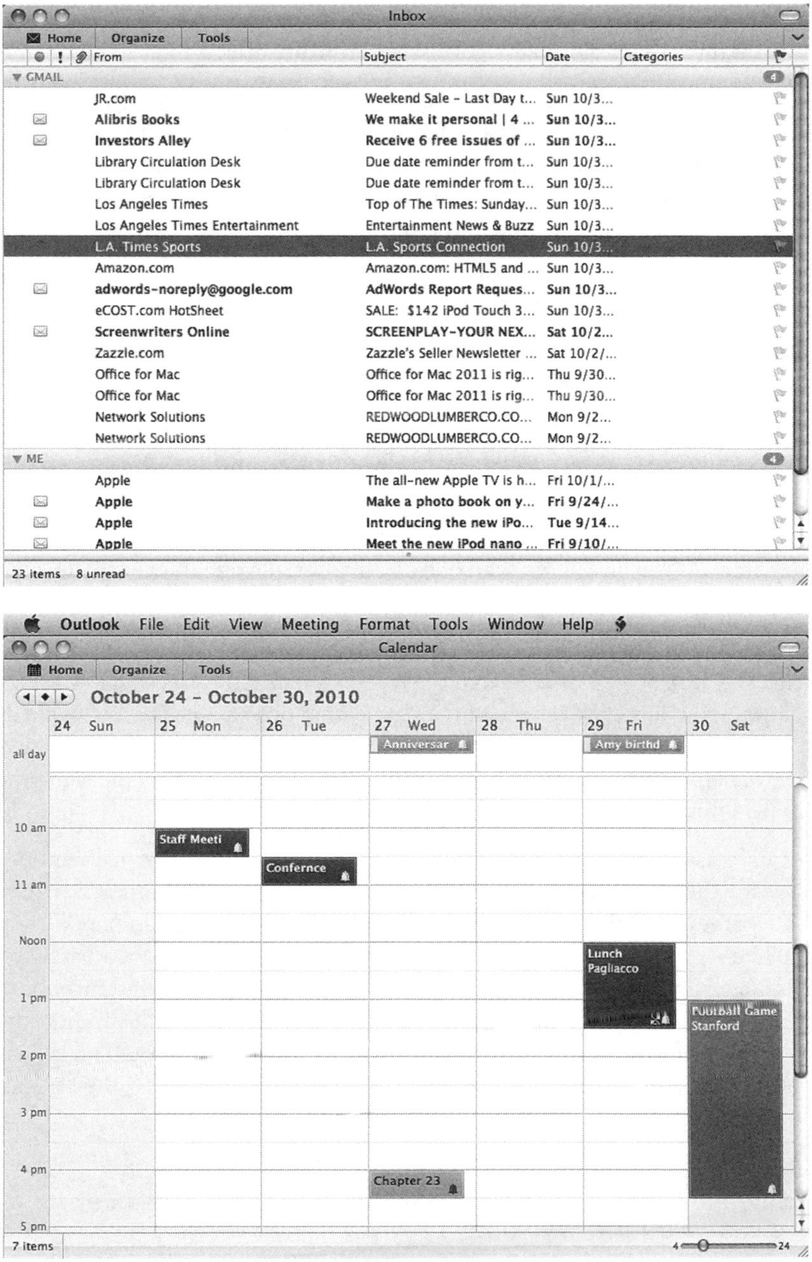

Figure 8-4:
It's possible to reduce Outlook's clutter with the View commands. Here's the mail and calendar view with some of the toolbars and panes turned off.

Sending Emails with Outlook

At its heart, Outlook is an email tool. That's the feature that draws most people to Outlook to begin with. There's a big benefit to handling all your email from a single program. With every message you send in one spot, you can use your computer to organize those messages. And when you're trying to find an address Aunt Rosemary sent to you three years ago, you've got some significant search tools to help.

Today, email is probably as vital to business as the desk. The beauty of email is its speed. It takes only seconds to dash off a message. On the other end, your boss can read and respond to your message at her convenience. Unlike a phone call, you don't both have to be available at the same moment to deal with an important issue. As always, Microsoft gives you multiple ways to begin your email message:

- **Using menus,** go to File→New→Email message. This command is convenient when you're working in the Calendar or some other view rather than Mail.

- **Using the ribbon**, when you're in Mail view, click Home | Email. When you're in one of the other views, click Home | New→Email message.

- **Using keyboard shortcuts,** when you're in Mail view, press ⌘-N. If you're in one of the other views, Option-⌘-N creates a new email message.

A new, as of yet untitled, email window appears. All you need to do is fill in the blanks labeled: To, Subject, and Message. At the very top, the From field shows your email identity. If you have more than one email account, you can choose the one you want to use.

In the To field (shown top Figure 8-5), start to type the name of the person you want to write. Outlook does a quick search of your contacts and starts suggesting recipients as you type. Just click on one of the names that pop up, or if your fingers don't want to leave the keyboard, you can use the arrow and Return keys. If you need a little extra help finding the right address, click the address book on the right end of the To field to search for a name.

You can add as many people as you want to the To field, but if you're just sending the message for their information, you may want to put their name in the Cc field. The term Cc comes from the prehistoric days when offices used carbon paper to make copies. If your name was in the Cc field of a memo it meant you got a barely readable smudged up carbon copy. Now, if your name was in the Bcc (blind carbon copy) field, that meant you got a copy but no one else except you and the author knows you're getting a copy. To add a Bcc to your email, click the options tab on the email form and choose Bcc (see Figure 8-6). The field appears right below the To and Cc fields.

Tip: The Bcc field is often used by folks who distribute newsletters by email. Suppose you send a newsletter to all your customers, they may not want everyone in the universe seeing their name and email address. And you don't necessarily want everyone to know who's on your customer list. If you put those names in the Bcc list, then you can put your own name in the To field, that way you'll get a copy yourself.

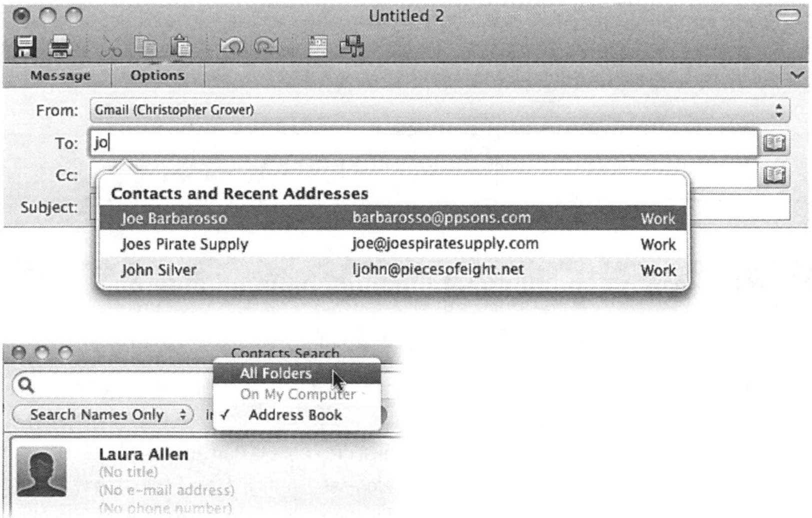

Figure 8-5:
Top: Outlook is quick to find contact names and email addresses, all you have to do is start typing and you'll get suggestions.

Bottom: If you need to do a major search, click the button on the right end of the To field. A search tool pops up that lets you search in your Mac address book, folders or your entire computer.

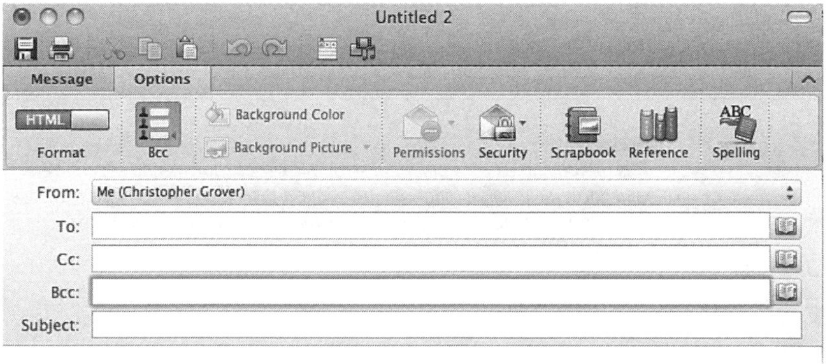

Figure 8-6:
Your email form has its own ribbon. Hidden under the tabs are goodies like the Bcc button and the switch that lets you choose between HTML or Plain format for your email.

Of course, the body of your email can be as simple or elaborate as you like. The formal conventions used in both personal and business letters aren't used as rigorously in email. It's common for coworkers to shoot email with just a few sentences back and forth as they work out an issue. No "Dears." No "Sincerelys." On the other hand, if you're applying for a job or writing to someone you want to impress, there's nothing wrong with writing a letter with all the accoutrements.

When you're finished writing your email, just click the Send button in the upper-left corner. Outlook closes the email form and sends your email on its way. If you want to save your email but not send it right now, you can press ⌘-S or click the Save icon in the toolbar. It looks like a disk. Your saved email is stored in the Drafts folder. You can leave it there until you're ready to edit it or send it.

Tip: Use ⌘-K to force Outlook to send and receive all email. If you only want to send email, use Shift-⌘-K.

Using Outlook's Reference Tools

Outlook puts a bundle of reference tools right there on the Options tab on the ribbon that at the top of the email form. The most useful of these is Options | Spelling, which runs a spell check on your email message. It works a lot like the spell checker in Word, described on page 57. This humble button can save you from the embarrassment of sending messages with typos.

The other two buttons, Scrapbook and Reference, lead to different tabs on the same toolbox. The scrapbook is just what the name implies. It's a great place to keep photos, company logos, or anything that you frequently pop into your emails. Just drag objects from the scrapbook into your email. The reference tab includes a Dictionary (with definitions), a Thesaurus, Bilingual Dictionaries, a Translation Tool (Figure 8-7), and (if all else fails) a Web Reference search tool.

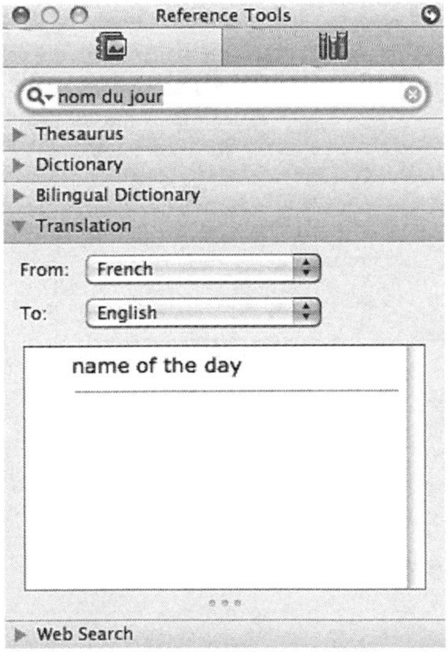

Figure 8-7:
This toolbox holds your personal scrapbook (not shown) and several reference tools including a language translation tool shown here. Type a phrase at the top, and then choose the source language and the language you want displayed.

Email Fancy Formatting

As you can tell by the sales pitches that appear in your inbox, it's possible to create email messages that are as elaborate as web pages complete with photos, headings, and other page layout features. You can compose your email in one of two formats—HTML or Plain. HTML (hypertext markup language) is the same language that's used to create web pages. When you choose the HTML option, you can format your text, create big bold headings, and use lots of color. You can even pop photos right inside the body of the message. If you choose Plain, your email is limited to plain text of a single size, and you can't even use bold or italics. When your recipient gets the message, it is displayed in whatever font he chooses. Why wouldn't you always use the fancy formatting capabilities of HTML? Well, some people don't like getting HTML email. In the bad old days, hackers used HTML email to sneak malware onto computers. These days, we're all a little smarter and our computers, web browsers, and firewalls are better at catching these kinds of attempts. Still, there are plenty of people who turn some or all the HTML features off. (The tip below explains how you can do just that.) So, the rule of thumb is, use HTML formatting for email that needs it, but it's best if you know the preferences of the people you're writing to. To switch between HTML and Plain text, click the Options tab on your email window and click the button on the left end of the ribbon. The keyboard shortcut is Shift-⌘-T.

Tip: Out of the box, Outlook is set to use HTML formatting unless you manually turn it off. You can change this behavior in your preferences. Go to Outlook→Preferences→Email→Composing and turn off the box for "Compose messages in HTML by default". You'll still be able to turn on HTML formatting, but Outlook will start off with Plain text emails. It's good to keep the next option in the preferences turned on: "When replying or forwarding, use the format of the original message." That way, your replies and forwarded messages match those sent to you.

When you have HTML turned on, you can format your email using the options on Outlook's Format menu (Figure 8-8). It's the standard drill, select the text you want to change and then choose an option like Format→Size or Format→Color. The standard keyboard shortcuts work for Bold (⌘-B), Italics (⌘-I), Underline (⌘-U), and Strikethrough (Shift-⌘-X).

Formatting your emails is similar to formatting a Word document, but you'll notice a difference here and there because HTML plays by slightly different rules. For example, there are no left and right margins in HTML formatting. Text fills the available space and recipients can change the page width in their email readers or web browsers. You can choose any font that's on your computer, but if it's not on your recipient's computer, she'll see something different.

Slide to switch between HTML and Plain text

Embedding a Picture in Your Email

You can always send photos by attaching them to an email, as explained on page 275; but to embed a photo in your email, you have to use the HTML format (Options | HTML). When it comes to finding the photo you want to send, Outlook lets you use Office's media browser or helps you search through your folders. When you embed a picture in your message, it's positioned within the flow of the text, rather than floating over the words. That means you have to plan a little to put your pic exactly where you want it. Often it's best to write your email first and then drop in pictures where you want them.

With the email you're writing open, follow these steps to place a photo in your email:

1. **Click the Options tab and choose HTML.**

2. **Write your email and then place the insertion point where you want to add a picture.**

   Sometimes it's best if your photos are placed in their own paragraph. You can do that by pressing Return to put the insertion point on a line by itself.

3. **Using the ribbon on your email form, go to Message | Picture and then choose Media Browser or Picture from Files.**

   - **Media Browser option.** The Media Browser is the same tool you use in Word and all the Office applications. It's described in detail on page 599. When you see a picture you like in the Media Browser, you can drag it to any spot in your email.

- **Picture from Files option.** If you choose the files option, you can use a Finder-style tool complete with a spotlight search box to zero in on your photo (Figure 8-10). When you select the photo and click Open, the photo is placed in your email at the insertion point.

After the picture is in your email message, you can drag it to a new location, or you can select it and delete. To select it, drag the cursor over the picture from side to side. When it's selected, the picture shows a bluish highlight. If you add more text, the picture moves, staying in position with the adjacent text.

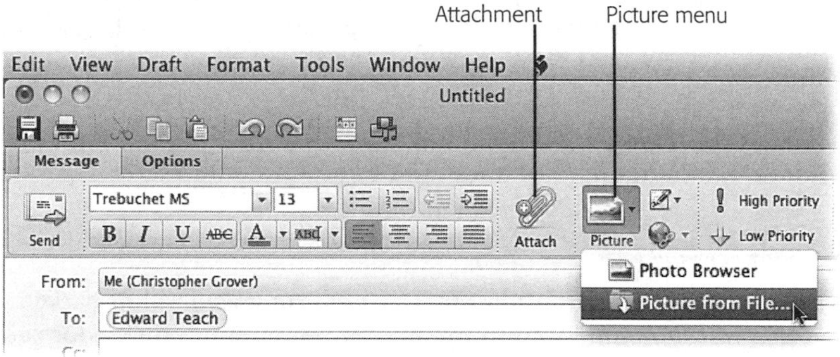

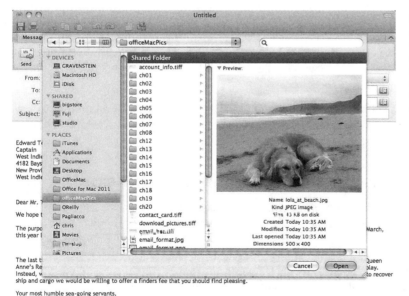

Figure 8-9:
Use the ribbon at the top of your email form (Message | Picture) to pop photos or other graphics into your message. Just make sure they aren't too big, as explained in the box on page 274.

Figure 8-10:
If you choose the "Picture from Files" option, you can browse to any photo or graphic on your computer. If you need to search for a photo, use the Spotlight box in the upper-right corner of the window.

EMAIL ETIQUETTE

Don't Send Huge Photos via Email

The cameras we use today create huge files. It's all those megapixels. That's great when you're making prints, but it's not needed when your recipient is simply looking a picture on their computer. There's no reason for the photo to have more pixels than a computer screen. In most cases, there's no need for your embedded photo to be more than 800 or 1000 pixels wide or tall. And there are plenty of reasons why they shouldn't be bigger than that.

Many email systems have a limit on the amount of space each person can use. The limit varies but with many systems,

there's a five megabyte limit. If an email and its attachments exceed the limit, they're rejected. It's entirely possible to send a photo that's so big that it consumes all the space allowed. In that case, your boss, friend, or relative won't be able to receive any more email from anyone! In lots of cases, it fouls up their inbox so much they won't even be able to open their inbox to delete the offending message. They'll have to get help from the person that manages their email server.

Adding a Background Picture or Color

You can create a watermark effect by putting a photo or graphic in the background of the email. Use Options | Background Picture. You must use HTML formatting (Options | HTML) and you should choose the image carefully so it doesn't fight with the message in your letter. Often it helps if you lighten the picture and reduce contrast before inserting it in the background. If the picture is smaller than the email window, Outlook automatically tiles the image. So, in this case you may want to use an image that's about the same size as a computer screen. For comparison, a MacBook pro 15-inch screen is 1440 × 900 pixels. A background image adds to the file size of email so you still want to keep the file size of the image to a minimum. That's something you can do with image-editing software like Adobe Photoshop Elements or Adobe Fireworks.

To add a color background to your email, choose Option | Background Color and then choose a color from the Mac's standard color picker tools. Be kind to your readers and choose a color that doesn't make it hard to read the text.

Getting Photos from Cameras, Scanners, and Screenshots

If your photo isn't on your computer yet, you can import it directly into your email from a camera or scanner. Right-click (Control-click) on the body of your email and choose Import from the shortcut menu. Make sure you don't have any text selected, or you may not see the Import option on the shortcut menu. A window appears where you can choose the device you want to use. If it's a camera, you can search through the available photos. If it's a scanner, you'll need to scan the image using the scanner's standard software.

Capturing screenshots to drop into your emails is easy, too. Right-click (Control-click) an empty spot in your email and choose Capture Selection from Screen. At this point, your arrow cursor is a loaded camera. You drag a box around anything that you want to capture in your picture as shown in Figure 8-11.

It helps to plan ahead a bit when you're capturing screen shots. You want to arrange the object that you're shooting so it's ready to go when you choose Capture Selection from Screen option. In some cases, you can drag your email to one side to make room for your screenshot subject. Or you may want to use your Mac's Spaces feature to set up the shot in another window. That way you can have your email in one space and your subject in another. After you choose the Capture command, you can use Option with the arrow keys to swap spaces. (For more details on your Mac's extremely handy Spaces feature, get a copy of David Pogue's *Mac OS X Snow Leopard: The Missing Manual.*)

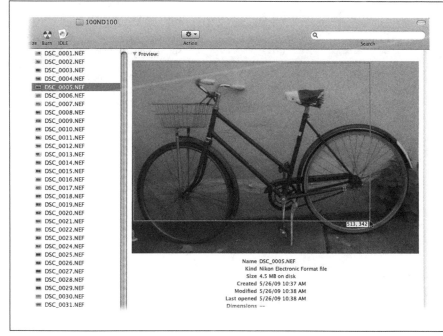

Figure 8-11:
Capturing an image from your computer screen is as easy as dragging a rectangle around the subject. Outlook can automatically place the captured image in your email. Screen captures are a quick and easy way to resize photos so they're suitable for email.

Sending Attachments with Your Email

You can attach one or more documents, photos or just about any file to an email. Attachments don't appear in the body of the letter, but they're identified by name and perhaps a paperclip icon in the email, as shown at the bottom of Figure 8-12. The person on the other end needs to have a program that can open the file. So if you send a Word document, they'll need Word or at least a program that can view Word files. As with photos, you don't want to send files that are so big they foul up your friend's email box. For the full story, see the box on page 274.

To attach a file to your email, use the ribbon on the email form and choose Message | Attach. A window opens where you can use Finder tools to locate your file. After you click the Choose button, the file is officially attached (as a glance at the email's header confirms). There's a new attachment field with a paperclip icon, listing the name of the attached file and its size. You can continue writing, or you can add more attachments.

Tip: Often the easiest way to attach a file to your email is with drag-and-drop. Just drag a photo or document onto the email and let go of the mouse button.

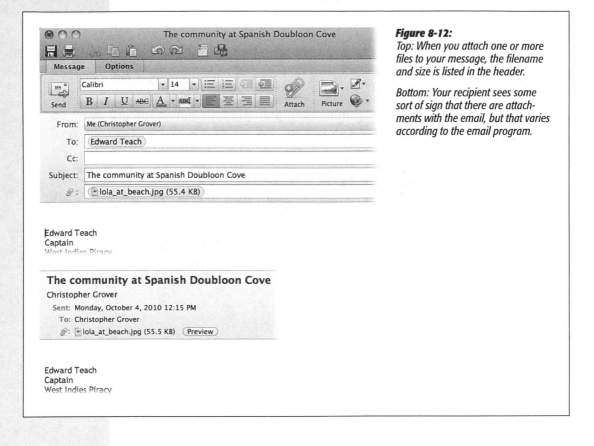

Figure 8-12:
Top: When you attach one or more files to your message, the filename and size is listed in the header.

Bottom: Your recipient sees some sort of sign that there are attachments with the email, but that varies according to the email program.

Adding Hyperlinks to Your Email

There are a couple of ways to add links to web pages and other resources to the body of your email. Unlike photos, you can add hyperlinks even if your message is formatted using the Plain Text option. The easiest way to add a link is to drag the page address from your browser right onto the email, as shown in Figure 8-13. You can also cut and paste addresses. If you use the Message | Hyperlink command, you can type or paste an address in the box at the top and then type the text you want to show in the message in the bottom box.

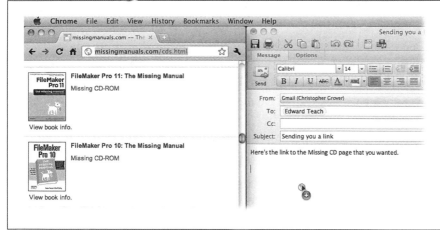

Figure 8-13:
The easiest way to add a web page link to your email is to drag the address from your browser (left) onto the body of the email (right). This method is great for those really long hyperlinks that you can't possibly enter without a typo.

Creating and Using Email Signatures

Often email between close friends and colleagues is very informal and dispenses with salutations and signatures. After all, it's perfectly easy to see the sender and the recipient at the top of the email. In that way, email messages are often more like office memos than they are formal letters. However, if you're in business and you want a little self-promotion, you may want to develop a signature that appears at the end of your email. A signature can include anything. Often it's a name, company name, and phone number, since those details don't appear in an email header. Some people like to include a complete address or a picture, such as a scan of their handwritten signature. Naturally, if you use images in your signature, you need to use the HTML format for your email (see page 272). Whatever you want to use, the process of creating it is the same.

1. **With your email open, using the ribbon in the email form, go to Options | Signature→Edit Signatures.**

   The signature button looks like a pen over a piece of paper and displays a tooltip that says "Add a signature to this message". The signatures box appears as shown in Figure 8-14. If this is your first signature, Outlook automatically names it Standard.

2. **In the box on the right, type your name and any other text you wish to use.**

   You can use multiple lines, and if you're using HTML formatting, you can use different fonts, bold, italic, and all the other formatting features available in Outlook and the Format menu.

3. **To add an image (optional): Right-click in the signature box and choose Import Picture or Capture Selection from Screen.**

   Follow the steps explained on page 272 to add photos and graphics. If you prefer, you can always copy and paste pictures from another program.

4. **To rename a Signature, double-click the name under Signature name.**

   These names appear in the Signature menu.

5. **To make a signature that automatically appears at the bottom of every message, click the Default Signatures button.**

   Use the menus to select an email account and the signature you want to use with it.

6. **Click the red button in the upper-left corner to close the Signature box.**

When you want to use a signature, go to Message | Signature and choose it from the menu by name. If you ever want to add or delete signatures, go to Message | Signature→Edit Signatures and use the + and – buttons in the lower-left corner.

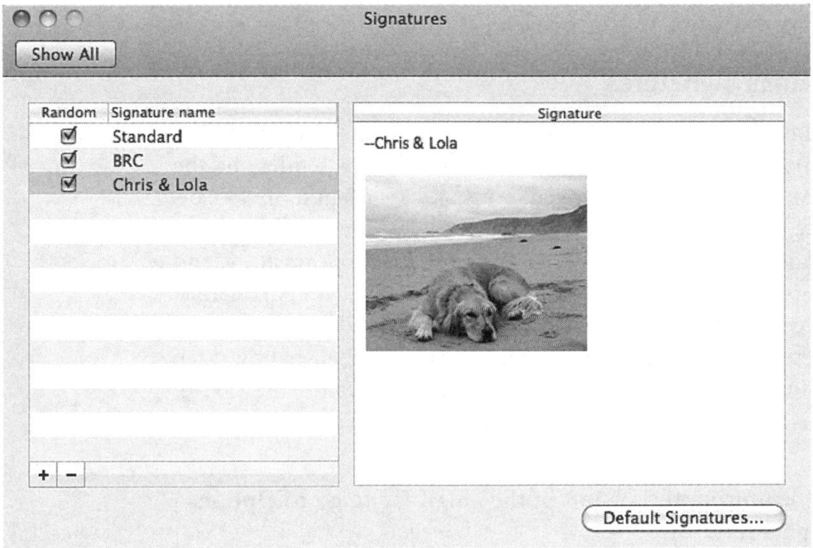

Figure 8-14:
In the Signatures window, the box on the left lists any signatures that have already been created. Choose one from the list and a preview appears in the box on the right.

Tip: If you want to draw attention to your email you can click the toolbar buttons for High Priority (!) and Low Priority (Down Arrow). If your recipient uses Outlook, they'll see high or low priority icons next to the email names. If he uses a different email program, the priority icons may or may not be visible.

About Digitally Signed and Encrypted Email

Outlook uses an Internet standard called S/MIME to provide an added level of security to email messages, but to use these features you need to acquire a certificate from a third party service like Thawte (*www.thawte.com*). You'll find they aren't cheap—about $300 for a year or $550 for two years. The certificate is added to the security keychain on your Mac. It's possible to have more than one certificate on your computer. For example you may have one issued by your company and a different certificate for personal use.

Tip: If you have a .Mac or MobileMe account, you can get a certificate for that account for "free" as part of your yearly subscription. Login to MobileMe mail, then in the upper-right corner, open the menu under your name and select Account. When the page with your account details opens, you can select Security Certificates from the list on the left.

Digital signatures can be used with your emails as you would a handwritten signature—a verification that you are who you say you are and that you're not 16 year-old Todd, aka GrimHackerOfAnarchy. To digitally sign an email, go to Options | Security→Digitally Sign Message.

Encrypted emails work when both the sender and recipient have certificates on their computers. If you are sending an encrypted letter, you must have a copy of each recipient's certificate saved with the contacts' entries in Outlook. Make sure you're sending your email from an account that's verified by a certificate. For details on saving contacts, see page 289. To send an encrypted email, choose Options | Security→Encrypt Message.

Note: For more details about security, digital signatures and encryption in Outlook, choose Tools→ Accounts. When the Accounts window opens, click the Advanced button in the lower-right corner, then click the Security tab. Finally, click the Learn about mail security link in the lower-left corner as shown in Figure 8-15.

Receiving Email

Your email is stored in those folders on the left side of the Outlook's Mail view (⌘ 1). If you want to make sure you have all your current email, press ⌘-K, the command to send and receive all email from all your accounts. Unless you've set up special rules, as explained on page 336, all the email appears in the Inbox at the top of the Navigation pane. The only exception is email that Outlook immediately identifies as Junk (see page 287). If you have more than one email account, Outlook also shows copies in individual folders with the account name. Figure 8-16 shows Outlook folders for two accounts.

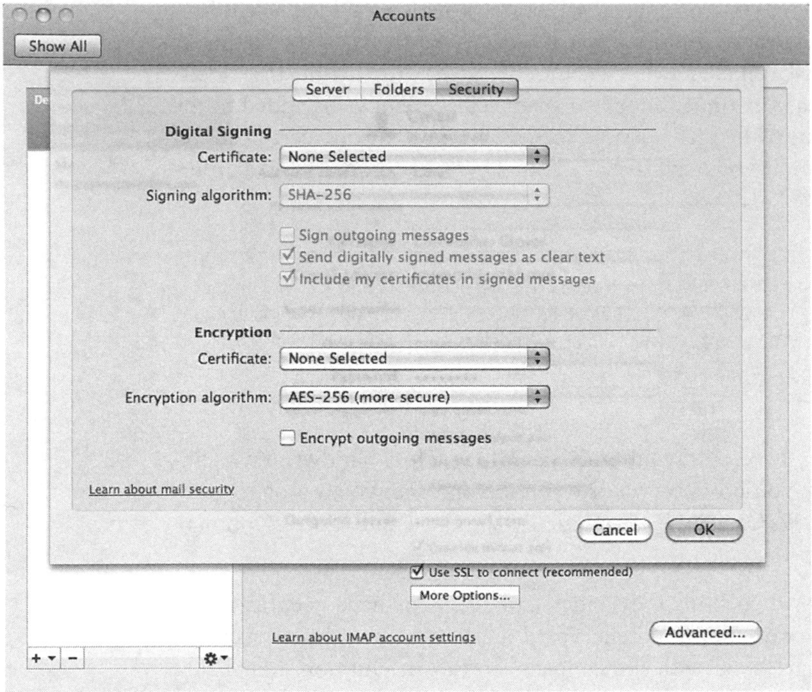

○ ○ ○   Accounts

Show All

Server   Folders   Security

Digital Signing

Certificate: None Selected

Signing algorithm: SHA-256

☐ Sign outgoing messages
☑ Send digitally signed messages as clear text
☑ Include my certificates in signed messages

Encryption

Certificate: None Selected

Encryption algorithm: AES-256 (more secure)

☐ Encrypt outgoing messages

Learn about mail security

Cancel   OK

☑ Use SSL to connect (recommended)
More Options...

Learn about IMAP account settings   Advanced...

+ ▼   −   ✿ ▼

Figure 8-15:
To send digitally signed or encrypted emails you need to get a third party certificate that verifies your identity. Once you have a certificate in your Mac's keychain, you can choose your security options in this window (Tools→Accounts→ Advanced→Security).

Figure 8-16:
Here's an Outlook navigation pane showing folders for a Gmail account and an Apple MobileMe account. All the incoming emails appear in the very top Inbox. Below, the Gmail folder holds copies of the email sent to the Gmail address. The Me folder holds mail sent to the MobileMe account.

Once mail arrives in the inbox, there are a number of things you may want to do with it. If your inbox looks like most folks', the Delete key comes into play. Many of the commands to work with your messages are on the Home tab when you're in Mail view. They also appear on a shortcut menu when you right-click (Control-click) a message (see Figure 8-17). Here's a list of all your email options:

- **Read your email**. Click a folder in the navigation pane to display a list of emails. Unread messages are bold, while ones that you've opened are listed with regular type. Click a message in the list to display it in the reading pane, or double-click it to open it in its own window. Sometimes you may want to change a message's Read/Unread status. Perhaps you want it to show as unread so you'll remember to come back to it later. Click Home | Read or Home | Unread to change the status of a message.

- **Reply to your email** (⌘-R). While viewing your email, click Home | Reply to send a message back to the sender. Click Home | Reply All (Shift-⌘-R) to send your reply to the sender and anyone who was on the Cc list. When replying to an email message, it's common to include a copy of the original message. It may be indented or labeled with the name of the person who sent the message and the date. You can tweak those settings by going to Outlook→Preferences→ E-mail→Composing.

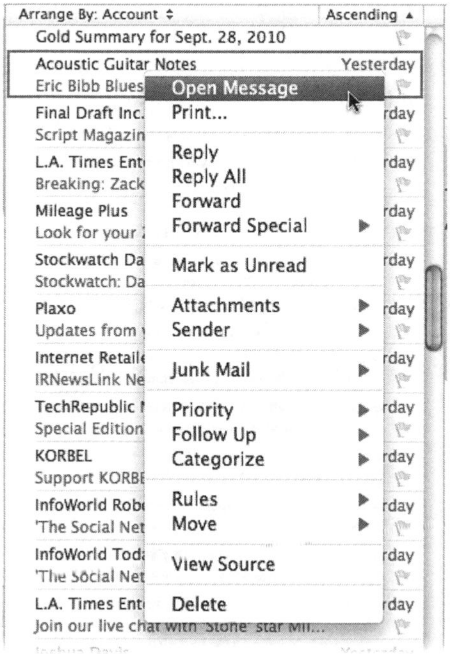

Figure 8-17:
Right-click (Control-click) on email headers in Outlook and this shortcut menu pops up loaded with the things you can do with your email. Your options include opening email for reading, moving it to a different folder, or marking it as junk.

- **Open attachments**. Click the Preview button in the message's header to sneak a quick peek at an attachment. Double-click an attachment to open it in the appropriate program. For example, Word docs open in Word; photos open in Preview. It's best not to open attachments from people you don't know. That's one of the ways the bad guys sneak malware on to your computer.

- **Delete your email**. Don't be afraid to exercise the Delete key. No one will know if you don't read that email. Deleted email goes to your Deleted mail folder where you can retrieve it you have a change of heart.

- **Move your email to another folder** (Shift-⌘-M). Email doesn't really take up much room on your computer unless there are lots of humongous photos and attachments. For this reason many people keep all their non-junk mail forever. They keep it organized by sorting it into folders: family, business, finances, soccer team, and so on. To move mail to a folder, go to Home | Move (Shift-⌘-M) and then choose a folder. If the folder you want isn't displayed, you can search for it by typing its name. Once you've moved mail to a folder, the folder name is added to the Move menu. If you want to leave a copy of the email in your Inbox as a reminder, you can copy mail to folders instead of moving it. Page 336 explains how to set up rules to automatically move emails to specific folders.

- **Flag your email for follow-up action** (Home | Follow Up). There's a line in a Gillian Welch song that goes "I wanna do right, but not right now." That's kind of the philosophy behind flagging messages. When a message contains something that you really need to deal with, but you don't have the time to tackle it now, you can flag it and tell Outlook when you want to follow up on the message. When the moment arrives, Outlook will remind you with a pop-up message like the one shown at the bottom of Figure 8-18. Outlook gives you several options for follow-up including: Today (Control-1), Tomorrow (Control-2), This Week (Control-3), Next Week (Control-4), No Due Date (Control-5), and Custom Date (Control-6). When you want to remove a Follow-up flag, select it and press Option-'.

- **Apply filters to show or hide messages**. When your folder is filled with tons of messages you can use a filter to show only the messages you want. For example, you can apply a filter that only shows messages that you've flagged for follow-up.

Figure 8-18:
Top: Got a message you're not ready to deal with? Flag it and Outlook will remind you later. You can choose a specific time or day to tackle that chore.

Bottom: When the moment arrives you can handle it, procrastinate, or decide it really wasn't that important.

Downloading Pictures

Using its initial settings, Outlook doesn't even download images embedded in an email. If you want to see the pictures, click the "Download pictures" button in the upper-right corner of the email (Figure 8-18). To change this setting, go to Outlook→Preferences→Reading→Security→"Automatically download pictures from the Internet". At the bottom of the Preferences window, choose between these options:

- **In all messages.** Choose this when you want to see pictures no matter who sends them.

- **In messages from my contacts.** A middle of the road security measure, you only automatically download and display pictures if the sender is listed in your Outlook contacts.

- **Never.** The paranoid's favorite option and Outlook's default. Never download pictures automatically. You have to use the download button described above. Why avoid pictures? Sometimes spammers put programs called *beacons* in pictures, so when your computer downloads the image, the spammers know they have a live one. In which case, you can count on getting more spam.

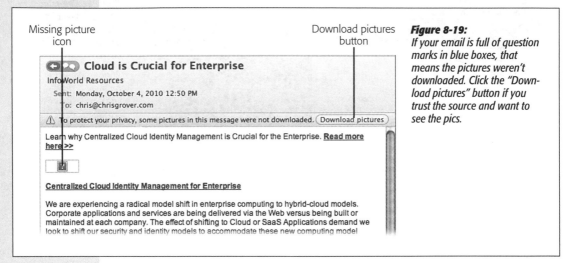

Missing picture icon

Download pictures button

Figure 8-19:
If your email is full of question marks in blue boxes, that means the pictures weren't downloaded. Click the "Download pictures" button if you trust the source and want to see the pics.

Categorize and Arrange Your Emails

Managing hundreds or maybe even thousands of emails is a big job. Fortunately, Outlook comes with lots of easy-to-use tools that can help you. Go to Home | Categorize to open the menu (shown in Figure 8-20) that you use to assign categories to your messages. Outlook comes with several common categories like: Family, Friends, Holiday, and Travel, but you're not limited to categories dreamed up at Microsoft. Click the Edit Categories option, and you can create your own categories and assign colors. Use the + and – buttons in the lower-left corner of the Categories window to add and remove categories. Double-click a category name to change it.

Categories are color-coded, and Outlook uses those colors in the email lists, which makes it easy to zero in on messages that belong to a certain category. You can also use categories with the Filter described on page 30. That way, you can hide all the messages in a folder except the ones in a chosen category.

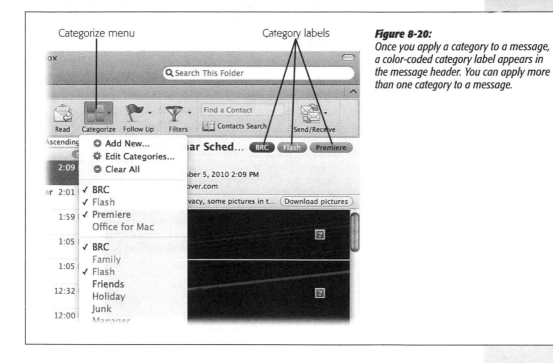

Categorize menu   Category labels

Figure 8-20:
Once you apply a category to a message, a color-coded category label appears in the message header. You can apply more than one category to a message.

In addition to categories and filters, Outlook offers a couple of tools that rearrange the way emails are displayed in the folder list. Use the Conversation button Organize→Conversation to group messages and their replies into collapsible conversation lists. This is especially handy for email because it's not unusual to discuss an issue or topic over several back-and-forth emails. Outlook uses the subject when it groups messages into conversations, so you'll sometimes find unrelated emails grouped together if the subject is the same. Next to the Conversation button is the "Arrange by" menu (Organize→Arrange by). There's a long list of ways Outlook can sort and arrange your emails, including: Date sent or received, Status, Flag Status, Attachments, or email accounts. If you have a better plan for arranging emails, click the Custom Arrangements option where you can create your own.

Instead of using the ribbon menu, you can use the little mini-menus at the top of the email list pane. The menu on the left is identical to the "Arrange by" menu. The menu on the right lets you specify an ascending or descending sort.

Setting Up a Schedule to Send and Receive Email

How do you like your email served? Do you want to check it at nine, noon, and five each day? Do you want to check your mail server every ten minutes? Is it more important to check your business email account frequently or your family account? With Outlook, you can build a schedule that matches your needs.

For example, here are the steps to set up a schedule that checks an email account on that nine, noon, and five schedule on business days:

1. **Go to Tools→Run Schedule→Edit Schedules.**

   When you first use Outlook, the Schedules window opens with a couple of schedules already listed. They are named Empty Deleted Items Folder, Send & Receive All, and Send All. The schedules with checkmarks are activated. The Send & Receive All schedule is not. If you double-click on a schedule, it opens for editing as shown in Figure 8-21.

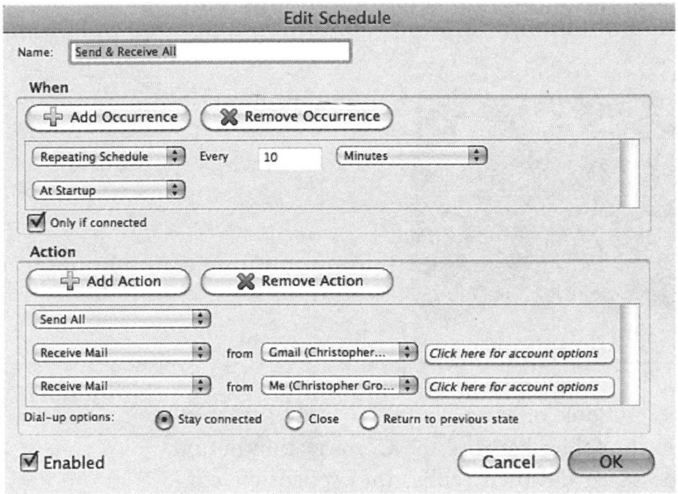

Figure 8-21:
Here are the innards of the Send & Receive All schedule. If it is activated, it downloads your email from all accounts every ten minutes. If you want to turn it on, just check the box in the Schedules window (not shown here).

2. **Click the + button in the lower-left corner of the Schedules window.**

   The Edit Schedule box opens. There are two main parts to the box. The When group at the top is where you choose how frequently or which event triggers the actions. The Actions group is where you choose the Outlook actions you want to take place.

3. **In the Name box at the top of the window, type a name for your schedule.**

   It's okay to include spaces, numbers, and symbols in your schedule name.

4. **Under When, set the menu to Timed Schedule, and then click the button labeled "Click here for timed schedule options".**

   A box opens where you can choose days of the week and times during the day.

5. **Click the five days of the week Monday through Friday. Then, click the three times of the day you want to download mail. Close the box by clicking the square in the upper-left corner.**

   The buttons appear pushed in when they're selected as shown in Figure 8-22.

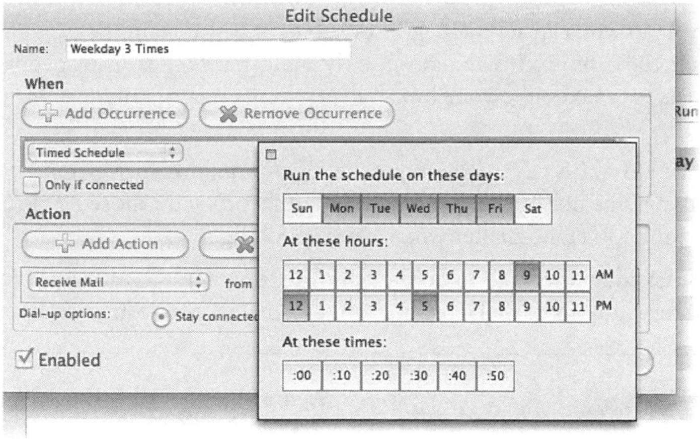

Figure 8-22:
You use this box to set up a cus-
tom schedule. This schedule is set
to run five days a week at 9 am,
12 noon, and 5 pm.

6. **Under Action, set the menu to Receive Mail.**

   This menu has several options like Send All and Delete Junk Mail.

7. **Use the From menu to choose the email account you want to check.**

   If you want to download mail from specific folders of your email account, click the "Click here for account options" button.

8. **Make sure the Enabled box is turned on and click OK**

   Your schedule is saved and enabled to run automatically. You can turn it on and off using the checkbox in the Schedules window.

When it's complete, your named schedule appears in a couple of places. It's listed in the Tools→Run Schedule menu and it also appears on the ribbon (Tools | Schedules).

Managing Junk Mail

Junk email can drive you crazy! Worse than that, if your inbox gets filled with junk mail, you might not notice some of the important messages that are in there. Outlook gives you a couple of weapons in the battle against junk mail. Mail that Outlook considers junk is stashed in a folder, appropriately named Junk E-Mail. Also appropriately, it's at the bottom of the folder list in the navigation pane. It's a good idea to check the folder occasionally, especially when you first start using Outlook. It's possible that your idea of junk mail and Outlook's aren't the same. If you find a message in the junk folder that you don't think deserves that status, right-click (Control-click) on the message and choose Junk Mail→Mark as Not Junk. With a little guidance, Outlook learns your preferences.

If you want to tweak the junk mail settings, go to Tools→Junk E-mail Protection. The window shown in Figure 8-23 opens with three tabs.

- On the **Level** tab, you can set the degree of protection you want: Low, High, or None. If you click the Exclusive option, only mail that comes from people in your Contacts list makes it to your Inbox. Everything else goes right to the junk folder.

- Click the **Safe Domains** tab to tell Outlook who you want to receive email from. Add a domain name like "apple.com" and Outlook won't send those Apple missives to the junk folder, no matter what they're pitching.

- Click the **Blocked Senders** tab to do the opposite. If you never, ever want to be pestered by the minions of Evil Corporation, list "evilcorporation.com" here.

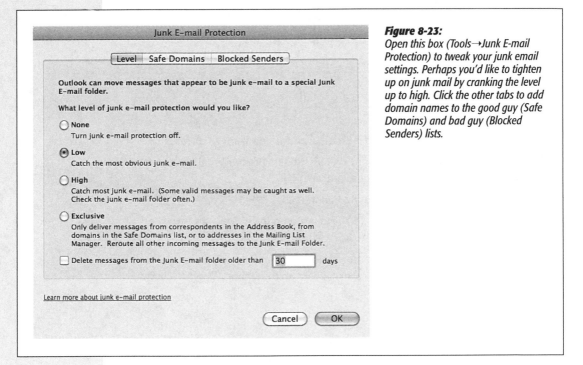

Figure 8-23:
Open this box (Tools→Junk E-mail Protection) to tweak your junk email settings. Perhaps you'd like to tighten up on junk mail by cranking the level up to high. Click the other tabs to add domain names to the good guy (Safe Domains) and bad guy (Blocked Senders) lists.

Managing Your Contacts

Once upon a time, people kept the names, addresses, and phone numbers of everyone they knew in real books with pages that had lettered tabs. Depending on your family names, there might have been lots of people on your D, M, and S pages, but not so many on your Q, U, and Z pages. If someone moved or a phone number changed, you'd scrawl out the outdated details and write in the new ones. Needless to say, these books got a little messy. Then, personal computers and iPhones came along. Now you've got more details than ever to keep track of: email addresses, web pages, and instant message (IM) names. Fortunately, along with those gadgets, you've got some smart tools to manage your contacts.

Outlook comes with contact tools that are designed to work smoothly with your Office programs. Surprisingly, they're also designed to play well with your Mac Address Book and other applications that don't come from that big blue Windows company. This chapter shows you how to add contacts and create groups of contacts for easy mailing. If you already use your Mac Address Book, Gmail, or some other contact manager, you'll learn how to import the contacts you've already created there. Along the way, you'll discover loads of tips to help you manage all the addresses and numbers attached to your friends, family, and colleagues.

Creating New Contacts

Creating new contacts is a fill-in the blanks affair. Most of your work with contacts takes place in the Contacts view and there are three ways to get there:

- The shortcut key is the fastest method: ⌘-3.
- On the menu, choose View→Go to→Contacts.
- In the lower-left corner of the Outlook window, click Contacts.

The contacts view is similar to the email view in that you make selections moving from the left to right across the window. As you work through that process, you zero in on the details. There's a navigation pane on the left. Choose a contact source such as Address Book or one of the smart folders, and you see a list of contact names in the center pane. Choose a name, and the details for that contact are displayed in the reading pane on the right.

Tip: You can change the position or hide the reading pane by choosing View→Reading Pane and then choosing one of the options: Right (⌘-\), Below (Shift-⌘-\) or Hidden (Option-⌘-\). Those are back slashes, not the more common forward slash. If you're in the clean-view, hide-the-reading-pane crowd, you can always view the contact details by double-clicking the contact, in which case they're displayed in a new window.

To add a contact, press ⌘-N, and a new contact form appears, like the one at the top of Figure 9-1. The contact name, company, and other major details are in the header at the top of the form. If you want, you can add pictures for your contacts; just double-click the little silhouette and then, in the pop-up window, click the Choose button to find a suitable pic. The bottom portion of the form is where you store email addresses, web pages, phone numbers, and street addresses for home and work. You can add as much or as little as you please. If the form doesn't display the blanks that you need, click one of the + buttons to see a pop-up list with more, as shown at the bottom of Figure 9-1. It's also possible to change, say a work address to a home address, by clicking on the label.

When you're finished adding details, click the Save and Close button on the form. If you simply click the red Close button, Outlook won't save the details and it won't even give you an "Are you sure?" warning.

The contact form has five tabs but if you're like most people you'll focus on the first General tab. The Organization and Details tabs work when you're connected to an LDAP server, which may be the case if you work in a large Windows focused office. These tabs connect you to your corporate directory. For more details, see the box on page 292. The notes tab is a good place to put the odd detail that doesn't fit into the General form. "Mary likes mountain biking and salmon fishing. Not a Giants fan." (Sales people make their living remembering the odd details and then bringing them up in conversation.) The last tab is used for security certificates like the ones mentioned on page 279. These certificates are used to verify an individual's computer identities. If you and one of your contacts both have certificates, you're able to use Outlook to send encrypted messages back and forth—a favorite for spies and people involved in creating the next great consumer gadget.

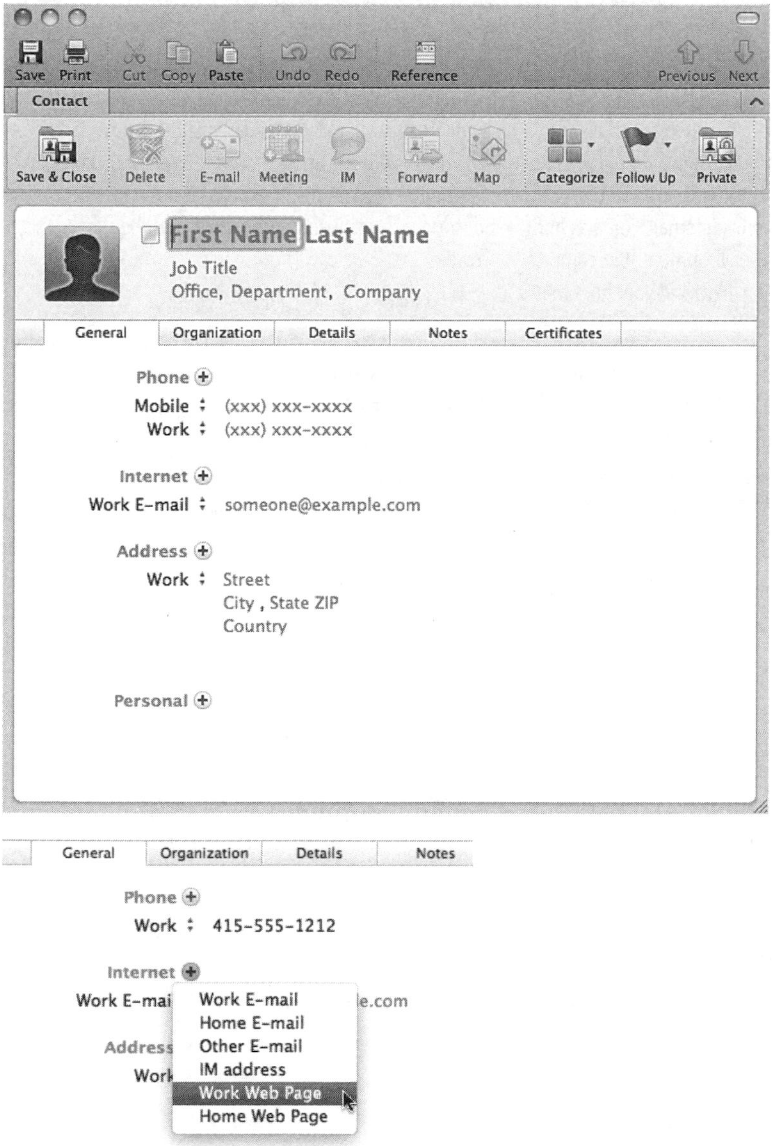

Figure 9-1:
Top: With lots of blanks and five tabs, the contact form may look like a lot of work, but you only have to fill in the details that are important to you.

Bottom: If you don't see the form labels you need, click the plus buttons to display additional options.

Working with Microsoft Exchange

If you work in a big Windows-centric office, you and your colleagues may be using Microsoft Exchange on the company network. Exchange is made up of software that runs on your company servers and client software like Outlook. The purpose of Exchange is to provide email, contacts and scheduling services in a secure environment. Big companies don't like outsiders spying on them and your boss may not want you poking around in her email either.

Undoubtedly, if your office is big enough to use Exchange, you've got one or more dedicated IT (information technology) people to set it up and assist you with your company practices and policies. Those same IT folks have probably read books like *Microsoft® Exchange Server 2010 Best Practices* by Siegfried Jagott and Joel Stidley (O'Reilly).

On your end, you can use Outlook as described throughout these chapters to work securely with your colleagues.

That will give you access to the company contacts directory, calendars and shared documents. Surely, those IT experts will set up your computer to work with your company's exchange server. At the most, you'll have to set up your individual account using these steps and the details they'll provide:

1. In Outlook, go to Tools→Accounts.
2. In the lower-left corner of the Accounts dialog box click the + button to add an account.
3. Choose Exchange from the menu to open the window shown in Figure 9-2.
4. Fill in the blanks with the details your company IT administrators provide. This will include: your assigned email address, the server's domain, and the Authentication method used by your company.

Figure 9-2:
In the event that you have to set up your own Exchange account, you can do that from Outlook by going to Tools→Accounts and then clicking the + Add Accounts button to open this dialog box. You'll still need to get the technical details about your company server from the powers that be.

Adding Email Senders to Your Contacts

It's often an email from a new acquaintance that spurs you on to create a contact card. Outlook makes it easy. When an email arrives, point to the contact name in the header of the email. A little menu pops up like the one shown in Figure 9-3. You're given several options, but there's no text so you may have to point at the icons to coax up tooltip explanations. The address card on the far right opens the contact form for the person. If you don't already have a contact form for that individual, Outlook helps you start one by opening a form and adding the name and email address. If the spirit moves you, you can cull a few more details from the email or a quick web search.

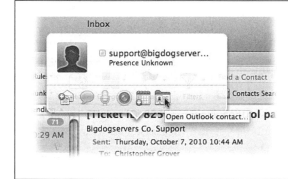

Figure 9-3:
Pause with your mouse over a contact name in an email and a menu displays several options via icon. From left to right they are: send email, send an instant message, start a voice conversation via Messenger or Communicator, start a video call, schedule a meeting and open Outlook contact.

Adding contact vCards

Another popular method for distributing contact details is the vCards. It's the email equivalent of paper-clipping a business card to a snail mail letter. If someone adds a vCard to an email, it appears as an attachment in the header. vCards always have a .vcf extension at the end of the file name. Click the preview button to check out the details. If you want to add the contact, right-click (Control-click) the attachment and choose Save As. You might want to save it to your desktop, because this is just a temporary stop before you suck that data into your Outlook address book. Then, to add the contact to Outlook, just drag the vCard file from your desktop onto Outlook's contact list.

You'll probably want to sync your Outlook contacts with your Mac's address book as described on page 295. That way all your contacts appear in both spots and you don't have to do updates twice. However, if you want to keep two separate lists of contacts where only a few individuals are on both lists, you can use the vCard format to shuffle a name or two back and forth. You can drag contacts directly from Outlook to your Mac Address Book and vice versa. If it's easier to use your desktop or some other folder as an interim location, that works, too. Dragging cards from either list doesn't delete the contact from the list: it makes a duplicate.

Tip: You can forward a vCard as an email to someone. Press ⌘-J or go to Contact→Forward as vCard, and Outlook creates an email with the vCard attached. All you have to do is choose a recipient and add a message.

Editing, Adding and Deleting Contacts

Unlike your pen and paper address book, you can make changes without ugly strike-outs in the midst of your contacts. Simply click on the contact to display the details in the reading pane and type over the addresses and phone numbers that need to be changed. And of course, you can add new fields to an address card any time by clicking on the + buttons in the form.

Occasionally you may try to add a new contact when you've already got that person's information stored in the list. Outlook is a little hit or miss at catching duplicates when you import or even when you create a new contact, so it's worth double-checking if you want to avoid duplicates.

To delete a contact, select it in the list and press Delete. You can also choose Home→Delete if you want to use Outlook's stylish wire wastepaper can.

Putting Contacts on the Map

Click the Home→Map button while you're viewing a contact and Outlook finds the location on a Bing map. If you're familiar with Google Earth or Yahoo Maps, you won't have any trouble using Microsoft's brand (shown in Figure 9-4). With Bing maps, you can toggle between street maps and actual aerial photographs. Depending on the location and your web browser, you may be able to see 3D views and street views.

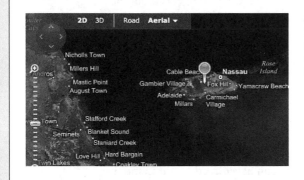

Figure 9-4:
With a click of a button (Home→Map), Outlook will show you a contact's location on a map. Using Microsoft's Bing maps, you can also get driving, or in the case shown here, boating directions.

Tip: You can also trigger the map an address feature by clicking the little globe next to addresses on your contact form.

Syncing Outlook Contacts with Your Mac Address Book

For most of us mere mortals, the promise of a computer means being able to get more done while doing less work. Choosing a Mac is a good step in that direction, but there are still times where it seems computers make us do more work rather than less. Keeping track of contacts in multiple programs and on home and office computers and handhelds is time consuming. One Outlook feature that helps cut through the confusion is the ability to sync your Mac address book and your Outlook address book. That means that if you create a contact in Outlook, it's automatically added to your Mac address book. You don't have to choose one over the other, and you don't have to do double the work to keep them in sync.

1. **Click Outlook→Preferences→Other→Sync Services.**

2. **Select Turn on Sync Services for contacts.**

3. **Under "Select the accounts to sync", choose On My Computer.**

4. **In the bottom menu choose On My Computer/Address Book.**

If you use an iPhone, Touch, iPad or the Mobile Me online service, you can synchronize your contacts and calendar with those devices and services, too. You use iTunes to sync your contacts and Calendars. In iTunes, select your device in the navigation pane on the left. Then, click the Info tab on the far right. You'll find separate settings for contacts, calendars and mail accounts.

Once your Outlook and Mac Address Books are synced, you can also sync those accounts with online accounts such as MobileMe and Gmail contacts. You can do that using your Mac Address Book preferences. In Address Book, go to Preferences→ Accounts and then use the checkboxes to synchronize the accounts that you have. You'll need to provide your account name and password. In the case of MobileMe, you have quite a few choices under the Sync tab for which services you want synced between your computer and your online services. For example, in addition to syncing contacts and calendars, you can choose dashboard widgets, keychains and dock items, as shown in Figure 9-5.

Importing Contacts

Outlook is very cooperative when it comes to working with your Mac's Address book. You can drag contacts directly from the Address Book list to Outlook and vice versa. Even better, as explained in the previous section, you can sync Outlook and Address Book on your computer. If you want to share contacts with other Mac using colleagues, the easiest way is to exchange data as vCards, as explained on page 293.

Figure 9-5:
If you use Apple's MobileMe online services, you can sync your contacts, calendars and many other features. The main advantage to MobileMe is that you can look up your contacts and calendars from any computer that has a web browser.

If you want to use contacts from other mail tools, the best option is to save the information in one of the universal data sharing formats called: comma separated values (CSV) or tab separated values (TSV). Any computer (Mac, Windows, or Linux) can read and write these type of files, so they're often used to exchange data across computers and programs that wouldn't normally speak with each other. The idea behind these file formats is that they have the same number of fields (name, address, phone number) for every record (contact), and they use either a comma or a tab character to signal the end of each field. You don't have to sweat the details, all you have to do is choose one format, like CSV, and use it to export the data from one program like Gmail's online mail program and then import it into Outlook.

As an example, here are the steps for exporting contacts from Gmail in the CSV format:

1. **Using your web browser, open your Gmail account.**

   The mail, contacts and tasks buttons are in the upper-left corner.

2. **Click the Contacts button.**

   Gmail displays the list of contacts you've stored in Gmail. Above the names there are a few drop-down menus that help you work with contacts.

3. **Use the "More actions" menu above your contact list and choose Export.**

   The Export contact box opens, displaying several options as shown in Figure 9-6.

Figure 9-6:
Gmail is set up to export your contact database in CSV (comma separated values) or as vCards. Use the Outlook CSV format when you want to send the data to Outlook. Use the vCard format when you want to bring the data into your Mac's Address Book.

4. **Choose the Outlook CSV format.**

   Gmail also offers the vCard format if you're exporting data to your Mac's Address Book.

5. **Click Export.**

   Outlook exports the data and it's downloaded on your computer, stashed in the directory where your browser usually stores downloaded files (usually your Downloads folder).

That's the first half of the process. You now have a data file stored on your computer in the CSV format. The next steps show how to import that data into Outlook.

1. **In Outlook, go to File→ Import.**

   The import dialog box opens showing a few options.

2. **Choose "Contacts or Messages from a text file". Then, in the lower-right corner, click the forward arrow.**

   Files stored in the CSV or TSV format are ordinary text files that can be read by most computers or programs. When you click the arrow, the dialog box shows the next step.

3. **Choose "Import contacts from a tab- or comma-delimited text file" and click the "next" arrow.**

   A window opens where you can navigate to the Download directory where your Gmail file is stored with the name *google.csv*. When you click the arrow, Outlook opens the data and shows you the Import Contacts window. There are two boxes in the window. The box on the left shows the field names that Outlook uses. The box on the right lists unmapped fields. Translation: these are fields from the incoming file that Outlook doesn't know what to do with, because Outlook doesn't use the same field names. If you don't help as explained in the next steps, Outlook will just ignore these fields.

4. **Compare the fields listed in the box on the left with the fields listed in the box on the right. If necessary, drag fields from the right to matching fields in the box on the left.**

   The sad truth is, these next steps can be a bit of work because Gmail and Outlook don't use exactly the same names for things like Work Email 1 and First Name. Outlook tries its best to map (match up) the incoming names with the names it uses. When it maps a field, you see the rectangular symbol and the matched names in the box on the left as shown in Figure 9-7. If it doesn't map the field, you need to do so manually as described in the next step.

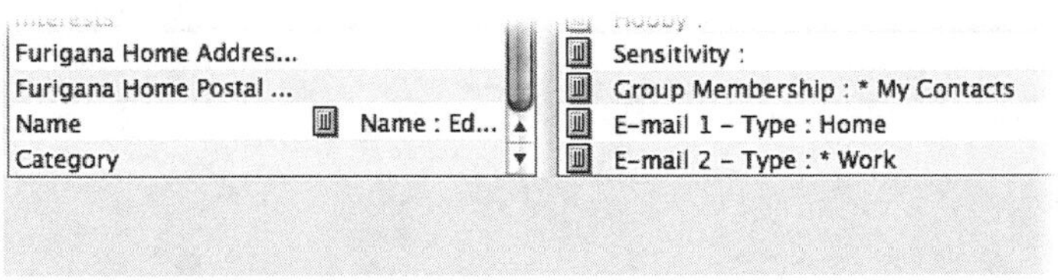

Figure 9-7:
In the box on the left side of the Import Contacts window, Outlook displays the little rectangle and field next to names it has mapped. If it makes a mapping mistake, you can drag the field to a new spot. If it doesn't map a field, you can do it manually.

5. **Drag unmapped fields from the box on the right to correct field name in the box on the left.**

   All the fields in the box on the right are not yet mapped and you may be surprised at the number of them. You don't have to manually map them all, just make sure you get the fields that are important to you. Outlook shows some data next to the field names in the box on the right. This helps you understand the type of data in the field. Use the Prev and Next buttons to see different contact records. This is helpful when you have a lot of records that don't have complete sets of addresses and numbers.

   You need to drop the fields onto the right side of the box. When you do it correctly, you see a blue highlight like the one in Figure 9-8. When you let go of the mouse button, you should see the rectangle and mapped name. The name disappears from the column on the right, because it's now a mapped field name.

6. **Click Import.**

   Outlook displays a box that asks if you'd like to save the settings. If you think you may import from Gmail again and you don't want to go through all that mapping names business, save the settings as Gmail CSV or some other memorable name. Then the next time you import a similar file, you can choose that name from the menu at the top of the Import Contacts box.

   Whichever option you choose, Outlook imports the data and shows you a dialog box to let you know the import was successful.

7. **Click Finish.**

   The process is complete and the Import windows close.

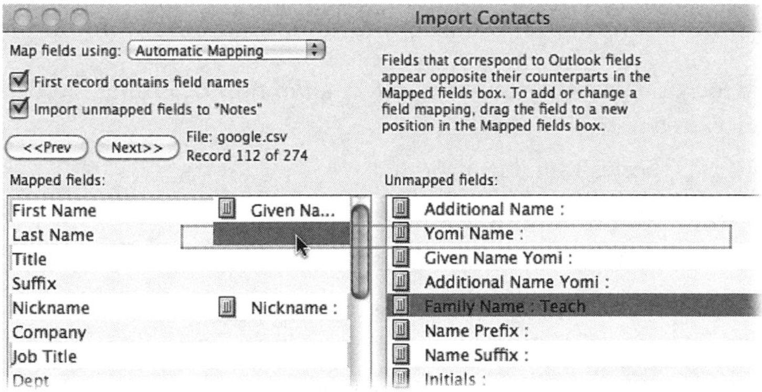

Figure 9-8:
Outlook has a field name called Last Name while Gmail calls the same name Family Name. It's up to you to map the two by dragging Family Name from the box on the right so that it's next to Last Name in the box on the left. When you're in the right spot, you'll see a blue highlight.

Importing Contacts and Other Data from Outlook for Windows

Office 2008 for Macintosh didn't have Outlook, it had a program called Entourage. Many Mac users complained that it made them feel like second-class citizens around the office, because it didn't have all the features that Windows users got with Outlook. One of the areas that got the most complaints had to do with Exchange services and the ability to import data saved in Outlook's PST file format. The Windows version of Outlook stores contacts, messages, calendars, and other data in one monster file known as the PST file. Folks that work on more than one computer sometimes export a copy of this file, and then import it to transfer data and keep a home and office computer in sync. Now that Outlook is part of Office for Mac, things are better and hopefully they'll continue to improve. Outlook can import data from several different sources including Outlook PST files.

On the Windows side, you can export Outlook PST files that hold contacts and other Outlook data. Then, you can import that PST file into Outlook on your Mac.

Note: There are still a few areas where Outlook doesn't provide everything that you'll find in the Windows version. For example, it's not as easy to set up a timed delivery for an email message. (As a workaround, you can make a special schedule [page 285] and a special folder for the job.) You also can't request a receipt when an email is delivered or read.

On the PC end you need to follow these steps:

1. **Open Outlook and go to File→Import and Export. A window opens that takes you through the export process.**

2. **In the "Choose an action to perform box", choose Export to a file. Click Next.**

3. **In the "Create a file of type" box, choose Personal Folder File (PST) and click Next.**

4. **In the "Select the folder to export from" box, choose the Contacts folder. Click Next.**

5. **Choose a location and file name and select an option regarding duplicates. Your choices are:**

    * Replace duplicates with item exported.

    * Allow duplicates to be created.

    * Do not export duplicate items.

Outlook creates a copy of the PST file that you can move to your Mac. On the Mac side, follow these steps:

1. **In Outlook, go to File→Import to open the Import box that walks you through the steps.**

2. **Choose Outlook Data File (.pst or .olm) and click the next button in the lower-right corner.**

3. **In the next window, choose Outlook for Windows Data File (.pst) and click next.**

4. **In the Finder window, select the PST file you exported from the PC.**

5. **Click the Import button and Outlook imports the data from the PST file.**

Tip: Sometimes when Outlook imports a Windows .pst, it suffers from indigestion. The symptoms include messages that Outlook has to restart and the disappearance of the main Outlook window. The cure? Take an antacid and follow the steps for creating a new identity on page 338. But instead of deleting or creating an identity, click the Rebuild button in the lower-right corner.

Creating Contact Groups

Often, you'll want to send one email to a bunch of people. Perhaps you're sending out an invitation to a family reunion or you're writing to everyone on the Rugby team. If you work in a big office, it's likely that you tackle big projects as a team and you want to keep everyone up-to-date on the developments. Email makes it downright easy to send messages to groups of people. You create contact groups by naming a group and then adding the contacts that are already in your contact list. The individuals in your contact list can belong to more than one group. If you delete a group, you're not removing those people from the main contact list.

To create a group, press ⌘-3 to switch to the Contacts view. Then, on the ribbon, click Home | Contact Group. An untitled Group Box appears like the one shown in Figure 9-9. Give your group a name at the top. Then double-click under the name field. Start to type in the name of a contact and Outlook searches through your contacts and offers suggestions. Click on a name and it's added to the list. You can also add names to a list by dragging them from your contact list to the group in the reading pane.

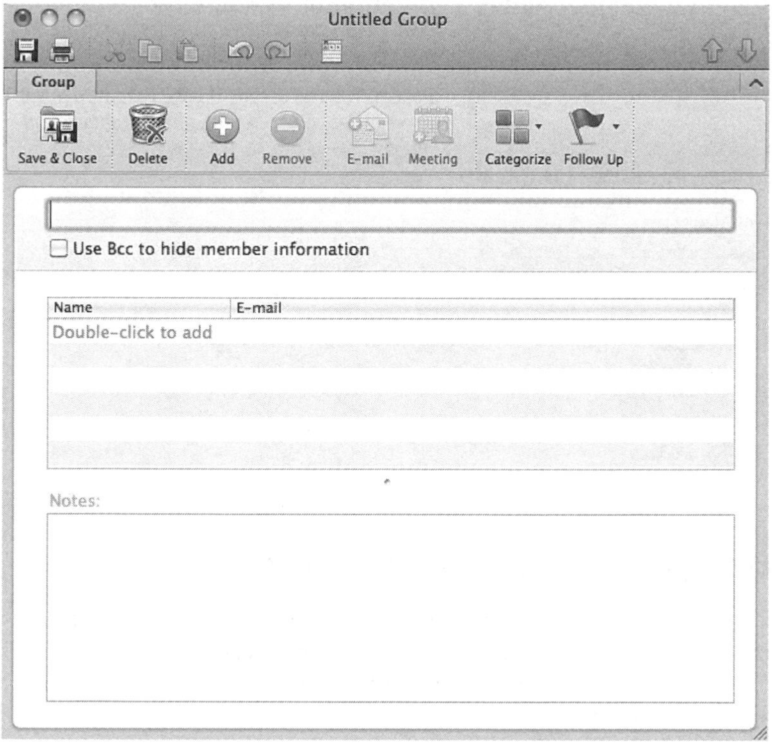

Figure 9-9:
Create a group of contacts to make it easier to send emails to everyone and schedule meetings. Creating a group entails giving the group a name and then adding contacts.

You can keep on adding names. Group lists can be quite big if you're creating something like a newsletter mailing list, or they can be small if it's for a small committee or group of friends that gather on Friday for lunch. If it helps, you can add notes to describe the group in the box at the bottom. Sometimes you won't want to broadcast the names and email addresses in a group to the other members. This is common if you're writing to a bunch of customers or sending a newsletter far and wide. If you want to keep identities of the group private, click the box labeled "Use Bcc to hide member information". Then, when you email the group, their names are hidden in the "blind carbon copy" field as explained on page 268. In these cases, you normally address the email to yourself.

You can do most of the things that you'd do with individual contacts with a group. For example, you can use the Categorize menu to apply a category to the group. You can flag the group for Follow Ups as covered on page 282. When it's time to send an email, open a new email form and then type the name of your group in the To field as shown in Figure 9-10. Before you're done, Outlook will suggest the group name. One click and you've addressed your email to the entire group.

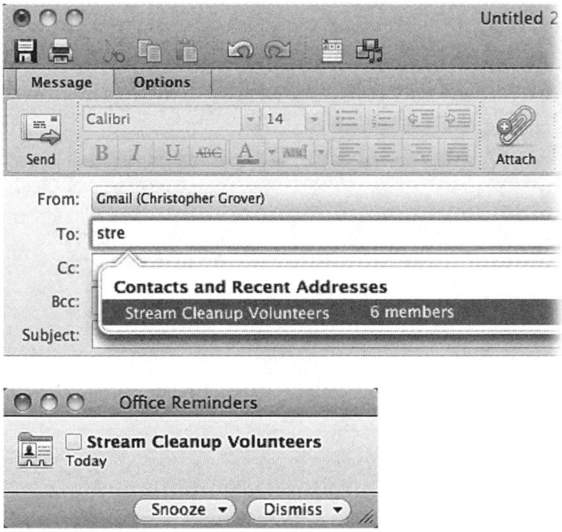

Figure 9-10:
Top: To send an email to everyone in a group, just put the group name in the To field. Use the Bcc field if you want to hide the names and email addresses of the people in the group.

Bottom: You can use the Home | Follow Up menu to create reminders like this one for contacts and groups.

Organizing and Searching for Contacts

The tools you use to organize your contacts and groups are similar to the ones you use to manage your emails. For example, you can categorize contacts using the Home | Categorize menu. A label appears in the header of the contact and it adopts the category color in the list.

If a contact needs your attention, but you don't have time to deal with it at the moment, you can flag the contact for follow-up. With the contact selected, go to Home→Follow Up and choose one of the options like tomorrow or next week. If you want to follow up later in the day, use the Custom option to set the time. For a quick way to check up on flagged contacts, use the smart folder in the navigation pane that's called Flagged Contacts. A second smart folder holds Updated Contacts.

You can search for specific contacts in a couple of ways. For a quick search, press ⌘-3 to switch to Contacts view, then use the search box in the upper-right corner (see Figure 9-11). Like the other search tools, the contact search examines each letter you type and immediately shows matching names next to the search box. The contact list is filtered to display matching contacts. A special Search tab appears in the ribbon with additional search tools and filters. For example, you can limit the search to contacts that have addresses or phone numbers. You can search for contacts flagged for follow-up or you can specify a time period when the contact was modified. If you want to search for text in a specific field, click the Advanced button. A new box appears above your contacts where you can choose a field and enter the text you're looking for. The name, email and company buttons automatically open this box with the search field already selected.

Figure 9-11:
Top: Type a few letters in the search field in the upper-right corner of the contact view, and Outlook starts to suggest contact names and automatically filters the list to display matching contacts.

Bottom: When you start a search, this search tab appears to help you fine-tune the hunt.

Printing Contacts

Sometimes you may want to print your contacts list. Perhaps you're going on a trip without your trusty laptop. With Outlook, you can choose the contact fields sent to the printer. Maybe all you need are names, email addresses, and phone numbers. If you don't want to print your entire contact list, you can do one of two things. Before you go to Home | Print select the contacts you want to print or flag (Home | Follow Up) the contacts.

1. **Press ⌘-3 to switch to the Contacts view.**

   The Print window opens as shown in Figure 9-12. The thumbnail in the upper-left corner gives you a preview of a page with contacts printed.

2. **At the top, choose the your printer and presets and make sure the menu is set to Outlook.**

   See page 141 for details.

3. **Use the Print box to choose the contacts you want to print.**

   Your choices are Selected Contacts, All Contacts or Flagged Contacts.

4. **Use the Style menu to choose the page layout.**

   Your choices are Phone List or Address Book.

5. **Choose the name format (Last First, or First Last) and choose whether you want to sort by name or company.**

   A drop down menu shows you the options.

6. **Use the checkboxes to pick the fields you want included in the printout.**

   Often it's a paper saver to turn off pictures and notes.

7. **Choose your page options.**

   If you're printing a long list for a permanent directory, you may want to have page breaks between letters. It's often helpful to print the date on a page so later you know how up-to-date your list is.

8. **Click Print to send contacts to the printer, or click the PDF button to print to an Acrobat document.**

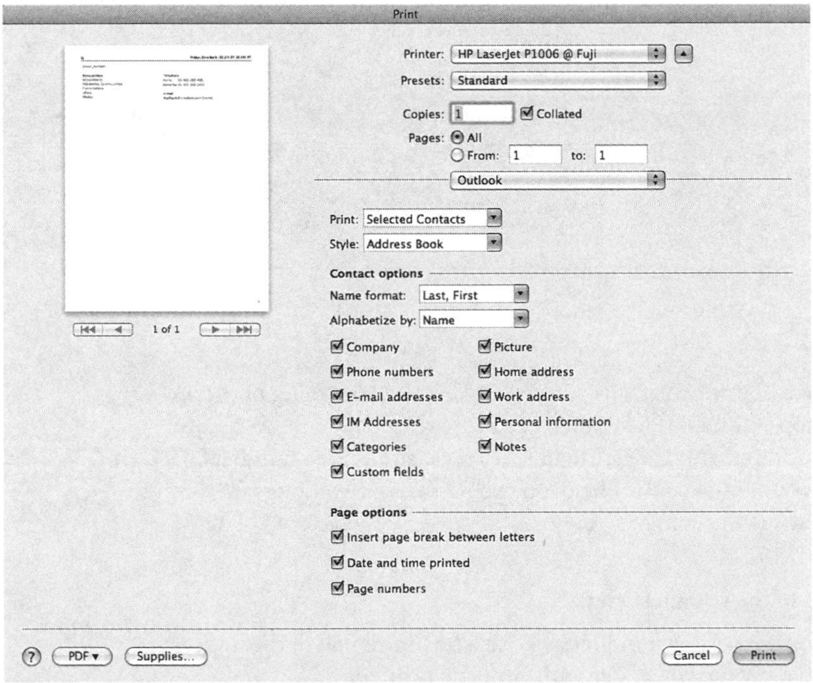

Figure 9-12:
Go to the Contacts view and then go to File→Print to open this window where you can choose how to print your contact list. You can choose which contacts and which fields you print.

Calendar: Meetings, Tasks, and Notes

L ife gets complicated. You probably have a ridiculous number of responsibilities each with their own appointments, meetings, and assignments. As you work through your daily to-do list, does that list get smaller? Not necessarily, because in all likelihood, you're adding new appointments, meetings, and tasks at the same time you're striking old ones off the list. Outlook understands and helps you in one very important way. If you put all those responsibilities in one place, at the very least you'll know where to find them. At best, it'll help you prioritize and organize those responsibilities in a way that helps you avoid conflicts.

This chapter begins with the calendar, showing you how to add appointments and coordinate meetings. Master some quick and easy techniques, and you'll go a long way towards efficient time management and meeting planning. Two other Outlook tools—Tasks and Notes—help you keep tabs on the details of a busy life. By spending a few moments listing tasks as they come up, you can make sure nothing slips through the cracks and that high priority jobs get done first. Outlook notes are perfect for capturing those great ideas that you'd otherwise forget and lose.

Creating Appointments and Meetings

To see your Outlook calendar, press ⌘-2 or choose View→Go to→Calendar. In Calendar view, the navigation pane on the right shows a mini-calendar that you use to select dates. Use the buttons on either side of the current month name to move back and forth through the calendar. To select a day, just click the date in the mini-calendar. The larger calendar in the reading pane changes its view based on your choices in the navigation pane and it displays headers for the appointments, meetings, and holidays that are marked on your calendar. You can change the calendar to view a single day, a work week, a complete week or a complete month. Use the ribbon commands like Home | Day or Home | Month as shown in Figure 10-1. Each view has its own shortcut key, so if you jump between views a lot, it's helpful to memorize your favorites:

- **Day** (Control-⌘-1). The reading pane displays your day as a scrolling list of events (Figure 10-2). The work day portion is shaded differently from the rest, as if work never spills into your private time.

- **Work Week** (Control-⌘-2). The work week view shows you Monday through Friday, without those pesky weekends that impeded our work efficiency. Each day is a column so you can size up just how hectic that week is likely to be.

- **Week** (Control-⌘-3). This displays every day of the week but the columns get a little narrower to squeeze in those extra weekend days.

- **Month** (Control-⌘-4). Shows your schedule in a calendar grid like the one your insurance agent sends you each year (Figure 10-3).

Tip: Outlook starts out displaying 9 to 5 bankers' hours as your work week, but you don't have to settle for that. Go to Outlook→Preferences, and click Calendar to set the time your work day starts and stops. While you're in Preferences, you can also choose the days you work and the first day of your week.

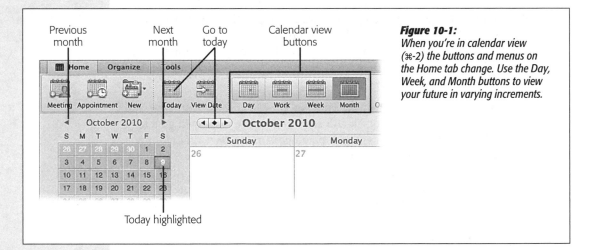

Figure 10-1:
When you're in calendar view (⌘-2) the buttons and menus on the Home tab change. Use the Day, Week, and Month buttons to view your future in varying increments.

Just like the paper calendar you keep tacked on a cupboard door in your kitchen, your Outlook calendar shows holidays and keeps a record of any notes you add.

There are a few extra advantages with your computer calendar. For one thing, there's room for everything. If you have meetings, you can keep records of everyone who's coming and who declined to come (page 311). If you want to add a really long note to particular appointment, you won't run out of room. Outlook does its best to show you the details of particular dates using categories and colors. When you need more detail, it's just a click away to drill down. There are two types of events you can add to the calendar:

- **Appointments** are things like a dentist appointment or taking your car in for repairs. You need to remember the time, date and location.

- **Meetings** involve other people. If you're scheduling a meeting, you need to invite others and keep track of who's going to show up.

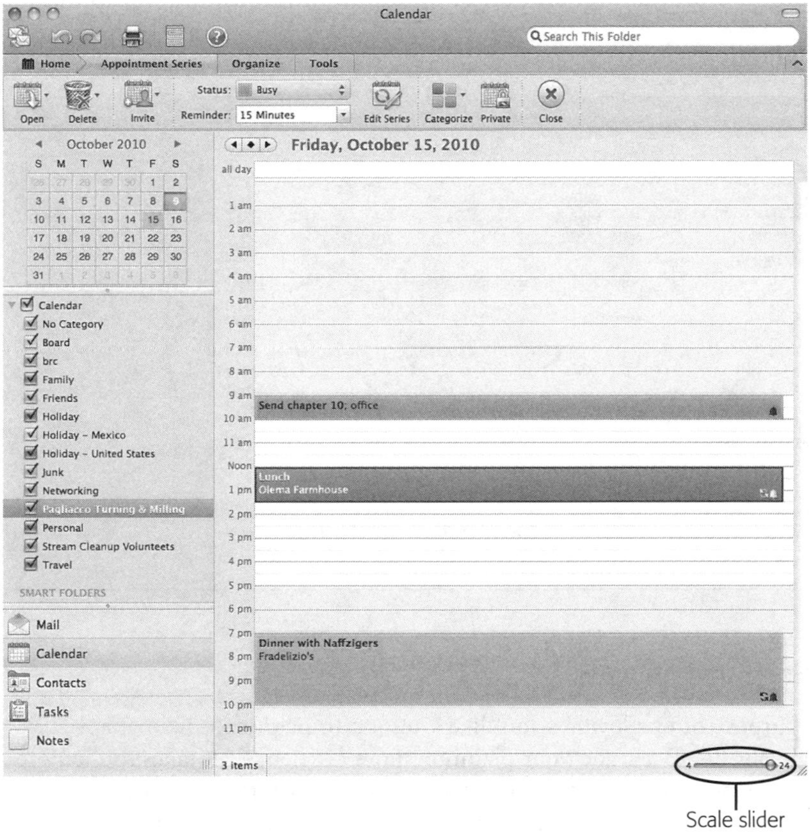

Figure 10-2:
The Day view (Control-⌘-1) shows you your day in a single column. Events are displayed as blocks color-coded according to the categories you assign. You can use the scale slider (circled) to zoom in and out, displaying fewer or more hours of the day

Figure 10-3:
Top: In month view, Outlook shows a snippet of the subject for your meetings and appointments. If you want to see more detail, double-click the item.

Bottom: You can also choose Calendar→ List to display only your appointments and hide the un-scheduled days and hours.

Adding Appointments

The purpose of employing a tool like Outlook to help with life management is to make your life easier and your planning more efficient. If it takes too long to add appointments, tasks, and meetings, you probably won't do it. You want to save time, not waste it. Learning a few Outlook techniques at the outset can save lots of time over the long haul. For example, if you preselect a date or time before you create a new appointment or meeting Outlook enters the details for you. Otherwise, it's up to you set things up manually using the little date and time widgets.

Here are the speedster steps for adding an appointment:

1. **In Outlook, press ⌘-2 for Calendar view.**

   Outlook usually displays the view you most recently used.

2. **In the navigation pane, click on a date on the mini-calendar.**

   If you're creating an all-day event, you don't need to do anything else to zero in on a time period. Just press ⌘-N and create your appointment using the form, as described on page 310.

3. **Using shortcut keys or the View menu, choose a view for the reading pane calendar.**

   The Day view (Control-⌘-1) or one of the Week views (Control-⌘-2) are best for setting up appointments with specific start and stop times. The Month view (Control-⌘-4) is fine for all-day events.

4. **In the reading pane, on the day for your appointment, click and drag to set the start and end time.**

   Outlook shows a color highlight as you drag as shown in Figure 10-4. When you release the mouse button, Outlook names your event New Appointment but it's already selected so you can change it to something better.

5. **Type in the subject for your event.**

   For many events, if you put enough info in the subject, you won't need to spend time adding more details.

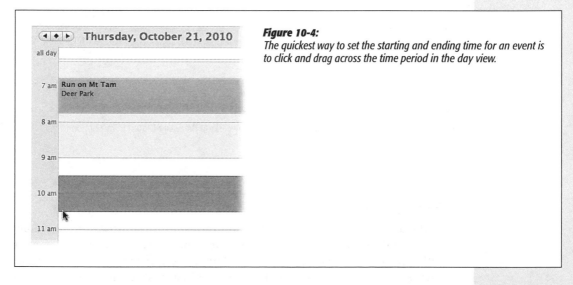

Figure 10-4:
The quickest way to set the starting and ending time for an event is to click and drag across the time period in the day view.

Of course, you can add more to your appointments as explained in the next section, but often all you need is a reminder and you want to block out the time to avoid conflicts.

Editing and Deleting Appointments

Our "best laid schemes" oft go kablooey, to misquote the poet Robert Burns. If you're using Outlook to lay those schemes, you'll know right where to go to make adjustments. To make changes to an appointment that you've already created, just double-click on the item in your calendar. The appointment opens in its own window with the subject at the top. As Figure 10-5 shows, there are text boxes where you can edit the subject and location for the meeting. Use the Starts and Ends time widgets to make adjustments. If you click All Day Event, the time widgets are disabled. The duration changes based on the Starts and Ends settings, but you can use it like a menu to choose time periods from five minutes to two weeks.

To delete an appointment, select it in any of the reading pane views and press Delete. If you prefer you can use the other usual suspects of deletion: Home | Delete, Edit→Delete, or right-click (Control-click)→Delete.

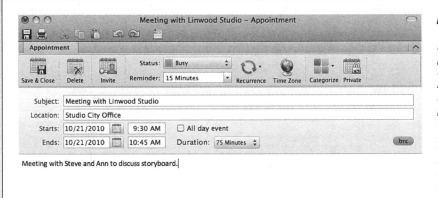

Figure 10-5:
You see this window if you start an appointment using the File→New→ Appointment command (⌘-N). It also pops up if you double-click an appointment for editing. You can add extensive notes to your appointments and change any of the details that Outlook stores.

Tip: You can turn any appointment into a meeting by clicking the Invite button in the Appointment window's ribbon.

Creating Recurring Appointments

It's not unusual to have appointments that occur on a regular basis. Maybe you belong to a birdwatcher's club that meets for lunch on the second Thursday of every month. The Recurrence menu is on the ribbon in the appointment form, as shown in Figure 10-6. You can set recurrence when you first create an appointment or you can go back and add it later. The menu gives you several options, but if you don't see the one you need, click Custom. An extremely flexible dialog box opens; with it, you can set recurring appointments for events like the second Tuesday of every month or the last Friday of the month, every other month.

After you click OK, Outlook inserts the recurring appointments in your calendar. If you need to make changes, just right-click on the event. The shortcut menu gives you the option to change a single occurrence or edit the series.

Figure 10-6:
Outlook's tools to create recurring appointments and meetings are extremely flexible. You can choose an option from this menu, or click Custom to handle special cases.

Adding Meetings

In many ways Outlook meetings work just like appointments. The main difference is that with meetings, you've got the tools to email attendees and keep track of who's coming. If you've ever been responsible for setting up committee or Board of Director's meetings, you'll love the way Outlook manages the details.

Case example: you're the Executive Director of an association of 16 restaurant owners. The group meets once a quarter, but the actual date moves around a bit to accommodate members' schedules. In the interest of unity, you try to accommodate all your members. You send a meeting invitation to all 16 members. Eight confirm that they can attend. You don't hear anything from three. Two members have gotten together and suggested an alternative date for the meeting, otherwise they can't attend. One person who said she could make the meeting sends another email changing their confirmation to a "maybe I can attend." You move on to round two, with the new suggestion, which involves just as many details and messages.

Outlook helps you coordinate events whether there are 16 attendees or 250. It gives you an easy way to send the same details to everyone and keep track of their responses. In some cases, you may have attendees who absolutely must be there or it's not worth holding the meeting. If you have to change the date or time for the meeting, you can change the date, but keep all the other details intact. It all starts with creating a list of invitees from your contacts.

There are several ways to add a meeting to your calendar. First, press ⌘-2 to change to the Calendar view, then:

- On the ribbon, go to Home | Meeting.
- On the menu, choose File→New→Appointment.
- With shortcut keys, press ⌘-N.
- Create an appointment. Double-click the appointment to open the form and then click Invite.

You'll notice a couple of differences in the Meeting form, which takes on the appearance of an email with your name in the From field. However, you fill in the blanks on your meeting form just as you do with appointments. You still have a subject and location fields. You set the Starts and Ends time in the same manner. The biggest difference is when you click the Scheduling Assistant tab at the bottom of the form. As shown in Figure 10-7, that's where you add names of the people you're inviting, creating a list that you can go back to time and again as the invitees respond, change their minds, and finally confirm. Add a name in the Scheduling Assistant, and their email address is automatically added to the To field.

Here are the scheduling chores you can manage with the help of the scheduling assistant:

- **To add an Attendee** to your meeting, click Add New and start typing a name. Immediately Outlook starts suggesting names from your contacts. Click a name, and the person is added to your list and their email address is added to the To field at the top of the form.

- **To delete an attendee,** click the button to the left of their name and choose Remove, the option at the bottom of the list. His name is removed from the list and his email address is removed from the To field.

- **To set an attendee's status,** click the button to the left of their name and choose Required, Optional, or Resource. Truth is, some people play a more vital role than others when it comes to meetings. If an individual's attendance is vital, set her status to Required. If they can't make it, you'll know it's time to reschedule. If someone is providing the room, the projector, or cupcakes, you can mark her as a resource. If she cancels, you'll have to find your cupcakes elsewhere.

- **To track attendee responses** click the button to the right of the name. The available options are No Response, Accepted, Tentative, and Declined.

Once you've added the names of the Attendees and set the time and place, you may want to add a message to your meeting invitation. It always helps if you let people know what's expected. You may want to prime the pump with a few questions or ask them to bring ideas. If you're going to be deciding major questions, let them know. "We intend to vote on the 3-year strategic plan." Perhaps you need to give them driving directions. In any case, click the message and type a message to go along with the invitation.

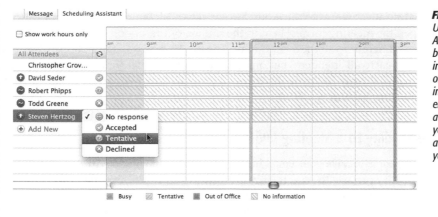

Figure 10-7:
Use the Schedule Assistant found at the bottom of the Meeting form to keep track of the people you've invited. Buttons on either side of the attendee's name help you set their status and their response to your invitation.

When you're happy with everything, click the Send button in the upper-left corner. Your invitation speeds on its way to all the people listed in the To field.

Tip: You can change the Starts and Stops time within the Schedule Assistant tab. Simply drag the green Starts bar or the red Ends bar to a new spot.

Sending Updates and Canceling Meetings

When things change, as they often do, Outlook is there to help. After you've sent your initial invitation, you close the meeting form and go on about your business. As you collect responses, you may want to adjust the time, add an attendee, or tweak the meeting in a variety of ways. Just go to Calendar view and double-click the meeting to open the form and make your changes. Then when you're done, click the Send Update button. Outlook sends the changes to everyone on the Attendee list, keeping everyone in sync. Likewise, if you click Cancel, a message goes out to everyone. Outlook automatically names all the messages so meeting attendees can identify them. For example, if the subject for the original meeting is "P&L Meeting," then the subject for a change is "Update: P&L Meeting."

It's worth noting that Outlook is a little dictatorial about the way you manage your meetings. If you make changes to the form, you must send an update to everyone if you want to save those changes. There are no Save options when you're editing a meeting. The icons and commands are grayed out. If you click the Close button on the meeting form, Outlook gives you three choices: Discard Changes, Continue Editing, and Send Update.

As your meeting approaches, you may want to send additional items to the group—an advance agenda, reports, budgets, or other plans. The easiest way to send an email including attachments to the group is to double-click the meeting on your calendar to open the meeting form. Then, in the middle of the ribbon, click the email icon. (This is different from the Send Update icon on the far left of the ribbon.) The "Send a new email to all attendees" button opens a standard email window with the attendees' names already in the To field. You can use whatever subject you want, and you can add attachments.

Responding to a Meeting Invitation

When people receive your email invitation, it looks like Figure 10-8, complete with menus they can use to send their responses. If an attendee uses Outlook, the meeting is automatically added to her calendar when she receives the email. This happens courtesy of an attachment that travels along with the email that's in the iCalendar format. For more details, see the box on page 315. In the attendee's calendar, the meeting appears with its name, location, and the email address of the person who sent the invitation. Attendees can open the meeting to see the specifics, including the names of the other attendees. If one of the attendees needs to change their status, say from Accept to Tentative, he can always do so by selecting the meeting in his calendar. That opens a special purple Meeting tab in the ribbon. Then, using the Accept, Tentative, and Decline buttons, he can change his status. Outlook automatically creates and sends emails to the meeting organizer. If they're using Outlook, attendees also have the ability to email the other people invited to the meeting via the Meeting | Reply All button.

Note: If you and your meeting colleagues work in an office that uses Microsoft Exchange, you'll find even more automated features when you schedule meetings in Outlook. For example, the Attendee status is automatically updated for the meeting planner without having to search for email replies. Also, if you have shared calendars, the meeting planner may be able to check on attendees availability prior to choosing a date.

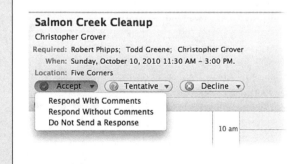

Figure 10-8:
When you or others respond to a meeting invitation sent via Outlook, you can choose Accept, Tentative, or Decline. You may also opt to add a comment with any of these options. Outlook automatically sends the response unless you specifically choose "Do Not Send a Response".

The iCalendar Format for Date Exchange

Outlook is certainly not the only application that handles meetings and appointments. The people you're trying to coordinate may be using some program you've never heard of. It was clear relatively early on in the information age that there would be a benefit to all of us if our calendars shared a common language. A few smart folks got together and agreed on a standard that's used by programs such as Microsoft Outlook, Google Calendar, Lotus Notes, and Apple's iCal program. (Yes, the iCal program on your Mac is compatible with the iCalendar file format, but they're actually two different things.)

Thanks to the adoption of the iCalendar standard, you can email all or part of your calendar to colleagues and they can import those details into their own calendar. That's exactly what's going on when invitations are sent and accepted with Outlook. Look at the attachments to an invitation and you see a file with an .ics extent, that identifies it as a file in the iCalendar format.

Adding Holidays to Your Calendar

When you first install Outlook, it may not display the holidays that you need to keep track of. Perhaps you work in the United States, but spend most of your vacations in Mexico, or maybe your business takes you China on a regular basis. Whatever your needs, Outlook can place big red labels on the holidays you celebrate or dread, as the case may be.

To add a new set of holidays to Outlook, follow these steps when you're in the Calendar view (⌘-2):

1. **Go to File→Import.**

   The Import window opens with buttons in the lower-right corner to move through the steps of the process (see Figure 10-9).

Figure 10-9:
You can display holidays on your calendar from a long list of countries. Once imported, holidays are individual all-day events that you can move, edit, or delete.

2. **Choose Holidays, and click the Next button.**

   When you click Next, Outlook builds a list of holidays for different countries. At most, this takes a few seconds.

3. **Scroll through the list and choose the holidays you want to show on your calendar.**

   Put checkmarks next to the countries you want to add. You can add more than one country's holidays.

4. **Click Next.**

   Outlook adds the holidays to your calendar as individual all-day events and creates a category for the holidays, such as Holiday – Mexico or Holiday – Finland. You can apply the category as you would any other to contacts, emails, and events.

   Outlook notifies you that the holidays were added successfully.

5. **Click OK to close the success notice and click Finish to close the Import window.**

Removing Holidays

Removing holidays from the calendar is a little trickier than adding them because each holiday is added as an independent all-day event. You can move, rename, re-categorize and delete each holiday individually. But if Finnish holidays are no longer of interest to you, you probably don't want to go through your calendar and remove them one by one. Mass removal is a job for advanced search techniques.

1. **In the upper-right corner of the Calendar view, click in the Search box.**

   A special purple tab called Search appears in the ribbon.

2. **Click the Advanced button.**

   A new menu and text box appears between the ribbon and the calendar. You can use the menu to choose search topics and type criteria in the text box.

3. **Choose Category from the menu.**

   The advanced search bar changes, giving you two menus to work within a category search.

4. **Leave the second menu set to Is.**

   You're building a statement. So far you've got "The category is…". Other options with this menu are: Is Not, Exists, and Does Not Exist.

5. In the third menu, choose your holiday's category: Holiday – Mexico or Holiday –Finland.

   The chosen holidays appear in the reading pane as shown in Figure 10-10.

6. **Click one of the holidays in the reading pane, then press ⌘-A to select them all.**

   You can also use the Edit→Select All menu command.

7. **Press Delete.**

   A message appears to make sure you want to permanently delete all these events at once.

8. **Click Delete.**

   The holidays are removed from the calendar.

After you've removed holidays from your calendar (you Grinch, you!), you may also want to remove the holiday category. If you're in the Calendar view, you can do that by going to Meeting | Categorize→Edit Categories. Then, in the Categories window, choose the categories you want to delete. In the lower-left corner, click the – button to remove the categories.

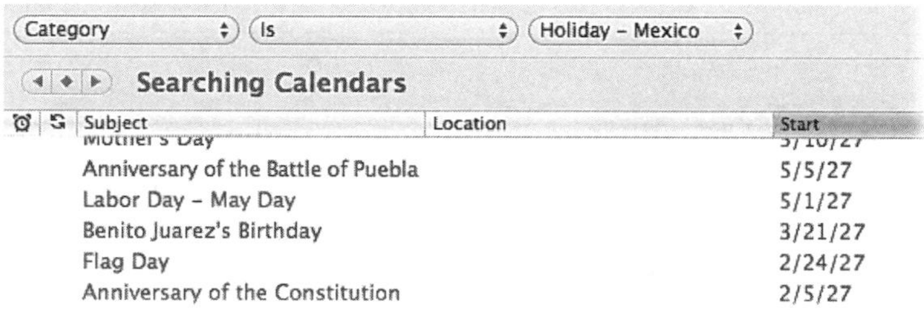

Figure 10-10:
To remove all the holidays for a particular country from your calendar, use Outlook's advanced search tools.

Filtering the Displayed Events

If you've got a busy schedule, it may be hard to zero in on specific events. Using Outlook's categories, you can filter out some events, making it easier to find others. Under the mini calendar in the upper-left corner of the Calendar view (⌘-2), there's a collapsible list of categories. Check the categories that you want displayed on the calendar, as shown in Figure 10-11. There are more details on using categories and filters in Chapter 11.

Figure 10-11:
Use the category checkboxes to filter the events displayed in your calendar. These filters also come in handy when you want to print calendars with some, but not all of your events.

Printing Calendars

There are lots of reasons why you might want to print your calendars. Maybe you want to print out a year's worth of meeting dates for a committee you chair. Maybe you want a hard copy of this month's events to stick on your refrigerator. With Outlook, you can print any of the calendar views—Day, Week, Work Week, and Month—and you can print any range of dates. You can print hard copies from your printer or you can print PDF copies of calendars.

If you've printed Word documents or a contact list from Outlook, the procedure won't come as much of a surprise. In Outlook, start off by going to File→Print to open the Print window (Figure 10-12), where you see a decent sized preview in the upper-left corner. The standard Printer, Presets, Copies, and Pages settings appear at the top. For a refresher on those details, see page 143. With the subpanel menu (in the middle) set to Outlook, there are a number of settings you can use to design your calendar print job. For example, you can choose to print all events or just selected events. So, if you're printing a meeting schedule for the Board of Directors, you can deselect the golf and fishing dates in your calendar using the Categories as explained on page 330.

No matter which Day, Week, or Month view you were in when you hit the File→Print command, you can choose any of the view options from the print window. You can also specify the range of days you want to print with the Start date and End date menus. Under task options you can choose to include or exclude specific tasks based on their status. For more on tasks, see the next section in this chapter.

If you want to print a hard copy, hit the Print button on the right. If you're creating PDF files, use the PDF menu on the left.

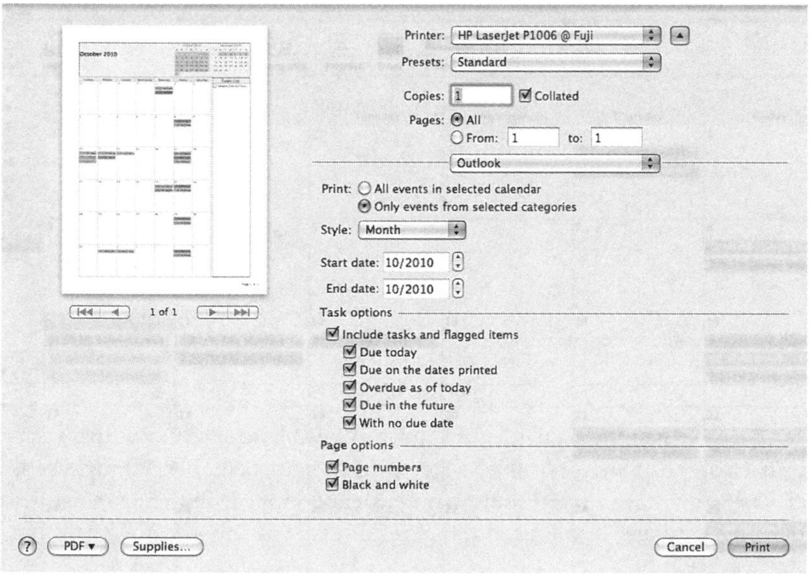

Figure 10-12:
This Print window gives you lots of control over how you print calendars. Make sure the subpanel menu, in the middle, is set to Outlook and you can choose views, a range of dates and other details.

Be Your Own Task Master

Tasks! The very word is enough to send a chill down the spine. Something must be done and you're the one to do it. If you've got so much to do that you sometimes let something slip through the cracks, it may be time to track those tasks with Outlook. If you invest a few moments providing details about a task, Outlook will pay you back by providing reminders and helping you choose which is the most important task to tackle at the moment.

You manage your many tasks in the Tasks view (⌘-4) and once you're there, press ⌘-N to add a new task to the list. An untitled Task window appears like the one in Figure 10-13, where you can provide the details including the due date, start date, priority, and how you wanted to be reminded.

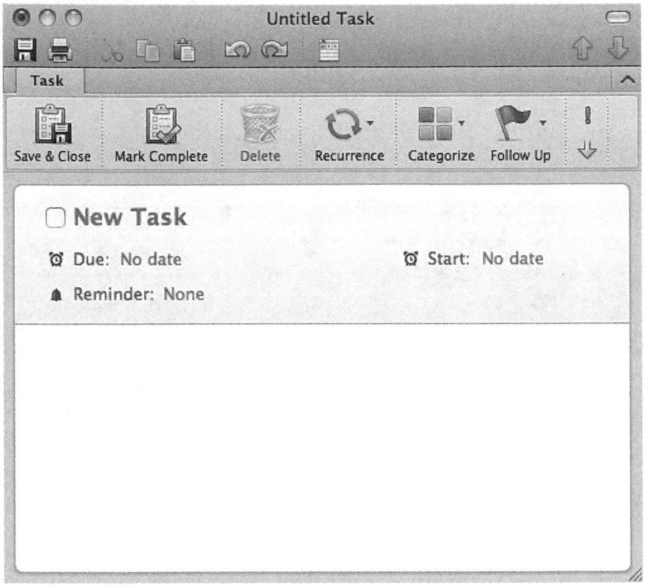

Figure 10-13:
Give your task a name and use any of the other tools you need to set a due date, a category and a reminder. In many cases, just having all your tasks in a list is enough to keep things from slipping through the cracks.

You have to give your task a name, or you won't be able to save it. But that's the only thing that you absolutely, positively have to give your task. Everything else is optional. Tasks that have a name, but no other details, appear in the tasks list with no due date, but perhaps all you need is that reminder. The other features you can add to your task are:

- **Due Date**. If your task has a deadline, you might as well fill in this blank and set the reminder to send you a message.

- **Start Date**. For many tasks, the Start date isn't as important as the Due date.

- **Reminder**. Choose the exact moment that Outlook should remind you about this chore.

- **Category**. Use the same categories that you've created for emails, contacts, and events to categorize your tasks.

- **Follow Up Flag**. Use follow up flags to help you procrastinate until the last possible moment.

- **Priority Flag**. All tasks were not created equal. Use a high or low priority flag to distinguish between them.

Tip: You can create new tasks from any of Outlook's views—just go to File→New→Task.

When the moment arrives, Outlook flashes a reminder on your computer screen like the one in Figure 10-14. Outlook doesn't have to be running to send you your reminder. If there are a few reminders pending, they'll all be listed in the box. You can customize your reminder options. For example, you can turn off the sound reminder, but keep the message. Go to Outlook→Preferences→Personal Settings→Notifications and Sounds. Then, under Sounds, deselect Reminder.

Figure 10-14:
If you set a specific time for a reminder, Outlook plays a tone and flashes a message like this on your screen. You can choose to dismiss the reminder, or choose one of the Snooze options, which range from five minutes to two weeks.

Nothing lasts forever, and fortunately that's true of the tasks on your list. When you're ready to remove a task from your to-do list, go to Tasks view (⌘-4) and then choose Mark Completed.

Taking Note

The oft-ignored Notes can store any random thought and odd thing that you want to copy and paste or write down. You can categorize your notes, using the same menu you use for emails, contacts, and events. This means you can associate notes with particular subjects and filter the view (as described on page 330) to choose which notes are visible. Notes are good for storing random thoughts and tidbits you don't want to lose, like these:

- The driving directions to an event you've added to your calendar.

- A record of a follow-up phone call you had with a contact to an email message.

- Ideas for the novel you're planning on writing.

- Keeping track of clever quotes or word definitions that you may want to use in the future.

- Creating miscellaneous notes you might otherwise write on a piece of paper, for example, a birthday gift idea that pops into your head, a scrap of info you discover while Web browsing, a packing list for taking your presentation on the road, or the name of a new song you hear on the radio.

Creating Notes

To create notes, switch to Notes view: ⌘-5 or View→Go to→Notes. Then, press ⌘-N and the minimalist Note form appears as shown in Figure 10-15. If you want to drop a picture into your note, use the Home | Picture menu on the ribbon. You can choose to open the photo tab of the media browser, or you can use the Picture From File option to browse through your folders. Once a picture is in a note, you can drag it to a different position in relation to the text. You can also import images or capture screenshots as explained on page 274. Just right-click (Control-click) on an empty spot in your message and choose one of the options at the bottom of the shortcut menu. Make sure you don't have any text selected or you'll see a different menu.

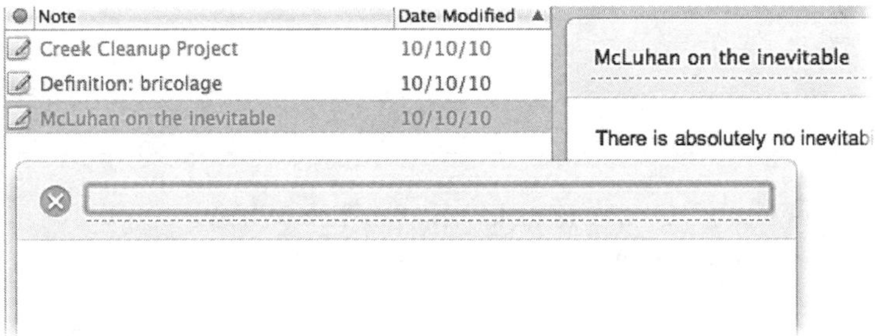

●	Note	Date Modified ▲
📝	Creek Cleanup Project	10/10/10
📝	Definition: bricolage	10/10/10
📝	McLuhan on the inevitable	10/10/10

McLuhan on the inevitable

There is absolutely no inevitab

Figure 10-15:
Not a lot of widgets here; all that's expected is a title and the content of your note. Notes can include pictures and they can be as short or long as needed to do the job.

You can't attach the notes in Outlook 2011 to tasks, contacts, or other objects, so it's a little like writing a bunch of notes and sticking them in a shoe box. You need to make the most of Outlook's Categorize tool and folders to organize your notes. And after you've created bunches of notes, you'll probably want to use the Search tool to help you find the note you wrote three years ago. You apply categories to notes in the same way that you apply them to Messages or Contacts. Select the note in the list and then go to Home→Categorize and choose one of the options. Once a category is applied, you can use the checkboxes in the navigation pane to filter the notes that are displayed.

Below the categories, is the On My Computer collapsible list where you can create folders. right-click (Control-click) On My Computer and choose New Folder. Give your folder a name and you can use it to hold specific notes. When you want to put a note in the folder, just select the note and then right-click (Control-click). Choose Move from the shortcut menu, and select the folder as shown in Figure 10-16.

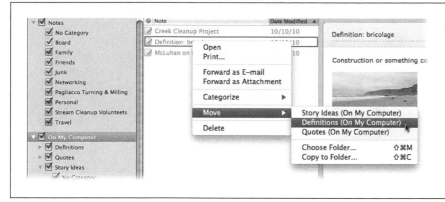

Figure 10-16:
If you write a lot of notes, you'll need to use Outlook Categories and folders to help you organize them. Here a right-click (Control-click) on a note brings up a shortcut menu, and the note is being moved to the Definitions folder.

Emailing and Forwarding Notes

You can send your best notes to friends and relatives. While you're in Notes view (⌘-5), use the ribbon command Home | Email to open an email window. The subject of your note is listed as the email subject, and the body of the note appears as the message. As an alternative, you can send your note as an attachment to an email. The attachment is saved in the HTML format that's used to describe web pages, so the recipient can open the note in her web browser.

Printing Notes

To print a note, Control-click (or right-click) a note in the list and choose Print from the pop-up menu, choose File→Print, or click the Print button in the toolbar of an open note. Outlook displays Notes' Print window, where you can choose to print all notes or just the selected ones. You can also specify whether the printed copy should include pictures or not. Checkboxes let you add date and time and page numbers.

CHAPTER 11

Customizing Outlook and Managing Data

O ut of all the tools you find in Office, Outlook is the most personal. It's where
you keep the names of your friends and it's where you schedule the important events in your life. It makes sense to shape Outlook to work the way you
like to work. The easier it is for you to use, the more you'll be inclined to add your
contacts, events, tasks, and notes to Outlook. That time spent customizing Outlook
to match your needs pays dividends in the long run. You'll avoid scheduling conflicts
and missed appointments. When you need to find the address, driving directions, or
random note you jotted down two weeks ago, you'll know where to look and you'll
have powerful tools to help with the search.

This chapter starts off with a list of ways you can change Outlook's appearance. Hide
the features you don't need all the time, and it's easier to focus on the ones you want.
You'll learn how to arrange emails, events, contacts, tasks, and notes in the order you
want and how to use advanced search tools to find the items you want. Categories
are the primary organizing feature in Outlook, in part because you can apply multiple categories to an item. Here you'll learn how to customize categories so they
match your needs. You can minimize the time you spend searching for details by
using folders and smart folders wisely. This chapter shows you how. Last but not
least, if you don't want to have Outlook open all the time, you can use the My Day
tool to see the most important bits of personal data in a small floating palette that's
always at the ready.

Changing the Look of Outlook

More than the other office tools, Outlook is a chameleon. You can show, hide, reposition and modify the different panes and tools that help you get a grip on the details

of your life and business. As shown in Figure 11-1, most of the views have three parts: a navigation pane, an items list, and a reading pane. As explained below, you can show and hide the navigation pane and the reading pane.

Figure 11-1:
All the views except for the Calendar view have three parts: the navigation pane, the items list and the reading pane. Calendar view doesn't have a reading pane. You can customize Outlook by showing, hiding, or repositioning these panes.

- **To hide the navigation pane,** go to View→Navigation Pane. You use the Navigation pane to select different folders or items that are then displayed in the list and the reading pane. In some cases, you may prefer to hide the navigation pane. For example, if you are only interested in your incoming mail, you can select your Inbox and then hide the navigation pane.

- **To hide or reposition the reading pane,** go to View→Reading Pane and choose Right, Below, or Hidden. Click an email, task, or note in the middle list, and it's immediately shown in the reading pane on the right. You can reduce Outlook's native clutter by hiding the reading pane. Then when you want to read the details about an item, just double-click it. Another thing happens when you hide the reading pane, extra details show up on the list and, as explained below, you can choose which items the list displays. You can quickly toggle the reading pane on and off using the keyboard shortcut Option-⌘-\.

- **To sort items in the list pane,** click the labels at the top of the list pane, as shown in Figure 11-2. Some of the labels, such as the "Arrange by" label in the Email list, provide several options. Often, on the right you'll also see an Ascending and Descending option, which lets you reverse the sort order.

- **To add columns to the list pane,** close the reading pane (Option-⌘-\) or position it Below (Shift-⌘-\). Then, right-click (Control-click) the bar above the listed items and choose the fields you want to show and hide (see Figure 11-2, bottom). It's hard to tell what tidbit of information is most important at a given moment. Perhaps you want to sort your Notes by category or zero in on an email you sent a year ago September. Once a field is added to the list view, you can sort the list on that particular field.

- **To rearrange columns in the list pane,** just drag them to a new location.
- **To show and hide tools in the ribbon,** click the tabs at the top of the ribbon. Unlike some of the other office tools, you can collapse the ribbon, but there is no way to hide it entirely.
- **To hide or modify the toolbar,** choose View→Hide Toolbar or View→Customize Toolbar. There aren't a lot of tools on Outlook's toolbar, but that "email send and receive button" is probably a good reason to leave the entire toolbar visible. If you right-click (Control-click) the toolbar, you can choose to display tools as Text, Icons, or both. If you choose to Customize the toolbar, you'll find that the only button Microsoft doesn't already have displayed is the Customize button itself.

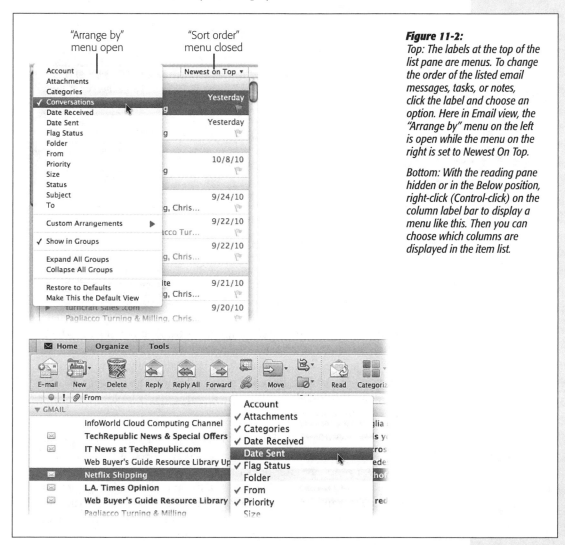

Figure 11-2:
Top: The labels at the top of the list pane are menus. To change the order of the listed email messages, tasks, or notes, click the label and choose an option. Here in Email view, the "Arrange by" menu on the left is open while the menu on the right is set to Newest On Top.

Bottom: With the reading pane hidden or in the Below position, right-click (Control-click) on the column label bar to display a menu like this. Then you can choose which columns are displayed in the item list.

- **To open another Outlook window,** choose File→New→Open New Main Window (see Figure 11-3). Why would you want more than one window open at once? Perhaps you'd like to see both your calendar and your email messages at the same time as you're composing a message. Or maybe you'd like to copy text from an email into a note. Today's Macs have beautiful wide screens for working with multiple windows.

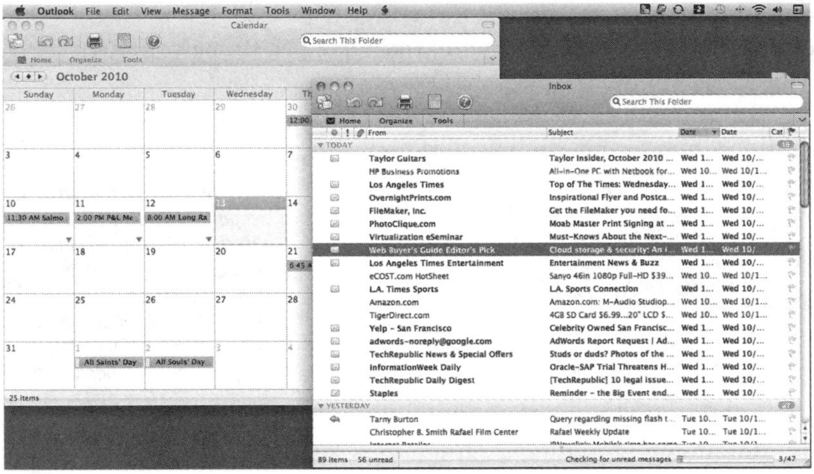

Figure 11-3:
You can make Outlook work the way you like to work. For example, here's a setup with two Outlook windows. One displays an uncluttered calendar and the other is a simple list showing the Email inbox. As always on your Mac, the ⌘-H command hides Outlook and both windows. ⌘-Tab lets you bring them back.

Creating Your Own Categories

The primary tool for organizing the data in Outlook is the category, which consists of two elements: a bit of text and a color. In one way, categories are like those little colored stick-on tabs they sell at Staples. You use those colored tabs to identify pages in a book or the random bits of paper you collect in your office. Perhaps you use blue tabs to identify all the paperwork that accumulates from your work with the Stream Cleanup Volunteers. Each letter, schedule, memo, and lunch receipt gets a blue tab. You use a red tab to mark receipts that may be helpful when tax day comes. Because you tag receipts as you collect them, the stream cleanup lunch receipt has two colored tabs, red, and blue. So on April 14, when you're madly looking for receipts, it's easy to zero in on all those red tabs.

Outlook works in a similar way, but it actually gives you a much greater ability to find emails, events, contacts, tasks or notes when you need them. Best of all, categorizing an item is so easy, it's foolish not to do it when you create new items. Just right-click (Control-click) the item in the list and choose Categorize from the shortcut menu. You can also use the Categorize menu in the item's window when you're creating it. The Notes item window is the only one that doesn't have a Categorize menu, so you need to use the Home | Categorize command or the right-click (Control-click) method.

Creating a new category is almost easy as applying a category. Just go to Home | Categorize→Add New. A box appears, like the one in Figure 11-4, where you can provide a category name and a color.

Note: The Categorize menu is in the Home tab for all the items except the Calendar, where it's in the special purple tab that appears when you select a meeting or appointment.

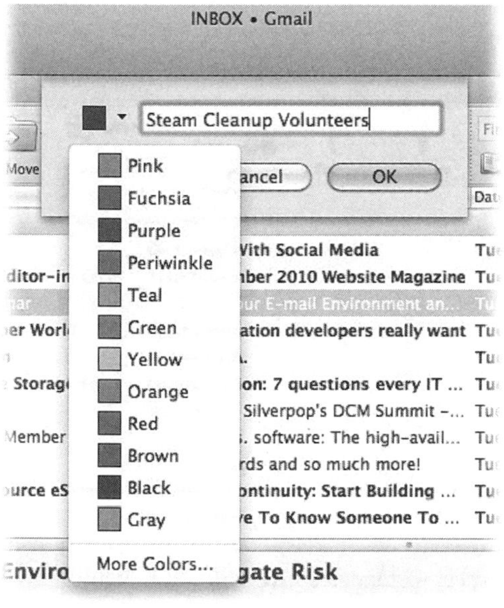

Figure 11-4:
To create a new category, all you have to do is give it a name and pick a color. Once you assign a category to an email, contact or event, they'll be color-coded in the lists and on the calendars for easy identification.

When you're in the mood for a major category reorganization, open the Categories window by going to Home | Categorize→Edit Categories. As you can see in Figure 11-5, the Categories window gives you + and – buttons to add and remove categories. Use the checkboxes on the right to choose which categories you want displayed in the Navigation pane. If you want to rename a category, double-click its name and type in a new one. There are two checkboxes at the bottom of the Categories box. Initially, both boxes are checked but you can turn them off:

- **Assign message to categorized contacts**. Choose this option if you want Outlook to automatically tag messages with categories. For example, if the Jean Ainsworth contact is tagged with the Board label, because she's on your Board of Directors, when you get a message from Jean, it will also have a Board category label.

- **Show new categories in the navigation pane**. When you create new categories, they're automatically displayed in the Navigation pane unless you turn this option off. You can also control which categories appear in the Navigation pane by using the checkboxes on the right side of the Categories box.

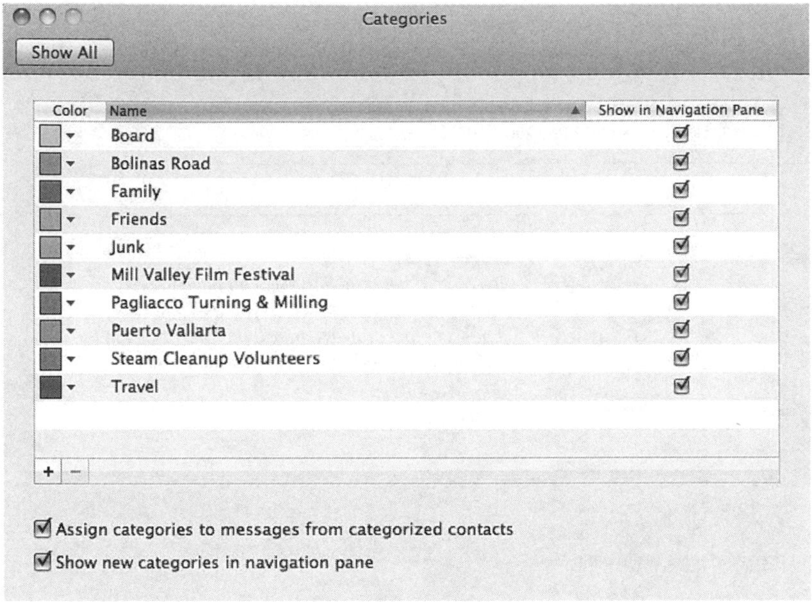

Figure 11-5:
Outlook's system for using and customizing categories is simple and straightforward. That's a good thing. You can add, remove and rename categories from this one window. Use the checkboxes on the right to choose which categories show up in the Navigation pane.

Using Categories to Filter the View

After you apply categories to emails, events, contacts, tasks, and notes, you can use them to view the items you want to see. Categories give you a quick and easy way to filter your view so you can focus on what's important at the moment. As shown in Figure 11-6, you select and deselect the categories you want to see in the navigation pane. It works the same for all the views except the Email view, which is slightly different. You can choose different categories in different views. For example, you can have your Notes set to view the Friends category, while your Calendar is set to Travel. Outlook remembers the categories you checked, so, for example, the next time you come back to the Calendar view, you'll see the same selection.

Working with categories in E-mail view

The navigation pane in Outlook's E-mail view is pretty busy with mailboxes, folders, and smart folders. As a result, there's no room for the Categories filter over there. Instead, you use the Home | Filters→Categories menu to show and hide items in your email list.

Figure 11-6:
*In the Navigation pane for the Calendar view, there are checks next to
Friends and Mill Valley Film Festival, so only the events in these categories
are displayed in the list.*

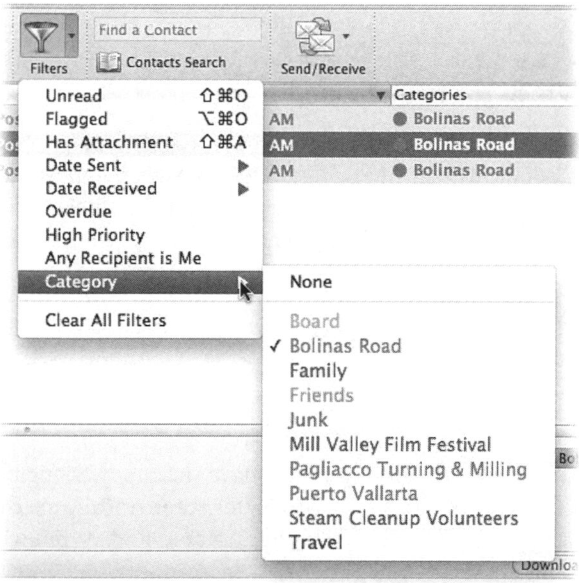

Figure 11-7:
*For your email, use the Home | Filters menu
to set Category filters. There are several other
items on this menu besides Categories that
make handy filters for your email messages.*

Using Folders and Smart Folders

When you have an office with waterfalls of paper pouring from desks and countertops, what do you do? You can start putting those letters, memos, reports, and receipts into folders. It works the same way in Outlook, as shown in Figure 11-8. In two of the views Email and Notes you can create your own folders. All of the five views in Outlook also have a feature called Smart Folders. Smart folders automatically collect copies of items that are stored elsewhere. For example, Email has a smart folder that holds all mail that's been flagged for follow-up. Both your manually created folders and your smart folders live in the navigation pane.

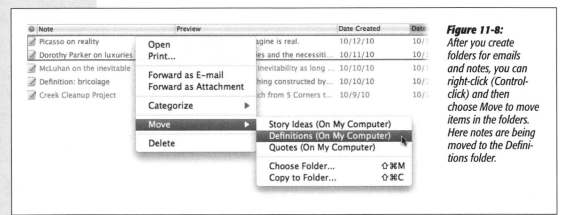

Figure 11-8:
After you create folders for emails and notes, you can right-click (Control-click) and then choose Move to move items in the folders. Here notes are being moved to the Definitions folder.

Manually Adding Folders in Notes and Email

Creating folders is a little simpler in the Notes view, so that's a good place to start. The navigation pane in Outlook has an item called On My Computer. To create a new folder, right-click (Control-click) on or below On My Computer and then choose New Folder. Type in a new name for the folder. If you ever need to rename a folder, double-click the name to open it for editing.

Note: If On My Computer isn't displayed in Outlook go to Outlook→Preferences→General and turn off the option labeled "Hide On My Computer folders".

The On My Computer list and each folder you create have the flippy triangle that expands and collapses folders. The folders you add to Notes automatically have subfolders that match your Categories. So, not only are your notes in folders, but within those folders, you can zero in on specific categories.

The basic procedure is the same for your email folders: right-click (Control-click) and choose New Folder. The difference is that the navigation pane for your email is most likely a lot more cluttered. If you have more than one email account, Outlook displays folders for each account. So if you have both a Gmail account and a MobileMe account, they'll both appear in the navigation pane. Outlook also creates mailboxes and folders that combine mail from accounts at the top of the navigation pane as shown in Figure 11-9. It's handy to see all your arriving mail in a single Inbox, but if you'd prefer, you can hide the combined inbox, drafts, sent mail, and deleted items folders. Go to Outlook→Preferences→General and turn off "Group similar folders, such as inboxes from different accounts". That will remove one block of clutter from the navigation pane, but if you have multiple accounts, you'll have to remember to check the inboxes for each one.

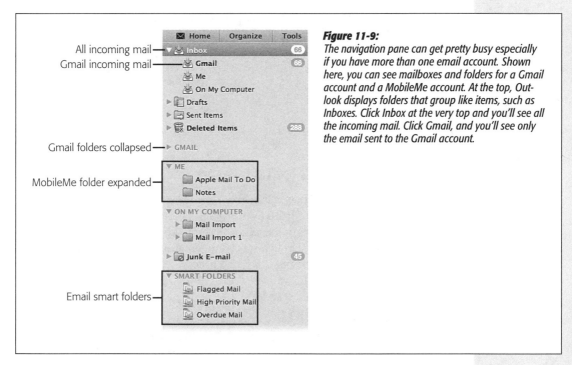

Figure 11-9:
The navigation pane can get pretty busy especially if you have more than one email account. Shown here, you can see mailboxes and folders for a Gmail account and a MobileMe account. At the top, Outlook displays folders that group like items, such as Inboxes. Click Inbox at the very top and you'll see all the incoming mail. Click Gmail, and you'll see only the email sent to the Gmail account.

Creating Smart Folders

The manual folders described above hold your email and notes. If you move an email from the inbox to a folder named Nigerian Scam Emails, it no longer lives in your inbox. Smart folders are a little different. Smart folders hold copies of email messages, while the original still exists someplace else. Smart folders are simply a tool to help you find what you need. Each view, except for the Calendar view, has smart folders that were automatically created by Outlook. Here's the list:

- **E-mail Smart Folders.** Flagged Mail, High Priority Mail, Overdue Mail
- **Contact Smart Folders.** Flagged Contacts, Updated Contacts
- **Tasks Smart Folders.** Due Today, High Priority, Overdue, Recently Completed
- **Notes Smart Folders.** Updated Notes

You don't have to do anything special to use any of these smart folders. Copies of your mail, contacts, tasks, and notes automatically appear in the folders when they meet the criteria. For example, if you want to see a list of overdue tasks you know exactly where to look. Go to the Tasks view and then in the Navigation pane, check out the Overdue smart folder shown in Figure 11-10.

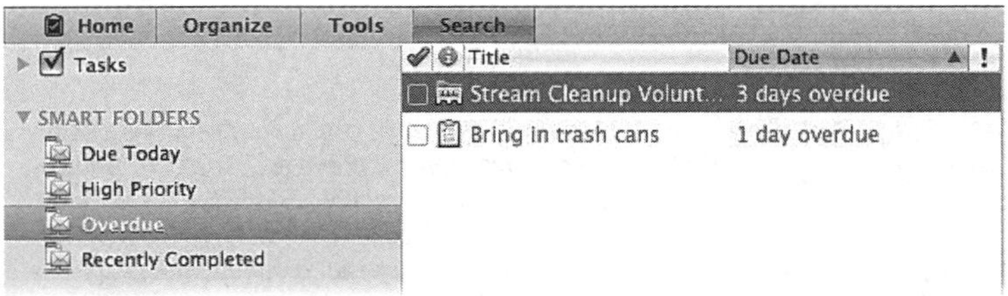

Figure 11-10:
Your overdue tasks smart folder relentlessly keeps track of the chores you haven't done. It's one of the smart folders that are automatically created when you install Outlook.

Using Advanced Searches to Create Smart Folders

The standard smart folders that come with Outlook are pretty useful, but you can probably think of a couple of items you'd like to automatically capture into smart folders. Perhaps you'd like to capture all the tasks in the Board of Directors category that are Overdue and store them in a special folder. You can create your own smart folders for emails, events, contacts, tasks, and notes. It's a two-step process. First you perform an advanced search, and then you save the rules of the search. So, in essence, a smart folder is a saved search.

Suppose you keep track of all the lunches you have with friends. You'd create a search that looks for appointments and meetings that are tagged with the "Friend" category and you could look for the word "Lunch" in the event's subject. Here's how you'd create that search:

1. **In the Calendar view (⌘-2), click the search box in the upper-right corner.**

   The special purple Search tab appears on the ribbon. Because you're in the Calendar view, Calendar is already selected on the ribbon as shown in Figure 11-11.

Figure 11-11:
The Search tab appears as soon as you begin a search in Outlook. Here the Calendar item on the far right is selected so the search will zero in on the events listed in the Calendar.

2. **On the ribbon, click the Advanced button.**

   A new panel appears below the ribbon with a menu and a text box. You use these tools to build an advanced search.

3. **Click the menu that says Item Contains and choose Category.**

   The panel changes to display two more menus.

4. **Leave the second menu set to Is and change the last menu to Friends.**

   You build rules for an advanced search by creating statements that define the items you're looking for. So far, you're searching for calendar events that are categorized as friends.

5. **At the right end of the panel, click the + button.**

   A new menu and text box appears. You can add another criterion to the search.

6. **Change Item Contains to Subject. Then type *lunch* in the text box.**

   In the list, Outlook shows the events that are categorized as Friends and have the word "lunch" in the subject. If necessary, you can continue to add criteria to your search by clicking the + button.

7. **On the ribbon, next to the Advanced button, click Save.**

   Outlook creates a new smart folder and puts your cursor in the name box.

8. **Type a name for your smart folder, such as *Lunch with Friends*.**

   Your smart folder is created. It holds the same items that were discovered during the advanced search. When you create more lunch dates with friends, they'll automatically show up in this folder.

At any time, you can rename your smart folder by double-clicking the name. If you want to tweak the search criteria for a smart folder, right-click (Control-click) the folder and choose Edit. Outlook opens the original search, and you can change the already defined criteria and add new rules.

Creating Email Rules

If you only get a couple of emails a day you probably don't need to worry about creating special rules that automate your email chores. However, if you're one of those lucky people who gets hundreds or thousands of emails, then email rules can help you do things like presort mail into appropriate folders, flag messages from your boss as high priority and automatically delete all the messages sent by your ex. Building email rules is similar to creating smart folders described in the previous section. You build up statements that define the criteria and then you build up statements that define the action you want taken. In other words, rules take the form of "If this criteria exists, then do that."

Suppose you're a guitar player and you're on several guitar makers' mailing lists. You don't need your inbox cluttered every day with sales pitches from the guitar companies, but you'd like to read the emails when you've got time. As described on page 332, you manually created a folder named Guitar to hold these emails. Now you want to create a rule that moves incoming emails from guitar companies to that folder. They'll remain marked as unread, so you'll know which emails are new.

Follow these steps to create an email rule to deal with guitar messages:

1. **In the Email view (⌘-1), on the ribbon go to Organize | Rules→Edit Rules.**

   The Rules window (Figure 11-12) appears showing the different types of email accounts you have. As the box on page 339 explains, your accounts are probably IMAP or POP.

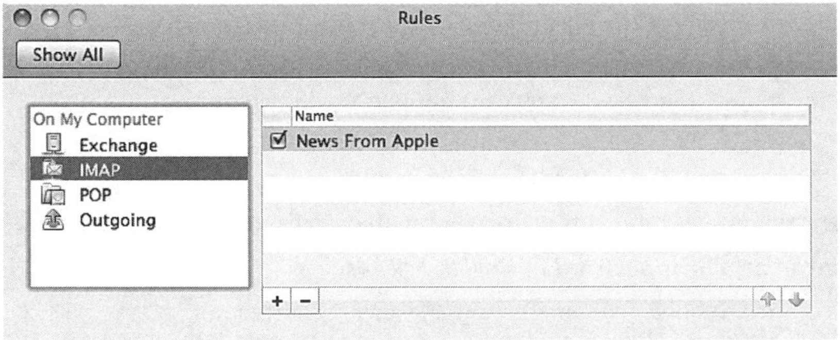

Figure 11-12:
The email rules window works like some of the other windows you come across in Outlook. Click the + and – buttons to add and remove rules from the list. To open an existing rule for changes, double-click it.

2. **Click the + button.**

   The Edit Rule window opens as shown in Figure 11-13, where you set the criteria using tools in the If group at the top. You describe the actions you want to take place in the Then group at the bottom.

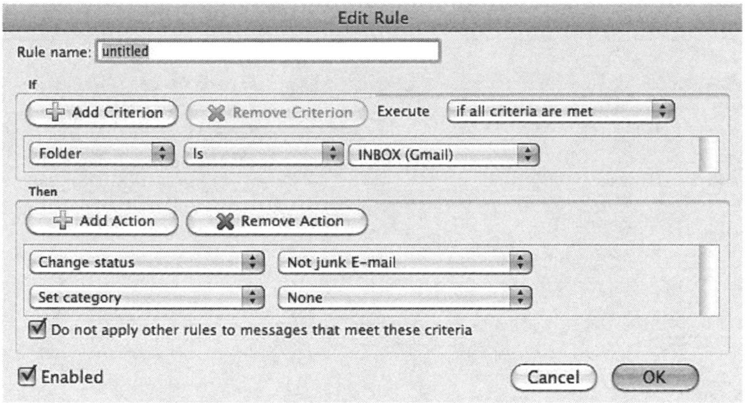

Figure 11-13:
The Edit Rule window shown here looks a little complicated at first glance; however, if you work from top to bottom it's not that bad. Just keep in mind you're creating a statement that says If these conditions exist Then perform these actions.

3. **In Rule Name, type *Guitar Makers*.**

   When you're done creating your new rule, this is the name that appears in the Rules list.

4. **Using the menus under "If", set the first criterion to read: From Contains @ martinguitars.com.**

   It takes three menus to craft the statement. Translation: if an email has *@martinguitars.com* in the From field, bingo! The end of the email address has to match perfectly, but the part in front of the @ sign could be anything like *sales@ martinguitars.com* or *support@martinguitars.com*.

5. **Optional: Add more guitar makers.**

   Use the same form: From Contains and then part of the email sender's address.

6. **In the top right corner set the Execute menu to *If any criteria are met*.**

   You're not going to get an email with all these addresses in the from field so you want the action to take place if any of the addresses show up.

7. **Under Then, leave the first criterion set to Change Status and Not junk E-mail**

   This setting keeps messages from these email addresses from getting tagged as junk mail and moved to your junk email folder. For more details, see page 287.

8. **Create a second criterion that reads Move Message Guitar, as shown in Figure 11-14.**

   You choose the move action in the first menu and the destination folder in the second.

9. **At the bottom of the Edit Rule window, make sure the Enabled checkbox is turned on, and then click OK.**

   The Edit Rule box closes.

10. **In the Rules box, click the red Close button in the upper-left corner.**

    The Rules window closes.

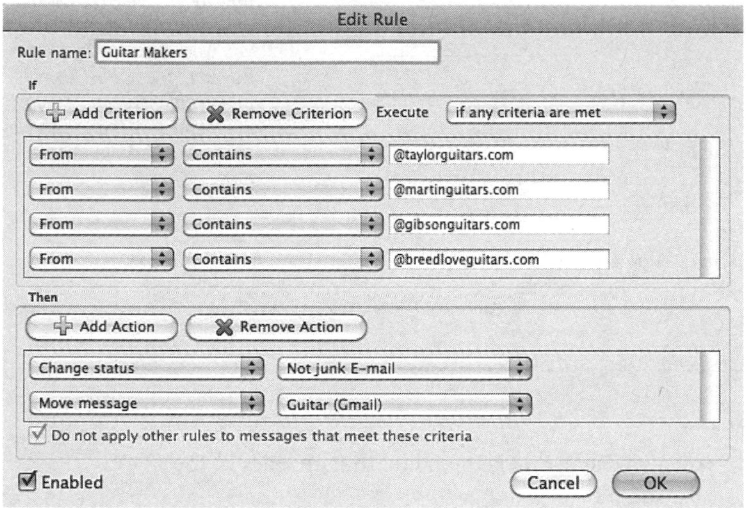

Figure 11-14:
Here's a completed rule that looks for email from four different guitar makers and moves the messages to the Guitars folder for later study.

Now when email arrives from any of the guitar makers, it will get shuttled off to the Guitars folder. The rule can be run manually from the Organize→Rules menu where it's already listed at the bottom.

Create Multiple Outlook Identities

If you prefer to keep your personal life separate from your business life or if you have a freelance business that you want to keep separate from your day job, you may want to create more than one Outlook Identity. Keep in mind, while you have your "work" identity open, you won't be able to access your "personal" email, events, and contacts. Also, identities are not intended as a way to create secure accounts for more than one person. If you share a computer with another person, it's much better to create separate user accounts with password protection, as described in *Mac OS X Snow Leopard: The Missing Manual* by David Pogue.

Follow these steps to create another identity:

1. **Close all your Office programs.**

   You have to close your Office applications to create a new database or later when you want to switch between databases.

2. **In the Finder, go to Applications→Microsoft Office 2011→Office and double-click the application named Microsoft Database Utility.**

   The database utility opens and it looks like Figure 11-15.

POP, IMAP, and Web-based Mail

When it comes to email, there are three flavors of accounts: POP (also known as Post Office Protocol or POP3), IMAP (also known as IMAP4), and Web-based. Although the lines between them are often blurry, each has its own distinct nature, with different strengths and weaknesses.

POP accounts are the most common kind. This type of account usually transfers your incoming mail to your hard drive before you read it, which works fine as long as you're using only one computer to access your email.

If you want to take your Outlook email world along with you on the road, you have to copy the Documents→Microsoft User Data folder on your desktop Mac's hard drive—or, at the very least, the Documents→Microsoft User Data→Office 2011 Identities folder—into the corresponding location on your laptop's hard drive. Then, when you run Outlook on the laptop, you'll find your messages and attachments already in place.

(Another travelers' tip: Outlook can leave your POP mail on the server so that you can read it while on the road, but still find it waiting on your home Mac when you return. Go to Outlook→Preferences→Accounts. Then select your email account and click the Advanced button. Turn on "Leave a copy of each message on server".)

IMAP accounts are most often found among educational institutions and corporations, but are becoming more popular for personal use because of services like .Mac and

Gmail. Unlike POP, where your mail is stored on your hard drive, IMAP keeps your mail on the remote server, downloading it only when you want to read or act on a message. Thus, you can access the same mail regardless of the computer you use. IMAP servers remember which messages you've read and sent, too.

The downside to this approach, of course, is that you can only work with your email when you're online, because all of your mail is on an Internet mail server, not on your hard drive.

Web-based servers are similar to IMAP servers, in that they store your mail on the Internet; you use a Web browser on any computer to read and send messages. Although Web-based accounts are convenient, most free Web-based accounts put ads in your email page, and you may find it awkward to compose and manage messages using a Web browser.

The only downside to POP and IMAP accounts is that if you switch Internet service providers (ISPs), you have to switch your email address as well. To prevent this problem, you can use Gmail or Apple's .Mac service, which give you a permanent email address. If your "real" email address changes, these services simply forward your mail to whatever new address you specify. That way, you'll never have to send out a change-of-email-address again.

3. **Click the + button and then type a name for a new identity.**

   The new identity appears in the list with the one originally created when you installed Outlook. That database is named Main Identity, but you can change it by double-clicking and typing in a new name.

4. **Choose the database you want Outlook to use the next time you start it, and then click the gear shaped button and choose Set as Default.**

   Outlook can only access one database at a time. It always starts the database you choose as the default. The default database is shown bold in the list. Later, when you want to change identities, you need to come back to this spot and set a new default.

5. **Optional: Click the red button in the upper-left corner to close the Microsoft Database Utility.**

The database utility closes. However, you don't have to close the database utility to open and use your Office applications—you can leave it open. As explained earlier, vice versa is not true. To switch identities or rebuild identities, you need to close all your Office applications.

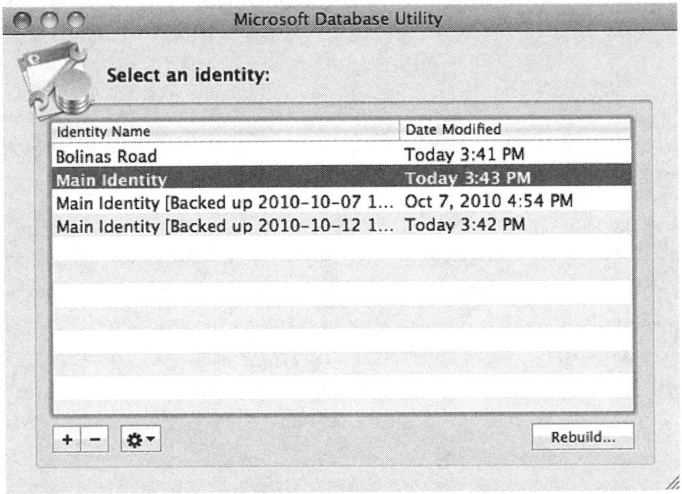

Figure 11-15:
You can create multiple identities using the Microsoft Database Utilities. Kind of makes you feel like a master spy, doesn't it? Use the + and – buttons to add and remove identities. Use the gear shaped button to set the Default Identity. That's the one Outlook will use when it starts.

The first time you open your new Outlook identity is similar to the first time you started Outlook. You need to set up email accounts (as described on page 263) and you need to make all the other changes described in this chapter to make Outlook work the way you want to work.

You now have two different identities. To switch back and forth between them, you need to close all your Office applications and then open Microsoft Database Utility as described above.

Tip: If you're going to be jumping back and forth between Outlook identities on a regular basis, you'll probably want to add the database utility to your Mac's dock. While you have it open, right-click (Control-click) the Microsoft Database Utility in the dock, then choose Options→Keep in Dock. Even after you close the utility, there will still be an icon in the dock you can use to launch it the next time you're ready to change identities.

Using My Day As Outlook Lite

All in all, Office 2008 was not the most-loved version for the Mac. There were lots of complaints about the lack of features that were available in the Windows version, like Visual Basic. Office 2011 marks a major do-over in many respects and this version of Office is probably closer to the Mac version than any other. One exception is the My Day tool, which is in essence a mini version of Outlook on a little palette. This option has never been available in the Windows version, but evidently Microsoft worried if they removed it from the Mac version of Office, folks that got used to it while they were working with Entourage would miss it.

Don't expect My Day to do everything Outlook does. For one thing, it doesn't really do email. It focuses on your schedule, tasks and contacts as shown in Figure 11-16. As the name implies, the main purpose of My Day is to show you the events and tasks you scheduled for the day.

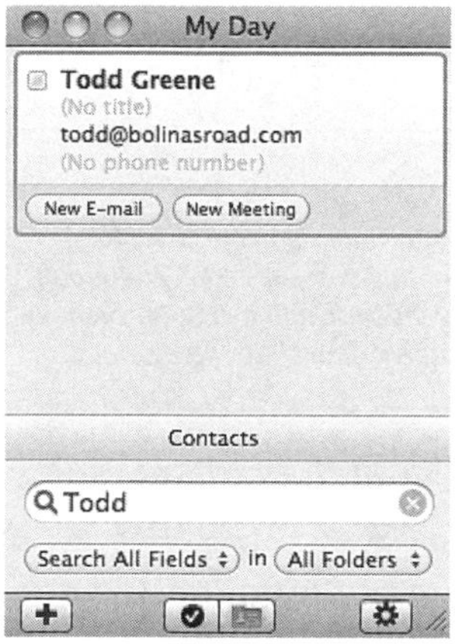

Figure 11-16:
The My Day app that comes with Outlook doesn't do everything that the full-blown program does. But if you don't want to run Outlook 24/7, but you'd like to keep track of your schedule, tasks, and contacts, give My Day a test drive.

My Day lets you keep an eye on your most urgent project elements—your current schedule and tasks—without opening or even launching Outlook. You don't have to confront your full calendar, your entire To Do List, or your email, giving you a fighting chance at concentrating on today's tasks without getting sucked into the E-maelstrom.

My Day is a mini-application that acts like a Mac OS X Widget emigrated from the Dashboard to the desktop. The small My Day window provides a quick view of your day's schedule and To Do List.

Initially, the top section of the My Day window shows scheduled events; the bottom section shows Tasks items and icons showing the type of the item and whether it's past-due (Figure 11-17). Click the date display at the top to open the Go To Date window and jump to a different date. You can also use the left and right arrow buttons to move day by day, or click the diamond button between the arrows to come back to today. Buttons at the bottom of the window let you create new tasks, change the view of the bottom pane from tasks to contacts, and open the My Day preferences.

There are lots of different ways to set up My Day. If you're a big fan, you can have My Day run every time you start your computer and you can put the icons on your menu bar and your dock. You change these settings in the preferences. Go to My Day→Preferences to open the window shown in Figure 11-18. The preferences are divided into three tabs:

- In the **General** tab, you can choose to show My Day in the menu bar and the dock. You can set a shortcut key that opens the applet. Check "Open My Day when computer starts" if you want to run it automatically. Choose "Always display My Day on top" if you want the window to always be visible when it's open.

- The **Calendars** tab gives you a way to choose the Calendar used in My Day.

- In the **Tasks** tab, you can choose the type of messages that are displayed in the task pane. For example, you can select flagged messages, overdue items, or items with no due date. You can also set the date and folder used to display tasks.

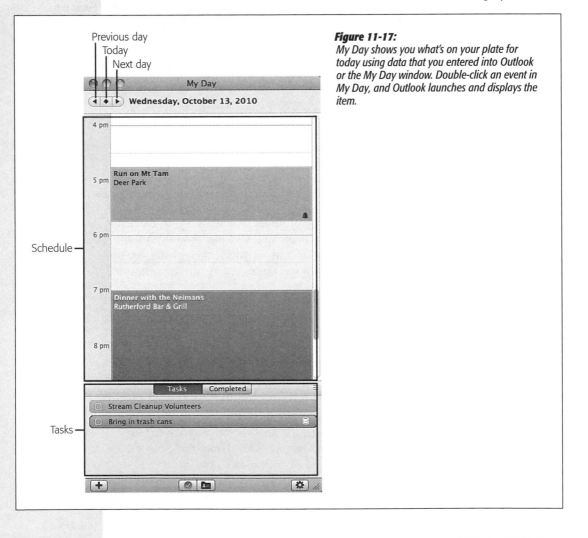

Figure 11-17:
My Day shows you what's on your plate for today using data that you entered into Outlook or the My Day window. Double-click an event in My Day, and Outlook launches and displays the item.

Figure 11-18:
Top: The My Day preferences window gives you control over how and when the program appears and what it displays. If you click the radio button marked "Show on Mac OS menu bar," the My Day application menu disappears and all menu items—including My Day Preferences—appear under the menulet icon in the menu bar.

Bottom: The To Do List preferences window lets you choose which To Do items to display.

Part Three: Excel

3

Basic Excel

Spreadsheets and Apple computers have long had a symbiotic relationship. Stories abound about business-types going to their bosses and demanding a "VisiCalc Machine." They'd heard about them, but didn't know they really wanted an Apple II computer and VisiCalc software, the granddaddy of all spreadsheet software. Fast-forward to today and you're talking about your Mac and Excel. However, today's Macs and Excel 2011 bear about as much relationship to VisiCalc as the Wright Brothers' first airplane to a Boeing 787.

Excel 2011 includes a bunch of new, helpful features topped off with a ribbon that makes it easier to find the tool you need.

Spreadsheet Basics

You use Excel, of course, to make a *spreadsheet*—an electronic ledger book composed of rectangles, known as *cells*, laid out in a grid (see Figure 12-1). As you type numbers into the rectangular cells, the program can automatically perform any number of calculations on them. And although the spreadsheet's forte is working with numbers, you can use them for text, too; because they're actually a specialized database, you can turn spreadsheets into schedules, calendars, wedding registries, address books, and other simple text databases. For details on Excel as a database, see Chapter 14.

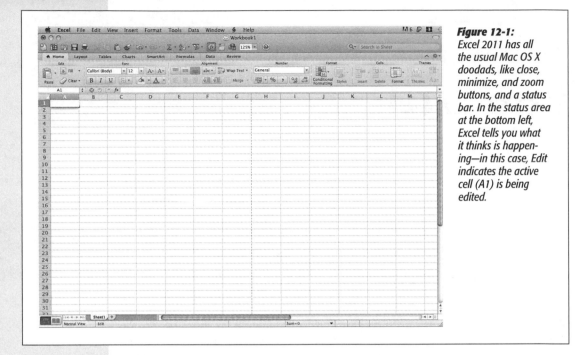

Figure 12-1:
Excel 2011 has all the usual Mac OS X doodads, like close, minimize, and zoom buttons, and a status bar. In the status area at the bottom left, Excel tells you what it thinks is happening—in this case, Edit indicates the active cell (A1) is being edited.

Opening a Spreadsheet

A new Excel document, called a *workbook*, is made up of one or more pages called *worksheets*. (You'll find more on the workbook/worksheet distinction in Chapter 388.) Each worksheet is an individual spreadsheet, with lettered columns and numbered rows providing coordinates to refer to the cells in the grid.

You can create a plain-Jane Excel workbook, like the one in Figure 12-1, by going to File→New Workbook (⌘-N), or by choosing File→New from Template (Shift-⌘-P) to open the Excel Workbook Gallery. The Gallery, and the commands to get there, are just like the Word and PowerPoint template galleries. A template can be a real timesaver if you find one that fits your immediate project. Templates are grouped in categories like Personal Finance, Business Essentials and Time Management. You can choose from address lists, gift lists, check registers, budgets, invoices, expense reports, portfolio trackers. Templates provide more than pretty formatting. For example, the Invoice template shown in Figure 12-2 includes all the formulas needed to tally items sold, calculate subtotals, and apply tax. All you have to do is drop in things like your company name, your customer's name, product descriptions, and unit prices.

Tip: Once you've opened a spreadsheet from a template, you can use it as-is or customize any part of it. Even without any spreadsheet skills, you can start filling in these preformatted sheets without having to think about cell formatting, cell references, or formulas—and still take advantage of Excel's data- and number-crunching prowess. (But you'll still find this chapter helpful when it comes time to customize a spreadsheet—or if you're interested in how it's doing what it does.)

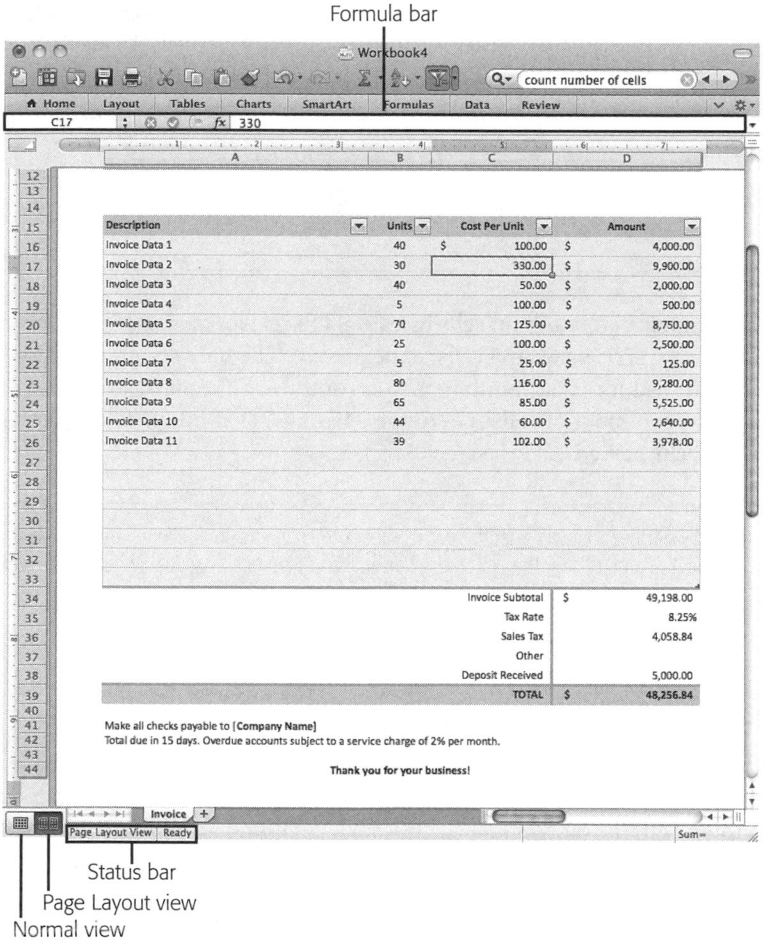

Figure 12-2:
Use Excel templates to get a jump on your project. Spreadsheets like this invoice form provide both attractive formatting and built-in formula smarts. In many cases, all you need to do is fill in the blanks. Click a cell and start typing to enter your data. Use Tab or Return to move to the next column.

Whether it starts out plain or preformatted, each worksheet can grow to huge proportions—about 16,000 columns wide (labeled A, B, C… AA, AB, AC… AAA, AAB, AAC, and so on, and on, and on), and more than one million rows tall (see Figure 12-3). Furthermore, you can get at even more cells by adding more worksheets to the workbook—click the plus-sign button next to the worksheet tabs at the bottom left or by choose Insert→Worksheet. Switch between worksheets by clicking their tabs.

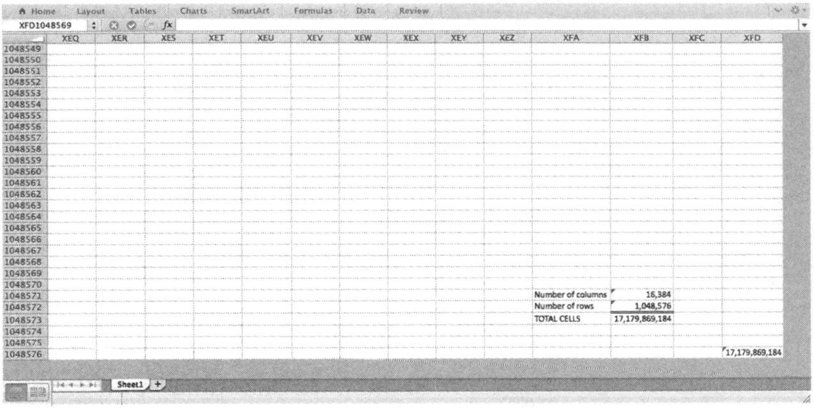

Figure 12-3:
You can't scroll all the way to cell XFD1048576 in a new spreadsheet (well, you can, but it may take several days), but you can leap to that far-distant cell by typing XFD1048576 in the Name box on the left side of the Formula bar and pressing Return.

In total, you can have 17.18 billion cells in a single Excel worksheet; 16,384 columns × 1,048,576 rows = 17,179,869,184 cells, to be precise. The only company that needs more space than *that* for its accounting is Microsoft itself. (Want to see the formula that calculates the number of cells? Go to the Missing CD at *http://missingmanuals. com/cds*. The file is named 12-1_last_cell.xlsx)

Tip: Newly minted worksheets always bear the name Sheet1, Sheet2, and so on. To rename a worksheet, double-click the sheet's name (it's on the tab on the bottom) and type in a new one. Sheet names can be as long as 31 characters.

Data Entry

Each cell acts as a container for one of two things: data or a formula. *Data* can be text, a number, a date, or just about anything else you can type. A *formula*, on the other hand, does something with the data in *other* cells—such as adding together the numbers in them—and displays the result. (There's more on formulas later in this chapter.)

Excel refers to cells by their coordinates, such as B23 (column B, row 23). A new spreadsheet has cell A1 selected (surrounded by a thick border)—it's the *active* cell. When you start typing, the cell pops up slightly, apparently hovering above your screen's surface, with a slight shadow behind it. Whatever you type appears in both the active cell *and* the Edit box on the right side of the Formula bar, shown in Figure 12-2. If you prefer, you can click in the Formula bar and do your typing there. When you finish typing, you can do any of the following to make the active cell's new contents stick:

- Press Return, Tab, Enter, or an arrow key.
- Click another cell.
- Click the Enter button (checkmark) in the Formula bar.

If you change your mind and want to leave a cell without changing its contents, press Esc or click the X button in the Formula bar.

There's another way to add data to a cell. You can cut (⌘-X) or copy (⌘-C) the data in one cell and then paste it into another (⌘-V). For the most part it works like cutting and pasting text in a Word document or an e-mail message, but there are a few special circumstances related to the way spreadsheets work. For example, when you paste data into a cell, you may see a smart button pop up in the immediate vicinity (Figure 12-4). Clicking the button's arrow reveals a shortcut menu with a number of formatting options specific to the information you're pasting and where you're pasting it.

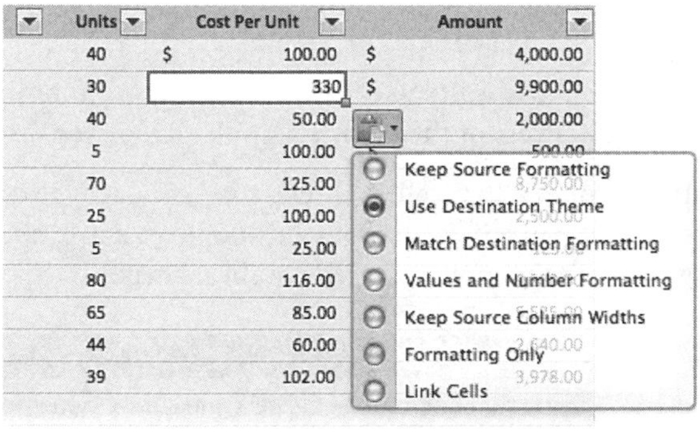

	Units		Cost Per Unit		Amount	
	40	$	100.00	$	4,000.00	
	30		330	$	9,900.00	
	40		50.00		2,000.00	
	5		100.00		500.00	
	70		125.00		8,750.00	
	25		100.00		2,500.00	
	5		25.00		125.00	
	80		116.00		9,280.00	
	65		85.00		5,525.00	
	44		60.00		2,640.00	
	39		102.00		3,978.00	

- Keep Source Formatting
- Use Destination Theme
- Match Destination Formatting
- Values and Number Formatting
- Keep Source Column Widths
- Formatting Only
- Link Cells

Figure 12-4:
A smart button often appears just after you paste data into a cell. Click its arrow to display a small menu from which you can choose to retain the source formatting (so that the text keeps the formatting it had in its original location) or match the destination formatting (in which Excel automatically adjusts the text to the formatting in the current workbook). Variations include pasting just the values and number formatting, pasting the source column width, pasting just the cell formatting, and creating a link to the source cell (see page 398). Since Excel isn't psychic, the smart button gives you a chance to tell it whether you had the old or new formatting in mind.

UP TO SPEED

Change Your Point of View

Page Layout view first appeared in Excel 2004 and its benefit is obvious—you can now see how your printed page will look without looking at a print preview of your work. In fact, some people work in this view from the get-go, so they can design their spreadsheet to fit on whatever size paper they'll eventually print it on. You no longer have to construct a spreadsheet, print it, and then be surprised by the results. Working in Page Layout view provides gloriously instantaneous feedback on how your numerical creation will look when it goes to hard copy. On the downside, in Page Layout view, you get to see less of your creation onscreen, due to all those blank page margins (but what better excuse to invest in a new 30" monitor?).

It's easy to switch views while you're working. Just click one of the buttons in the window's lower-left corner. Whichever view you choose, it affects only your onscreen view—your spreadsheet prints the same way no matter what.

You can choose which view you'd like to see when Excel creates a new spreadsheet. Visit Excel→Preferences→View and then choose either Normal or Page Layout from the "Preferred view for new sheets" menu.

Working in an Excel sheet is simple at its heart: You enter data or a formula into a cell, move to the next cell, enter more information, and so on. But before entering data in a cell, you have to first *select* the cell. Clicking is the easiest method; after you click a cell, the cell border thickens and as soon as you start typing, the cell does that popping-up thing.

Tip: When you double-click a cell, it pops up from the spreadsheet and you find yourself again in the editing mode. If, perhaps due to an over-eager mouse-button finger, you keep landing in this "in-cell editing" mode accidentally, choose Excel→Preferences→Edit panel, turn off "Double-click allows editing directly in the cell", and click OK. Now you can only edit cell contents in the Edit box on the Formula Bar.

To select a cell far away from the current active cell, enter the cell's *address* (the column letter followed by the row number) in the Name box on the Formula bar (Figure 12-2) and press Return. Or choose Edit→Go To (or press F5), to summon a dialog box where you can enter the address of the lucky cell in the Reference field.

But the fastest means of getting from cell to cell is to use the keyboard. Excel is loaded with keyboard shortcuts that make it easy to plow through an entire sheet's worth of cells without having to touch the mouse. Here's the cheat sheet:

Keystroke	What Happens
Arrow key	Selects a different cell—the next one above, below, to the left, or to the right of the current one.
Shift-arrow key	Selects the current cell and the one above, below, to the left, or to the right. Hold the Shift key down and press the arrow key more than once to extend the selection.
Control-Page Up or Control-Page Down (for MacBooks FN-Control-Up Arrow or FN-Control-Down Arrow)	Makes the previous or next sheet in the workbook active.
Control-arrow key	Moves the active cell to the next non-empty cell in the direction indicated by the arrow key.
Return	Accepts the entry and moves the active cell down one row. (Unless you've changed that behavior in Excel→Preferences→Edit.)
Shift-Return	Accepts the entry and moves the active cell up one row. (Unless you've changed that behavior in Excel→Preferences→Edit.)
Tab	Accepts the entry and moves the active cell right one column (or to the first cell in the next row in a multiple-cell selection).
Shift-Tab	Accepts the entry and moves the active cell left one column.
Control-Option-Return	Starts a new line within the same cell.

Control-Return	Fills each selected cell with the same entry. (First select the cell range, type the data that you want repeated in each cell, and then hit Control-Return to fill all of the cells.)
Esc	Cancels an entry.
Delete	Deletes cell contents.
Control-D	Fills the active cell with the contents of the cell directly above it.
Control-R	Fills the active cell with the contents of the cell directly to the left of it.
Control-'	Fills the active cell with the formula in the cell directly above it, and leaves the cell in Edit mode.
Control-;	Enters the current date.
⌘-;	Enters the current time.
Control-Shift-:	Enters the current time (to the nearest minute).

Tip: Return doesn't have to select the next cell down; it can select any of the four neighboring cells, or do nothing at all. You change what the Return key does in the Excel→Preferences→Edit panel.

UP TO SPEED

Window Tricks

Because spreadsheets can be wide, sprawling affairs, Excel is filled with window-manipulation tools that let you control how the program uses your precious screen real estate.

For example, when you need to see a few more rows and columns, choose View→Full Screen. Excel hides all of its toolbars, status bars, and other nonessential items. Your precious cells fill your monitor. Choose View→Full Screen again (or click Close Full Screen on the tiny, one-button toolbar) to bring back the bars, ribbon and so forth.

Another example: As shown in Figure 12-5, Excel's scroll bars have vertical and horizontal split boxes, which you can double-click or drag to split a sheet into independently scrolling sections, as shown here. (Note the discontinuity in the lettering and numbering of rows and columns in this illustration; the result of scrolling each pane to a different part of the spreadsheet.) To remove the split, just double-click the split box or the split bar that separates the panes. (Or choose Window→Remove Split.)

You don't have to split the window if all you want to do is keep the row and column names in view while scrolling the rest of the document, however. Excel has a much more streamlined means of locking the column and row labels: Click in the cell just below and to the right of the row/column label intersection, and then choose Window→Freeze Panes. Now scrolling affects only the body of the spreadsheet; the row and column labels remain visible.

If, on the other hand, you wish you could split your spreadsheet into six or more panes in order to work on widely separated bits of data, open additional Windows by choosing Window→New Window. Open as many additional windows as you, your monitor, and your multitasking abilities require. Each window is a separate view of the same spreadsheet; make a change in one window and it affects them all.

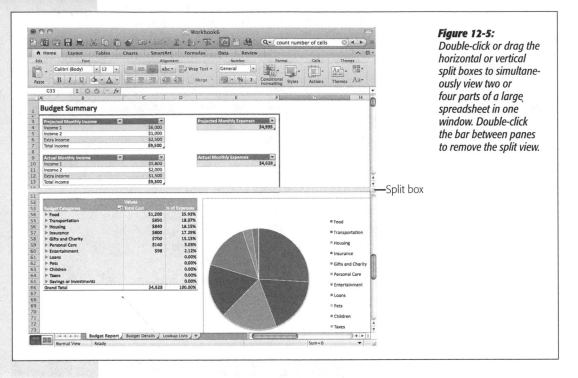

Figure 12-5:
Double-click or drag the horizontal or vertical split boxes to simultaneously view two or four parts of a large spreadsheet in one window. Double-click the bar between panes to remove the split view.

Excel is positively brimming with keyboard shortcuts—the table on page 352 is just the tip of the iceberg. For a complete list, open Excel Help and search for "Excel keyboard shortcuts." (By not including the entire list in this book, we're saving a small forest somewhere in Oregon.)

Basic Formatting

The way numbers are formatted serves as a kind of code that indicates what the numbers mean. For example, you can probably identify the following: $12.99, 415-555-3232, 11/16/11 and 43/64 as money, a phone number, a date, and a fraction simply by the way they're formatted. The dollar, decimal point, commas, and slash marks tell the story. You'll want to use formatting in your spreadsheet to communicate the purpose of your numbers.

Formatting plays an important role in Excel because it's used to present so many different types of data, not to mention charts, graphs, and other heavily formatted objects. In fact, Chapter 16 is completely devoted to the subject. For now, all you need to know is where to turn when you want to apply basic formatting to an object, to display currency, to display general numbers, or to add or remove numbers to the right of the decimal point. You handle these basic formatting needs from the Home | Number group. Select a cell or a range of cells, and then click one of the buttons. If there are numbers in the cells, you see the change immediately.

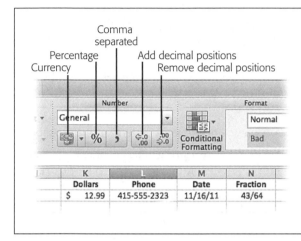

Figure 12-6:
The buttons on the Home ribbon are the quickest way to apply standard formatting to the numbers in your spreadsheet. A single click displays a number as currency or a percentage. Other buttons add comma separators and set the number of decimal places.

If the basic buttons don't complete the formatting job, open the menus in the Number group. The Number format menu gives you several choice for dates, times, scientific notation and fractions. As you learn next, formatting can have a dramatic and sometimes unexpected effect on the way numbers are displayed.

Note: For all the details on advanced formatting, see page 459.

Kinds of Data

You can enter four kinds of data into an Excel spreadsheet: numbers, text, dates, or times (not including formulas, which are described beginning on page 372). Mostly, entering data is as straightforward as typing, but exceptions lurk.

Numbers

- There are only 21 characters that Excel considers numbers or parts of numbers: 1 2 3 4 5 6 7 8 9 0 . , ( ) + - / $ % e and E. Anything else is treated as text, which is ineligible for performing most calculations. For example, if Excel sees *three* in a cell, it sees a bunch of typed characters with no numerical value; when it sees *3.14*, it sees a number.

- Depending on the formatting of the cell where you're entering numbers, Excel might try to do some work for you. For example, if you've applied *currency formatting* to a cell, Excel turns *3/2* into $1.50. But if you've formatted the same cell as a Date, Time, or General, Excel turns *3/2* into a date—March 2 of the current year.

- When you've formatted a cell to accept General input, and the number you've entered is longer than 11 digits (such as *12345678901112*), Excel converts it to scientific notation (*1.23457E+13*).

- Excel's number precision is 15 significant digits—anything over 15 will be lost.

Text

- Text can be any combination of characters: numbers, letters, or other symbols.

- To make Excel look at a number as if it were a string of text (rather than a number with which it can do all kinds of mathematical wizardry), you have to either precede the number with an apostrophe or *format* the cell as a text-based cell. To format the cell, choose Text from the Format menu in the Formatting Palette's Number pane. Alternatively, select the cell and choose Format→Cells (or right-click the cell and choose Format Cells from the shortcut menu). Click the Number tab and then select Text from the Category list. Click OK.

Dates

- You can perform math on dates, just as though they were numbers. The trick is to type an equal sign (=) into the cell that will contain the answer; then enclose the dates in quotation marks and put the operator (like + or *) between them. For example, if you click a cell, type = *"12/30/2007"-"5/25/1963"*, and then press Return, Excel fills the cell with 16290, the number of days between the two dates.

Tip: If you're trying to determine someone's age with this calculation, you probably want to write it as =*("12/30/2007" –"5/25/1963")/365* which gives a result in years: 44.63013699.

This math is made possible by the fact that dates in Excel *are* numbers. Behind the scenes, Excel converts any date you type into a special date serial number, which is composed of a number to the left side of a decimal point (the number of days since January 1, 1900) and a number on the right (the fraction of a day).

- When entering dates, you can use either a slash or a hyphen to separate months, days, and years. Usually it's OK to format date and time numbering at any time. However, you'll avoid occasional date recognition problems by applying date or time formatting *before* you enter the data in the cell.

The Beginnings of Time

The original Macintosh used a starting date of January 1, 1904–which lingers on to this day. Windows PCs, by contrast, use a starting date of January 1, 1900. Excel workbooks can now support either date system, but you may run into problems when linking or copying dates between workbooks based on different date systems. Out of the box, Excel uses the January 1, 1900 as the beginning of time, but you can change that by choosing Excel→Preferences→Calculation and turning on the checkbox for "Use the 1904 date system".

If copying or linking between workbooks gives you results that are 1462 days off from what you expect, you'll need to add a correction formula. Visit *www.support.microsoft.com/kb/214330* to read Microsoft's knowledge-base article that describes the problem in detail and supplies formulas for correcting it.

Times

- Excel also treats *times* as numbers—specifically, as the fractional part of a date serial number, which is a number representing the number of days since midnight on January 1, 1904.

- Excel bases times on the 24-hour clock, or military time. To enter a time using the 12-hour clock, follow the number with an *a* or *p*. For example, to Excel, *9:34* always means 9:34 a.m., but *9:34 p* means 9:34 p.m.—and *21:34* also means 9:34 p.m. Whether you type *9:34 p* or *21:34*, Excel displays it in the spreadsheet as 21:34 unless you format the cell to display it in the AM/PM format.

- As with dates, you can perform calculations on times by entering an equal sign and then enclosing the times in quotation marks and typing the separator in the middle. For example, = *"9:34"*-*"2:43"* gives you 0.285416667, the decimal fraction of a day between 2:43 a.m. and 9:34 a.m. If you format the cell with time formatting, as described on page 470, you instead get a more useful 6:51, or six hours and 51 minutes' difference.

Note: If the times in a calculation span midnight, the calculation will be wrong, since times reset at midnight. Fix it by adding 24 hours to the calculation—or even better by using the MOD function. (See page 375 for more on functions.)

Tedium Savings 1: AutoComplete

Excel 2011 is teeming with features to save you typing. The first, *AutoComplete*, comes into play when you enter repetitive data down a column. Find out more in Figure 12-7.

WORKAROUND WORKSHOP

When Excel Formats Numbers as Dates

If you enter what looks like a date to Excel (say, May 3, 1999), and then later, in the process of revising your spreadsheet, enter a number containing a decimal (such as 23.25), Excel converts your decimal into a date (23 becomes January 23, 1904).

What's going on?

All cells start out with a generic format. But when you enter what Excel interprets as a date or time, Excel automatically applies date or time formatting. In this example, when Excel interpreted the first entry as a date, it applied date formatting to the cell.

Later, when the first entry was replaced with a decimal number, Excel retained the date formatting—and merrily

displayed the number as a date. You don't have to let Excel guess at what format you want, though. Take charge! Select the cells in question and choose Format→Cells (or right-click the cells and choose Format Cell from the shortcut menu). Use the Number tab to select the appropriate format, and your troubles are over.

Similarly, to keep Excel from turning two numbers separated by a forward slash into a date, and keep it as a fraction instead, put a 0 and a space in front of the fraction (enter 0 1/4)—or just format the cell with the *Number* category. Excel now understands that you intended to enter a fraction.

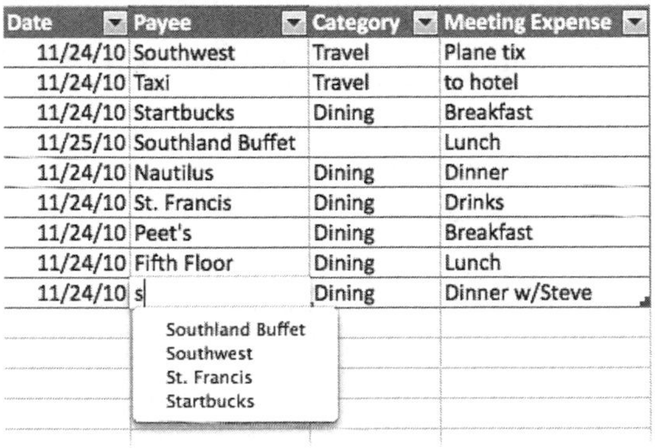

Date		Payee		Category		Meeting Expense	
11/24/10		Southwest		Travel		Plane tix	
11/24/10		Taxi		Travel		to hotel	
11/24/10		Startbucks		Dining		Breakfast	
11/25/10		Southland Buffet				Lunch	
11/24/10		Nautilus		Dining		Dinner	
11/24/10		St. Francis		Dining		Drinks	
11/24/10		Peet's		Dining		Breakfast	
11/24/10		Fifth Floor		Dining		Lunch	
11/24/10		s		Dining		Dinner w/Steve	

Southland Buffet
Southwest
St. Francis
Startbucks

Figure 12-7:
Excel's AutoComplete function watches as you type in a given cell. If your entry looks as though it might match the contents of another cell in the same column, Excel shows a pop-up menu of those possibilities. To select one, press the down arrow until the entry you want is highlighted, and then press Return. Alternatively, just click the entry in the list. Either way, Excel finishes the typing work for you.

Tedium Savings 2: Formula AutoComplete

Formula AutoComplete is a great, time-saving feature in Excel 2011, extending the AutoComplete concept to the chore of writing formulas. Instead of having to remember all the elements for a formula, Excel prompts you with valid function names and syntax as you type.

Tedium Savings 3: AutoFill

Excel's AutoFill feature can save you hours of typing and possibly carpel tunnel surgery, thanks to its ingenious ability to fill miles of cells with data automatically. The Edit→Fill submenu is especially useful when you're duplicating data or typing items in a series (such as days of the week, months of the year, or even sequential apartment numbers). It has seven options: Down, Right, Up, Left, Across Sheets, Series, and Justify.

Here's how they work. In each case, you start the process by typing data into a cell and then highlighting a block of cells beginning with that cell (see Figure 12-8). Then, choose any of the following:

- **Down, Up**. Fills the selected block of cells with whatever's in the top or bottom cell of the selected block. You might use one of these commands when setting up a series of formulas in a column that adds a row of cells.

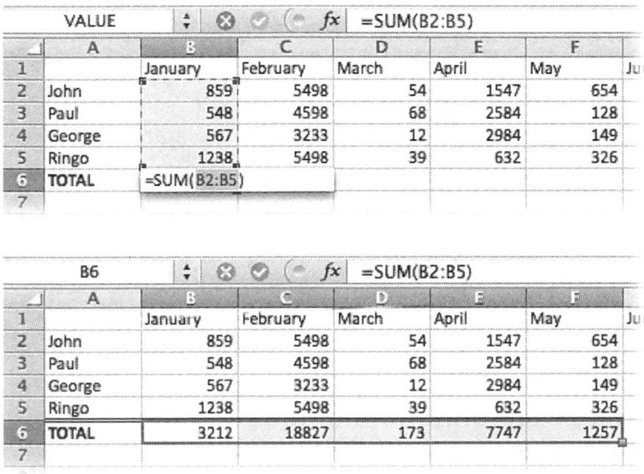

Figure 12-8:
Filling a range of cells with formulas is where AutoFill really shines. You can drag the formula in cell B6 through cells to the right and then choose Edit→Fill→Right (top). Excel fills the cell with totals of the columns above them (bottom).

- **Right, Left**. Fills the selected range of cells with whatever's in the leftmost or rightmost cell. For example, you'd use this feature when you need to put the same total calculation at the bottom of 23 different columns.

- **Across Worksheets**. Fills the cells in other sheets in the same workbook with the contents of the selected cells. For example, suppose you want to set up worksheets that track inventory and pricing over different months in different locations, and you want to use a different worksheet for each location. You can fill in all of the general column and row headings (such as part numbers and months) across worksheets with this command.

To make this work, start by selecting the cells whose contents you wish to copy. Then select the sheets you want to fill by Shift-clicking a group of sheet tabs or ⌘-clicking non-contiguous sheet tabs at the bottom of the window. (If you can't see all the tabs easily, drag the slider between the tabs and the horizontal scroll bar. When you drag it to the right, the scroll bar shrinks, leaving more room for the tabs.)

Choose Edit→Fill→Across Sheets. A small dialog box (see Figure 12-9) asks whether you want to copy data, formats, or both across the selected worksheets. Make your choice by clicking one of the radio buttons, and then click OK.

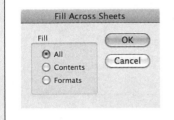

Figure 12-9:
You can copy three ways into other worksheets: All (both the formats and data), Contents (the data or formulas), or Formats (just the formats in the worksheet).

- **Series**. Fills the selected cells with a *series* of increasing or decreasing values based on the contents of the topmost cell (if the selected cells are in a column) or the leftmost cell (if the cells are in a row).

  For example, suppose you're about to type in the daily statistics for the number of dot-com startups that went out of business during the first two weeks of 2011. Instead of having to type 14 dates into a row of cells, you outsource this task to Excel.

  Enter *1/1/2011* in a cell. Then highlight that cell and the next 13 cells to its right. Now choose Edit→Fill→Series. The Series window appears, where you can specify how the fill takes place. You could make the cell labels increase by months, years, every other day, or whatever. Click OK; Excel fills the cells with the date series 1/1/2011, 1/2/2011, 1/3/2011, and so on.

Tip: The above example reflects the way Americans write dates, of course. If you use a different system for writing dates (perhaps you live in Europe or Australia), and you've used the Mac's International preference pane (choose ⌘→System Preferences) to specify that you like January 14, 2011 written *14/1/2011*, the next time you launch Excel, it automatically formats dates the way you like them.

The other options in this dialog box include Linear (adds the amount in the Step field to each successive cell's number), Growth (*multiplies* by the number in the Step field), and AutoFill (relies on the lists described in the next section).

- **Justify**. Spreads the text in a single cell across several cells. You'd use this function to create a heading that spans the columns beneath it. If the cells are in a row, this command spreads the text in the leftmost cell across the selected row of cells. If the cells are in a column, it breaks up the text so that one word goes into each cell.

Tip: At this writing, the Justify command doesn't work in the current version of Excel (version 14.0.0). Until Microsoft fixes it, you can achieve the same effect by selecting the group of cells, choosing Format→Cells→Alignment, and choosing Center Across Selection from the Horizontal pop-up menu.

Using the Fill handle

You don't have to use the Edit→Fill submenu to harness the power of Excel's AutoFill feature. As a timesaving gesture, Microsoft also gives you the *fill handle* (see Figure 12-10), a small square in the lower right of a selection rectangle. It lets you fill adjacent cells with data, exactly like the Fill commands—but without a trip to a menu and a dialog box.

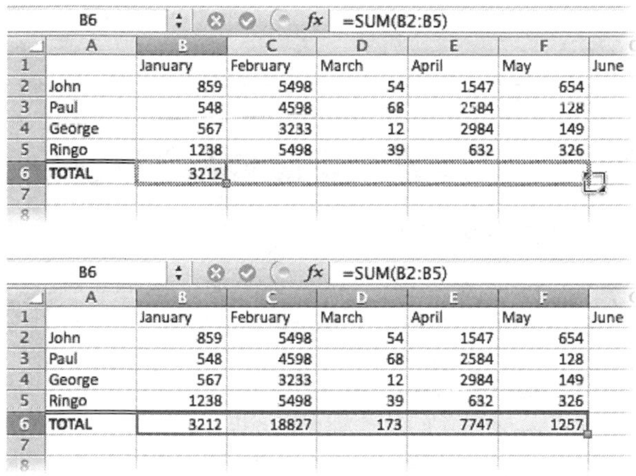

Figure 12-10:
To use the fill handle, select the cell containing the formula or values you want to replicate and drag the tiny fill handle at the lower-right corner of the selection across the cells you want to fill. When you release your mouse, Excel fills the cells and displays the smart button, giving you the option to fill with or without formatting, or with formatting only.

To use it, select the cells containing the data you want to duplicate or extend, then drag the tiny fill handle across the cells where you want the data to be, as shown in Figure 12-10. Excel then fills the cells, just as though you'd used the Fill Down, Right, Up, or Left command. (To fill a series, Control-drag the handle and choose an option from the shortcut menu.)

Tip: Excel can perform some dramatic and complex fill operations for you if you highlight *more than one* cell before dragging the fill handle. Suppose, for example, that you want to create a list of *every third* house number on your street. Enter *201 Elm St.* in the first cell, then *204 Elm St.* in the next one down. Highlight both of them, and then drag the fill handle at the lower-right corner of the second cell downward.

Excel cleverly fills the previously empty cells with *207 Elm St., 210 Elm St., 213 Elm St.*, and so on.

What's more, the fill handle can do *smart filling* that you won't find on the Edit→Fill submenu. For example, if you type *January* into a cell and then drag the fill handle across the next bunch of cells, Excel fills them with February, March, and so on; ditto for days of the week. Drag beyond December or Saturday, and Excel starts at the series over again. In fact, if you type January, March, drag through both cells to select them, and then drag the fill handle across subsequent cells, Excel fills them in with May, July, and so on. How cool is that?

What's more, you can teach Excel about any other sequential lists you regularly use in your line of work (NY Office, Cleveland Office, San Diego Office, and so on). Just choose Excel→Preferences→Custom Lists panel; click Add and then type the series of items in order, each on its own line. Click OK; the AutoFill list is now ready to use.

Tip: You can also type the list in a column of cells, select the cells, and then choose Excel→Preferences→Custom Lists→Add.

Invasion of the ######s

A few of my numbers have been replaced by ##### symbols. Do I have a virus?

A string of number signs in a cell means, "The cell isn't wide enough to show whatever text or number is supposed to be here. Widen the column—or use a smaller font—if you ever hope to see your numbers again."

As noted later in this chapter, the quickest way to fix the problem is to double-click the divider line between the gray column-letter headings—the one to the right of the column containing the ######s. Excel instantly makes the column wide enough to show all the numbers inside of it.

That's not the only error notation you might see in a cell, by the way. Excel might also react to faulty formulas by showing, for example, #DIV/0! (your formula is attempting to divide a number by zero, which, as you remember from third grade, is a mathematical no-no); #VALUE! (you've used unavailable data in a formula, by referring to an empty cell, for example); #REF (a bogus cell reference); and so on.

Selecting Cells (and Cell Ranges)

Selecting a single cell in Excel is easy. Just click the cell to select it. Often, though, you'll want to select more than one cell—in readiness for copying and pasting, making a chart, applying boldface, or using the Fill command, for example. Figure 12-11 depicts all you need to know for your selection needs.

- **Select a single cell**. To select a single cell, click it or enter its address in the Name box in the Formula bar (which is shown in Figure 12-2) or press F5.

- **Select a block of cells**. To select a rectangle of cells, just drag diagonally across them. You highlight all of the cells within the boundaries of the imaginary rectangle you're drawing. (Or click the cell in one corner of the block and then Shift-click the cell diagonally opposite.)

- **Select a noncontiguous group of cells**. To select cells that aren't touching, ⌘-click (to add individual independent cells to the selection) or ⌘-drag across cells (to add a block of them to the selection). Repeat as many times as you like; Excel is perfectly happy to highlight random cells, or blocks of cells, in various corners of the spreadsheet simultaneously.

- **Select a row or column**. Click a row or column *heading* (the gray label of the row or column).

- **Select several rows or columns**. To select more than one row or column, *drag through* the gray row numbers or column letters. (You can also click the first one, then Shift-click the last one. Excel highlights everything in between.)

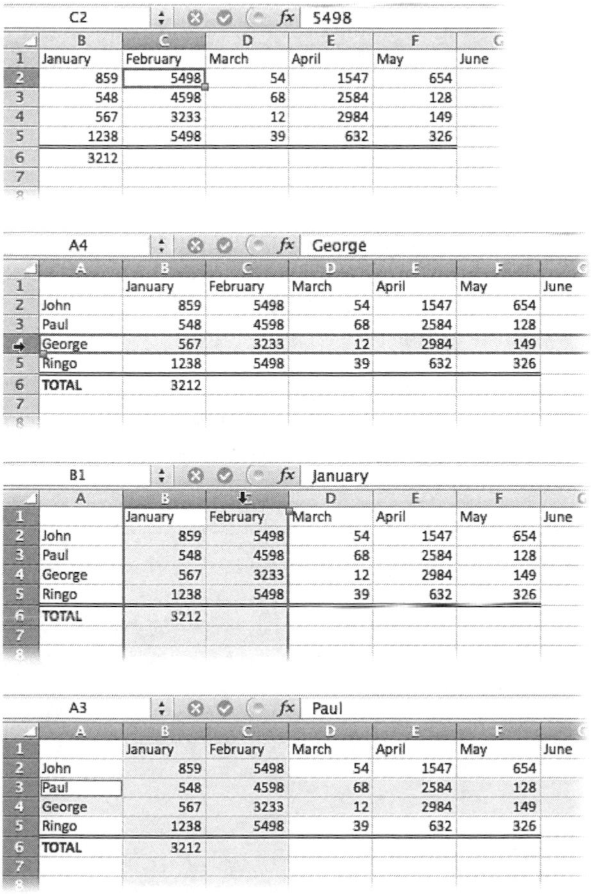

Figure 12-11:
You can highlight spreadsheet cells, rows, and columns in various combinations. You can copy using rectangular-shaped selections, but you can apply cell formatting changes to any group of selected cells.

Top: Click a cell (or arrow-key your way into it) to highlight just one cell.

Second from top: Click a row number or column letter (row 4, in this case) to highlight an entire row or column.

Third from top: Drag to highlight a rectangular block of cells; add individual additional cells to the selection by ⌘-clicking.

Bottom: ⌘-click row headings and column headings to highlight intersecting rows and columns.

- **Select noncontiguous rows or columns**. To select two or more rows or columns that aren't touching, ⌘-click or ⌘-drag through the corresponding gray row numbers. You can even combine these techniques—highlight first rows, then columns, and voilà! Intersecting swaths of highlighting.
- **Select all cells**. Press ⌘-A to select every cell on the sheet—or just click the gray, far upper-left rectangle with the triangle in it.

Tip: To select within the *contents* of a cell, double-click the cell and then use the I-beam selection tool to select the text you want.

Moving Things Around

Once you've selected some cells, you can move their contents around in various ways—a handy fact, since few people type everything in exactly the right place the first time. Excel only lets you copy groups of cells that are basically rectangular in shape or that share the same rows and multiple columns or the same columns in multiple rows. Figure 12-12 shows some acceptable and unacceptable selections for copying.

Cutting, copying, and pasting

Just as in any other Mac program, you can use the Edit menu commands—Cut (⌘-X), Copy (⌘-C), and Paste (⌘-V)—to move cell contents around the spreadsheet—or to a different sheet or workbook altogether. When you paste a group of cells, you can either select the same number of cells at your destination, or select just one cell—which becomes the upper-left cell of the pasted group.

But unlike other Mac programs, Excel doesn't appear to cut your selection immediately. Instead, the cut area sprouts a dotted, *moving border*, but otherwise remains unaffected. It isn't until you select a destination cell or cells and select Edit→Paste that the cut takes place (and the shimmering stops).

Tip: Press the Esc key to make the animated dotted lines stop moving, without otherwise affecting your copy or cut operation. One more piece of advice: Check the status bar at the bottom of the window to find out what Excel thinks is happening ("Select destination and press ENTER or choose Paste," for example).

B2		fx	859			
A	B	C	D	E	F	G
1		January	February	March	April	May	June
2 John	859	5498	54	1547	654	
3 Paul	548	4598	68	2584	128	
4 George	567	3233	12	2984	149	
5 Ringo	1238	5498	39	632	326	
6 TOTAL	3212	18827	173	7747	1257	
7						
8						

Figure 12-12:
Thou shalt copy multiple cells by selecting a rectangular group of cells, an entire row or column, multiple rows or columns, or matching groups of cells in various rows or columns. The three upper examples are acceptable, the bottom one is not. If you try to copy a group of cells and don't follow these selection rules, Excel informs you of your error: "That command cannot be used on multiple selections."

D1		fx	March			
A	B	C	D	E	F	G
1		January	February	March	April	May	June
2 John	859	5498	54	1547	654	
3 Paul	548	4598	68	2584	128	
4 George	567	3233	12	2984	149	
5 Ringo	1238	5498	39	632	326	
6 TOTAL	3212	18827	173	7747	1257	
7						
8						

B5		fx	1238			
A	B	C	D	E	F	G
1		January	February	March	April	May	June
2 John	859	5498	54	1547	654	
3 Paul	548	4598	68	2584	128	
4 George	567	3233	12	2984	149	
5 Ringo	1238	5498	39	632	326	
6 TOTAL	3212	18827	173	7747	1257	
7						
8						

D5		fx	39			
A	B	C	D	E	F	G
1		January	February	March	April	May	June
2 John	859	5498	54	1547	654	
3 Paul	548	4598	68	2584	128	
4 George	567	3233	12	2984	149	
5 Ringo	1238	5498	39	632	326	
6 TOTAL	3212	18827	173	7747	1257	
7						
8						

Paste Special

The Edit→Paste Special command summons a dialog box inquiring about *how* and *what* to paste. For example, you might decide to paste the formulas contained in the material you copied so that they continue to do automatic math—or only the *values* (the results of the calculations as they appear in the copied material).

Tip: This dialog box also contains the mighty Transpose checkbox, a tiny option that can save your bacon. It lets you swap rows-for-columns in the act of pasting, so that data you input in columns winds up in rows, and vice versa. This kind of topsy-turvy spreadsheet modification can be a great help if you want to swap the orientation of your entire spreadsheet, or copy a group of cells between spreadsheets which have juxtaposed rows and columns.

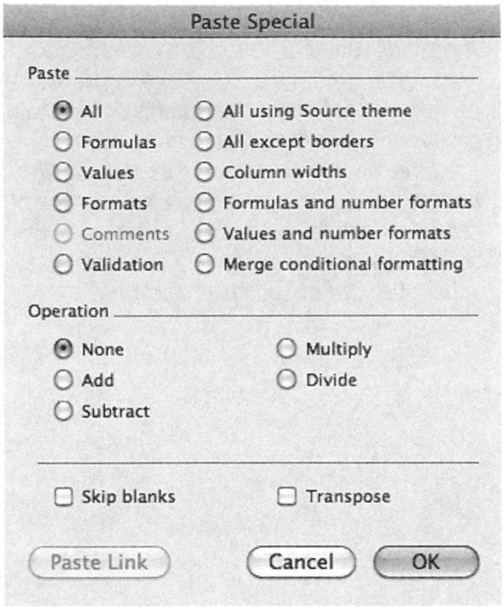

Figure 12-13:
The Paste Special command lets you paste formulas, comments, and formatting independently. The Operations options let you perform a mathematical operation as you paste, such as adding what you've copied to the contents of the cells you're pasting over.

Drag-and-drop

Excel also lets you grab a selected range of cells and drag the contents to a new location. To do this, select the cells you want to move, then point to the thick border on the edge of the selection, so that the cursor changes into a little hand that grabs the cells. You can now drag the selected cells to another spot on the spreadsheet. When you release the mouse button, Excel moves the data to the new location, exactly as though you'd used Cut and Paste.

You can modify how dragging and dropping items in Excel works by holding down these modifier keys:

- **Option**. If you hold down the Option key, Excel *copies* the contents to the new location, leaving the originals in place.

- **Shift**. Normally, if you drag cells into a spreadsheet area that you've already filled in, Excel asks if you're sure you want to wipe out the cell contents already in residence. If you Shift-drag cells, however, Excel creates enough new cells to make room for the dragged contents, shoving aside (or down) the cell contents current occupants in order to make room.

- **Option and Shift**. Holding down both the Option *and* Shift keys as you drag copies the data *and* inserts new cells for it.

- **Control**. Control-dragging yields a menu of 11 options when you drop the cells. This menu lets you choose whether you want to move the cells, copy them, copy just the values or formulas, create a link or hyperlink, or shift cells around. It even lets you cancel the drag.

- **Command.** If you want to drag cells to a different worksheet in your workbook, select the cells, hold down the Command (⌘) key, and point to the tab of the destination worksheet. Once the view changes to the new sheet, continue to drag the cells to their new home.

Inserting and Removing Cells

Suppose you've just completed your spreadsheet cataloging the rainfall patterns of the Pacific Northwest, county by county, and then it hits you: You forgot Humboldt County in California. Besides the question of how you could possibly forget Humboldt County, the larger question remains: What do you do about it in your spreadsheet? Delete the whole thing and start over?

Fortunately, Excel lets you insert blank cells, rows, or columns into existing sheets through the Insert menu. Here's how each works.

- **Cells**. The Insert→Cells command summons the Insert dialog box. It lets you insert new, blank cells into your spreadsheet, and lets you specify what happens to the cells that are already in place—whether they get shifted right or down. See Figure 12-14.

- **Rows**. If you choose Insert→Rows, Excel inserts a new, blank row above the active cell.

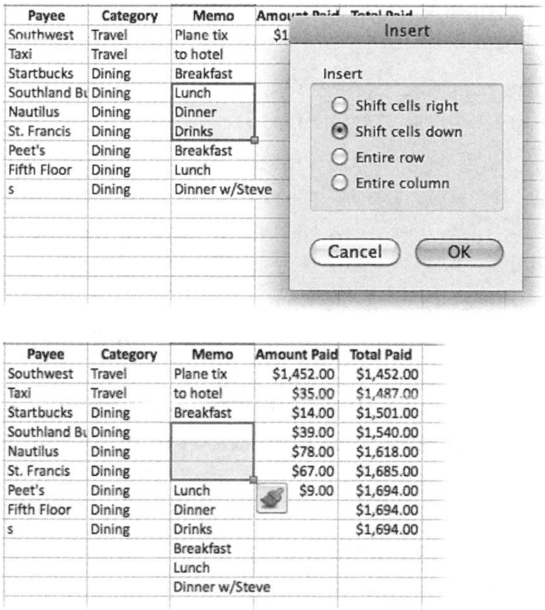

Figure 12-14:
When you select cells and then choose Insert→Cells, Excel asks where you want to put the new cells (top). The two buttons at the bottom let you insert entire rows or columns. Excel then inserts the same number of cells as you've selected in the location selected, and moves the previous residents of those cells in the direction that you specify (bottom). In addition, the Format smart button appears, giving you three choices: format your new cells to match those above, those below, or without formatting at all.

Tip: If you select some cells before using the Insert→Cells command, Excel inserts the number of rows equal to the number of rows selected in the range. That's a handy way to control how many rows get added—to add six blank rows, highlight six rows, regardless of what's in them at the moment.

- **Columns**. If you choose Insert→Columns, Excel inserts a new blank column to the left of the active cell. If you've selected a range of cells, Excel inserts the number of columns equal to the number of columns selected in the range.

Warning: If the cells, columns, or rows that you send shifting across the spreadsheet by inserting cells already contain data, you can mangle the entire spreadsheet in short order. For example, data you entered in the debit column can suddenly end up in the credit column. Proceed with extreme caution.

Find and Replace

Exactly as in Word, Excel has both a Find function, which helps you locate a specific spot in a big workbook, and a Replace feature that's ideal for those moments when your company gets incorporated into a larger one, requiring its name to be changed in 34 places throughout a workbook. The routine goes like this:

1. **Highlight the cells you want to search.**

   This step is crucial. By limiting the search range, you ensure that your search-and-rescue operation won't run rampant through your spreadsheet, changing things you'd rather leave as is.

2. **Choose Edit→Find. In the resulting dialog box, specify what you want to search for, and in which direction (see Figure 12-15).**

   You can use a question mark (?) as a stand-in for a single character, or an asterisk (*) to represent more than one character. In other words, typing *P?ts* will find cells containing "Pats," "Pots," and "Pits"; while typing *P*ts* will find cells containing "Profits," "Prophets," and "Poltergeists."

   The "Find entire cells only" checkbox means that Excel will consider a cell a match for your search term only if its entire contents match; a cell that says "Annual profits" isn't considered a match for the search term "Profits."

3. **If you intend to *replace* the cell contents (instead of just finding them), click Replace; type the replacement text into the "Replace with" box. Click Find Next (or press Return).**

   Each time you click Find Next, Excel highlights the next cell it finds that matches your search phrase. If you click Replace, you replace the text with the "Replace with" text. If you click Replace All, of course, you replace *every* matching occurrence in the selected cells. Use caution.

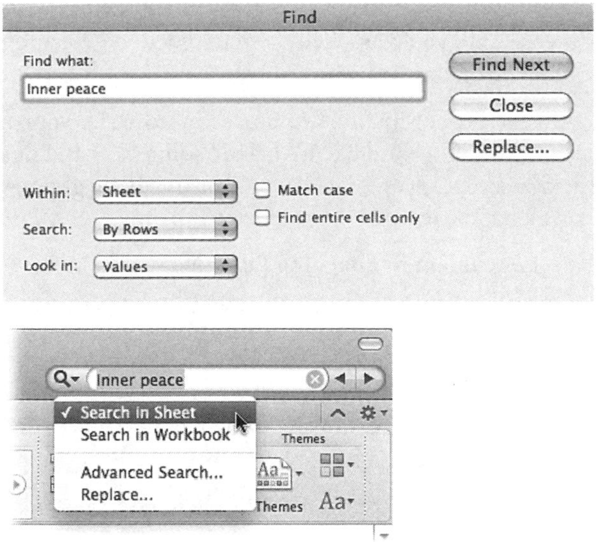

Figure 12-15:
Top: Using the Search pop-up menu, you can specify whether Excel searches the highlighted cells from left to right of each row ("By Rows") or down each column ("By Columns"). Use the "Look in" pop-up menu to specify which cell components are fair game for the search: formulas, values (that is, the results of those formulas, and other data you've typed into the cells), or comments. Turn on "Match case" if you're trying to find "Bill" and not "bill."

Bottom: For quick and easy search missions, you may want to use the standard Search box in the upper-right corner of the document window.

Erasing Cells

"Erase," as any CIA operative can attest, is a relative term. In Excel, the Edit→Clear submenu lets you strip away various kinds of information without necessarily emptying the cell completely. For example:

- **Edit→Clear→All** truly empties the selected cells, restoring them to their pristine, empty, and unformatted condition. (Control-B does the same thing.)

- **Edit→Clear→Formats** leaves the contents, but strips away formatting (including both text and number formatting).

- **Edit→Clear→Contents** empties the cell, but leaves the formatting in place. If you then type new numbers into the cell, they take on whatever cell formatting you had applied (bold, blue, Currency, and so on).

- **Edit→Clear→Comments** deletes only electronic yellow sticky notes (see page 438).

None of these is the same as Edit→Delete, which actually chops cells out of your spreadsheet and makes others slide upward or leftward to fill the gap. (Excel asks you which way you want existing cells to slide.)

Tutorial 1: Entering Data

If you've never used a spreadsheet before, the concepts described in the previous pages may not make much sense until you've applied them in practice. This tutorial, which continues with a second lesson on page 379, can help.

Suppose that you, Web marketer extraordinaire, are preparing to write your next bestseller, *The Two-Hour Workweek*, and you'd like to include some facts and figures about your remarkable rise to success. So you cancel your morning hang gliding lesson and crank up Excel to get a handle on your years of part-time toil.

1. **Create a new spreadsheet document by choosing File→New (⌘-N).**

   Excel fills your screen with the spreadsheet grid; the first cell, A1, is selected as the active cell, awaiting your keystrokes.

2. **Begin by typing the title of your spreadsheet in cell A1.**

   Profit and Loss Statement: Time is Not Money might be a good choice. As you type, the characters appear in the cell and in the Edit box in the Formula bar.

3. **Click outside of cell A1 to get out of the entry mode, click back on cell A1 to highlight it, and then press ⌘-B.**

   Excel inserts your text into cell A1. Since all the cells to the right of A1 are empty, Excel runs the contents of cell A1 right over the top of them. When you press ⌘-B, Excel formats the first cell's text in bold, to make a more impressive title for your spreadsheet.

4. **Press Return three times. And then press ⌘-S.**

   Excel moves the active cell frame down a couple of rows, selecting cell A4. Even if you haven't entered any data yet, save the spreadsheet by pressing ⌘-S (or choosing File→Save), naming it, and then choosing a suitable destination. Now as you continue to work on your spreadsheet, periodically press ⌘-S to save your work as you go along.

5. **Type *January*.**

   You need to track expenses over time: to track the project by calendar year, name the first column *January*. You could now tab to the next cell, enter *February*, and work your way down the spreadsheet—but there's an easier way.

   As noted earlier, Excel can create a series of months automatically for you, saving you the effort of typing *February, March*, and so on—you just have to start it off with the first entry or two.

6. **Click once outside cell A4 to get out of entry mode, and then click cell A4 again to select it. Carefully click the tiny square at the lower-right corner of the highlighted cell; drag directly downward through 11 more cells.**

   Pop-out yellow screen tips reveal what Excel intends to autofill into the cells you're dragging through. When the screen tip says *December*, stop.

   Excel enters the months and highlights the cells you dragged through. Figure 12-16 shows this step.

   Now it's time to add the year headings across the top.

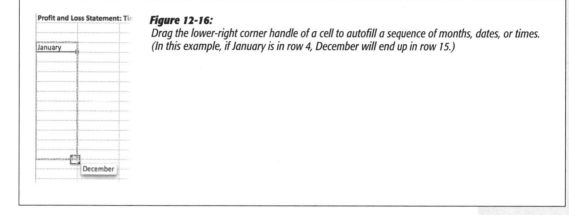

Figure 12-16:
Drag the lower-right corner handle of a cell to autofill a sequence of months, dates, or times. (In this example, if January is in row 4, December will end up in row 15.)

7. **Click cell B3 to select it. Type *2006*. Press Tab, type *2007*, and then press Return.**

   You'll use the same AutoFill mechanism to type in the names of the next four years. But just dragging the tiny square AutoFill handle on the 2006 cell wouldn't work this time, because Excel wouldn't know whether you want to fill *every* cell with "2006" or to add successive years. So, you've given it the first *two* years as a hint.

8. **Drag through the 2006 and 2007 cells to highlight them. Carefully click the tiny square at the lower-right corner of the 2007 cell; drag directly to the right through three more cells.**

   Excel automatically fills in *2008, 2009,* and *2010,* using the data in the first two cells to establish the sequence.

   If you like, you can now highlight the year row, the month column, or both, and then press ⌘-B to make them boldface (see Figure 12-17). Chapter 16 has more details on formatting your spreadsheets.

   Now that the basic framework of the spreadsheet is in place, you can begin typing in actual numbers.

Profit and Loss Statement: Time is Not Money					
	2006	**2007**	**2008**	**2009**	**2010**
January	-1895	2323	12151	21979	30659
February	-1470	3142	12970	22798	29684
March	-1109	3961	13789	23616	32984
April	-752	4780	14608	27436	31597
May	-321	5599	15427	25255	31449
June	-648	6418	16246	26074	30945
July	-288	7237	17065	26893	34697
August	-305	8056	17884	29712	32458
September	-96	8875	18703	28531	33125
October	59	9694	19522	31350	35698
November	298	10513	20341	30169	34254
December	1697	11332	21160	30988	35412

Figure 12-17:
You can make the headings stand out from the data you'll soon put in the cells by changing the font style and alignment (see Chapter 16). In this example, the row and column headings are bold, and the column headings are centered.

9. **Click cell B4, January 2006. Enter a figure for your January income.**

   Your first several months of operation showed a loss since you were investing in lots of "Get Rich Quick on the Internet!" programs. You invested heavily at the beginning, and your losses in January were $1,895. Since this is a loss, enter it as a negative number, and leave off the dollar sign—just type *-1895*.

10. **Press Return (or the down arrow key).**

    Excel moves the active cell frame to the next row down.

11. **Type another number to represent your loss for February; press Return. Repeat steps 9 and 10 until you get to the bottom of the 2004 column.**

    For this experiment, the exact numbers to type don't matter too much, but Figure 12-16 shows one suggestion. Perhaps, toward the end of that first year, you started making money instead of losing money.

12. **Click in the January 2007 column (C4); fill in the numbers for each month, pressing Return after each entry. Repeat with the other years.**

    Remember, this is a success story, so type ever-increasing numbers in your columns, because once you started making money, it was an ever-upward trend. But then your income kind of leveled off toward the end of 2010 as you cut back your work week to two hours.

    When you've successfully filled your spreadsheet with data, save your work one more time. You'll return to it later in this chapter—after you've read about what Excel can *do* with all of these numbers.

Formula Fundamentals

Without *formulas*, Excel would just be glorified graph paper. With them, Excel becomes a number-crunching powerhouse worthy of its own corner office. Excel formulas do everything from basic arithmetic to complex financial analysis. And

Excel 2011 makes working with formulas easier than ever. Formula AutoComplete helps you write formulas even if you can't remember all the arcane elements of particular formula. As you type, Excel presents valid functions, names, and named ranges for you to choose from. In addition, the new Formula Builder joins the toolbox, where you can search for, learn about, and build formulas by following simple instructions.

Basic Calculations

A *formula* in a cell can perform calculations on other cells' contents. For example, if cell A1 contains the number of hours in a day, and cell A2 contains the number of days in a year, then you could type =A1*A2 into cell B3 to find out how many hours there are in a year. (In spreadsheet lingo, you'd say that this formula *returns* the number 8760.)

After typing the formula and pressing Return, you'd see only the mathematical answer in cell B3; the formula itself is hidden, though you can see it in the Formula bar if you click the cell again (Figure 12-18).

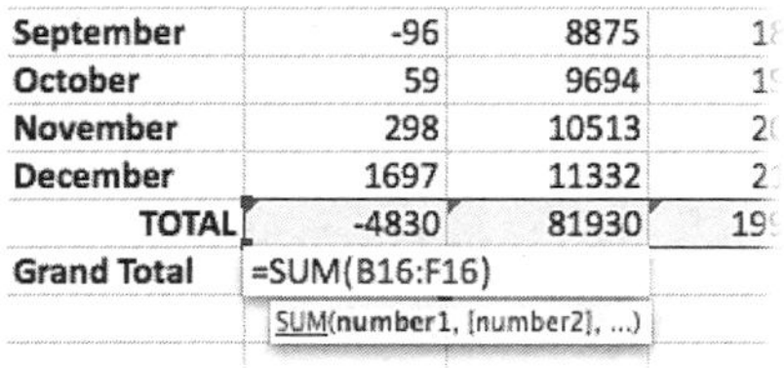

September	-96	8875	1
October	59	9694	1
November	298	10513	2
December	1697	11332	2
TOTAL	-4830	81930	19
Grand Total	=SUM(B16:F16)		
	SUM(number1, [number2], ...)		

Figure 12-18:
The Rangefinder highlights each cell that's included in the formula you're currently typing. Furthermore, the color of the outline around the cells matches the typed cell reference.

Formulas do math on *values*. A value is any number, date, time, text, or cell address that you feed into a formula. The math depends on the *operators* in the formula—symbols like + for addition, – for subtraction, / for division, * for multiplication, and so on.

Tip: Your formulas don't have to remain invisible until clicked. To reveal formulas on a given sheet, press Control-` (the key in the upper-left corner of most keyboards). This command toggles the spreadsheet cells so that they show formulas instead of results. (Excel widens your columns considerably, as necessary, to show the formulas.) To return things to the way they were, press Control-` again.

Consider that keystroke a shortcut for the official way to bring formulas into view: Excel→Preferences→ View panel. Under Window options, click Formulas; click OK. Repeat the whole procedure to restore the results-only view. Aren't you glad you've now memorized the Control-` shortcut?

Error checking

If you make a mistake when you're typing in a formula, Excel's error-checking buttons attempt to return you to the straight and narrow. For example, if you type =*suum*

E3:E6, Excel displays "#NAME?" in the cell. Click the cell to display the error-checking button, as shown in Figure 12-19. Clicking the tiny arrow on the right of the button displays several options and bits of information, like the following:

- **Error Name**. The name of the error heads the list. Fortunately, it's a descriptive name of the error, like Invalid Name Error.

- **Help on this Error**. Click here to view the Excel Help screen on this particular error. This information may help you understand where you went wrong.

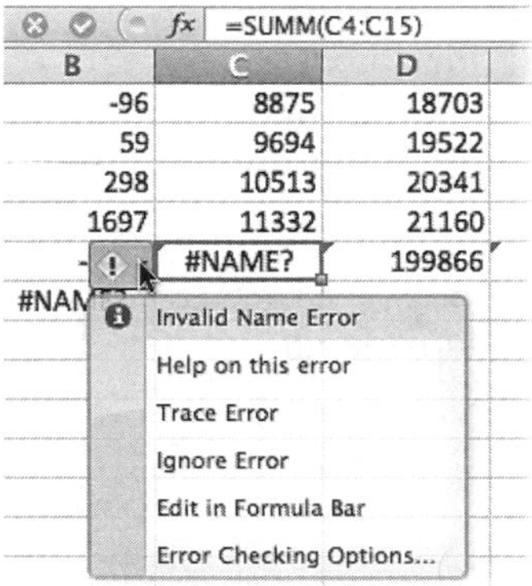

Figure 12-19:
If you choose to edit the formula in the Formula bar, the alleged formula becomes active in the Formula bar. There you can edit it, and with any luck, fix the problem. Note that when presented in the Formula bar, the formula's cell references are color-coded to indicate which color-coded cell they apply to.

- **Trace Error**. Draws lines to the cells that might be causing the errors. Examine the cells in question to determine what you might have done incorrectly.

- **Ignore Error**. The computing equivalent of saying "never mind." Choosing this item tells Excel to leave the formula as you entered it. (Excel obeys you, but let's hope you know more than Excel does—there's no guarantee that the formula will work.)

- **Edit in Formula Bar**. This option lets you edit the formula in the Formula bar as described in Figure 12-19.

- **Error Checking Options**. Opens the Excel→Preferences→Error Checking tab. Here you can turn error checking on and off, and tell Excel which kinds of errors to look for, like empty or missing cells in formulas.

To enter a simple formula that you know well, just double-click the cell and start typing (or click the Edit box in the Formula bar, shown in Figure 12-19, and type there). The cursor appears simultaneously in the cell and in the Edit box, signaling that Excel awaits your next move.

Your next move is to type an equal sign (=), since every formula starts that way. Then type the rest of the formula using values and operators. When you want to incorporate a reference to a particular cell in your formula, you don't actually have to type out B12 or whatever—just *click* the cell in question. Similarly, to insert a range of cells, just drag through them.

Tip: If you mess up while entering a formula and want to start fresh, click the Cancel button at the right end of the Formula bar. (It looks like an X.)

To complete a formula press Enter, Return, Tab, or an arrow key—your choice.

Functions

When you tire of typing formulas from scratch (or, let's be honest, when you can't figure out what to type), you can let Excel do the brainwork by using *functions*. Functions are just predefined formulas. For example, the SUM function adds a range of specified values [=SUM(B3:B7)] so you don't have to type the plus sign between each one [=B3+B4+B5+B6+B7]. Excel 2011 adds Formula AutoComplete and the Formula Builder to help you find and enter functions properly. In addition, Excel Help is a veritable Function University with detailed information and examples for all of its functions.

Function screen tips and AutoComplete

Screen tips (Figure 12-20) for function help are a real boon to spread-sheeting neo-phytes and dataheads alike. As you start to type a function into a cell, AutoComplete pops up a list of function names matching what you've typed so far. Click one to add it to the cell. Then a screen tip displays the syntax of the function in a pale yellow box just below where you're typing. Not only does the screen tip show you how to cor-rectly type the function it believes you have in mind, but you can also use the screen tip in other ways. For example, you can drag the screen tip to reposition it (to get a better look at your worksheet), click a piece of the tip to select it, or click the function to open up its Help topic in a separate window.

Tip: If you want to turn off function screen tips, choose Excel→Preferences→View and then remove the checkmark next to "Show function ScreenTips".

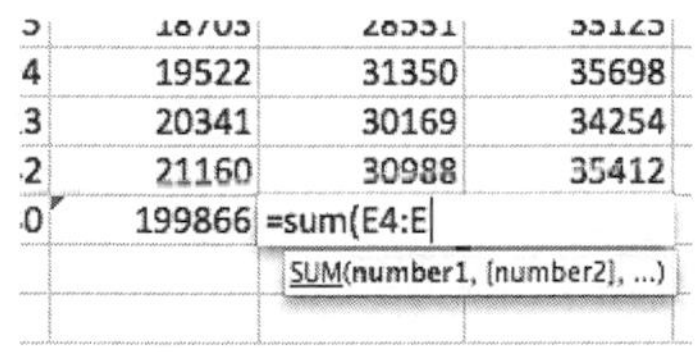

5	18705	28551	33123
4	19522	31350	35698
3	20341	30169	34254
2	21160	30988	35412
0	199866	=sum(E4:E	
		SUM(number1, [number2], …)	

Figure 12-20:
Excel's Function screen tips make an educated guess at what you're trying to do—usually a pretty darn good one—and provide the correct syntax for doing it. Here, the SUM screen tip explains how to add a series of numbers.

The AutoSum button

You don't need access to Microsoft's reams of focus-group studies to realize that the most commonly used spreadsheet function is *adding things up*. That's why Excel comes equipped with a toolbar button that does nothing but add up the values in the column directly above, or the row to the left of, the active cell, as Figure 12-21 shows. (The tutorial that resumes in "Tutorial 2: Yearly Totals" also shows why AutoSum is one of the most important buttons in Excel.)

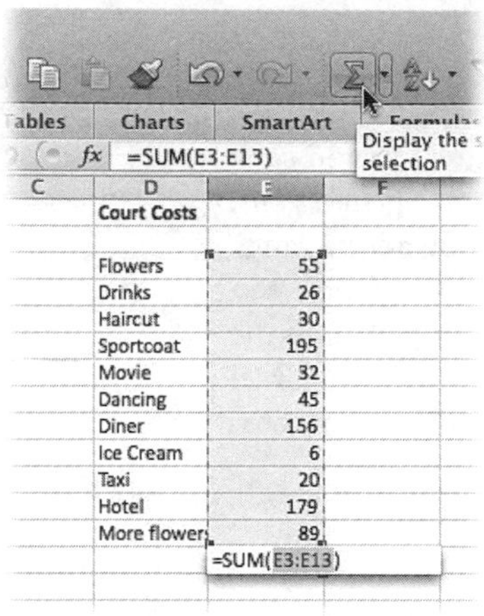

Figure 12-21:
The powerful AutoSum button on the Standard toolbar (upper-right) is the key to quickly adding a row or column. A click of the button puts a SUM function in the selected cell, which assumes that you want to add up the cells above it. Note that it doesn't write out C3+C4+C5+C6+C7+C8+C9, and so on; it sets up a range of numbers using the shorthand notation C3:C13. When you press Return, you see only the result, not the formula.

The flippy triangle to the right of the AutoSum button reveals a menu with a few other extremely common options, such as the following:

- **Average.** Calculates the average (the arithmetic mean) of the numbers in the column above the active cell. For example, if the column of numbers represents your website revenues for each month, then using this function gives you your average monthly income.

- **Count Numbers.** Tells you *how many* cells in a selected cell range contain numbers.

- **Max** and **Min.** Shows the highest or lowest value of any of the numbers referred to in the function.

- **More Functions.** When you choose this command, the Formula Builder appears, described shortly.

Tip: After you click the AutoSum button (or use one of its pop-up menu commands), Excel assumes that you intend to compute using the numbers in the cells just *above* or *to the left of* the highlighted cell. It indicates, with a moving border, which cells it intends to include in its calculation.

But if it guesses wrong, simply grab your mouse and adjust the selection rectangle by one of its corner handles or just drag through the numbers you *do* want computed. Excel redraws its border and updates its formula. Press Return to complete the formula.

The Anatomy of a Function in a Formula

Like web-page and email addresses, formulas with functions have a regular form. If you understand that anatomy, you'll find working with formulas much easier.

The first element in a formula is the equal sign (=), which signals to Excel that what follows is a formula, not plain old data. Next comes the function name, like SUM. After the function name comes a left parenthesis, which tells Excel that the function's *arguments* are coming next.

Arguments in this case have nothing to do with the validity of the entries in your expense report, and everything to do with telling the function what *values* to process—values being the numbers or text in a cell.

Some functions have one argument, others have more, and a few have none. To use more than one argument,

separate them with commas. Finally, finish the function with a closing parenthesis. Each function expects its arguments to be listed in a very specific manner, or *syntax*.

For example, the formula =SUM(B4:B8,20) adds the contents of cells B4, B5, B6, B7, and B8, and then adds 20. *SUM* is the function, *(B4:B8,20)* are the arguments.

Given the many functions and operators Excel provides, you can do more number crunching in an hour with Excel than you probably did in your entire grade-school experience. (Unless, of course, you used spreadsheets in grade school, in which case you're probably not reading this section anyway.)

Looking up functions with the Formula Builder

Whipping up the sum or average of some cells is only the beginning. Excel is also capable of performing the kinds of advanced number crunching that can calculate interest rates, find the cosine of an arc, find the inverse of the one-tailed probability of the chi-squared distribution, and so on. It's safe to say that no one has all of these functions memorized.

Fortunately, you don't have to remember how to write each function; save that brainpower for the Sunday Times crossword. Instead, you can use Excel's new Formula Builder to look up the exact function that you need. To call up the Formula Builder, click the fx button on the formula bar, choose View→Formula Builder, or click the Toolbox button on the Standard toolbar and then click the *fx* button.

No matter how you get there, the Formula Builder toolbox appears, ready to simplify your search for and use of functions. The top of the Formula Builder displays a search field (see Figure 12-22) where you can type any bit of information relating to the function you're looking for. You can type *cosine*, for example, and the Formula Builder displays in its main panel the six functions which somehow relate to cosine. Click any of the functions to read a brief description and the syntax for that function. Double-clicking the function does two things: it inserts the function in the active cell of your spreadsheet and opens the Arguments pane of the Format Builder where it displays the arguments (if any) it's extracted from your spreadsheet, and at the bottom of the window displays the result.

Just like when you use the AutoSum button, if Excel guesses wrong and highlights the wrong cells in your spreadsheet, either readjust the selection rectangle or click the appropriate cells. Press Return to enter the function into your spreadsheet.

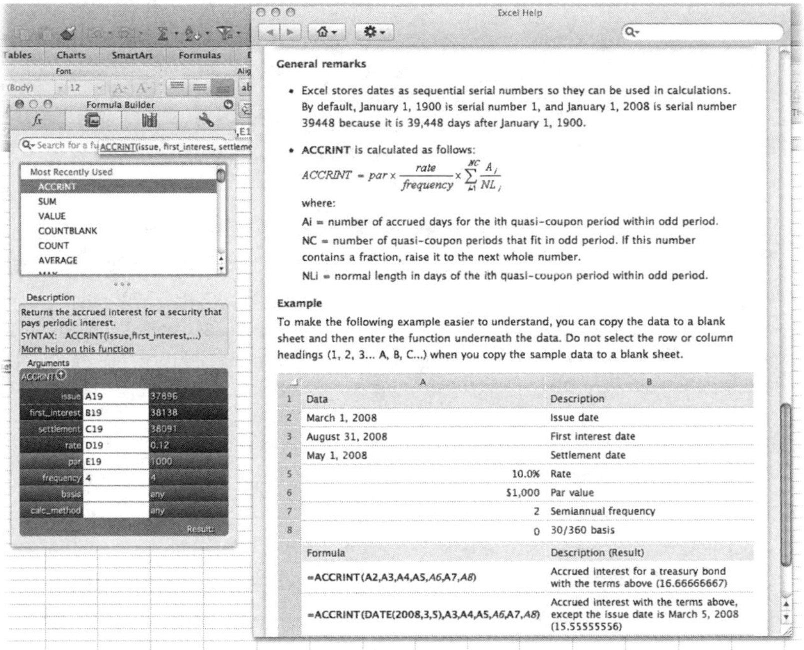

Figure 12-22:
Using the Formula Builder (left) you can focus your hunt for the correct one from among the hundreds offered by using the search field at the top of the window. Double-click a function to open the arguments pane, where you can fill in the arguments by clicking cells and making entries directly in this window. When complete, the Formula Builder displays the result at the bottom. To learn more about any specific function, for more assistance with the arguments, or to view sample examples, click "More help on this function" to summon the Excel Help window for that function (right).

Order of Calculation

As you no doubt recall from your basic algebra class, you get different answers to an equation depending on how its elements are ordered. So it's important for *you*, the purveyor of fine Excel formulas, to understand the order in which Excel makes its calculations.

If a formula is spitting out results that don't jibe with what you think ought to be the answer, consult the following table. Excel calculates the operations at the top of the table first, working its way down until it hits bottom. For example, Excel computes cell references before it tackles multiplication, and it does multiplication before it works on a "less than" operation.

Table 12-1. *Excel's calculation order*

Computed First		
:	Colon, reference operator (such as a series of cells)	
,	Comma, reference operator	
	Single space, reference operator	
-	Negation (multiplying the number by -1)	
%	Percent	
^	Exponents	
* and /	Multiplication, division	
+ and −	Addition, subtraction	
&	String concatenation	
- < > < - > - < >	Comparison (equals, less than, and so on)	
Computed Last		

For example, Excel's answer to =2+3*4 is not 20. It's 14, because Excel performs multiplication and division within the formula *before* doing addition and subtraction.

You can exercise some control over the processing order by using parentheses. Excel calculates expressions within () symbols before bringing the parenthetical items together for calculation. So in the above example, =(2+3)*4 returns 20. Or, the formula =*C12*(C3-C6)* subtracts the value in C6 from the value in C3 and multiplies the result by the value in C12. Without the parentheses, the formula would read =*C12*C3-C6*, and Excel would multiply C12 by C3 and *then* subtract C6—a different formula entirely.

Tip: Excel does its best to alert you to mistakes you make when entering formulas manually. For example, if you leave off a closing parenthesis (after using an open parenthesis), Excel pops up a dialog box suggesting a fix—and sometimes just fixes it without asking.

Tutorial 2: Yearly Totals

Suppose you've entered a few numbers into a spreadsheet, as described in the tutorial earlier in this chapter. Finally it's time to put these numbers to work. Open the document shown in Figure 12-17.

Now that it has some data to work with, Excel can do a little work. Start with one of the most common spreadsheet calculations: totaling a column of numbers. First, create a row for totals.

1. **Click cell A17 (leaving a blank row beneath the month list). Type** *Total*.

   This row will soon contain totals for each year column.

2. **Click cell B17, in the Total row for 2006. Click the AutoSum button on the Standard toolbar.**

    In cell B17, Excel automatically proposes a *formula* for totaling the column of numbers. (It's =*SUM(B3:B16)*, meaning "add up the cells from B3 through B16.") The moving border shows that Excel is prepared to add up *all* of the numbers in this column—including the year label *2004!* Clearly, that's not what you want, so don't press Return yet.

3. **Drag through the numbers you *do* want added: from cell B4 down to B15. Then press Return.**

    Excel adds up the column.

    Now comes the real magic of spreadsheeting: If one of the numbers in the column *changes*, the total changes automatically. Try it.

4. **Click one of the numbers in column B, type a much bigger number, and then press Return.**

    Excel instantly updates 2006's total to reflect the change.

Tip: The AutoSum feature doesn't have to add up numbers *above* the selected cell; it can also add up a *row* of cells. In fact, you can even click the AutoSum button and then drag through a *block* of cells to make Excel add up all of *those* numbers.

You *could* continue selecting the Total cells for each year and using AutoSum to create your totals. Instead, you can avoid repetition by using the Fill command described earlier in this chapter. You can tell Excel to create a calculation similar to the 2006 total for the rest of the columns in the spreadsheet.

5. **Click the cell containing the 2006 total (B17) and drag the selection's Fill handle (see page 359) to the right, all the way over to the 2010 column (F17).**

    As you drag, Excel highlights the range of cells for column totals, and when you release your mouse, it fills those cells with column totals as shown in Figure 12-23.

    You could've accomplished the same thing by first just selecting the range of cells and then choosing Edit→Fill→Right—but why would you want to?

    Either way, Excel copies the contents of the first cell and pastes it into every other cell in the selection. In this example, the first cell contains a *formula*, not just a total you typed yourself. But, instead of pasting the exact same formula, which would place the 2004 total into each column, Excel understands that you want to total each column, and therefore enters the appropriate formula in each cell of your selection. The result is yearly totals calculated right across the page.

    Finally, to make the yearly totals in the tutorial example more meaningful—and see just how much money you actually made—calculate an overall total for the spreadsheet.

6. **Click cell A19, type *Grand Total*, and then press Tab.**

   Excel moves the active cell to B19.

   To calculate a lifetime total for the spreadsheet, you need to tell Excel to add together all the yearly totals.

7. **Click the AutoSum button on the Standard toolbar.**

   In this case, the cells you want to add aren't lined up with the Grand Total cell, so the AutoSum button doesn't work quite right; it proposes totaling the column of numbers above it.

8. **Drag across the yearly totals (from B17 through F17).**

   As you drag across the cells, Excel inserts the cell range within the formula and outlines the range of cells. In this example, the function now reads, =SUM(B17:F17)—in other words, "add up the contents of the cells B17 through F17, and display the result."

9. **Press Return (or Enter).**

   Excel performs the calculation and displays the result in cell B19, the grand total for the rags to riches story of an Internet marketer.

Profit and Loss Statement: Time is Not Money					
	2006	**2007**	**2008**	**2009**	**2010**
January	-1895	2323	12151	21979	30659
February	-1470	3142	12970	22798	29684
March	-1109	3961	13789	23616	32984
April	-752	4780	14608	27436	31597
May	-321	5599	15427	25255	31449
June	-648	6418	16246	26074	30945
July	-288	7237	17065	26893	34697
August	-305	8056	17884	29712	32458
September	-96	8875	18703	28531	33125
October	59	9694	19522	31350	35698
November	298	10513	20341	30169	34254
December	1697	11332	21160	30988	35412
TOTAL	-4830				

November	298	10513	20341	30169	34254
December	1697	11332	21160	30988	35412
TOTAL	-4830	81930	199866	324801	392962

Figure 12-23:
Top: To total all of the columns in the spreadsheet quickly, drag the Fill handle from the cell containing the total for the first column (B17) all the way over to the last column.

Bottom: When you release the mouse, Excel creates a total for each of the selected columns.

Note: For comparison, you can download a copy of this completed tutorial from the Missing CD at *http://missingmanuals.com/cds*. The file is named *12-2_Profit_Loss.xlsx*.

Building Advanced Workbooks

Congratulations, you've mastered enough of Excel to input numbers, apply basic formatting and perform basic arithmetic on cells, rows and columns. In fact—you already have far more spreadsheet ability than most people.

If, on the other hand, you're the kind of person who needs more than a glorified calculator, whose business depends on the flow of numbers, analysis, and projections, there's still more to learn. This chapter covers the eerie realms of power in Excel, where spreadsheets and the workbooks that hold them become more complex. You'll learn some tricks to help you work with very large spreadsheets and how to manage workbooks that hold several related spreadsheets in a single document. The exploration begins with named cells and ranges of cells. When you name a cell, you don't have to remember its column/row address, but, as you'll learn, there are even greater benefits to naming parts of your spreadsheet.

Naming Cells and Ranges

Computers are fine with numbers and codes, but we homo sapiens tend to prefer words. That's why websites use domain names instead of Internet protocol numbers (their true addresses). Once your spreadsheet grows beyond the confines of your screen, you may find it difficult to scroll your way back to areas within it that you work on the most frequently. By designating a cell or group of cells as a *named range*, you can quickly jump to a certain spot without having to scroll around for it. You can use named cells as a quick way to navigate a large spreadsheet. Once you've created a named range, click the Name pop-up menu in the Formula bar and choose it from the list. Excel instantly transports you to the correct corner of your spreadsheet, where you'll find the named range selected and waiting for you, as shown in Figure 13-1.

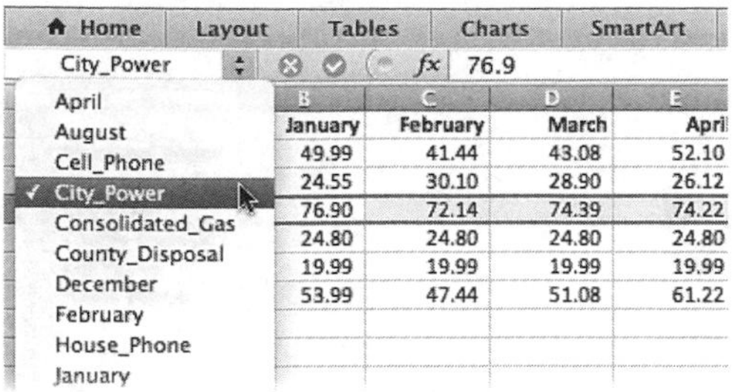

Figure 13-1:
Excel keeps track of all the cells that you name in an alpha-betized list. To jump to a named location anywhere in your workbook, just choose the name from the list. Excel displays the location and highlights it for good measure.

As you create formulas, you may find yourself referring over and over to the same cell or range of cells. For example, in the profit and loss spreadsheet from the previous chapter, you may need to refer to the 2006 Total in several other formulas. So that you don't have to repeatedly type the cell address or click to select the cell, Excel lets you give a cell, or range of cells, a name. After doing so, you can write a formula in the form of, for example, *=Total2008-Taxes* instead of *=B17-F27*. Or, you may find yourself doing the same operation on the same range of cells over and over, for example, totaling or averaging your monthly expenses. By designating monthly expense totals as a named range, you can create surprisingly readable formulas that look like *=SUM(Expenses)* or *=AVERAGE(Expenses)*.

To create a named cell or range, simply select the cell or range, enter a name for it in the Formula bar's Name box, and press Return (or choose Insert→Name→Define) as shown in Figure 13-2.

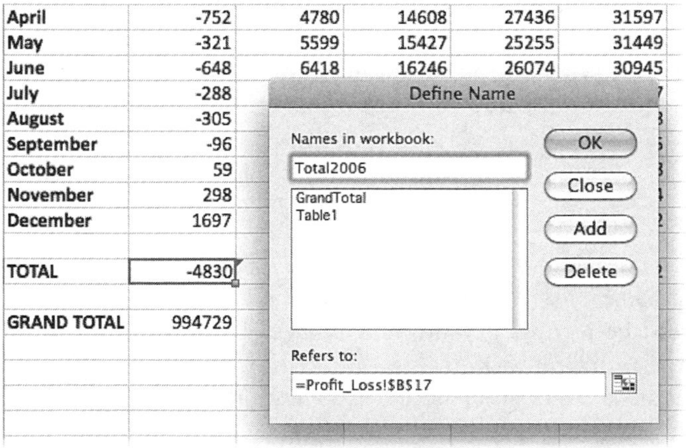

Figure 13-2:
To name a cell or range of cells, select it, enter a name for it in the Formula bar's Name box, and press Return. From now on, you can use the Name box pop-up menu to jump directly to that point in your spreadsheet.

Note: Named ranges take one-word names only: Excel doesn't accept spaces or hyphens. And, as you'd expect, no two names can be the same on the same worksheet: Excel considers upper- and lowercase characters to be the same, so *profit* is the same as *PROFIT*. Additionally, the first character of a name has to be a letter (or an underscore); names can't contain punctuation marks (except periods) or operators (+, =, and so on); and they can't take the form of a cell reference (such as B5) or a function (such as SUM()).

From now on, the cell's or range's name appears in the Formula bar's Name pop-up menu. The next time you want to go to that cell or range or use it in a formula, you need only click that pop-up menu and select it from the list. In addition, Excel displays the name instead of the cell address whenever you create a formula that refers to a named cell or range.

If you need to change or remove a name, choose Insert→Name→Define to display the Define Names dialog box. From there, you'll find it easy to delete, create, or edit names.

Creating Names Quickly

Names are so handy that Excel has an easy way to create named regions in your spreadsheet, using information you've already provided as headings for your rows and columns. In this little exercise, you'll see how easy it is to name rows and columns in your spreadsheet and then use those names to zero in on your data. Suppose you keep track of your monthly expenses on a spreadsheet. Each month you dutifully enter your bills for things like water, electricity, phone, and recycling. You end up with a spreadsheet that looks something like Figure 13-3.

Note: You can try this out on one of your own spreadsheets, or you can grab *13-1_Named_Ranges.xlsx* from the Missing CD at *http://missingmanuals.com/cds*. The completed exercise is called *13-2_Named_Ranges_done.xlsx*.

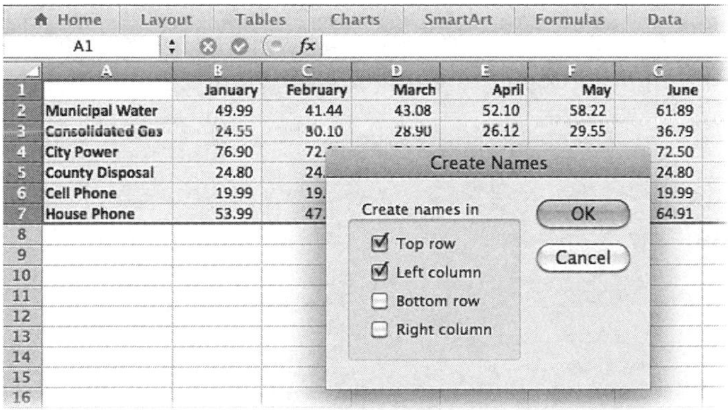

Figure 13-3:
Many spreadsheets look like this one. Each column represents a month and each row represents some value (expense or income). Excel can create named ranges using the words you've already typed into your spreadsheet.

To create names that correspond to the rows and columns in your spreadsheet, first select all of the text and numbers. Then go to Insert→Name→Create and you see the small Create Names window shown in Figure 13-3. You've already got headings for each column, like January, February and so on. The rows also have headings for each expense: City Power, Cell Phone, and the like. These headings are in the top row and the left column of your selection, so turn on the corresponding boxes in the Create Names window and then click OK. Then go up to the Names list and choose a month or an expense. Excel highlights the range of values, but not the labels. Pretty smart and pretty easy to name all those ranges.

As mentioned earlier, names must be a single word. In this example, the expenses were more than one word, so Excel automatically separated the words using the underscore (_) character. So, City Power became City_Power.

Using Names to Look Up Data

Once you've named ranges in rows and columns, it's easy to pinpoint a value in that grid of cells. Best of all, you don't have to remember cell addresses, you can use real words. For example, using the table described in this section, you can zero in on an expense for any month, using the handy *intersection operator*, which is simply a space. For example, the formula to look up the City Power for March looks like this:

    =City_Power March

When you type the equal (=) symbol, Excel knows that a formula will follow. If you type *city_power* (remember Excel doesn't concern itself with upper or lowercase letters), Excel highlights the City_Power range of cells. Type a space to separate the arguments in the formula and then type *march*. Excel highlights the range named March, and you can see exactly where the two named ranges intersect. When your formula is complete, the cell shows your City Power expenses for March.

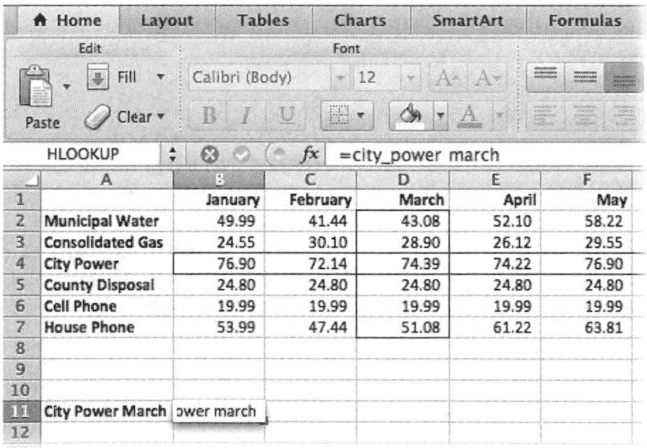

Figure 13-4:
Once you've named the data in rows and columns, you can use the LOOKUP() function to zero in on specific data. Want to know how much you spent on power in March? Here's the formula.

Tip: Sections coming later in this chapter discuss working with multiple worksheets in a single workbook (Excel document file). One of the great things about named cells and ranges is that you can use them on any worksheet in workbook. For example, if you had a separate worksheet devoted to City Power issues, you could use the same formula =City_Power March to retrieve that data.

References: Absolute and Relative

When you create a formula by typing the addresses of cells or by clicking a cell, you create a *cell reference*. However, rather than always meaning *B12*, for example, Excel generally considers cell references in a *relative* way—it thinks of another cell in the spreadsheet as "three rows above and two columns to the left of this cell," for example (see Figure 13-5). In other words, it remembers those cell coordinates by their position relative to the selected cell.

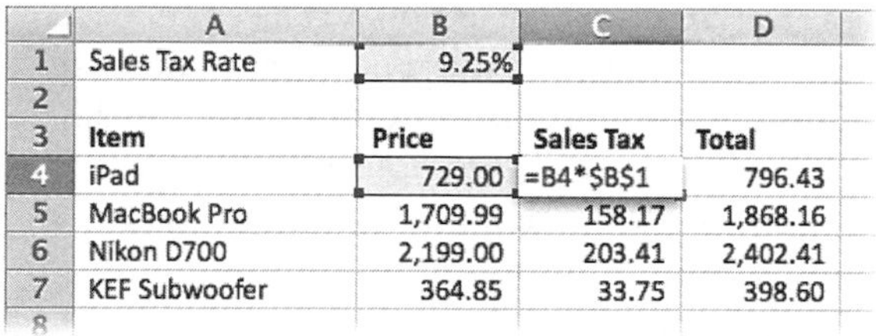

	A	B	C	D
1	Sales Tax Rate	9.25%		
2				
3	Item	Price	Sales Tax	Total
4	iPad	729.00	=B4*B1	796.43
5	MacBook Pro	1,709.99	158.17	1,868.16
6	Nikon D700	2,199.00	203.41	2,402.41
7	KEF Subwoofer	364.85	33.75	398.60
8				

Figure 13-5: *The formula in cell C4 calculates the sales tax for the item priced in B4. The sales tax rate is stored in B2. Thus, the formula in C4 multiplies the price (B4) by an absolute reference to the sales tax rate (expressed B1). When you copy this formula, it always refers to the fixed cell B1.*

Relative cell references also make formulas portable: When you paste a formula that adds up the two cells above it into a different spot, the pasted cell adds up the two cells above *it* (in its new location).

The yearly totals in the Profit and Loss spreadsheet (Figure 13-2) show how this works. In Chapter 12, when you "filled" the Total formula across to the other cells, Excel pasted *relative* cell references into all those cells that say, in effect, "Display the total of the numbers in the cells *above this cell*." This way, each column's subtotal applies to the figures in that column. (If Excel instead pasted absolute references, then all the cells in the subtotal row would show the sum of the first-year column.)

Absolute references, on the other hand, refer to a specific cell, no matter where the formula appears in the spreadsheet. They can be useful when you need to refer to a particular cell in the spreadsheet—the one containing the sales tax rate, for example—for a formula that repeats over several columns. Figure 13-5 gives an example.

You designate an absolute cell reference by including a $ in front of the column and/or row reference. (For the first time in its life, the $ symbol has nothing to do with money.) For example, A7 is an absolute reference for cell A7.

You can also create a *mixed reference* in order to lock the reference to *either* the row or column—for example, G$8, in which the column reference is relative and the row is absolute. You might use this unusual arrangement when, for example, your column A contains discount rates for the customers whose names appear in column B. In writing the formula for a customer's final price (in column D, for example), you'd use a *relative* reference to a row number (different for every customer), but an *absolute* reference to the column (always A).

Tip: There's a handy shortcut that can save you some hand-eye coordination when you want to turn an absolute cell reference into a relative one, or vice versa. First, select the cell that contains the formula. In the Formula bar, highlight only the cell name you'd like to change. Then press ⌘-T. This keystroke makes the highlighted cell name cycle through different *stages* of absoluteness—for example, it changes the cell reference B4 first to B4, then to B$4, then to $B4, and so on.

Workbooks and Worksheets

A *workbook* is an individual Excel file that you save on your hard drive. Each workbook is made up of one or more *worksheets*, which let you organize your data in lots of complex and interesting ways. Try thinking of a workbook as a bound ledger with multiple paper worksheets. Although most of the work you do is probably in an individual sheet, it's often useful to store several spreadsheets in a single workbook document—for the convenience of linking multiple Excel worksheets.

Working with Multiple Worksheets

Although it doesn't offer quite the heart-pounding excitement of, say, creating a beautiful 3D Chart, managing the worksheets in a workbook is an important part of mastering Excel. Here's what you should know to get the most out of your sheets:

Tip: Several of the techniques described here involve selecting more than one worksheet. To do so, ⌘-click the tabs of the individual sheets you want—or click the first in a consecutive series, then Shift-click the last.

- **Adding sheets**. With Excel 2011, Microsoft makes a noble effort to save virtual paper—and in turn preserve a virtual forest. Instead of the three sheets of Excel's past, workbooks now starts out with one sheet, bearing the inspired name Sheet1. (You can set the number of sheets in a new workbook in Excel→Preferences→General panel.)

  To add a new sheet to your workbook, click the plus-sign tab at the bottom of the worksheet or choose Insert→Sheet→Blank Sheet. A new sheet appears on top of your current sheet, with its tab *to the right* of the other tabs; it's named Sheet2 (or Sheet3, Sheet4, and so on).

Tip: To insert multiple sheets in one swift move, select the same number of sheet tabs that you want to insert and *then* click the plus-sign tab or choose Insert→Sheet→Blank Sheet. For example, to insert two new sheets, select Sheet1 and Sheet2 by ⌘-clicking both tabs, and then click the plus-sign tab. Excel then inserts Sheet4 and Sheet5 (to the right of all the other sheets if you click the plus-sign tab, to the right of the selected sheet if you choose Insert→Sheet→Blank Sheet).

- **Deleting sheets**. To delete a sheet, click the doomed sheet's tab (or select several tabs) at the bottom of the window, and then choose Edit→Delete Sheet. (Alternatively, Control-click the sheet tab and choose Delete from the contextual menu.)

Warning: You can't bring back a deleted sheet. The Undo command (Edit→Undo) doesn't work in this context. If you make an error, the best that you can do is close your workbook without saving and then reopen it. Naturally, you'll lose any unsaved work in the process.

- **Hiding and showing sheets**. Instead of deleting a worksheet forever, you may find it helpful to simply hide one (or several), keeping your peripheral vision free of distractions while you focus on the remaining ones. To hide a sheet or sheets, select the corresponding worksheet tabs at the bottom of the window, then choose Format→Sheet→Hide. To show (or *unhide*, as Excel calls it) sheets that have been hidden, choose Format→Sheet→Unhide; this brings up a list of sheets to show. Choose the sheet that you want to reappear, and click OK.

Note: You can unhide only one sheet at a time.

- **Renaming sheets**. The easiest way to rename a sheet is to double-click its tab to highlight its name, and then type the new text (up to 31 characters long). Alternatively, you can select the tab of the sheet you want to rename and then choose Format→Sheet→Rename. You can also Control-click the sheet tab and choose Rename from the contextual menu.

- **Moving and copying sheets**. To move a sheet (so that, for example, Sheet1 comes after Sheet3), just drag its tab horizontally. A tiny black triangle indicates where the sheet will wind up, relative to the others, when you release the mouse. Using this technique, you can even drag a copy of a worksheet into a different Excel document.

Tip: Pressing Option while you drag produces a copy of the worksheet. (The exception is when you drag a sheet's tab into a different workbook; in that case, Excel copies the sheet regardless of whether the Option key is held down.)

Adding Background Pictures to Sheets

Every now and then, it's easy to feel sorry for Microsoft programmers; after umpteen revisions, what possible features can they add to Excel? They must rack their brains, lying awake at night, trying to figure out what else they can invent.

Surely, the ability to add a graphics file as a background image behind your cell grid is an idea that sprang from just such a late-night idea session.

Start by choosing Format→Sheet→Background. An Open dialog box pops up, where you can choose the graphics file (JPEG, GIF, Photoshop, and so on) that you want to use as a background. Once you've selected it and clicked Insert, the image loads as the spreadsheet's background. If the image isn't large enough to fill the entire worksheet, Excel automatically tiles it, placing copies side by side until every centimeter of the window is filled.

Clearly, if this feature is ever successful in improving a worksheet, it's when the background image is extremely light in color and low in contrast. Most other images succeed only in rendering your numbers and text illegible.

If, after adding an image to a sheet, you decide that it makes things much, much worse, choose Format→Sheet→Delete Background. Your normal white Excel sheet background returns. By the way, the background doesn't print. It's a screen-only thing. Go figure.

As usual, there are other ways to perform this task. For example, you can also select a sheet's tab and then choose Edit→Move or Copy Sheet, or Control-click the sheet tab and choose Move or Copy from the contextual menu. In either case, the Move or Copy dialog box pops up. In it, you can specify which open workbook the sheet should be moved to, whether you want the sheet copied or moved, and where you want to place the sheet relative to the others.

- **Scrolling through sheet tabs**. If you have more sheet tabs than Excel can display in the bottom portion of the window, you can use the four tab scrolling buttons to scoot between the various sheets (see Figure 13-6). Another method is to Control-click any tab-scrolling button and then choose a sheet's name from the contextual menu.

- **Showing more or fewer sheet tabs**. The area reserved for Sheet tabs has to share space with the horizontal scroll bar. Fortunately, you can change how much area is devoted to showing sheet tabs by dragging the small, gray, vertical tab that sits between the tabs and the scroll bar. Drag it to the left to expand the scroll bar area (and hide worksheet tabs if necessary); drag it to the right to reveal more tabs.

Exporting Files

Every now and then, you may find it useful to send your Excel data to a different program—FileMaker, for example, or iWork (if you're collaborating with somebody who doesn't have Office). You'll find a lot of programs can read Excel's file formats. For example, the iWork spreadsheet program Numbers '09 can import files in either .xls or .xlsx format and export in .xls format. In addition, Microsoft engineers have built in many different file formats for your Excel conversion pleasure.

To save your Excel file in another file format, choose File→Save As; then select the
file format you want from the Format pop-up menu. Figure 13-7 shows a few of the
most useful options in that pop-up menu.

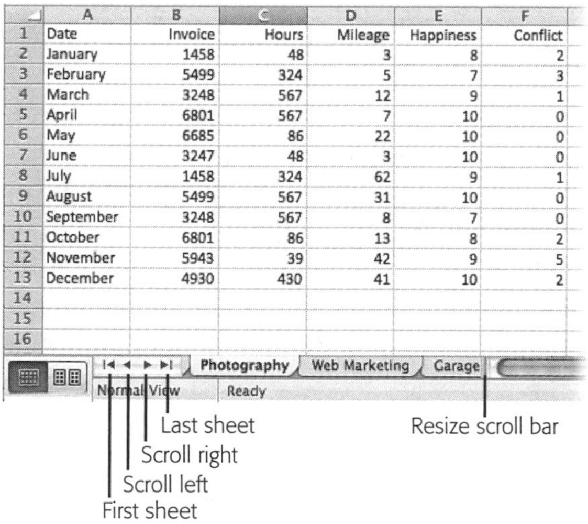

	A	B	C	D	E	F
1	Date	Invoice	Hours	Mileage	Happiness	Conflict
2	January	1458	48	3	8	2
3	February	5499	324	5	7	3
4	March	3248	567	12	9	1
5	April	6801	567	7	10	0
6	May	6685	86	22	10	0
7	June	3247	48	3	10	0
8	July	1458	324	62	9	1
9	August	5499	567	31	10	0
10	September	3248	567	8	7	0
11	October	6801	86	13	8	2
12	November	5943	39	42	9	5
13	December	4930	430	41	10	2
14						
15						
16						

Photography / Web Marketing / Garage

Normal View   Ready

Last sheet
Scroll right
Scroll left
First sheet

Resize scroll bar

Figure 13-6:
The sheet scrolling buttons become active only when you become so fond of sheets that you can no longer see all their tabs at once. (Or maybe you just have a 13-inch PowerBook.) From left to right, the four sheet scrolling buttons perform the following functions: scroll the tabs to the leftmost tab, scroll the tabs to the left by one tab, scroll the tabs to the right by one tab, and scroll the tabs all the way to the right. Control-click any of the buttons and choose the sheet to go to from the pop-up menu. You can also make room for more tabs beneath your spreadsheet by dragging the left end of the lower scroll bar.

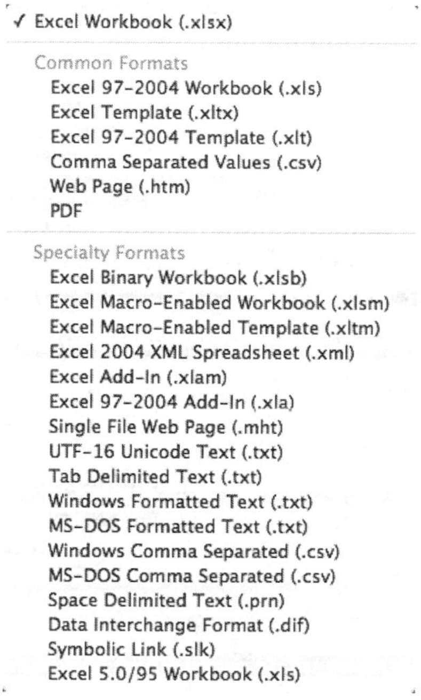

✓ Excel Workbook (.xlsx)

Common Formats
  Excel 97–2004 Workbook (.xls)
  Excel Template (.xltx)
  Excel 97–2004 Template (.xlt)
  Comma Separated Values (.csv)
  Web Page (.htm)
  PDF

Specialty Formats
  Excel Binary Workbook (.xlsb)
  Excel Macro–Enabled Workbook (.xlsm)
  Excel Macro–Enabled Template (.xltm)
  Excel 2004 XML Spreadsheet (.xml)
  Excel Add–In (.xlam)
  Excel 97–2004 Add–In (.xla)
  Single File Web Page (.mht)
  UTF–16 Unicode Text (.txt)
  Tab Delimited Text (.txt)
  Windows Formatted Text (.txt)
  MS–DOS Formatted Text (.txt)
  Windows Comma Separated (.csv)
  MS–DOS Comma Separated (.csv)
  Space Delimited Text (.prn)
  Data Interchange Format (.dif)
  Symbolic Link (.slk)
  Excel 5.0/95 Workbook (.xls)

Figure 13-7:
Excel gives you a long list of file formats when you use Save As. If you're like most spreadsheet artists, you'll rarely use most of these, but they are there when you need them.

Excel 97-2004 Workbook (.xls)

If you're sharing your document with Excel fans who have yet to upgrade beyond Excel 2004 for the Mac or Excel 2003 for PC (or if you're uncertain), be sure and save your spreadsheet in this.xls format. The new (.xlsx) file format can *only* be read by Excel 2008 and later. (On the Windows side, the new file format began with Excel 2007.)

Comma separated values (.csv)

The *comma-separated* file format is a popular way of getting your Excel sheets into other spreadsheets or databases (AppleWorks, FileMaker, Outlook, non-Microsoft word processors, and so on). It saves the data as a text file, in which cell contents are separated by commas, and a new row of data is denoted by a "press" of the Return key.

Saving a file as a comma-separated text file saves only the currently active worksheet, and dumps any formatting or graphics.

Tab delimited text (.txt)

Like comma-separated values, the *tab-delimited* file format provides another common way of getting your Excel sheets into other spreadsheets or databases. It saves the data as a text file, in which cell contents are separated by a "press" of the Tab key, and a new row of data is denoted by a "press" of the Return key.

Saving a file as a tab-delimited text file saves only the currently active worksheet, and dumps any formatting or graphics.

Excel template (.xltx)

The Template file format is a special kind of Excel file that works like a stationery document: When you open a template, Excel automatically creates and opens a *copy* of the template, complete with all of the formatting, formulas, and data that were in the original template. If you use the same kind of document over and over, templates are an awesome timesaver. (For more on Excel templates, see page 348.)

To save an Excel workbook as a template, choose File→Save As and then select Template in the pop-up menu of the Save window. Excel proposes storing your new template in the Home→Library→Application Support→Microsoft→Office→User Templates→My Templates folder on your hard drive. Any templates you create this way appear in the My Templates portion of the Project Gallery and in the My Templates portion of the Sheets tab of the Excel Workbook Gallery (see page 348).

Tip: When you share templates, play it safe by saving it as an Excel 97-2004 Template (.xlt) unless you're absolutely sure your cohort's Office software is up-to-date.

Web page

Where would a modern software program be without the ability to turn its files into web pages?

Sure enough, Excel can save workbooks as web pages, complete with charts, and with all sheets intact. In the process, Excel generates the necessary HTML and XML files and converts your graphics into web-friendly file formats (such as GIF). All you have to do is upload the saved files to a web server to make them available to the entire Internet. Once you've posted them on the Internet, others can look through your worksheets with nothing but a web browser, ideal for posting your numbers for others to review. That's the *only* thing they can do, in fact, since the cells in your worksheet aren't editable.

To save a workbook as a web page, choose File→Save as Web Page. At this point, the bottom of the Save window gives you some powerful settings that control the web page creation process:

- **Workbook, Sheet, Selection**. Using these buttons, specify how much of your workbook should be saved as a web page—the whole workbook, the currently active sheet, or just the selected cells. (If you choose Workbook, all of the sheets in your workbook will be saved as linked HTML files; there'll be a series of links along the bottom that look just like your sheet tabs in Excel. Here again, though, these features won't work smoothly for everyone, because not all web browsers understand JavaScript and frames, which these bottom-of-the-window tabs require.)

- **Automate**. This button brings up the Automate window, which lets you turn on a remarkable and powerful feature: Every time you save changes to your Excel document, or according to an exact schedule that you specify, Excel can save changes to the web-based version automatically. Of course, you'll still be responsible for posting the HTML and graphics files to your web server.

  To set up a schedule, click "According to a set schedule" and then click Set Schedule. In the Recurring Schedule window, set the Web version to be updated daily, weekly, monthly, or yearly. You can also specify the day of the week, as well as a start and end date for automatic updating. Updating happens only when the workbook is opened in Excel.

- **Web Options**. The Web Options dialog box lets you assign appropriate titles and keywords to your web pages. (The title appears in the title bar of your visitors' browser windows and in search results from search engines like Google and Yahoo; search engines also sometimes reference these keywords.)

  On the Pictures tab, you can also turn on *PNG* (Portable Network Graphics) *graphics*, which makes smaller graphics that download more quickly.

Tip: You can test the workbook-saved-as-web-page feature by dropping the HTML file on your web browser's icon. If you prefer, you may also choose File→Web Page Preview to view the web page.

Spreadsheet properties

Excel gives you the chance to attach additional information to your files through something called *properties*. To call up the Properties dialog box for a worksheet, select File→Properties. In the resulting dialog box, you'll see five tabbed subject areas with all kinds of information about your file:

- **General**. This subject area tells you the document type, its location, size, when it was created and last modified, and whether it's read-only or hidden.

- **Summary**. This feature lets you enter a title, subject, author, manager, company, category, keywords, comments, and a hyperlink base for your document (the path you want to use for all the hyperlinks you create in the document).

Tip: Excel automatically inserts your name and company in the summary. If you don't want these details included in a workbook, go to Excel→Preferences→Security and turn on the box "Remove personal information from this file on save".

- **Statistics**. This tab shows when a document was created, modified, and last printed, as well as who last saved it. It also displays a revision number and the total editing time on the document.

- **Contents**. Here, you'll see the workbook's contents—all of its sheets, even the hidden ones.

- **Custom**. Finally, this tabbed area lets you enter any number of other properties to your workbook by giving the property a name, type, and value. You can enter just about anything here.

Advanced Formula Magic

Chapter 12 covered the fundamentals of formulas—entering them manually, using the Formula Builder, and so on. The following section dives deeper into the heart of Excel's mathematical power—its formulas.

Note: Technically, there's a difference between formulas and *functions*. A *formula* is a calculation that uses an arithmetic operator (such as *=A1+A2+A3+A4+A5*), while a *function* is a canned formula that saves you the work of creating a formula yourself (such as *=SUM(A1:A5)*).

Because there's no difference in how you *use* them, this chapter uses the terms interchangeably.

Nested Formulas

A *nested* formula is a formula that's used as an argument (see the box on page 377) to another formula. For example, in the formula *=ABS(SUM(A1:A3))*, the formula

SUM(A1:A3) is nested within an absolute-value formula. When interpreting this formula, Excel first adds the contents of cells A1 through A3, and then finds the absolute value of that result—that's the number you'll see in the cell.

Nested formulas keep you from having to use other cells as placeholders; they're also essential for writing compact formulas. In some cases (such as with the logical IF function), nesting lets you add real sophistication to your Excel spreadsheets by having Excel make decisions based on formula results.

The Formula Builder

The Formula Builder is a quick way of building powerful mathematical models in your spreadsheets. When activated, the Formula Builder shows every imaginable aspect of a formula: the value of the cells used in it, a description of what the formula does, a description of the arguments used in the formula, and the result of the formula.

To use the Formula Builder, click the Toolbox button in the toolbar and click the Toolbox's fx tab. When the Formula Builder pops up (Figure 13-8), it shows one of two things:

- If the currently active cell doesn't contain a function, the bottom of the Formula Builder says "To begin, double-click a function in the list." Use the Search field or scroll through the Formula Builder's long, long list to find your function.

- If the currently active cell contains a function, or if you type a function into your formula, the Formula Builder opens fully and tries to help you with the function.

Once the Formula Builder appears, you can use it to construct your formula. It provides a text box for each function parameter. Typing the parameter in the text box effectively inserts it into its proper place in the formula. You can also click cells or drag through cells in the spreadsheet to insert the cell reference or range in the Formula Builder. If you've named cells and ranges, you can use the names as cell references.

As you fill out the formula in the Formula Builder, the formula's result appears in the bottom of the palette, as well as in the active cell. When you're done creating the formula in the Formula Palette, press Return to enter it in the cell.

Although the Formula Builder might seem like overkill when it comes to simple formulas (such as a SUM), it's a big help when you're dealing with more complex formulas. It outlines the parameters that the formula is expecting and gives you places to plug in those parameters. The rangefinder feature (page 373) also makes it easier to track your calculations. (The rangefinder highlights each cell cited in the calculation with the same color used to denote the cell in the calculation. It's a sharp way to keep track of what you're doing, and which cells you're doing it with.)

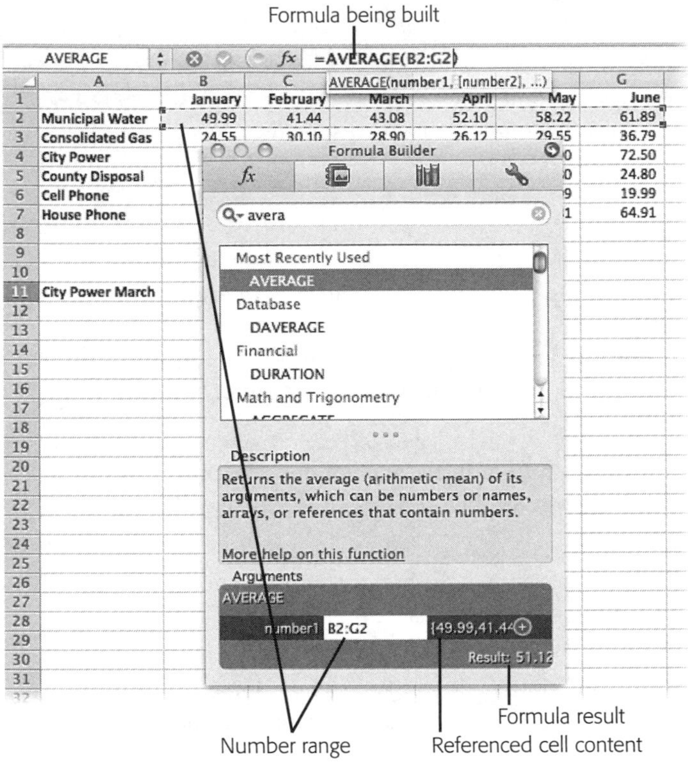

Formula being built

Figure 13-8:
Excel's Formula Builder conveniently presents an amazing amount of information about a selected cell's formula. It's especially helpful for times when you know something about the formula that you're entering, but you need a little help with the details. The Formula Builder not only shows the result of the formula but also lists the arguments and the referenced cell contents. It gives a short description of the function and shows its syntax. Click "More help on this function" to open the functions page in Excel Help for a more detailed description and further examples. You can modify your function by editing directly in this window; click the plus-sign button to add more arguments.

Number range

Formula result

Referenced cell content

Circular References

If you create a formula that, directly or indirectly, refers to the cell *containing* it, beware of the *circular reference*. This is the spreadsheet version of a Mexican standoff: The formula in each cell depends on the other, so neither formula can make the first move.

Suppose, for example, you type the formula =*SUM(A1:A6)* into cell A1. This formula asks Excel to add cells A1 through A6 and put the result in cell A1—but since A1 is included in the range of cells for Excel to add, things quickly get confusing. To make matters worse, a few specialized formulas actually *require* that you use formulas with circular references. Now, imagine how difficult it can be to disentangle a circular reference that's *inside* a nested formula that *refers* to formulas in other cells—it's enough to make your teeth hurt. Fortunately, Excel can help.

For example, when you enter a formula containing a circular reference, Excel immediately interrupts your work with a dialog box that explains what's happening. You may enter a formula that doesn't itself contain a circular reference, but instead completes a circular reference involving a group of cells. Or the formulas in two different cells might refer to each other in a circular fashion, as shown in Figure 13-9. To leave the formula as is, click Cancel. For help, click OK, which brings up a Microsoft Office Help window loaded with directions and the Circular Reference toolbar. (Excel also overlays circles and tracer arrows on the cells of your spreadsheet.)

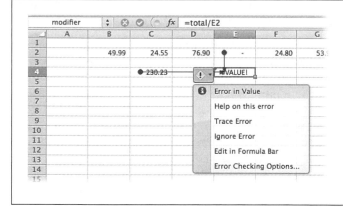

Figure 13-9:
Excel alerts you to errors including the dreaded circular reference. right-click (Ctrl-click) on the erring cell and choose Trace Error to see these helpful arrows. Double-click the tracer arrow to jump to the next cell involved in the circular reference. With these tools, Excel reveals the various cells involved in the circular reference; eventually, you should be able to untangle the problem.

Excel flags errors with the exclamation point (!) warning symbol. Click the symbol to see a menu with different error-fixing options as shown in Figure 13-9.

Iterations

On the other hand, certain functions (mostly scientific and engineering) *need* circular references to work properly. For example, if you're doing a bit of goal-seeking (page 429), you can use circular references to plug numbers into a formula until the formula is equal to a set value.

In these cases, Excel has to calculate formulas with circular references repeatedly, because it uses the results of a first set of calculations as the basis for a second calculation. Each such cycle is known as an *iteration*. For example, suppose you want to figure out what value, when plugged into a formula, will produce a result of 125. If your first guess of 10 gives you a result of 137 when plugged into the formula, a circular reference can use that result to *adjust* your guess (say, reducing it to 9.5), then make a second pass at evaluating the formula. This second pass is a second iteration. If 9.5 doesn't do the trick, Excel can make a third iteration to get even closer, and so on, until it reaches a level of accuracy that's close enough.

To turn iteration on (and set some of its parameters), choose Formulas→Calculations →Settings→Calculation Options. Then, in the preference panel, turn on Limit Iteration, and change the number of iterations and, if you like, a maximum change value. Excel automatically stops after 100 iterations, or when the difference between iterations is smaller than 0.001. If you make the maximum number of iterations larger or the maximum change between iterations smaller, Excel can produce more accurate results. Accordingly, it also needs more time to calculate those results.

Connecting to Other Workbooks

Formulas aren't necessarily confined to data in their own "home" worksheet; you can link them to cells in other worksheets in the same workbook, or even to cells in other Excel documents. That's a handy feature when, for example, you want to run an analysis on a budget worksheet with your own set of Excel tools, but you don't want to re-enter the data in your workbook or alter the original workbook.

To link a formula to another sheet in the same workbook, start typing your formula as you normally would. When you reach the part of the formula where you want to refer to the cells in another worksheet, click the sheet's tab to bring it to the front. Then select the cells that you want to appear in the formula, just as you normally would when building a formula. When you finish clicking or dragging through cells, press Return and Excel instantly returns you to the sheet where you were building the formula. In the cell, you'll find a special notation that indicates a reference to a cell on another sheet. For example, if a formula on Sheet 3 takes the sum of G1 through G6 on Sheet 1, the formula looks like this: *=SUM(Sheet1!G1:G6)*. When a worksheet name has more than one word, Excel places the name in single quotes. For example, if you named Sheet1 Household Expenses, the formula would look like this: *=SUM('Household Expenses'!G1:G6)*

To link a formula in Document A to cells in another workbook (Document B), the process is almost identical. Start typing the formula in Document A. Then, when it's time to specify the cells to be used in the formula, open Document B. Select the cells you want to use by clicking or dragging; when you press Return, they appear in the formula. Excel returns you to the original document, where you'll see the Document B cells written out in a *path notation* where the file name appears in square brackets as shown in Figure 13-10.

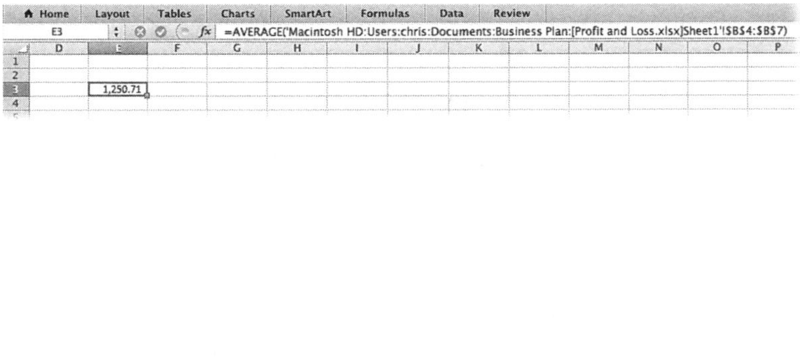

Figure 13-10:
External cell references display the path to the worksheet of the external spreadsheet between single quotation marks in the formula bar. If you move the file or rename any volumes or folders along the path, you'll break the link. You can manually update the external reference in the formula bar, but it's often easier to just double-click the cell, press Return, navigate back to the external document, and let Excel update the reference. (And you won't risk a path-breaking typo.)

Once you've set up such a cell reference, Excel automatically updates Document A each time you open it with Document B already open. And if Document B is closed, Excel asks if you want to update the data. If you say yes, Excel looks into Document B and grabs whatever data it needs. If somebody has changed Document B since the last time Document A was opened, Excel recalculates the worksheet based on the new numbers.

Tip: If you want Document A updated automatically whenever you open it (and don't want to be interrupted with Excel's request to do so), choose Excel→Preferences, click Edit, and then *turn off* "Ask to update automatic links". Excel now automatically updates the link with the data from the last saved version of Document B.

TROUBLESHOOTING MOMENT

Keeping Track of References

The problem with referring to other workbooks in formulas is that things change—and cause confusion. Suppose, for example, that one Excel workbook, Document A, contains a formula in reference to a cell in Document B. But if somebody renames Document B, renames the disk it's on, or moves the file to a different folder, Excel can't find Document B. The link to the external workbook is broken.

When you try to update those references, Excel tells you that it can't find the sheet containing the data it needs and it displays an Open dialog box, asking you to locate the missing data. Now all you need to do is navigate to Document B—even if it has a new name or it's on a new hard drive—and click OK. Excel fixes the reference so that everything works normally.

For the curious (or the coders), there's a manual way to fix such a broken link, too. Click the cell with the external reference; the formula—complete with the external reference—appears in the Formula bar. Inside the formula, there's a series of names with colons and brackets, as shown in Figure 13-10.

Think of this path notation as a street map to the location of the external file on your hard drive. The first phrase after the left parenthesis and single quote is the name of the hard drive (Macintosh HD, in this illustration). Then come a series of folder names separated by colons; in this illustration, the file is in the Chris user directory, in the Documents folder, and then in a folder called Business Plan. Finally, you'll find the file's name (Profit and Loss.xlsx, in this example) inside the brackets.

The phrase to the right of the right bracket identifies one worksheet name inside the file (Sheet1). After that, there's another single quote and an exclamation point, which marks the end of the external reference. Then, finally, there's the name of the cell (expressed as absolute cell references with $ signs, as described on page 387) used in the formula.

Armed with this information, you can repair a broken external cell reference. If you renamed the hard drive, correct the problem by changing the first name in the list to match the new hard drive name. If you've changed the folder location of Document B, you can correct the situation here by typing the proper folder path. If you've renamed Document B, simply enter the new file name in the space between the brackets.

Auditing

Every now and then, you'll find a formula whose cell references are amiss. If the formula references another formula, tracing down the source of your problems can be a real pain. Excel's Auditing tools can help you access the root of formula errors by showing you the cells that a given formula references and the formulas that reference a given cell. Brightly colored *tracer arrows* (these won't appear in an Excel workbook saved as an HTML file) appear between cells to indicate how they all relate to each other.

You'll find auditing tools on the ribbon (Formulas→Audit Formulas) and in the Tools→Auditing submenu, which has five submenu choices:

- **Trace Precedents** draws arrows from the currently selected cell to any cells that provide values for its formula.

- **Trace Dependents** draws arrows from the currently selected cell, showing which *other* formulas refer to it.

- **Trace Error** draws an arrow from an active cell containing a "broken" formula to the cell or cells that caused the error.

- **Remove All Arrows** hides all the auditing arrows.

CHAPTER 14

Excel Data Magic

After spending years loading up Excel with advanced number-crunchy features like pivot tables, database queries, and nested formulas, in 1999, Microsoft decided to step back and conduct some studies to see how its customers were enjoying their NASA-caliber spreadsheet program.

And what were 65 percent of Excel fans doing with all this power?

Making lists.

That's right—most people use the software that drives uncounted businesses and statistical analyses for nothing more than building lists of phone numbers, CD collections, and so on. That's why Microsoft, which never met a feature it didn't like, has been building sophisticated list-making features into Excel ever since.

This chapter shows you how to use Excel tables, which are in essence multifeatured lists that give you the power to sort and filter the rows of your worksheet. You'll also learn about some of Excel's more advanced features that approach the border of a true database program like FileMaker Pro. Why use Excel, a number cruncher, instead of a database program for these tasks? If you already have Excel on your Mac and you might not be inclined to buy and learn a new application. Certainly, if your needs are very complicated, you may have to move up to FileMaker, but read on to see if Excel meets your data storage needs. You may be surprised.

Excel Tables, the New List Maker

Excel's data-handling tools have gone by a few different names. At first they were databases. Then the Redmond gang started calling them Lists and they gave us List Maker wizards to tackle the job. Now the nom du jour is Tables. Well, the moniker doesn't matter. The fact is it's easier than ever to store, manipulate, and retrieve data in Excel. Tables are great for all types of list-making tasks and they don't necessarily have to crunch numbers. For example:

- Build a list of all of the DVDs in your vast collection and sort them by genre, rating, number of stars in reviews, whether discs have director's commentaries—the possibilities are endless.

- Create a restaurant list for every city you visit, complete with names, categories, comments, and telephone numbers. When leaving for a trip to Detroit, you can filter that list so that it shows only the names of eateries in Detroit.

- Make an inventory list, with prices, part numbers, and warehouse location; you can later add a column to that list when you remember that you should have included something to indicate availability. Plus, you can format your list with alternating row colors that still alternate properly when you add a new column.

You can turn worksheet cells into a table, whether they're empty or already contain data. Usually, it's easier to create headers and a few rows of data, and then select a range to convert into to a table. Suppose you're a DVD wholesaler and you want to create a table to keep track of your products, their unit prices and a discount price for quantity orders. First you create headings for the data that describes each DVD: a unique product number, a DVD title, a unit price, and a quantity price. These headings appear in the first row. After you've added the data for a few titles, it might look like Figure 14-1, top. At that point, you select the cells and go to Insert→Table. Excel formats the cells automatically. Don't worry if you don't like the look, it's easy to change later as explained on page 460. More significant, the headings at the top become drop-down menus, giving you the tools to work with the data.

If you've dabbled in database black arts in the past, you probably recognize the basic elements of a table. Each row (except for the top one) is a *record* and each cell in those rows represents a *field* within the record. A record holds related chunks of information and each one of those is known as a field. The words in that top row that have been transformed into menus are *field names*.

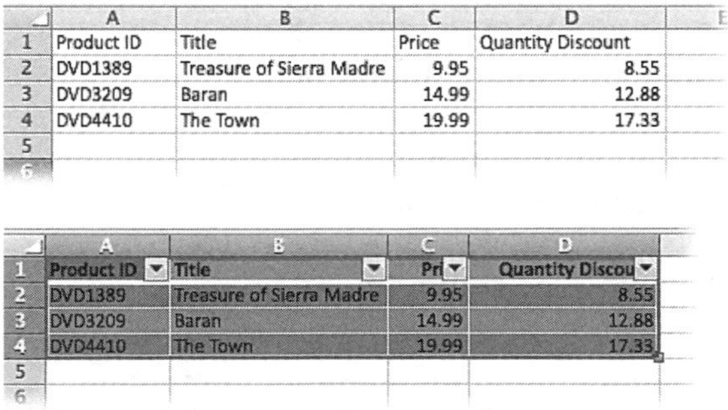

Figure 14-1:
Top: Here a table starts life as a collection of worksheet cells with names at the top of the columns identifying DVD titles and prices.

Bottom: After being converted to a table, these cells are automatically formatted with background colors. The headers at the top now sport drop-down menus leading to tools to sort and filter the data.

Here are some special features that make tables different from your run-of-the-mill worksheet cells:

- **Excel automatically formats table cells.** This is Excel's way of distinguishing a table from regular cells on a worksheet. Even if the fancy formatting is removed, you can still identify a table as shown in Figure 14-2.

- **Sort data.** You can sort the entire table on the contents of one or more columns. In the DVD example, you may want to sort alphabetically based on the titles. When working with a list of addresses, you may want to sort on the Zip codes.

- **Filter data.** After you've added a few hundred records to your table, it may be hard to zero in on the items you want. By applying filters, you display the records you want to work with and hide the rest. For example, a filter could hide the DVDs with a unit price of less than $12.

- **Headings are kept separate from the data beneath them.** As a result, they won't disappear when the table gets sorted or filtered.

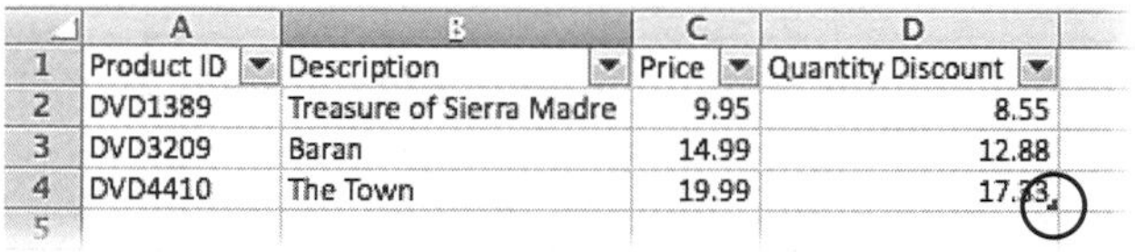

Figure 14-2:
Remove the colorful formatting from a table, and there are still two features that identify a worksheet range as a table: the drop-down menus mark the top row and the marker (circled) in the corner of the cell in the lower-right cell of the table.

Building Your Table

You can turn any group of cells into a table, and you can have more than one table on a worksheet. But generally, life is easier if you put each table on a worksheet by itself. That way, if you add or remove rows and columns, you won't mess up your work in another table. And if you follow that one table per worksheet guideline, you might as well place it in the upper-left corner to make it easy to find.

Here are the steps to create a new table. In keeping with the DVD/movie theme, this table will keep track of a personal movie collection.

Note: If you're not interested in typing in a lot of data, you can download a worksheet with movie data in place ready for conversion to a table. Download *14-1_Create_Table.xlsx* from the Missing CD at *http://missingmanuals.com/cds*.

---

1. **In a new worksheet, click in the upper-left corner (cell A1) and type *Title*.**

   Your first column header or field name is in place.

2. **Press Tab and type** *Genre.*

Pressing the Tab key moves the cursor to the next cell where you can enter another field name.

3. **Continue pressing Tab and adding the headings that you want to use for your table.**

You may want to add headings for the screenwriter, one or more actors, the film's language, and its release date. As you create fields for your table, think about the items you're cataloging. For example, your DVDs are likely to have a single title and a single release date, but most of them will have more than one actor. It's probably a good idea to create more than one field for actor's names.

4. **Starting in Row 2, add three or four rows of data to your table.**

Start with a movie title. Press Tab to move to the next field and add a Director's name. When you want to add a new DVD, start on a new row. At this point, you haven't created a table, you're just adding data to worksheet cells. It's okay if some of the cells are empty. When you're finished it may look like the top of Figure 14-4.

5. **Select all the cells that you've modified so far, including the headings and then choose Insert→Table.**

Excel transforms your DVD list into a table. The top row with Title, Genre, and the other headings change to drop-down menus and the entire table is automatically formatted with background colors as shown at the bottom of Figure 14-4.

When you create a table, Excel automatically uses the top row to create field names. In most cases that's exactly what you want. However, there's another option you can use if you haven't yet defined the field names for your table. On the ribbon, go to Tables | New→Insert Table without Headers as shown in Figure 14-3. Excel creates a table and automatically adds a row at the top with generic headers: Column1, Column2, and so on. You can rename these headers later, as explained next.

Figure 14-3:
You can create tables using the Table | New ribbon menu. Choose the "Insert Table with Header" *option when you've already created headings at the top of your data. Choose* "Insert Table without Header" *if you haven't yet defined your headings (field names).*

Tip: When you're working with tables, the Window→Freeze Frames command is particularly helpful. If you want the header row and first column to always be visible, click the cell beneath your headers and to the right of your first column. Then choose Window→Freeze Frames. To turn Freeze Frames off, go to Window→Unfreeze Frames.

Naming Your Table and Renaming Headers

If plan to perform some advanced data magic, it's a good idea to name your table. That way you can use the table's name in formulas and references. Click on any cell within your table, and then on the ribbon, choose Table | Tools→Rename. Excel automatically selects the entire table and places your cursor in the Name box on the Formula bar. Type a new name and press Return. Now the table has a range name that can be used in formulas and references. (You can learn more about naming cells and ranges on page 383.)

If you followed the steps in the previous exercise, you typed header names in the top row before you created your table. If you want to edit one of the names, or if you want to turn Excel's Column1, Column2 names into something more useful, just double-click on the name and type a new one.

Adding New Records and Fields

Most tables grow over time, so it's common to add new records. In the case of your DVD collection table, it's likely to grow. When it's time to add a new DVD to the list, follow these steps:

1. **Click the cell in the lower-right corner of your table and press Tab.**

   Excel automatically expands the table, creating room for another record. Instead of moving to the next cell on the right, the cursor moves down a row and jumps to the Title column (Column A).

2. **Continue to add new DVDs to your table.**

   As you work, Excel continues to add new records, complete with formatting and all the rights afforded to a table cell.

As you type in a cell, Excel checks the column above to see if you've already entered the same data. A tooltip may appear with options you can click to AutoComplete your data entry. A small, but helpful timesaver.

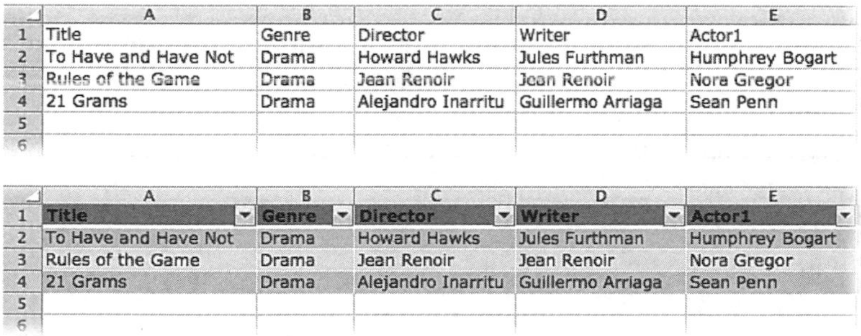

	A	B	C	D	E
1	Title	Genre	Director	Writer	Actor1
2	To Have and Have Not	Drama	Howard Hawks	Jules Furthman	Humphrey Bogart
3	Rules of the Game	Drama	Jean Renoir	Jean Renoir	Nora Gregor
4	21 Grams	Drama	Alejandro Inarritu	Guillermo Arriaga	Sean Penn
5					
6					

	A	B	C	D	E
1	Title	Genre	Director	Writer	Actor1
2	To Have and Have Not	Drama	Howard Hawks	Jules Furthman	Humphrey Bogart
3	Rules of the Game	Drama	Jean Renoir	Jean Renoir	Nora Gregor
4	21 Grams	Drama	Alejandro Inarritu	Guillermo Arriaga	Sean Penn
5					
6					

Figure 14-4:
Top: Before your data is converted to a table, it looks and behaves like any other group of worksheet cells. Excel aligns text to the left and numbers to the right.

Bottom: After your data becomes a table, it's formatted with color backgrounds and you have menus at the top of each column that you can use to sort and filter your data.

In many respects, the cells in your table behave like those in any worksheet. That's true when it comes to adding rows (records) or columns (fields). For example, suppose you'd like to add a Producer or a Rating field to your DVD table. You insert columns into the table just as you would any other worksheet. Click one of the column letters: A, B, C, and so on. With the entire row selected, right-click (Control-click) and choose Insert. Excel creates a new column with a header initially labeled Column1 or something similar. It's up to you to give it a more useful name, as described in the previous section.

You can insert rows (records) into your table using a similar technique. Click a row number to select the entire row. Right-click the row and choose Insert.

Here are some tips to keep in mind when you add columns or rows to your table:

- Initially, you must select a row or column within the table. If you choose a row or column below or to the right of your table, the insertion won't be part of the table.

- To insert more than one row or column, start off by selecting more than one row or column. For example, want to insert five new records? Select five rows before choosing the Insert command.

- You can't insert or delete a few cells in the middle a column or rows for reasons explained on page 369.

Using a Form to Add Records

Often, when you're working with the kind of data that appears in tables, you only need to see one record at a time. All the excess rows and the grid-like, worksheet structure make everything appear more complicated than it really is. If you simplify the view, you and your coworkers are less likely to make errors. What you need is a data input form.

Click anywhere in your table and then go to Data→Form. A form appears, floating over your table like the one in Figure 14-6.

To create a new record, click the New button at the top and start typing. If you want to browse through the table, you can use the scroll bar, including the buttons at the bottom that move through the table one record at a time. The numbers at the top of the form show you your position in the database. For example, 1 of 63 means you're on the first record of a table with 63 records.

You can even apply a simple filter to the records shown in the form. Click Criteria and a blank form appears. Type the criteria you want to match in the appropriate fields. For example, if you want to see the movies directed by John Huston, type *John Huston* in the Director field and press Return. Immediately, the form displays a movie directed by John Huston. If you click the Find Prev or Find Next buttons, you'll see another movie directed by the master. If you've got a really big table, it may be helpful to enter criteria in more than one field. When you're through with your filter, click Criteria again and click Clear to remove all the filters. Then click Form to see all the table entries displayed in the form.

When you're through with the form, click Close. The form disappears, but any additions or changes you made in the form are now a part of your table.

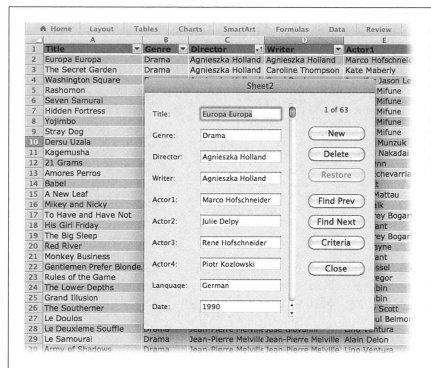

Figure 14-5:
Data forms like this one simplify data entry and make it less likely that you'll make a mistake. When you use a data form, you don't have to click on any cells or create new rows in your table. The form and its buttons manage those details for you.

Rearranging Rows and Columns

If you want to move a row or a column in your table, you need to create an empty spot for the data. If you simply drag a row or column to a new place in the table, Excel thinks you want to replace those cells with the new content. Fortunately, a dialog box appears, checking to see if that's your intention.

The workaround is to insert empty rows or columns as described on page 367, and then drag your row or column to that spot. When you're done, you may need to delete some empty rows or columns as described next.

Deleting Records, Fields, and Entire Tables

There aren't any major surprises if you want to delete rows or columns from your table. For example the quickest way to delete a record from your table is to click on the row number to select the entire row, as shown in Figure 14-6. Then, just right-click (Control-click) anywhere on the row and choose Delete. As usual, if you select multiple rows, you can delete them all at once and if you have a change of heart, press ⌘-Z to undo.

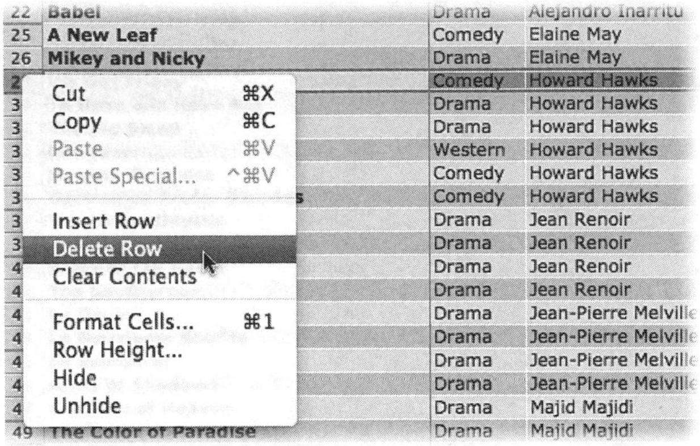

22	Babel		Drama	Alejandro Inarritu
25	A New Leaf		Comedy	Elaine May
26	Mikey and Nicky		Drama	Elaine May

	Cut	⌘X		Comedy	Howard Hawks
	Copy	⌘C		Drama	Howard Hawks
	Paste	⌘V		Drama	Howard Hawks
	Paste Special...	^⌘V		Western	Howard Hawks
				Comedy	Howard Hawks
				Comedy	Howard Hawks
	Insert Row			Drama	Jean Renoir
	Delete Row			Drama	Jean Renoir
	Clear Contents			Drama	Jean Renoir
				Drama	Jean Renoir
	Format Cells...	⌘1		Drama	Jean-Pierre Melville
	Row Height...			Drama	Jean-Pierre Melville
	Hide			Drama	Jean-Pierre Melville
	Unhide			Drama	Jean-Pierre Melville
				Drama	Majid Majidi
49	The Color of Paradise		Drama	Majid Majidi

Figure 14-6:
When you click one of the row numbers on the edge of your worksheet, it selects and highlights the entire row all the way out to the end of the worksheet. Then with a right-click (Control-click), you can insert a row or delete the highlighted row.

Excel has strong opinions about what constitutes a proper table and it's not about to let you break the rules. For example, you can't merge two cells in the middle of a table. The Home | Alignment→Merge command is grayed out. Likewise, if you select a cell or two in the middle of a table and right-click (Control-click) the Delete command reads Delete Columns. You can't remove individual cells in the middle of a table, but you've got the opportunity to remove then entire column if you want.

Converting and Deleting a Table

There are different ways to get rid of a table. In some cases, you may want to keep the data and its fancy formatting. In other cases you may want to get rid of the table and all the data it holds.

- **To remove a table but keep its data**. In this instance you're removing the "table features" from the cells but keeping their contents and formatting. Click on any cell in the table and then on the ribbon choose Tables | Tools→Convert to Range. A dialog box appears, asking: "Do you want to convert the table to a normal range?" Click yes and the table cells are demoted to plain-Jane status.

- **To delete a table and its data**. Select the cells that make up the table. (You can select the specific table cells or you can select entire rows and columns.) Then right-click (Control-click) and choose Delete. Depending on the selection technique the command may read Delete Columns or Delete Rows, but any of the options will do the trick.

Table Formatting Tricks

Excel uses fancy formatting as a way to separate tables from other cells in your spreadsheet. In fact, you might think that Microsoft has gone overboard in its table formatting features, but some of these features come in handy when you're working with large tables with lots of records and fields.

You don't have to select an entire table to apply a table style or use the table options—just click any cell within the table. To apply a style, click one of the thumbnails in Tables | Table Styles. You can scroll through the styles or click the button at the bottom to see all the styles in a window. To see a different option, click on a thumbnail. The table styles take their cue from the selected Theme. So, if you don't like the color choices you see, go to Home | Themes and choose new colors. If all those colors become too much, check out the None option as shown in Figure 14-7.

In addition to Table Styles, you can use the usual Format Cells dialog box, where you can set up this column's type and formatting characteristics: number formatting; text alignment, rotation, and indentation; font size, style, and color; cell borders; fill patterns and colors; and whether a cell is locked or hidden. (Chapter 16 gives you much more on these possibilities.) You may want to use the Format Cells box to manually highlight random cells within a table. However, if your plan is to highlight all the cells above, below, or equal to a certain value, check out the conditional formatting coming up next.

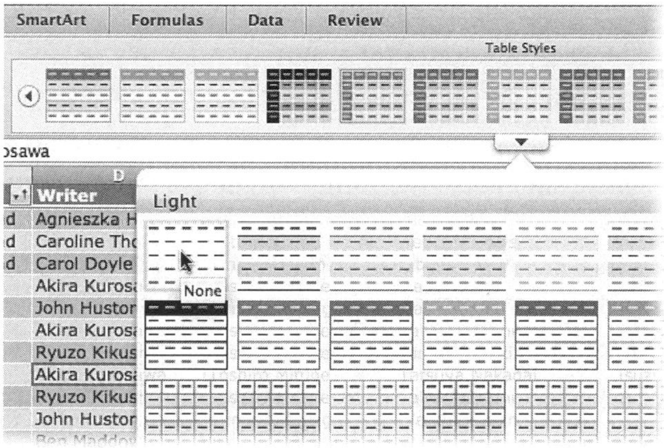

Figure 14-7:
Chase those blues away. Choose the None option in the table styles to remove colored cell backgrounds. The result is a bit drab, but sometimes make it easier to focus on the underlying data.

Automatic Formatting with Table Options

To the left of the styles, the Table Options help you fine-tune your table. For example, if you want to highlight the DVD titles in the table, turn on the First Column check, and the Title column is formatted differently from the rest of the cells in the table. Here's a description of all the Table Options including some common uses:

- Use the **Header Row** checkbox to show or hide the Header row that displays the field names and provides access to the Sort and Filter tools described on page 411.

- The **Total Row** option adds a row at the bottom of the table and totals the numeric data (if there is any) in the column.

- The **Banded Rows** command is strictly a formatting feature adding alternating colors to the cell backgrounds. This makes it easier to identify data in long rows.

- Use the **First Column** option to highlight the cells in the first column. This option works well when the first column is an ID number or the primary description of the item as in a DVD title or product name.

- The **Last Column** option highlights that last column in a table. This option is helpful when individual records have sums or other mathematical operations that are expressed in the final column.

- The **Banded Columns** option is similar to the banded rows command except that it creates alternating columns.

Conditional Formatting for Cells

You can use Excel's smarts to explain what's going on in your table. For example, suppose you want to identify all the movies in your list that were released before 1960. You can create a rule that tells Excel to highlight all the cells in the Date field where the value is less than 1960. Here are the steps to apply some simple color formatting to cells that meet a certain criteria:

1. **Select the range of cells you want to format, but don't select the headers.**

   Most of the time you won't want to apply the highlights to your header cells.

2. **Go to Home | Number→Conditional Formatting→Highlight Cell Rules→Less Than.**

   The New Formatting Rule box appears as shown in Figure 14-8. The Style menu at the top of the box determines which formatting tools are displayed.

3. **From the Style menu, choose Classic.**

   The Classic option displays the simplest tools for conditional formatting, but give you enough firepower to highlight those dates. The other style options include:

   - Use **2 Color Scale** to apply high and low value options to your data.
   - Use **3 Color Scale** to designate minimum, midpoint and maximum values.
   - Use **Data Bar** to display numeric values as shading within the cell.
   - **Icon Sets** to express data difference using a variety of mini-graphics like dots and arrows.

4. **Create your rule using the following options:**

   In the top menu choose: "Format only cells that contain".

   Next choose: "Cell value" and "less than".

   Type *1960* in the text box.

   Choose "yellow fill with dark yellow text to set the highlight color".

   When you put it all together, it almost makes an understandable sentence.

5. **Click OK.**

   Excel highlights the cells with numbers less than 1960.

   The great thing about creating conditional formatting rules is they continue to work if you as you add new records to your table. If you enter a number less than 1960 in the date column, it gets highlighted.

Tip: In this example, the movie release years were entered into the table as general numbers, not dates with days and months. If you find conditional formatting isn't working as expected, use the Format Cells box (Format→Cells) to double-check the cell's number type and the formatting. Make sure the numbers in the formatting rules and the cells are the same type.

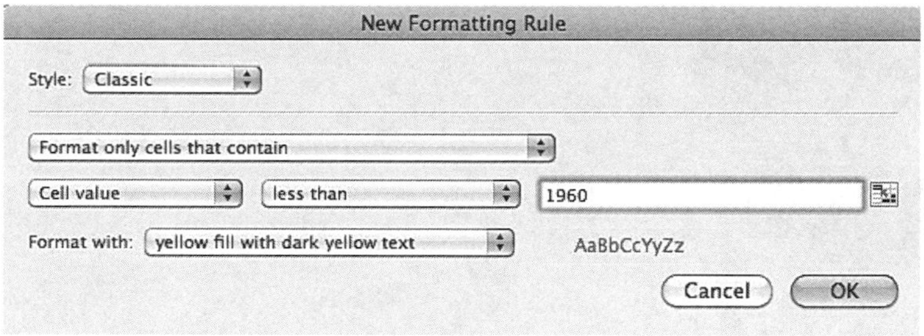

Figure 14-8:
The New Formatting Rule box shown here is set to Classic, the simplest of the cell formatting options. Use the menus in the box to build a sentence that describes the formatting rule you want to apply to your data.

Sorting and Filtering Your Table

Formatting, whether it's manual or conditional, is just a matter of eye-candy. You really make your data dance when you sort and filter it. Sorting is the easiest and quickest so it makes sense to examine it first.

Note: For these explorations, you can continue using your file from the previous exercises, or you can download *14-2_Data_Sort.xlsx* from the Missing CD at *http://missingmanuals.com/cds*.

Each column in your table has a header that appears to be a drop-down menu. When you click the header, instead of a menu, a dark, semi-transparent dialog box appears like the one in Figure 14-9. The title at the top of the box matches the column's header text. Click either Ascending or Descending, and Excel sorts the entire table. Naturally, it keeps the rows of data intact so it doesn't mess up your DVD records. The box stays open in case you want to try a different sort or filter option. To close the box, click the X button in the upper-left corner. After you've sorted your data, a small arrow icon appears on the column's menu button to indicate that it was last sorted on that field.

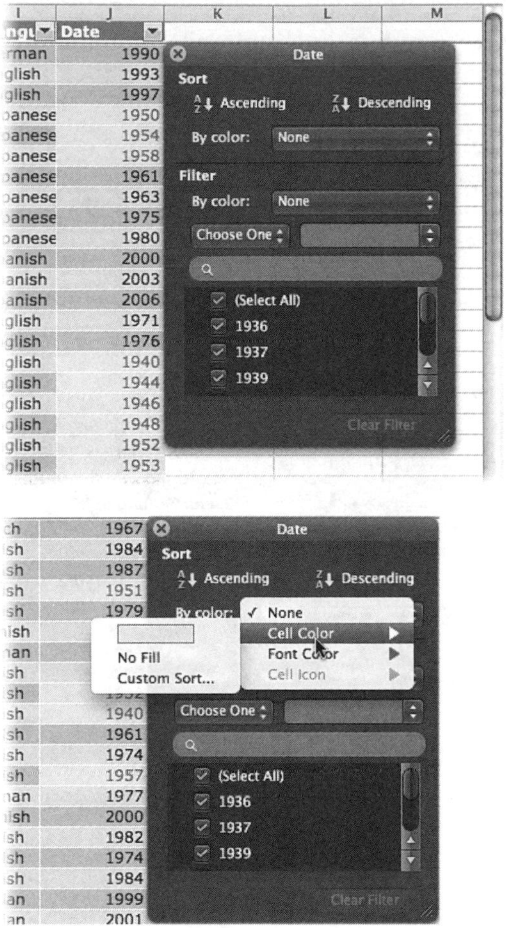

Figure 14-9:
After you click the column header, this box appears. To sort the entire table, click the Ascending or Descending button at the top. You can almost see through this box to read your data beneath, but if it really gets in the way, simply drag the box to a new spot.

You can apply multiple sorts to the same table; for example, if you want to sort your list by alphabetically by director and see each director's movies from the most recent to the oldest. Click Date and then click Descending. Then, click Director and click Ascending.

If you applied colors to your data using either manual or conditional formatting, you can also use that criteria to sort your data. Use the "By color" menu shown at the bottom of Figure 14-9.

Hide and Seek with Table Filters

Sorting determines the order in which the data is displayed. Filters determine which rows (data records) are visible. You can use these tools in combination to help you zero in on your data. The easiest way to apply filters to your table is to use the check-list that appears in the sort and filter box as shown in Figure 14-10.

Figure 14-10:
The sort and filter box shown here was expanded by dragging the lower-right corner. It now shows all the Directors listed in the table. Female directors, a sadly under-represented breed, are selected in the list and consequently displayed in the table.

Excel shows the results of your filters immediately and leaves the box open so you can tweak it some more. Each of the buttons in the list acts as a toggle. That includes the Select All button, which functions as both a Select All and a Select None button. To close the filter box, click the X button in the upper-left corner.

Once the table has been filtered, a filter icon appears on the column's menu button as an indication. When you want to see all of your data again, click the Select All button or click the Remove Filter button at the bottom of the box. Keep in mind, the Remove Filter button only works one column at a time. If you've applied filters in multiple columns, you'll need to remove them individually.

Tip: When you apply a filter and hide the rows (records) in your table, you create gaps in the sequence of row numbers on the left side of the worksheet. Excel doesn't change the numbering to match the visible items, it simply hides both the rows and the row numbers. So, a quick glance at the numbering next to your table can tell you whether a filter is hiding records.

Applying Multiple Filters

When you use the checkboxes to apply filters, you're actually applying multiple filters. However, the floating boxes give you some other powerful ways to apply multiple filters to your table. Suppose you want a list of all the movies created by directors named Jean, but you don't want to include Jean Renoir's movies in the list.

1. **Click the menu at the top of the Director column.**

    A Director filter and sort box appears, like the one in Figure 14-11.

2. **In the first menu in the Filter section, choose** *Begins With.*

    Your cursor is automatically placed in the text box next to the menu so you can enter the filter criteria.

3. **Type** *Jean* **and press Return.**

    When you press return, Excel applies the filter to the table and a new row appears where you can add a second filter.

4. **In the second menu, choose** *Does Not End With* **and type** *Renoir* **in the text field.**

    The list displays any director whose name begins with Jean, but keeps Jean Renoir off the premises.

Who would want to exclude Jean Renoir or his movies from anything? That's anybody's guess. But it does show the power of applying multiple filters. Also consider the multiplying factor that you can apply filters to more than one column in your table. The options on the filter menus include: Equals, Does Not Equal, Begins With, Ends With, Does Not Begin With, Does Not End With, Contains, and Does Not Contain. For example, you can filter out all French films whose director's name begins with J.

Figure 14-11:
In addition to the checkboxes, you can build filters using the menus and text boxes. The menus give you the power to analyze the data to see if they equal, contain, begin with *or* end with *the criteria you supply in the text box.*

The Calculating Table

Tables certainly aren't limited to text-type lists—not when you have all the power of Excel at your fingertips. You can perform calculations in your table and still take advantage of the all the sorting and filtering functions. For example, check out the file named *14-3_Table_Math.xlsx* in the Missing CD at *http://missingmanuals.com/ cds*. This table is just a simple shopping list, but it demonstrates the power of tables, formulas and table's Total row.

1. **Open** *14-3_Table_Math.xlsx*.

    At the top, the table has headers named: Item, Quantity, Unit Cost, SubTotal, Tax, and Total. On the left are the ingredients for a good burrito lunch including liquid refreshment. The unit cost for each item is already entered in the table.

    The table has already been named "BurritoLunch", using the Tables→Tools→ Rename command.

2. **Click in the SubTotal row and then type the equals symbol =.**

    Excel knows that a formula will follow.

3. **Click the row to the left, Unit Cost, and then type an asterisk *.**

    Excel automatically uses a reference for the Unit Cost cell. It looks like this: [@ [Unit Cost]]. The asterisk (*) is the multiplication operator, so Excel knows it will be multiplying the unit cost with the next number referenced.

4. **Click Quantity and then press Return.**

    Excel displays the complete formula as: =[@[Unit Cost]]*[@Quantity] and copies the formula to all the cells below in column, saving you some copy and paste work. If in other circumstances, you don't want the formula copied to the cells below, you can press ⌘-Z or click the lightning bolt menu and choose Undo Calculated Column.

Note: Why the double brackets around Unit Cost and not around Quantity? Unit Cost is two words and Excel uses the brackets to contain multiple words, so they can be handled mathematically as a single element.

---

5. **In the Tax column, enter = and click the SubTotal. Then type** ** .09*.

    You and Excel have just applied a 9% tax to all your grocery items. If you prefer lower taxes, here's a golden opportunity.

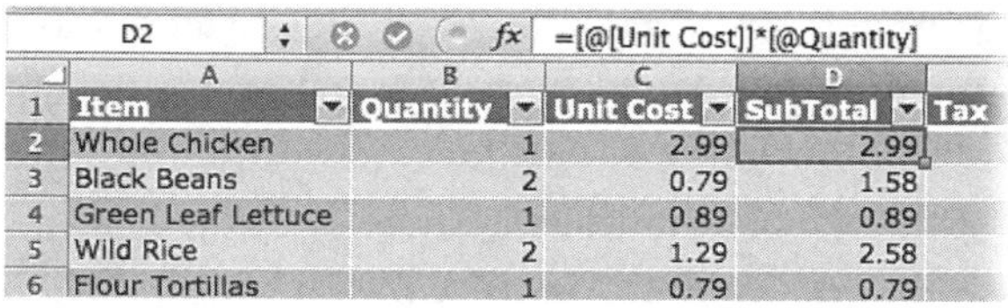

Figure 14-12:
You build the SubTotal formula through a combination of point and click and typing. The complete formula is shown here in the Formula bar.

6. **In the Total column, type = and click the Tax cell. Then type + and select the SubTotal cell.**

   Quicker than a supermarket checkout clerk, Excel calculates totals for your entire shopping list.

7. **Select any cell in the table and then go to Tables | Table Options→Total Row.**

   Excel adds a row to the bottom of your spreadsheet and automatically applies a Sum function to the last column in the table. You now know the grand total for your shopping excursion.

That's not all you can do with the Total Row tool. Click the menu button and you see several other functions tucked away like Average, Minimum, Maximum, and Count. Also, if you'd like to apply any of these formulas to one of the other columns, just click on the cell in the Total row. Then choose a function from the menu. For example, click at the bottom of the Unit Cost column and choose Average to find out the average unit price for the items you're purchasing.

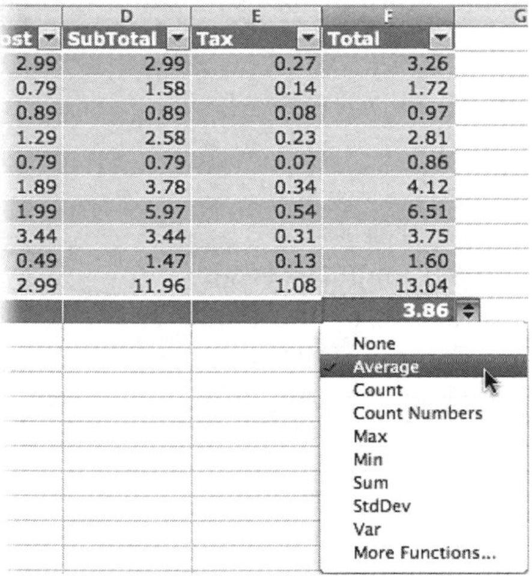

Figure 14-13:
Choose the Total Row option in Tables | Table Options to automatically calculate the grand total for your shopping list. Use the menu to apply other functions to your table.

Building a Lookup Formula for Your Table

If you've followed the examples up to this point, you can see the power of tables to store, manage, and display records. The data in your table is available to any of the cells in your workbook; all you have to do is build a formula that references a specific chunk of data. As explained on page 405, if you name your tables, you can use the name in a reference. Sadly, you can't use column names in references that are outside of your table, so instead you need to use a number that references the column.

Here's a formula that works with the burrito lunch table. It looks up the Tax charged on the 2 jars of olives and can be placed in any cell, on any sheet in the workbook that holds the BurritoLunch table:

```
=VLOOKUP("Olives",BurritoLunch,5,FALSE)
```

"V" for vertical lookup searches for a value (Olives) in the leftmost column of a named data range (BurritoLunch) and then finds the value in another column (in this case the 5th column) in the data range. The word FALSE at the end of this formula tells Excel to find an exact match for Olives.

In this case, because the table is named BurritoLunch, you don't have to enter specific range coordinates like A1:F11.

Note: For all the gory details on the VLOOKUP and its fellow lookup functions LOOKUP and HLOOKUP go to Help→Excel Help. When the Excel Help window appears, type one of the terms in the search box in the upper-right corner.

Working with Databases

Excel isn't a database but it does have much in common with full-powered database programs. Both kinds of software keep track of a list of *records* (like cards in a card catalog—or rows of a spreadsheet), and let you browse through those records and even perform some calculations on them. No wonder Excel is so adept at incorporating database files into its spreadsheets; Excel 2011 can access data in web pages and FileMaker Pro databases, and may be able to use *open database connectivity* to access data from additional databases such as Microsoft SQL Server. Open database connectivity, usually called ODBC (pronounced "oh-dee-bee-see"), is a standard set of rules for transferring information among databases, even if the databases are in different programs from different companies.

POWER USERS' CLINIC

Open Database Connectivity (ODBC)

In order to use ODBC to import data, you need to install a driver for the database you want to query. Microsoft doesn't supply drivers to Office 2011 customers; instead, you have to purchase a driver from another company, such as Actual Technologies (*www.actualtechnologies.com*) or OpenLink Software (*www.openlinksw.com*).

Excel 2011 comes equipped with the necessary smarts to use Microsoft Query—software that puts a graphical user interface on the task of creating database queries. With this program, you can create and modify queries in Excel 2011—if you have the driver installed, that is. Look for it in the Applications→Microsoft Office 2011→Office folder.

Once you've rounded up and installed all the required ODBC software, you can get started with ODBC by scanning the Microsoft Query Help files, investigating the commands listed on the Data→Get External Data submenu, playing with the External Data toolbar (View→Toolbars→External Data)—and perhaps by speaking to your corporate IT department. However, the full rundown on using ODBC to connect to these industrial-strength databases is beyond the scope of this book. (But if you're an ODBC expert, consider writing *ODBC: The Missing Manual* yourself.)

Fetching FileMaker Pro Data

Excel loves to import data from FileMaker Pro databases directly into its work-sheets—no muss, no fuss, no messy translation workarounds.

Here's how to go about it:

Note: Excel can only work with FileMaker databases if you actually *have* FileMaker on your Mac.

Step 1: Import the database

You can import a FileMaker Pro database in either of two ways. First, you can bring the data into Excel once, where you continue to work on it (this is called a *one-time* import). Second, the data can remain connected to FileMaker, and updates itself in Excel when it's updated in FileMaker (this is called an *updating* import).

- **For a one-time import**, which puts data into Excel as a *table sheet* (a sheet containing nothing except a table object, as described on page 403), choose File→ Open, then navigate to, and double-click, the FileMaker file's icon in the Open dialog box.

  If you make changes in FileMaker and want the changed data to come into Excel, you have to reimport the entire database.

- **For an updating import**, which places data in an Excel worksheet and lets you control how often cells update (reflecting changes made in FileMaker), choose Data→ External Data Sources→ FileMaker. (You need to have a workbook open in Excel for this menu option to be available.)

In either case, an amazing thing happens: Excel triggers FileMaker Pro to launch, opening the specified database. Then the FileMaker Pro Import Wizard window appears. On the first screen, specify which of the FileMaker file's fields you want to import (Name, Address, Phone, or whatever). You can also specify the end order for them to appear in Excel, as shown in Figure 14-14.

Click Next to continue.

Step 2: Choose only the data you want

The next screen in the FileMaker Import Wizard offers to *filter* (screen out) the records that you import into your Excel workbook (see Figure 14-15). The wizard lets you specify three criteria to help eliminate unwanted data from the import process. (If you want *all* of the data, skip this step by clicking Finish.)

Click Finish to continue. Excel launches into importing the data from your FileMaker file.

Figure 14-14:
If one of the FileMaker file's layouts contains the fields you want, click the Layouts button and select its name from the pop-up menu. Otherwise, click the Tables button and select the database file name from its pop-up menu (which also displays the names of other linked FileMaker files) to display the list of every field in the database. Next, choose the fields you want by double-clicking each in the "Available fields" pane on the left. (Move all fields at once by clicking the Add All button.) This action adds each selected field to the pane on the right. You can then rearrange the order of the fields in the right-hand list by selecting one and then clicking the up and down arrow buttons on the right.

Note: This process may take a long time (depending, in part, on how much data you're importing). Because there's no progress bar, spinning cursor, or any other sign that Excel is working, you might assume that the program has crashed. Go brew a fresh pot of coffee or stick your head out the door for some air, but don't switch out of Excel; the program is communicating with the database and constructing the spreadsheet.

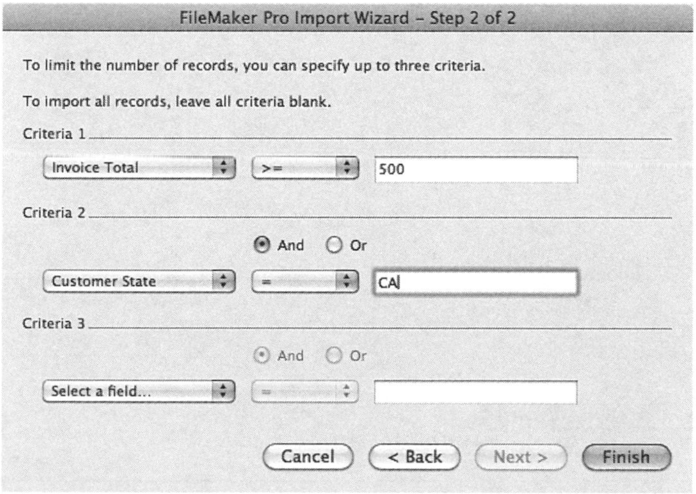

Figure 14-15:
Suppose you want to import only the records for clients who have spent more than $500 and live in California, so that you can thank them and invite them to your annual goal-setting retreat. Set the Criteria 1 pop-up menu to Invoice Total, set the middle pop-up menu to >=, and type 500 into the final field. After filling in Criteria 1, you can set up additional requirements in the Criteria 2 and Criteria 3 rows, such as Customer State = CA.

If you began this process by choosing File→Open, you're all set; Excel creates a new workbook and places the imported data on a new worksheet named after the imported database. The imported data goes into a table that displays the usual drop-down menu tools described on page 411. So once you've imported the data, you can sort and filter to your heart's desire.

If, on the other hand, you chose Data→Get External Data→Import from FileMaker Pro, Excel now asks you exactly where you'd like the imported data to be placed. You can specify a cell or opt to create a new worksheet (Figure 14-16).

After telling Excel where and how to place the data, click Finish. Excel imports the data and shows the External Data toolbar. If you turned on the "Use Table" checkbox in the Properties section of the FileMaker Import Wizard, that data is converted to a table when it's imported.

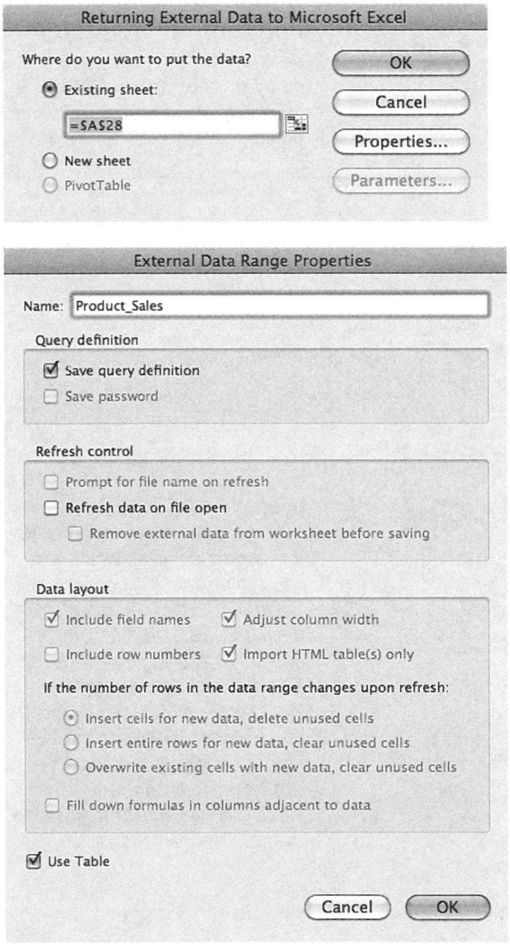

Figure 14-16:
The last step in bringing in FileMaker Pro data is choosing where the data goes (top). With the click of a radio button, it can be delivered into the worksheet currently open or into a new worksheet. Clicking Properties brings up the External Data Range Properties dialog box (bottom), whose options include "Refresh data on file open" (sets whether Excel receives fresh data every time the file opens) and "Use Table" (puts data into a table). The table object offers easy sorting and filtering. But to use the data layout controls in this dialog box, you have to first turn off "Use Table" and forgo the extra features it provides. (See page 411 for table details.)

Note: You may encounter an error message when Excel attempts to open a FileMaker database: "Microsoft Office is not able to run FileMaker Pro at this time." Of course, there are many reasons why Office might not be able to run FileMaker–it's not installed, it's compressed, or it's out on a lunch break. You can solve the problem, though, by launching FileMaker on your own–just double-click its icon in the Finder.

Grabbing Data from the Web

If pulling data from a database on your computer or network isn't exciting enough, Excel also has the ability to grab data from certain websites (and FTP or intranet sites). Excel comes with three sample Web queries that help show the power of this little-known feature. To see how it works, give the sample queries a try (actually, they can be very useful if you're creating spreadsheets to track your portfolio).

- **MSN MoneyCentral Currencies**. This query grabs the current currency value for about 50 countries on an open exchange. Check it before you head out on an international trip, so you'll know what to expect when you exchange your currency—and help you understand why you only paid €5 for a beer.
- **MSN MoneyCentral Major Indices**. This query grabs data for around 20 stock exchanges, including the Dow, S&P 500, FTSE 100, and NASDAQ.
- **MSN MoneyCentral Stock Quotes**. This query looks up data including last value, close value, volume, and change for a stock symbol you specify (Figure 14-17). (If you're among the thousands of people who use Excel to track your stock market holdings, behold the dawn of a new era—you no longer need to type in the latest stock prices. Your software can do it automatically.)

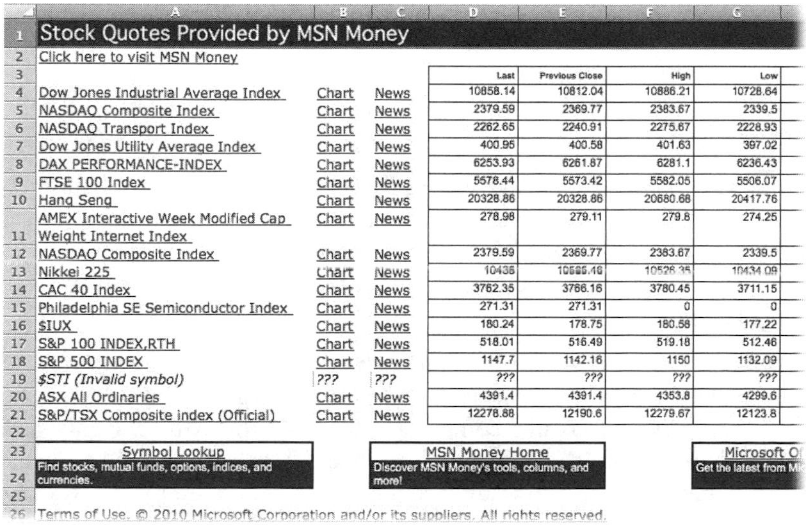

	A	B	C	D	E	F	G
1	Stock Quotes Provided by MSN Money						
2	Click here to visit MSN Money						
3				Last	Previous Close	High	Low
4	Dow Jones Industrial Average Index	Chart	News	10858.14	10812.04	10886.21	10728.64
5	NASDAQ Composite Index	Chart	News	2379.59	2369.77	2383.67	2339.5
6	NASDAQ Transport Index	Chart	News	2262.65	2240.91	2275.67	2228.93
7	Dow Jones Utility Average Index	Chart	News	400.95	400.58	401.63	397.02
8	DAX PERFORMANCE-INDEX	Chart	News	6253.93	6261.87	6281.1	6236.43
9	FTSE 100 Index	Chart	News	5578.44	5573.42	5582.05	5506.07
10	Hang Seng	Chart	News	20328.86	20328.86	20680.68	20417.76
11	AMEX Interactive Week Modified Cap Weight Internet Index	Chart	News	278.98	279.11	279.8	274.25
12	NASDAQ Composite Index	Chart	News	2379.59	2369.77	2383.67	2339.5
13	Nikkei 225	Chart	News	10436	10585.46	10526.35	10434.09
14	CAC 40 Index	Chart	News	3762.35	3766.16	3780.45	3711.15
15	Philadelphia SE Semiconductor Index	Chart	News	271.31	271.31	0	0
16	$IUX	Chart	News	180.24	178.75	180.58	177.22
17	S&P 100 INDEX,RTH	Chart	News	518.01	516.49	519.18	512.46
18	S&P 500 INDEX	Chart	News	1147.7	1142.16	1150	1132.09
19	*$STI (Invalid symbol)*	???	???	???	???	???	???
20	ASX All Ordinaries	Chart	News	4391.4	4391.4	4353.8	4299.6
21	S&P/TSX Composite index (Official)	Chart	News	12278.88	12190.6	12279.67	12123.8
22							
23	Symbol Lookup			MSN Money Home			Microsoft O
24	Find stocks, mutual funds, options, indices, and currencies.			Discover MSN Money's tools, columns, and more!			Get the latest from Mi
25							
26	Terms of Use. © 2010 Microsoft Corporation and/or its suppliers. All rights reserved.						

***Figure 14-17:** Using the saved MSN MoneyCentral Major Indices Web query, you can call up current information on a number of major stock market indices directly in your Excel worksheet. Now you can work with those numbers just like any others in your spreadsheet—except these numbers will stay up-to-date with the markets.*

To use one of these predesigned Web queries, choose Data→Get External Data→Run Saved Query, which brings up an Open dialog box. Double-click one of the queries listed here. (You can find the saved queries in the Microsoft Office 2011→Office→Queries folder.)

Excel then asks you where in the spreadsheet you want to put the information that it downloads from the Web. (This modest dialog box calls itself Returning External Data to Microsoft Excel.) After you select a location and click OK, Excel connects to the Internet, downloads the information, and inserts it into the spreadsheet.

Importing Data from a Text File

Databases and the World Wide Web both make effective data sources, but sometimes you just want to pull some information out of a text file and into your Excel worksheet. For example, you might have a tab-delimited list of contacts that your marketing guru emailed you, and you'd like to get it into Excel. Here's how to do it:

Choose Data→Get External Data→Import Text File; in the resulting Open dialog box, navigate to, and double-click, the text file that you want to import. Alternatively, choose File→Import, click the Text file button, and click Import. Either way, the Text Import Wizard appears and walks you through a three-step process to choose the delimiter type, choose which columns to import, and set the column data format before Excel sucks the data into the current worksheet

Analyzing and Viewing Your Data

Like a good piece of Swiss Army Software, Excel provides tools that go beyond the basics. Using features like PivotTables, Scenarios, and Goal Seeking, Excel lets you sharpen your powers of visualization as you look at your data in new and interesting ways.

Making a PivotTable

A *PivotTable* is a special spreadsheet entity that helps summarize data into an easy-to-read table. You can exchange the table's rows and columns (thus the name PivotTable) to achieve different views on your data. PivotTables let you quickly plug different sets of numbers into a table; Excel does the heavy lifting of arranging the data for you.

PivotTables are useful when you want to see how different-but-related totals compare, such as how a retail store's sales per department, category of product, and salesperson relate. They let you build complicated tables on the fly by dragging various categories of data into a premade template. PivotTables are also useful when you have a large amount of data to wade through, partially because Excel takes care of subtotals and totals for you.

The following steps show you how to create a PivotTable from data in an Excel sheet.

Note: Both the raw data file to start this exercise and a finished copy are available from the Missing CD at *http://missingmanuals.com/cds*. The filenames are *14-4_Pivot_Table.xlsx* and *14-5_Pivot_Table_done.xlsx*.

Step 1: Choose the data source

Suppose, for example, that you're the Executive Director for a community non-profit, trying to decide which fundraisers bring in the most donors for the time and money spent. You have a spreadsheet showing four years' worth of data on five different fundraisers (such as each event's revenue, number of new donors, and hours of staff and volunteer time). But you can't yet see the trends that identify which fundraisers bring in the most new donors for the least time investment while achieving the highest revenues. A PivotTable, you realize, would make the answer crystal clear.

Select a cell in the data range from which you want to create a PivotTable. On the ribbon choose Data→Analysis→PivotTable→Create Manual Pivot Table, which brings up the Create Pivot Table dialog box, which asks for details about the pivot table you're creating.

In the first step, select the data from which you want to create a PivotTable (Figure 14-18, top). If you already selected a range in your spreadsheet, the "Use table or range in this workbook" option is selected and the address for the range appears in the box. If you need to, you can click the range button and select a new range. You can also choose "Use an external data source". If you've installed the necessary ODBC-related software (see the box on page 417), you can also use data from an external data source.

In this example, you want to create a PivotTable from the data range you selected at the beginning.

Step 2: Choose the cells

The bottom of the Create Pivot Table box wants to know where to put your Pivot-Table. "New worksheet", the choice that's initially selected, is often the best. Your other option is to place the PivotTable on the same worksheet as the raw data. If you want to do that, click in the range box and then click in a cell.

Step 3: Pivot

At this point, Excel has dropped a blank PivotTable into the specified location, but its poor cells are empty. To help you insert data, Excel provides tools, which you can use to add elements to your blank slate shown at the bottom of Figure 14-18.

The PivotTool Builder is command central for designing your PivotTable. At the top there's a checklist with field names. At the bottom there are four boxes named Report Filter, Column Labels, Row Labels, and Values.

	A	B	C	D	E	F	G
1	Date	Fundraiser	Net Revenue	Staff Hours	Volunteer Hours	New Donors	
2	2007	Raffle	34892	92	1254	65	
3	2007	Concert	9854	49	170	33	
4	2007	Direct mail	21578	51	89	72	
5	2007	Cookbook sale	2481	49	181	11	
6	2008	Raffle	40587	121	1058	79	
7	2008	Concert	11009	64	184	29	
8	2008	Direct Mail	20593	46	98	102	
9	2008	Cookbook Sale	1987	32	168	9	
10	2009	Raffle	44817	93	1332	48	
11	2009	Concert	10502	51	192	42	
12	2009	Direct mail	26314	41	79	114	
13	2009	Cookbook sale	2671	21	141	6	
14	2010	Raffle	48369	102	1009	65	
15	2010	Concert	13067	44	167	46	
16	2010	Direct Mail	21258	37	71	98	
17	2010	Cookbook Sale	2499	18	129	17	
18							
19							
20							

Figure 14-18:
Top: To finish your PivotTable, fill in the blank table with field items from the Pivot-Table toolbar. Drag these items onto the column to the left, the row across the top, or the data field in the middle to complete your PivotTable.

Bottom: Excel gives you some brief tips and displays the PivotTable Builder box, which holds a list of fields from the original table and four boxes named Report Filter, Column Labels, Row Labels, and Values.

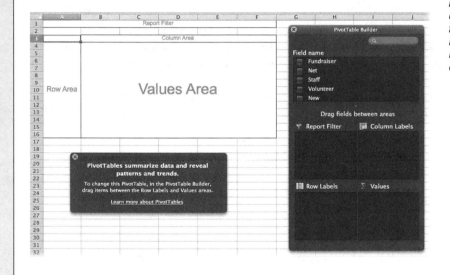

Step 4: Build the table

You, the weary executive director, now want to build a table relating how much revenue each fundraiser brought in to the staff time it ate up.

1. **Click the checkbox next to Date, Fundraiser, and Staff Hours.**

   With each checkmark, Excel tries to guess your intentions by placing the selected item into one of the four boxes at the bottom of the PivotTable Builder.

2. **Drag the Date filed to the Row Labels box.**

   Following your instructions, the PivotTable uses the Date as the source for row labels.

3. **Drag Fundraiser to the Column Labels box and drag Staff Hours to the Values box.**

   Your pivot table takes shape and presents some useful data regarding staff hours and fundraisers as shown in Figure 14-19. The table displays how many staff hours each fundraiser required, and adds the totals for each fundraiser (at the bottom) and for each year (at the right).

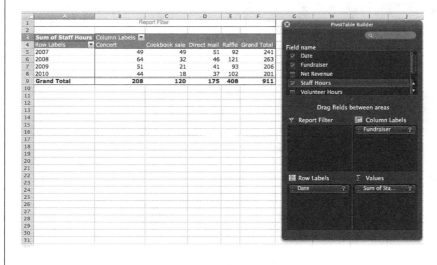

Figure 14-19:
Check off the fields you want to include in your PivotTable. Excel tries to guess your intentions, but you can modify the Pivot-Table by dragging the fields into different boxes at the bottom of the PivotTable Builder box.

Step 6: Massage the data

Now that you've created your simple PivotTable, you can quickly rearrange it to glean the juicy results from it by dragging field names to different areas in the Pivot-Table, or you can add a new dimension by selecting yet another field name (in the case of the executive director, the number of new donors) onto the table. If you add a new field to the data area, Excel divides each row into two, showing how the data for each date interrelate. The more field names you drag into the data area, the more complex your table becomes, but the more chance you'll have to spot any trends (Figure 14-20). Field names can also be added to the row and column axes for an entirely different kind of table.

Though PivotTables start out *totaling* rows and columns you needn't stop there. Control-click (or right-click) any of the totals and choose Field Settings. In the Pivot-Table field dialog box you can choose other functions for your summaries, such as Average, Max, Min, and so on. Click the Options button if you'd like your summaries expressed as percentages or differences.

Note: If you're wrestling with PivotTables and would like to see a working example from this exercise, download *14-5_Pivot_Table_done.xlsx*.

Sum of Staff Hours	Column Labels				
Row Labels	Concert	Cookbook sale	Direct mail	Raffle	Grand Total
2007	49	49	51	92	241
2008	64	32	46	121	263
2009	51	21	41	93	206
2010	44	18	37	102	201
Grand Total	**208**	**120**	**175**	**408**	**911**

Sum of New Donors	Column Labels				
Row Labels	2007	2008	2009	2010	Grand Total
Concert	33	29	42	46	150
Cookbook sale	11	9	6	17	43
Direct mail	72	102	114	98	386
Raffle	65	79	48	65	257
Grand Total	**181**	**219**	**210**	**226**	**836**

	Column Labels				
Row Labels	Concert	Cookbook sale	Direct mail	Raffle	Grand Total
2007					
Sum of New Donors	33	11	72	65	181
Sum of Staff Hours	49	49	51	92	241
Sum of Volunteer Hours	170	181	89	1254	1694
2008					
Sum of New Donors	29	9	102	79	219
Sum of Staff Hours	64	32	46	121	263
Sum of Volunteer Hours	184	168	98	1058	1508
2009					
Sum of New Donors	42	6	114	48	210
Sum of Staff Hours	51	21	41	93	206
Sum of Volunteer Hours	192	141	79	1332	1744
2010					
Sum of New Donors	46	17	98	65	226
Sum of Staff Hours	44	18	37	102	201
Sum of Volunteer Hours	167	129	71	1009	1376
Total Sum of New Donors	**150**	**43**	**386**	**257**	**836**
Total Sum of Staff Hours	**208**	**120**	**175**	**408**	**911**
Total Sum of Volunteer Hours	**713**	**619**	**337**	**4653**	**6322**

Figure 14-20:
These three PivotTables were created using the same data source—the only difference is that the fields from the PivotTable toolbar were dragged to different areas on the blank Pivot-Table. In the case of the complicated PivotTable (bottom), three different fields were dragged to the data field, creating three totals at the bottom of each column and grand totals at the right. Exercise this option with caution, since dragging multiple fields to the same axis can quickly render a PivotTable unreadable. If your table turns to hash, press ⌘-Z repeatedly to undo your steps.

What If Tools Analyze Your Data

PivotTables aren't the only way to analyze your Excel data. In fact, if you're the type who loves to answer those "what if" questions posed by board members or your spouse, then Excel has some great tools for you: *data tables, goal seek*, and *scenarios*.

Data tables

Data tables let you plug several different values into a formula to see how they change its results. They're especially useful, for example, when you want to understand how a few different interest rates might affect the size of a payment over the life of a five-year loan.

Note: Don't confuse *data tables* with the ordinary old *tables* described on page 403.

Data tables come in two flavors: one-variable tables (where you can change one factor to see how data is affected) and two-variable tables (where you can change two factors). The only hard part about using a data table is setting it up. You'll need to insert the formula, the data to substitute into the formula, and an *input cell* that will serve as a placeholder for data being substituted into the formula.

To create a one-variable table, arrange the data in your cells so that the items you want plugged into your calculation (the interest rate, for example) are in a continuous row or column; then proceed as shown in Figure 14-21. If you choose a row, type the formula you want used in your table in the cell that's *one column to the left* of that range of values, and one row below it. If you choose a column, type the formula in the row above the range of values, and *one row to the right* of it. Think of the values (the interest rates) as row or column heads, and the formula's location (the payment amount) as the heading of an actual row or column in your soon-to-be-formed table. You'll also need to decide on the location of your input cell; it should be outside this table.

	A	B	C	D	E
2			Rate	Payment	
3	Happy Home Mortgage			1,476.26	
4	Interest rate	5.00%	5.00%		
5	Term	360	5.25%		
6	Loan amount	275,000.00	5.50%		
7			5.75%		
8			6.00%		
9			6.25%		
10			6.50%		

	A	B	C	D	E
1	One Variable: Rate				
2			Rate	Payment	
3	Happy Home Mortgage			$1,476.26	
4	Interest rate	5.00%	5.00%		
5	Term	360	5.25%		
6	Loan amount	275,000.00	5.50%		
7			5.75%		
8	Data Table		6.00%		
9			6.25%		
10	Row input cell:		6.50%		
11			6.75%		
12	Column input cell:	B4			
13					
14	Cancel	OK			
15					
16					
17					

	A	B	C	D
1	One Variable: Rate			
2			Rate	Payment
3	Happy Home Mortgage			1,476.26
4	Interest rate	5.00%	5.00%	1,476.26
5	Term	360	5.25%	1,518.56
6	Loan amount	275,000.00	5.50%	1,561.42
7			5.75%	1,604.83
8			6.00%	1,648.76
9			6.25%	1,693.22
10			6.50%	1,738.19
11			6.75%	1,783.64
12				

Figure 14-21:
Top: To create a single-variable What-If data table, start by entering one set of data and a formula to calculate your result. Column B contains the values needed to calculate loan payments. Cell D3 contains the PMT formula to calculate monthly payments. Enter your set of substitute values in a column starting one column to the left and one row below the cell containing the formula (or one column to the right and one row above for a row-oriented data table).

Middle: Select the group of cells containing your substitute values and the formula and choose Data→Data Table to summon the Data Table dialog box. Since this is a column-oriented table, click the Column input cell field and then click cell B4—the cell containing the value in the formula to be replaced by the substitute values.

Bottom: When you click OK, Excel builds the table, calculating the payment for each interest rate.

For example, to see the effects of different rates of interest on a proposed loan, set up a table similar to the one at the top of Figure 14-21, where column B contains one possible interest rate, the loan term, and the loan amount. Column C contains a list of other possible loan rates, while D3 contains the formula to calculate payments based on the values in column B: =PMT(B4/12,B5,-B6).

If one "what if" is good, two has got to be better—and Excel is happy to oblige by creating a two-variable data table. Using the same example, you can compute payments based on different rates *and* a different number of monthly payments in much the same way as a single-variable data table.

To create a two-variable table, enter a formula in your worksheet that refers to the *two* sets of values plugged into the formula. Now proceed as shown in Figure 14-22.

	A	B	C	D	E	F
1	Two Variables: Rate and Term					
2						
3	Happy Home Mortgage		$1,476.26	180	240	360
4	Interest rate	5.00%	5.00%			
5	Term	360	5.25%			
6	Loan amount	275,000.00	5.50%			
7			5.75%			
8			6.00%			
9			6.25%			
10			6.50%			
11			6.75%			
12						

	A	B	C	D	E	F
1	Two Variables: Rate and Term					
2						
3	Happy Home Mortgage		$1,476.26	180	240	360
4	Interest rate	5.00%	5.00%			
5	Term	360	5.25%			
6	Loan amount	275,000.00	5.50%	Data Table		
7			5.75%			
8			6.00%	Row input cell: B5		
9			6.25%			
10			6.50%	Column input cell: B4		
11			6.75%			
12				Cancel OK		
13						
14						

	A	B	C	D	E	F
1	Two Variables: Rate and Term					
2						
3	Happy Home Mortgage		$1,476.26	180	240	360
4	Interest rate	5.00%	5.00%	2,174.68	1,814.88	1,476.26
5	Term	360	5.25%	2,210.66	1,853.07	1,518.56
6	Loan amount	275,000.00	5.50%	2,246.98	1,891.69	1,561.42
7			5.75%	2,283.63	1,930.73	1,604.83
8			6.00%	2,320.61	1,970.19	1,648.76
9			6.25%	2,357.91	2,010.05	1,693.22
10			6.50%	2,395.55	2,050.33	1,738.19
11			6.75%	2,433.50	2,091.00	1,783.64

Figure 14-22:
Top: In a two-variable data table, one set of data serves as one axis, and the second set serves as the second axis (top). The formula sits in the upper-left corner (C3), and it refers to two input cells outside of the table (B4 and B5). Enter one set of values in a column starting just below the formula, and the second set of values in a row starting just to the right of the formula. Select the range of cells containing the formula and all of the input values that you just entered, and choose Data→Data Table.

Middle: Enter the addresses for the row input cell (B5 for the term) and the column input cell (B4 for the rate) and click OK.

Bottom: Excel creates a beautiful table of payments based on how two variables interact showing you payments for a variety of interest rates for a 15-, 20-, or 30-year term.

If you still don't see the information you really need after Excel creates one of these tables, you can simply replace values in the table—for example the loan amount, terms, or interest rates—and Excel updates the results in the table.

Goal seek

When you know the answer that you want a formula to produce but you don't know the values to plug into the formula to *get* that answer, then it's time for Excel's *goal seek* feature.

To use it, choose Tools→Goal Seek. It you prefer the ribbon route, you can go to Data→Analysis→What If→Goal Seek. In the resulting dialog box (Figure 14-23), fill in the following three fields:

- **Set cell**. Specifies which cell to start from—the cell containing the formula you're using to seek your goal. For example, Figure 14-23 shows a mortgage calculation. The Sct cell (the upper-right cell), which shows the amount of the monthly payment, is D3. The purpose of this exercise is to find the amount you can mortgage if the most you can pay each month is $1,200.

- **To value**. Specifies the value that you want to see in that cell. In the example of Figure 14-23, the To value is $1,200—that's what you and your spouse agree you can pay each month.

- **By changing cell**. Tells Excel which cell it can tinker with to make that happen. The key cell in Figure 14-23 is B6, the loan amount, since you want to know how much you can spend on a house with a $1,200 mortgage payment.

Click OK to turn Excel loose on the problem. It reports its progress in a Goal Seek Status dialog box, which lets you step Excel through the process of working toward your goal. There are a couple of caveats: You can select only single cells, not ranges, and the cell you're tweaking has to contain a value, not a formula.

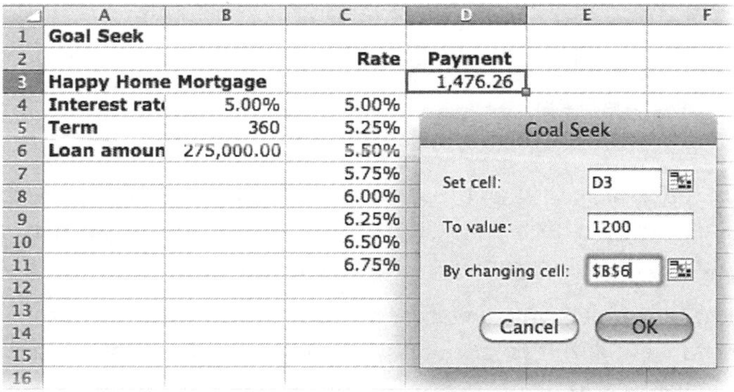

Figure 14-23:
By letting Excel determine how much the financed amount will be, you can keep your loan payment to $1,200. Using the same data from the data tables example, Excel informs us that for $1,200 per month we can afford a $223,537.94 loan at 5% for 360 months.

Scenarios

Scenarios are like little snapshots, each containing a different set of "what if" data plugged into your formulas. Because Excel can memorize each set and recall it instantly, scenarios help you understand how your worksheet model is likely to turn out given different situations. (You still have to enter the data and formulas into your spreadsheet before you play with scenarios, though.) In a way, scenarios are like saving several different copies of the same spreadsheet, each with variations in the data. Being able to quickly switch between scenarios lets you run through different situations without retyping any numbers.

To create a scenario, on the ribbon, go to Data | Analysis→What If→Scenario Manager to bring up the Scenarios Manager, where you can add, delete, edit, and merge different scenarios, as shown in Figure 14-24.

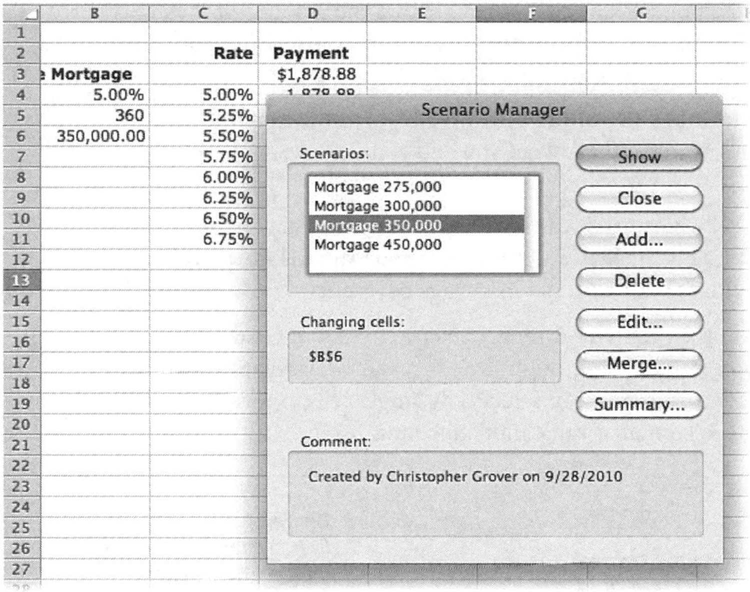

Figure 14-24:
In the Scenario Manager dialog box, you can switch between saved scenarios, add new ones, edit existing ones, merge scenarios from other worksheets into the Scenarios list, and even summarize your scenarios to a standard summary or PivotTable. The Scenarios list displays all of the scenarios that you've created and saved, and by selecting a scenario and clicking Show, Excel plugs the scenario values into the worksheet and shows the results.

The listbox on the left side displays all of the scenarios that you've saved. By selecting a scenario and then clicking a button on the right, you can display your scenarios in your spreadsheet, or even make a summary. Here's what each does:

- **Show**. The Show button lets you switch between scenarios; just select the scenario you want to view, and then click Show. Excel changes the spreadsheet to reflect the selected scenario.

- **Close**. As you expect, this button simply closes the Scenario Manager.

- **Add**. Click this button to design a new scenario, courtesy of the Add Scenario dialog box (Figure 14-25). It lets you name your scenario and specify the cells you want to change (either enter the cell references or select them with the mouse). Excel inserts a comment regarding when the scenario was created. You can edit this comment to say anything you like, making it a terrific place to note exactly what the scenario affects in the spreadsheet.

After clicking OK, you're taken to the Scenario Values dialog box, where you enter new values for the cells you specified in the previous window. Once you're done entering your new values, click OK. The new scenario appears in the Scenario Manager.

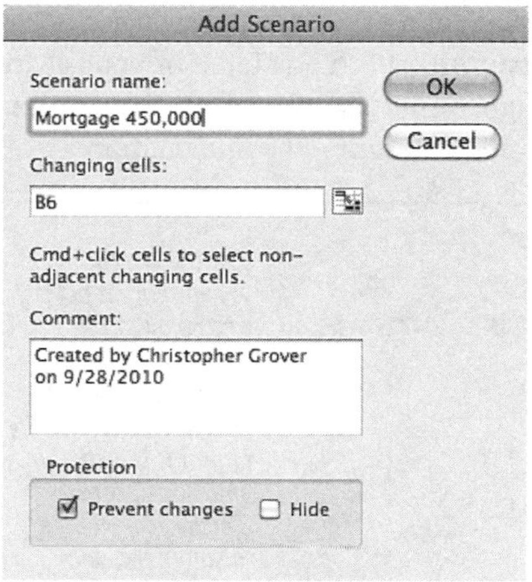

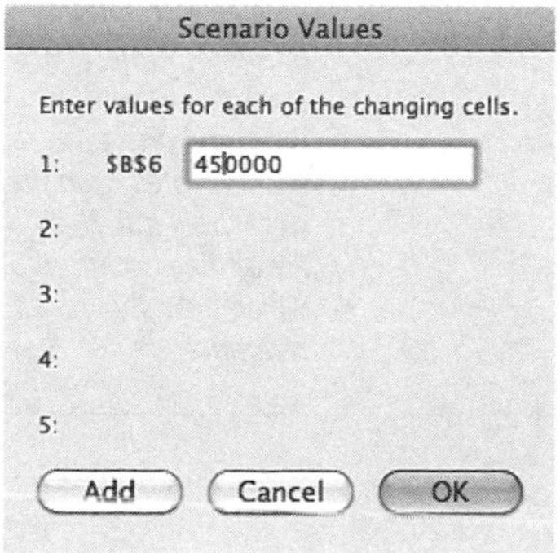

Figure 14-25:
Top: Clicking Add in the Scenario Manager calls up the Add Scenario dialog box, shown here. (It changes to say Edit Scenario when you fill in the "Changing cells" field.) In this box, you name your scenario and tell Excel which cells to change when showing it.

Bottom: Once you click OK, you see the Scenario Values dialog box, where you enter the new values for the cells that you specified in the previous window.

- **Delete**. This button deletes the currently selected scenario.

- **Edit**. The Edit button opens the Edit Scenario dialog box, which looks just like the Add Scenario box. Use this box to edit a previously saved scenario.

- **Merge**. This command merges scenarios from other worksheets into the Scenario list for the current worksheet. To merge scenarios, open all of the workbooks that contain scenarios that you want to merge, and then switch to the worksheet where you want the merged scenarios to appear. This is your destination worksheet for the merge.

Open the Scenario Manager (Tools→Scenarios) and click Merge, select the workbook that has the scenarios to merge, and then select the sheet containing the actual scenarios.

Tip: When you're merging scenarios, make sure that your destination worksheet is the same as all of the scenarios. Otherwise, merged data will still appear in the proper cells, but if those cells aren't properly placed or formatted, it'll look strange.

- **Summary**. When you click the Summary button, the Scenario Summary dialog box appears. It has two radio buttons: one for a standard summary (which creates a table) and one for a PivotTable summary (a PivotTable of your changes *really* lets you tweak the numbers). Figure 14-26 shows a standard summary, complete with buttons for expanding and contracting the information.

Scenario Summary

Changing Cells:	Current Values:	Mortgage 275,000	Mortgage 300,000	Mortgage 350,000	Mortgage 450,000
B6	350,000.00	275,000.00	300,000.00	350,000.00	450,000.00
Result Cells:					
D4	1,878.88	1,476.26	1,610.46	1,878.88	2,415.70
D5	1,932.71	1,518.56	1,656.61	1,932.71	2,484.92
D6	1,987.26	1,561.42	1,703.37	1,987.26	2,555.05
D7	2,042.50	1,604.83	1,750.72	2,042.50	2,626.08
D8	2,098.43	1,648.76	1,798.65	2,098.43	2,697.98
D9	2,155.01	1,693.22	1,847.15	2,155.01	2,770.73
D10	2,212.24	1,738.19	1,896.20	2,212.24	2,844.31
D11	2,270.09	1,783.64	1,945.79	2,270.09	2,918.69

Notes: Current Values column represents values of changing cells at time Scenario Summary Report was created. Changing cells for each scenario are highlighted in gray.

*Figure 14-26:
A summary report shows all of the scenarios in your worksheet. Click the + and - buttons in the margins to expand and contract rows. Once Excel creates a summary, you can edit it, to dress it up or just make it more readable. For example, you could copy and paste the interest rates from the worksheet into the Result Cells column which now shows cell references.*

Tapping the Data menu

Granted, PivotTables and databases are some of the most powerful elements found in the Data menu, but they're not the only ones. A few other commands in the Data menu let you perform additional tricks with your data.

- **Sort**. This powerful menu command lets you sort selected data alphabetically or numerically. It's similar to sorting tables, but you can select any range of cells. You can perform several levels of sorting, just as you can when sorting database items—for example, sort by year, then by month *within* each year. As shown in Figure 14-27, the beauty of the Sort command is that it sorts entire *rows*, not just the one column you specified for sorting.

Tip: Clicking "My list has headers" avoids sorting the top-row column labels into the data—a common problem with other spreadsheet software. Excel leaves the top row where it is, as shown in Figure 14-27.

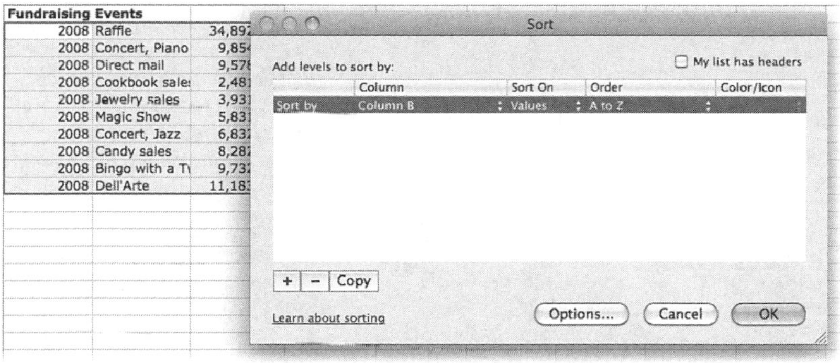

Figure 14-27:
A table sorted alphabetically by event. Highlight the table (including the header row of across the top), and then choose Data→Sort. In the Sort dialog box, specify (using the Sort by pop-up menu) that you want to sort the rows according to the text in column B. turn on the radio button for "Header row" to exclude that row from the sorting. When you click OK, Excel sorts the rows into the proper order.

- **Filter**. You can apply filters to groups of cells even if they aren't in a table. Select the range of cells you want to change, and then go to Data→Filter. Excel places drop down menus at the top of the cells and you can summon the sort and filter dialog box (Figure 14-28) that works just like the one described on page 411.

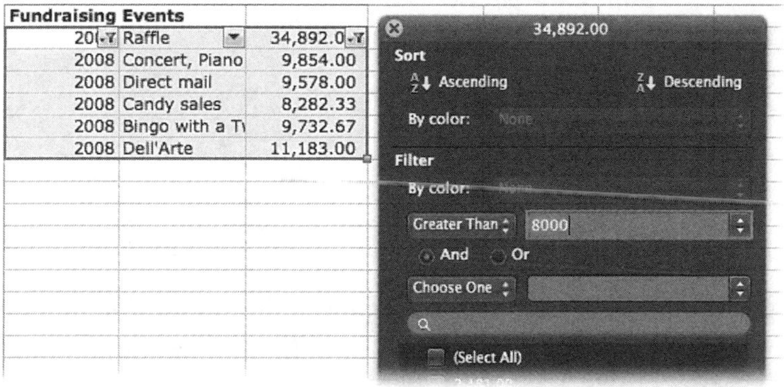

Figure 14-28:
You can quickly and easily filter any group of cells without making them into a table. Select the cells and go to Data→Filter. Then, click on the header submenu to display this familiar toolbox where you can set criteria through menus or check-boxes.

- **Subtotals**. This command automatically puts subtotal formulas in a column (or columns). The columns need to have headings that label them (Figure 14-29 shows an example).

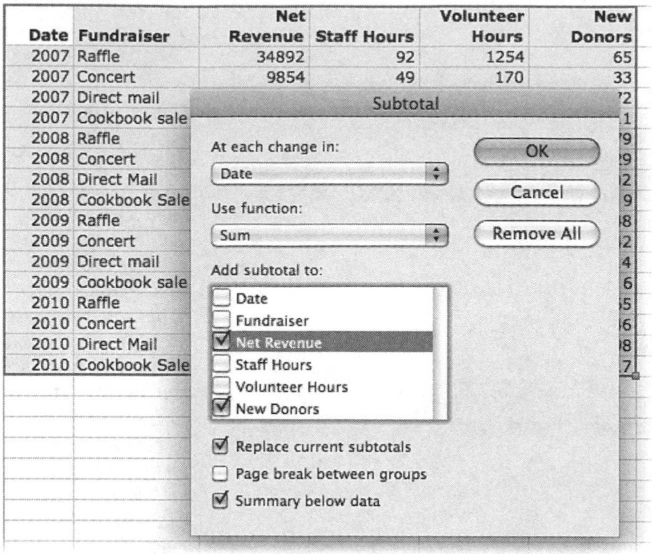

Date	Fundraiser	Net Revenue	Staff Hours	Volunteer Hours	New Donors
2007	Raffle	34892	92	1254	65
2007	Concert	9854	49	170	33
2007	Direct mail				'2
2007	Cookbook sale				1
2008	Raffle				'9
2008	Concert				'9
2008	Direct Mail				2
2008	Cookbook Sale				9
2009	Raffle				8
2009	Concert				2
2009	Direct mail				4
2009	Cookbook sale				6
2010	Raffle				5
2010	Concert				6
2010	Direct Mail				8
2010	Cookbook Sale				7

Subtotal

At each change in:

[Date ⇅]

Use function:

[Sum ⇅]

Add subtotal to:

☐ Date
☐ Fundraiser
☑ Net Revenue
☐ Staff Hours
☐ Volunteer Hours
☑ New Donors

☑ Replace current subtotals
☐ Page break between groups
☑ Summary below data

(OK)
(Cancel)
(Remove All)

Figure 14-29:
Top: Select a set of data that could stand some subtotals. When you choose Data→Subtotals, the Subtotal dialog box appears. In this box, you can choose the column that determines where subtotals go (in this case, at each change in the date), which function is used, and in which columns the subtotal appears.

Bottom: When you click OK, the subtotals appear in your data, grouped appropriately according to the column you selected in the Subtotal dialog box. (Excel uses its outlining notation, as described on page 436, making it easy to collapse the result to show subtotals only.)

Date	Fundraiser	Net Revenue	Staff Hours	Volunteer Hours	New Donors
2007	Raffle	34892	92	1254	65
2007	Concert	9854	49	170	33
2007	Direct mail	21578	51	89	72
2007	Cookbook sale	2481	49	181	11
2007 Total		68805			181
2008	Raffle	40587	121	1058	79
2008	Concert	11009	64	184	29
2008	Direct Mail	20593	46	98	102
2008	Cookbook Sale	1987	32	168	9
2008 Total		74176			219
2009	Raffle	44817	93	1332	48
2009	Concert	10502	51	192	42
2009	Direct mail	26314	41	79	114
2009	Cookbook sale	2671	21	141	6
2009 Total		84304			210
2010	Raffle	48369	102	1009	65
2010	Concert	13067	44	167	46
2010	Direct Mail	21258	37	71	98
2010	Cookbook Sale	2499	18	129	17
2010 Total		85193			226
Grand Total		312478			836

To use this feature, select the relevant columns, including their headings, and then choose Data→Subtotals. In the Subtotal dialog box that pops up, you can tell Excel which function to use (your choices include Sum, Count, StdDev, and Average, among others) and whether to include hidden rows or columns in the subtotal. If you've selected more than one column, you can add the selected function to whichever column or columns you choose.

- **Text to Columns**. Suppose you've pasted a phrase into a single cell, and now you'd like to split each word into a separate column. Or maybe a cell contains several cells worth of text, each separated by a nonstandard delimiter (such as a semicolon) that you'd like to split in a similar fashion. "Text to Columns" is the solution, as shown in Figure 14-30.

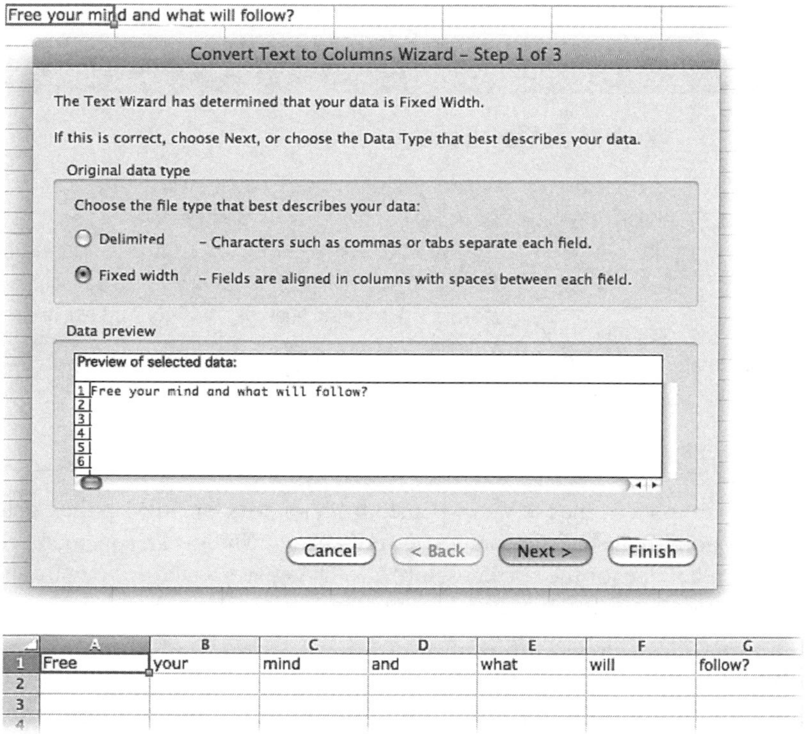

Figure 14-30:
Top: To split delimited text into several columns, select the cell and choose Data→Text to Columns to summon the three-step Convert Text to Columns Wizard. Excel asks what kind of split you'd like to perform, what punctuation serves as the delimiter, and what the data and cell formatting looks like.

Bottom: Click Finish, and Excel splits the data into columns.

- **Consolidate**. The Consolidate command joins data from several different worksheets or workbooks into the same area, turning it into a kind of summary. In older versions of Excel, this command was important; in Excel 2011, Microsoft recommends that you not use it and instead simply type the references and operators that you wish to use directly in the consolidation area of a worksheet. For example, if you track revenues for each region on four different worksheets, you can consolidate that data onto a fifth worksheet. (If you insist on going old-school, learn more by reading the "Consolidate data" entry in Excel's online help.)

Viewing Your Data

Excel worksheets can grow very quickly. Fortunately, Excel has some convenient tools to help you look at just the data you want.

Custom views

Excel can memorize everything about a workbook's window: its size and position, any splits or frozen panes, which sheets are active and which cells are selected, and even your printer settings—in a *custom view*. Custom views are snapshots of your view options at the time that the view is saved. Using custom views, you can quickly switch from your certain-columns-hidden view to your everything-exposed view, or from your split-window view to your full-window view.

POWER USERS' CLINIC

Validating Data

To ensure that the right kind of data is entered in a cell or cells, use a built-in Excel feature called Data Validation. This feature makes sure that dates, for example, don't end up in cells meant for currency.

To set up data validation for a cell or cells, select them and then choose Data→Validation, which brings up the Data Validation dialog box. This box has three tabs: Settings, Input Message, and Error Alert.

In the Settings tab, you can choose which data types are allowed to be entered (such as whole numbers, decimals, or lists). In the Input Message tab, you can enter a message that will pop up when you (or whoever uses this spreadsheet) select the cell in question. The Error Alert tab, meanwhile, lets you specify which error message Excel should display when someone enters the wrong kind of data.

To create a custom view, choose View→Custom Views, which brings up the Custom Views dialog box. To make Excel memorize your current window arrangement, click Add (and type a name for the current setup); switch between custom views by clicking a view's name in the list and then clicking Show.

Outlining

In Excel, *outlines* help to summarize many rows of data, hiding or showing levels of detail in lists so that only the summaries are visible (see Figure 14-31). Because they let you switch between overview and detail views in a single step, outlines are useful for worksheets that teem with subtotals and details. (If you're unfamiliar with the concept of outlining software for word processing, consult page 173, which describes the very similar feature in Microsoft Word.)

You can create an outline in one of two ways: automatically or manually. The automatic method works only if you've formatted your worksheet in a way Excel's outliner can understand:

- Summary *columns* have to be to the right or left of the data they summarize. In Figure 14-32 at top, the D column is a summary column, located to the right of the data it summarizes.

- Summary *rows* have to be immediately above or below the cells that they summarize. For example, in Figure 14-32 at bottom, each subtotal is directly below the cells that it adds together.

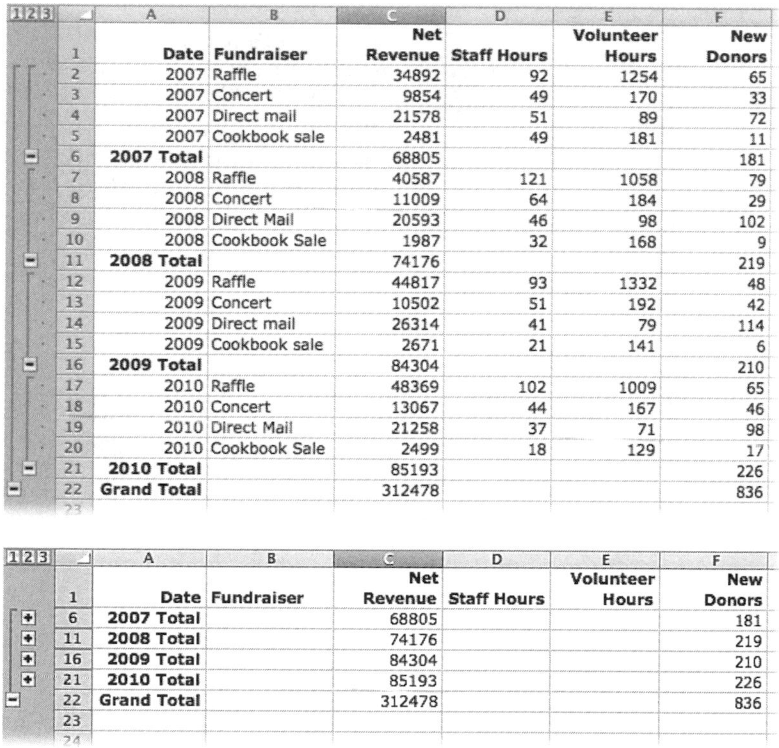

Figure 14-31:
Top: An outlined spreadsheet fully expanded.

Bottom: The same spreadsheet partially collapsed. Clicking a + or - button opens or closes detail areas, while clicking the number buttons in the upper-left corner displays just the first, second, or third levels of detail for the entire outline. This example shows three levels, but Excel allows up to eight levels of detail in outlines.

	Date	Fundraiser	Net Revenue	Staff Hours	Volunteer Hours	New Donors
1						
2	2007	Raffle	34892	92	1254	65
3	2007	Concert	9854	49	170	33
4	2007	Direct mail	21578	51	89	72
5	2007	Cookbook sale	2481	49	181	11
6	**2007 Total**		68805			181
7	2008	Raffle	40587	121	1058	79
8	2008	Concert	11009	64	184	29
9	2008	Direct Mail	20593	46	98	102
10	2008	Cookbook Sale	1987	32	168	9
11	**2008 Total**		74176			219
12	2009	Raffle	44817	93	1332	48
13	2009	Concert	10502	51	192	42
14	2009	Direct mail	26314	41	79	114
15	2009	Cookbook sale	2671	21	141	6
16	**2009 Total**		84304			210
17	2010	Raffle	48369	102	1009	65
18	2010	Concert	13067	44	167	46
19	2010	Direct Mail	21258	37	71	98
20	2010	Cookbook Sale	2499	18	129	17
21	**2010 Total**		85193			226
22	**Grand Total**		312478			836

	Date	Fundraiser	Net Revenue	Staff Hours	Volunteer Hours	New Donors
1						
6	**2007 Total**		68805			181
11	**2008 Total**		74176			219
16	**2009 Total**		84304			210
21	**2010 Total**		85193			226
22	**Grand Total**		312478			836

If your spreadsheet meets these conditions, creating an outline is as easy as selecting the ribbon command Data→Group and Outline→Group→Auto Outline.

If your data isn't so neatly organized, you'll have to create an outline manually. Select the rows or columns of data that you want to group together into one level of the outline; choose Data→Group and Outline→Group. A bracket line appears outside the row numbers or column letters, connecting that group. Keep selecting rows or columns and grouping them until you've manually created your outline.

Outlines can have eight levels of detail, making it easy to go from general to specific very quickly. Thick brackets connect the summary row or column to the set of cells that it summarizes; a + or - button appears at the end of the line by the summary row or column.

To expand or collapse a single "branch" of the outline, click a + or - button; if you see several nested brackets, click the outer + or - buttons to collapse greater chunks of the outline. Also, the tiny, numbered buttons at the upper-left hide and show outline levels and correspond to Level 1, Level 2, and so on, much like the Show Level buttons on the Outlining toolbar in Word (see page 177).

	A	B	C	D	E
1		Fairfax	San Anselmo	Woodacre	**Subtotal**
2	January	2,343	2,388	2,298	**7,029**
3	February	6,445	6,479	6,382	**19,306**
4	March	6,532	6,596	6,499	**19,627**
5	April	5,536	5,592	5,493	**16,621**
6	May	4,356	4,422	4,332	**13,110**

	A	B	C
1	**Date**	**Fundraiser**	**Net**
2	2007	Raffle	34892
3	2007	Concert	9854
4	2007	Direct mail	21578
5	2007	Cookbook sale	2481
6	**2007 Total**		68805
7	2008	Raffle	40587
8	2008	Concert	11009
9	2008	Direct Mail	20593
10	2008	Cookbook Sale	1987
11	**2008 Total**		74176
12	2009	Raffle	44817
13	2009	Concert	10502
14	2009	Direct mail	26314
15	2009	Cookbook sale	2671
16	**2009 Total**		84304
17	2010	Raffle	48369
18	2010	Concert	13067
19	2010	Direct Mail	21258
20	2010	Cookbook Sale	2499
21	**2010 Total**		85193
22	**Grand Total**		312478
23			

Figure 14-32:
Top: Because the column of subtotals (column E) is to the right of the data to which it refers, this spreadsheet can be automatically outlined.

Bottom: Each subtotal is beneath the cells it summarizes, making this spreadsheet, too, a fine candidate for automatic outlining.

Tip: Although outlines were originally designed to hide or reveal detail, you can use them to hide *any* rows or columns that you like.

Flag for Follow-Up

Sometimes, when you're presenting the contents of a workbook to someone else—or when you're up battling a bout of insomnia by going through your old Excel workbooks—you come across something in a spreadsheet that needs updating, research, explanation, or some other kind of follow-up. Excel's "Flag for Follow Up" feature (Figure 14-33) lets you attach a reminder to a file, which you can program to appear (as a reminder box on your screen) at a specified time.

Adding a Comment

Here's another way to get your own attention (or somebody else's): Add a *comment* to a cell—a great way to annotate a spreadsheet. A note might say, for example, "This figure is amazing!—Congratulations!," or "I had no idea that old cookbook was still selling so well!" See Figure 14-34 for details.

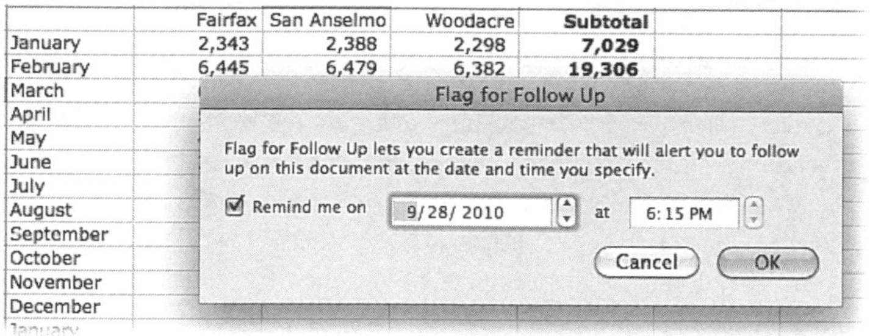

	Fairfax	San Anselmo	Woodacre	**Subtotal**	
January	2,343	2,388	2,298	**7,029**	
February	6,445	6,479	6,382	**19,306**	
March					
April					
May					
June					
July					
August					
September					
October					
November					
December					

Flag for Follow Up

Flag for Follow Up lets you create a reminder that will alert you to follow up on this document at the date and time you specify.

☑ Remind me on   9/28/ 2010   at   6:15 PM

Cancel   OK

Figure 14-33:
To flag a file for follow-up, choose Tools→"Flag for Follow Up", which produces the "Flag for Follow Up" dialog box (inset). In this box, you can set a time and date to be reminded that you need to attend to your worksheet. (Press Tab if you have trouble moving the insertion point around in the dialog box.) Click OK and save the document. Excel creates a task in Outlook; the reminder pops up at the specified time—as long as your computer is on. Otherwise, you'll see the reminder the next time you turn on your Mac.

To edit a comment that already exists, select the cell and then choose Insert→Edit Comment. To *delete* a comment, select the cell with the comment and choose Edit→Clear→Comments. You can also reveal all comments on a worksheet at once by choosing View→Comments.

Tip: Like the Stickies program on every Mac, Excel comment boxes lack scroll bars. If you have a lot to say, keep typing past the bottom boundary of the box; Excel expands the note automatically. You can press the up and down arrow keys to walk your insertion point through the text, in the absence of scroll bars. (Alternatively, drag one of the blue handles to make the box bigger.)

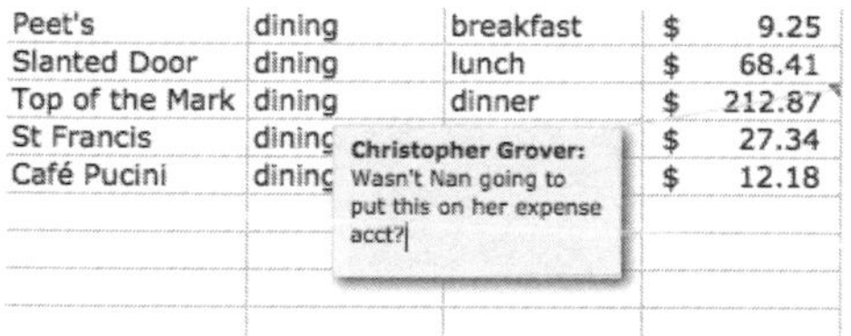

Peet's	dining	breakfast	$	9.25
Slanted Door	dining	lunch	$	68.41
Top of the Mark	dining	dinner	$	212.87
St Francis	dining		$	27.34
Café Pucini	dining		$	12.18

Christopher Grover:
Wasn't Nan going to put this on her expense acct?|

Figure 14-34:
To add a note to a cell, click the cell and then choose Insert→Comment. A nice yellow "sticky note" opens with your user name on the top (as it appears in the Excel→Preferences→General tab). Type your comment in the window. When you click elsewhere, the note disappears, leaving only a small triangle in the upper-right corner of the cell. To make the comment reappear, let the cursor hover over the triangle. (If you prefer to see comments all the time, change that setting in Excel→Preferences→View.)

Proofing Tools

A spelling error can ruin the credibility of an otherwise brilliant spreadsheet, especially when you've gone through the trouble of getting it to look just right. Running a spell check on your spreadsheet before you show it to others can prevent just such an embarrassing mishap. Fortunately, Excel is part of the larger Office suite—which includes spelling tools.

To run a spell check on your spreadsheet, choose Tools→Spelling. Excel scans the text in your spreadsheet; if it comes across a suspect word, the Spelling dialog box appears. It works much like the Word spell checker described on page 57, and, in fact, relies on the same spelling dictionaries. There's probably not much call for a definitions dictionary in spreadsheets these days, but if you run across a term in a spreadsheet that you don't know (taxable, for example), you can access Office's definitions dictionary by selecting the word and opening the Reference Palette in the Toolbox (or choosing Tools→Dictionary) or by typing in the word you'd like defined.

CHAPTER 15

Excel Macros and Visual Basic

If you find yourself doing the same thing over and over, that's the perfect moment to ask yourself, "Shouldn't my Mac be doing this work?" Invariably, the answer is yes. That's particularly true if you're using an Office program that has built-in macros supported by Visual Basic for Applications (VBA). This chapter shows you how to record and run macros and introduces some of the basic concepts behind Visual Basic.

Turn on the Macro recorder, and it watches your actions, keeping track of the cells you change, and the menu or ribbon commands you use. After you stop the recorder, those details are stored in a macro. Whenever you want to do the same thing, you can play back that recorded macro.

Visual Basic for Applications is a scripting language. Think of it as the junior version of a full-blown programming language. VBA was designed from the ground up to work with Office programs. When you combine its programming power with the features already built into features of Excel, Word, and PowerPoint, you can tackle a whole slew of projects. Programming pros design sophisticated custom programs using VBA and Office applications. You could write three books this size and not cover everything there is to know about Visual Basic for Applications, so this chapter is simply a dip-your-toe-in-the-water introduction.

One of the greatest things about macros and Visual Basic is their relationship. When you record a macro, your actions are transcribed into the Visual Basic programming language. When you play the macro, you're playing a snippet of VBA code. Best of all, you can open the macros you've recorded and read the code that makes them work. This chapter shows you how. It's a great way to start learning VBA.

Recording and Playing Macros

The first step down this geeky programming trail is as easy as recording a voice memo on your iPhone. The basic steps are: Turn on the recorder—a simple menu command as shown in Figure 15-1. Do something. Turn off the recorder.

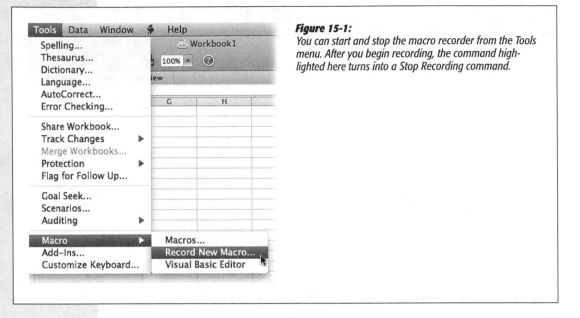

Figure 15-1:
You can start and stop the macro recorder from the Tools menu. After you begin recording, the command highlighted here turns into a Stop Recording command.

Suppose you always add an address block at the top of your spreadsheets: company, street, city, and so forth. Instead of typing those same details over and over, you decide to create a macro to do the job with a single keystroke.

Here's a walk through that creates a letterhead for the Critter Clipper Dog Grooming company.

1. **Go to Tools→Macro→Record New Macro.**

   The Record Macro box appears, which, as you can see in Figure 15-2, is mercifully simple—just one menu and three text boxes.

2. **In the Macro Name box, type *LetterHead* and then type a short description in the Description box.**

   You can't use spaces in your macro names, so it's best to follow one of nerdy conventions for multiple words: LetterHead or Letter_Head. If you don't give your macro a name, Microsoft calls it Macro1 or something equally memorable. So, it's good to give your macros descriptive names. That way, you can identify them later. When you want to run your macro, you'll be picking it from a list of macros.

   You're not required to add a description and if the name is descriptive enough, maybe you don't have to.

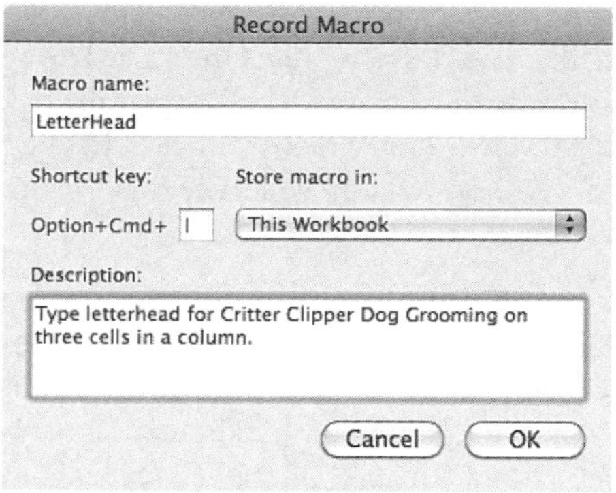

Figure 15-2:
The Record Macro box is pretty simple. In fact, you could just click OK and record a macro. But, in most cases, you'll want to at least give your macro a name and a shortcut key. Use the "Store in" menu to determine whether this macro is available in a single workbook or in all the workbooks you use, as explained on page 449.

3. **Type a letter, such as *l* for letterhead, in the Shortcut key box.**

   Since macros are all about doing something quickly, you want to give your macro a shortcut key. That way you won't have to mess around with menus and dialog boxes when its time to play the macro. Excel automatically sets up macros to use the Option and ⌘ keys, all you have to do is provide a letter. In this case, Excel keeps track of upper and lowercase letters. So if you press the Shift key while entering your shortcut key, you'll need to press it when you run the macro.

4. **For this example, leave "Store macros in" menu set to *This Workbook*.**

   Macros have to be stored in a workbook. By saving the macro in This Workbook, it will be available to any worksheet that's created by this workbook. Page 449 explains how to save macros where they can be used in all your workbooks.

5. **Click cell A1, and then type the business name: *Critter Clipper Dog Grooming*.**

   When you're recording a macro, you can work in Excel as you normally would. It doesn't matter if you go fast or slow. You can correct typos using the delete key. Explore menus if you want. The macro recorder doesn't notice menu browsing until you actually click a command. For the most part, the macro recorder doesn't take note if you click a cell but don't make any changes.

6. **Press Return and type a street address for your business. Then press Return again and finish the letterhead with a city, state, and Zip code.**

   The Macro recorder keeps track of any changes you make to cells, including the text that you type.

7. **Go to Tools→Macro→Stop Recording.**

   The recorder is turned off and your macro is stored in your workbook.

Playing and Saving Macros

You probably want to take your shiny new macro out for a test drive. Before you do, delete the text you created while making the macro. Then press Option-⌘-l. In most cases, macros run so fast you can't see them do their magic. That's especially true of a short macro like this. All you see are the results. Open a new worksheet by clicking the + sign down near the sheet tabs. Press Option-⌘-l and you'll see that the macro works in any of the sheets in your workbook.

If you forget the keyboard shortcut for your macro, or you never applied one, you can run your macros from the Macros box. Go to Tools→Macro→Macros to open the box shown in Figure 15-8. The available macros are listed in the large pane in the middle of the box. If the macro is stored in a different workbook, the name of the workbook precedes the macro name. To run a macro, double-click its name, or select it and then click the Run button.

The LetterHead macro changes the contents of cells. If there happens to be something else in those cells, your macro doesn't care. It goes ahead and replaces it. When you're typing away, you can always press ⌘-Z to undo any mistakes. Not so with your macros. You can't undo a macro, so it pays to be cautious. If disaster strikes, you may want to close your workbook without saving. The only problem with that workaround is that you'll lose your unsaved work.

If you want to save this workbook with your recorded macro, you need to use the special macro-enabled file format that ends in *.xlsm*. If you try to save it in the standard file format, you'll see a warning like the one in Figure 15-3. (Why is there a special file format for macros? See the box on page 445 for the story.)

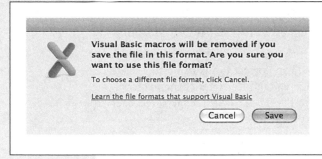

Figure 15-3:
Sorry. It's a matter of security. Excel won't let you store macros in any old document file. You have to use the macro-enabled file format, as explained in the box on page 445.

Absolute vs. Relative Cell References

The first macro example in this chapter is fine for a start. It saves a few keystrokes by typing text into three cells in the upper-left corner of your worksheet. The example used a business address, but you can easily use anything you want. Perhaps you'd like to put your name, a date, and an email address on your spreadsheets. It's easy to see how you can do that.

Macro and Macro-free Excel Documents

Sadly there are nasty folks out there who want to mess up your work, and they're pretty creative at turning your own tools against you. That's what happened with Office macros and Visual Basic. Microsoft handed hackers the perfect tools to foul up our office work. As a result, Word and Outlook in particular got a bad reputation. Innocent people opened documents or clicked email links, and bad things happened.

In an effort to fix the problem, Microsoft came up with several security measures. For starters they removed macros and VBA from Outlook, because it was the most common delivery method for malware. Then they developed new file formats that won't store macros or VBA programs. No way, no how. Excel documents that end in *xlsx* don't support macros. So, you can open these Excel files without worrying that something bad will happen. If you want to create an Excel document that stores macros, you have to save it in the .xlsm format. The same convention is true with Word and PowerPoint documents. If the filename extension ends in an "m", it stores macros. If it doesn't, it won't.

Bottom line, if you open an Office macro-enabled document make sure you know that it came from a friendly source. Here are the file format extensions to look for:

Excel: .xlsm (documents) .xltm (templates).

Word: .docm (documents) .dotm (templates).

PowerPoint .pptm (documents) .potm (templates) .ppsm (show).

The last measure of defense that Microsoft added were warning dialog boxes. When you open a document with macros, you'll see a message like the one in Figure 15-4. You're given three options. If you trust the source, go ahead and open the workbook with the Enable Macros button. If you're not sure about the source, you can open the document, but leave the macros turned off with the Disable Macros button. If you're really in doubt, you can hit the Do Not Open button.

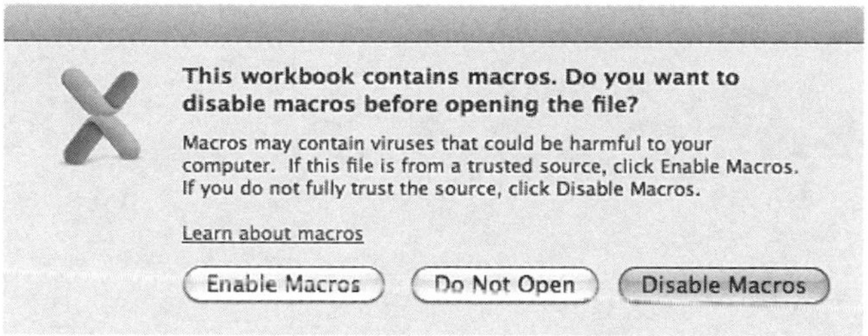

Figure 15-4:
When you open a workbook that contains macros, Excel is likely to flash this warning. Microsoft wants you to be aware that the document you're opening contains macros. Some of these macros may run without you doing anything. If you don't know who created this workbook, beware!

If you play around with that first macro, you'll begin to see one of its limitations. It always puts the words in exactly the same cells. That may be okay if you're creating an address header, but there are plenty of cases where you might want to write a macro that adds to or changes cells that might be anyplace on a worksheet. Maybe you'd like to create a macro that automatically lists the twelve months of the year. Maybe your company has seven divisions and you're constantly labeling columns with their names.

In those cases, you'd like to be able to click on a cell and have the macro type the text in the cells to the right. In that case, you need to use relative cell references when you record your macro, instead of absolute references like A1 or B3.

For relative references, you need the help of the Developer tab. Don't worry, you won't have to start wearing a pocket protector and a propeller beanie, but yeah, you're getting into computer geek territory. On the right end of the ribbon, click the button that looks like a gear, and choose Ribbon Preferences. In the Ribbon Preferences window (shown in Figure 15-5), scroll the tab or group title all the way to the bottom and turn on Developer. Click OK to close the window. Now at the end of your ribbon, you've got the Developer tab, which holds some controls that help you work with macros.

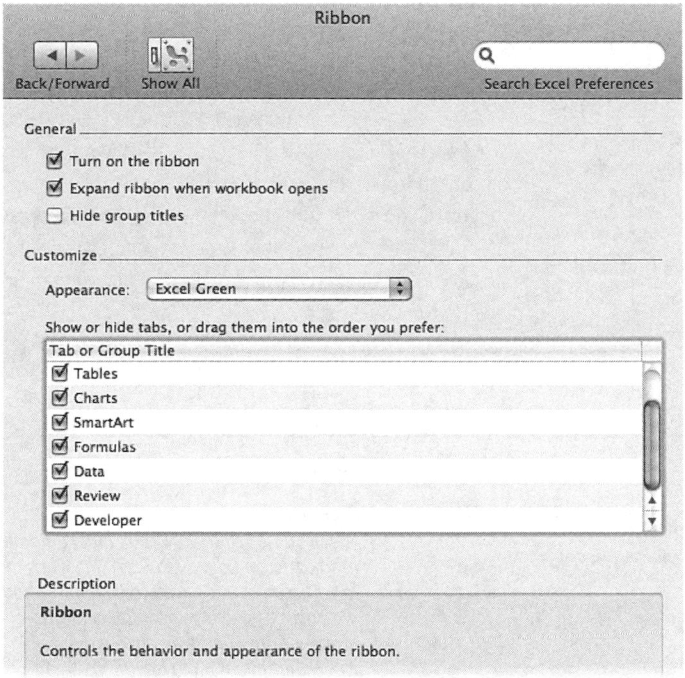

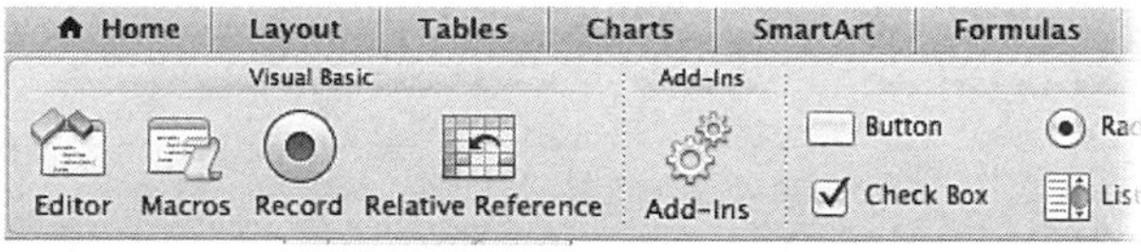

Figure 15-5:
Turn on the Developer tab in your ribbon preferences to display some new tools that help you create macros. In addition to buttons that stop and start macro recording, you can toggle the Relative Reference mode on and off as needed.

You can take your new macro tools for a test drive by creating a macro that writes the months of the current year horizontally across twelve cells.

1. **Click somewhere in a worksheet where you have twelve empty horizontal cells.**

2. On the ribbon, click Developer | Visual Basic→Record button.

3. Name your macro Months and, if you want, give it a shortcut key like Option-⌘-Y. (Y for year, because Option-⌘-M is already taken by OS X. It's the Finder command to minimize all windows).

4. Click the Relative Reference button so that it looks pushed in.

5. Type January in the current cell.

6. Drag the expand button in the lower-right corner of the cell to fill in all twelve months.

7. Click stop.

Click somewhere else in your spreadsheet and press the shortcut key. This macro will work on any cell on any sheet in this workbook. Instead of references to specific cells like B3 and C2, the macro uses relative references. It's more like saying, now move one cell to the right. Now, move up two cells. More often than not, you're going to want to use relative references because they make your macros more portable and usable.

Using Formulas in Macros

When you're working in Excel, you're certainly not limited to text. You'll soon want to create macros that add formulas to cells. Here's another good example of relative references that handles a common sales tax chore. Suppose you often create invoices for sale items. Your invoices include the quantity and unit price of each item. You want to create a macro that multiplies the quantity by the unit price creating a subtotal and then applies a sales tax and posts the total for the sale of that item.

Your spreadsheet might look something like Figure 15-6. In fact, your worksheet can look exactly like that if you download *15-1_relative_address.xlsm* from the Missing CD (*http://missingmanuals.com/cds*). If you're creating your own spreadsheet for this project, the important point is that you have a cell with the Quantity and to the right of that, you have a cell with the Unit Cost.

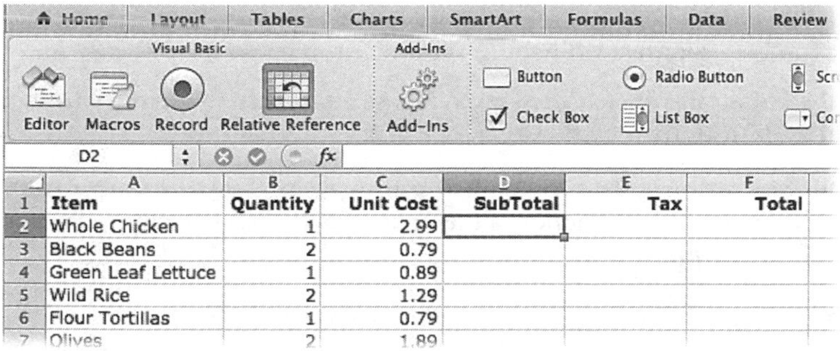

Figure 15-6:
If you're looking at an invoice that looks like this one, you can create a macro that fills in the columns. Just make sure that you make the cell references relative as explained on page 444. That way you can use the macro over and over in different places.

1. **Click on a cell to the right of unit cost.**

    Figure 15-6 shows the proper starting position.

2. **Click Developer→Visual Basic→Record and give your macro a name like
    SubAndTax and shortcut key like Option-⌘-X.**

    Your macro starts recording when you click OK in the Record Macro box.

3. **Toggle Relative by clicking Developer | Visual Basic→Relative.**

    Use relative references so you can use this same macro in other locations on a
    worksheet.

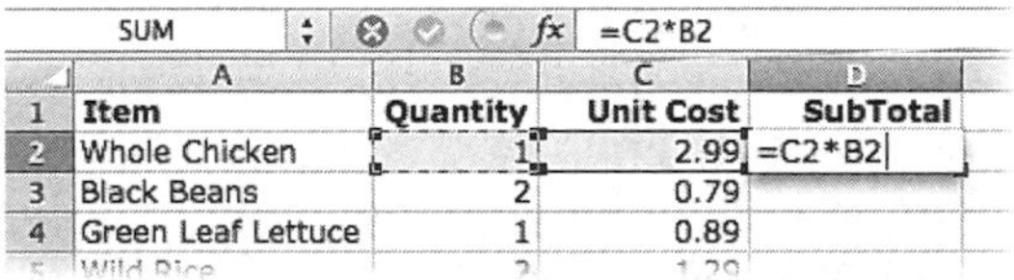

Figure 15-7:
*This is the starting point for creating a macro that
calculates a subtotal, applies a tax and posts the total.
As you can see from this exercise, your macros aren't
tied down to a single cell in your worksheet.*

4. **Type = and then click in the *Unit Cost* cell.**

    The Unit Cost cell is one cell to the left on the same row.

5. **Type * and then click the Quantity cell. Press Return.**

    The entire formula is displayed in the formula bar as *=C2*B2*. Even though
    these are absolute cell references, your macro is recording something slightly
    different. It's recording a formula that says something like: reference the cell one
    space to the left and multiply it by the cell two spaces to the left.

6. **Click the Tax cell in the same row and create a formula that looks like
    =D2*0.09. Press Return to save the formula.**

    Your formula should multiply the subtotal by a tax rate. This example applies a
    9% rate. Your mileage may vary depending on location.

7. **In the last cell under Total, type in a formula that adds the SubTotal and Tax
    cells. Something like *=E2+D2* does the trick. Press Return to save the formula.**

    Macros will handle any formula you want to use, whether they're ones that you
    build as in this exercise, or functions that you drop in.

8. **With the Total cell still selected, go to Home | Number→Currency to format
    the cell to show dollars.**

    You can use just about any command in your macros. It doesn't matter whether
    you trigger them with the ribbon, a menu or a keyboard shortcut.

9. **Click Developer | Visual Basic→Stop.**

    Your macro stops recording and is stored in your workbook.

Now that your macro is complete, go ahead and try it out in one of the other rows. Click in one of the empty SubTotal cells and press the shortcut key. As an alternative, you can run the macro from the Macros box. Go to Developer | Visual Basic→Macros to open the box an then choose your macro from the list.

Making Macros Always Available

When you go to all the trouble of planning and then recording a macro that saves you time and typing, you'll probably want to use it in more than one workbook. Well, here's a helpful tip: You can run macros from any workbook that's open at the moment. To test this theory, open the workbook with the SubAndTax macro, then open a brand new workbook. Type in some dummy numbers for a quantity and a unit cost. Then, click in the cell to the right and go Developer | Visual Basic→Macros to open the Macros box. In the Macros list, double-click on the macro that has Sub-AndTax at the end of the name. The beginning of the name refers to the workbook where the macro is stored.

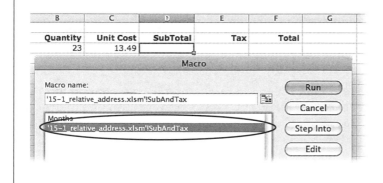

Figure 15-8:
You can have more than one Excel workbook open at once and you can run macros from any open workbook. By opening the Macros box (Developer | Visual Basic→Macros) this workbook is about to run the SubAndTax macro (circled) that's been stored in the 15-1_relative_address.xlsm *workbook.*

In general, you may not want to go around opening up workbooks just so you can use the macros that are stored inside. Fortunately, there's an easier way to get at those macros. Remember, the rule is that you can run a macro from any workbook that is open. Well, there's a special workbook whose primary task is to hold macros that you want to use all the time. Once you store macros in your Personal Macro Workbook, Excel opens it every time you start Excel. You won't see the workbook though, because it's automatically hidden.

To make the macro that you're recording always available, you need to store it in your Personal Macro Workbook. You can do this right after you click the Record button (Developer | Visual Basic→Record). After you click the Record button in the ribbon or go to Tools→Macro→Record New Macro, the Record Macro box appears. Click the "Store macro in" menu on the right and choose Personal Macro Workbook, as shown in Figure 15-9.

Tip: Macros stored in your Personal Macro Workbook are always available to you in any workbook that you open. However, they aren't necessarily available to anyone else. That's why it's called your *Personal* Macro Workbook. If you're creating a workbook for fellow coworkers and want them to be able to use the macros, you should save them in the workbook that you're distributing.

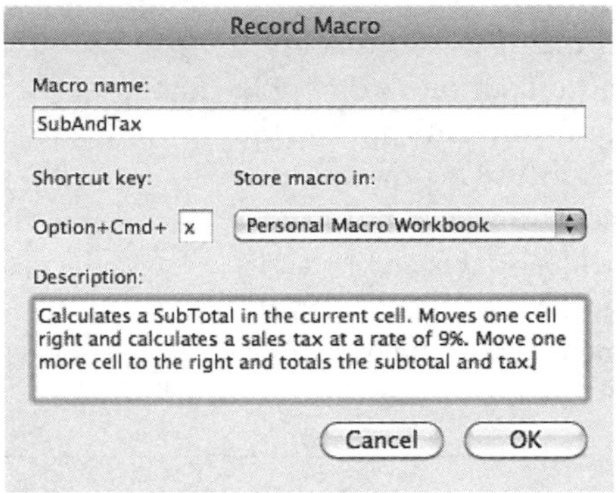

Figure 15-9:
When you create macros, if you change the "Store macro in" menu to Personal Macro Workbook, they'll always be available to you in any workbook. This doesn't make the macro available to any other coworkers, though.

Introducing Visual Basic for Applications

Macros are fine for recording keystrokes, menu, and ribbon commands and those kind of tasks. They're easy to use and play back. But what if you want to make a minor tweak to a macro you recorded? Everything's perfect except you'd like that SubAndTax macro to apply a little formatting to the cells. You have to go back and repeat all the steps perfectly and remember to apply the formatting changes. But there must be an easier way to tweak your macro. Or suppose, your invoice includes some items that are taxable and some that aren't. How do you explain to your macro that you want to apply tax only when a product is taxable? Visual Basic, enter stage left. When you're recording macros, you're actually creating Visual Basic for Applications (VBA) code. When the macro recorder stores your macros in a worksheet, it writes those actions in the Visual Basic. If you learn to read and modify VBA code, you can tweak code that you record in macros and you can code situations like: If this item is taxable, apply a 9% tax and enter that value in this cell.

Note: There's more than one flavor of Visual Basic. The rest of this chapter discusses Visual Basic for Applications, which is a scripting language that lives and operates inside of Office applications. You can't create standalone programs in VBA. That's a job for its grow-up sibling Visual Basic 2010. As you might guess, the two share many of the same concepts, so if you learn VBA, you can transfer those skills to full-blown Visual Basic.

Opening a Recorded Macro in Visual Basic

The best way to start to learn and understand Visual Basic for Application (VBA) code is to open a macro that you've recorded and try to decipher the way the macro recorder transcribed your actions. Why not start off easy? Here's an experiment you can do to learn the VBA command for changing a selected cell's format to bold.

1. **In a brand new workbook type** *Make me bold* **in any cell and make sure that cell remains selected.**

2. **Go to Developer | Visual Basic→Record.**

3. **In the Record Macro box, name your macro Bold and store it in This Workbook.**

4. **Press ⌘-B to make the "Make me bold" text bold.**

5. **Click Developer→Visual Basic→Stop.**

You've recorded a macro that performs a single action: It turns the contents of the selected cell bold. That shouldn't be too hard to parse in Visual Basic. To see your massive programming effort, click Developer | Visual Basic→Macros. Choose Bold (the name of your macro) and click the Edit button. A new application opens on top of Excel. This is the Visual Basic for Applications working environment, shown in Figure 15-10. With its multiple windows, it may seem a little intimidating, but if you explore a little bit at a time, you'll learn your way around. Right now focus on the largest of the windows that has the same name as your workbook. If you haven't saved your workbook, the window has a name like "Workbook1 – Module1 (Code)." Inside the window is a little bit of code as shown in Figure 15-11. Not too scary. At least it's short!

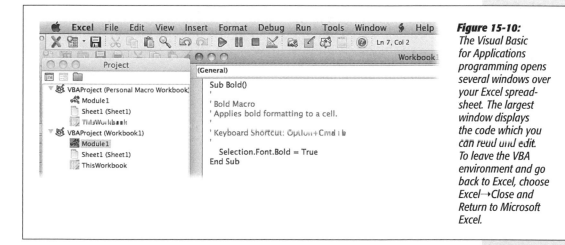

Figure 15-10:
The Visual Basic for Applications programming opens several windows over your Excel spreadsheet. The largest window displays the code which you can read and edit. To leave the VBA environment and go back to Excel, choose Excel→Close and Return to Microsoft Excel.

You'll find some of the same elements in every recorded macro and Visual Basic program, so it's worth taking the time to look at your Bold code line by line.

- **Sub Bold().** This is the first line of your macro. All macros are *subroutines*, so the word *Sub* always introduces a subroutine. It's followed by the title of the sub-routine, in this case *Bold*. The parentheses are always part of a subroutine intro-duction, too. In this case there's nothing inside them. Sometimes, subroutines pass information back and forth by putting the details inside of the parentheses.

- **Lines preceded by ' (apostrophe) are comments.** They don't have any function as far as the program is concerned, but programmers use comments to explain how a program works and to write notes to themselves when they're working on a project. In this case, the macro recorder automatically added comments that explain this is a macro named Bold and that you can use the Option-⌘-B shortcut key to trigger it. The VB editor uses green text for comments to make it easy to separate comments from the real code.

- **Selection.Font.Bold = True**. This is the heart of your program—a single line of almost understandable English. It's saying set the selection's font to bold. In Visual Basic, Font is an object and Bold is a property. You can change the ap-pearance of text by changing the font properties. For example, you can assign a different font name, or change its size or color. One of those properties is Bold. Bold is expressed by one of two values; it's either True or False. You'll find lots of properties that use True or False as a kind of toggle switch. Other properties might use words or a numbers to set their values. For example, font names are expressed as words while colors may be expressed as either words or numbers.

- **End Sub**. You guessed it! These two words mark the end of a subroutine.

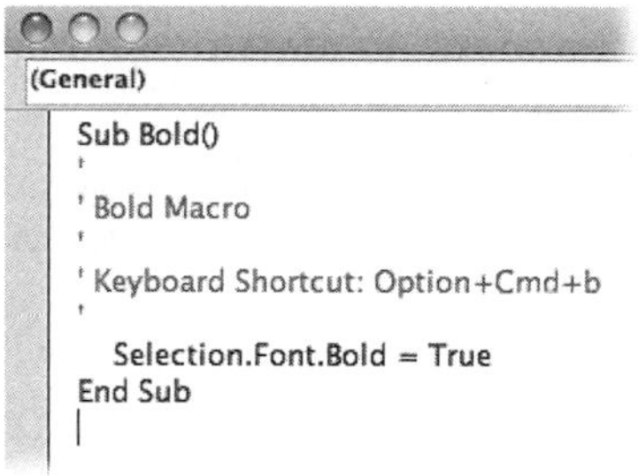

Figure 15-11:
Each macro that you record is considered a subroutine in Visual Basic geek-speak. When you open the Macros window, choose a macro and click Edit, you see the subroutine displayed in the VBA editor.

```
(General)

Sub Bold()
'
' Bold Macro
'
' Keyboard Shortcut: Option+Cmd+b
'
    Selection.Font.Bold = True
End Sub
|
```

You can edit macros that you've recorded. Don't worry, you won't break anything. You can select, delete and add text just as you'd do with a Word document. Most of the same techniques work in the Visual Basic editor. As an experiment, change the line that reads:

```
Selection.Font.Bold = True
```

to

```
Selection.Font.Italic = True.
```

You just tweaked Visual Basic code. Close the Visual Basic programming environment by going to Excel→Close and Return to Microsoft Excel. Now, if you select a cell and run your Bold macro, it turns the text italic. That's just wrong, you mad hacker you!

From the experiment it's clear that you can apply formatting to a selection with a single command. If you continue to record macros and read the code, you learn that other formatting expressions are very similar. Here are some other examples that change the format of the selected cell:

```
Selection.Style = "Currency"
Selection.Style = "Comma"
Selection.Style = "Percent"
```

Referencing Cells the VB Way

It's easy to see how you could apply this same technique to almost any Excel command that you want translated into Visual Basic lingo. Record the simplest macro you can that involves the command and then dissect it. Moving from cell to cell and referencing cells is a big deal in Excel, so it's another interesting area to explore. If you're going to fiddle with Visual Basic code, it's good to understand the difference between an absolute reference to a cell and a relative reference. (If you need a refresher on the differences between absolute and relative references, see page 387.)

Here's the code that was recorded when a cell was selected and the contents of that cell was set to bold. This action was performed with the Relative button toggled off:

```
Sub MoveLeft()
'
' MoveLeft Macro
'

'
    Range("E15").Select
    Selection.Font.Bold = True
End Sub
```

The important line reads: *Range("E15").Select*. That's the absolute reference to the cell E5 in Visual Basic code. It selects and highlights that particular cell. Any actions performed immediately after that, such as changing the bold property, affects the contents of that cell. As you can see, the bold command is identical to the earlier example. *Range* is Excel's term for a bunch of cells. A range can be as small as a single cell or as large as an entire worksheet. When you build formulas in the formula bar, Excel expresses ranges like this: C2:E12. That reference means all the cells from C2 to E12. With this tidbit in your VB toolbox, it's easy to figure out that you can select a range of several cells. For example: *Range("C2:E12").Select*.

Tip: Programming languages like Visual Basic are stricter than your 3rd Grade grammar teacher. They want everything just so. For example, the Range command expects both the parentheses and the quotes. If they aren't there, you've got a broken VB subroutine.

Making a selection using a relative reference is more complicated than an absolute selection. When you click on that Relative button, Excel thinks of the currently se-lected cell as the center of the universe. It even refers to that cell as A1. (This is not the same A1 that you know and love in the upper-left corner of your workbook. And it's not the same cell you'd find in an absolute reference to A1.) Any movement from that cell to the right or down is considered a plus move. Any movement to the left or up is considered a minus move. The Visual Basic term for a this kind of a move is Offset and it's expressed like this: *Offset(0, 2)*. The numbers in the parentheses indicate the number of cell in the relative move. The first number (in this case, 0) shows the number of rows that were moved (none). The second number shows the number of columns that were moved (2). If the move had been 2 columns to the left, the expression would use a negative number like *Offset(0, -2)*. Check out Figure 15-12, if you want to see a visual representation of the Offset method.

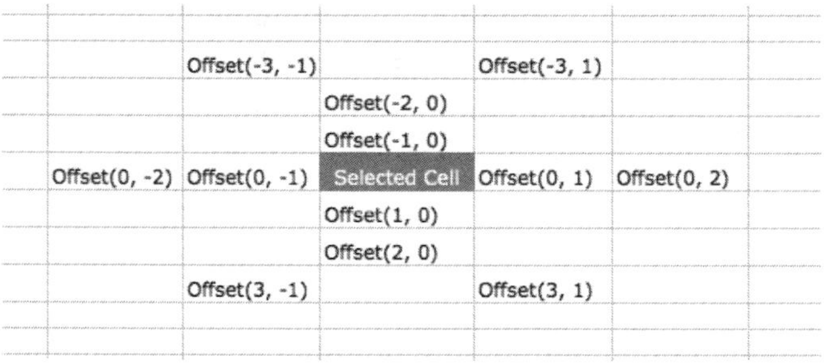

Figure 15-12:
The Offset() method is used for relative references to other cells in a worksheet. In this case, the selected cell is in the middle. Other cells show the Offset expression that you'd use to reference those cells. The numbers in parentheses represent (rows, columns). Movement to the right or down are positive num-bers. Movement left or up are negative numbers.

Here's a complete line of code that moves the selection 2 cells to the left and then selects a range of several cells:

```
ActiveCell.Offset(0, 2).Range("A1:C6").Select
```

It starts with the *ActiveCell*—the currently selected cell. The *Offset()* moves the selection 2 cells to the right. Keep in mind that the Relative button is toggled to record relative references. So, the newly selected cell is considered A1, the center of the universe. The reference A1:C6 starts from the newly selected cell and moves down six rows and right three columns.

Changing the Contents of a Cell

What's the fun in moving from cell to cell if you don't change their content? You can write a simple subroutine that selects a specific cell and then changes the value of the selection. It's the same thing you'd do with your mouse and keyboard if you're working inside of Excel, and it looks like this:

```
Sub SetValue()
    Range("C3").Select
    Selection.Value = "I am a VB genius!"
End Sub
```

One of the fun things about VB scripting is you don't always have to do things the way you'd do it in the real world. For example, in VB you can make changes to a cell without selecting it first. All you need to do is reference the object and the property you want to change. Here's a simpler way to set the value of C3:

```
Cells(3, 3).Value = "I am a VB genius!"
```

You certainly don't have to limit your changes to text. You can change the value of a cell to a formula. Just put the formula inside of the quotes and write it the same way you'd write it in the formula bar. Like so:

```
Cells(3, 3).Value = "=C1+C2"
```

This statement adds the values in C1 and C2 and places the total in C3.

Getting More Visual Basic Help

Visual Basic looks at the elements it manipulates as objects. Perhaps that's unkind, but that's the way it is in the cruel VB world. Objects have properties. For example, Bold and Italic are properties of the Font object. Sometimes you'll hear programmers talk about *object-oriented* programming. It's a big subject. See the box on page 158 for some more details.

As you work in VB, you often make changes by assigning new values to an object's properties. So, when you want to accomplish something, you need to know what property you want to change and what type of values you can use to accomplish the deed. The example from page 451 shows one tried and true way to identify properties and values. You record a macro and then dissect the code written by the macro recorder. If you're serious about learning Visual Basic, you'll find the tutorials in Michael Halvorson's *Microsoft Visual Basic 2010 Step by Step* (Microsoft Press) very helpful.

You can also turn to some of the help tools provided by Microsoft, but be fore-warned, they're the kind of documents that are written by programmers for pro-grammers. In fact, at the time this was written, just finding help documentation for Visual Basic is a bit of a journey. Perhaps it will be easier in the future. Follow these steps to get help with the Visual Basic language as it relates to Excel:

1. **Go to Developer | Visual Basic→Editor to open the editor.**

2. **Click the Visual Basic help button on the toolbar. It's a purple circle with a question.**

3. **In the Excel Help window, click the link that says "To view the documentation, see Visual Basic Editor Help".**

    The online help page opens as shown in Figure 15-13. Finding your way around Microsoft's documentation can be challenging. For example, there are links that provide help for using the Visual Basic Editor and links that lead to a reference for the Visual Basic language. When you're trying to learn about the objects, properties and methods, your best bet is the link that says Visual Basic Language Help.

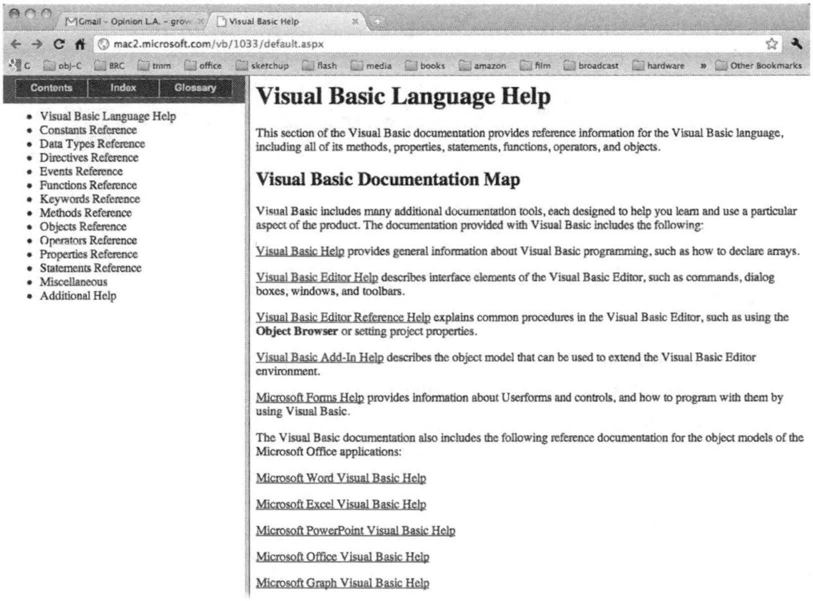

Figure 15-13:
Microsoft's online help can be a bit puzzling for the beginner. There are several links to different sections. At the bottom of this page, there are links to VB documentation for Word, Excel, and PowerPoint.

4. **If you're working on an Excel Visual Basic project, click the link at the bottom of the page: Microsoft Excel Visual Basic Help.**

To use this reference, you click topics on the left to display information in the main window. Initially the left pane displays the Contents, but you can also choose an alphabetized Index or a Glossary of Terms. When you use the Contents, you can pick a subject like Objects Reference to study up on the Font object. Once you zero in on the topic you want, the explanations are pretty good and they often include examples. Object definitions lead to the properties and methods that are members of the object.

There's one more tool that can help you understand the relationship between objects, properties and methods. It's called the Object Browser. When you're in the Visual Basic editor, go to View | Object Browser. A new window opens that looks like Figure 15-14.

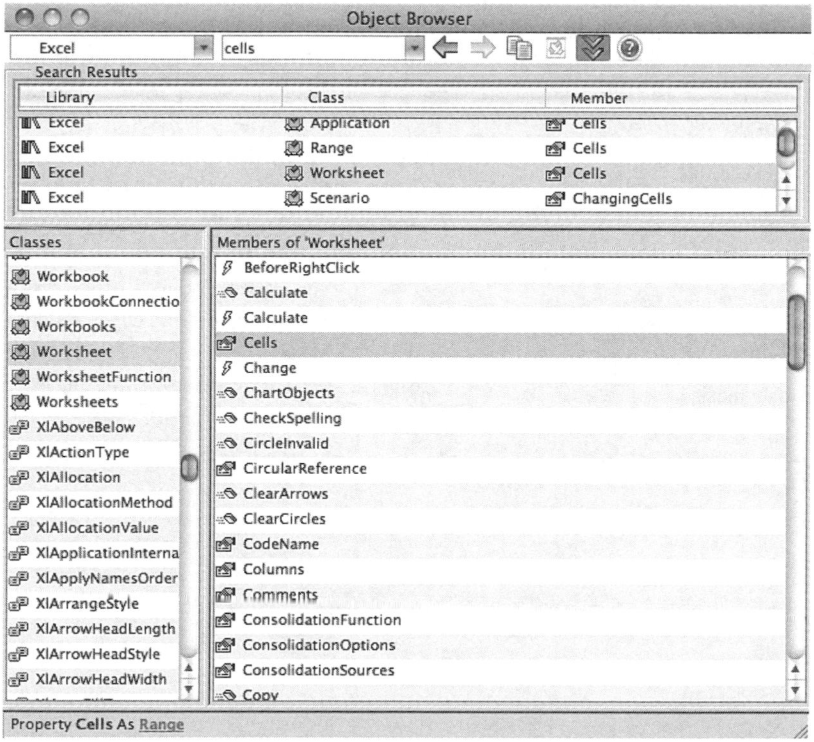

Figure 15-14:
The object browser is available when you're working in Visual Basic. Use the menu at the top to choose categories like Excel or Word. You can search for a word, such as Cells, to display related details. Here, in the pane on the left, Worksheet is selected so the large pane displays the properties and methods related to the worksheet class of objects.

Object-Oriented Thinking

What does object-oriented programming mean, anyway?

When programmers talk about object-oriented programming, they're referring to specific programming techniques— a way of looking at the parts of a program and the overall design. The idea is to create chunks of programming code that do a specific job. If you design them all correctly, those chunks can fit together with other pieces of code. Think for a second about a typical home theater system that has an amplifier/receiver, a DVD player, a TV screen, and maybe a cable box. Each unit is an object. The folks who designed the DVD player don't have to know how to build a TV screen, they just have to make a DVD player that can plug into a TV. You can plug the same DVD player into another home theater system, and it'll work perfectly well. Programmers strive for that kind of modularity when they build objects.

The benefits are obvious. As long as the objects have an agreed-upon way of interacting, different programmers can work on different objects. When they all come together, they'll play well with each other. If the objects are truly useful and flexible, you can reuse them in future projects. Future programmers won't have to understand how the DVD player works, all they need to know is how to plug it in and how to send and receive signals from it.

In addition to reusability, there are a handful of other concepts that define object-oriented programming. Some of them don't make a lot of sense until you've had some experience with VBA, but here are a few of the basics for reference:

- **Objects.** Objects are the building blocks of an object-oriented program. In VBA, a workbook is an object. A worksheet is an object that's inside of a workbook. You manipulate objects through their properties and methods. In VB-speak, properties and methods are considered "members" of objects.

- **Properties.** Properties are the characteristics that define an object. For example, if the object is an iPod, then color might be one of its properties. The color value of the iPod could be white, silver, or hot pink. In VBA, you spend a lot of time setting values for various properties. That's how you change the formula in a cell and how you format numbers and text.

- **Methods.** Methods are actions that an object can perform. To continue with the iPod example, Play and Pause are methods for the iPod object. Methods, are part of the object's definition. The Select method appeared in several of the examples in this chapter in statements like: *Range("C3").Select*.

CHAPTER 16

Formatting and Charts: Well-Dressed Spreadsheets

When many of us mere mortals see row after row and column after column of numbers, our eyes glaze over and a certain portion of our brain goes numb. There are others who insist that numbers are exciting when you see the dramatic stories they tell about success and failure. This chapter shows you how to make those columns of numbers tell their story in a way that's immediately accessible and understandable.

For starters, you'll learn how to dress up your worksheets with attractive fonts, background and colors border styles. Now, these techniques don't generally wring the story out of your numbers, but something like banded background colors will make it easier for the Board to read your numbers.

Excel's charts (sometimes called graphs) are the key to making your numbers give up their secrets. A good chart pinpoints the moment when your business went from losing money to making it, or (gulp) vice versa. A chart can point out that your variegated flachitometer sells best in the winter months and that sales to the Lake States have grown steadily for the last 7 quarters. Excel 2011 adds a new charting feature called Sparklines. These mini-charts fit in a cell right next to your data. They don't have the eye-popping visual impact of full blown charts, but they play a role in revealing the story hidden in those numbers.

Excel offers so many different styles of charts, it may be hard for you pick the right one to tell your story. However, once you read this chapter, it won't be hard at all for you to create, customize, and print a chart.

Formatting Worksheets

When it comes to spreadsheets, the term *formatting* covers a lot of ground. It refers to the size of the cell, its background color, how its borders look, as well as how the *contents* of the cell are formatted (with or without dollar signs or decimal points, for example)—anything that affects how the cell looks. There are a lot of tools to handle these chores and they're grouped on different tabs on the ribbon. Here's an overview of the tabs the type of tools they hold:

- The **Home** tab holds the standard font settings like size and color, including cell background color. The Number group provides styles for showing data as currency, dates and other options. The Format group gives you a sophisticated way to format cells based on the underlying data. It goes way beyond showing negative numbers in red. Last and perhaps least, the Themes in the group at the far end of the Home tab make it easy to choose matching fonts and colors.

- The **Layout** tab gives you the tools you need if you're printing your spreadsheet. Will the pages have headers and footers? Do you want to print gridlines? You can insert page breaks to make sure different portions of your spreadsheet print on different pages. These features are covered in the chapter on printing (page 499).

- The **Tables** tab turns portions of your worksheets into data tables (as explained on page 403) and gives you lots of ways to format them with borders and background colors.

- It's no surprise that the **Charts** tab is command central for adding charts and making them look good.

- Likewise, the **SmartArt** tab holds Microsoft's customizable graphics that show relationships like organization hierarchies and processes. (SmartArt picks up the fonts and colors from themes.)

Excel offers two ways to add formatting to your spreadsheet: by using Excel's automatic formatting capabilities or by doing the work yourself. Odds are, you'll be using both methods.

Automatic Formatting with Table Styles

If you want to quickly add background colors and border formatting to your spreadsheet, the tools on the Table tab are your best option. As explained in Chapter 14, tables let you turn your rows and columns into data that you can sort and filter.

In addition, tables give you some automatic formatting eye candy. By using different background colors and font styles, you can visually separate the cells with descriptive words from the cells that hold numbers. When you have long rows and columns of numbers you can help readers find their way by using alternating background colors called bands.

If you have a worksheet that looks like the one in the top of Figure 16-1, follow these steps to dress it up:

Note: If you need a practice spreadsheet for your formatting experiments, you can download *16_1_For-matting_Worksheets.xlsx* from the Missing CD at *http://missingmanuals.com/cds*.

---

1. **Select the cells you want to format.**

2. **Tables→New→Insert Table with Headers.**

   Excel turns the selected range into a table and applies automatic formatting. The top row in the range turns into drop-down menus. (If that annoys you, you'll see how to change that in later steps.)

3. **Use the Table Options to change the background colors for specific rows and columns in your sheet.**

   For example, if you have descriptive text in the first column like the example in Figure 16-1, then turn on the first column box. Excel highlights the column by applying different font styles and cell colors. The Total Row option goes beyond formatting by creating a row with formulas that total the numbers above them.

4. **Choose a Table style.**

   The center of the Tables ribbon is taken up with table styles that apply colors and borders to your table, using theme colors. If you click the button at the bottom of the group to view all the styles, you'll see they are arranged by Light, Dark, and Medium. Dark options may look great on your computer but, depending on your printer, might not look as good on the page. The darker options also consume more of that expensive printer ink.

5. **Optional: Select any cell in the table and then choose Convert to Range.**

   If you don't need or want the table functions, you can convert your table back to ordinary spreadsheet cells but keep the fancy formatting. A warning box appears to confirm the action; click OK and the deed is done.

After you convert the table back to normal cells, you can't use any of the table option checkboxes to format the cells. Instead, you need to use some of manual formatting methods, described next.

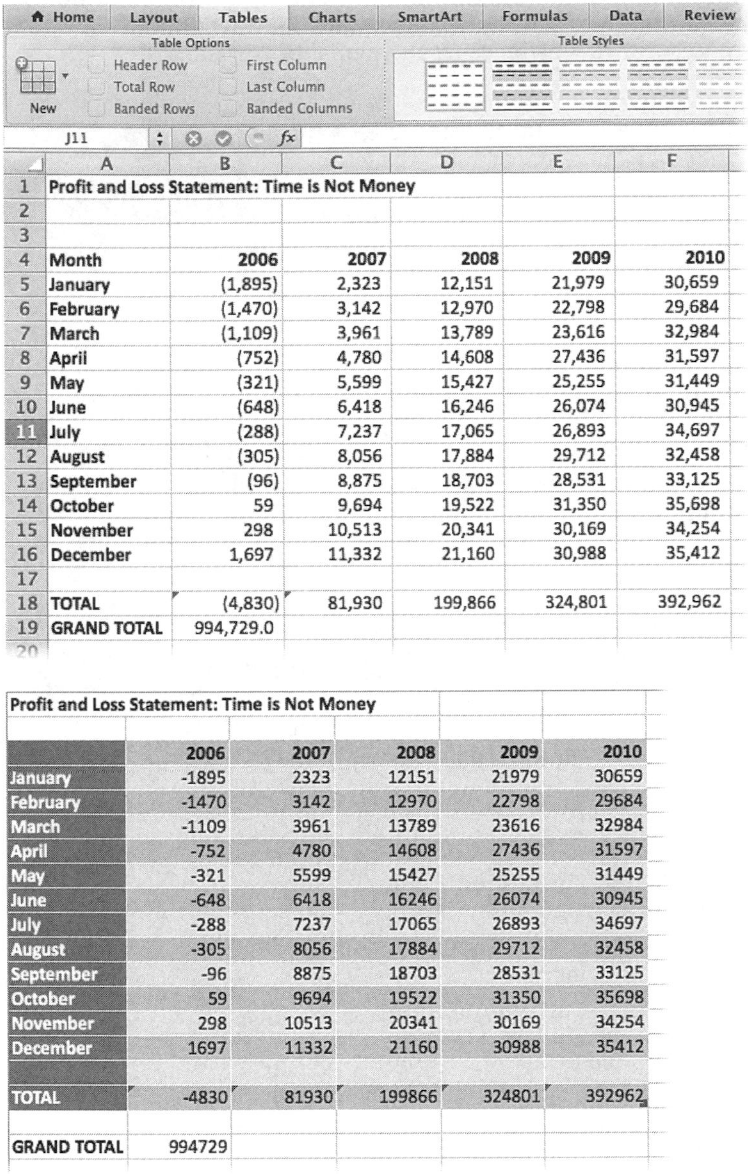

| Home | Layout | Tables | Charts | SmartArt | Formulas | Data | Review |

Table Options

- Header Row
- Total Row
- Banded Rows
- First Column
- Last Column
- Banded Columns

New

Table Styles

J11   fx

	A	B	C	D	E	F
1	Profit and Loss Statement: Time is Not Money					
2						
3						
4	Month	2006	2007	2008	2009	2010
5	January	(1,895)	2,323	12,151	21,979	30,659
6	February	(1,470)	3,142	12,970	22,798	29,684
7	March	(1,109)	3,961	13,789	23,616	32,984
8	April	(752)	4,780	14,608	27,436	31,597
9	May	(321)	5,599	15,427	25,255	31,449
10	June	(648)	6,418	16,246	26,074	30,945
11	July	(288)	7,237	17,065	26,893	34,697
12	August	(305)	8,056	17,884	29,712	32,458
13	September	(96)	8,875	18,703	28,531	33,125
14	October	59	9,694	19,522	31,350	35,698
15	November	298	10,513	20,341	30,169	34,254
16	December	1,697	11,332	21,160	30,988	35,412
17						
18	TOTAL	(4,830)	81,930	199,866	324,801	392,962
19	GRAND TOTAL	994,729.0				
20						

Figure 16-1:
You can use Table Styles to turn plain Jane spreadsheets into something with a bit more style. Once you've used the Table tools to format the cells, you can go to Table→Tools→Convert to Range to remove the table data features and keep the formatting.

Profit and Loss Statement: Time is Not Money					
	2006	2007	2008	2009	2010
January	-1895	2323	12151	21979	30659
February	-1470	3142	12970	22798	29684
March	-1109	3961	13789	23616	32984
April	-752	4780	14608	27436	31597
May	-321	5599	15427	25255	31449
June	-648	6418	16246	26074	30945
July	-288	7237	17065	26893	34697
August	-305	8056	17884	29712	32458
September	-96	8875	18703	28531	33125
October	59	9694	19522	31350	35698
November	298	10513	20341	30169	34254
December	1697	11332	21160	30988	35412
TOTAL	-4830	81930	199866	324801	392962
GRAND TOTAL	994729				

Automatic formatting bonus

Sooner or later, another year will roll by, and it'll be time to update the sheet shown at the bottom of Figure 16-1. So, you head over to the column with the years and you type in 2011. When you hit Enter, a little formatting magic takes place: Excel formats the entire column to match the others. It's a handy little timesaver if that's what you want. If it's not what you want, press ⌘-Z, and Excel removes the formatting but leaves your number in place.

The Format Painter

Another way to quickly apply formatting to a group of cells is the Format Painter. Suppose you've painstakingly applied formatting—colors, cell borders, fonts, text alignment, and the like—to a certain patch of cells. Using the Format Painter, you can copy the formatting to any other cells—in the same or a different spreadsheet.

To start, select the cell(s) that you want to use as an example of good formatting. Then click the Format Painter button (the little paintbrush) on the Standard toolbar. Now, as you move the cursor over the spreadsheet, it changes to look like a paintbrush with a + sign.

Next, drag the cursor over the cells (or click a single cell) you'd like to change to match the first group. Excel applies the formatting—borders, shading, font settings, and the like—to the new cells (Figure 16-2).

Tip: To format discontinuous areas without going back to the paintbrush, double-click the paintbrush button. Now you can apply the format multiple times. To stop, click the paintbrush button again.

Formatting Cells by Hand

If the table styles are a bit too canned for your purposes, you can always format the look of your spreadsheet manually. When formatting cells manually, it's helpful to divide the task up into two concepts—formatting the cells themselves (borders and backgrounds), and formatting the *contents* of those cells (what you've typed).

Changing cell size

When you open an Excel worksheet, all the cells are the same size. Specifically, they're 1.04 inches wide (the factory-set width of an Excel column) and 0.18 inches tall (the height of an Excel row). The good news is that there are several ways to set a cell's height and width. Here's a rundown:

Note: If you use the Metric system, you can switch to centimeters or millimeters on the Excel→ Preferences→General tab. Choose from the "Measurement units" pop-up menu. Unfortunately, 4.59 millimeters is just as hard to remember as 0.18 inches.

Profit and Loss Statement: Time is Not Money

	2006	2007	2008	2009	2010
January	-1895	2323	12151	21979	30659
February	-1470	3142	12970	22798	29684
March	-1109	3961	13789	23616	32984
April	-752	4780	14608	27436	31597
May	-321	5599	15427	25255	31449
June	-648	6418	16246	26074	30945
July	-288	7237	17065	26893	34697
August	-305	8056	17884	29712	32458
September	-96	8875	18703	28531	33125
October	59	9694	19522	31350	35698
November	298	10513	20341	30169	34254
December	1697	11332	21160	30988	35412
TOTAL	-4830	81930	199866	324801	392962
GRAND TOTAL	994729				

Monthly Income from Day Job

	2006	2007	2008	2009	2010
January	987	1152	876	1289	1894
February	987	1152	876	1289	1894
March	987	1152	876	1289	1894
April	987	1152	876	1289	1894
May	987	1152	876	1289	1894
June	987	1152	876	1289	1894
July	987	1152	876	1894	2015
August	987	1152	1289	1894	2015
September	987	1152	1289	1894	2015
October	987	876	1289	1894	2015
November	987	876	1289	1894	2015
December	987	876	1289	1894	2015
TOTAL	-4830	81930	199866	324801	392962

Figure 16-2:
The Format Painter can take everything but the data from the cells on the top, and apply it to the cells on the bottom.

- **Dragging the borders**. Obviously, you can't enlarge a single cell without enlarging its entire row or column; Excel has this funny way of insisting that your cells remain aligned with each other. Therefore, you can't resize a single cell independently—you can only enlarge its entire row or column.

  To adjust the width of a column, drag the divider line that separates its *column heading* from the one to its right, as shown in Figure 16-3; to change the height of a row, drag the divider line between its row and the one below it. In either case, the trick is to drag *inside the row numbers or column letters*. Your cursor will look like a bar between two arrows if you drag in the right place.

Note: Excel adjusts row heights automatically if you enlarge the font or wrap your text by turning on the Wrap text control in Format→Cells→Alignment (unless you've set the height manually, as described above).

- **Menu commands**. For more exact control over height and width adjustments, choose Format→Row→Height, or Format→Column→Width. Either command pops up a dialog box where you can enter the row height or column width by typing numbers on your keyboard.

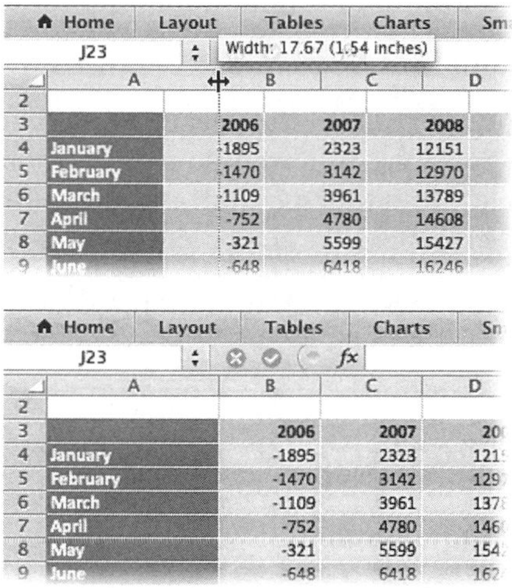

Figure 16-3:
Changing the width (top) of a column or height of a row is as simple as dragging its border inside the column letters or row numbers. A small yellow box pops up as you drag, continually updating the exact size of the column or row. When you let go of the mouse, the column or row assumes its new size, and the rest of the spreadsheet moves to accommodate it. If you select multiple columns or rows, dragging a border changes all of the selected columns or rows—a lovely way to keep consistent spacing.

- **Autosizing**. For the tidiest spreadsheet possible, highlight some cells and then choose Format→Row→AutoFit, or Format→Column→AutoFit Selection. Excel readjusts the selected columns or rows so they're exactly as wide and tall as necessary to contain their contents, but no larger. That is, each column expands or shrinks just enough to fit its longest entry.

Tip: You don't have to use the AutoFit command to perform this kind of tidy adjustment. You can also, at any time, make an individual row or column precisely as large as necessary by double-clicking the divider line between the row numbers or the column letters. (The column to the *left* of your double-click, or the row *above* your double-click, gets resized.) When using this method, there's no need to highlight anything first.

Hiding and showing rows and columns

There are any number of reasons why you may want to hide or show certain columns or rows in your spreadsheet. Maybe the numbers in a particular column are used in calculations elsewhere in the spreadsheet, but you don't need them taking up screen space. Maybe you want to preserve several previous years' worth of data, but don't want to scroll through them. Or maybe the IRS is coming for a visit.

In any case, it's easy enough to hide certain rows or columns. Start by highlighting the rows or columns in question. (Remember: To highlight an entire row, click its gray row number; to highlight several consecutive rows, drag vertically through the row numbers; to highlight nonadjacent rows, ⌘-click their row numbers. To highlight certain columns, use the gray column letters at the top of the spreadsheet in the same way.)

Next, choose Format→Row→Hide, or Format→Column→Hide. That's all there is to it: The column or row disappears completely, leaving a gap in the numbering or letter sequence at the left or top edge of the spreadsheet. The row numbers or column letters surrounding the hidden area turn blue.

Making them reappear is a bit trickier, since you can't exactly highlight an invisible row or column. To perform this minor miracle, use the blue-colored row numbers or column headers as clues. Select cells on either side of the hidden row or column. Then choose Format→Row→Unhide, or Format→Column→Unhide.

Alternatively, you can also select a hidden cell (such as B5) by typing its address in the Name box on the Formula bar, and then choosing Format→Row→Unhide, or Format→Column→Unhide.

Conditional Formatting

Cell formatting doesn't have to be static. With Conditional Formatting, you can turn your cells into veritable chameleons, changing colors or typography on their own, based on their own contents.

A common example is setting up income-related numbers to turn bold and bright red when they go negative, as is common in corporate financial statements. Another common example is using this feature to highlight in bold the sales figures for the highest-earning salesperson listed in a column.

To use conditional formatting, select the cell(s) that you want to change on their own, and then choose Format→Conditional Formatting. In the Conditional Formatting dialog box, set up the conditions that trigger the desired formatting changes.

For example, to set up a column of numbers so they'll turn red when negative, use the first pop-up menu to choose "Cell Value Is" and the second to choose "less than." Finally, type 0 into the text field, as shown in Figure 16-4. Then click Format to specify the typographical, border, and pattern changes you want to see if a highlighted cell's contents fall below zero. For example, in the Font tab, choose

red from the Color pop-up menu and Bold from the Font Style list. Click OK.

By clicking the Add button at this point, you can even add a second set of conditions to your cells. For example, you might want your monthly income spreadsheet to show numbers over $10,000 with yellow cell shading.

You can apply up to three conditions to the same selection, but if more than one condition applies, Excel uses the first one to apply. In other words, if condition one doesn't apply, but conditions two and three do, Excel uses the second condition.

The dialog box previews how your cells will look if a condition is met. If everything looks right, click OK. You return to the spreadsheet, where numbers that meet your conditions now display their special formatting.

If you want to take conditional formatting to the next level, check out the options in the Conditional Formatting button on the Home tab. The Data Bar options use background shading to turn each cell into a data graph. The Color Shading options use shades of colors to represent data values.

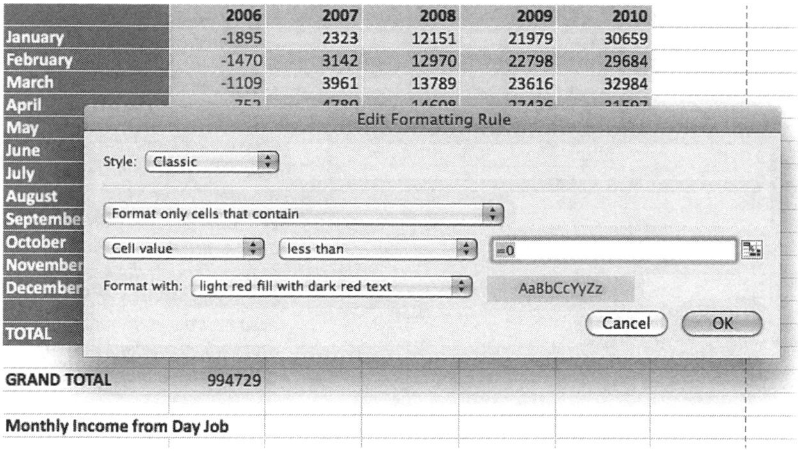

	2006	2007	2008	2009	2010
January	-1895	2323	12151	21979	30659
February	-1470	3142	12970	22798	29684
March	-1109	3961	13789	23616	32984
April	753	4780	14608	27426	31597
May					
June					
July					
August					
September					
October					
November					
December					
TOTAL					
GRAND TOTAL	994729				
Monthly Income from Day Job					

Edit Formatting Rule

Style: Classic

Format only cells that contain

Cell value   less than   =0

Format with: light red fill with dark red text   AaBbCcYyZz

Cancel   OK

Figure 16-4:
Choose Format→ Conditional Formatting to make cells style their contents according to the conditions you set in this dialog box. Let Excel tell you when your finances are "in the red" by formatting any negative numbers with that eye-catching color. Use the pop-up menus in the first line to set the condition, and then click the Format button to tell Excel how to format the cell when that condition is met.

Format Cells with Borders and Fill Color

The light gray lines that form the graph-paper grid of an Excel spreadsheet are an optical illusion. They exist only to help you understand where one column or row ends and the next begins, but they don't print (unless you want them to; see page 505).

If you'd like to add solid, printable borders to certain rows, columns, or cells, select them and then open the versatile Format Cells dialog box with Format→Cells (or press ⌘-1). The Format Cells dialog box appears; now click the Border tab to show the border controls. In this tab, you'll see three sections: Presets, Border, and Line (see Figure 16-5).

1. **If you don't want to use the default line style and color, choose new ones in the Line section.**

   Excel loads your cursor with your desired style and color.

2. **To create a border around the *outside* of your selection, click the Outline preset button; to create borders for the divisions *inside* your selection, click the Inside button; and click both buttons for borders inside and around your selection.**

   As you click the buttons, Excel displays a preview of your work in the Border section. If you change your mind, click None to remove the option.

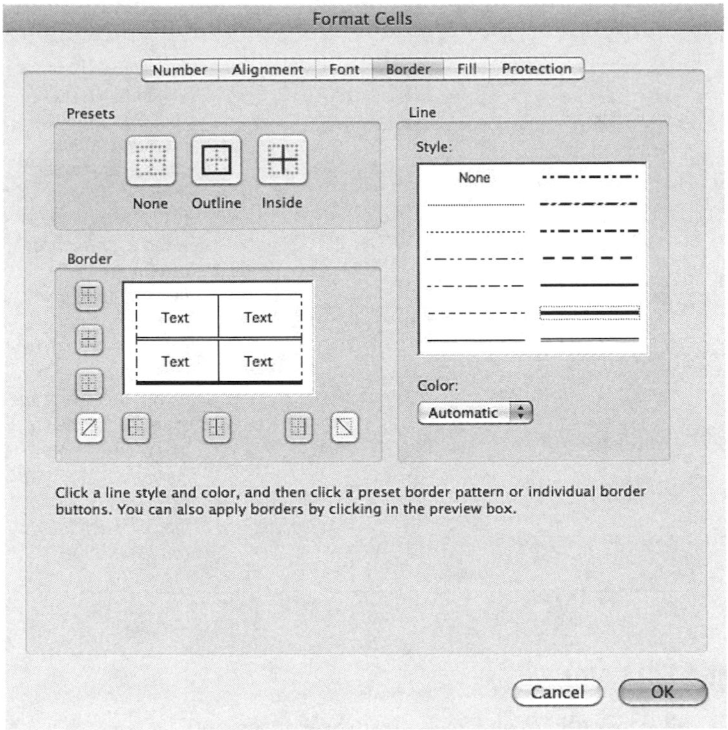

Figure 16-5:
Click directly in the preview area inside the Border section to place borders where you want them. First, select the style and color of line on the right side, and then click in the preview area to place the line. Or if you're feeling more button-oriented, use the eight buttons around the left and bottom edges of the preview area to draw your horizontal and vertical borders, and the oft-overlooked diagonals.

3. **If the Outline and Inside presets aren't what you have in mind, apply custom borders. Click directly between the guides in the preview pane to add or delete individual borderlines, or use the buttons that surround the preview.**

   To change a line style, reload the cursor with a new style from the Line section and then click the borders in the preview area you wish to change.

   If you mess up, click None in the Presets area and start again.

4. **Once the borders look the way you'd like, click OK.**

   Excel applies the borders to the selection in your spreadsheet.

Removing borders

On the Home tab in the Font group, there's a button that changes cell borders. Click it to display a long list of options like All Borders, Top and Bottom Border and Thick Bottom Border. Each option includes a little icon that shows its effect. Perhaps the most useful in the bunch is the No Border option, which quickly removes borders from the selected cells.

Protecting the Spreadsheet Cells

Excel's Format Cells dialog box is a real workhorse when it comes to applying a bunch of formatting changes to a sheet. The first five of its tabs—Number, Alignment, Font, Border, and Patterns—let you exercise pinpoint control over how your spreadsheet—both cells and text—looks and feels, as described in this chapter.

The last tab—Protection—is the exception to the formatting rule. The Protection tab has only two options, presented as checkboxes: Locked and Hidden. These two options let you protect selected cells from changes or hide formulas from view.

But be warned: Neither of these options takes effect unless you also protect the sheet through the Protection feature, which is nestled in the Tools menu.

Setting Cell Fill Colors

For each cell, there's a background color and a foreground color. The background applies a shade to the cell, while the foreground color is applied to patterns. All these color options appear behind the cell content—numbers, letters, and symbols. To change cell colors, go back to your old friend the Format Cells dialog box and click on the Fill tab. There are two menus where you can choose colors and one menu for patterns.

Changing How Text Looks

Borders and fills control how cells look whether or not they actually contain anything. Excel also gives you a great deal of control over the appearance of your text—which in spreadsheets is often numbers. The text controls in Excel are divided into three major categories: number formatting, font control, and text alignment.

Adding number formats

Number formats in Excel add symbols, such as dollar signs, decimal points, or zeros, to whatever raw numbers you've typed. For example, if you apply Currency formatting to a cell containing 35.4, it appears in the spreadsheet as $35.40; if you apply Percentage formatting, it becomes 3540.00%.

What may strike you as odd, especially at first, is that this kind of formatting doesn't actually change a cell's contents. If you double-click the aforementioned cell that says $35.40, the trappings of currency disappear instantly, leaving behind only the 35.4 that you originally entered. All number formatting does is add the niceties to your numbers to make them easier to read.

To apply a number format, select the cells on which you want to work your magic, and then select the formatting that you want to apply. Excel comes prepared to format numbers using eleven broad categories of canned formatting. The easiest way to get at all the options is through the ribbon Home→Number→Number Format menu (Figure 16-6) but you can also use the Number tab in the Format Cells box. Either method gives the same broad categories of formatting. For the most popular options, such as currency, you can click buttons on the ribbon.

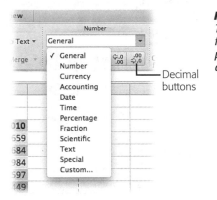

Figure 16-6:
The Number Format menu provides quick access to common number formatting options. Buttons below this open menu let you quickly apply popular number formats and increase or decrease the number of decimal places.

The following descriptions identify which additional controls are available in the Format Cells dialog box:

- **General**. This option means "no formatting." Whatever you type into cells formatted this way remains exactly as is (see Figure 16-7).

- **Number**. This control formats the contents as a generic number.

    Format Cells dialog box extras: You have the option to specify exactly how you want negative numbers to appear, how many decimal places you want to see, and whether or not a comma should appear in the thousands place.

- **Currency**. A specific kind of number format, the Currency format adds dollar signs, commas, decimal points, and two decimal places to numbers entered in the selected cells.

    Format Cells dialog box extras: You can specify how many decimal places you want to see. You also get a Currency Symbol pop-up menu that lists hundreds of international currency symbols, including the euro. You can also set how Excel should display negative numbers.

- **Accounting**. A specific kind of *currency* format, the Accounting format adds basic currency formatting—a $ sign, commas in the thousands place, and two decimal places. It also left-aligns the $ sign and encloses negative numbers in parentheses.

    Format Cells dialog box extras: You can opt to use a different currency symbol and indicate how many decimal places you'd like to see.

Figure 16-7:
Here's how the 11 different number formats make the number 35396.573 look. Some of the differences are subtle, but important. The contents of Text formatted cells are left-justified, for example, and the Number format lets you specify how many decimal places you want to see. Date and Time formats treat any number you specify as date and time serial numbers—more a convenience for Excel than for you.

A Number of Options	
35396.573	General
35396.57	Number
$35,396.57	Currency
$ 35,396.57	Accounting
11/27/96	Date
1:45:07 PM	Time
3539657.30%	Percentage
35396 4/7	Fraction
3.54E+04	Scientific
35396.573	Text
35397	Special

- **Date**. Internally, Excel converts the number in the cell to a date and time *serial number* (see page 356) and then converts it to a readable date format, such as 11/22/2011.

  Format Cells dialog box extras: You can specify what date format you want applied, such as 11/22/11, November-11, or 22-Nov-2011.

- **Time**. Once again, Excel converts the number to a special serial number and then formats it in a readable time format, such as 1:32.

  Format Cells dialog box extras: The dialog box presents a long list of time-formatting options, some of which include both the time and date.

- **Percentage**. This displays two decimal places for numbers and then adds percent symbols. The number 1.2, for example, becomes 120%.

  Format Cells dialog box extras: You can indicate how many decimal places you want to see.

- **Fraction**. This option converts the decimal portion of a number into a fraction. (Carpenters and people who still aren't used to a stock market statistics represented in decimal form will especially appreciate this one.)

  Format Cells dialog box extras: You can choose from one of nine fraction types, some of which round the decimal to the nearest half, quarter, or tenth.

- **Scientific**. The Scientific option converts the number in the cell to scientific notation, such as 3.54E+04 (which means 3.54 times 10 to the fourth power, or 35,400).

  Format Cells dialog box extras: You can specify the number of decimal places.

- **Text**. This control treats the entry in the cell as text, even when the entry is a number. (Excel treats *existing* numbers as numbers, but after you format a cell as Text, numbers are treated as text.) The contents are displayed exactly as you entered them. The most immediate change you'll discover is that the contents of your cells are left-justified, rather than right-aligned as usual. (*No special options are available in the Format Cells dialog box.*)

- **Special**. This option formats the numbers in your selected cells as postal Zip codes. If there are fewer than five digits in the number, Excel adds enough zeros to the beginning of the number. If there's a decimal involved, Excel displays it rounded to the nearest whole number. And if there are more than five digits to the left of the decimal point, Excel leaves the additional numbers alone.

  Format Cells dialog box extras: In addition to Zip code format, you can choose from several other canned number patterns: Zip Code + 4, Phone Number, and Social Security Number. In each case, Excel automatically adds parentheses or hyphens as necessary.

- **Custom**. The Custom option brings up the Format Cells dialog box, where you can create your own number formatting, either starting with one of 39 preset formats or writing a format from scratch using a small set of codes. For example, custom formatting can be written to display every number as a fraction of 1000—something not available in the Fraction formatting.

Add or remove decimal places

To add or remove decimal places, turning *34* and *125* into *34.00* and *125.00*, for example, click the Decimal buttons on the ribbon (you can see them in Figure 16-6). Each click on the Increase Decimal button (on the left) adds decimal places; each click on the Decrease Decimal button (on the right) decreases the level of displayed precision by one decimal place.

Changing fonts

Excel lets you control the fonts used in its sheets via the Font portion of the ribbon. As always on the Macintosh, highlight what you want to format, and then apply the formatting—in this case using the ribbon.

Of course, you can highlight the cell(s) you want to format using any of the techniques described on page 467. But when it comes to character formatting, there are additional options; Excel actually lets you apply different fonts and font styles *within* a single cell (but not for formulas). The trick is to double-click the cell and then use the I-beam cursor to select just the characters in the cell that you want to work with—or select the characters in the Edit box of the Formula bar. As a result, any changes you make in the Formatting Palette affect only the selected characters.

Once you've highlighted the cells or text you want to change, go to the Fonts group on the ribbon (Figure 16-8) to reveal its four main controls:

- The **Name** pop-up menu lets you apply any active font on your Mac to the highlighted cell(s).

Tip: If your Mac has numerous fonts installed, you may find it faster to specify your desired font by typing its name in the Name field rather than by using the pop-up menu. As you type, Excel's AutoComplete guesses your intention and produces a pop-up menu for you to choose from. As soon as the correct font name appears, click it (or select it using the up and down arrow keys), and press Return.

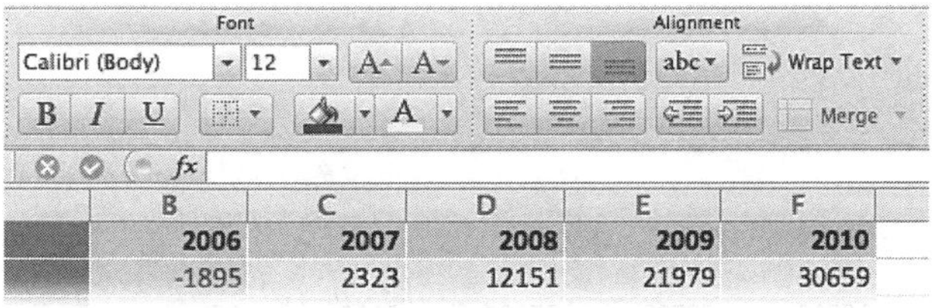

Figure 16-8:
Left: By tweaking the controls in the Font group on the ribbon, you can quickly create your own custom text look.

Right: The Alignment group provides precise control over how text fills a cell; it can even be used to join cells together.

- The **Size** pop-up menu lets you choose from commonly used font sizes (9-point, 18-point, and so on). If the size you want isn't listed, type a number into the Size field and then press Enter or Return. (Excel accommodates only whole- and half-number point sizes. If you type in any other fractional font size, such as 12.2, Excel rounds it to the nearest half-point.)

- Use the **font style** buttons to apply bold, italic, underline, or strikethrough (or any combination thereof).

Tip: As you've no doubt come to expect, you can apply or remove these font styles to selected characters or cells without even visiting the ribbon; just press ⌘-B for bold, ⌘-I for italic, ⌘-U for underline, or Shift-⌘-X for strikethrough. In fact, you can use keyboard shortcuts to apply shadow and outline styles, which don't even appear in the Formatting Palette (probably because they look terrible). Try Shift-⌘-W for shadowed text, and Shift-⌘-D for outlined text.

- The **font color** control lets you choose from theme colors, standard colors or, if that's not enough of an artist's palette for you, use the Mac's standard Colors tool to mix up your own hue.

- Finally, two last buttons allow you to change the selected text to **superscript** or **subscript**—which only works in cells formatted as text.

Changing the standard fonts

Whether you want a funky new font to lighten up your serious number crunching, or you want to switch back to the 9-point Geneva of your childhood, you can make that your default font choice with a quick trip to the Excel→Preferences→General panel (Figure 16-9). After you change the Standard font and Size (the controls are right in the middle of the General panel) and click OK, Excel displays a warning message, noting that you have to quit and restart Excel before the new formatting takes effect in new worksheets.

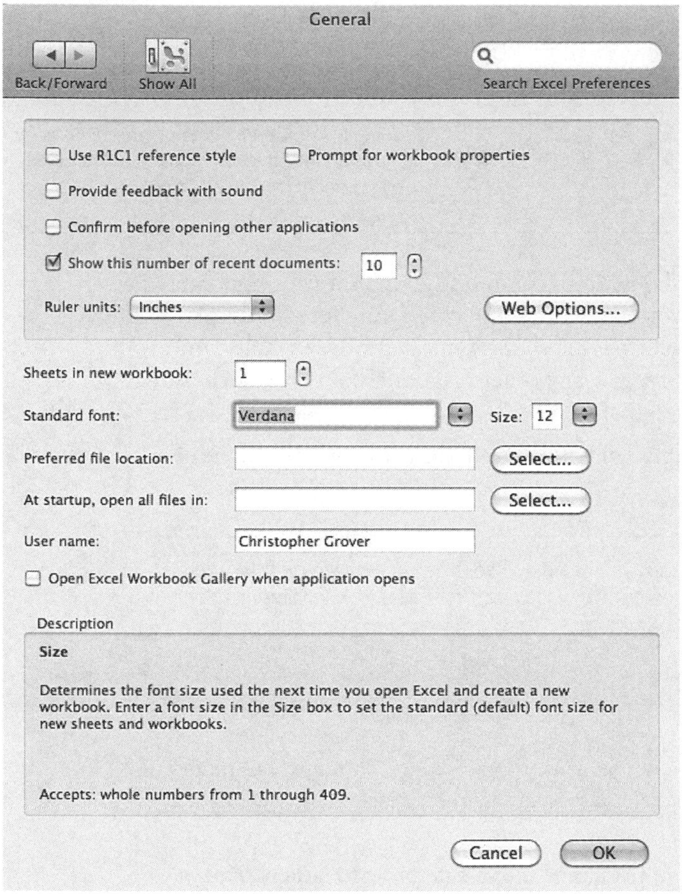

General

Back/Forward   Show All   Search Excel Preferences

☐ Use R1C1 reference style   ☐ Prompt for workbook properties

☐ Provide feedback with sound

☐ Confirm before opening other applications

☑ Show this number of recent documents: 10

Ruler units: Inches   (Web Options...)

Sheets in new workbook: 1

Standard font: Verdana   Size: 12

Preferred file location: (Select...)

At startup, open all files in: (Select...)

User name: Christopher Grover

☐ Open Excel Workbook Gallery when application opens

Description

Size

Determines the font size used the next time you open Excel and create a new workbook. Enter a font size in the Size box to set the standard (default) font size for new sheets and workbooks.

Accepts: whole numbers from 1 through 409.

(Cancel)   (OK)

Figure 16-9:
The Excel Preferences→General pane lets you set what you'd like to see every time you start Excel. You can control the number of sheets in a new workbook, the font and font size, your preferred location to save Excel files, and even have an entire folder full of Excel documents open all at once. (Microsoft appears to be betting on the popularity of bigger and bigger monitors—you can choose font sizes up to 409 points!)

Tip: To change fonts in old worksheets, press ⌘-A to select the entire sheet, and then change the formatting in Home→Fonts.

To make broader changes that you can use optionally, instead of every time, you can create another template—a generic document that can be used over and over to start some of your new Workbooks. Because a template can hold formatting and text, it's a great base for a Workbook that you redo regularly (such as a monthly report).

To make a template, create a new workbook or a copy of one that already looks the way you like it. You can select the entire sheet or specific sections of it, apply formats (as described in this chapter), and even include text (column headings you'll always need, for example). When you finish formatting the sheet, choose File→Save As.

In the Save dialog box, enter a name for the template in the "Save As" field, and then choose Excel Template (.xltx) from the Format menu. Excel gives your file an .xltx extension and switches the Where pop-up menu to "My Templates." Click Save.

Back in Excel, close the template workbook.

Thereafter, whenever you'd like to open a copy of the template, choose File→New from Template. Click the My Templates category, and double-click your template.

Aligning text

Ordinarily, Excel automatically slides a number to the right end of its cell, and text to the left end of its cell. That is, it right-justifies numbers, and left-justifies text. (*Number formatting* may override these settings.)

But the ribbon gives you far more control over how the text in a cell is placed. In the Alignment section of the Home ribbon (Figure 16-8, right), you'll find enough controls to make even a hard-core typographer happy:

- **Vertical alignment**. Use the top three buttons to align text to the top, middle or bottom of a cell.

- **Horizontal alignment**. The three buttons handle left, right and center alignment of the text within its cell. There are other less common horizontal alignment options that you'll only find using the menu command Format→Cells→Alignment.

- **Indent** buttons increase or decrease the indent from the edges of a cell border. Each time you click the up arrow button, Excel slides the text approximately two character widths to the right.

  It's especially important to use this control when you're tempted to indent by typing spaces or pressing the Tab key. Those techniques can result in misaligned cell contents, or worse.

- **Orientation** rotates text within its cell. That is, you can make text run "up the wall" (rotated 90 degrees), slant at a 45-degree angle, or form a column of right-side-up letters that flow downward. You might want to use this feature to label a vertical stack of cells, for example.

- **Wrap text** affects text that's too wide to fit in its cell. If you turn it on, the text will wrap onto multiple lines to fit inside the cell. (In that case, the cell grows taller to make room.) When the checkbox is off, the text simply gets chopped off at the right cell border (if there's something in the next cell to the right), or it overflows into the next cell to the right (if the next cell is empty).

- **Shrink to fit** attempts to shrink the text to fit within its cell, no matter how narrow it is. If you've never seen 1-point type before, this may be your opportunity.

- **Merge cells** causes two or more selected cells to be merged into one large cell (described next).

Making Your Own Styles

If you format spreadsheet cells in the same ways over and over again, you can save a lot of time and tedium by defining a particular set of formatting attributes as a style.

Exactly as in Word (see page 96), a *style* is a chosen set of formatting characteristics, which you can apply to a selection with just a couple of clicks, saving time and ensuring consistency. Excel doesn't have nearly as many ways to apply styles as Word does; style sheets simply aren't as critical in spreadsheet formatting as they are in word processing. Excel comes with a few preset styles, but there's room for more.

To create your own style the quick way, apply any of the formatting characteristics described in this chapter to a selected cell or block of cells. Now choose Format→Style, which calls up the Style dialog box. Enter a new style name.

You'll see that Excel has already recorded the formatting exhibited by the selected cells: the number format, the text alignment, the font, the border, the cell pattern, and the cell protection. If you're happy with the formatting, click the Add button on the right.

Or, if you want to further change any of the settings, click Modify to summon the Format Cells dialog box. In fact, if you failed to highlight some already-formatted cells before choosing Format→Style, this is how you would define your style characteristics from scratch.

To apply a style to selected cells in the spreadsheet, choose Format→Style. In the Style dialog box that appears, select the style name you want to apply, and then click OK. Excel applies your chosen Formatting to the selected cells.

Merging cells

Every now and then, a single cell isn't wide enough to hold the text you want placed inside—the title of a spreadsheet, perhaps, or some other heading. For example, the title may span several columns, but you'd rather not widen a column just to accommodate the title.

The answer is to *merge cells* into a single megacell. This function removes the borders between cells, allowing whatever you put in the cell to luxuriate in the new space. You can merge cells across rows, across columns, or both.

To merge two or more cells, select the cells you want to merge, verify that the Text Alignment portion of the Formatting Palette is open, and then turn on the Merge Cells checkbox, shown in Figure 16-10.

Warning: Merging two or more cells containing data discards *all* of the data except whatever's in the upper-left cell.

To unmerge merged cells, go to the Home→Alignment→Merge menu and choose Unmerge. Note, however, that although the combined space returns to its original status as independent cells, any data discarded during the merge process doesn't return.

Profit and Loss Statement: Time is Not Money					
	2006	2007	2008	2009	2010
January	-1895	2323	12151	21979	30659
February	-1470	3142	12970	22798	29684
March	-1109	3961	13789	23616	32984
April	-752	4780	14608	27436	31597
May	-321	5599	15427	25255	31449
June	-648	6418	16246	26074	30945
July	-288	7237	17065	26893	34697

Figure 16-10:
Because Excel treats merged cells as one big cell, you can align the contents of that cell any way you'd like; you don't have to stick to the grid system imposed by a sheet's cells. One typical use for this is centering a title over a series of columns. Without using merged cells, centering doesn't do the job at all. When you merge those cells together and apply center alignment, the title is happily centered over the table.

You can also merge and unmerge cells by using the Format Cells dialog box. To do this, select the cells to merge, then press ⌘-1 (or choose Format→Cells or Control-click the cells and choose Format Cells from the contextual menu). In the Format Cells dialog box, click the Alignment tab, and then turn on (or turn off) the Merge cells item in the Text control section.

Tip: Often when you're merging cells to create titles like the one in Figure 16-10, you'll want to split lines of text within the cell. The keyboard shortcut to add another line to a single cell is Ctrl-Option-Return.

Adding Pictures, Movies, and Text Boxes

Although you probably won't want to use Excel as a substitute for Photoshop (and if you do, you have to be seriously creative), you *can* add graphics and even movies to your sheets and charts. Plus, if you're artistically inclined, you can use Excel's drawing tools to create your own art.

When using Excel for your own internal purposes—analyzing family expenditures, listing DVDs, and so on—the value of all this graphics power may not be immediately apparent. But in the business world, you may appreciate the ability to add clip art, fancy legends, or cell coloring (for handouts at meetings, for example). You can even add short videos explaining how to use certain features of your product—or even of the spreadsheet itself.

Although you can add text to cells, and merge cells to create larger text cells, you may often find it helpful to add larger blocks of text to a spreadsheet for explanatory paragraphs, descriptions of your services, or disclaimers reminding your clients that past performance is no guarantee of future results. Enter the Text Box, a mini text document or sidebar that you can place anywhere in a spreadsheet.

Excel gives you two ways of embellishing your spreadsheets with graphic elements of all kinds, the Insert menu options: Photo, Audio, Movie, and so on. Or you can use the Media Browser that's available to all Office programs. All these tools work precisely as explained in depth in the Word section of this book.

When you add one of these graphic objects to Excel, it floats on top of the grid rather than inside a cell. You can resize and reposition these objects—and you'll usually want to position them over empty cells. However, Excel lets you cover up any parts of your spreadsheet data with these graphic objects without so much as a warning murmur. Consider yourself forewarned.

Objects in Excel spreadsheets feature a couple of extra options (or properties) you won't see in Word or PowerPoint. Since you're often adding rows and columns to spreadsheets as you work, graphic objects in Excel move along with whatever cells they happen to be sitting on top of. (If they didn't, you'd risk inadvertently covering your data-filled cells with a picture as you add new columns, for example.)

But if you don't like this behavior, you can change it—you can fasten the objects to a place on the page instead of in the cell grid. Here's how: Select the object and choose Format→Photo (or Object, Shape, or Text) and click the Properties tab, and then choose one of the three Object positioning buttons:

- **Move and size with cells**. This option keeps the object tied to the cells beneath it no matter how many columns or rows you add in front of it in the spreadsheet. Additionally, if you resize the columns or rows under this object, it automatically resizes along with them, so it always covers the same number of cells.

- **Move but don't size with cells**. This option keeps the object tied to the cells beneath (it's actually locked to the cell that its upper-left corner touches) it but the object remains the same size no matter how you resize the columns or rows beneath it.

- **Don't move or size with cells**. This option connects the object to a spot on the page, completely ignoring the cell grid. If you add or remove rows or columns the object stays in the same place on the page.

Inserting by the Insert menu

Here's a summary of the different objects you can pop into your spreadsheet via the Insert menu or the Media Browser:

- **Insert→Photo.** Use this command to search for photos using Finder or the Media Browser. In this context, a photo is any graphic saved in JPEG, GIF, TIFF, PICT, PNG, PDF or Photoshop format.

- **Insert→Audio.** Use this command to add MP3s or AIF files to your spreadsheet, perhaps a verbal explanation of that story behind the numbers.

- **Insert→Movie.** If you want them to remember your face, add a talking head video clip. Keep in mind that videos dramatically increase the size of your Excel file.

Choose Insert→Movie to open the Insert Movie dialog box with which you can locate any QuickTime movie on your Mac to make part of your worksheet. Select it, and then click Choose. The movie appears with its upper-left corner in the selected cell. You can then resize and reposition it, and then double-click the cinematic masterpiece to play it (see page 75). You can insert a sound file in exactly the same way—it lands on your spreadsheet as a loudspeaker icon.

- **Insert→Clip Art**. Use the Gallery option to open a database containing hundreds of images in 31 categories. You can also search for specific images using the built-in search feature (see page 604).

- **Insert→Symbols**. Adds the © (copyright) symbol and scores of other possibilities, saving you a trip to the Insert→Symbol dialog box.

- **Insert→Shape**. Choose this command to summon the Media Browser's Shapes pane, from which you can insert many different automatically generated shapes—arrows, boxes, stars and banners, and so on (see page 605).

- **Insert→Text Box**. Excel transforms your cursor into a letter A with a crosshair icon. Drag it diagonally anywhere on your spreadsheet to create a text box. When you release the mouse button, the insertion point begins blinking inside, awaiting your text entry. Move your cursor toward any of the text box's edges until it takes on a four-arrow shape—then you can drag and reposition the box. Surprisingly, unlike text boxes in Word, Excel text boxes feature the green rotating handle sprouting from their top. Drag it to rotate the box.

  Excel text boxes are ready for text editing with one click. If you want to change the look of the text box itself—its fill color, line, shadow, and so on—you have the entire ribbon at your disposal.

- **Insert→SmartArt**. When you choose this menu item, Excel opens the SmartArt tab where you can choose organization chart types of graphics.

- **Insert→WordArt**. The WordArt menu command adds a text box with placeholder text to your worksheet and opens the usually hidden Format tab. Use the tools on the Format tab to sculpt your WordArt creation.

- **Insert→Object**. As explained on page 626, you use the Insert→Object command to embed objects created by other Microsoft programs such as the Equation Editor or the Graph add-in program.

- **Insert→Hyperlink**. This command works as it does in the other Office programs; you can attach links to web pages or documents. You can also create a "mailto" hyperlink, an easy way for people to contact you regarding the spreadsheet. If the cell already has content, the hyperlink is indicated by a highlight. If there isn't any content in the cell, the address for the link appears.

Charts

To paraphrase the old saying, "a graph is worth a thousand numbers." Fortunately, Excel can easily turn a spreadsheet full of data into a beautiful, colorful graphic, revealing patterns and trends in the data that otherwise might be difficult or impossible to see.

Excel 2011 repackages the program's already strong charting capabilities, putting the tools you need on the ribbon. You can quickly scan through and choose a chart type from Excel's abundance of styles—and then make it your own by modifying it. After you choose a type of chart, the ribbon options change, making customization easy.

The keys to making an effective chart are to design your spreadsheet from the beginning of charthood, and then to choose the right chart type for the data (see Figure 16-11).

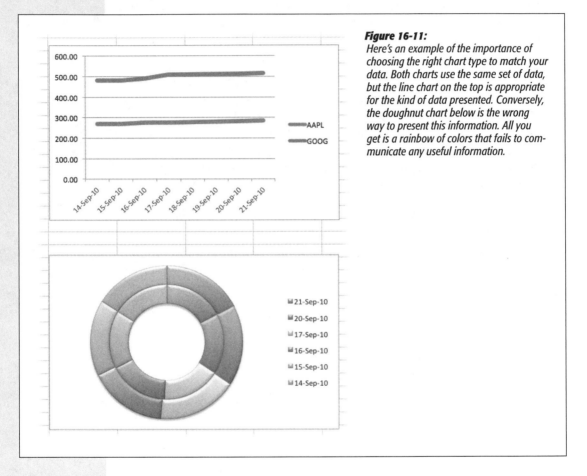

Figure 16-11:
Here's an example of the importance of choosing the right chart type to match your data. Both charts use the same set of data, but the line chart on the top is appropriate for the kind of data presented. Conversely, the doughnut chart below is the wrong way to present this information. All you get is a rainbow of colors that fails to communicate any useful information.

Chart Parts

Most charts share the same set of features to display your spreadsheet information as shown in Figure 16-12.

- **Axes**. An *X axis* (or category axis) and a *Y axis* (or value access) are the horizontal and vertical rulers that provide a scale against which to plot or measure your data. One axis corresponds to the row or column headings—in Figure 16-12, the row headings for date intervals. The other axis is the scale determined by the data *series*—in this case, dollars. 3-D charts may include a third Z axis (or series axis), at right angles to the other two, appearing to protrude from the plane of your screen right at you. Excel sometimes calls this the Depth axis.

- **Axis labels**. This term may refer either to the tick mark labels ("January, February, March…") or to the overall title of the horizontal or vertical scale of your chart ("Income, in millions" or "Months since inception," for example).

Note: The X axis is the horizontal axis; the Y axis is the vertical. (Only pie charts and doughnut charts don't have axes.) Having trouble remembering? Remember that the letter Y has to stand upright, or vertically. The letter X looks like an X even if it's lying on its side.

- **Series**. Each set of data—the prices of Apple stock, for example—is a *data series*. Each datum (or data point) in the series is plotted against the X and Y axes of the chart (except for pie and doughnut charts that don't have axes). On a line chart, each data point is connected to the next with a line. In a bar chart, each data point is represented by a bar. In Figure 16-12, column B of the spreadsheet contains the data series for Apple, and column C contains the series for Google. The chart data series can be drawn from either columns or rows of a spreadsheet.

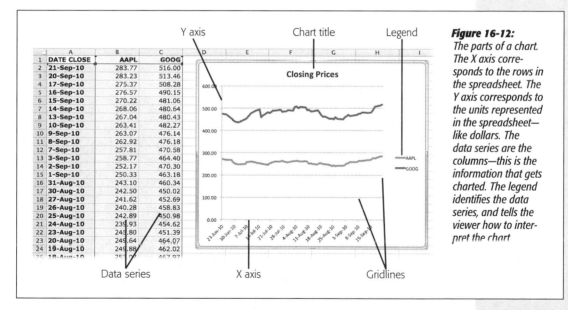

Figure 16-12:
The parts of a chart. The X axis corresponds to the rows in the spreadsheet. The Y axis corresponds to the units represented in the spreadsheet—like dollars. The data series are the columns—this is the information that gets charted. The legend identifies the data series, and tells the viewer how to interpret the chart.

- **Legend**. Just like the legend on a map, this legend shows what the lines or symbols represent. The legend displays the headings of the columns containing the data series and can also display the symbol used for the data points on the chart.

- **Gridlines**. To help readers align your chart data with the scales of one or both of the chart axes, you can choose to display gridlines extending from the axis across the chart. Gridlines come in two flavors: major gridlines line up with each unit displayed on the axis, minor gridlines further break up the scale between the major gridlines.

UP TO SPEED

Understanding Data Series

To master Excel charts, you'll have to first master the concept of a *data series*. Put simply, a data series is a group of numbers or data points that represent a single row or column of numbers from a spreadsheet (such as monthly revenues). In a simple bar or column chart, Excel turns each data series into its own set of bars or columns and assigns a different color to each.

For example, suppose you have a chart with two data series—that is, the numbers begin life as two spreadsheet columns, as shown here with Revenue and Profit columns.

When you create the chart, each month's revenue might show up as a blue bar, and each month's expenses as a green bar. Each set of like-colored bars came from the same data series.

One more tip: When you make a chart from a selection of cells, whichever there is fewer of—rows or columns—becomes the data series. You can always switch this arrangement, swapping the horizontal and vertical axes of your chart, once the chart is born.

Step 1: Select the Data

The first step is to select the data that you want to chartify. You select these cells exactly the way you'd select cells for any other purpose (see page 350).

Although it sounds simple, knowing which cells to select in order to produce a certain charted result can be difficult—almost as difficult as designing the spreadsheet in the first place. Think ahead about what you want to emphasize when you're charting, and then design your spreadsheet to meet that need.

Here are a few tips for designing and selecting spreadsheet cells for charting:

- When you're dragging through your cells, include the labels you've given to your rows and columns. Excel incorporates these labels into the chart.

- Don't select the *total* cells unless you want them as part of your chart.

- Give each part of the vital data its own column or row. For example, if you want to chart regional sales revenue over time, create a row for each region, and a column for each unit of time (month or quarter, for example).

- It's usually easier to put the data series into columns rather than rows, since we tend to see a list of data as a column. Furthermore, the numbers are closer together.

- Keep your data to a minimum. If you're charting more than 12 bars in a bar chart, consider merging some of that data to produce fewer bars. For example, consolidating a year's worth of monthly sales data into quarterly data uses 4 bars instead of 12.

- Keep the number of data series to a minimum. If you're charting more than one set of data (such as gross revenues, expenses, and profits), avoid trying to fit six different data series on the same chart. Use no more than three to avoid hysterical chart confusion. (A pie chart can't have more than *one* data series.)

- Keep related numbers next to each other. For example, when creating an XY (Scatter) chart, use two columns of data, one with the X data and one with the Y data.

- You can create a chart from data in nonadjacent cells. This technique is handy when you have labels at the top of a column but want to use data from the middle. To select the cells, hold down the ⌘ key while clicking or dragging through the cells to highlight them. When you finally click one of the thumbnails on the ribbon, Excel knows exactly what to do.

Step 2: Choose a Chart Style

When you click the Charts tab or choose Insert→Chart, Excel 2011's Charts ribbon appears, with its rows of icon buttons for choosing different chart types (see Figure 16-13). Click one of the buttons like Column and a pane opens beneath the ribbon showing variations on the Column chart theme: Clustered Columns, Stacked Columns, 3D Columns, and Stacked Pyramid.

Your first challenge is to choose the kind of chart that's appropriate for the data at hand. You don't want to use a pie or doughnut chart to show, say, a company's stock price over time (unless it's a bakery). Excel makes it easy to preview how your selected data looks in the various chart types. Choose one of the chart options, and Excel inserts that style chart in your spreadsheet. As you click other options, the chart display changes to the new style. Once you've got the correct chart type, you can resize it and drag it into position, just as you would with a picture. If you later decide you'd like a different style, select the chart and click a different style in the ribbon.

Here are your chart style options, each of which gives several variations:

- **Area** charts are useful for showing both trends over time or across categories *and* how parts contribute to a whole. **3-D area** charts are the way to go when you want to compare *several* data series, especially if you apply a transparent fill to reduce the problem of one series blocking another.

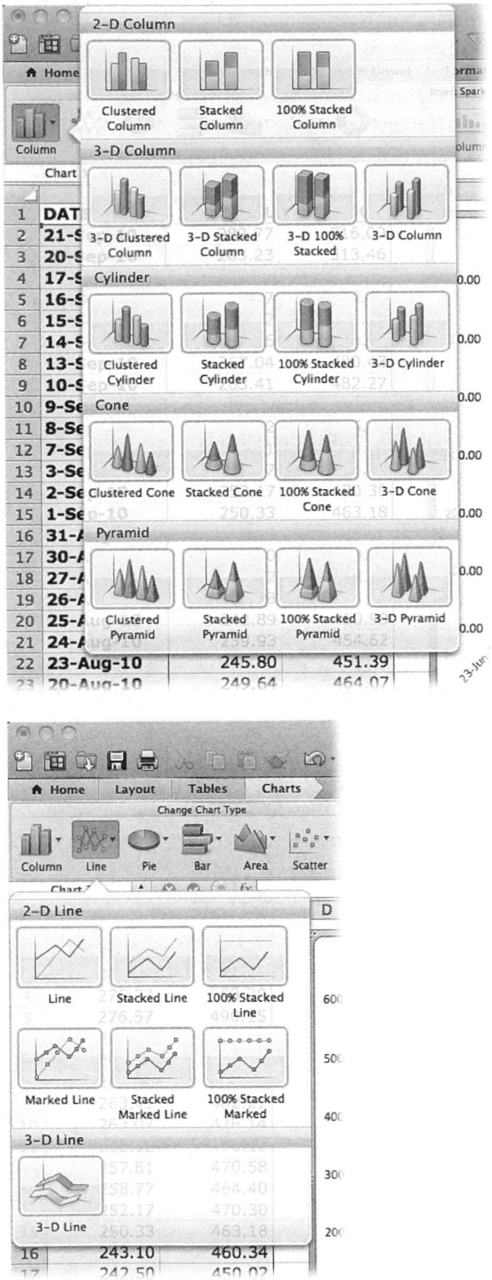

Figure 16-13:
Use the Chart tab on the ribbon to choose the various chart types. Inserting a chart into your worksheet is a two-step process. Click one of the chart types like Column (top) or Line (bottom) and a pane appears with different forms of Column or Line charts. Make a selection from the pane and a chart appears in your worksheet.

- **Column** charts are ideal for illustrating data that changes over time—each column might represent, for example, sales for a particular month; or for showing comparisons among items. As you'll see in the Chart Gallery, Excel offers 18 variations of this chart type. Some are two-dimensional, some are three-dimensional, some are stacked, and so on.

  Stacked-column charts reveal totals for subcategories each month. That is, the different colors in each column might show the sales for a particular region, while 3-D charts can impart even more information—sales over time plotted against sales region, for example.

  3-D Column charts let you compare two sets of data. You can apply a transparent fill applied to the front data series to make it easier to see the ones behind it.

  Cone, cylinder, and pyramid charts are simply variations on basic column and bar charts. The difference is that, instead of a rectangular block, either a long, skinny cone, narrow cylinder, or a triangular spike (pyramid) represents each column or bar.

- **Bar** charts, which resemble column charts rotated 90 degrees clockwise, are as good as column charts for showing comparisons among individual items—but bar charts generally aren't used to show data that changes over time. Again, you can choose stacked or 3-D bar chart variations.

- **Bubble** charts are used to compare three values: the first two values form what looks like a scatter chart, and the third value determines the size of the "bubble" that marks each point.

- **Doughnut** charts function like pie charts, in that they reveal the relationships of parts to the whole. The difference is that the various rings of the doughnut can represent different data sets (data from different years, for example).

- **Line** charts help depict trends over time or among categories. The Line sub-type has seven variations; some express the individual points that have been plotted, some show only the line between these points, and so on.

- **Pie** charts are ideal for showing how parts contribute to a whole, especially when there aren't very many of these parts. For example, a pie chart is extremely useful in showing how each dollar of your taxes is spent on various government programs, or how much of your diet is composed of, say, pie. The Pie subtype has six variations, including "exploded" views and 3-D ones.

- **Radar** charts exist for very scientific and technical problems. A radar chart features an axis rotated around the center, polar-coordinates style, in order to connect the values of the same data series.

- **Stock** charts are used primarily for showing the highs and lows of a stock price on each trading day, but it's also useful for indicating other daily ranges (temperature or rainfall, for example).

- **Surface** charts act like complicated versions of the Line chart. It's helpful when you need to spot the ideal combination of different sets of data—the precise spot where time, temperature, and flexibility are at their ideal relationships, for example. Thanks to colors and shading, it's easy to differentiate areas within the same ranges of values.

- **XY (Scatter)** charts are common in the scientific community; they plot clusters of data points, revealing relationships among points from more than one set of data.

Excel creates the chart floating as a graphic object right in your spreadsheet with a handsome, light-blue selection border. Charts remain linked to the data from which they were created, so if you change the data in those cells, the chart updates itself appropriately.

Step 3: Check Your Results

Make sure your chart represents the range of cells you intended. If not, you can go back to Step 1 and start over again, or click Charts | Data→Select (or right-click the blue chart border and choose Select Data from the pop-up menu). The Select Data Source window appears, displaying the current chart data range and the included data series (see Figure 16-14).

If you need to adjust the data range you can edit the contents of the "Data range" fields, where the spreadsheet, starting cell, and ending cell are represented with absolute cell references (see page 387). The easier way to do it is to click the cell-selection icon to the right of the "Chart data range" field. This icon, wherever it appears in Excel, always means "Collapse this dialog box and get it out of my way, so that I can see my spreadsheet and make a selection."

Now is also your opportunity to swap the horizontal and vertical axes of your chart, if necessary, by clicking the Switch Row/Column button (also available in the ribbon as Charts | Data→Switch Plot).

The bottom section of the Select Data Source dialog box displays the data series included in the chart, and it also lets you add or remove a data series. To add another series, click Add. Name the new series by clicking in the Name field, and clicking the spreadsheet cell that labels a series. Then click the Y Values field and indicate the value a range by dragging through the data cells in your spreadsheet (see Figure 16-14).

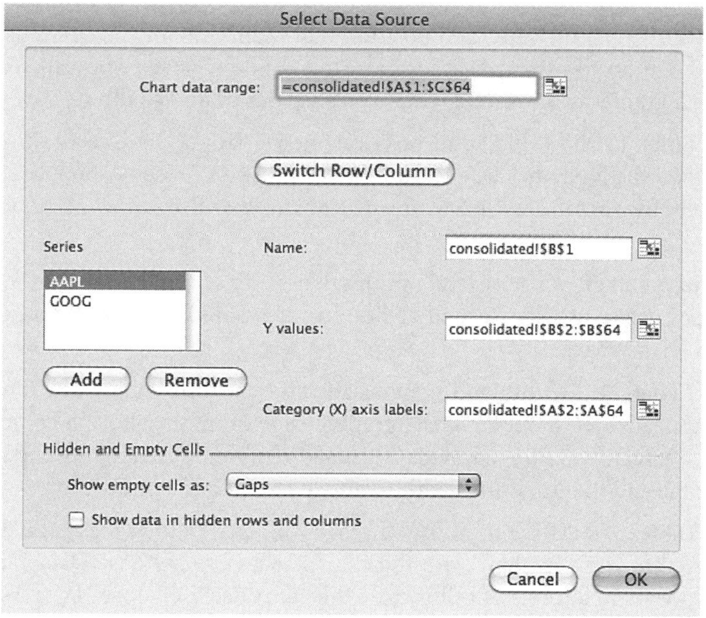

Figure 16-14:
The cell-selection icon just to the right of each of the three fields, appears in dozens of Excel dialog boxes. When you click it, Excel collapses the dialog box, permitting access to your spreadsheet. Now you can select a range by dragging. Clicking the cell-selection icon again returns you to the dialog box, which unfurls and displays, in Excel's particular numeric notation, the range you specified.

Step 4: Design the Chart Content

With the correct style chart in place, representing the correct range of spreadsheet data, you can now turn your attention to fine-tuning the various chart parts. Turn first to the Chart Layout tab on the ribbon (see Figure 16-15). These settings let you change the look of every conceivable chart element, including the chart and axes titles, how gridlines are displayed, where the legend is placed, how data is labeled, and whether the spreadsheet cells used to make the chart are displayed.

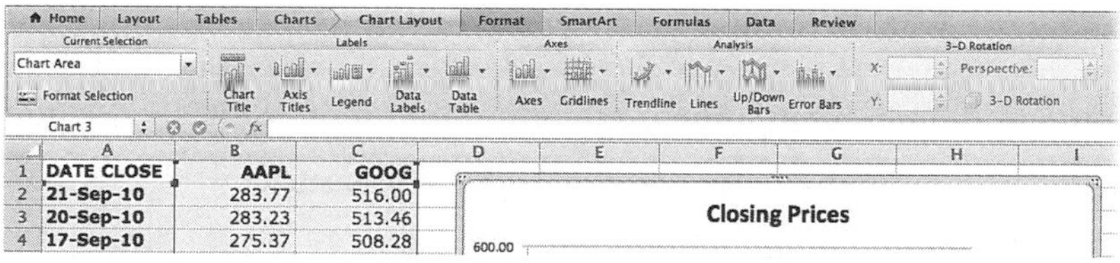

Figure 16-15:
The Chart Options and Chart Data panes of the Formatting Palette contain most of the controls you need to set up your chart's contents. Once the content is in place, you can move along to tweaking its appearance.

When you want to show, hide, or reposition chart parts, use the menus in the Labels and Axes group to make your changes.

- Use **Chart Title** to show, hide, and position that main title for the chart. Click the options button to display the Format Title window, where you can select fonts, colors, gradients, and effects such as transparency and shadows.

- Use **Axis Titles** to show, hide and position the horizontal and vertical axes. Depending on the type of chart and your data, you can choose to show or hide the Vertical, Horizontal, Depth, Secondary Vertical, and Secondary Horizontal axes.

- The **Legend** menu gives you several options: No Legend, Legend at Right, Legend at Top, Legend at Left, Legend at Bottom, Legend Overlap at Right, and Legend Overlap at Left.

- Use **Data Labels** to identify and emphasize values within your chart. These numbers appear directly on the chart graphics; for example, above a column. Because the information they provide is usually redundant, make sure the values are legible and that they don't add too much clutter and confusion.

- The **Data Table** menu lets you choose whether your chart shows the actual data that was used to build it, along with the chart itself. If you choose Data Table, this data appears in a series of cells below the chart itself. Choose "Data Table with Legend Keys" to make Excel reveal how each data series appears on the chart. You might find this option helpful should you display your chart separately from the spreadsheet—in a linked Word document, for example.

- The **Axes** section lets you choose which of your charts and axes appear on the chart. You can also use the axes menu to provide information about the scale. For example, in a financial chart, you might choose the Axis in Thousands to simplify the numbers.

- Use the **Gridlines** buttons to show the Vertical, Horizontal, or Depth gridlines for the Major units—and the same options for the Minor units (see page 482).

Step 5: Refine the Chart's Appearance

Like so many computer constructions, creating the content is just the beginning. Once your chart appears onscreen, it's time to cozy up to your mouse and gleefully putter with its appearance using Excel's abundance of alluring formatting options.

When modifying your chart, start with the most urgent matters:

- **Move the chart** by dragging it around on a sheet.

- **Resize the chart** by dragging any of its corner or side handles. (If you don't see them, the chart is no longer selected. Click any area inside the chart to select the whole chart, bringing back its blue border.)

- **Delete some element of the chart** if you don't agree with the elements Excel included. For example, for a simple chart you might not need a legend. Get rid of it by clicking it and then pressing the Delete key.

- **Reposition individual elements in the chart** (the text labels or legend, for example) by dragging them.

- **Convert a chart from an object to a chart sheet (or vice versa)** by selecting the chart and then choosing Chart→Move Chart and making the appropriate choice in the resulting dialog box.

- **Rotate a 3-D chart** by double-clicking the blue chart selection border to open the Format Chart Area dialog box. Click the 3-D rotation tab and use the up and down arrow buttons or type new numbers into the X, Y, and perspective fields (see Figure 16-16).

- **Move series in a 3-D chart** to put smaller series in front of larger ones. Start by double-clicking any data series to open the Format Data Series dialog box, and then click the Order tab. Watch the chart as you click Move Up or Move Down.

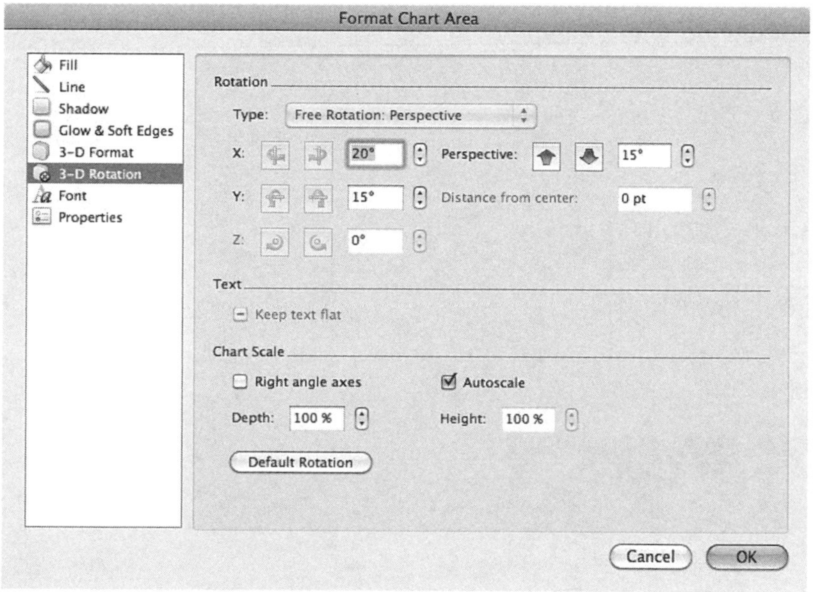

Figure 16-16:
Double-click a chart's blue border to open the Format Chart Area dialog box (top). Among other things, this box is home to the 3-D rotation controls for 3-D charts; you can use them to turn, tilt, and twist, and add perspective to 3-D charts (bottom).

To quickly change the appearance of a chart, choose from the options in Charts | Quick Styles and Chart→Styles groups. The color options displayed take their cue from the Themes, so if you don't see a color combination you like, head down to the Home→Themes and choose a different set.

To change the look of individual elements on your chart (see Figure 16-17), go to the Charts | Current Selection menu to choose an element then click the Format Selection button. The Format dialog box appears where you can change the fonts, colors, gradients, and effects such as transparency and shadows.

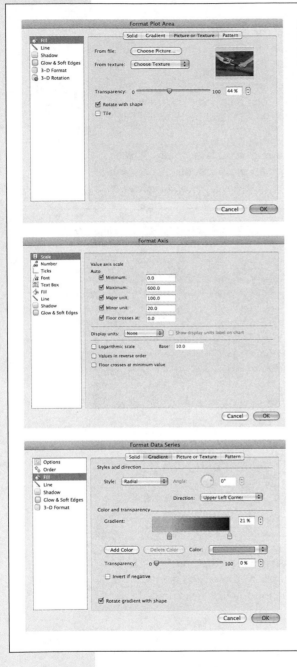

Figure 16-17:
By double-clicking the individual elements in a chart, you open a multitabbed dialog box that lets you change every conceivable aspect of them.

Top: The dialog box that appears when you double-click a chart background.

Middle: The choices that appear when you double-click an axis.

Bottom: Additional choices that appear when you double-click a chart bar.

For example, when working with a bar chart, you have the following options:

- **Change the border or interior color** of the chart by double-clicking within the body of the chart.

- **Change the font, color, or position of the legend** by double-clicking it.

- **Change the scale, tick marks, label font, or label rotation of the axes** by double-clicking their edges or slightly outside their edges.

- **Change the border, color, fill effect, bar separation, and data label options of an individual bar** by double-clicking it. You can even make bars partially transparent, revealing hidden series at the rear, as described in the next section.

Tip: For a simpler but less complete set of formatting tools, use the special Format tab that appears on the ribbon when a chart is selected.

You'll also notice that when you select a chart, the Formatting Palette has specialized formatting controls relevant to your selection. Using the palette, you can change the chart type, gridline appearance, legend placement, and so on.

Tip: You can copy a selected chart into another program either by dragging it or by using the Copy and Paste commands in the Edit menu.

Transparent Bars

Individual bars or areas of a chart can be partially or completely see-through, making it much easier to display 3-D graphs where the front-most bars would otherwise obscure the back ones.

You can apply transparent fills to most chart types, but their see-through nature makes the most sense in charts with at least two data series, where the front series blocks a good view of the rear (Figure 16-18, top).

Begin applying a transparent fill to a data series by double-clicking the series (the bar, column or area, for example). The Format Series dialog box opens. To make transparency available, you first have to change the Fill color. You can't use transparency with the Automatic option. Once you've selected a color you can then use the Transparency slider to adjust the opacity.

To format a multiseries 3-D chart for maximum "wow" factor, you may also wish to rotate it (by double-clicking the blue chart selection border, clicking the 3-D rotation tab and typing new numbers into the X, Y, and perspective fields) or change the series order (double-click a series and work in the Order tab).

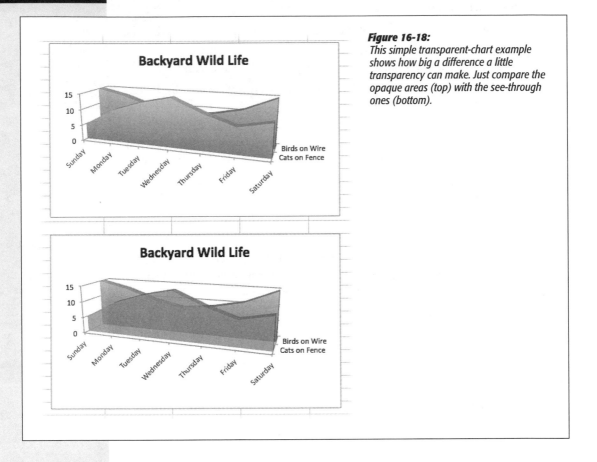

Figure 16-18:
This simple transparent-chart example shows how big a difference a little transparency can make. Just compare the opaque areas (top) with the see-through ones (bottom).

Advanced Analysis Charting

The standard charts suffice for many projects. But every now and then, you may have special charting requirements; fortunately, Excel can meet almost any charting challenge that you put before it—if you know how to ask.

Error bars

On some charts—such as those that graph stocks and opinion polls—it's helpful to graph not only the data, but also the range of movement or margin of error that surrounds the data. And that's where *error bars* come in. Error bars let you specify a range around each data point displayed in the graph, such as a poll's margin of error (Figure 16-19).

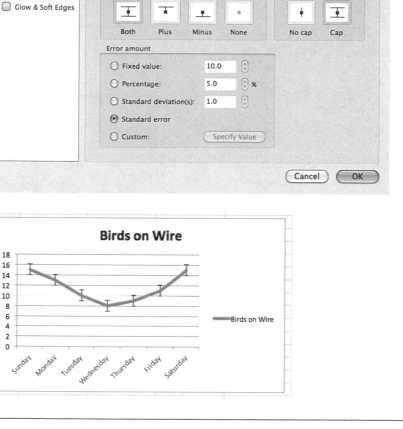

Figure 16-19:
Top: Error bars are easy to add to a data series once the Format Data Series dialog box is open to the Y Error Bars tab. In the "Error amount" area, you can select one of several options.

Bottom: After you've set up error bars and clicked OK, the range bars appear on the graph.

To add error bars to a chart, first select the data series (usually a line or bar in the chart) to which you want to add error bars. Choose Chart Layout | Analysis→Error Bars. The menu gives you three ways of expressing errors: Error Bars with Standard Error, Error Bars with Percentage and Error Bars with Standard Deviation. To make changes after you've added error bars, select the chart, and then go to Chart Layout | Analysis→Error Bars→Error Bars Options.

Note: You can add error bars to 2-D area charts, bar charts, bubble charts, column charts, line charts, and scatter charts. In fact, X axis error bars can even be added to scatter charts. (You'll see this additional tab in the Format Data Series dialog box.)

Trend lines

Graphs excel at revealing trends—how data is changing over time, how data probably changed over time before you started tracking it, and how it's likely to change in the future. To help with such predictions, Excel can add *trend lines* to its charts (Figure 16-20). Trend lines use a mathematical model to help accentuate patterns in current data and to help predict future patterns.

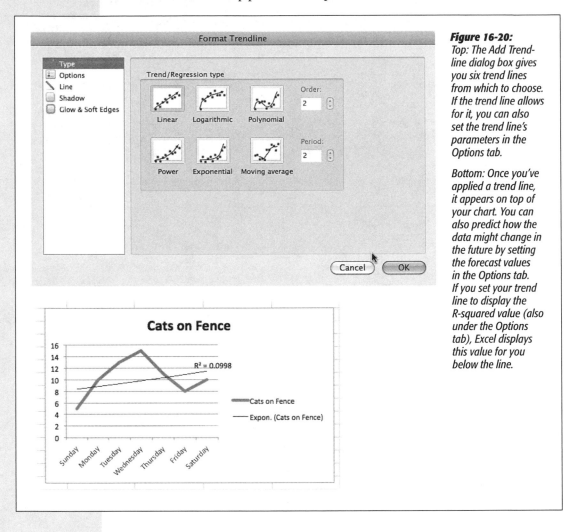

Figure 16-20:
Top: The Add Trend-line dialog box gives you six trend lines from which to choose. If the trend line allows for it, you can also set the trend line's parameters in the Options tab.

Bottom: Once you've applied a trend line, it appears on top of your chart. You can also predict how the data might change in the future by setting the forecast values in the Options tab. If you set your trend line to display the R-squared value (also under the Options tab), Excel displays this value for you below the line.

Note: You can use trend lines only in unstacked 2-D area charts, bar charts, bubble charts, column charts, line charts, scatter charts, and stock charts.

To add a trend line to your chart, click to select one of the data series in the chart—typically a line or a bar—and then choose Chart Layout | Analysis→Trendline and choose one of the options described below.

The Type tab lets you choose one of these trend-line types:

- **Linear**. This kind of trend line works well with a graph that looks like a line, as you might have guessed. If your data is going up or down at a steady rate, a linear trend line is your best bet, since it closely resembles a simple straight line.

- **Logarithmic**. If the rate of change in your data increases or decreases rapidly and then levels out, a *logarithmic* trend line is probably your best choice. Logarithmic trend lines tend to have a relatively sharp curve at one end and then gradually level out. (Logarithmic trend lines are based on logarithms, a mathematical function.)

- **Polynomial**. A *polynomial* trend line is great when graphed data features hills and valleys, perhaps representing data that rises or falls in a somewhat rhythmic manner. Polynomial trend lines can also have a single curve that looks like a camel's hump (or an upside-down camel's hump, depending on your data). These trend lines are based on polynomial expressions, familiar to you from your high school algebra class.

- **Power**. If the graphed data changes at a steadily increasing or decreasing rate, as in an acceleration curve, a *power* trend line is the way to go. Power trend lines tend to curve smoothly upward.

- **Exponential**. If, on the other hand, the graphed data changes at an ever-increasing or decreasing rate, then you're better off with an *exponential* trend line, which also looks like a smoothly curving line.

- **Moving Average**. A *moving average* trend line attempts to smooth out fluctuations in data, in order to reveal trends that might otherwise be hidden. Moving averages, as the name suggests, can come in all kinds of shapes. No matter what the shape, though, they all help spot cycles in what might otherwise look like random data.

The Chart Layout | Analysis→Trendline→Trendline Options, on the other hand, lets you name your trend line, extend it beyond the data set to forecast trends, and even display the R-squared value on the chart. (The R-squared value is a way of calculating how accurately the trend line fits the data; you statisticians know who you are.)

Incidentally, remember that trend lines are just models. As any weather forecaster, stockbroker, or computer-company CEO can tell you, trend lines don't necessarily predict *anything* with accuracy.

Sparklines: Small, Intense, Simple Datawords

The concept and name for sparklines comes from statistician Edward Tufte, who's well known for his writings on innovative ways to display data. He describes sparklines as "small, intense, simple datawords." That's exactly what they are in Excel. Sparklines fit in the space of a single cell, yet they express data relationships. For example, a sparkline might tell a doctor how a patient's glucose level or respiration changes over time. For a meteorologist, a sparkline might express temperature or barometric changes.

Full-blown charts are great for comparing the values of different elements. Sparklines are better for tracking the changes in a single element. Suppose you kept track of the cost for the ingredients of a burrito lunch over a six month period. You'd use a standard Excel chart to compare the cost of beans and rice over that period. You'd use a sparkline to see the fluctuations in the price of beans.

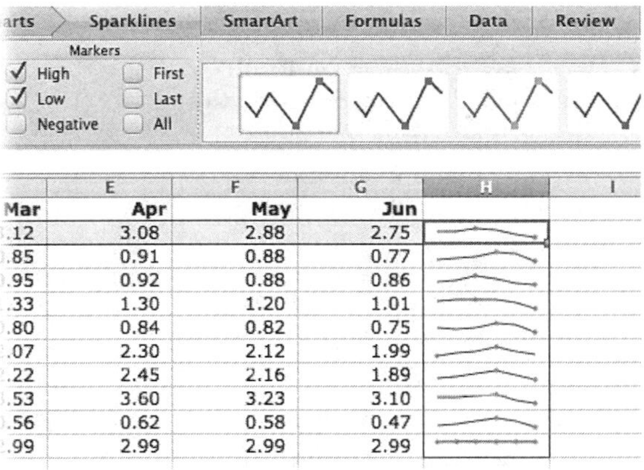

Figure 16-21:
Sparklines are compact graphs that fit in a cell. They're normally placed right next to the data that they represent.

Mar	E Apr	F May	G Jun	H	I
.12	3.08	2.88	2.75		
.85	0.91	0.88	0.77		
.95	0.92	0.88	0.86		
.33	1.30	1.20	1.01		
.80	0.84	0.82	0.75		
.07	2.30	2.12	1.99		
.22	2.45	2.16	1.89		
.53	3.60	3.23	3.10		
.56	0.62	0.58	0.47		
.99	2.99	2.99	2.99		

Here are the steps to create sparklines for that burrito lunch. If you haven't been tracking the costs for the last six months, you can download *16-2_sparklines.xlsx* from the Missing CD at *http://missingmanuals.com/cds*.

1. **Open *16-2_sparklines.xlsx*.**

   The spreadsheet already contains the data for several burrito ingredients and has a standard line chart. You'll see how sparklines differ from their big brother.

2. **Select the cells with numbers that represent the cost of ingredients (B3 to G12).**

   Sparklines are all about numbers and values, so you don't want to select the labels in your worksheet.

3. **On the menu choose Insert→Sparklines.**

   The Insert Sparklines dialog box appears with two text boxes for cell ranges. The top box is for the range that holds the data you want to map. You use the bottom box to tell Excel where to place the sparklines.

4. **Click the "range" button to the right of bottom box and then select the cells at the end of the prices: H3:H12.**

   If you make a mistake, select and delete all the text in the box and try again. If you don't specifically delete your mistake, the range box remembers it and you'll get a message about an invalid range.

5. **Click OK.**

   Excel creates mini sparkline graphs in the cells next to the price data. Each ingredient has its own little trend line or as Professor Tufte would say: a dataword.

Your burrito ingredient sparklines aren't great for determining specific values. They're too small for that. They don't tell you the cost of beans in March, but they do show how that cost rises and falls. Sparklines are great for expressing trends. With sparklines next to each ingredient, you can quickly determine whether there are similarities in those changes.

Click one of the sparkline cells and Excel puts a box around the data that's expressed in the sparkline. You don't always have to put your sparklines close to the data, but usually, they're more useful if you do. When a sparkline cell is selected, the ribbon displays the purple Sparklines tab (Figure 16-22) where you can choose different styles and format your datawords in different ways.

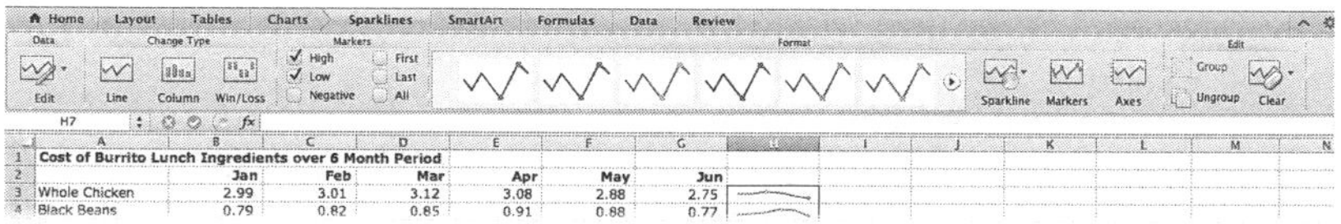

Figure 16-22:
The Sparklines tab gives you several options for changing the appearance of the sparklines in your worksheet. You can choose between three different styles—Line, Column, and Win/Loss—and then set formatting options.

Formatting Sparklines

The sparklines in the burrito lunch example express price trends, so it might be helpful to highlight the high and low prices over the six month period. To do that, click one of the sparkline cells then on the ribbon turn on Sparklines | Markers→High and Sparklines | Markers→Low. Small markers appear on the lines.

Like all the other graphic elements in Office, sparklines take their color cues from Themes. In the case of sparklines, these colors may be too subtle. You might want your High and Low markers to jump out a bit more. You can choose sparkline styles from the thumbnails in the Sparkline | Format group or you can explicitly choose colors. For lines go to Sparkline | Format→Sparklines. To change the marker colors go to Sparkline | Format→Markers. Because you created all your sparklines at once, Excel automatically placed them in a group. Formatting changes made with a single cell selected affect all the sparklines in the group. If you want to format them individually, you need to ungroup them first by going Sparklines | Edit→Ungroup.

Moving and Removing Sparklines

You can move sparklines around your worksheet just like any other cell. Move your cursor over the edge of a cell or group of cells. When the cursor changes to a hand, you can grab and drag those datawords to a new home.

The standard Edit→Clear commands don't work with sparklines, you need to use special commands to send sparklines to the bit bucket. Use the shortcut menu right-click (Control-click)→Sparklines→Clear Selected Sparklines to remove individual sparklines that you've preselected. Use (Control-click)→Sparklines→Clear Selected Sparkline Groups to get rid of entire groups. If you'd rather use a ribbon command, there's a Clear menu on the right end of the Sparklines tab.

CHAPTER 17

Printing and Sharing Spreadsheets

S ome spreadsheets are simply a personal tool, used by one person, but more frequently, spreadsheets are communication devices. Beam me up, CFO. You share a worksheet with your Board of Directors to describe the financial well-being of your corporation or you share a pie chart with your husband to highlight the portion of the family treasure spent on golf-related expenses.

Sure, you can share your spreadsheets and chart by printing them and handing out the pages; but if you share workbooks electronically, you'll save money, save time and save the world a bunch of resources. There are a number of ways you can go the electronic document route. If you just want to show off numbers and charts, print to a PDF file. Then you can distribute your document via email, USB thumb drive, disc, or on a website. If you want to get input from others and let them make changes to your workbooks, then you need to use Excel's sharing features, described at the end of this chapter. You can give others access to your workbooks by emailing them or making them available by on a network.

Printing Worksheets

Once you've gone through the trouble of making your sheets look their best with killer formatting and awe-inspiring charts, you're set to print them out and show them off.

Print Preview

Viewing a print preview before you send your spreadsheet to the printer can save you time and frustration, and help save an a tree or two. If you've used Excel 2004 or earlier versions, you may recall that both Excel and Mac OS X had similar print-preview functions. In Excel 2011, the print-preview function is now entirely up to Mac OS X.

Tip: To check out your page-break preview without doing a print preview first, just choose Layout | View→Page Layout or click the Page Layout View button at the bottom-left of the Excel window.

As in any Mac OS X–compatible program, you turn a document into a print-preview file by choosing File→Print (⌘-P) and then, in the Print dialog box, clicking the Preview button at the bottom. Your Mac fires up the Preview program, where you see the printout-to-be as a PDF. Use the commands in the Display menu to zoom in, zoom out, scroll, and so on. Each page appears as a separate page image, with thumbnails of all the pages lined up in Preview's drawer at the side of the window.

Tip: To print just a certain portion of your spreadsheet, select the cells that you want to print and then choose File→Print Area→Set Print Area. This command tells Excel to print only the selected cells. To clear a custom print area, select File→Print Area→Clear Print Area. Alternatively, you can set a print selection for just a current print job by selecting the cells you want to print and then clicking the Selection option button in the Print What section of the Print dialog box.

If you've been working on your spreadsheet in Page Layout view, then any print preview may be a bit redundant. Instead, you can quickly flip through the Quick Preview right in the Print dialog box to get a general idea of your spreadsheet's pagination (see Figure 17-1).

Print to PDF Files

Don't miss the best part of the Print dialog box—the PDF button. Choose "Save as PDF" from its menu to turn your printout into a PDF—also called Acrobat—file that you can send to anyone with a computer, so he can open, read, and print your handiwork. (Your recipient's computer must have Acrobat Reader, which is free, or Preview, which comes on the Mac.) Other options in this menu let you, among other things, fax a PDF, save it into your iPhoto library, or attach it to an email message (but only if you're using Apple Mail—see the box on the next page for a workaround).

If you're not seeing what you'd like to in the Quick preview window, click the Cancel button to cancel the print job and go back to configuring your document.

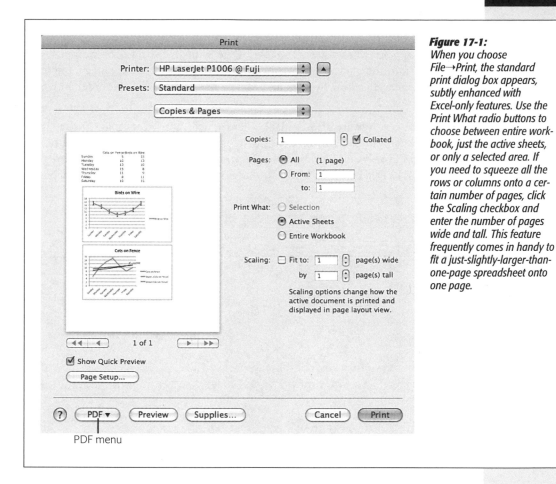

Figure 17-1:
When you choose File→Print, the standard print dialog box appears, subtly enhanced with Excel-only features. Use the Print What radio buttons to choose between entire workbook, just the active sheets, or only a selected area. If you need to squeeze all the rows or columns onto a certain number of pages, click the Scaling checkbox and enter the number of pages wide and tall. This feature frequently comes in handy to fit a just-slightly-larger-than-one-page spreadsheet onto one page.

PDF menu

WORKAROUND WORKSHOP

Emailing Without Mail

If you choose Mail PDF from the PDF button in the Print dialog box, the Apple Mail program automatically opens to do the deed. If you don't use Apple Mail—perhaps you use, oh, Outlook—you can change the behavior of your Mac's Mail PDF function. To do so, you have to edit the Automator Workflow that's responsible for the handoff of a PDF to your email program, which isn't as complicated as it sounds.

Open the folder [Hard Drive]→Library→PDF Services and then double-click *Mail PDF.workflow*. The Automator window

appears, with the New Mail Message action showing in the right pane. Delete that action by highlighting it and pressing Delete. Type *Outlook* in the Search field, press Return, and double-click Create New Outlook Mail Message. The Outlook action appears in the right pane. Choose File→Save and then choose Automator→Quit. From now on when you choose Mail PDF from the print dialog box, Outlook handles the task.

Page Setup

Excel's Page Setup dialog box (Figure 17-2) is far more comprehensive than the Page Setup that appears when you choose File→Page Setup in TextEdit, for example. In it, you can control how pages are oriented, how spreadsheets fit on a page, the print quality, the margins, how headers and footers are printed, and the order in which pages are printed.

These same controls are also available—and much more accessible—through the ribbon's Layout tab. The Layout | Page Setup group has commands for orientation, size, margins, breaks, background and page headers and footers. The "Fit to" page command is Layout | Print→Fit To. Use the text boxes to specify the number of pages.

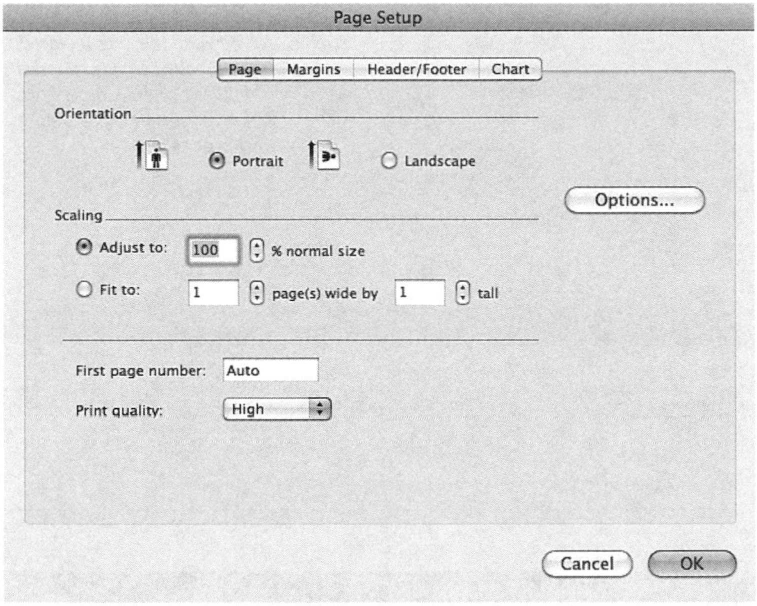

Figure 17-2:
The Page tab of the Page Setup dialog box is another place to start if you want a spreadsheet to print on one page. A click in the "Fit to" radio button (in the Scaling area) automatically adjusts your spreadsheet's print size to fit on a sheet of paper. If you want it to fit on more than one sheet, adjust the numbers in the "Fit to" area.

Page orientation

In the Page tab of the Page Setup box, you can change the orientation for the print job (Portrait for the usual up-and-down style or Landscape for a sideways style—often the preferred spreadsheet format), reduce or enlarge the printout by a certain percent, or—using the "Fit to" radio button—force the spreadsheet to fit onto a certain number of printed pages. (Using this control, of course, affects the printout's type size.) If you don't want the pages of your spreadsheet numbered 1, 2, and so on, then type a different number into the "First page number" field. This is how you force Excel to number the pages beginning with, say, 5 on the first printed sheet.

Note: Setting the starting page number in the Page tab won't make page numbers appear on your sheets; you have to also initiate page numbering in the Header/Footer tab. The easiest technique is to choose a page number option from the Header or Footer pop-up menu.

An Options button on the right brings up the more familiar Page Setup dialog box for your printer, where you can set more of your printer's options (such as paper size).

Margins tab

You can use the ribbon Layout | Page Setup→Margins command to choose Normal (1/2 inch), Wide (1 inch) or Narrow (1/4 inch) margins. If you have more specific margin needs click the Custom Margins option on the same menu to open the Margins tab of the page setup dialog box (Figure 17-3, top). These settings let you specify the page margins individually for each edge of the page and for headers and footers. You can also tell Excel to center the printout on the page horizontally, vertically, or both. The Options button, once again, summons the standard Page Setup dialog box for your printer.

Header/Footer tab

If you want something printed on the top or bottom of every page (such as a title, copyright notice, or date), it's time to visit the Header/Footer tab (Layout | Page Setup→Header & Footer) as shown in Figure 17-3, bottom.

Here, you can use the Header or Footer pop-up menu to choose from a selection of prepared headers and footers—"Page 1 of 7," "Confidential," and so on.

If the header or footer message you want isn't there, click the Custom Header or Custom Footer buttons to bring up a customization dialog box. In it you can enter your own header or footer text; click the Font button to format the text; and use the remaining buttons to insert placeholder codes for the current page number, the total number of pages, the current date, the current time, the file name, and the tab name.

You can combine these codes with text that you type yourself. For example, in the "Center section" box, you could type, *DVD Collection Status as of*, and then click the fourth icon. Excel inserts the code *&[Date]*. Now whenever you print this document, you'll find, across the top of every page, "DVD Collection Status as of 9/15/08," or whatever the current date is.

Sheet tab

The last section of the Page Setup dialog box, called Sheet, gives you yet another way to specify which portions of the sheet are to be printed (Figure 17-4). You can type starting and ending Excel coordinates—separated by a colon—into the "Print area" box, or click the cell-selection icon to return to the spreadsheet to select a region of cells you want to print.

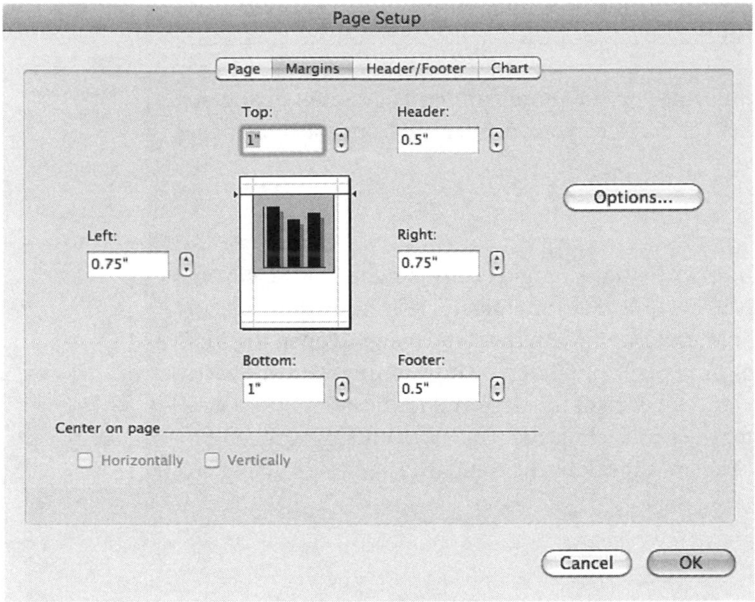

Page Setup			

Page | Margins | Header/Footer | Chart

Top:
`1"`

Header:
`0.5"`

Options...

Left:
`0.75"`

Right:
`0.75"`

Bottom:
`1"`

Footer:
`0.5"`

Center on page
☐ Horizontally   ☐ Vertically

Cancel   OK

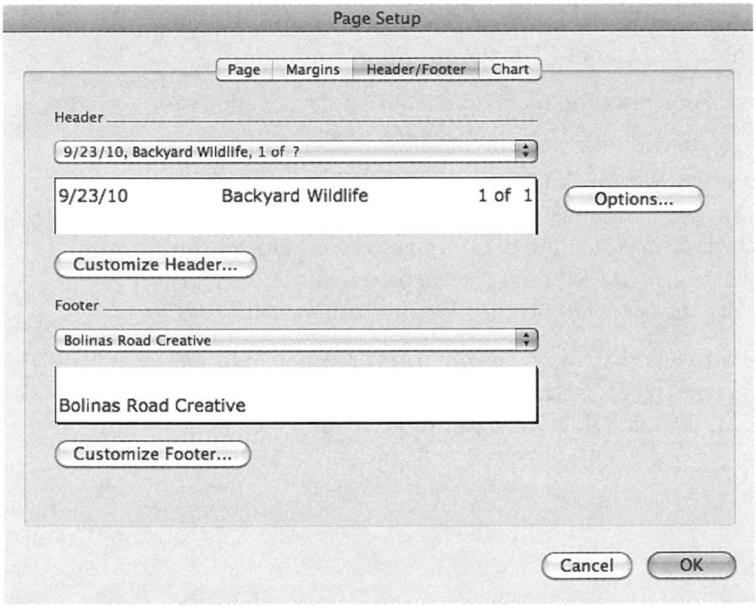

Figure 17-3:
Top: The Margins portion of the Page Setup window gives you power over your sheet's margins when printed, naturally. It lets you set top, left, right, and bottom margins, and it gives you the chance to determine how much top and bottom space is left over for headers and footers—useful if you have particularly large headers and footers. The checkboxes at the bottom of the box let you set how—and whether—your printouts are centered on the page.

Bottom: The Header/Footer part of the Page Setup dialog box is where you can set text to be printed on the top or bottom—or both—of every page.

Page Setup			

Page | Margins | Header/Footer | Chart

Header
9/23/10, Backyard Wildlife, 1 of ?

9/23/10	Backyard Wildlife	1 of 1

Options...

Customize Header...

Footer
Bolinas Road Creative

Bolinas Road Creative

Customize Footer...

Cancel   OK

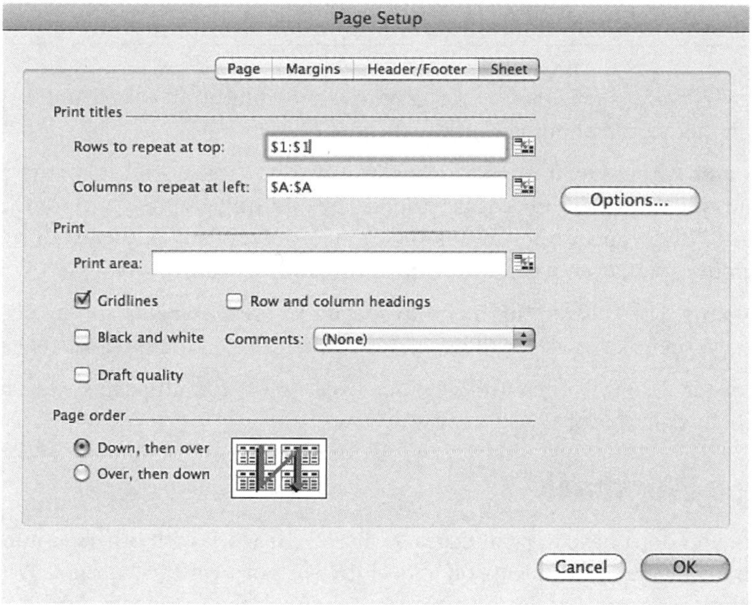

Figure 17-4:
The Sheet portion of the Page Setup window lets you set a print area (if you haven't already done so). If you want to display a certain range of data on every page, you can specify that certain rows repeat at the top of each page and/or columns repeat on the left of each page. It gives you five print options, letting you choose to print gridlines, row and column headings, print in black and white or draft quality, and print comments you may have added to the spreadsheet. Finally, you can choose print order: whether pages are printed down and then over, or over and then down.

You'll also find the following in the Sheet tab:

- **Rows to repeat at top, Columns to repeat at left (Layout | Print→Repeat Titles).** If you've carefully typed the months of the year across the top of your spreadsheet, or product numbers down the left side, you'll have a real mess on your hands if the spreadsheet spills over onto two or more pages. Anyone trying to read the spreadsheet will have to refer all the way back to page 1 just to see the labels for each row or column.

  Excel neatly avoids this problem by offering to reprint the column or row labels at the top or left side of *each* printed page. To indicate which row or column contains these labels, click the appropriate "Print titles" field, and then type the desired row number or column heading directly in the spreadsheet. Or click the cell-selection icon just to the right of each field; this shrinks the dialog box so you can more easily select the repeating cell range.

- **Gridlines, Row and column headings (Layout | Print→Gridlines and Layout | Print→Heading).** For years the answer to one of the world's most frequently asked spreadsheet questions—"How do I get the gridlines to print?"—was buried here in the fourth tab of a buried dialog box. And it still is—but you can more easily access this control via the ribbon's Layout | Print→Gridlines option.

Note: There are two gridlines options on the layout tab. One option (Layout | View→Gridlines) toggles gridlines on and off on your computer screen, but doesn't affect printing. If you're not getting what you want when you print, make sure you checked the right box on the ribbon.

Excel never prints gridlines or the gray row and column headings unless you turn on their corresponding checkboxes here.

- **Black and white, Draft quality**. Use these two checkboxes when you're in a real hurry. Draft quality speeds up printing by omitting graphics and some formatting. "Black and white" means that your printer won't bother with time-consuming color, even if color appears in the spreadsheet.

- **Comments**. Use this pop-up menu to specify where *comments* appear on the printout—on its last page, or right where you put them in the spreadsheet itself.

- **Page order**. Use this to control whether Excel prints a multipage spreadsheet column by column (of pages), or row by row.

Sharing a Workbook

These days, you don't have to print pages to share your work with others. You have lots of options to share documents on a local network or over the Internet. With a little preparation, several Excel fans on the same network can work on a single worksheet at the same time. (If you want to share a workbook, but prevent others from accessing it, read about protection on page 508 first. Bear in mind, some protection commands have to be applied *before* you turn on sharing.) To share a workbook, choose Tools→Share Workbook, which brings up the Share Workbook dialog box. On the Editing tab (Figure 17-5), turn on "Allow changes by more than one user at the same time". Click the Advanced tab for the following options:

- **Track changes**. This section lets you set a time limit on what changes are tracked (see "Tracking Changes" on page 510). If you don't care what was changed months ago, you can limit the tracked changes to 60 days. You can also tell Excel not to keep a change history at all.

- **Update changes**. Here, you specify when your view of the shared workbook gets updated to reflect changes that others have made. You can set it to display the changes that have been made every time you save the file, or you can command it to update at a specified time interval.

  If you choose to have the changes updated automatically after a time interval, you can set the workbook to save automatically (thus sending your changes out to coworkers sharing the workbook) and to display others' changes (thus receiving changes from your coworkers' saves). Or you can set it not to save your changes, and just to show changes that others have made.

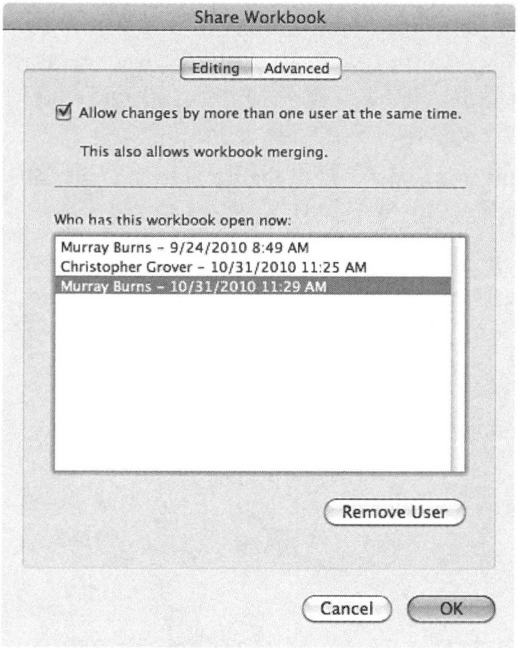

Figure 17-5:
The Share Workbook dialog box reveals exactly who else is using a shared workbook. If you worry that one of your fellow network citizens is about to make ill-advised changes, click his name and then click Remove User. Your comrade is now ejected from the spreadsheet party. If he tries to save changes to the file, he'll get an error message explaining the situation. Please note that there's little security in shared workbooks. As you can see, two people are logged in and able to make changes from two different Macs at the same time. Of course, if you password protect the sheet before sharing it, you'll achieve a basic, keeping-honest-people-honest level of security.

- **Conflicting changes between users**. This section governs whose changes "win" when two or more people make changes to the same workbook cell. You can set it so that you're asked to referee (which can be a *lot* of work), or so that the most recent changes saved are the ones that win (which can be risky). Clearly, neither option is perfect. Since each person can establish settings independently, it's worth working out a unified collaboration policy with your coworkers (see Figure 17-6).

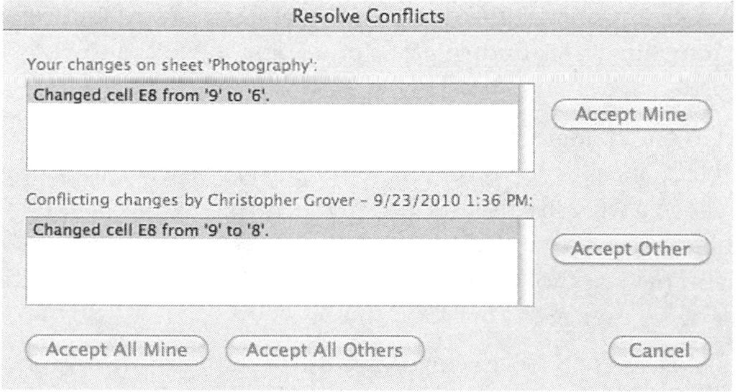

Figure 17-6:
The Result Conflicts dialog box appears when two people try to change the same cell. You're given the option of accepting one change or the other. If Excel lists more than one conflict, you can also choose to accept either all of your changes or all of your coworker's.

- **Include in personal view**. These two checkboxes—Print settings and Filter settings—let you retain printing and filtering changes that are independent of the workbook. They can be set independently by anyone who opens the workbook.

When you click OK, Excel prompts you to save the workbook—if you haven't already. Save it on a networked disk where others can see it. Now, anyone who opens the workbook from across the network opens it as a shared book.

Shared workbooks have some limitations, detailed in the Excel help topic, "Share a workbook." Here's a summary of things that you *can't* do with a shared workbook:

- Assign, change, or delete a password that protects a worksheet.
- Insert charts, hyperlinks, objects, or pictures.
- Make or change PivotTables, or make or refresh data tables (page 416).
- Merge, insert, or delete blocks of cells; delete worksheets.
- Use automatic subtotals or drawing tools.
- Use or create conditional formats or data validation (page 466).
- View or edit scenarios (page 430).

Protecting the Spreadsheet

Fortunately, there's no need to give everyone on the network unfettered access to your carefully designed spreadsheet. You can protect your spreadsheet in several ways, as described here, and your colleagues can't turn off these protections without choosing Tools→Unprotect Sheet (or Unprotect Workbook)—and *that* requires a password (if you've set one up).

- **Protect a workbook from changes**. Choose Tools→Protection→Protect Workbook, which brings up the Protect Workbook dialog box. By turning on Structure and/or Windows, you can protect the workbook's *structure* (which keeps its sheets from being deleted, changed, hidden, or renamed) and its windows (which keeps the workbook's windows from being moved, resized, or hidden). Both of these safeguards are especially important in a spreadsheet you've carefully set up for onscreen reviewing. You can also assign a password to the workbook so that if someone wants to turn *off* its protection, he needs to know the password.

- **Protect a sheet from changes**. Choose Tools→Protection→Protect Sheet to bring up the Protect Sheet dialog box. Turn on the Contents checkbox to protect all *locked* cells in a worksheet (described next). Turn on Objects to prevent changes to graphic objects on a worksheet, including formats of all charts and comments. Finally, turn on the Scenarios checkbox to keep scenario definitions (page 430) from being changed.

  The top of the dialog box lets you assign a password to the worksheet; this password will be required from anyone who attempts to turn off the protections you've established.

- **Protect individual cells from changes**. Excel automatically formats all cells in a new worksheet as locked, so if you protect the contents of a sheet you've been working in, all the cells will be rendered unchangeable. If you want *some* cells in a protected sheet to be editable, you have to unlock them while the sheet is unprotected. Unlock selected cells by choosing Format→Cells. In the resulting dialog box, click the Protection tab, turn off the Locked checkbox, and then click OK.

- **Require a password to open a workbook**. Open the workbook you want to protect and choose File→Save As (or, if you've never saved this workbook before, choose File→Save). In the Save dialog box, click Options. In the resulting dialog box (Figure 17-7), enter one password to allow the file to be opened and, if you desire, another to allow file modification.

Tip: Alternatively, choose Review | Protection→Password and assign a password to open or to modify the workbook, and use the two buttons to access the Protect Workbook dialog box and the Protect Sheet dialog box.

Figure 17-7:
Entering a password in the top text box prevents others from opening your workbook without the password. If you specify only the second password, people can open the file, but can't make changes without the password.

Warning: Remember these passwords! If you forget them, you've locked yourself out of your own workbook. There's no way to recover them without buying a password cracking program.

- **Hide rows, columns, or sheets**. Once you've hidden some rows, columns, or sheets (page 412), you can prevent people from making them reappear by choosing Tools→Protection→Protect Workbook. Turn on Structure and then click OK.

- Protecting a **shared workbook**. To protect a shared workbook, choose Tools→ Protection→Protect Shared Workbook, which brings up the Protect Shared Workbook window. This window presents you with two protection choices. If you turn on "Sharing with track changes" and enter a password, you prevent others from turning off change tracking—a way of looking at who makes what changes to your workbook. Turning on this checkbox *also* shares the workbook, as detailed previously.

Tracking Changes

When people make changes to your spreadsheet over the network, you aren't necessarily condemned to a life of frustration and chaos, even though numbers that you input originally may be changed beyond recognition. Exactly as in Word, Excel has a *change tracking* feature that lets you see exactly which of your coworkers made what changes to your spreadsheet and, on a case-by-case basis, approve or eliminate them. (The changes, not the coworkers.)

To see who's been tiptoeing through your workbook, choose Tools→Track Changes→Highlight Changes, which brings up the Highlight Changes dialog box (Figure 17-8). In it, you can choose how changes are highlighted: by time or by the person making the changes. To limit the revision tracking to a specific area on the worksheet, click the spreadsheet icon at the right of the Where field, select the area, and then click the icon again.

Note: The Review tab on the ribbon holds some of the most commonly used tools for tracking changes. For example, Review | Share→Track Changes→Highlight Changes brings up the same dialog box shown at the top of Figure 17-8.

As life goes on with this spreadsheet on your network, Excel highlights changes made by your coworkers with a triangular flag at the upper-left corner of a cell or block of cells (Figure 17-8, middle).

Once you've reviewed the changes, you may decide that the original figures were superior to those in the changed version. At this point, Excel gives you the opportunity to analyze each change. If you think the change was an improvement, you can accept it, making it part of the spreadsheet from now on. If not, you can reject the change, restoring the cell contents to whatever was there before your network comrades asserted themselves.

To perform this accept/reject routine, choose Tools→Track Changes→Accept or Reject Changes. In the Select Changes to Accept or Reject dialog box, you can set up the reviewing process by specifying which changes you want to review (according to when they were made, who made them, and where they're located in the worksheet). When you click OK, the reviewing process begins (Figure 17-8, bottom).

Merging Workbooks

In many work situations, you may find it useful to distribute copies of a workbook to several people for their perusal and then incorporate their changes into a single workbook.

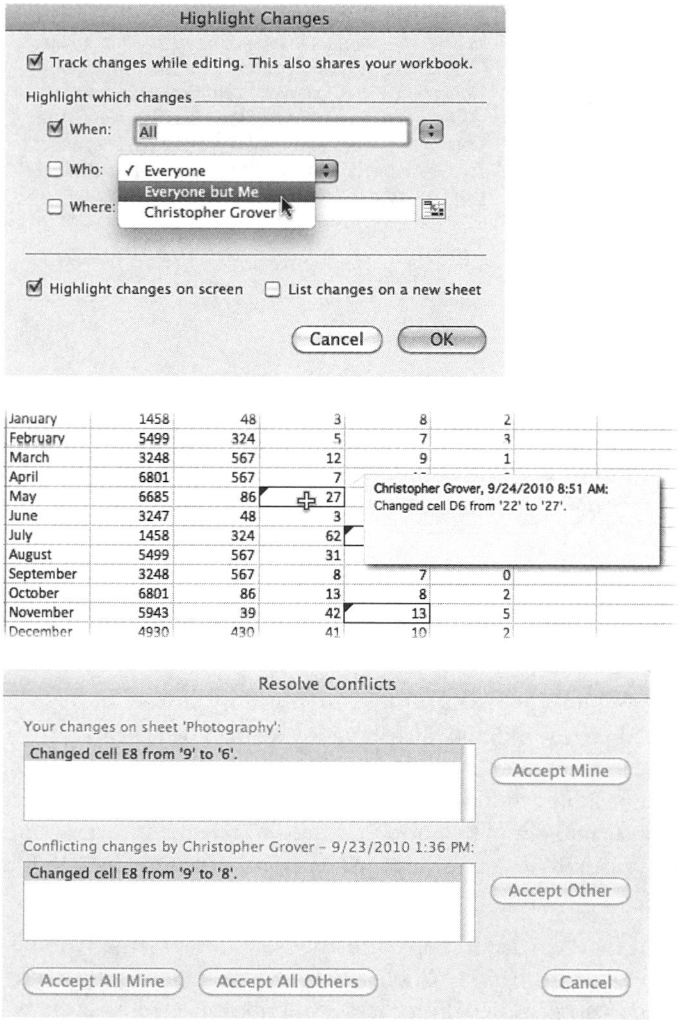

Figure 17-8:
Top: This dialog box lets you turn on change tracking and specify whose changes are highlighted. By turning on Where, clicking the tiny spreadsheet icon next to the box, and dragging in your worksheet, you can also limit the tracking feature to a specific area of the worksheet.

Middle: The shaded triangle in the upper-left corner of a cell indicates that somebody changed its contents. A comment balloon lets you know exactly what the change was.

Bottom: Using this dialog box, you can walk through all the changes in a spreadsheet one at a time, giving each changed cell your approval or restoring it to its original value.

Performing this feat, however, requires some preparation—namely, creating a shared workbook (see the previous section), and then configuring the workbook's *change history*. You'll find this option by choosing Tools→Share Workbook and then clicking the Advanced tab (Figure 17-9). The number that you specify in the "Keep change history for" box determines how old changes can be before they become irrelevant. The theory behind this feature contends that you'll stop caring about changes that are older than the number of days that you set. (Tracking changes forever can bloat a file's size, too.)

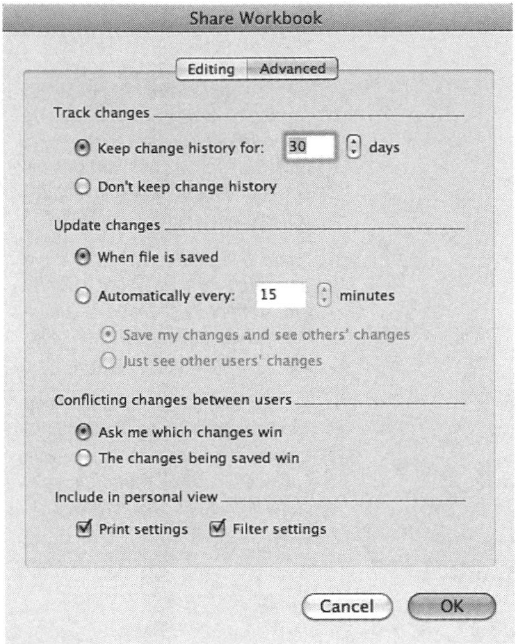

Figure 17-9:
To prep your workbook for later merging, turn on the "Keep change history" option in the Share Workbook dialog box. You also have to complete your merge within the time limit that you set in the "Track changes" area. Once you're ready to bring everything together, choose Tools→Merge Workbooks and select the first workbook that you want to merge into the current workbook.

Once you've prepared your workbook, distribute it via email or network. Ask your colleagues to make comments and changes and then return their spreadsheet copies to you (within the time limit you specified, as described in the previous paragraph). Collect all of the copies into one place. (You may need to rename the workbooks to avoid replacing one with another, since they can't occupy the same folder if they have the same names.)

Now open a copy of the shared workbook and choose Tools→Merge Workbooks, which brings up an Open dialog box. Choose the file you want to merge into the open workbook, and then click OK. This process has to be repeated for every workbook you want to merge.

Part Four: PowerPoint

4

Planning and Creating Great Presentations

Communication takes many forms, from smoke signals to web pages; from rude gestures to polished oratory; from an order at the drive-through to a speech at the podium. And whether you're a Great Communicator or a first-time speaker, what you're really doing in any of these instances is making a *presentation*: you're delivering information to others to get your point across.

PowerPoint's a great tool to help you make presentations. But it's only a tool. Don't fall into the trap of thinking the computer presentation is the star of the show. *You* are the star of the show. PowerPoint, your handouts, your guest speakers, and your sharp new suit are all playing supporting roles.

Before you even boot up your computer, it's worth spending some time thinking about your presentation's goal (convince Mom and Dad to let you go away to camp, for example) and who your audience is (two people who know you very well). As a wise man once said, "Scratch 'em where they itch." To succeed, your presentation has to resonate with the audience's needs, expectations, and assumptions. The first two parts of this chapter help you plan an effective presentation tailored to your audience. The last section deals with presentation nuts and bolts—picking out laptops, projectors, and so on.

If you're an award-winning member of the dinner-speech circuit and you just bought this book to learn how to use Office and PowerPoint, then by all means skip ahead to the next chapter to learn the ins and outs of the program. But if you have limited or no experience giving knock-'em-dead presentations, this chapter's loaded with advice that can help you plan, prepare for, and deliver your pitch.

Planning the Presentation

It doesn't matter if you're planning on talking one-on-one—teaching your daughter how to operate the lawnmower—or speaking to thousands of Macworld attendees: if you care about the message you're about to deliver, it's worth spending time organizing your thoughts before you begin composing your presentation. See Figure 18-1 for a flowchart to help you plan.

Tip: While you're planning your presentation, don't forget to make a contingency plan too. Identify parts of your presentation you could simplify, gloss over, or cut out completely in case your guest speaker rambles on for ten minutes instead of three; audience questions take much longer than anticipated; or you have to send someone to find the janitor when you turn on your projector and trip a circuit breaker.

The Goals of Your Presentation

Begin by thinking through what you want your presentation to accomplish. There's nothing worse than being on the receiving end of an aimless talk. In other words, what do you want your audience to walk away with? Here are some examples:

- Gain knowledge or skills.
- Understand a new concept.
- Be inspired or moved.
- Change their behavior.
- Change their belief system.
- Take action.
- Approve your plan or budget.
- Buy something.
- Donate to your organization or invest in your company.
- Become involved in a process or a cause.
- Get media coverage for your business or organization.

Know Your Audience

In order to increase the likelihood of achieving your goal, you need to learn as much as you can about the kind of people who'll be in the audience. Put yourself in their shoes and figure out how you can make your presentation interesting and relevant to them. Sometimes you'll know exactly who you're talking to: the members of your project team, the Board of Directors, or your fellow Rotary members. In these cases, you've probably already got a pretty good idea of who these people are, what interests them, what their group culture is like, and what the norms are for typical presentations.

At other times the audience may be much more of an unknown quantity: the attendees at a conference you've never been to before, reporters at a press conference, a brand new client, or the circuit court judge. In this case, make an effort to learn about your audience to give yourself a better chance of really connecting with them.

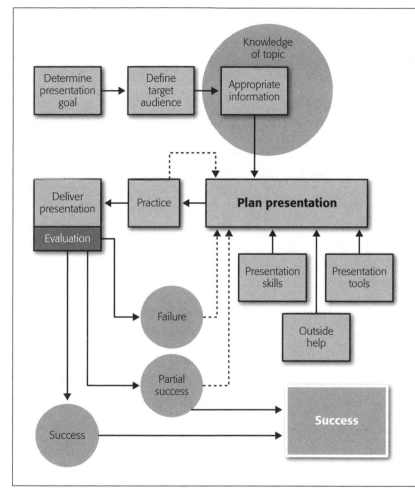

Figure 18-1:
As you plan and present your presentation, you'll have to deal with lots of details—but always keep the big picture in mind and tackle the tasks in the proper order. There are many steps between determining your desired outcome and celebrating a successful presentation. Most vital is defining your target audience as clearly as possible, and then figuring out the appropriate information to give this group. The evaluation and the resulting feedback loops (shown by the dotted lines) provide important opportunities for you to tailor the design of your presentation. See page 523 for advice on how to create evaluation forms.

Tailor the Presentation to the Audience

With your presentation goal and target audience clearly in mind, you can tailor what you're going to say to this particular group.

- What language do they speak?
- Do they use a colloquial language or jargon?
- How might their culture—their regional, ethnic, class, or corporate culture—affect how you communicate with them?

- What kinds of presentations are they accustomed to viewing?
- What would this audience consider appropriate dress for a presenter?
- What would make this topic important to this audience?

Tip: Interview potential audience members or other people who've presented to this group previously and ask for advice on how to make your presentation succeed.

Outline the Presentation

Start by creating an outline of your presentation on paper or in Word—but save PowerPoint's Outline view for later, when it's actually time to start working on your slides. Start rough with the high points of what you want to say and refine your outline as you go. If your presentation is part of a larger event, then outline your part from the time you take the podium to the time you leave the stage. A PowerPoint presentation may be all or only a small part of this outline.

Tip: Using Word's outlining feature (page 173) will save you time later, since you can transfer it right into PowerPoint, as described on page 540.

Build Your Presentation

Work from your outline to create your PowerPoint presentation. The following chapters cover the mechanics of working with PowerPoint. But before you start creating slides, refine your outline so you'll know how and where to make use of those slides.

It's certainly not the only way to do it, but an old favorite structure for speeches is the overview, the presentation, and the review. In other words, tell them what you're going to tell them, then tell them, and then tell them what you told them. That may sound excessively simple, but it's a wonderfully easy way to keep your audience oriented.

You might find it useful to start with a joke, a quip, or humorous anecdote—especially a self-deprecating one—that somehow relates to your topic. If skillfully delivered, this kind of icebreaker helps lower the audience's defenses and can endear you to them. But if you can't tell jokes, or if you're sure you're going to be so nervous you could never pull it off, don't attempt it. You certainly don't want to start off with a poorly-told joke that falls flat.

Remember as you design your presentation—and later as you make it—your job is to communicate your information clearly, simply, and interestingly. Your mission is to engage the audience and keep their attention for the duration. Keep these points in mind when you're sketching out what you want to say:

- Know your subject thoroughly—but don't feel you have to tell everything you know.

- Use as many slides as you need—and no more. Slides are supporting materials—use them where they do the most good. It's possible you could give an hour-long talk and use five slides. Some slides may be up for several minutes each, while others may be onscreen for only a few seconds.

- Slides are especially good for tables and charts, pictures, and strong bullet points.

- Don't fill your slides with text. Use a larger font than you think you need.

- If you have several bullet points on a slide, build them in one at a time as you discuss each one. Otherwise, your audience will be reading ahead and not listening.

- Try to approximately balance your use of slides containing bullet points, charts, and pictures.

- Try to make your presentation interactive. For example, present a problem or question to the audience and open it up for discussion. Alternatively, ask them to discuss the question with their neighbor for a few minutes and then gather responses from the room.

- Vary the pace of the presentation—especially if it's a long one—by pulling audience members up for demonstrations, bringing out surprise guests, giving attendees one minute to furiously scribble responses to your question, and so on.

- Use every different communication method at your disposal: auditory, visual, and direct experience. Involve the right brain by using stories, movement, or song.

- Be careful with how much color you use in your slides. You don't want color to distract from the point you're making, and you always want your slides to be legible.

- Don't use slide animations or fancy transitions just because it's easy to do so. These features should serve the presentation, not distract from it.

- Your presentation should keep the audience involved by keeping them thinking or reacting emotionally; by generating questions, new thoughts, and new dreams.

Practice

Practice giving your presentation to a coworker, an indulgent spouse, or an attentive dog, and listen carefully to any feedback—from the humans anyway. Watch yourself in the mirror or shoot a video of yourself as you practice. Pay special attention to your gestures, expressions, and body language. Be yourself, but remember you're essentially "on stage"—even if your audience is composed of only two people. Don't fake it, but let yourself be naturally enthusiastic. And in order to reach an audience you need to project not only your voice, but your movements and gestures as well.

Have someone else proofread your slides. If you have to proofread them yourself, print out the slides so you can see the words on paper instead of onscreen. Misspelled words or incorrect punctuation that you read over a dozen times onscreen will jump out at you on a printed page. Double- and triple-check the spelling of people's names or product names that appear in your slides. One of the best ways to proof is to read aloud while someone else views your slides.

Tip: At this point, you can use your watch to get an idea of how long it takes to do your presentation, factoring in time for introductory comments and any question-and-answer period. Once you've finalized your script and typed out your slides, you can use PowerPoint's rehearsal mode (page 580) to determine the exact timing.

Delivering the Presentation

If you're responsible for the whole event, it's up to you to deal with a handful of tasks that seemingly have nothing to do with your presentation. Factors like lighting and furniture can have a huge impact on your audience's experience. Unfortunately, if you're late or equipment fails, your audience may be less receptive to your message.

Try to take care of the following ahead of time so you can solve any problems before the audience arrives:

- Know how to unlock the doors, adjust the lights, and control the temperature. If you have to dim the lights in order to see the screen, make sure there's a light projecting on you whenever you're speaking so your audience can see you.

- If you have control over the way the room is set up, place the podium at center stage and your screen off to the side. The slides are for speaker support—what you're saying is the main attraction.

- Set up and test the equipment, or coordinate with your tech support people who'll be running the lights and the public address system.

- If your audio person needs to manage inputs—say, from your laptop's sound output and your microphone—print a slide list for her (see page 594) with all the audio cues clearly indicated. For example, she might need to fade out the "walk-in" music and turn on your microphone input; or she may need to turn up the sound from your computer's audio during a part of the presentation while turning off your mic.

- Set up tables or set out information packets or programs.

- Make sure there are clear signs prominently posted to help attendees find the room so they know they've come to the right place.

- Figure out the parking situation, handicapped access, and restroom locations.

- Greet people as they come in to make them feel welcome and help them get oriented.

Welcome Your Audience

When it's time to start and your audience is seated, don't launch right into your program. Welcome the audience, introduce yourself, and tell them what presentation they're attending so they know they're in the right room. Make sure everyone has a seat and a program. Tell them how long the session will run, if there will be a break, and where the bathrooms are. Explain how you'd like to handle questions from the audience—whether they should shout them out at any time, save them until the end, line up at a microphone, or whatever. If you've brought printed handouts (page 591) or posted your slides on the Web, let the audience know they don't need to take notes.

Explaining these seemingly simple things to your audience may seem like a waste of time, but it actually serves to increase their comfort level, lower their defenses, and make them feel like they're part of the group—all of which will make them better and more receptive listeners.

Introduce Your Presentation

The time has come to finally talk about your topic. Try to open with a bang—catch people's attention and tell them how this presentation is going to be valuable to them, and what they're going to take away from it.

Note: A speaker at a forum on the future once started his presentation with "Many of the people in this room will be alive 100 years from now." That's the kind of sentence that makes an audience pay attention.

At this point you may want to query your listeners to see how they relate to your topic—both for your own benefit and theirs. Ask for a show of hands: "How many of you are running Mac OS X Server?" "Who's had, or has a loved one who's had breast cancer?" "How many of you are parents of seventh or eighth graders?"

Choose your questions so all the audience members see themselves as part of one or another of these groups. The responses you get will give you a better idea of the makeup of the audience—and it helps everyone feel like they belong as they identify with others who respond similarly.

Now that your audience has told you something about themselves, tell them something about yourself. For example: don't brag, but explain why you're qualified to speak on your topic.

Making the Presentation

After all your preparation, planning, and practice, giving your presentation should be a piece of cake. You've got great information, you know it inside out, and you've tailored it to this particular group of people. Relax and enjoy the process of sharing. During your talk keep these points in mind:

- If you don't feel relaxed, fake it. Your audience will never know the difference. Never make apologies for being nervous.

- Speak to the audience—don't just read from a script or recite. Look your listeners in the eye—in all parts of the room.

- Don't stare at your laptop or look behind you at the screen.

- Enthusiasm is contagious—smile! Let the audience see how enthusiastic you are about your topic.

- Vary your cadence when speaking—pauses can be very powerful.

- Don't read your slides (unless there's a compelling need to for the benefit of blind or foreign-language speaking members of the audience).

- If you have a slide full of text, it probably doesn't need to be there—that's what should be in your speech. In fact, don't even use complete sentences in your slides—sentences belong in your speech.

Review

Wrap up your presentation with a review. Now's when you "tell them what you told them." Let audience members know what you hope they've gained from this presentation and what you expect them to do with it—buy your product, sign up for a time share, host a foreign-exchange student, or whatever.

Make any other concluding statements, put up a slide with your contact information, and remind them where you'll be after the presentation if they have more questions. Explain how you sincerely want their feedback on this presentation so that you can improve it in the future. Urge them to take a moment to fill out feedback forms, assuming you've chosen to prepare them as described in the next section.

Finally, thank them for coming and for their attention—and take a bow as the audience applauds and cheers.

Evaluating the Presentation

You've completed your presentation. You think you did a pretty good job—the audience applauded, no rotten fruits or vegetables hit the stage, and several people told you, "Nice job." But how can you be sure? Getting feedback is a step that's often overlooked, and while not appropriate for every presentation, it's a vital tool for judging your success using something other than guesswork. Audience feedback can tell you whether you succeeded in getting your message across, how useful the information is to the audience, and how you might improve the presentation—or similar presentations—next time.

The quickest, most direct—and least accurate—feedback method is to simply question your listeners and ask for a show of hands (see the box below). If you go this route, design your questions carefully because you can only ask about three or four without annoying most folks.

Feedback Fundamentals

Gathering feedback from your audience shouldn't be an afterthought. It's the only way you'll know how well you're doing and how you can do better in the future. Whether you just ask for a show of hands or provide an evaluation form, the information you receive can be invaluable.

For example, say your presentation is entitled *Controlling Gophers in Your Yard and Garden.* You're presenting to a group of organic gardeners, many of whom you know object to killing animals. Your goal is for the members of the audience to learn about and choose from different methods of gopher control appropriate to their situation and their ethical values.

If you only have time for raised-hands feedback, you might want to ask your audience the following questions—and be sure to write down your estimate of their responses:

- **Question:** Do you now know what approach you want to take to deal with your gopher problem? (Show of hands for yes, show of hands for no.)

- **Question:** For those of you who raised your hand *yes*, do you know enough to feel you can succeed with your chosen method? (Show of hands if you do know enough, show of hands if you don't know enough.)

- **Question:** If you raised your hand *no* to the first question, have you gained useful information that will be helpful in choosing an approach to gopher control in the future? (Show of hands for yes, show of hands for no.)

Tip: Consider using instant feedback. Throw out some raised-hand feedback questions part way through your presentation. You'll be able to gauge how well you're doing, and be able to modify your presentation to make the best use of your remaining time.

Designing an evaluation form

If you have a lot riding on the outcome of your presentation, consider hiring a professional evaluator to design evaluation forms and help you interpret the results. There are many different approaches to designing these forms. The type of presentation you're giving and the type of outcome you're hoping for will determine the kinds of questions you need to ask.

You can design evaluation questions as review questions (to see if your listeners recall the points you made) or you can ask participants what they got out of the presentation. Questions can be answered with a simple yes or no, with a set of multiple choice answers, or according to a rating scale. People are likely to skip open-ended, essay-type questions that take too long to complete.

Design your evaluation questions carefully in order to judge your success and target ways to improve your presentation next time. Use a mix of simple yes/no or checkbox questions along with open-ended questions and rating scales. One side of one page is about as much as you can ask of your audience—remember, they're doing you a favor by filling this out.

Tip: There's an excellent example of an evaluation form you can download at *www.missingmanuals.com/cds* named *18-1_Evaluation_Form.pdf*.

When you ask your listeners to fill out an evaluation, you're turning the tables on them—asking them to give *you* information. It's not always easy to get your audience to cooperate. In some cases, it may be best to let them comment anonymously. In other cases, consider using some kind of incentive. For example, you could give a small gift in exchange for completed evaluation forms or use the forms in a drawing for door prizes.

Tip: Whether you ask questions or prepare a questionnaire, make sure to budget time for the evaluation. Evaluations need to be completed immediately after your presentation. Don't expect your participants to turn them in later in the day or mail them to you—it just won't happen.

Presentation Hardware

If you're lucky, you'll have complete control over every aspect of your presentation—including the computer, the projector, and all the other technical bits and pieces that are required.

Often, though, you'll be using others' equipment; plugging your laptop into a video projector at a conference; or just showing up with your presentation on a USB thumb drive or a CD and running it on someone else's computer. When the equipment isn't your own, you have to be more flexible and ready to improvise. Whether you're using your own projector or someone else's, it's a good idea to make a checklist and pack items that might be needed. Consider bringing extra extension cords and AC adapters, gaffer's tape (to tape down cords), batteries (for remotes and pointers), a pocket flashlight, a USB thumb drive, an extra projector lamp, and a variety of cables and adapters to connect computers to projectors.

Laptops

You can run PowerPoint 2011 presentations on any of the current crop of MacBooks and MacBook Pros. As explained on page 651, Office 2011 requires an Intel processor, so that leaves out older G4 machines. To get the best performance, use JPEG's for image files, MP3s for audio files, and don't use 3-D or shadow effects. Presentations intended for single viewers—like self-paced lessons—are well-suited to a desktop computer. But for most presentations, the portability of a laptop makes it the computer of choice.

Projectors

Depending on the size of your audience, the type of room you're in—and the size of your budget—you can show your PowerPoint presentations right on your laptop, on an external monitor, or with a video projector.

If you're presenting to a group and you're able to dim the lights, a projector is usually your best bet. The video projector market is booming, fueled by home theater buffs and computerized presenters like you. Prices are falling and new models are emerging weekly—resulting in a bewildering array of projectors to choose from. Prices start at about $500, but plan on at least $800 as a minimum price for a bright, high-resolution projector.

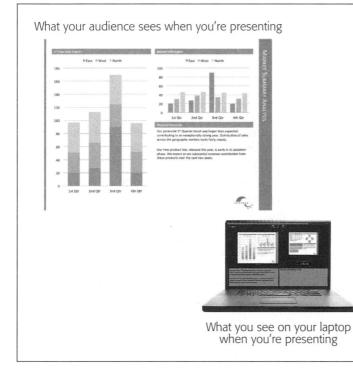

What your audience sees when you're presenting

What you see on your laptop when you're presenting

Figure 18-2:
While the audience sees your slides on the big screen, your MacBook can help you keep your place in the presentation—and keep you from looking over your shoulder to see what's on the screen. It can display the current slide and the next slide, your slide notes, and a clock or timer telling you either elapsed time or the remaining time in your presentation. If you need to rush to the finish, or go back to the beginning, the thumbnails on the left let you jump to any slide in the presentation. You'll learn how to display these onscreen features in the next chapter.

Tip: If you're not familiar with video projectors and you're considering dropping $1000 or more to purchase one, you should really find a store where you can compare the models you're interested in under lighting conditions that are similar to the way you'll be using it. Get a head start on your comparison shopping by visiting *www.projectorcentral.com* or *www.projectorpeople.com* where you can read reviews and buyer guides, and post projector-related questions on their forum.

Figure 18-3:
Top: When your audience starts bumping heads as a result of leaning in to look at your laptop screen, it's time to consider a video projector. The variety of sizes and prices available is growing rapidly, and though the prices are coming down, it's still a big investment. Consider renting a projector if you need one infrequently. Then when you're ready to buy, you'll better understand the features you need (and by then you'll get even more for your money).

Bottom: Today's projectors usually give you several different ways to connect to your computer. Second from the left is the VGA connector.

Choosing a projector

If the thought of shopping for a new digital camera gives you a frisson of excitement, then deciphering the specs of video projectors should be right up your alley. There are three basic types of video projectors: LCD (liquid crystal display), DLP (digital light processing), and LCOS (liquid crystal on silicon). Most of the time the projector type is less important than its key specifications. After you figure out your budget and how large and heavy a projector you're willing to carry around, consider these important criteria:

- **Resolution.** This figure represents the number of pixels the projector can display, and should match your computer's video output. Most business projectors are designated SVGA (800 × 600 pixels), XGA (1,024 × 768 pixels) or WXGA (1280 × 800). More pixels give you a sharper screen image and—surprise, surprise—cost more. All MacBooks and MacBook Pros can handle any of these resolutions.

- **Brightness.** Like slide or movie projectors, video projectors produce an image on the screen by projecting it with a very bright light. The intensity of that light is measured in ANSI lumens. Methods of measuring lumens vary from manufacturer to manufacturer, so consider these specifications as only ballpark figures. Less than 1000 lumens is fine when projecting on smaller screens or in darkened rooms, but will be too dim on larger screens or under brighter lighting conditions. 1500 lumens is a good minimum for rooms that can't be darkened—but you'll only know for sure by trying out a projector under similar projection conditions.

- **Inputs.** Projectors designed for a home theater system may feature only HDMI, S-video or composite video inputs. Mac laptops can output in this format—if it's your only option. Projectors designed for computer presentations usually have either a VGA connector, a DVI connector, or both (and quite possibly S-video and composite video inputs as well). Connect your laptop using the VGA connection (Figure 18-3, bottom) or, if available, the DVI connection. Some newer, higher-end projectors have only a DVI connection.

Tip: When you're buying a projector, also consider the cost and expected lifetime for the lamps/bulbs it uses. They're notoriously expensive and the projected life can be from 1000 to 3000 hours.

Renting projectors

If you don't find yourself giving PowerPoint presentations at the drop of a hat, you may be better off renting a projector. Look in the Yellow Pages under Audio-Visual Equipment to find a local outlet. And if you don't have a local AV house, you can even rent equipment by mail (or at least, by UPS). When you rent, you can take advantage of the newest technology, get a projector that suits the requirements for your particular presentation space, and let somebody else worry about repairs and bulb replacement.

Projection screens

The screen is an often overlooked element of projection quality. A poor screen—or wall—can make the best projector's image look terrible. There are as many different kinds of screens available as there are projectors, starting at about $100 for rollup screens. Any screen will be better than a regular wall, although you can get very good results in a darkened room with a smooth, matte white painted wall.

Projection screens come in a wide variety of surfaces which provide varying amounts of *gain,* enhanced brightness attained by directing the light from the projector back to the audience instead of allowing it to scatter in all directions. High-gain screens have a lower viewing angle. In other words, they reflect more light to viewers closer to the centerline of the screen. A matte white screen—or a flat, white wall—provides the widest viewing angle and the least gain.

Remote Controls

Using a remote control for your PowerPoint presentation gives you the freedom to move away from your laptop—and you'll appear much more professional when you're not reaching for the computer to advance each slide. Even if you like the security of the podium and want to keep an eye on your speaker's notes on your PowerBook's screen, by using a remote control you can advance slides while gesturing or with your hand in your pocket. When you're ready to break free of the podium, the remote lets you stroll the stage or amble through the audience—while still controlling your presentation.

Figure 18-4:
Plug this remote's USB receiver into your computer and you needn't be tied to the lectern to change slides. Whether you're seated at a table or mingling with the audience, a handheld remote lets you spend more time connecting with your audience, and less time connected to your computer.

If you've got a MacBook or MacBook Pro, you've already got the remote control that came with your laptop, intended mostly as a way to control Apple's Front Row feature. The Apple Remote communicates with your computer via infrared (just like a TV remote)—so you do have to point it at your computer and it won't function if it's in your pocket.

Tip: Be sure to *pair* your Apple Remote with your computer so it can be controlled only by that particular remote. Otherwise, a jokester in the audience could control your presentation with *his* Apple Remote. To create this bond of remote-control monogamy, make sure you're logged in as an Admin user. Then, from a few inches away, point the remote at the IR sensor on the front of the computer, and press and hold the Menu and Next/Fast-forward buttons simultaneously for five seconds. (If you ever need to unpair, choose Apple→System Preferences→Security and click Unpair.)

Most other remote controls use RF (radio frequency) to communicate with a receiver plugged into your laptop's USB port. Because they use radio waves, there's no need to point the remote control at your laptop. But when you *do* need to point something out on one of your slides, some remotes have a built-in laser pointer, so you don't have to fumble with more than one handheld device.

Some remotes can also function as a mouse, or control your iTunes and DVD playback. However, when you're in the midst of the presentation, you may find that simpler is better—and the only buttons you really need are forward and backward. The winner of the simplicity competition is the Power Presenter RF, sporting only forward and back buttons and a laser pointer (*www.powerremote.com*). The sleek and popular Keyspan Presentation Remote (or its more powerful sibling, the Presentation Remote Pro) adds a mouse controller to the mix (*www.keyspan.com*).

There's also the possibility that you already own a RF remote control—albeit one with *lots* of buttons: your cell phone. Salling Clicker software lets you use certain Bluetooth mobile phones and PDAs to control your computer. If your Mac has built-in Bluetooth—or you've added a Bluetooth adapter—then this $20 piece of software is all you need to turn your phone into a remote control for PowerPoint and many other programs. Learn more at *www.salling.com*.

CHAPTER 19

Building a PowerPoint Presentation

S lideshows derive their power from their simplicity. By displaying a single static image at a time, slide shows can present information simply and clearly—and often with more impact than you could achieve with a moving picture—whether you're teaching geography to a class of third-graders or pitching an ad campaign to a Fortune 500 CEO.

PowerPoint gives you the ability to create very basic, simple slides—for example, just words on a plain background or a single picture—or a complex blend of photographs, animation, movies, and sound, to create dazzling presentations that grab and hold your audience's attention. Whether you opt for simple or fancy, PowerPoint helps you build a presentation with a clean, consistent look. Templates and themes determine the appearance of your presentation, while layouts position the elements on individual slides. As with many Office projects, the easiest way to build a presentation is to start with one of PowerPoints predesigned templates.

Step 1. Choose a Template

When you launch PowerPoint, your first stop is probably the PowerPoint Presentation Gallery shown in Figure 19-1, which looks and works a lot like the window you use to choose a Word or Excel template. Use the categories on the left to filter the templates viewed in the main pane. Before you open a template, you can change the color, fonts, and slide size. You'll be able to make some of these same changes even after you've started your presentation.

The template names hint at their intended purpose with words like: photo album, status report, quiz show, or five rules. Templates include slide layouts specific to their purpose. For example, a photo album template makes it easy to display photos. To see the individual slide layouts included in a template, expand the right pane, and use the arrow buttons. Templates include boilerplate material in the form of text and graphics that you'll usually replace when you build your presentation. When you've made your selections, click Choose, and PowerPoint opens your presentation in the Normal view (Figure 19-2).

Tip: If you've changed your preferences by turning off PowerPoint→Preferences→General→"Open PowerPoint Presentation Gallery when application opens", you'll see the PowerPoint work area shown in Figure 19-2. In that case, you can open the gallery by pressing Shift-⌘-P (or choosing File→New from Template).

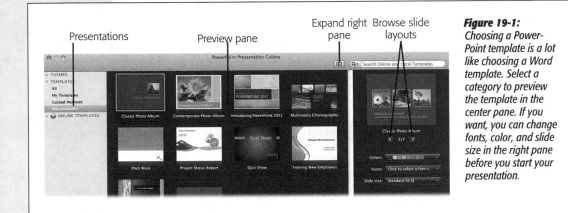

Figure 19-1:
Choosing a Power-Point template is a lot like choosing a Word template. Select a category to preview the template in the center pane. If you want, you can change fonts, color, and slide size in the right pane before you start your presentation.

The Three-Pane View

When the PowerPoint window opens, you see the first slide of your chosen theme in the main *slide pane*. PowerPoint's three-pane Normal view lets you concentrate on one slide at a time, yet lets you quickly navigate through your slides or add notes. The largest pane shows you exactly what your audience will see (apart from animations and other special effects). The pane on the left gives you an overview of the entire presentation in thumbnail or outline format. When a presentation is brand-new, it shows only one slide. As you add more slides to the presentation, they appear in the outline pane—where you can reorder them by dragging the thumbnails.

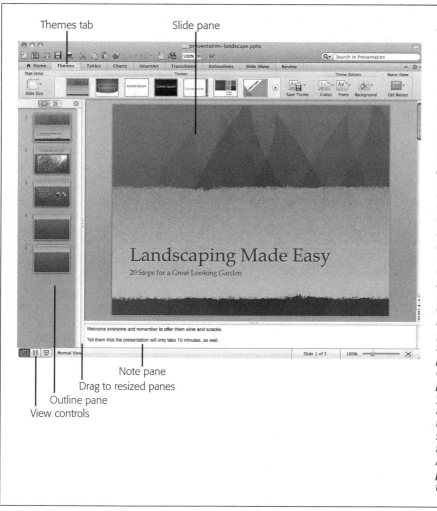

Themes tab   Slide pane

Figure 19-2:
*Topped by the
toolbar, and the rib-
bon, the PowerPoint
window displays
three panes. The
slide you're editing
occupies center stage
on the slide pane.
Here you can edit
the slide's text; add
pictures, charts, and
other objects; change
backgrounds; and so
on. The Outline pane
displays thumbnail
images of each slide
in the presentation
(when in Slides view)
or an outline of your
slides' text when in
(Outline view). You
can enter random
notes to yourself or
your presentation
script in the Notes
pane. If you use an
external monitor or
projector to present
your show, Power-
Point can display
these notes on your
screen and hide them
from the audience.
Adjust the size of the
panes by dragging
the divider bars.*

Note pane
Drag to resized panes
Outline pane
View controls

The third pane, below the slide, is never going to be seen by the audience—it's for your own notes, visible on your computer display during your presentation—while the audience sees only your slide on the room's main screen. The Notes pane is also handy while you're creating your presentation for "notes to self" about the slide you're creating—for example, to remind yourself to double-check a fact or replace a product photo with a new version. Although the slide area is the biggest when you start a new presentation, you can resize the panes by dragging their dividers. In fact, you can hide the outline and notes panes by dragging the dividers all the way to the edges of the window.

At the top of the window you'll find the familiar Standard toolbar and ribbon.

- **To view Templates and create a brand new presentation**, go to File→New from Template (Shift-⌘-P).

- **To view Themes**, click the Theme tab on the ribbon, as shown at the top in Figure 19-3.

- **To view Slide Layouts**, go to Home | Slides→Layout, as shown at bottom in Figure 19-3.

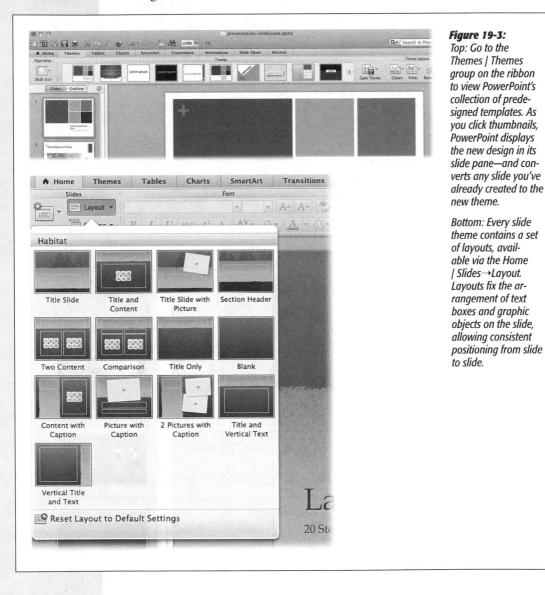

Figure 19-3:
Top: Go to the Themes | Themes group on the ribbon to view PowerPoint's collection of prede-signed templates. As you click thumbnails, PowerPoint displays the new design in its slide pane—and con-verts any slide you've already created to the new theme.

Bottom: Every slide theme contains a set of layouts, avail-able via the Home | Slides→Layout. Layouts fix the ar-rangement of text boxes and graphic objects on the slide, allowing consistent positioning from slide to slide.

Starting from Scratch

Although templates and themes save you hours of work, there's a downside to using them, too. Since you'll be choosing from the same repertoire as millions of other PowerPoint fans, your slideshow just may look just like someone else's—maybe even the speaker who came before you. The only surefire way to guarantee a unique look is to design your presentation yourself. Fortunately, it's not as hard as it sounds. To create a relatively blank presentation, go to File→New Presentation (⌘-N).

PowerPoint creates a new presentation using the White template, which you can customize to your heart's content. You'll still have access to some slide layouts to position

elements, but it's up to you to give your presentation character. Design your own backgrounds, add your company logo, create your own combinations of colors and fonts. You can use PowerPoint's various text and drawing tools to build each slide from scratch. Although designing slides this way involves a lot more work than simply choosing a template, you'll be rewarded with a presentation that doesn't *look* like it came out of a can. Even if all you do is create a different slide background color, pattern, or image, you can have a completely unique look with minimal effort, since you can still use all of PowerPoint's predesigned layouts.

Step 2: Specify a Theme

Even though your slides may display different kinds of information—text, charts, tables, and pictures, for example—it's usually best if they follow a consistent design that uses the same fonts, background graphics, color scheme, and so on. The design sets the overall tone for the presentation, so choose a theme that suits the topic and audience. Unlike templates, themes don't change your presentation's content; they just change the appearance of what's already there. They let you build your slideshow without spending time testing out color combinations, designing backgrounds, and choosing fonts. When project deadlines are looming and you have a million things to do (including creating a presentation), you'll welcome these timesaving features.

Tip: If you want to start with the most basic, blank, white slideshow, click the All category and choose the White template. Or, if the gallery isn't open, you can choose File→New (⌘-N). For more information on starting from a clean slate, see the box above.

PowerPoint 2011 includes more than 50 slide themes. As you build each slide, the theme and template keep your designs consistent, and your text and objects aligned, from slide to slide. You'll find Slide Themes on the ribbon's Themes tab. Scroll through the themes, or click the triangle button at the bottom to reveal the entire lineup. If a theme looks like it might work, click it to instantly apply it to your slideshow. If you change your mind, press ⌘-Z—or simply choose another theme. Because themes don't change your presentation's content, there's no downside to exploring the different looks.

Adding Your Own Templates

In many corporations, PowerPoint slideshows are an everyday occurrence—as are rules and regulations. You may be required to use a PowerPoint template, designed and approved by your company, as the basis for all slideshows you give. (Don't worry if your company is Windows-based: templates for the Windows version of PowerPoint work just fine on Macs.)

If you're working with a required template, you can make it ready for easy access each time you begin to create a slideshow. Just drag the template file into Home→Library→Application Support→Microsoft→Office→User Templates→My Templates folder. From then on, it'll show up in the Presentation Gallery under the My Templates group. In fact, you

can transform *any* PowerPoint file into a template by dragging it into this folder. If you're creating your own template, choose File→Save As and choose PowerPoint Template (.potx) from the format pop-up menu. PowerPoint tucks it into the My Templates folder unless you tell it to do otherwise. (Consider saving your templates in the .pot format if you might be sharing them with people who have yet to upgrade to Office 2007 or later.)

When you open it, you'll get a blank copy of that file (called Presentation1, for example), even if it wasn't a PowerPoint template to begin with. PowerPoint is smart enough to figure: "If it's in the Templates folder, I'm probably supposed to treat it as a template."

Step 3: Add Slides and Choose Layouts

Add some of your own text to your first slide by clicking where it says "Click to add title" and then start typing. Then add a new slide to the presentation in any of the following ways:

- Click the Home | Slides→New Slide button in the ribbon.
- Choose Insert→New Slide.
- Press Shift-⌘-N.
- Right-click (Control-click) in the Outline pane or Slide pane, and from the pop-up menu, choose New Slide.

PowerPoint creates the new slide, displays it on the slide pane, and adds its thumbnail to the outline pane directly beneath the selected slide.

Note: When PowerPoint creates a second slide in the show, it automatically uses the second slide layouts for the new slide—but any other time you create a new slide, PowerPoint creates it in the same style as the selected slide.

With the new slide selected in the outline pane, go to Home | Slides→Layout to see the layouts you can apply to your slide. Click any of the layouts and the selected slide takes on this new appearance, ready for you to plug in text and images. If you don't like its looks, click another to choose a different design.

Take a moment to create four or five slides from various layouts and add some text so you have some slides with which to experiment.

OFFICE 2011 FOR MACINTOSH: THE MISSING MANUAL

Changing Themes in Midstream

Unlike, say, home decorating, changing your presentation's color scheme and other elements requires nothing more than a few quick mouse clicks. Just click the Themes tab to return to PowerPoint's trove of themes. Click one to apply it to your presentation. If you don't like the change, choose Edit→Undo Document Theme (⌘-Z) to revert, or just click another theme.

When you change themes, PowerPoint changes all the slides in your presentation to the new theme. If you'd like to change the theme for just part of your presentation, select two or more slides in the outline pane (by Shift-clicking or ⌘-clicking) and then click a new theme in the gallery. PowerPoint changes your selected slides to the new theme. You may find switching from one thing to another helpful to differentiate different segments of the presentation.

Each PowerPoint theme has a set of colors chosen to provide contrast between its various elements while maintaining a uniform color palette. If you don't agree with any of these colors, choose Themes | Theme Options→Colors→Create Theme Colors to display the Create Theme Colors window. Double-click any of the color swatches to change that color using the Color Picker (page 616). PowerPoint displays the results of your meddling in the small Preview diagram (see Figure 19-4). Click Apply to All to see your color change reflected throughout the presentation. Your new custom color collection is added to the Colors palette in the Formatting Palette's Document Theme pane. You can also make a wholesale change to the theme colors by selecting a different collection from this pop-up menu. (Be sure to make note of the collection you start with so you can always return if you decide you're making things worse.)

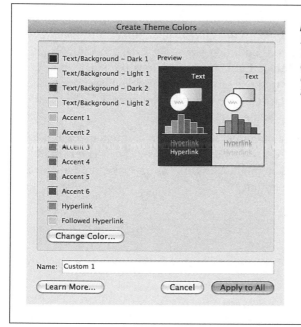

Figure 19-4:
If you want to create your own color collection, choose Themes | Theme Options→Colors→Create Theme Colors. In the resulting Create Theme Colors dialog box, you can choose new colors for the slide's background, text, fills, accents, and links.

You can also change the slide background, choosing from a dozen variations for each theme. Open the Slide Background pane of the Formatting Palette and click any of the background thumbnails to apply that background to your theme. Many of the theme designs have background graphics as well—frames or images. Click Themes | Theme Options→Background→Hide Background Graphics to remove them from the theme. (See page 537 for more on backgrounds.)

Step 4: Writing the Outline

A picture may be worth a thousand words, but it's the rare presentation that doesn't include at least some text. Deciding how to transform possibly boring facts into compelling word slides is often the most challenging part of creating a presentation, so words are a good place to begin before you get too hung up on design. If you've already worked up an outline in Word, skip ahead to page 540 to import it into PowerPoint.

Otherwise, open PowerPoint's Outline view by clicking the Outline tab at top of its pane. When you do so, the pane gets wider to accommodate your text, and the thumbnails are reduced to mere specks.

Each numbered slide icon at the left of the Outline pane represents an individual slide. Whatever you type adjacent to the slide icon becomes that slide's title, whether or not there's a title placeholder in the slide's layout (see Figure 19-5). Indented lines below the title correspond to the slide's subtitle and bullet text. (Bullet text refers to lines of text denoted by special *bullet* markers—see page 44).

To generate more outline text, you can do any of the following:

- **Add a slide**. Press Return after typing a title to start another title—and another slide. Each title corresponds to a slide.

- **Demote text**. Press Tab to *demote* a title into a bullet point under the previous title or bullet point. (Demote is outlining jargon for "make less important," or "move down one level in the outline.") If you continue pressing Tab, you can continue the demotion, down to five levels below the title. PowerPoint indents the line of text farther and farther to the right as you press Tab. Alternatively, you can drag the slide or text to the right.

- **Promote text**. Press Shift-Tab to *promote* a bullet point into a more important bullet point or—at the top level—to a slide title. Or you can drag text to the left to promote it. (Promote, as you might guess, means to "make more important," or "move up one level in the outline.")

Tip: When you use the Tab key in the Outline pane, it doesn't matter where in the line of text you place your insertion point—at the end, at the beginning, or somewhere in the middle.

- **Create another bullet point**. Press Return after typing a bullet point to start another bullet point.

- **Add a slide beneath a bullet point**. Press Shift-⌘-N after typing a bullet point to start a title for a new slide.

- **Expand or contract the slide outline text**. Right-click (Control-click) a slide's text and choose Collapse→Collapse to collapse the subtext of the selected slide or slides. Choose Collapse→Collapse All to hide the subtext of the entire outline—leaving only the slide titles visible. Right-click and choose Expand→Expand (or Expand All) to again reveal the slides' subtext.

- **Show formatting**. To display the outline in the same fonts used in the slides, Right-click (Control-click) any of the slide text and choose Show Formatting.

- **Delete a slide**. Select one or more slides, and then press Delete; Right-click (Control-click) the slide title and choose Delete Slide; or choose Edit→Delete Slide.

- **Move a slide**. Drag the slide icon up or down the list, and drop it when the blue line is directly above the slide you want to move it above.

- **Duplicate a slide**. Choose Edit→Duplicate slide, press ⌘-D, or Right-click (Control-click) the slide title and choose Duplicate Slide. PowerPoint creates the duplicate slide just below the original.

Tip: You can select more than one slide by Shift-clicking or ⌘-clicking additional slides, or by dragging up or down through the slide text, or to the right of it. Then you can apply any of the above techniques to add, delete, move, or duplicate the selected slides.

If you'd rather push buttons than drag slides around directly in the Outline pane, choose View→Toolbars→Outlining to summon the Outlining toolbar (see Figure 19-5). It has buttons for promoting, demoting, moving, expanding and contracting, and showing formatting.

As you're creating slide text, remember that your audience will probably be reading everything for the first time, so it's important not to pack too much text into each frame. Generally, it's best to limit your slides to about seven lines, with no more than seven words on each line. Simpler is always better. As you type your slideshow's outline, you can watch the slide being built in the Slide pane—handy feedback to avoid typing too much text for a bullet. (You can also type directly in the slide, as described on page 553.)

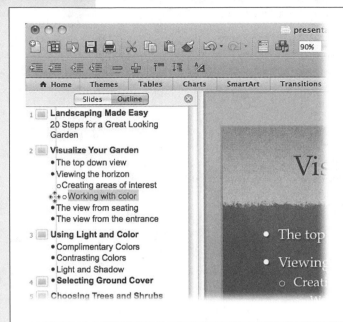

Figure 19-5:
You can drag topics or bullet points into a different order as you build your outline. The cursor changes to crossed arrows when you mouse over a draggable slide or bullet icon. A horizontal line indicates where PowerPoint thinks you want to place the item when you drag up and down to reorder; a vertical line indicates the indent level where PowerPoint intends to place the item. As you work on your outline in the left-hand Outline pane, you get to see your work in the Slide pane. Choose View→Toolbars→Outlining to call forth the Outlining toolbar. Its button collection lets you promote, demote, or move items up and down the outline; collapse or expand subordinate items for one slide, or the whole outline; or hide or show the font formatting in the outline view.

Using a Word Outline

The PowerPoint outliner isn't the only outliner in Office 2011. If, having cuddled up with Chapter 5 for several evenings, you're already proficient with the outliner in Word, you may prefer to write up your slideshow in Word. Fortunately, you can transfer your outline into PowerPoint, but it requires a couple of not so obvious steps. In Word, you need to save your outline in a special format that PowerPoint can read. So once your outline is complete, go to File→Save As and then choose Rich Text Format (RTF).

In PowerPoint, you insert the outline into an open PowerPoint presentation as if the outline were a series of slides. You can use the ribbon command Home | Slides→New Slide→Slides from Outline, or you can use the New Slide button on the Home tab, as shown in Figure 19-6. After you insert your Word outline, PowerPoint produces one slide for every level 1 heading in your outline, and creates bullet points for every subheading.

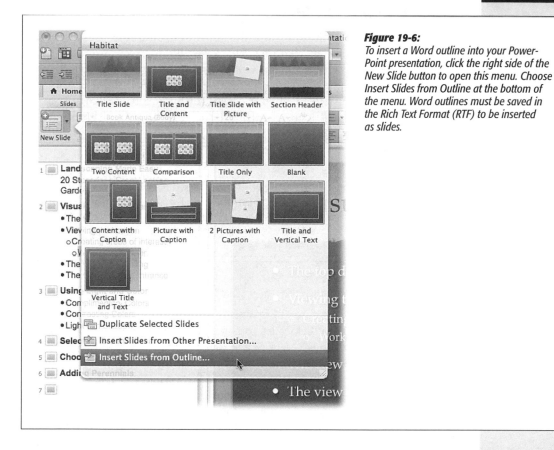

Figure 19-6:
To insert a Word outline into your Power-Point presentation, click the right side of the New Slide button to open this menu. Choose Insert Slides from Outline at the bottom of the menu. Word outlines must be saved in the Rich Text Format (RTF) to be inserted as slides.

Typing Directly into Your Slides

Not everybody uses the Outline pane to hash out the shape of a presentation. Lots of people prefer to type their text directly onto the slides themselves.

If you fall into this category, begin the slideshow by choosing a theme, as described at the beginning of this chapter. Go to Home | Slides→New Slide and then just click one of the layouts. PowerPoint adds it to your slideshow following the currently selected slide.

Now start filling in the details by clicking the various text or graphics placeholders and then typing or importing text and graphics.

Step 5: Building the Show

It's much better to show blank white slides containing an effective message than fancy graphics that don't say anything. That's why it's an excellent idea to begin your presentation planning with the Outline pane. Once the outline's in good shape, it's time to start thinking about the cosmetics—how your slides look. Power-Point's tools make it easy to adapt your design (or Microsoft's design) for all the slides simultaneously.

Warning: Choose Themes | Page Setup→Page Size and set the Size options *before* you design your slides. A radical change to these options later in the game may result in cut off graphics or unintended distortions, as though your slides were being projected through a fun-house mirror. PowerPoint's standard setting, On-screen Show (4:3), is the one most often used with a video projector. Your projector may also be able to use the widescreen options On-screen Show (16:9) is a proportion used by widescreen TVs. The On-screen Show (16:10) setup perfectly fits a MacBook screen. If possible, it's always best to test at least a slide or two with the equipment you'll use for the actual presentation.

Using Masters

In the same way that slide themes let you alter the look of your presentation in a flash, *slide masters* save time by letting you make changes that apply to the entire theme, or just certain layouts (Figure 19-7). *Background master items* appear on every slide, unless you specify otherwise (see page 551). When you add, delete, move, or replace a background master item, you see the change reflected in all of your slides that use it. For example, if you want to add a company logo to all your slides, just place it on the *slide master;* PowerPoint updates all the slides instantly. Other master items serve as placeholders for the title and bullet text. Changes you make to them on the slide master—the size and color of the font, or the appearance of the bullets, for example—are automatically reflected throughout the presentation.

Once you have a slide master, you can create slide layouts based on it. Layouts act as mini-masters, so you can have a wide collection of related looks for your slides. You can delete master items from layouts and add more text boxes or text and graphic placeholders that don't appear on the master slide.

In fact, PowerPoint has three types of master items: slides, handouts, and notes. Here's how they work:

Slide master

The *slide master*—or, as most people would call it, the master slide—is a special slide whose background, font size and style, bullet style, and footer (whatever appears at the bottom of every slide) determine the look of these elements on every slide it controls.

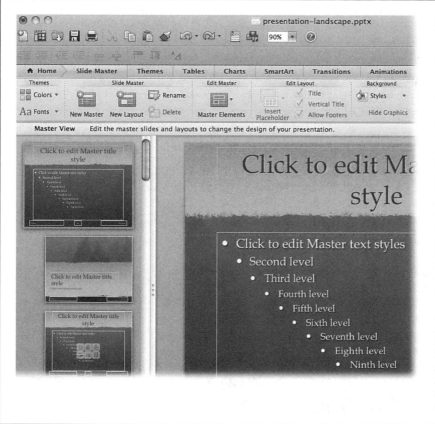

Figure 19-7:
*When you choose
Themes | Master
Views→Edit Master→
Slide Master, Pow-
erPoint reveals the
blueprints hidden be-
hind every one of the
theme's slide layouts.
PowerPoint shows the
slide master at the
top of the stack, and
each layout displayed
beneath. Click the
slide master, and any
changes you make
in the slide pane
cascade through all
the layouts. Make
changes on a layout,
and they apply only
to that one layout.
When you switch
to Master view,
PowerPoint displays
the Master ribbon: its
tools let you create
new masters, new
layouts, and insert
every possible kind of
content placeholder.*

Editing the slide master

To look at and change the slide master, choose Themes | Master Views→Edit
Master→Slide Master. PowerPoint displays the slide master at the top of the Outline
pane and—befitting its sovereignty—larger than the layouts below (see Figure 19-8).
The slide pane gives you a closer view of this monarch and its component master
items, each staking out their area with a pale outline.

- **Title Area**. This area usually contains some dummy text in the large title font—
  a placeholder for your real text.

- **Object Area**. The settings you make in this area determine how the body of
  your slides—text, charts, pictures, and media clips—will look and where they
  will sit.

- **Date Area, Footer Area, and Number Area**. These boxes at the bottom of the slide master show where the date and time, slide number, and miscellaneous footer text will appear on each slide. (These same boxes appear in the preview when you go to Themes | Page Setup→Slide Size→Header/Footer→Slide.)

Tip: In Themes | Master Views→Edit Master→Slide Master mode, the placeholder text (such as "Click to edit Master title style") is irrelevant. Don't bother editing it; doing so has no effect on your actual slides.

By changing the font size, style, color, and placement of these items, you can change how PowerPoint draws those elements on your slides. For example, if you want all of your slides' titles to be in 24-point Gill Sans Ultra Bold, just click once inside the placeholder text to select the box; then use the Formatting Palette to change the font to 24-point Gill Sans Ultra Bold. Now, any existing slides that have titles (and any *new* slides you make) will display the title in 24-point Gill Sans Ultra Bold.

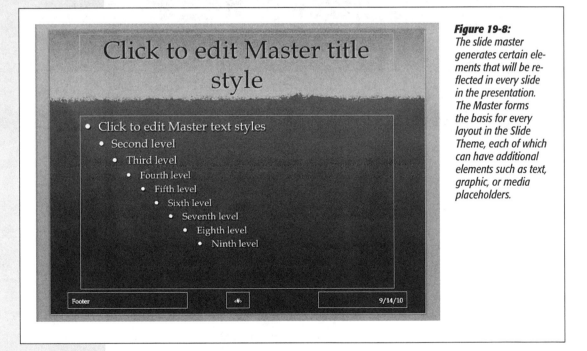

Figure 19-8:
The slide master generates certain elements that will be reflected in every slide in the presentation. The Master forms the basis for every layout in the Slide Theme, each of which can have additional elements such as text, graphic, or media placeholders.

Adding new elements to a slide master

The title, bulleted text items, and various footers revealed on your slide master can appear on every slide; all you have to do is fill them in. But if you need *additional* text to appear on each slide (such as your department or project name), you can create additional default text blocks on your slide master.

To do so, go to Slide Master→Insert Placeholder→Text. Click the slide master where you want the new text box to appear, type some dummy placeholder text, and then use the Formatting Palette to set its font, color, and style.

When you start creating slides, you won't base any new slides directly on the slide master. Instead, you create slides based on slide layouts—which are themselves based on the slide master.

Slide layouts

When you're in the Slide Master view, PowerPoint displays slide layouts beneath the master slide in the outline pane. Each slide layout is based on the master slide, though it doesn't necessarily contain all the master objects, and possibly contains other objects or placeholders not found in the master. You can think of the master slide as the blueprint for all the slide layouts, and a slide layout as the blueprint for the slide you create.

When you're in Normal view or Slide Sorter view, you'll choose layouts by going to Home | Slides→Change the layout. From the menu, you choose from all the available layouts. Click one of the layout thumbnails to apply it to the selected slide.

Modifying slide layouts

Choose Themes | Master Views→Edit Master→Slide Master and click any layout in the outline pane to display it in the slide pane. Here you can add, delete, resize, rotate, or reposition any of the slide elements. Any changes you make affect slides you've already created using that layout in the presentation—as well as those you make from now on. (Working with slide elements is discussed beginning on page 555.)

Handout master

A PowerPoint *handout* is a special page design that lets you place several slides on a single sheet for printing and distributing to your audience. Set up the design of your handouts by choosing Themes | Master Views→Edit Master→Handout Master, and then adding or editing the elements you want. (You can read more about handouts on page 595.)

Notes master

In PowerPoint terminology, a *note* is another form of handout—one that features a miniature slide at the top half of the page, and typed commentary at the bottom (see page 595). Once again, you can specify the basic design of your notes printouts by choosing Themes | Master Views→Edit Master→Notes Master, and then editing the design you find here (such as altering the font, resizing the notes field or slide image, or adding graphics). Predictably, those changes appear on every notes page in the presentation.

View Controls

Becoming familiar with PowerPoint's View controls, which are in the lower-left corner of the PowerPoint window (see Figure 19-2), will help you get the most out of the program. These three buttons let you switch among PowerPoint's three main view modes: Normal, Slide Sorter, and Slideshow. The View menu contains two additional view modes: Notes Page and Presenter Tools. Here's a rundown on them all:

- **Normal view** is the standard three-pane view, as shown in Figure 19-2. You control what you see using buttons at the top of the outline pane: Slides displays thumbnails of each of your slides, while Outline displays the outline text of your slides. The Slides mode makes it easy to find your way around your presentation visually, but the text in those slides is too small to read. Outline mode is great for presentations that contain a lot of text. This view shows all the text—the slide titles, subtitles, and each bullet point—but not an image of what the slide looks like. You can edit slide text directly in the outline, making it a great way to create slides and enter text quickly (see page 538).

Tip: In any multipane view, you can drag the boundaries between the panes to make individual panes larger or smaller. (A row of three dots in the center of these lines denotes a draggable boundary—but you don't have to put your cursor on the dots themselves.)

- **Slide Sorter view**. Back in the day, slideshow producers had to don white gloves to sort actual 35mm slides by hand and load them into projector trays. This process was impossible without a *light table* to lay the slides on, shuffle them around into different orders, and decide which ones to cut from the show and which ones to send to the lab for duplication. PowerPoint's Slide Sorter View is your virtual light table (Figure 19-9). Here you can reorder, delete, or duplicate your virtual slides; or designate slides for PowerPoint to skip during a presentation. Now you need white gloves only if you want to make a fashion statement.

  You can drag either a single slide or several at once; click the gray margin between slides and drag through several slides or Shift-click the first and last in a range. You can select more than one slide in any noncontiguous group by ⌘-clicking. When you drag slides to a new spot, a gap conveniently appears, showing you where the slides will go.

  Slide Sorter View makes a handy navigational aid. Double-clicking a slide in Slide Sorter view opens the slide in the Normal view.

Figure 19-9:
You can rearrange slides in the Slide Sorter view by dragging them, or delete slides by selecting and then pressing Delete (or choosing Edit→Delete Slide). You can also work with transitions (page 563) in Slide Sorter view; a small slide and arrow icon below a slide represents a transition. Click the icon to see a high-speed preview of the transition. Use the Zoom slider in the windows lower-right corner to vary the slide size.

- **Notes Page**. If you find the notes pane at the bottom of Normal view too confining, choose View→Notes Page to see the current slide and a large Notes field displayed on a single page—the very same page you can print as a handout. The Notes page derives its layout from the Notes master.

- **Presenter Tools**. If you choose this view, PowerPoint displays the presenter tools on your screen as it begins your slideshow. (Your audience sees just the current slide projected before them.) See page 584 for more on using Presenter Tools.

- **Slideshow**. When you choose this view, PowerPoint actually begins the slideshow. See page 582 for more detail.

Navigation

No matter which view you're using, moving among the slides in your show is easy. For example:

- **Normal view**. The outline is always on the left of the slide; all it takes to move to a slide is a click anywhere within or alongside its outline text. If, for example, you want to go to the fourth slide in the presentation, just click somewhere in the fourth outline text. PowerPoint displays that slide in the slide pane.

When you're looking at slide thumbnails when the outline pane is in Slides mode, you can use the scroll bar or the up and down arrow keys to move through the slides. (In Outline mode, those same keys move through each line of text).

- **Slide Sorter view**. In the Slide Sorter view, you can move from slide to slide by clicking the slide, or by using the arrow keys to move the selection rectangle around. If you double-click a slide, PowerPoint switches to Normal view.

- **Slideshow**. When you're in Slideshow view, each individual slide takes up the entire screen or window—no menus, no scroll bars, no controls. There are lots of key combinations that help you move around while in Slideshow view (see page 584). For example, you can use the right or down arrow key to move to the *next* slide in a slideshow, or the left or up arrow key to move to the *previous* slide. Press the Esc key to exit the show and return to the previous view.

Manipulating Your Slides

As you construct the show, new ideas will inevitably pop into your head. Topics you originally expected to fill only three bullet points on a single slide may expand to require several slides—or vice versa. Fortunately, it's no problem to adjust the slide sequence as you go.

Inserting new slides

Inserting a new slide into the lineup once you've created a few is easy. Just click any-place in the outline topic or the slide *before* the spot where you want the new slide to appear, and then choose Home | Slides→New Slide (Shift-⌘-N). PowerPoint inserts a new slide in the layout of the selected slide. You can also use the menu command Insert→New Slide.

Inserting slides from other presentations

You can reduce your work, reuse entire slides, and recycle great layouts from other presentation files simply by choosing Home | Slides→New Slide→Insert Slides From Other Presentation. The "Choose a File" dialog box appears; locate and single-click the PowerPoint file whose slides you want to import.

The Slide Finder window appears where you can choose individual slides to import, or if you want them all, click Insert All. As usual, a Shift-click selects slides in a se-quence and ⌘-click lets you select slides that aren't next to each other.

Tip: You can also import slides by opening both presentations and dragging thumbnails from one to the other.

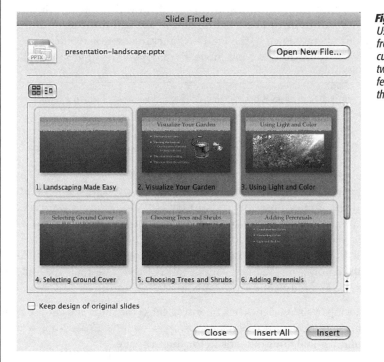

Figure 19-10:
Use this window to import slides from another presentation into your current project. Don't worry if the two presentations' themes are different, the imported slides take on the look of the current presentation.

Duplicating a slide

You can duplicate a slide—including its contents—so you can use it in another part of the presentation, or modify it to create a new version of the slide. Select a slide and choose Edit→Duplicate or press ⌘-D. You can also use the pop-up menu by right-clicking (Control-clicking) a slide and choosing Duplicate Slide. PowerPoint creates the duplicate slide just below the original. If you press the Option key while you drag one or more slides, the cursor sprouts the green-ball-with-plus-sign that indicates you're copying the item. Release the mouse button when the cursor is over your intended destination, and PowerPoint duplicates the selected slide or slides, and drops them into that spot.

Deleting a slide

In Normal or Slide Sorter view, click the slide and then press Delete, right-click (Control-click) a thumbnail and choose Delete Slide from the pop-up menu, or choose Edit→Delete Slide.

Moving slides around

The easiest ways to rearrange your slide sequence are by dragging thumbnails around in Slide Sorter view, dragging the slide thumbnails in the outline pane, or dragging the tiny slide icons up and down in the Outline pane. In addition, you can use the Cut, Copy, and Paste commands to copy, move, or remove slides or groups of slides.

Tip: The pasting trick in Slide Sorter view is to select the slide just *before* the spot where you want the pasted slides to appear.

Hiding slides

PowerPoint can skip slides you want to remove from the presentation without actually deleting them. You can use this trick to try out two different versions of a particular slide you're working on, or to modify presentation for certain audience. You can hide a slide or an entire section of the presentation for one audience and then turn it back on for another. For example, your travelogue on Amsterdam could feature the beautiful flower markets and your canal cruise for one audience—and its famous coffee shops and red-light district for another.

Select a slide or group of slides, right-click (Control-click) the slide, and choose Hide Slide from the pop-up menu. PowerPoint superimposes a little crossed-out symbol over the slide's number and dims the slide in the outline pane.

During a presentation, hidden slides appear dimmed in the Presenter Tools slide gallery. If you want to show a hidden slide, click it or press H when you're on the preceding slide.

Bring skipped slides back into the show by selecting them, right-clicking, and choosing Hide Slide again, which removes the checkmark from the menu command.

Tip: If you have to deliver similar presentations to two or more groups repeatedly, save yourself the trouble of remembering to reconfigure the presentation by creating a Custom Show (see page 585) or by just duplicating the entire PowerPoint file. Then either delete or skip slides to tailor the duplicate presentations to the specific audience.

How to Build a Slide

The outliner is an excellent tool for creating the text and the overall flow of your slideshow. But sooner or later, you'll want to work on the slides themselves—to add charts or other graphics, modify text that doesn't fit quite right—and perhaps edit your concluding slide when new data becomes available five minutes before your meeting.

Using Backgrounds

Creating a PowerPoint slide is much like creating a page in a page-layout program. In fact, it's very similar to creating a page in Word 2011's Publishing Layout View.

Starting off, PowerPoint lets you set a background color, gradient, pattern, or graphic for your slide or you can create a backdrop by adding shapes and importing graphics. Then on top of that background you'll add text boxes, pictures, tables, charts, and other graphics—and possibly movies and sounds. PowerPoint shares many of the techniques for creating and manipulating layout objects with Word, as discussed in Chapter 2.

Changing backgrounds

Every slide begins life with a backdrop, courtesy of its slide master. If you'd like to override or enhance that backdrop on a particular slide, however, choose Themes | Theme Options→Background, or right-click (Control-click) the slide and choose Format Background from the pop-up menu, to summon the Format Background dialog box (Figure 19-11). Click the Fill tab on the left and the Solid tab at the top to change the background color. Click the pop-up menu and choose any color variation from the palette of Theme Colors; one of the ten more-intense Standard Colors; or click More Colors to choose any color at all, via the Color Picker (page 616). You can tone down the background by using the Transparency slider.

PowerPoint adjusts the slide as you make your choices. The checkbox marked "Hide background objects" lets you hide any objects, such as background pictures or text, that may be present on the slide master. Click Apply to apply your changes to the background of the selected slide only, or "Apply to All" to change the backgrounds for all the slides in the presentation.

Warning: The Background dialog box has two buttons: *Apply* changes only the background of the current slide; *Apply to All* changes every slide in the presentation, even slides with customized backgrounds—use it with caution.

If you want something more elaborate than a solid background color, choose one of the Format Background dialog box's other three tabs: Gradient (a smoothly shifting color blend), Picture (a graphics file from your hard drive), Texture (a realistic image of some natural material, such as wood grain, marble, or burlap). See Chapter 21 for much more on these special tabs.

Tip: Be careful with this feature. Photos, textures, and gradients can make your text very difficult to read. Assuming you want your slides to be legible, make judicious use of the Transparency slider to reduce the opacity of these backgrounds.

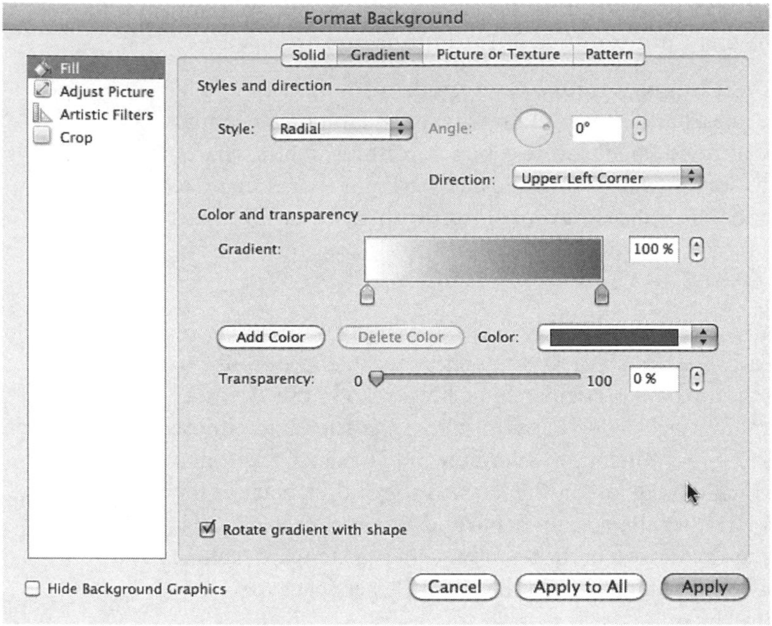

Figure 19-11:
The Format Background dialog box lets you add or change background colors or add gradients, pictures, or textures to the background. Working with the Transparency slider is essential—especially with pictures and textures—to ensure your text is still readable.

WORKAROUND WORKSHOP

Shutting Off Two Annoying PowerPoint Features

If, as you add text to a box, you notice that the words and paragraphs are shrinking, don't panic. PowerPoint is just trying to help, trying to make your text fit into the place-holder text box. PowerPoint makes the text spill over onto another line only if shrinking the font size and line spacing fails.

If you find this feature annoying, you can turn it off eas-ily enough: Just choose PowerPoint→Preferences, and, in the dialog box, click the AutoCorrect button. Click the Auto Format As You Type tab, turn off the option called "Autofit body text to placeholder," and then click OK.

Another feature that sometimes annoys: When you se-lect more than one word and end your selection halfway through a word, PowerPoint selects the rest of that word for you. (This feature may sound familiar—the same thing happens in Word.)

This quirk can be frustrating when all you want to do is get rid of an errant suffix. To turn this feature off, choose PowerPoint→Preferences→Edit tab and turn off "When selecting, automatically select entire word". Now you can select as much or as little of a word as you like.

Working with Text

There are two straightforward ways to add text to your slides. First, if your slide master includes text placeholders, as shown in Figure 19-8, you can click the individual placeholder text items (which typically read something like "Click to Add Text"), and then type in your own words. Because these placeholders are linked to the slide master, they reflect its font characteristics.

The other method is to add new text boxes (with no corresponding placeholders on the master) to a particular slide. Simply select Home | Insert→Text→Text Box (Figure 19-12), and then click the slide where you want to add text (the text box grows as you type). Alternatively, drag on the slide to create a text box of the desired size before you start typing.

Editing and formatting text

Adjusting the type characteristics of any kind of text box is easy—click the text you want to adjust. You've just activated the text box. Now you can select part or all of the text to change its font, size, or style, using the Formatting Palette or the Format menu.

Note: The outline only shows text inside placeholders (titles, subtitles, and bullet points), so it doesn't display text that you add using the Text Box tool. You can change the formatting of text in the outline, but the changes appear only on the slide—after all, an outline with 72-point bold text would look really odd.

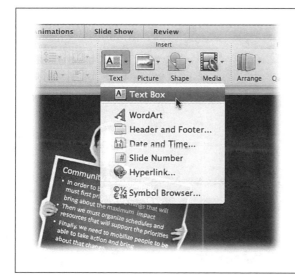

Figure 19-12:
Choose Home | Insert→Text→Text Box and drag to position a text box on your slide. Text boxes begin life only one line tall, but expand as you type more. Drag the box to reposition it, drag one of its handles to resize it, or drag its green stalk to rotate it.

To format text, click to select the text box and then use the tools on the Home or the special purple Format tab that appears when you select a text box. The Home tab provides the usual suspects: size, color, and style. The Format | Text Styles→Effects menu gives you some snazzy visual options including: Shadows, Reflections, and several 3D effects.

Formatting bullets

Traditionally, bullet-point lists play a huge role in business presentations. And just as being able to prescribe the silver bullet is an important CEO's skill, learning how to format bullets is a key PowerPoint skill.

To change the bullet style, click to put the insertion point in the text where you want the change to happen. Then right-click (Control-click) and choose Bullets and Numbering.

Other characters as bullets

You needn't be content with the mundane dot, box, or checkmark as your bullet symbol. Choose "Bullets and Numbering" from the Style pop-up menu of the "Bullets and Numbering" pane (or choose Format→"Bullets and Numbering") to call up the "Bullets and Numbering" section of the Format Text dialog box. Here you can choose from an assortment of other preset buttons or click the Custom Bullet pop-up menu to see others. Choose Character from that menu to reveal the Character Palette, from which you can choose any character—including all the optional symbols and dingbats—from any font on your Mac (see Figure 19-13).

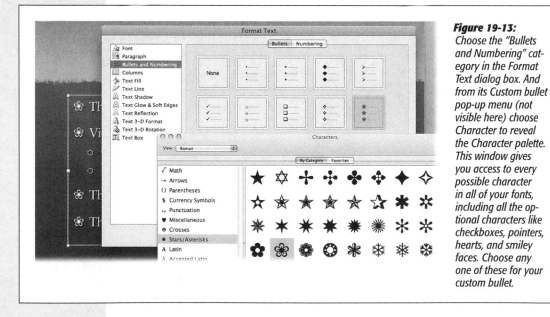

Figure 19-13:
Choose the "Bullets and Numbering" category in the Format Text dialog box. And from its Custom bullet pop-up menu (not visible here) choose Character to reveal the Character palette. This window gives you access to every possible character in all of your fonts, including all the optional characters like checkboxes, pointers, hearts, and smiley faces. Choose any one of these for your custom bullet.

Graphics as bullets

You can even use a little graphic as the bullet—a JPEG file showing a flag, a map, or your boss's head, for example.

To specify a graphics file on your hard drive that you want to use as a bullet, proceed like this:

1. **Click the text of the bullet that you want to modify.**

   The insertion point flashes next to the bullet point.

2. **Choose Format→"Bullets and Numbering"→Bullets and select Picture from the "Custom bullet" pop-up menu.**

   The Choose a Picture dialog box appears.

3. **Navigate to and double-click the graphic you want to use as a bullet.**

   PowerPoint replaces the bullet with your chosen picture at the same size as the text. To adjust the bullet size, enter a new percentage in the "Size: _% of text" box.

Adding Graphics, Charts, and Tables

Even if you're delivering the greatest news, a text-only presentation is a surefire way to put your audience to sleep. By inserting graphics, charts, tables, movies, and other objects into your presentations, PowerPoint lets you add visual information to spice up your slideshow. After all, you'll probably be speaking along with your presentation, so the slides need to reinforce your spoken message and display information you can't put into words. For example, you may want to insert a video clip of your company president explaining why this year's sales numbers are so much higher than the forecast. Or, you want to include pictures of your products when giving a marketing presentation, along with the all-important tables and graphs. Here's how to go about using these specialized objects:

Graphics

PowerPoint gives you lots of options for bringing graphics into your slides. The Toolbox's Scrapbook (View→Scrapbook) holds photos that you've placed there, while the Media Browser (View→Media Browser) holds photos, sounds, videos, symbols and shapes. Adding a graphic from either of these sources is simply a drag-and-drop operation. You can insert photos or other pictures, clip art from Office's Clip Art collection, charts, tables, AutoShapes, SmartArt graphics, movies, and sounds. For the most part, working with objects in PowerPoint is exactly the same as working with objects in Word's Publishing Layout View; Chapter 21 covers object manipulation in depth. The following sections detail what's different about objects in PowerPoint.

Tables

Not surprisingly, building tables in PowerPoint is very similar to making tables in Word. The easiest way to insert a table is with the Tables | New menu shown in Figure 19-14. The ribbon's Tables tab reveals a whopping array of preformatted table colors and styles, displayed as thumbnails. Select a table on your slide and then click one of the styles to apply the formatting. The styles take their cue from the presentation's theme. You can continue clicking your way through the Styles until you find the ideal match for your table.

You can begin typing in that cell, or use the tab key to move from cell to cell. If you continue to tab after reaching the lower-right cell, PowerPoint adds another row to the table. To adjust the table's size by drag the resize handles at each corner, and you can move it or rearrange its interior by dragging the table's borders.

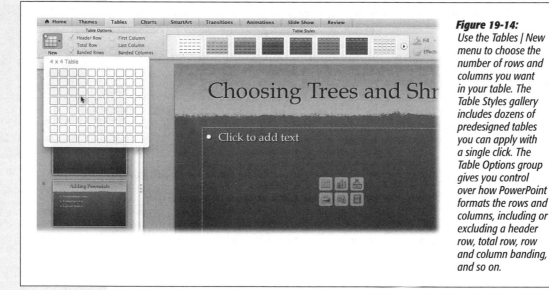

Figure 19-14:
Use the Tables | New menu to choose the number of rows and columns you want in your table. The Table Styles gallery includes dozens of predesigned tables you can apply with a single click. The Table Options group gives you control over how PowerPoint formats the rows and columns, including or excluding a header row, total row, row and column banding, and so on.

Tip: If you prefer to draw a table directly on the slide, you can use the techniques described on page 69.

All the tools you need to work with tables are found on the Tables and the Tables Layout tabs (Figure 19-15). These tools along with those found in the Table and "Borders and Shading" panes of the Formatting Palette cover the basics for making changes like these to your PowerPoint table.

- **Change border lines (Tables | Draw Borders).** To change a border's style, width, or color, use the menus.

- **Change text alignment (Table Layout | Alignment).** To change how text is aligned in a cell, select the cell (or cells); then click the Text Alignment buttons, which let you align text at the top, center, or bottom of the cell; as well as left, right, center, justified, or distributed horizontal alignment. Using the other buttons in this group, you can change the text direction to vertical.

- **Merge or split cells (Tables | Draw Borders).** By erasing the line between two cells using the Eraser tool, you can tear down the barrier between them, creating one larger cell. Use the pencil to draw a border, splitting a single cell in two.

- **Add or remove columns and rows.** Right-click (Control-click) a cell on the table to show the shortcut menu, where you can insert columns and rows as well as delete them. They also let you merge and split cells.

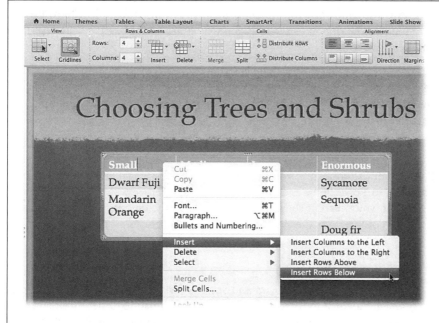

Figure 19-15:
The commands to work with tables live on the Tables and Table Layout tabs. You can also find helpful commands on the shortcut menu as shown here. Right-click (Control-click) a cell to display the shortcut menu.

Go to Tables | Table Styles→Effects to add preset shadows, glows, reflections, and 3-D effects to a table or individual cells. Select an entire table by clicking its frame—the insertion point disappears. The next formatting change you make applies to the whole table. If the insertion point is blinking in a table cell, the formatting change you make applies only to that cell.

For the last word in Table formatting, select a table, cell, or group of cells and choose Format→Table from the menu. This dialog box duplicates commands found in the purple Table Layout tab, but it also provides the only way to change cell fill colors, gradients, pictures, or textures (see page 613).

Charts

If your presentation is just crying out for a chart—and what presentation isn't?—click the Charts tab and choose any of the chart styles by clicking one of the thumbnails. Doing so launches Excel, and opens a spreadsheet containing a small amount of dummy information. Replace it with your own data and close the spreadsheet. Excel doesn't prompt you to save your spreadsheet, because PowerPoint *embeds* your chart and its data into the current slide. (Embedding puts the output of one program into a document belonging to another. In this case, Excel's output is appearing in a PowerPoint document.)

When you return to PowerPoint, you'll see your newly minted chart resting gracefully on your slide. Since it is, in fact, an Excel chart, you can double-click its various elements to change their appearance, size, or remove them all together. You can also change to a different chart type by clicking another thumbnail in the Charts | Insert Chart group on the ribbon—exactly as you would in Excel, and exactly as described starting on page 473.

If you need to change your chart's data, Control-click (or right-click) the chart and choose Edit Data from the pop-up menu—again launching the Excel spreadsheet containing your data. (The fact that you can edit it again in its parent program is the gift of an embedded object.)

You can also insert a graph that you've already created in Excel. Open the Excel document containing the chart and simply drag the chart from Excel onto the slide in PowerPoint. Alternatively, you can select the chart in Excel, choose Edit→Copy, switch back to PowerPoint and choose Edit→Paste. Either way, the chart ends up embedded in your current slide. If you later change the data in your Excel spreadsheet PowerPoint reflects the change in its copy of the graph.

Movies and Sounds

PowerPoint makes inserting movies and sounds just as easy as inserting still pictures, making it a cinch to insert a short movie of a climactic raffle drawing, a 360° view of your latest prototype, or a morale-building snippet from *30 Rock*. Via the Insert menu or the Media browser, PowerPoint can import movies and sounds, including recordings you make from your computer.

Drag a movie or audio clip from the Media Browser to drop it onto a slide. If your media doesn't show up in the browser, you can always go to Insert→Movie→"Movie from File" or Insert→Audio→"Audio from File" and then use the Finder to locate the file. When you inserts media into a PowerPoint slide, the clip includes the standard play controls like the ones shown in Figure 19-16. When the slide with the media appears in your presentation, you can start it playing with a single click. You can change this and other playback options on the Format Movie and Format Audio tabs. Some of the options for audio and movies are different.

Figure 19-16:
PowerPoint gives you a standard controls to Play, Pause and jump to a spot in your movie and audio files. Usually, a click makes your movie play, but you can change it to play when the mouse moves over the movie. Right-click (Control-click) and choose Action Settings to make changes.

Format Movie options

- **Format Movie | Start→On Click.** The standard setting.

- **Format Movie | Start→Automatically.** Saves you a mouse click when you're presenting. This option is also good when you're distributing a PowerPoint show—your audience may not realize they need to start the movie.

- **Format Movie | Playback Options→Play Full Screen.** Show your movie in its full glory.

- **Format Movie | Playback Options→Hide While Not Playing.** Hides your movie from view when it's not center stage

- **Format Movie | Playback Options→Loop Until Stopped.** A good option for short animations and movies.

- **Format Movie | Playback Options→Rewind After Playing.** Leaves your movie ready to go when the next time the slide is displayed.

Format Audio options

The Start options for audio clips include On Click and Automatically and they work just like the movie options. There's one additional option specific to audio:

- **Format Audio | Start→Play Across Slides.** Choose this option when you want the sound to continue even as you move on to the next slide. A nice choice for background music.

The Playback Options for audio files include Loop Until Stopped and Rewind After Playing which work as they do in movies. There's one additional option:

- **Format Audio | Playback Options→Hide Icon During Show.** Usually audio files display an icon to indicate there's an audio file embedded. Use this option to hide the icon.

Tip: In earlier versions of PowerPoint, movies and large audio files weren't stored inside of the Power-Point file because it creates files that were too huge for computers to handle gracefully. Today's computers are better able to handle large files, so movies and long audio clips are now copied and stored within your PowerPoint file, just like a photo.

Record your own audio

If you've got a mic connected to your computer, you can add your own recordings to your PowerPoint presentation. Go to Insert→Audio→Record Sound to open the window shown in Figure 19-17. On the ribbon, you can go to Slide Show | Presenters Tools→Record Slideshow. You'll find this most useful for recording narration—or voice-over as it's called. (See page 576 for more details on recording narration and the importance of using a good microphone.)

Tip: Before you record, you have to verify that your microphone or other sound input device is working. Go to →System Preferences→Sound→Input to see your mic options. Make sure that the correct device is selected, and adjust the input volume if necessary.

In the Record Sound window, click Record, speak or sing or squawk into your Mac's microphone, and then click Stop. You can play back the sound by clicking Play to make sure it's just what you want. If so, click Save. You'll find a little speaker icon on your PowerPoint slide; click it during a presentation to hear your recording.

Figure 19-17:
Choose Insert→Audio→Record Sound to open PowerPoint's built-in voice-over studio, where you can record narration, music, or any other sound to play back with the slide. The "Max record time" notation refers to the amount of space available on your entire hard drive.

Other Objects

The Insert→Object command is the first step to embedding several other kinds of visuals onto a PowerPoint slide. The objects can come from such other Office programs as Word, Excel, Microsoft Graph, or Microsoft Equation.

As shown in Figure 19-18, the resulting dialog box lets you either choose an existing document to install onto your slide, or create a new one. If you plan to insert an existing file into your slide, *first* choose the object type and then click "Create from file". The instant you turn on "Create from file," the standard Mac OS X Open File dialog box appears so that you can select the document you want. If you want to create a new file, PowerPoint conveniently starts the related program and opens a new document.

You need to make one more decision to successfully embed your object: you can choose to display the embedded file as a icon, like the one shown at the bottom of Figure 19-18, or you can display the actual contents of the file. In the case of charts, graphs and equations, you probably want to show the contents in your slide. However, when it comes to large Word documents or Excel Spreadsheets, you'll most likely want to show an icon. Then, you or anyone else watching your presentation, can open the file in the related program by clicking on the icon.

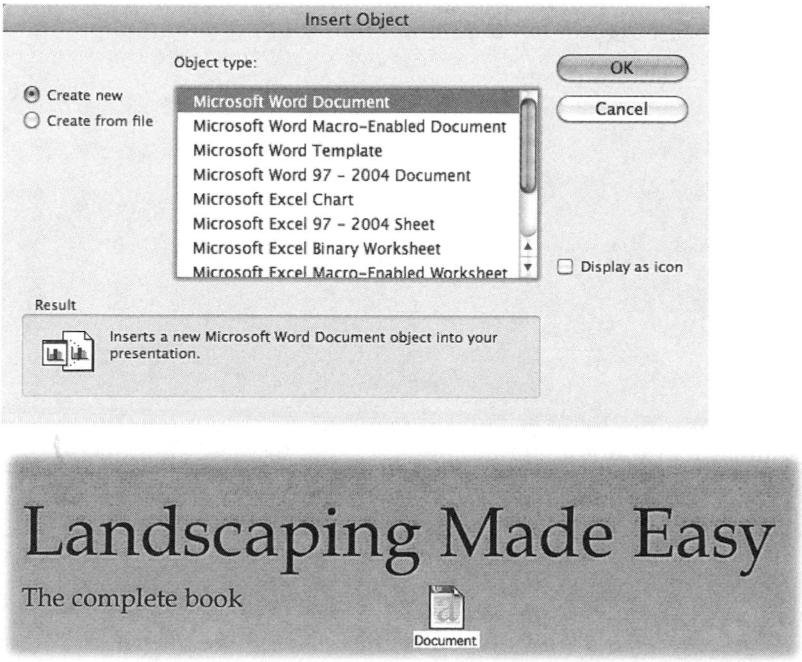

Figure 19-18:
Top: In the Insert Object dialog box, you can choose whether you want to bring in an existing document or create a new one on the spot. (If you click "Create from file", the "Choose a File" dialog box opens immediately, which is a bit disconcerting.)

Bottom: Turning on "Display as icon" plants a document icon on your slide instead of the document itself. Click it to open the document in the program that created it.

You may reasonably scratch your head at the prospect of placing an entire Word or Excel document onto a slide, especially if the document is larger than the slide itself. After scratching for a few moments, though, you'll probably realize that Microsoft has provided a dandy way to link supporting documents and reference materials to your PowerPoint presentation. When, during your pitch, some shortsighted co-worker objects, "I don't recall the marketing plan we talked about last month being quite so ambitious," you can click the Word document's icon that you've placed on the slide in anticipation of just such a protest—and smugly open the actual Word file, in Word, for all to see.

Note: Unfortunately, the "Display as icon" and, indeed, this whole object-embedding business, relies on a message technology called Object Linking and Embedding (abbreviated OLE and often pronounced "o-LAY"). As noted in the more complete discussion on "3-D Rotation" on page 237, Object Linking and Embedding has a reputation for behaving oddly. It works best when linking to very small documents on computers that have lots of memory.

Hyperlink

Insert→Hyperlink turns the selected text or graphic into a clickable link, capable of opening another PowerPoint file, any other Macintosh file, a specified web page on the Internet, or a preaddressed email message. You'll find a complete description of this feature on page 210.

CHAPTER 20

Putting On the Show

Building the outline and creating individual slides in PowerPoint are obviously necessary to produce a great presentation. But PowerPoint's real talent lies in its ability to pull those images together into a running slideshow. Although good taste sometimes suffers as a result, PowerPoint gives you the tools to enrich your slide presentations with transitions, builds, video, music, sound effects, and voice narration. You can then rehearse your PowerPoint shows to work out the split-second timing. You can even turn your masterpieces into printouts or a website for the benefit of those who missed the presentation, or save your slideshows as Quick-Time movies, then edit them again later (back in PowerPoint).

This chapter shows you how to harness these potent PowerPoint features.

Adding Movement

After you've created all your slides and put them in the proper order, the content part of your creation is done. Now it's time to add slide *transitions* to supply sophisticated smoothness—or gee-whiz glitz—as you move from slide to slide. You can also add *object builds*—animations within a slide. Besides adding some visual excitement to your slideshow, transitions and builds can help you present your information more clearly, add drama, signal changes in topic, and—if you use them wisely—give your slideshow a much more professional, polished appearance.

Transitions

If you don't add a transition, PowerPoint changes slides instantly—or *cuts*—from one slide to another. Besides the simple cut, PowerPoint has 64 other slide transition styles to choose from. They range from simple *dissolves* (where one slide melts into the next) and *wipes* (where one slide moves across the screen to replace the other) to striking pinwheels, checkerboards, and twirling 3-D cubes. You owe it to yourself to sample all the transitions once just so you know what's available. Even with all this variety, though, it's a good idea to rely on simple transitions and use the pyrotechnics sparingly. You don't want your audience to walk away impressed by your fancy transitions—and unable to remember your message.

Transitions serve two very different purposes in a slideshow: They can either create smooth segues from one slide to another, or they can provide a dramatic punctuation to highlight the break between slides. When you choose transitions, consider carefully whether you're trying to just move smoothly to the next slide, provide a noticeable break between topics, or startle the audience with your visual prowess. Always consider your message and your audience as you choose transitions. If your presentation is a pep booster for the cheerleading team, you almost can't have too much color and action. But if you own a funeral home and your presentation to the bereaved describes the various services you offer, stay away from the goofy pinwheel, checkerboard, or news flash transitions. Transitions are like fonts—you usually need only one or two styles in a single document. If you have any doubt about which transition to use, err on the side of simplicity.

Tip: When you add a transition to a slide, you're creating the transition *into* the current slide *from* the previous slide. You can't create a transition out of the last slide of a presentation. If you want to end with a transition—to fade to black, for example—you need to create a black slide for the ending of the show and transition *from* the last slide *to* the black slide.

Add a transition

Transitions, as the term implies, appear in the spaces between slides in a show. To add a transition in PowerPoint, you first need to specify the location by selecting the slide that *ends* the switcheroo. If, for example, you want to insert a transition between the fourth and fifth slides in a show, select slide five in one of the following ways:

- In Normal view, click in the outline heading or the slide thumbnail.
- In Slide Sorter view, click the slide thumbnail.
- In the Slide outline, click the slide thumbnail.

After selecting a slide, add a transition by choosing one from the Transitions tab on the ribbon (see Figure 20-1, top):

- Click the Transitions tab and click the transition you want to use.
- Choose Slide Show→Transitions and then click the transition you want to use.
- Control-click (or right-click) a slide in any view, and choose Transitions from the pop-up menu. Then click the transition you want to use.

When you add a transition to a slide, PowerPoint highlights the selected transition on the ribbon with an orange border and indicates its presence by placing a small transition icon beneath the lower-right corner of the slide thumbnail—in Slide Sorter view only (see Figure 20-1, top). In the Slides outline, you see a similar icon below the slide number. You can add transitions in Normal view, but you have to do so with blind faith. When doubts surface, switch to Slide Sorter view for reassurance.

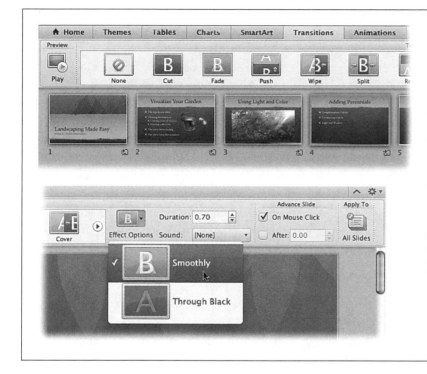

Figure 20-1:
Top: The Transitions tab is home to PowerPoint's salmagundi of transitions. When you click one to apply it to a slide, PowerPoint reminds you of what you've done by displaying a small icon at the lower-right corner of the slide in Slide Sorter view.

Bottom: At the right end of the Transitions tab you'll find setting to fine-tune your transitions. Here you can specify a sound effect, adjust the transition speed, and time the slide to advance automatically.

You can apply the same transition to several selected slides at once. Press ⌘ as you click an assortment of slides, or Shift-click to select a contiguous group of slides. You can even choose Edit→Select All to select all the slides in your presentation. Now when you click a transition, PowerPoint applies it to all those slides at once.

Tip: For the quickest way to apply the completely respectable "fade" transition to your entire presentation, do this: Click any slide in your presentation and then click the Fade transition (Transitions | Transition to this Slide→Fade). Then at the end of the ribbon, click the Apply to→All Slides button.

Choosing transition styles

Although your future audience members are crossing their collective fingers hoping that you'll end up using simple cuts and cross-fades over the course of your slide-show career, PowerPoint dangles before you a mouth-wateringly long list of special effects. When you click the Transitions tab, PowerPoint displays transition thumbnails. You can scroll through the list using the arrow buttons on either side of the list, or you can click the expand button at the bottom to see all the transitions grouped by category.

Along with the simple cut (essentially, no transition) and the zany Vortex, Power-Point gives you more transitions than you'll ever need. The best way to see how they work is to try them, but here's a description of a few:

Subtle

- **Cut**. The next slide in the show simply pops in place of the previous one. No frills, no fireworks. This is the most basic, and therefore the most useful, of all the transition types; it's also the "transition" you get if you don't specify *any* transition.
- **Fade**. The first slide fades away as the second one appears; what most people call a cross-fade or a dissolve.
- **Push**. The second slide pushes the first one away—from whichever direction you choose.
- **Wipe**. The incoming slide squeegees the previous slide off the screen as it comes into view. Like a talented window washer, you can wipe from any direction.
- **Split**. The first image splits into doors that open either horizontally or vertically to reveal the next slide. Or, doors showing the second image close in over the first image.
- **Random Bars**. Irregular horizontal or vertical slats appear across the image, quickly disintegrating and giving way to the next slide.
- **Uncover**. The existing slide moves offscreen to expose the next image lying behind it. Choose to uncover from any direction.
- **Cover**. The new slide scoots in from offscreen to cover the previous image with a framed, three-dimensional effect. The eight variations in this group match the directions from which the incoming slide can enter: top, bottom, left, right, and the four corners. This is the reverse of Uncover.

Exciting

- **Dissolve**. One slide fizzles out and morphs into another in a pixelated, fairy-dust fashion. Think of Captain Kirk beaming up and you've got the idea.
- **Checkerboard**. The first image breaks up into a pattern of adjacent squares, which turns into the next image as it sweeps across or down the screen.
- **Blinds**. The first slide closes like a set of Venetian blinds, either horizontally or vertically. As that image moves out, the next one emerges in its place.

- **Clock**. It's as if the hands of a clock wipe away the old slide as a new one comes into view.

- **Ripple**. Your new slide comes in as a blurry wave beginning in the center of the image.

- **Vortex**. Slides come and go as if they're being chased by a swarm of flies.

- **Flip**. Think of a chalkboard that pivots horizontally or vertically, and you'll know what this one does.

- **Cube**. The slide becomes the face of a 3-D cube, which rotates to reveal the upcoming slide.

Dynamic Content

- **Pan**. This looks as if the camera displaying your presentation rotates on its tripod to display a different image.

- **Ferris Wheel**. The old slide rotates out of view while the next one rotates in, as if they're connected by spokes somewhere outside of the picture.

- **Conveyor**. Imagine your slides on a conveyor belt moving horizontally across the screen.

- **Rotate**. A rotating cube effect.

- **Orbit**. One slide zooms out, away from the viewer while the next zooms in.

- **Fly Through**. A zoom-in effect where one slide disappears and the next appears behind it.

UP TO SPEED

Avoiding the Cheese Factor

PowerPoint makes it easy to load up your presentations with funky transitions, sounds, and other cheesy gimmicks. But with power comes responsibility. While you may be tempted to show off all the program's entertaining features in a single presentation, bear in mind that old design adage: Less is more. Please. It's usually best to keep your transitions and sounds simple (or absent) and your designs basic.

If PowerPoint contained only the cut and the fade you could live a full and happy presentation life—and so could your audience. With a simple transitions, you won't distract the audience from the important part of the presentation—your message—with a bunch of dazzling effects.

Customizing your transitions

Once you've chosen a transition effect, you can tinker with its settings to add variety or to make them conform to your presentation's overall style. Customizing transitions is also an effective way to set your slideshow apart from the efforts of other PowerPoint fans. PowerPoint displays different effect options for each transition under the Transitions | Transition to this Slide→Effect Options menu. For example, transitions with motion give you options that control the direction of the motion. Here are some of the options you'll find:

- **Smoothly** or **Through Black**. Transitions such as Cut, Fade and Dissolve give you the option to go directly from one image to the next (Smoothly) or to go from the first image to black and then to the next image.

- **From Right** or **From Left**. Transitions like Reveal and Uncover give you options to choose the direction of the motion: left, right, top or bottom. The options vary depending on the motion.

- **Horizontal** or **Vertical.** Transitions like Blinds can have a horizontal or vertical orientation.

- **Strips** or **Particles**. Choose a transition like Shred and you get a choice between strips, like those that come out of a paper shredder, or particles, more like the output from a tree shredder.

Other options, such as duration and sounds are available to all your transitions. The settings for these options are also found at the right end of the Transitions tab (Figure 20-1, bottom):

- **Duration**. Many effects, especially the more intricate ones, look more impressive at slower speeds, but be careful not to test the patience of your audience.

- **Sound**. In the gratuitous-bells-and-whistles department, nothing beats the Sound section. Using this pop-up menu, you can add a sound effect to your transition: applause, breaking glass, the ever-popular slide projector, or anything else you find in this lengthy pop-up menu. (You can also choose Other Sound to use a sound located elsewhere. PowerPoint recognizes sounds in many common file formats; search for "sound" in the online help to see the full list.)

Tip: You can add new sounds to the pop-up menu by dropping your own WAV (.wav) sound files into the Microsoft Office 2011→Office→Media→Sounds folder.

The occasional explosion or whoosh can bring comic relief, help you underscore a point, or draw special attention to an image. But for the sanity of those viewing your slideshow, go easy on the noise. Please resist applying sound to every transition, or the next sound you hear will be the silence of an empty auditorium. Avoid turning on the checkbox marked "Loop until next" which keeps the sound-effect snippet playing over, and over, and over, and over until you change the slide. Please.

Note: Don't confuse these sound effects with background music. For background sound, insert a sound object in a given slide using the Insert command, as described on page 558.

- **Advance slide**. Here's where you tell PowerPoint the method you want to use for advancing to the next image in your slideshow. You have two basic choices: advance when you click the mouse (or remote control, or arrow key, or space-bar), or advance automatically after a number of seconds that you specify (the preferred choice if you're designing a presentation to run unattended). You can also turn on both options, thereby instructing the program to change slides after a number of seconds *unless* you click the mouse first.

Multimedia Effects

PowerPoint pumps up your presentations with a Spielbergian selection of special effects. In addition to the transitions you insert between slides, the program lets you animate particular elements in an image. It also lets you add a soundtrack or voice narration to your slideshow—features that are especially useful if you want to save the presentation as a standalone presentation or movie.

Adding Animations

While slide transitions create animations *between* slides, *animations* (or builds) add animation *within* a slide. You can use animations to do things like make bullet points appear one by one; bring pictures, shapes, or other objects into the slide (singly, or in groups); or display a chart element by element. You can control animations with the mouse or spacebar during a presentation; or you can automate them, bringing in each object or element in a timed sequence.

You can choose from a variety of impressive animation styles that PowerPoint can apply when moving text or objects into a slide, or moving them out. As with transitions, discretion is advised when creating animations. It's nice to have all these options available, but not every slide needs its text to appear as if it's been shot from a machine gun or whirled in a Cuisinart.

Warning: You've been warned: Animations may not show up when you export your PowerPoint presentation as a QuickTime movie (as described on page 586), especially if you've also created transitions between slides.

Since every element of a PowerPoint slide—text boxes, pictures, shapes, and so on—is an *object*, you employ the same techniques to build *pictures* into or out of a slide as you do to build *shapes* into or out of a slide, for example. PowerPoint also gives you further building possibilities for text and charts—all of which are objects made up of many individual elements.

The basic procedure for creating animations on a slide is to select the objects on the slide—text boxes, pictures, shapes, and so on—one at a time, and use the Custom Animation pane in the toolbox to determine how and when each object appears on the slide, whether it does something special while it's on the slide, and then how and when each object disappears from the slide. The *Entrance Effect* (when objects appear on the slide), *Emphasis Effect* (what objects do for special emphasis while they're on the slide), and *Exit Effect* (when objects disappear from the slide) are completely separate operations. You can have any one, two, or all of them.

You can create dramatic animated effects by controlling the Entrance Effect, Emphasis Effect, and Exit Effect order, timing, and direction for various slide elements. Switch to Normal View and click the Animation tab on the ribbon to get started (see Figure 20-2, top). The other tool for controlling animations is the Custom Animation toolbox shown at the bottom of Figure 20-2.

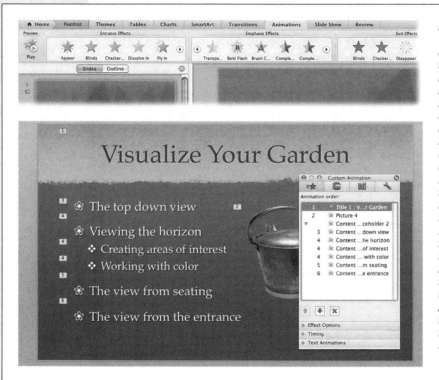

Figure 20-2:
The Animation tab is animation headquarters, your personal DreamWorks studio. Its panes and pop-up menus give you access to umpteen animation effects and options. To change the order of animations, click the Reorder button on the far right to open the custom animation toolbox shown here. Select an animation from the list and use the arrow buttons to move it up or down the list—or the X button to delete it. As you work, click the large Play button to preview the animation.

Note: You can only create animations in the Normal View—the only view that lets you click the various slide elements.

After you choose the text or graphic you want to give life to, click one of the effects in the ribbon. The effects are divided into three groups: Entrance Effects, Emphasis Effects, and Exit Effects. As usual, you can scroll through these panes on the ribbon or click the expand button at the bottom to see all the effects at once. If an effects group is dimmed out, that means those effects can't be applied to the selected object.

- **Entrance Effect**. Use this tab to select how the element makes its appearance on the slide.

- **Emphasis Effect**. This option lets you choose an effect that calls attention to an element that already appears on the slide. For example, Change Font Color changes the font to a contrasting color.

- **Exit Effect**. This tab lets you choose an effect to apply when an element disappears from the slide. Other than those options that don't apply to disappearing objects—and a few extra ones that do—the list is identical to the one in the Entrance tab.

Note: You can apply as many animations to an object as you like, so an element can appear in the Animation Order box more than once.

The Animation Effects window offers dozens of effects, ranging from the wild and wacky to the basic and restrained. A representative few from the restrained end of the spectrum include the following:

- **Appear**. In this, the simplest of all PowerPoint's animations, the selected item just pops into its predetermined spot on the slide.

- **Dissolve**. The selected object gradually materializes before your eyes, in a sparkly, pixelated way.

- **Fly In**. The selected object shoots in and comes to rest at its rightful spot in the layout.

- **Fly Out**. The selected object rockets off the slide.

- **Bold Flash**. The selected object simply flashes once in a silent, subliminal kind of way.

When you click one of the animations in the Animation Effects window, PowerPoint previews it for you on the slide. Want to see it again? Click the Play button on the left side of the ribbon. Continue adding effects until you strike the perfect balance between your playful yin and your business-like yang. In the Normal view, small numbers appear next to the elements that are animated. The numbers indicate the playing order. The Custom Animation toolbox also lists the animations showing the order in which they happen. To change the sequence, select an element and click the up or down arrow buttons beneath. You can also delete one or more animations by selecting them and clicking the X button.

At the far end of the Animation tab, other settings let you fine-tune the timing and behavior of your animations:

- **Start** lets you choose when the effect happens. The standard setting is *On Click*: the effect happens when you click your mouse or remote control. *With Previous* causes the effect to begin simultaneously with the effect directly above it in the list. If it's the first effect in the list, the effect happens as soon as the slide appears. *After Previous* triggers the effect automatically after the previous effect is finished.

- **Duration** lets you set how long an animated effect takes to complete.

- **Property** determines the main option for the animation itself, such as which side of the screen it starts from, or how much larger or smaller it makes the item. Many effects don't have an adjustable property.

- **Speed** lets you choose one of five durations for the effect, in tenths of a second up to 60 seconds. Only use the latter if you're inclined to torture your audience. One to two seconds is usually long enough for most effects.

Yet more animation options await in the lower panes of the Custom Animation toolbox:

- **Effect Options**. Use the Sound pop-up menu to choose a sound effect to accompany the animation effect or stop a previous sound playing from a previous effect. Select No Sound to maintain glorious silence.

  The "After animation" pop-up menu lets you turn the selected item a solid color when animation finishes, make it disappear from the slide after the animation (Hide After Animation), or disappear as soon as the next animation begins (Hide on Next Animation). The standard setting, Don't Dim, keeps it onscreen after the animation—in other words, does nothing.

- **Timing**. This section lets you set a Delay of so many seconds before the animation begins, and a Repeat for how many times the animation plays over again. Turning on the "Rewind when done playing" checkbox immediately returns the slide to its appearance just before the animation began playing.

- **Text Animations**. If you selected a text object, you'll see this pane appear in the Custom Animation toolbox. Use the "Animate text" pop-up menu to choose whether the text appears in the animation all at once, by the word, or by the letter. The "Group text" pop-up menu determines whether your lines of text appear as one object, or one line at a time (according to their level in the outline.) You can also determine whether the lines below a certain level in the outline appear as a group by choosing "2nd level," "3rd level," and so on.

  If the object you're animating is a shape with text inside (see page 605), turn on the "Animate attached shape" checkbox to make the shape and its text remain stuck to one another during the animation. Finally, if the text you're animating contains several lines, you can turn on the "In reverse order" checkbox to make the lines appear onscreen from last to first.

- **Chart Animations**. When you animate a chart object, this pane appears in the Custom Animation toolbox to give you control over how the chart appears on your slide. The "Group graphic" pop-up menu lets you choose whether the chart simply appears all at once (As one object), or by series or category, or by element in series or category. Turn on the checkbox at the bottom of the pane if you'd like the chart animation to begin with the appearance of the empty chart background.

Bullet by Bullet

I've seen smart, well-dressed, people do presentations where their bullet lists don't show up all at once. Instead, each point whooshes onto the screen on command. I've got my new suit—but how can I make my bullet points do that?

It's easy to animate the arrival of your bullets. Select the text box containing your bullets, and choose the Fly In effect from the Animation | Entrance Effects group. Open Custom Animation toolbox (View→Custom Animation). Make sure the animation is selected in the toolbox panel, then open the Effect Options pane and choose From Left in the Property menu. Then open the Timing pane, and choose Fast from the Speed menu. Leave the Start menu set to On Click if you want to control when your bullet points appear.

This is a great way to have them emphasize points as you speak. (For a more subtle effect, instead of Fly In, try Fade or Dissolve In.)

Click the Play button on the ribbon to preview the effect. Your bullet points fly in one at a time, each time you click the mouse (or press an advance key). If you instead want to automate their entrance, you can specify a certain number of seconds between bullet points in the Timing pane. And, in the Text Animation pane, you can choose the bullet level that you want to fly in together as a group—something that makes sense only if you've created bulleted lists within bulleted lists.

Putting Controls on Slides

If you need to jump to various parts of your slideshow during a presentation, or if you're creating self-paced learning modules that students run on their own computers, consider adding navigation buttons to the slides. When you require this kind of control, you can embed a host of useful command buttons—for advancing slides, jumping to the end of the show, and so on—right on the slide when you're preparing the show. You can place buttons on individual slides or many slides at once:

- If you want to add a button to just one slide, switch into Normal view (⌘-1) and bring up the slide in question.
- If you want to add a button to the same location in a group of slides—or all of them—place it on the slide master. Start by choosing Themes | Master View→ Edit Master→Slide Master. (See page 542 for a refresher on working with the slide master.)

Note: Don't try this shortcut if you'll be saving your presentation as a QuickTime movie. For QuickTime movies, you have to put the buttons on each slide individually.

Once the slide where you want to stick your button is displayed, go to Home | Insert→Shape and make a selection from the Action Buttons submenu as shown in Figure 20-3. The Action Buttons palette has 12 buttons. The four in the middle help you jump around during the show: Previous Slide, Next Slide, First Slide, and Last Slide.

To put an Action Button on your slide, click the button you want. Then drag diagonally on the slide. PowerPoint draws the button for you, and then opens up the Action Settings dialog box shown in Figure 20-3.

In this box, you can specify exactly what your newly created button will do. The proposed settings are fine for most purposes, so you can generally just click OK. It's worth noting, however, that you can use these controls to make your button do much fancier tricks, as described in Figure 20-3. (Normally, your action is triggered when you click the corresponding button. But if you click the Mouse Over tab in the Action Settings dialog box, you can also specify that something happens when you just point to it instead.)

Later, when the slideshow is running, press the A key to make the arrow cursor appear, and then click your newly created button to trigger the associated event.

Warning: Planning to save your show as a QuickTime movie? Watch out for action settings that don't work well with movies! For example, Microsoft recommends that you not use mouseovers, since they won't work. Also, don't set a button to run another program or to play a sound.

You can put any of eight other Action Buttons on your slides. Some come with preset icons and some have preset Action Settings that match their individual functions.

- **Custom** lets you customize your own action button (to launch a program, for example).
- **Home** zips back to the first slide in the show.
- **Help** lets you create a link to a help slide that you've designed.
- **Information** creates a link to an information slide that you've added.
- **Return** takes you back to the last slide you saw (which, if you've been jumping around, isn't necessarily the slide before this one in sequence).
- **Document** launches a Macintosh file or program that you specify.
- **Sound** triggers a sound, and its cousin **Movie** starts rolling a movie that you've set up beforehand.

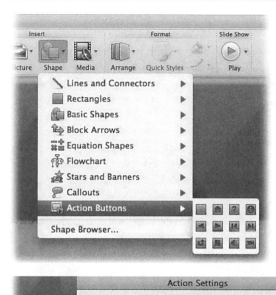

Figure 20-3:
Top: From Home | Insert→Action Buttons, click an action button to load your cursor with it. Drag to draw the shape of the button on your slide; when you release the mouse, PowerPoint presents you with the Action Settings dialog box.

Bottom: You can use the "Hyperlink to" pop-up menu to specify that a click of your button transports you to another slide, a website, or even another Macintosh file. Or you can check "Play sound" to create a button that, when clicked, plays the thunderous applause the occasional heartless audience may not provide.

If you want to change the *appearance* of an Action Button—or any other shape—right-click (Control-click) and choose Format Shape from the shortcut menu. To change a button's *action*, control-click (or right-click) it and choose Action Settings.

Tip: You don't have to use one of the predrawn shapes on the Action Buttons palette as your visible button—PowerPoint can turn *any* graphic object into a button. Just Control-click it and choose Action Settings from the shortcut menu, and then proceed as described in the preceding paragraphs.

Exit Gracefully

If you've given slideshow presentations with a slide projector, you probably used a solid cardboard "black slide" as the final slide in your tray. This opaque slide prevents a blindingly white screen appearing when you advance the final slide. In PowerPoint, the view of your desktop doesn't sear any retinas, but its appearance is at best unprofessional and at worst embarrassing. (Especially if you forgot to tuck away that *Geeks Gone Wild* folder before the presentation.)

To create a black slide at the end of your PowerPoint presentation, add a slide and choose the blank slide layout. Choose Format→Slide Background; turn on the checkbox at the bottom marked "Hide background objects"; in the Solid tab, change the Color pop-up menu to black; and then click Apply. Now choose ⌘-D to create a *second* black slide. From now on when you reach the end of your presentation the screen goes black—and stays black even if a nervous presenter gives the remote control an extra click.

The black slide is also the key to creating a fade-out transition at the end of your last slide. Select the black slide, add the Fade Smoothly transition to it, and set the Transition Options to Slow. While you're at it, you may as well put a black slide at the beginning of your presentation. That way, your audience won't see the first slide until you're really ready.

As an alternative to the black slide option, you may want to put a slide with something on it at the beginning or end of your presentation. After all, your audience may spend more time staring at the beginning and ending slides than any of the others. If you want them to remember your company, it's a great place to put your logo. If you want them to be drawn into your presentation, why not put an intriguing question on that first slide? It'll give them something to contemplate before you begin. If there's a single major point you want them to remember, try putting it at the end of your presentation. It may stay up through the entire question and answer period—not a bad way to burn it into their memory.

Adding Narration

If you're worried about laryngitis on the day of your presentation, if you're creating a self-running kiosk show, or if you have an unnatural fear of public *squeaking*, you might want to record voice narration for your slideshow ahead of time. This way, you can sit back and relax while your confident, disembodied voice (or the voice that you hired) plays along with the show.

To get your voice into the Macintosh, you'll need a microphone, of course. Some Macs have built-in microphones—but don't be tempted to use them to record narration. The quality is poor and they pick up a lot of noise from the operation of the computer. Mics very widely in quality and cost. For about $25, you can get a tie-clip microphone from Radio Shack, which delivers surprisingly good voice quality at a very low price. If you plan to do a lot of recording, you could step up to a desktop mic like the Blue Snowball (about $100) or the Audio Technica Studio Condenser

Microphone (about $150). If you already have a good quality mic, but it doesn't have a USB connector, you can get an adapter like the Shure X2U XLR to USB Signal Adapter (about $80).

When you've got your microphone hooked up, visit the Sound panel of System Preferences (⌘→System Preferences→Sound) to make sure that you've selected the correct microphone for input (Figure 20-4).

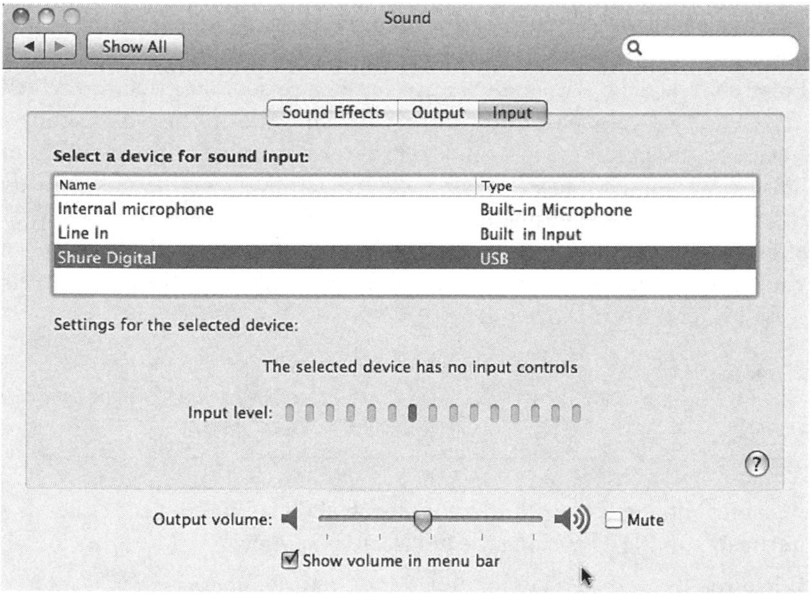

Figure 20-4:
The Sound preferences in your Mac's System Preferences help you to choose and adjust the microphones connected to your computer.

POWER USERS' CLINIC

Recording Narration the Careful Way

Although PowerPoint can record narration for the entire slideshow or a single slide, its recording abilities are pretty primitive—for example, you can't make any adjustments to the EQ, or mix in background music or sound.

You may already have the software you need to get the sound from the microphone onto your hard drive. Garage-Band can handle the task, as can the free, open-source, Audacity (*http://audacity.sourceforge.net*).

When you record, make a separate audio file for *each* slide that requires narration. Experiment with microphone placement and input levels, as well as with your delivery and pacing.

Listen to the playback through headphones or good external speakers—don't try to judge the sound quality using your laptop's built-in speakers. If you're not accustomed to recording narration, try to emulate your favorite radio or TV newscaster.

When you've got a good take, trim off any "dead air" at the beginning and end of the file before saving it—giving it a filename that includes the slide number. Then use the Insert→Audio→From File command to insert each narration into its respective slide (see page 558).

When you're ready to record, quit all other sound-recording programs, if any are running. Then, follow these steps:

1. **Choose Slide Show | Record Slide Show to bring up the Record Slide Show view.**

   This view shows a large image of the current slide and a smaller image for the next slide or step in an animation. A box shows the timing for the current slide and the entire slideshow.

2. **Record your narration.**

   Speak as you would to your audience and PowerPoint records your narration. PowerPoint attaches the audio you recorded as a sound object on each slide. Try to keep up your pace and your enthusiasm. And try to avoid getting distracted because there's no easy way to re-record just one flubbed slide; for most purposes, it's simplest to start a new take. To start over, end the slideshow using whatever method you normally use (press Esc, for instance). Then, choose Slide Show | Record Narration and begin again. (And if you're *really* having trouble, you can always record individual sound files for each slide, then attach them as described in the box above.)

Note: These voice clips override any other sound effects in the slideshow, so if you're using a recorded narration, any embedded sound effects (including transition sounds) won't play.

---

3. **Record whatever you want to say for each slide, advancing the slides as you normally would (by clicking the mouse, for example).**

   When you reach the end of the slideshow, PowerPoint asks if you want to save the timings (to record the amount of time you spent on each slide) along with your narration. If you click No, PowerPoint saves only the narration. If you click Yes, PowerPoint saves the timings along with the narration, overwriting any existing timings.

   If you choose not to include the timings, each sound will play when you manually advance to a given slide. This way, you can let the narration play, and then discuss each slide, moving on only when you're ready.

Note: Voice recordings can eat up a lot of disk space, so be sure you have enough room on your hard drive to hold the sound. If not, consider saving your voice files to an external hard drive or some other industrial-strength storage area.

Once you're done recording your narration, you've got a self-contained slideshow, suitable for parties or board meetings.

Adding a soundtrack

Instead of adding sound to each slide, you may want to add a soundtrack to an entire slideshow. For example, you may want background music or sound, which doesn't need to be synchronized with the slides, playing through the entire slideshow. On the other hand, you could also use a single soundtrack for an unattended kiosk-type presentation where you've set each slide to advance automatically.

If you want your sound track to start at the beginning of your presentation, make sure you're on the first slide. Then, use the Home Insert→Media→Audio from File command and choose the sound file. PowerPoint places the speaker icon on the current slide. To set up the options for this sound, select the speaker icon on the slide (Normal view) and then click the Format Audio tab on the ribbon. Under Audio Options, choose whether you want it to start Automatically or When Clicked. If you want the sound to play while you advance from slide to slide, choose Play Across Slides. If your soundtrack is shorter than your show, you can loop it so it plays continuously. Under Playback Options, choose Loop Until Stopped.

When you add a soundtrack in this fashion, it plays right along with any other sounds, narration, or sound effects you've attached to your slides or transitions.

Putting On the Show

Now that you've built your individual slides, folded in your transitions, and sprinkled it lightly with animations and sounds, it's time to bake it at 350° for 45 minutes while you run through your final checklist and get dressed.

Setting Up

Before you slick your hair and stride onto the stage, the first preparatory step is to choose Slide Show | Set up→Set Up Show. In the dialog box that appears (see Figure 20-5), you can choose the *type* of presentation you want it to be—a typical full-screen slideshow, a small show for an individual reader to browse, or a self-running kiosk-style show that keeps playing until you (or the police) shut it off.

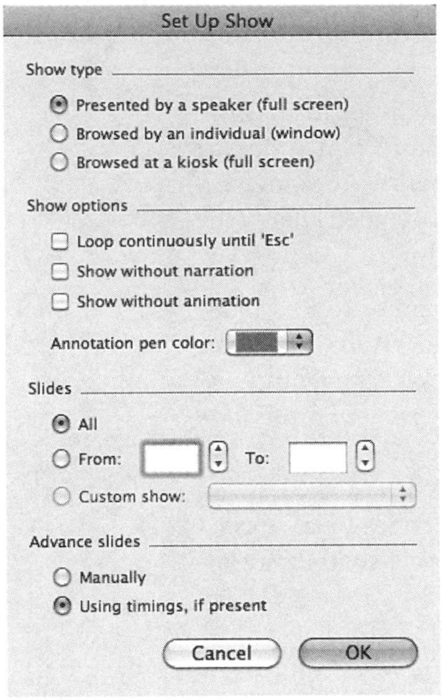

Figure 20-5:
The Set Up Show dialog box lets you select the type of show and show options, and choose which slides to use and how you want them to be advanced: manually, with a mouse click; or automatically, using preset timings.

Rehearsing Your Presentation

As P-Day (Presentation Day) draws near, you can use PowerPoint's *rehearsal mode* to run through the slideshow and work out the timing. It can be very helpful to know how long it takes to show each slide, especially if you have a tight presentation schedule. This handy feature even lets you factor in sufficient time for the laughter to subside after your well-rehearsed "off the cuff" jokes.

To begin the rehearsal, choose Slide Show | Presenter Tools→Rehearse Timings. You see the same view that's displayed when you record narration. A timer appears, ticking off the number of seconds the slide is spending onscreen. Each time you advance to a new slide, the timer resets itself to zero and begins the count anew for *that* slide.

When you've gone through the whole show, PowerPoint asks if you want it to record those timings for use later in an automated show. If you answer yes, PowerPoint logs the timings and then asks if you want it to note those timings in Slide Sorter view, as shown in Figure 20-6. You may as well do this; it's pretty handy to see those time allotments, even if you decide to ignore them and advance the slides manually.

Figure 20-6:
After you've completed your timing run, PowerPoint marks the slide duration beneath each slide in Slide Sorter view. The duration of transitions isn't factored into the timing of each slide, so if you've chosen some of the slower transitions, take their length into account when calculating the timing of your show. If you click the icon beneath the slide, PowerPoint displays the transition in the thumbnail at high speed; click the build icon beneath the slide to watch the build at closer to real time.

Choosing a Navigation Scheme

If you choose PowerPoint→Preferences→View tab, you'll find some useful preference settings that affect the appearance of the show you're about to give. In the Slide Show area, for example, you'll find a pop-up menu with these choices:

- **Pop-up menu button**. Turning on this option means that when you twitch the mouse during your slideshow, PowerPoint will make a subtle toolbar appear in the lower-left corner. Clicking it gives you the same pop-up menu of useful controls (Next, Previous, End Show, and so on) that you usually get only by right-clicking (Control-clicking) the screen (Figure 20-7).

- **[No Slide Show Controls]**. If you choose this option, your slides remain unsullied by any toolbar, no matter how twitchy your mouse hand is.

Note: The Preferences→View tab also has an "End with black slide" checkbox—however the black slide it creates isn't completely black. It creates a black slide emblazoned with the words "End of slideshow, click to exit." What part of *black slide* doesn't Microsoft understand? Take the time to create a real black slide as described in the box on page 576.

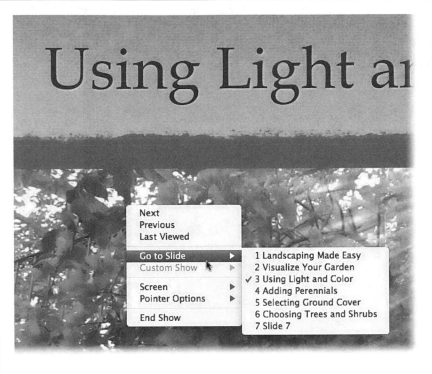

Figure 20-7:
To view the contextual menu in a slideshow, either Control-click a slide or click the pop-up menu button in the lower-left corner of the screen (if you've turned it on in the PowerPoint→Preferences→ View tab). The resulting menu (shown here) gives you a lot of power. For example, you can choose Pen from the Pointer Options submenu and then scribble circles, arrows, underlines, and other real-time doodles on your slides during the presentation. (You can later erase your additions by choosing Screen→Erase Pen from the contextual menu, or just move to the next slide—Power-Point doesn't save your scribbles.)

Presenting Onscreen

Your formal wear is clean and pressed. Now the moment has come—it's time to run your show. Any one of the following options starts the slideshow:

- Click the Slide Show view button in the lower-left corner of the main window. (It looks like an old-time home movie screen—the rightmost button.) The slideshow starts with the selected slide.

- Choose Slide Show | Play Slideshow→From Current Slide (⌘-Return). The slideshow starts playing from the selected slide.

- Choose Slide Show | Play Slideshow→From Start (Shift-⌘-Return). The slideshow starts with the first slide.

What happens next depends on your computer setup. If you have only one monitor, PowerPoint fills the screen with your first slide (or, if you clicked the Slide Show view button, with the slide that was previously selected). Unless you've chosen to use pre-set timings, the first slide stays on the screen until you manually switch to the next one (by clicking the mouse or pressing the space bar, for example).

If you have two screens, the slide only appears on the secondary monitor. The main display—typically your laptop's screen—turns into a command center called Presenter View (see page 584).

PowerPoint gives you several ways to move around inside a full-screen show. A simple mouse click or a press of the space bar moves you to the next slide, as does pressing the down arrow or right arrow key. (One exception: If you've set up an animation on a slide, these advance keys trigger the animation instead of summoning the next slide.)

After you've reached the end of the show, PowerPoint returns you to its previous view.

Note: If you rehearsed your slideshow and chose to save your timings, the show will play automatically to the end, displaying each slide for the predetermined number of seconds.

While your slideshow is running, you can right-click (Control-click) anywhere on the screen to bring up a contextual menu that gives you such self-explanatory navigation options as Next, Previous, and End Show (see Figure 20-7). It also gives you some less obvious options worth pointing out:

- **Black Screen** blacks out the screen during a discussion.
- **Pointer Options**, as you might imagine, let you pick the kind of onscreen cursor you want to use—Automatic, Hidden, Arrow, or Pen. (Automatic gives PowerPoint the authority to choose a pointer for you; Hidden makes the pointer go away; Arrow is the standard Mac arrow-shaped pointer; and Pen turns the pointer into a writing tool.)
- Finally, the **Screen** submenu's commands let you pause a running slideshow that's otherwise on autopilot, or erase any graffiti that you made with the aforementioned pen tool.

Controlling the Show

The following table gives you the rundown on helpful keystrokes you can use while the slideshow is running.

Table 20-1. Keystrokes for navigating slideshows

What to do	How to do it
Next slide (or start an animation)	Mouse click, space bar, Return, N, Enter, right arrow, down arrow, page down
Previous slide or animation	Left arrow, up arrow, page up, P, Delete
Jump to a certain slide number	Enter the slide number and then press Return
Jump to the first slide/last slide	Home, End (On a MacBook, FN-left arrow and FN-right arrow)
To/from a black screen	B, period
To/from a white screen	W, comma
Erase drawing onscreen	E
Show or hide arrow pointer	A, =
Change pointer to pen	⌘-P
Change pointer to arrow	⌘-A
Stop/restart a self-running slideshow	S, +
End the slideshow	Esc, ⌘-. (period), - (hyphen)
Go to the next hidden slide	H

Tip: A presenter's nightmare is to have everyone gathered in a room, but something's gone wrong. The last projector bulb blew. The power went out. The PowerPoint file is corrupt. It doesn't happen often, but the cautious presenter always has a plan B for presenting without a projected image. Printed handouts with page numbers are a good start. See page 595.

Using Presenter View

If you've ever had to rush through a presentation because you lost track of time or forgot what was coming up on the next slide, PowerPoint's Presenter View is a blessing. It looks very much like the view you use to record narration or rehearse timings. While the video projector or other external monitor shows a full-screen presentation, this feature displays the current slide, notes, and upcoming slides (Figure 20-8). A clock shows the time or counts the elapsed time since the beginning of the slideshow, so it's easy to pace yourself. Best of all, you don't even have to do anything extra to use Presenter View. If your computer supports non-mirrored video and you have a second monitor connected, this feature starts up automatically when you begin the slideshow.

All the shortcuts that work in full-screen mode also work in Presenter View. For example, you can advance to the next slide by pressing Return or space bar. Or if you prefer, you can also navigate by clicking the green arrows at the top of the screen.

Tip: To practice using Presenter View on a single monitor, Choose Slide Show | Presenter Tools→
Presenter View.

The Presenter View notes pane would be handy even if it only let you read your notes during a slideshow—after all, you can't be expected to remember *everything* when you're at the podium. But Presenter View goes a step further by letting you *edit* the notes during your presentation, too. It's the ideal way to keep track of which jokes work and which slides make your audience wince in pain.

Tip: If you move your mouse off the Presenter View screen onto the slideshow screen, you can Control-click to bring up the shortcut menu that includes the pen tool and other options.

Recycling Your Presentations

PowerPoint lets you create multiple *custom shows* in a single document. This feature comes in handy if, for example, you want to have both long and abbreviated versions of the same show, or if you want to tailor some material you've used before to a different audience.

Suppose you're going to address two different groups on the topic of deer. You have lots of engaging slides on the topic. But there's a good chance the Bambi Fan Club won't sit through the show you've got planned for Hunters Anonymous. You can solve this moral dilemma by creating a *customized* show for each group, each of whose slides are a subset of the complete deer presentation.

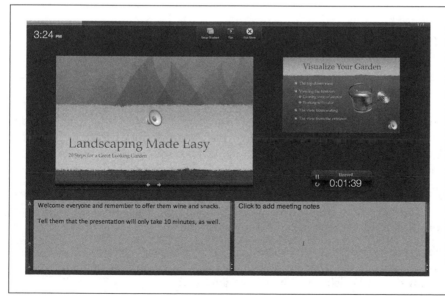

Figure 20-8:
Presenter View shows you exactly what the audience sees, in the largest pane. The smaller pane shows you the next slide or animation that's coming up. The notes pane at the bottom shows the reminder notes you made on the left. Use the space on the right to take notes as you give your presentation. You can pause and reset the Elapsed Time clock.

To build such a custom show, choose Slide Show | Custom Shows. The resulting dialog box gives you four choices: New, Edit, Remove, and Copy (Figure 20-9). When you click New, a dialog box pops up that lets you choose the slides you want to include in the custom show. You can also reorder the slides in your custom show and give your custom show a name.

Then, when it's time to give the actual presentation, choose Slide Shows | Play Slide Show→Custom Shows to bring up a window that lists the custom shows you've built. Click the one you want to present and then click Show; your custom show begins.

Saving Presentations as QuickTime Movies

PowerPoint 2011 retains previous versions' ability to save presentations as QuickTime movies. This is a nifty idea since anyone with QuickTime installed—Mac or Windows fans—can play these movies even if they don't have PowerPoint. This is a great way for your associates and underlings to give the same kinds of pitches you give without having to spring for a copy of Office—but proceed with caution.

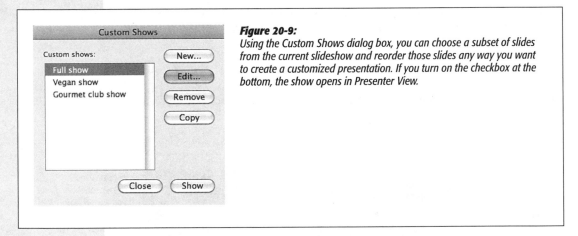

Figure 20-9:
Using the Custom Shows dialog box, you can choose a subset of slides from the current slideshow and reorder those slides any way you want to create a customized presentation. If you turn on the checkbox at the bottom, the show opens in Presenter View.

Remember that not every bell and whistle of a PowerPoint slideshow survives the conversion into a QuickTime movie. As noted here and there throughout this chapter, things like action buttons on master slides, many PowerPoint transitions, and certain actions (mouseovers, certain kinds of links, sound, and so on) won't work at all.

To turn an open PowerPoint presentation into a QuickTime movie, choose File→"Save as Movie". This brings up a Save dialog box, which you can use to name your movie file and choose a folder location for it.

Before you save your movie, PowerPoint gives you a chance to fine-tune some of its settings. To begin, click the Movie Options button. PowerPoint responds by opening the Movie Options dialog box shown in Figure 20-10.

The most important settings worth examining here are Movie Dimensions and the Optimization pop-up menu. The latter lets you specify which you value more: compact file size, smooth playback of animations, or picture quality. Depending on the complexity of your file and the screen size you've specified, these virtues may be mutually exclusive. If you want the highest quality animations, for example, the file won't be very small on your hard drive, and the quality of animated photos may suffer.

Tip: After you've saved your slideshow as a QuickTime movie, you may notice your transitions acting flaky. Because the PowerPoint Movie format doesn't actually support PowerPoint transitions, they get translated to a QuickTime equivalent that may be very different from what you intended. For the best results, use simple transitions like Fade Smoothly, or don't use any transitions at all.

The movie Options dialog box also lets you import a sound file to use as a soundtrack. Depending on your presentation, if chosen tastefully, music or some other nondistracting background sound (rainfall or ocean waves, perhaps) can make your movie a more well-rounded presentation. Tread carefully, though, to avoid crossing that fine line between "nondistracting" and "sleep-inducing." These background sound files can be in any number of formats, including AIFF, QuickTime audio, WAV, and MP3.

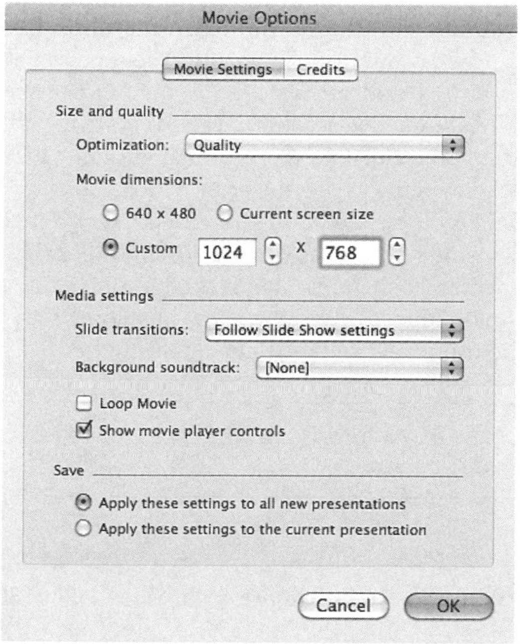

Figure 20-10:
This dialog box lets you specify the size of the QuickTime movie; 640 x 480 creates a tiny window on today's larger screens—1,024 × 768 is a good minimum size. Using the "Background soundtrack" pop-up menu, you can choose an MP3 file or another file to play during the whole slideshow—a handy option in self-running, kiosk situations. Notice the radio buttons in the Save area that let you select whether PowerPoint should use your new settings for just this presentation, or use them for future presentations you save as QuickTime movies as well.

Mac Presentations on Windows PCs

If you're really in demand as a speaker, you'll eventually have to bite the bullet and show a Mac PowerPoint presentation on a Windows computer. Although the QuickTime movie format offers one workaround, it's usually better if you can use the Windows version of PowerPoint 2011 to run your slideshow. When you're preparing your presentation, use fonts that you know will be installed on the Windows PC. If you stick with the fonts found in Themes | Theme Options→Fonts, you'll be in good shape. Import

graphics in cross-platform formats like JPEG and GIF, and convert movies to AVI format using Apple's QuickTime Pro program.

Finally, if you can, do a dry run on a PC (best-case scenario, the actual computer that you'll be using for your presentation) just to outfox any last-minute glitches. Copy your slideshow, along with movies and other linked files, to the PC's desktop and double-click the presentation file.

To add a background soundtrack, choose Select Soundtrack in the Background soundtrack pop-up menu. PowerPoint asks you to locate the sound file that you want to use, which it then attaches to your presentation when you click OK. PowerPoint will mix the soundtrack sound with any embedded sounds, including voice narration.

Broadcasting Presentations on the Web

Suppose the audience for your presentation is flung far and wide. Rather than having everyone burn jet-fuel to meet at a Holiday Inn, you can broadcast your presentation over the Internet. Here's how it works: To broadcast, you upload your pages to a server you can access through a free Windows Live account (page 740). Then, you invite your audience via instant messages or email messages containing a link to your presentation. From your computer, you start playing the presentation and everyone else views it from the comfort of their offices, bedrooms, or beach chairs. You're in control of the presentation, so they only see slides as you click to show them. As for sound, your only option is to synchronize the presentation with a conference call. (The broadcast doesn't play recorded sound, there's no way for you to broadcast live narration, though you can bet Microsoft will add this feature in the future.)

Note: Once you've ended the slideshow, it disappears into the Internet ether. There are no permanent pages that attendees can visit after you've ended the show.

To broadcast:

1. **Open your show in PowerPoint, and then choose Slide Show | Play Slide Show→Broadcast Slide Show.**

   A box appears, explaining that you need a Windows Live ID to use the service. You already have one if you use Hotmail, Messenger or have an Xbox Live account. If you don't already have an ID, you can get one at *http://home.live.com*.

2. **Once the ID issues are settled, click Connect.**

PowerPoint uploads your presentation to the Broadcast service. When it's done, you see the window shown in Figure 20-11, which gives you a couple of options for sending invitations.

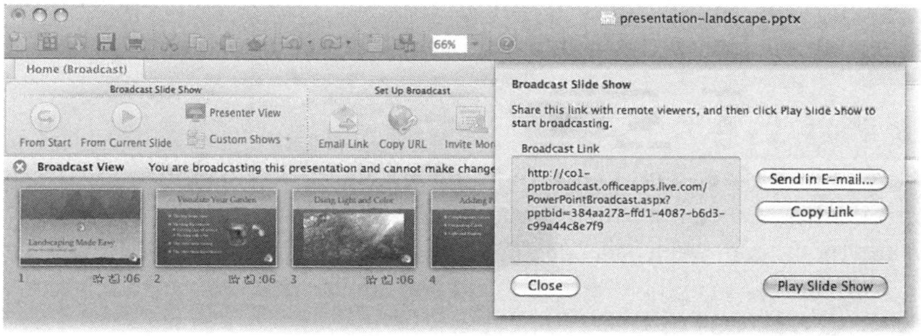

Figure 20-11:
If your audience is scattered across the globe, you can reach them with a real-time PowerPoint broadcast via Microsoft's Live.com service. All they need to view your presentation in their web browser is a web link that you provide via instant message or email after you've uploaded the presentation.

3. **Click Copy Link and paste it into an Instant Message invitation or click Send in Email.**

The instant message option works great as long as you can reach your whole audience. You can easily copy that link into an email, or if you click the Send in Email option, PowerPoint starts up your favorite email program and starts the message for you.

4. **Click Play Slide Show when you're ready to begin.**

Your slideshow appears on your computer, and everyone who's attending via web sees the same images. They won't see the shortcut menus or some of the other presenter's details, but they'll see what they'd see if they sat in an audience. You can choose to view the slideshow in Presenter view if you want to refer to your notes or the clock. In fact, if you need to fire up a different program on your computer, your audience will never know. They'll continue to see the slides.

5. **At the end of the show, click End Broadcast.**

This click ends the broadcast and your audience is returned to Facebook, You-Tube, or whatever they were doing before. The presentation is no longer available via the web link. Anyone who tries to visit the link sees a message that explains, "There is no broadcast at this location."

Saving Slides as Graphics

Among its many other gifts, PowerPoint lets you save individual slides—text and all—as graphics files. This can be a handy little feature whenever you want to make sharp-looking, high-resolution images of your presentation to pass along to your friends, your students, or your mom. When PowerPoint saves slides as graphics, you'll end up with an individual file for each slide. (As you undoubtedly surmise, transitions, animations, and sounds are all lost in translation.)

Send to iPhoto

The easiest way to save your slides as high-quality graphics is to send them to iPhoto. Once in iPhoto, you can use them in an iPhoto slideshow that you could put on a DVD, add them to an iWeb page, or import them to iMovie. Best of all, if you have a video iPod, you can load the slides on it and always have your presentation with you (see the box on page 592):

1. **Select the slides you want to export to iPhoto.**

   You can select one or more slides if you want to send just a portion of your slide-show to iPhoto. PowerPoint doesn't care what slides you select if you're going to send the entire slideshow.

2. **Choose File→Share→Send to iPhoto.**

   The "Send to iPhoto" dialog box appears; iPhoto is about to create a new album for your slides. Give the folder a different name if you don't want it to have the same name as your PowerPoint file.

3. **Click the Format pop-up menu to choose either JPEG or PNG format—your only choices.**

   Both can create visually identical, high-quality images—but JPEG is a more universal format and probably the better choice. This menu controls the format but not the quality.

4. **Choose to send all of the slides or just the selected group.**

   Click All to send the entire slideshow, no matter what slide or slides you've selected.

5. **Click "Send to iPhoto".**

   PowerPoint launches iPhoto, which then creates a new album and imports the slides. When it's done, iPhoto pops to the foreground to show off its newly created album.

Tip: Enable Disk mode on your iPod (in your iPod's Summary tab in iTunes) to make your iPod function like an external hard drive. Then drag your actual PowerPoint file to your iPod to copy it. Now you can plug your iPod into a Mac or Windows PC, launch PowerPoint, choose File→Open, and locate the file on your iPod. This way you can run the full PowerPoint slideshow with all its bells, whistles, animations, transitions, and so on—but without lugging around your own computer. (You can do the same thing, of course, with a USB flash drive, and the usual considerations with XML file format still apply.)

Save as Pictures

If you don't go the iPhoto route, PowerPoint is willing to save its slides in a wider variety of file types. To do so, first select the slide you want to convert, and then follow these few steps:

1. **Choose File→Save as Pictures (or File→Save As—which leads to the same dialog box).**

   A dialog box appears, offering several options.

2. **From the Format pop-up menu, select a graphics file format.**

   JPEG or TIFF are excellent choices for photos. Use GIF or PNG for smaller files, especially if you intend to use the resulting still images on a web page.

3. **Click Options.**

   At the bottom of the resulting Preferences window, you can choose whether you want PowerPoint to save *all* the slides in the show as graphics or just this one. In addition, you can set up the *file resolution* or *dimensions*. (Choose one or the other—they both adjust the file's pixel dimensions.) If you want high quality graphics for printing or viewing large onscreen, try 180 dpi or 1800 × 1350 pixels—either results in exactly the same size file. Finally, you can specify whether to compress the file (if you need to make it smaller for emailing, for example). The Image Quality pop-up menu's choices run from Least (high compression, small file size, and low quality) to Best (no compression, large file size, and high quality).

Tip: You don't need to set up these options time after time; you can set up your preferred settings only once, on the PowerPoint→Preferences→Save tab. There you'll find the identical graphics-saving options, which affect the proposed values for all your subsequent graphics-saving exploits.

---

4. **Change the settings as desired, click OK; then name the still image and click Save.**

   If you opted to save all of the slides, PowerPoint automatically creates a *folder* bearing your file's name. Inside the folder are the individual graphics files, with names like *Slide1.jpg*, *Slide2.jpg*, and so on.

Printing Your Presentation

Although PowerPoint is primarily meant to display images on a monitor or projected on a screen, you can also print out your slideshow on good old-fashioned paper—which is especially useful, of course, for printing handouts, overheads, and notes. Whatever the format, all printing is done through the same basic procedure: Open the presentation you want to print, make a few adjustments in the Page Setup dialog box and the Print dialog box, then print away.

Page Setup

Before printing your presentation, you should pop open the hood and take a peek at Themes | Page Setup→Slide Size→Page Setup (see Figure 20-12). After all, this important window is the engine that controls the size of your slides, whether they're for onscreen viewing or printing. Doing so brings you face to face with Microsoft's version of the Page Setup box, which presents you with a pop-up menu offering several preset slide sizes: On-screen show (multiple versions), US Letter, US Ledger, A3, A4, and so on. If you have a custom slide size in mind, you can set its width and height here as well.

As noted at the beginning of Chapter 19, be sure to make any size adjustments early in the game; if you fiddle with the knobs in Page Setup *after* the slide has been made, it'll stretch to fit, possibly giving the image a warped or distorted look, or knocking certain graphics off the edges altogether. It's worth noting however, that On-screen Show (4:3), Letter Paper (8.5 × 11 in), and Overhead all use the same size: 10 × 7.5 inches.

POWER USERS' CLINIC

A Presentation in Your Pocket

If you have an iPod, you have another option for presenting PowerPoint slideshows: you can ask everyone to gather round and watch a slideshow on your iPod screen. Or, more realistically, you can hook your iPod to a TV, monitor, or video projector and run your presentation straight from the iPod—no computer required.

What *is* required is an iPod that can do TV output, and the appropriate video output cable. In early 2011, that means the following iPod models:

- iPod Touch
- iPhone
- iPod Nano (3rd generation)
- iPod Classic
- iPod Video (a.k.a. 5th generation)
- iPod with color display (iPod Photo)

Begin by sending your presentation slides to iPhoto as described on page 590, which results in an album in iPhoto containing your slideshow.

Connect your iPod to your computer, triggering iTunes to launch. In the iTunes window, click your iPod's Photos tab and turn on the checkbox marked "Sync photos from iPhoto". Then click the "Selected albums" button and turn on the checkbox for the slideshow album in the scrolling list window. Finally, click the Sync button and iTunes sends your slides into the iPod.

Disconnect your iPod from your computer, and you'll find your slideshow in the Photos section. Visit the Slideshow Settings department and adjust such things as time per slide, music, and transitions. Set the TV Out setting to either Ask or On.

Connect your iPod to a TV, monitor, or video projector. If you're using a soundtrack, make sure to connect the iPod's audio output as well as video. Return to the iPod's Photos category and start the show. Use the Next/Fast-forward button to advance to the next slide, or the Previous/Rewind button to return to the previous slide. For further details on using your iPod to play slideshows launch iTunes and choose Help→iPod Help and search for slideshow.

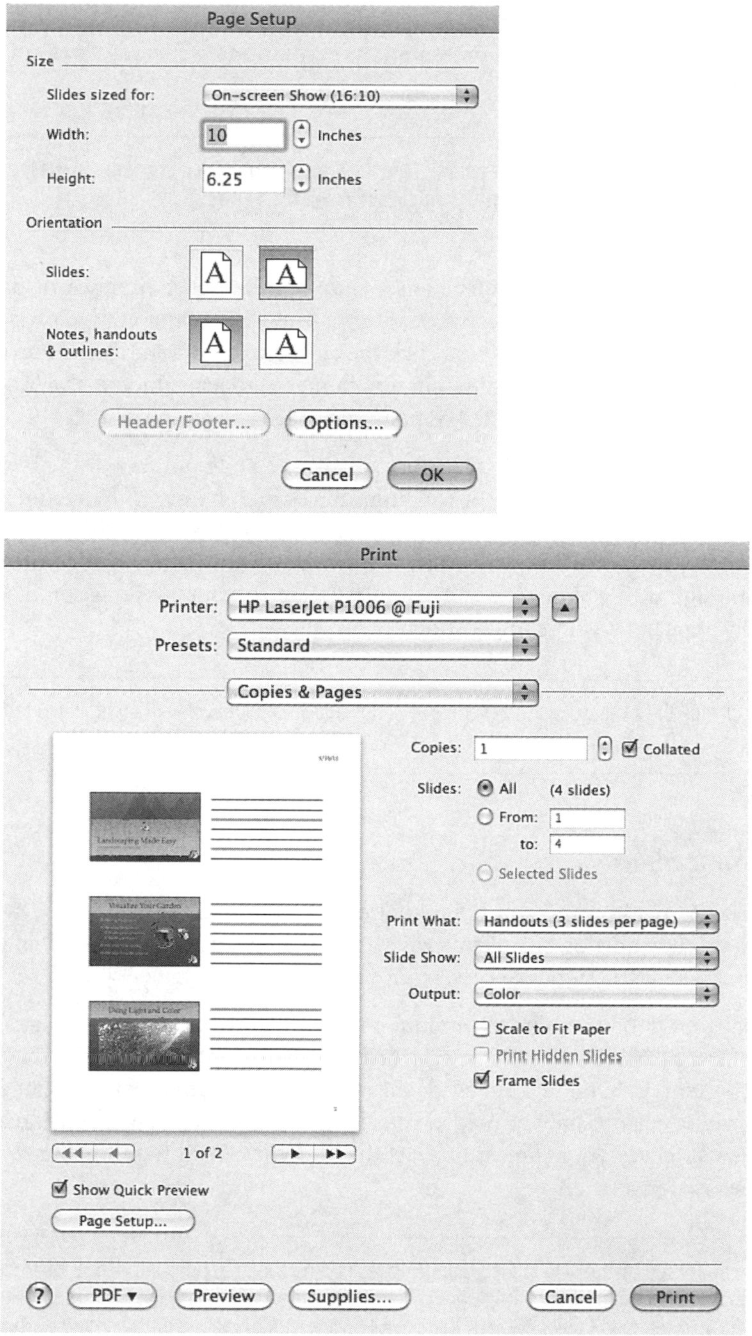

Page Setup

Size

Slides sized for: On-screen Show (16:10)

Width: 10 Inches

Height: 6.25 Inches

Orientation

Slides: A A

Notes, handouts & outlines: A A

Header/Footer... Options...

Cancel OK

Figure 20-12:

Top: The basic options in the Page Setup dialog box let you size your slides and set a separate orientation (portrait or landscape) for slides and other documents—notes, handouts, and outlines—that you want to print.

Bottom: In the Print dialog box, use the Print What drop down menu to print an outline, notes, various styles of Handouts—or full-page slides. The Output pop-up menu lets you save your color printer's ink—and your time—by choosing Grayscale or Black and White.

Print

Printer: HP LaserJet P1006 @ Fuji

Presets: Standard

Copies & Pages

Copies: 1 ☑ Collated

Slides: ⦿ All (4 slides)

○ From: 1

to: 4

○ Selected Slides

Print What: Handouts (3 slides per page)

Slide Show: All Slides

Output: Color

☐ Scale to Fit Paper

☐ Print Hidden Slides

☑ Frame Slides

◀◀ ◀ 1 of 2 ▶ ▶▶

☑ Show Quick Preview

Page Setup...

? PDF ▼ Preview Supplies... Cancel Print

You can use the settings in this dialog box to morph your slideshow into something appropriate for another format—taking it from an overhead projector to a Web banner, for instance. Also, if you want to send your presentation out to be printed at a real print shop, you can adjust the presentation's resolution by clicking the Options button in the File→Save As panel.

Tip: If you need the options available in the familiar Mac OS X Page Setup dialog box, you can get there quickly by clicking Options in Microsoft's version of the Page Setup dialog box.

Click Header/Footer to make text (such as a slide number, page number, or date) appear on the top or bottom of every slide, or every note and handout. On each tab in the "Header and Footer" dialog box, click the checkboxes and watch the Preview at the lower right to see where the different text elements appear. Once you've turned on a checkbox, select the box's related options and enter text as appropriate.

For example, working in the Slide tab, you can insert a slide number at the lower-right corner of each printed slide (or slide thumbnail on a handout) by turning on "Slide number" and then entering a starting slide number. Turn on "Don't show on title slide" at the bottom of the dialog box if you'd like that number hidden on *title* slides. (Although a title slide is usually the first slide in your presentation, it can theoretically appear anywhere in the show.)

Tip: You can change the locations of the footer boxes on the Slide tab by dragging them on the slide master (see page 542).

Printing Your Slides

When you're ready to commit your presentation to paper, choose File→Print (⌘-P) to bring up the Print dialog box. Here's where you tell PowerPoint exactly what you want to print—slides, handouts, notes, or an outline.

In the Print dialog box, you'll find unique PowerPoint-related print settings (see Figure 20-12, bottom). Here, you can select which chunks of your presentation you want to print (slides, handouts, notes, or the outline). From this spot, you can also choose to print a custom show, provided you created one earlier. When you're ready, click Preview to check your choices one last time, or click Print to send your document to the printer.

Tip: You can choose the Layout item in the Copies & Pages pop-up menu to print 1, 2, 4, 6, 9, or 16 slides per page. With Layout chosen, use the "Pages per Sheet" pop-up menu to choose the number of slides per page. If you now return to Copies & Pages, the Quick Preview window shows just one slide per page— never fear, however: you'll see the multislide layout you chose emerge from the printer.

Notes and Handouts

It didn't take the world long to dispel the myth of the paperless office, and that's evident every time your audience asks you for a hard copy of your presentation. PowerPoint can print out your notes and handouts or convert them to PDF files for electronic distribution.

Every PowerPoint slide can have *notes* attached to it: written tidbits to help you get through your presentation, or to clarify points for your audience. As you build your presentation, the Notes pane in PowerPoint's Normal view provides a place to type notes for each slide. (These notes appear on web pages if you leave "Include slide notes" turned on in the Appearance tab of the Web Options dialog box when saving your presentation as a web page.)

Handouts are printouts of your slides, usually featuring multiple slides per sheet of paper. They let your audience take your entire show away with them on paper, to spare them from having to take notes during the meeting. Handouts don't include notes; you'll have to print those out separately.

Note: Both notes and handouts have master pages, which work the same as slide masters; see page 542 for details.

To print your notes and handouts, choose File→Print (⌘-P). This summons a Print dialog box specific to PowerPoint. In the Print What pop-up menu, you can choose to print notes or handouts in layouts that show two, three, four, six, or nine slide miniatures per sheet (see Figure 20-12). Here again, if you click Preview, you'll be shown an onscreen preview of the printout-in-waiting, which you can then save as a PDF file as described above.

Tip: The beauty of the Mac OS X Preview function is that it lets you convert your PowerPoint document—or *any* document—into a PDF file (otherwise known as an Acrobat file). Anyone with almost any kind of computer (Mac, Windows, or Unix) can open the resulting document using the free Acrobat Reader program. (You can create a PDF file immediately by clicking PDF→Save As PDF in the Print dialog box.)

Of course, sending people a PDF file of your presentation isn't quite as exciting as sending them a Quick-Time movie complete with animations and multimedia. But a PDF document is compatible with far more computers. (Plus, it's less detrimental to forests than distributing printouts on paper.)

Part Five: Office As a Whole

5

Making the Most of Graphics and Media

Office comes with Word for text, Excel for numbers, PowerPoint for slides, and Outlook for email and scheduling. From reading the box, you might conclude that Office is therefore missing one of the cornerstone Macintosh features—graphics software.

In fact, however, Office comes with a herd of graphics tools, including Office 2011's SmartArt graphics, the Clip Art Browser, AutoShapes, WordArt, and more—built right in and shared among Word, Excel, and PowerPoint. As is almost always the case with Office, there's more than one way to open the same window or widget, and in the case of graphics, multiple tools seem remarkably similar. For instance, what's the difference between the Clip Art Gallery and the Clip Art Browser? For that matter, how is the Clip Art Browser different from the Media Browser? Should you look for your artwork in the media browser or the scrapbook? This section answers these and many other questions about popping artwork into your documents, presentations, spreadsheets, and email.

Inserting a Graphic or Media Clip

You can drag, paste, or insert pictures, drawings, and media clips into a Word, Excel, or PowerPoint document. The launch pad for any of these is the Media Browser, a tabbed window. If you have the Standard toolbar showing, the quickest way to open the media browser is by clicking the Show or Hide Media Browser button. As shown in Figure 21-1, the button's icon shows musical notes, a movie clip and a picture. Six buttons at the top of the media browser change the window's content to show: Photos, Audio, Movies, Clip Art, Symbols, and Shapes. If you don't work with the Standard toolbar displayed or if you want to go directly to a specific media window, use the Insert menu. For example, to open the media browser to shapes, go to Insert→Shape. For photos, go to Insert→Photo→Photo Browser. These commands work the same whether you're in Word, Excel, or PowerPoint.

Note: Outlook uses media a little differently than the other three programs. When you're writing an email, you can open the media browser from a button on the ribbon Message | Picture. You can cut and paste pictures into your notes and add pictures to your contact cards.

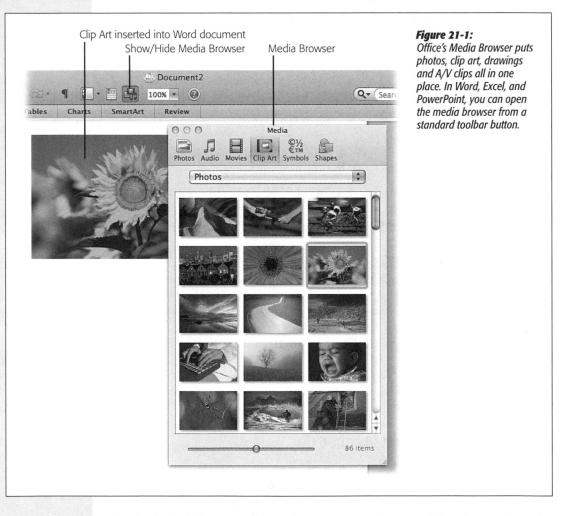

Clip Art inserted into Word document
Show/Hide Media Browser   Media Browser

Figure 21-1:
Office's Media Browser puts photos, clip art, drawings and A/V clips all in one place. In Word, Excel, and PowerPoint, you can open the media browser from a standard toolbar button.

So, what's the difference between photos, clip art, shapes, and the other media in the browser?

- Click the **Photos** button to you see your photos—the ones that you've added to iPhoto, for example. You can use the menu at the to choose iPhoto, specific iPhoto albums, or even Photo Booth photos from your Mac's iSight camera.

- The **Audio** button takes you to your iTunes library and Garage Band.

- Similarly, the **Movies** button shows you iMovie clips, your Movies folder, and Photo Booth.

- The **Clip Art** window also holds photos, but these are from the library of photos that comes with Office. In general, these are pretty good quality images that you might actually want to use to liven up a document or presentation. Subjects include people, animals, food, and artsy nature pictures.

- The **Symbols** window shows a variety of symbols or glyphs that you can't usually create using the keyboard. For example, you'll find a variety of currency or math symbols.

- The **Shapes** button displays Office's library of AutoShapes—predrawn graphics that you can easily resize and reshape for your own creative purposes.

The standard method for adding any of these media to your document is to drag them from the browser onto the page, spreadsheet, or slide. The differences between movie and sound clips is pretty obvious, but there are some more subtle differences between graphic files. Your photos and clip art files are stored as *pictures* while the shapes are stored as *drawings*. For the details on the differences, see the box below.

Some of these windows are so jam-packed with media, you'll want to make use of the Search box (Figure 21-2) at the bottom of the media browser to find your movie clip or photo. You can preview the audiovisual clips by clicking the Play button. If the photo, movie, or audio clip you want doesn't appear in the browser, you can use the "from File" menu command. For example, to find a photo that you know is on your computer, go to Insert→Photo→Picture from File.

UP TO SPEED

Pictures and Drawings

There are two distinct kinds of graphics in the computer world, which, in Office, are known as pictures and drawings.

Pictures include bitmap files, raster graphics, painting files, JPEG or GIF images, photographs, anything scanned or captured with a digital camera, anything grabbed from a web page, and Office clip art. What all pictures have in common is that (a) they're composed of individual, tiny colored dots, and (b) you can't create them using the tools built into Office. You *can* make pictures larger or smaller, but if you stretch something larger than its original size, it might look blotchy.

Drawings include AutoShapes, WordArt, and any graphics you create using Office's own drawing tools. Drawings, also known as *vector* or *object-oriented graphics*, are stored by the Mac as mathematical equations that describe their size, shape, and other characteristics. That's a fancy way of saying that you can resize, rotate, squish, or squeeze drawings as much as you like without ever worrying that they'll print jagged or blotchy.

Keeping these distinctions in mind will help you understand why your Office programs function like they do when you work with graphics.

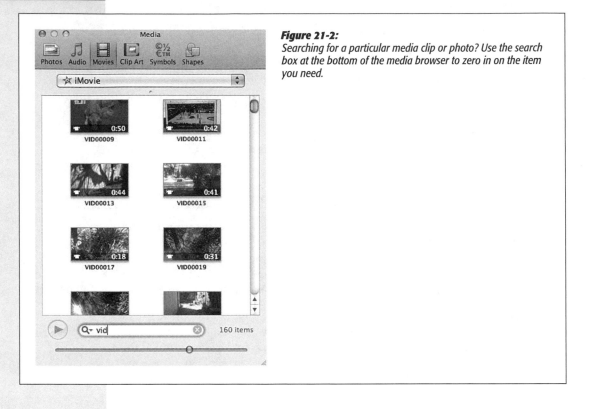

Figure 21-2:
Searching for a particular media clip or photo? Use the search box at the bottom of the media browser to zero in on the item you need.

The Clip Art Gallery

If you used earlier versions of Office, you may be familiar with the Clip Gallery. If you're used to working with it, you'll be pleased that it's still included in Office 2011 even though it duplicates some of the functions of the Clip Art browser. When this was written, the gallery held more images than the Clip Art Browser. The gallery also has a handy button that leads to an even bigger online library of images, shown in Figure 21-3.

In Office, the term clip art refers to photos or professionally-drawn illustrations designed for use in a wide variety of documents. Designing a birthday card for a child? You can count on finding a soccer ball or kite in any self-respecting clip art collection. Need a sketch of people at the office for a newsletter article about business travel? Off you go to the clip art collection. Office comes with hundreds of pieces of ready-to-use art in a collection called the Clip Art Gallery. And they're not all cartoon-like graphics either. You'll find dozens of stock photographs you can use in your documents without having to worry about securing copyright permissions— everything from flowers, cute animals, and babies to businesspeople, landscapes, and athletes. To review them, choose Insert→Clip Art→Clip Art Gallery. The Clip Art Gallery opens, as shown in Figure 21-4. From there you can simply drag thumbnails to your document.

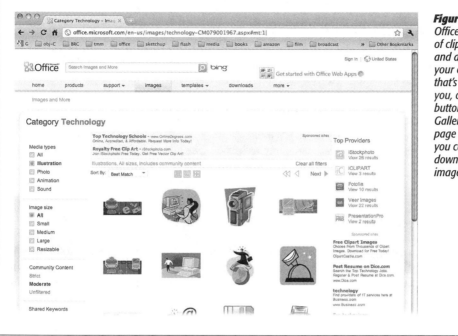

Figure 21-3:
Office places dozens of clip art photos and drawings on your computer, but if that's not enough for you, click the Online button in the Clip Art Gallery to open a web page like this where you can find and download even more images.

Figure 21-4:
Click a category in the list at the left to see thumbnails of the available clips. After you've done a keyword search, as shown here, your results appear in the Search Results category. Click a thumbnail and then click Insert (or just double-click the thumbnail) to place the full-size version in your document at the insertion point. (Turn on the Preview box to see the full-size image in a separate window.) When you've finished adding pictures, click Close to make the dialog box vanish.

Categories

The Categories button in the Clip Gallery window opens a dialog box where you can delete categories from, or add categories to, the Clip Gallery. Neither process deletes or adds any actual pictures; they stay where they always were—in the Applications→ Microsoft Office 2011→Office→Media→Clipart folder. You're just deleting or adding category names into which the pictures can reside.

Tip: Often a single photo or drawing is appropriate for more than one category. To choose the categories for any clip art, right-click (Control-click) the image and choose Clip Properties from the shortcut menu. Then, click the Categories tab, where you can use checkboxes to choose categories. You can also use the Properties window to describe the clip, providing keywords used for searches.

Online

If you click the Online button, Office launches your Web browser and connects to the Microsoft Office Online Clip Art and Media page (Figure 21-3), which offers thousands of additional clip art files in a searchable database. You can download them individually or in groups by "adding them to your basket." After doing so, you'll end up with a *.cil* file in your downloads folder; double-click it to add the images to the Clip Art Gallery, where they'll appear in the Favorites category.

Adding Your Own Clips

You're not limited to clip art from Microsoft. Not only can you transfer your own images into any Word document with the Home | Insert→Picture→ Insert→Photo→ Picture from File command, but you can also make them part of the Clip Art Gallery. This gives you the opportunity to use the Clip Art Gallery's search function and organizing features and see thumbnails of your own clip art, too. (iPhoto it ain't, but this feature can be handy.)

To do so, choose Insert→Clip Art→Clip Art Gallery to open the Clip Art Gallery, and then click Import. Use the Import dialog box to navigate to the graphics file you want to bring into the Clip Gallery. (Make sure the Enable menu shows "Clip Gallery Images"; the kinds of images you can import are JPEG, TIFF, PICT, GIF, PNG, or Photoshop files, as well as clip art from Microsoft.) Use the three buttons at the bottom of the window to copy, move, or create an alias for the image in the clip Gallery; then click Import.

The Properties window appears; you can give the image a new name to display in the Clip Gallery (instead of the file name) and assign categories or keywords. When you click OK, you'll find yourself back at the Clip Gallery, with your newly added image in its window.

Deleting Clips

If you want a clip out of your life forever, click it in the Clip Gallery and choose Edit→Clear. A dialog box asks for confirmation before expunging it. If you just want to remove the clip from a single category but leave the file on your computer, see the note on the previous page.

Search

When you enter a word in the Search box at the top of the Clip Gallery and click Search, Clip Gallery finds all the clips that match (or are related to) that keyword. For instance, if you type in *automobile*, Clip Gallery pulls up all the clips that have "automobile" as a keyword. Cooler yet, it also finds clips with "car" or "vehicle" as keywords—it relies on the Office 2011 Thesaurus to figure out which possible keywords mean the same thing as what you typed!

Working with Clip Art

After placing a piece of clip art into your document, you can click it to produce eight blue handles at its perimeter and one green stalk sprouting from its top. By dragging these handles, you can resize the illustration in a variety of ways:

- **Drag a side handle** to resize the figure in that dimension—drag the top one to make it taller, a side one to make it wider, and so on.
- **Dragging a corner handle** keeps an object in its original proportions as you resize it.
- **Option-drag a side handle to resize** the object from the center outward in the direction you're dragging.
- **Option-drag a corner handle** to resize an object from the center outward *and* maintain its proportions.
- **Drag the green stalk** to rotate the object (see page 613).
- ⌘-**dragging** any handle overrides the *drawing grid* (see page 612).

You can also move a graphic around the screen by dragging it freely.

AutoShapes, Lines, SmartArt, and WordArt

Your Office programs share several different types of artwork, including AutoShapes, Lines, SmartArt, and WordArt. This section explains how to choose and use each type of graphic.

AutoShapes

An AutoShape is a ready-made drawing object. As with the simple circle, square, and triangle of times past, you simply drag to size and place them in your document. However, you now have a plethora of new choices, courtesy of Office 2011.

To use an AutoShape in your document, choose Insert→Shapes or click the Media Browser button on the standard toolbar and then click Shapes.

As shown in Figure 21-5, you can use the Shapes menu to choose different categories. Then, drag the chosen shape to your document—you can always resize, reshape or move it later. As an alternative, you can select the shape in the browser, then click and drag in your document. Using this technique, you can adjust the dimensions of the shape as you add it. If you want to keep equal proportions, hold the Shift key as you drag. Once it is in your document, you can move or modify the shape. To move it, drag it to a new spot. To modify a shape, select it to display the handles. Drag the handles using the same options described on page 607. Shapes have special yellow handles that modify something unique about the shape. For example, there's a notched circle shape that looks like a pie chart. The yellow handles let you adjust the size of the slice that's missing. For a line with arrowheads, the yellow handles may let you change the proportions of the line or the arrowhead.

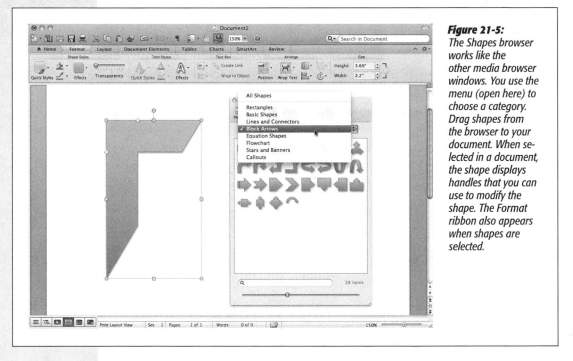

Figure 21-5:
The Shapes browser works like the other media browser windows. You use the menu (open here) to choose a category. Drag shapes from the browser to your document. When selected in a document, the shape displays handles that you can use to modify the shape. The Format ribbon also appears when shapes are selected.

Note: As you drag to create an AutoShape, press Shift to keep the shape in equal length-to-height proportion. For instance, select the rectangle shape and Shift-drag to create a square, or select the oval and Shift-drag to create a perfect circle. As noted earlier, you can also press Shift when dragging to resize such an object without distorting its original proportions.

Lines

Even with the immense variety of AutoShapes and WordArt, some days your own creative juices are flowing. With Office's line tools, you can draw free-form lines and combine them with arrows and AutoShapes to build your own masterpieces.

To get started, open the Shapes browser (Home | Insert→Shape→Shapes Browser) then choose the Lines and Connectors category. As shown in Figure 21-6, some of the lines work in the standard AutoShape manner, but others let you draw free-form lines and squiggles. (As usual, your lines and shapes lie *on top of* text in Word—and are invisible in Draft view—unless you wrap them around the text, as described on page 77.)

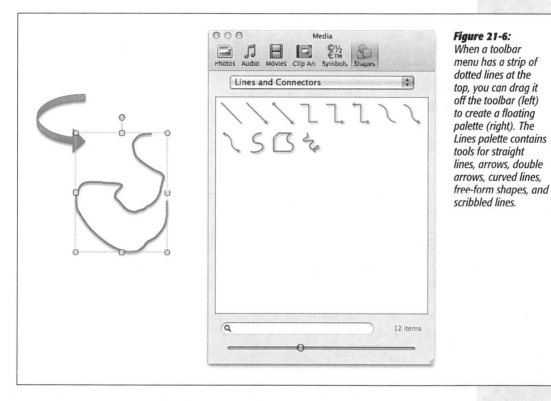

Figure 21-6:
When a toolbar menu has a strip of dotted lines at the top, you can drag it off the toolbar (left) to create a floating palette (right). The Lines palette contains tools for straight lines, arrows, double arrows, curved lines, free-form shapes, and scribbled lines.

You'll find that each of the options in the Lines pop-up button menu works a bit differently:

- **Line**. Drag for the position and length of the straight line you want; the cursor turns into a tiny cross. To resize the newly drawn line, drag the handles on each side, or reposition it by dragging the line itself (at which time the cursor turns into the four-arrow move cursor).

- **Arrow** and **Double Arrow** work just like lines. When you draw a single arrow, the point appears where you stop dragging; a double arrow automatically springs points on both sides.

- **Curve**. Unlike lines, you draw curves by clicking, not dragging. Click to create a starting point; as you move the mouse, the curve follows. When you click a second time, the line gently curves from the first point to the second. Continue in this same manner. (The curve tool works best for wiggles and waves rather than closed shapes.) When you're done, double-click to finish off the curve. To enclose the shape, click as close as you can to your starting point.

- The **Freeform** tool is a two-in-one special. When you drag with it, the cursor turns into a + crosshair and works like a pencil—you can draw lines with any bend and direction without the limitations of the Curve tool. The instant you let go of the mouse button, the cursor turns into a cross and becomes a line tool. Clicking the mouse again now draws a straight line, just as with the Line tool. Hold down the mouse button again to go back to freehand drawing.

- The **Scribble** tool is exactly like Freeform without the straight-line feature. You drag it to draw a freehand line; the line ends when you let go of the mouse button.

Tip: You can create closed shapes with the Curve, Freeform, or Scribble tools—just move the + cursor back to the beginning of the line. You can choose to fill your shape with a color or leave it empty using the special purple Format tab as described next.

Formatting and Editing Shapes and Lines

When you want to customize a shape or line that you've drawn, select the graphic and then turn to the special purple Format tab on the ribbon: Format | Shape Styles. If you're in a hurry, use one of the Quick Styles that apply combinations of the Theme colors to the selected graphic. If you have time to customize, use the paint bucket to choose a fill color or to leave a closed object empty. Use the pencil to set the color, weight, and line style for lines and outlines. The Effects menu lets you apply eye candy like drop shadows, reflections, or glow to lines and shapes. Using the transparency slider, you can give your graphics a ghostly, see-through effect.

Two other line options await only if you right-click (Control-click) the line and choose them from the shortcut menu:

- **Edit Points**. Don't worry if your line or drawn object doesn't come out perfect on the first try. Just do the best you can, and then right-click (Control-click) the shape and choose Edit Points from the shortcut menu. You can then drag the little dots to resize and reshape the line. This trick is especially useful for the Curve, Freeform, and Scribble tools.

- **Open Path**. This unusual command (available on the shortcut menu only) "disconnects" the point where you closed a Curve, Freeform, or Scribble object. Now you can use the edit points to reshape the object. Should you ever want to close the gap again, right-click the shape again and choose Close Curve.

SmartArt Graphics

Office 2011 comes packed full with a slew of SmartArt graphics. Like collections of AutoShapes choreographed by Busby Berkeley, SmartArt graphics let you visually communicate information in lists, processes, cycles, hierarchies, relationships, and so on. Starting with these graphical templates, you can fill in your text information, refine the formatting, and experiment with different layouts.

Click the SmartArt tab to display the ribbon of Smart Art tools shown in Figure 21-7. Use the menus on the Insert SmartArt Graphic group to to narrow your choices to List styles, Process styles, Relationship styles, and so on; and then click one option on the menu. The graphic appears in your document surrounded by a blue selection frame and accompanied by the dark gray Text Pane.

You can type directly on the graphic, or in the Text Pane. As you type, you'll see your words appear in the graphic. The Text Pane operates like a little outline. You can make a list of items of equal importance, or you can use the Demote button to move an item down one level of importance, or use the Promote button to elevate an item in importance. As you do, the text in your graphic reflects the new arrangement, with added or removed bullet points. Two more buttons let you add or remove items from your outline—which you can also accomplish with the Return key and the Delete key.

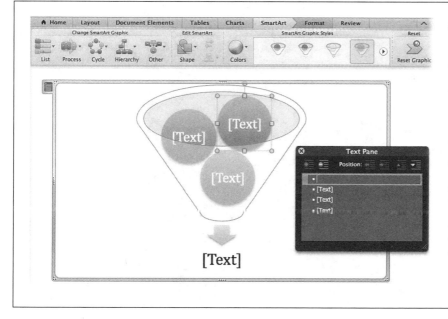

Figure 21-7:
Top: As you hold your cursor over a Smart-Art thumbnail in the Elements Gallery, a short description of the diagram appears at the left. Click a thumbnail to insert it in your document.

Bottom: You can enter text either directly in the diagram or in the Text Pane. The button on the upper-left corner of the selection frame hides or reveals the Text Pane.

As you add text to your outline, SmartArt's canniness becomes evident, as it automatically adjusts container size and font size to accommodate your words—always keeping the entire group balanced and in proportion.

When you're working with SmartArt graphics, the SmartArt Graphic Styles tab gives you tools that instantly transform your flat graphic into a variety of 3-D configurations. Similarly, the Colors tab gives a selection of colorization schemes, based on your Document Theme colors.

As you work with a SmartArt graphic, you can click other SmartArt thumbnails in the Change SmartArt Graphics group to see how your information would look in a different format—and always come back to your original design. For example, you might start out thinking your relationship comparison data would work well in a Balance diagram, but then discover that a simple opposing arrow chart gets your point across much more clearly (see Figure 21-8, bottom).

Although it appears in your document as one unit, a SmartArt graphic is actually collection of regular graphic objects. And like other graphic objects, you can select and modify them just as you would any other graphic—as described later in this chapter.

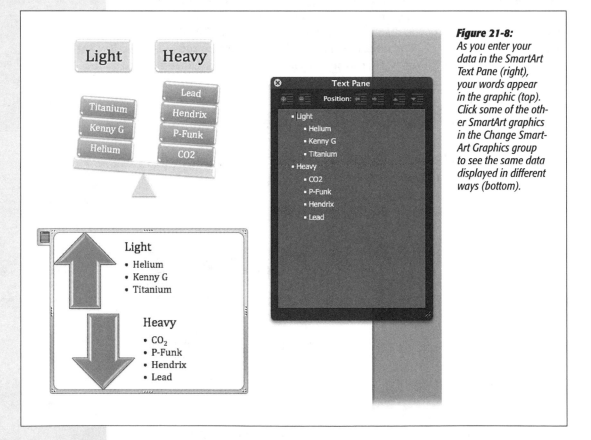

Figure 21-8:
As you enter your data in the SmartArt Text Pane (right), your words appear in the graphic (top). Click some of the other SmartArt graphics in the Change Smart-Art Graphics group to see the same data displayed in different ways (bottom).

WordArt

Like an AutoShape, a piece of WordArt is a type of ready-made drawing object. In this case, it's used for special text effects—3-D, wavy, slanting, colored, and various other permutations—that would be just right on a movie poster (but should be used sparingly in other situations). Figure 21-9 shows some examples.

To create some WordArt, choose Insert→WordArt. A drawing box appears with the hint: Your Text Here. Unless those were the words you planned on using, you'll want to type in some new words. You can tell by the handles this box is a hybrid—part text and part graphic. You can edit the text any time by clicking or double-clicking. You can move, modify, and rotate the box as you would any graphic in your documents. The Format tab gives you plenty of options to change the colors and add special effects. The Text Styles groups gives you options specially designed for WordArt. For some variety, on the Format | Text Styles→Effects menu, check out the Reflection, 3D Rotation, and Transform options.

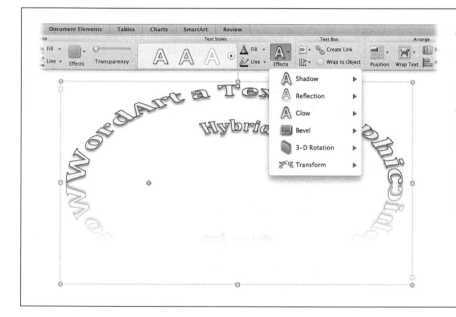

Figure 21-9:
WordArt is a text and graphic hybrid. The graphic box has handles to resize and shape the text inside. Any time you want to edit the text, just click or double-click to open it for editing. The Format→Text Styles→Effects menu, shown here, gives you lots of eye-popping effects.

Aligning Objects

When you have multiple objects on a page, you may want them to be equally spaced or evenly aligned by their top edges. Instead of working out the measurements and aligning them manually, use Office's built-in alignment features.

To do so, select the objects that you need to line up or arrange (Shift-click each one). Then, go to Format | Arrange→Align and choose one of the following options from the Align or Distribute menus.

- **Align Left, Align Center, or Align Right**. These commands bring the selected objects into perfect vertical alignment by their left or right edges, or centerlines.

- **Align Top, Align Middle, or Align Bottom**. These commands bring the selected objects into perfect *horizontal* alignment by their top or bottom edges, or centerlines.

- **Distribute Horizontally or Distribute Vertically**. Use these commands to spread your drawing objects across the page or from top to bottom—with an equal amount of space between each one.

You can also use the above commands on a single object, to place it at either side or in the center of a page.

The Drawing grid

Even without using the alignment commands, you might have noticed that it's fairly easy to pull objects into alignment with one another just by dragging. That's because each Word page has an invisible alignment grid that objects "snap to," as if pulled into line by a magnetic force.

To see the grid, select graphics in your document, then go to Format | Arrange→ Align→Grid Options. In the Grid Options dialog box, turn on "Display gridlines on screen"; specify a gridline separation in the "Horizontal every" box (and the "Vertical every" box too, if you like); and then click OK. Now you can see the grid's faint gray lines superimposed on your document.

Note: In Excel, the gridlines are the cell boundaries themselves. You can either snap to these gridlines or snap "To Shape" (see page 713).

Now that you know what the grid looks like, here's how to use the other Grid Options settings:

- To turn the grid off so that you can drag objects around with no spatial restriction whatsoever, turn off the appropriate option under the "Snap objects" section.

Tip: When the grid is turned off, ⌘-drag an object when you *do* want it to snap to the grid. Conversely, when the grid is turned on, ⌘-dragging a graphic moves it exactly where you put it, *without* snapping to the grid.

- You can use the "Snap objects to other objects" box with or without snapping to the grid. When this box is turned on, a dragged object snaps into alignment with the edges of the closest nearby object. If the grid is on, the nearest object overrides the grid.

- Change the default grid spacing (an eighth of an inch) by changing the measurements in the "Grid settings" boxes.

Click OK to apply the grid changes to your document.

Rotating drawing objects

You can rotate drawing objects in either of two ways: freely with the mouse, or in precise 90-degree increments.

- To rotate something, click the object, and then drag the green handle. A curved-around arrow appears while you rotate the object and a tooltip reports on the change in degrees.

Tip: Hold down the Shift key while you rotate to pivot in 15-degree increments.

- To rotate in 90-degree increments, click the object, and then go to Format→ Arrange and click the curved arrow, choose Rotate Left or Rotate Right from the Rotate menu. Repeat the process to continue rotating the object a quarter turn at a time.

- To flip a selected drawing object, click the object, and then go to Format→ Arrange and click the curved arrow. Choose Flip Horizontal or Flip Vertical from the Rotate menu. Flip Horizontal reverses the object from side to side; Flip Vertical turns it head-over-heels.

Modifying Graphics with the Format Dialog Box

Besides arranging a graphic's size and placement on the page, you can also adjust the way each object looks by adjusting its various properties. Formatting properties include things like fill color, line color and style, drop shadow, and transparency. The Format tab, the Format dialog box, and the Color Picker have the commands for making all of these adjustments.

- **The Format tab**. When you click a graphic, the purple Format tab on the ribbon provides a plethora of graphics controls (Fill, Line, Size, and so on), the assortment of which varies depending on the type of object at hand. You'll find many of the Format tabs commands duplicated in the Format dialog box. The purpose of the Format tab is to give quick and easy access to the options you use the most.

- **The Format dialog box**. When you right-click (Control-click) a graphic and choose the Format Shape (or Format Picture) command, this massive, multi-tab dialog box appears (see Figure 21-10). Its various panes let you specify every conceivable aspect of the selected object.

- **The Color picker**. In several places, the Format tab and the Format dialog box give you option to choose a color. When you're given that choice, Office usually presents a limited set of Theme colors along with a "more colors" option that opens your Mac's standard color picker tools.

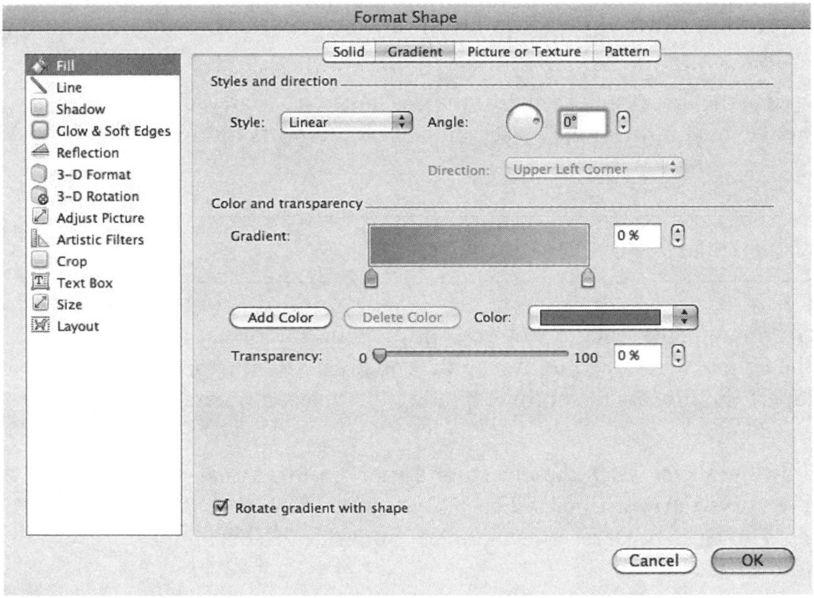

Figure 21-10:
The Format dialog box lets you massage the appearance of your inserted graphics in great detail, but using it takes time. Select one of the 13 categories on the left like Fill, Line or 3D format, then use the tools provided in the pane on the right. In some cases, like Fill and Line, there are multiple tabs within a category. This figure shows the formatting tools for a gradient fill.

Often when you're working with photos, shapes or other graphics you find yourself faced with the very Microsoftian-looking Format dialog box shown in Figure 21-10. This box with its tabs and panels and dozens upon dozens of fine-tuning widgets gives you complete control over graphic elements. The tools are divided into the categories shown along the left side of the box. The next few sections of this chapter explain how to use the tools in each of those categories: Fills, Lines, Glow & Soft Edges, Reflection, 3-D Format, 3-D Rotation, Adjust Picture, Artistic Filters, Crop, Text Box, Size, and Layout.

Formatting Fills

Shapes in Office have two parts: the fill (the inner portion) and the line (the border's outline). You can apply colors to either part or choose none, making the fill or line invisible. Using the Format dialog box, you can fill a shape or object with solid colors, gradients, pictures or textures, or patterns. You'll find tabs for each of those options at the top of the Fill pane. Click a tab, and you'll find the tools you need to select a color, adjust a gradient or choose pictures, textures and patterns.

Tip: If you select a shape in Word, Excel, or PowerPoint, the purple Format tab appears. Go to the Format | Shape→Shape Styles→Fill menu, and you can choose colors from the menu or choose Fill Effect to open the Format Dialog Box.

All the options except Pattern provide a transparency slider. This slider, found on the Colors and Lines tab and the Formatting Palette, changes whatever color you've chosen into a transparent version. The text or objects layered above or below it remain visible through the color, courtesy of Mac OS X's Quartz graphics technology. Drag the slider to the right to increase the transparency; drag left to make your graphics more opaque.

Note: The Fill settings are designed to fill in the background of *drawing objects* and *Office clip art*. The corresponding Fills options have no visible effect on normal pictures, but can provide a background layer that shows through if the picture has transparent areas.

Fill Color: Standard palette

Click one of the Color pop-up menus and Word displays its array of Theme Colors—an assortment chosen to coordinate with your template, or a different collection you've chosen in the Formatting Palette's Document Theme pane—and 10 standard colors. This colorful palette appears any time you have the option to change a color in Office. You can also use it to change font color. Click the color you want to apply.

Fill Color: More Colors

If none of the 70 colors meets with your artistic standards, choose More Colors from the Fill Color pop-up menu to open the Mac OS X color picker, which offers five different ways to select almost any color in existence. First of all, you can choose any color that you currently see on the monitor—like a sample from a favorite picture—by clicking the magnifying glass icon and then clicking anywhere onscreen, as discussed in Figure 21-11.

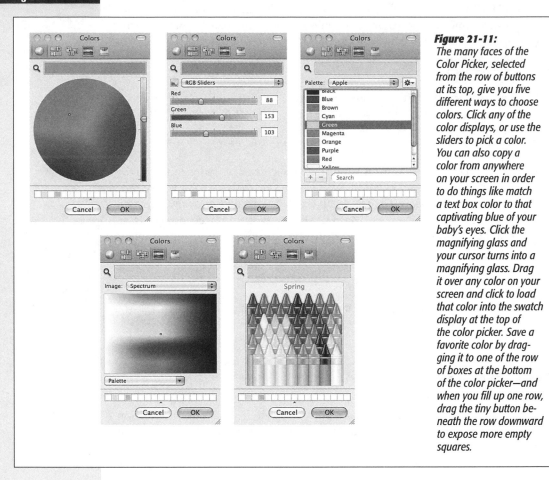

Figure 21-11:
The many faces of the Color Picker, selected from the row of buttons at its top, give you five different ways to choose colors. Click any of the color displays, or use the sliders to pick a color. You can also copy a color from anywhere on your screen in order to do things like match a text box color to that captivating blue of your baby's eyes. Click the magnifying glass and your cursor turns into a magnifying glass. Drag it over any color on your screen and click to load that color into the swatch display at the top of the color picker. Save a favorite color by dragging it to one of the row of boxes at the bottom of the color picker—and when you fill up one row, drag the tiny button beneath the row downward to expose more empty squares.

The five square buttons at the top of the color picker reveal different panels, each of which provides a unique way to see and even blend colors. Choose the one that best matches how you're used to looking at color. Here are the various color pickers you can try:

- On the **Color Wheel** panel, you can click anywhere in the circle to choose a color from the spectrum. Use the slide on the right to make the hues brighter or darker.

- The **Color Sliders** panel gives you access to traditional color systems, like CMYK, which lets you blend the ink color used in the printing business—Cyan, Magenta, Yellow, and BlacK; or RGB, the system computers use to describe colors with Red, Green, and Blue. Choose your favorite color system from the pop-up menu near the top of the panel, and then click the ColorSync pop-up menu (under the magnifying glass) to fine-tune your color palette for various devices—scanners, printers, and so on—or paper stocks.

- The **Color Palettes** panel lets you choose, from the pop-up menu, lists of color swatches such as Apple's standard palette or the set of colors that you can use on web pages. Scroll through the list and click your desired color.

- **Image Palettes** lets you select colors from the spectrum in the big square on the panel. You can also choose to import a graphics file into the square and then pick colors from it—helpful if you want to match colors for your interior design scheme or latest spring sportswear collection.

- **Crayons** is the simplest one to use—as easy as picking a Crayola out of a box. (The names—Asparagus, Spindrift, Bubblegum—are lots of fun, too.)

Format fill: Gradients

The Gradient tab lets you apply smoothly-shifting colors within the interior of the drawing object—for rainbow-like, shimmery effects. Choose the type of gradient you want to use: Linear, Radial, Rectangular, or Path. See Figure 21-12 for examples of each. The Gradient color box gives you a preview of the gradient and the colors it uses. Click the tabs to choose the three colors that blend to make your gradient, and then use them like sliders to fine-tune the blending effect. Depending on the type of gradient you choose, other widgets on the gradient panel come to life. For example, you can set the angle of a linear gradient with the dial in the upper-right corner. The Direction menu lets you set the focal point for Radial and Rectangular gradients.

Format fill: Picture or Texture

Don't let Office kid you—pictures and textures are pretty much the same thing. They both fill your shape or object with an image. You can choose a picture from your photo library or you can use one of Office's texture images, which are designed to look good when they repeat on a surface.

When you click the Choose Picture menu, a Finder style window opens where you can choose any picture file on your Mac, including, but not limited to, Office clip art. Click Insert to bring the picture into the Picture tab, where you can see what it will look like. Click OK to use the picture as a fill for your object. Unless they're really big, pictures are repeated over the surface of the fill. If you want background objects to show through, adjust the Transparency slider.

The From Texture menu is your personal Home Depot for marble, granite, burlap, and other building materials. When you need to dress up, say, a title or heading by mounting it on a stately, plaque-like rectangle, these squares are just the ticket.

Format fill: Pattern

The **Pattern** tab has a variety of two-color patterns. Using the pop-up menus at the bottom of the dialog box, you can specify which is the dark color and which is the light one.

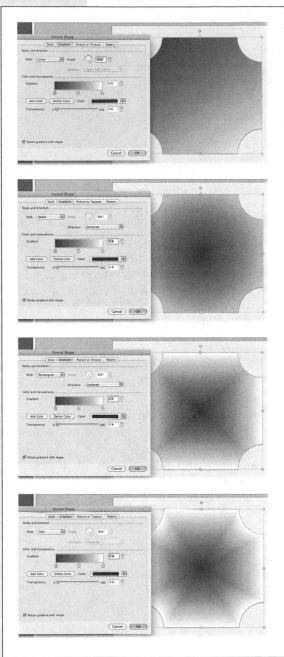

Figure 21-12:
There are four types of gradients you can apply to your graphics. Here, the gradients are applied to the Fill portion of a shape. From the top to bottom they are: linear, radial, rectangular, and path. Click the tabs under the large color swatch to choose the three colors used in the gradient. Then slide the same tabs to control the way one color blends into the next.

Drawing Lines

Lines can be solid or gradients, and they come in different weights (thickness) and with or without arrows. As explained on page 607, you draw lines by choosing Insert→Shape and using the Lines and Connectors option. If you want arrows on the end of your lines, you need to choose from the options in the Shapes Browser. You can't add arrowheads from the Format dialog box; you can only modify them.

Tip: In Word and PowerPoint, you can use the Home | Insert→Shape→Lines and Connectors menu to pop lines into your document. In Excel, you need to use the menu command Insert→Shape to open the Media Browser and then select Lines and Connectors. The Media Browser is available to all your Office applications and it often has more options than are shown on the Ribbon.

- Use the **Solid** tab to set the color and transparency for lines with a solid color.
- The **Gradient** tab gives you several options for gradients including: linear, radial, rectangular, and path. Depending on your choice, different tools are activated so you can fine-tune the gradient. For example, if you choose Linear, the circular tool comes to life where you can set the angle of the gradient in degrees.
- Use the **Weights and Arrows** tab to choose line weight and style (dotted, dashed). The Cap menu lets you choose end points for your lines and the Join type gives you options for the point where lines meet. If you've created a line with arrows, the Arrows options are activated and you can choose from different arrow styles.

Adding Shadows

Drop shadows are a great effect when you want to separate a graphic from the background. With the formatting options, you can create a subtle realistic shadow or a bright, glowing in-your-face shadow effect. You can choose from three different types of shadows, as shown in Figure 21-13.

- Use the **Style** pop-up menu to choose Outer, the traditional drop shadow style; Inner, to create a shadow that falls within the picture; or Perspective, to make it look like your picture object is illuminated by a Klieg light far above and to your right.
- Twist the **Angle** knob, enter the exact number of degrees, or use the up- and down-arrow button to determine the direction in which the shadow falls.
- Click the **Color** pop-up menu if you'd like your shadow to be something other than black or gray.
- The **Size** slider adjusts the size of the shadow, relative to the picture.
- Adjust the **Blur** control to affect the shadows and softness, mimicking the range from harsh, direct sun to soft window light.

- The **Distance** control determines how far from the picture the shadow falls.
- Adjust the **Transparency** control to affect the darkness of the shadow. If you have black selected as the shadow color, for example, this slider creates shadows from pure black to gray, all the way to nonexistent.

Tip: Shadow options are often available from the purple Format tab that appears on the ribbon when you select an object. Look under Format | Shape Styles or Format | Text Styles, depending on what you've selected.

Figure 21-13:
Here are the three shadow effects you can choose in the Format dialog box.

Left: Outer shadow is the most common choice for separating objects from the page.

Middle: Inner shadow places the shadow effect inside the selected object, sometimes creating a 3D effect.

Right: The Perspective option provides the most dramatic shadow.

Glow and Soft Edges Effects

The two effects in this group both soften the edges of a picture—but do it in very different ways.

- The **Glow** effect adds a soft frame of color around a picture—another technique to make a picture stand out on the page. Use the Color pop-up menu to choose a glow color, the Size slider to determine how wide a glowing frame to create, and the Transparency slider to soften the effect. Ribbon command: Format | Shape Styles→Effects→Glow or Format | Text Styles→Effects→Glow.

- The **Soft Edges** effect creates a soft or feathered edge to the picture, so it blends gradually into the page background. You'll often see this technique used in collages where one picture blends into another. Set the Glow pop-up menu to No Glow and then adjust the Soft Edges slider to see the effect. Ribbon command: Format | Shape Styles→Effects→Glow Options or Format | Text Styles→Effects→Glow Options.

Feel free to experiment using the Glow and Soft Edges effects together.

Creating Reflections

Turn on the Reflection checkbox to make your pictures appear to be standing on a highly polished surface, with a reflection extending from the bottom of the picture.

This is a modern look you are no doubt familiar if you've been hanging around Mac OS X—or especially Steve Jobs' keynote presentations—for very long.

- The **Transparency** control determines the intensity, or density, of the reflection.
- Use the **Size** slider to control how much of the picture is reflected below it, from none at zero, to the entire picture at 100%.
- When you slide the **Distance** adjustment to the right, the reflection moves away from the bottom of the picture—the same effect you'd see if you were to raise the picture above the reflective surface.

3-D Format

Pixar it isn't, but Word does its best to simulate three-dimensionality by giving you the option of adding 3-D effects to your pictures. Using these tools, you can transform a flat picture into what looks like a very thick picture, or a box with the picture wrapped around every side.

- The **Bevel** tab controls what the virtual sides and edges of the 3-D picture look like. Since the picture is turning into a 3-D "box," use the two pop-up menus to determine the kind of edge treatment for the top and bottom of the box. The Width settings control how far that edge intrudes into the picture; while the Height settings control the thickness or depth of the edge treatment.
- The **Depth & Surface** tab's **Depth & Contour** section controls the edge color and "thickness" of your 3-D box. Use the Depth Color pop-up menu to apply a color to the 3-D sides of your picture, and use the Depth setting to determine its thickness.

  You can use the Contour Color pop-up menu and Size box to apply a color to all the edges of your box as an additional way to highlight your picture's three-dimensionality.

- The **Surface** section of the Depth & Surface tab lets you choose the material that your virtual 3-D object is built from. Use the pop-up menu to choose from shiny metal, clear glass, a matte surface, and so on. Then use the Lighting pop-up menu to control the virtual illumination for your virtual object. Choose from simple flat lighting, warm sunset light, harsh contrast lighting, and many others; and then choose the direction for your light source using the Angle control.

3-D Rotation

Once you've built a 3-D object from a picture using the 3-D Format tab, make the most of it by using the 3-D Rotation tab to orient it on the page.

Use the **Rotation** section's Type pop-up menu to choose how your 3-D object appears as you rotate it. Choose Parallel to keep the sides of your object parallel with one another; choose perspective to make it look like the rotated object is receding into space. Then use the Perspective up- and down-arrow buttons to vary the perspective amount.

The four Oblique settings determine which corner your object rotates around. After choosing the type of rotation, use the X, Y, or Z buttons to perform the rotation. Click these rotation buttons to rotate in 5-degree increments in the direction indicated on the button, or use the up-and down-arrow button to move in 1-degree increments. Of course, you can also enter a measurement directly in the box.

You can move the rotation axis away from the plane of the object by the amount you enter in the "Distance from center" box—an effect that's especially visible if you've turned on the shadow or reflection options.

If your shape or object includes text, you may or may not want to spin the text with the object. If you want the text to stay put, check the "Keep text flat" box.

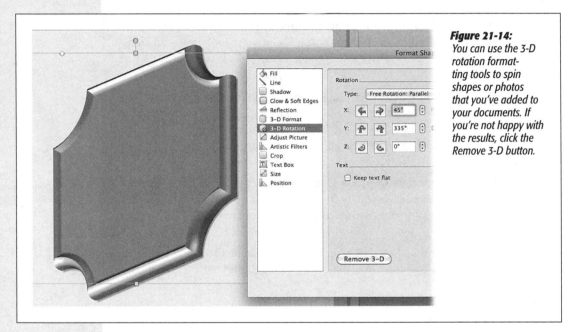

Figure 21-14:
You can use the 3-D rotation formatting tools to spin shapes or photos that you've added to your documents. If you're not happy with the results, click the Remove 3-D button.

Adjust Picture

Like the photographers who snapped the shots, pictures aren't always perfect. They may be too light or too dark. There may not be as much contrast as you'd like. In general, if a picture has a problem, you're best off editing the picture in iPhoto, Photoshop Elements, or some other photo-fixing tool. On the other hand, for special effects or some other reason, you may want to make changes to your photo inside of PowerPoint or a Word Publishing Layout. Office gives you some basic photo-fixing abilities, as well as some snazzy special effects. In the Format dialog box, click Adjust Picture, and you'll find a transparency slider and the photographer's friends: Brightness, Contrast, and Sharpen.

- The **Transparency** control lets you make a picture completely—or just slightly—transparent, so that whatever is behind it shows through. Combining transparency with a fill color is a good way to make a tinted background image.

- **Brightness** and **Contrast** are mainly useful for touching up photographs, but they do affect clip art and other images. Increase contrast for a crisper look; decrease it for a softer effect.

- The **Sharpness** slider can make a slightly out-of-focus picture look better, but it should be used sparingly. If you over-sharpen an image, it gets a grainy look.

- The **Recolor** menu lets you turn your color graphic into grayscale, black and white, or washout. (The washout setting produces an extremely faint image, light enough that you can still read text that flows over it.) In addition, you can choose from a batch of dark and light variations to colorize your picture based on the Document Theme colors.

Artistic Filters

The artistic filters are just plain fun to use. Take a photo or even a shape, and you can use a filter to make it look as if it were sketched with a pencil, drawn with pastels, or painted onto a rough, cement-like surface. For some examples, see Figure 21-15.

After you choose an effect from the menu, you can use two sliders to fine-tune the effect. The function of the sliders differ for each filter. There's really only one problem with the Artistic Filters—you'll waste way too much time trying them all out.

Figure 21-15:
Artistic filters change the appearance and mood of a photo.

Left: The original image from Office's clip art without any filter.

Middle: The image with the Pencil Sketch filter.

Right: The same image with the Watercolor Sponge filter applied.

Cropping Graphics

The crop tools affect the shape and look of your graphics in addition to removing the unwanted portions around the edges.

- Use the **Width** and **Height** settings to stretch and squash the image within the original graphic box.

- The **Offset X** and **Offset Y** controls shift the image within the same frame. As usual, X represents horizontal movement and Y represents vertical.

- The **Crop Position** tools trim the edges of your image from the top, bottom, left, and right edges.

Formatting Text Boxes

You may have noticed computers think differently from humans. For example, when you put text in a text box, you still think of it as text. To Office, it considers a text box another Shape. Oh, Office gives you some text-specific tools too, but for the most part, it thinks of text boxes as shapes. So, if you want to do fancy graphic things with text, put it in a text box. Right-click (Control-click) the box and choose Format Shape from the shortcut menu. At that point you can use most of the Format dialog box tools discussed in this chapter. For example, want to make the text look like the floating-away-from-you Star Wars text? Click 3-D Rotation and make adjustments to the Y axis.

For the text-specific formatting options, click Text Box near the bottom of the list on the left. You can choose the alignment for the text within the box: Top, Middle, Bottom, and a few centering options. The Text Direction menu lets you rotate the text box. Another menu controls the direction the text flows in the box. The oddest one in the bunch is Stacking, which displays each word in its own little vertical tower.

Use the AutoFit options to help Office decide how block of text relates to the text box. If you want the text box to retain its dimensions, and have the text change to fit the box, choose Resize text to fit shape. If you want the box to grow to accommodate the text, choose Resize shape to fit text.

Tip: When you want to add fancy formatting to the text within the text box, right-click (Control-click) the text and choose Format Text.

Size Adjustments

The size adjustment tools let you make the same kinds of changes you make when you grab the handles around a shape, photo, or text box. In most cases, it's easier to make changes to width, height and rotation by just dragging the handles to a new position. However, if you want to make change with numeric precision, you'll find the tools here. You can set width and height in inches or as percentages of the original object. Turn on the Lock Aspect Ratio box if you want the graphic to maintain its proportion as you change dimensions.

Note: Making bitmapped images (like digital photos) *larger* than they originally appear is a recipe for blotchiness, since you can't have more dots per inch than the image's original resolution. And if you intend to print such graphics, be aware that their standard screen resolution of 72 dots per inch looks good on the screen but isn't fine enough to produce high-quality prints. So if your document is destined for the printer, use digital images of 150 dots per inch or higher.

Adjust Position

Like the Size tools mentioned above, the Positions tools mimic what you do when you drag a graphic to a different place in your document. The difference is that you can make the move with numeric precision.

Storing Favorites in the Scrapbook

Think of the Scrapbook as, well…a scrapbook. It's a place where you can drag copied snippets from documents or pictures, or Excel spreadsheets for safekeeping.

After opening the Scrapbook, as described in Figure 21-16, copy your text (or whatever) into the Scrapbook window by dragging it or using any of the conventional cut, copy, and paste methods. To reuse the material, click the Paste button (near the middle of the Scrapbook) to paste the material shown in the Scrapbook window into your cursor's current location. There are three pasting options:

- **Paste**. This most common option pastes the material in the exact same format that you copied it.

- **Paste as Plain Text**. By golly, they weren't kidding. Use this button if you want to remove all the formatting and paste it as just plain text.

- **Paste as Picture**. This command pastes your snippet as a picture you can format using any of Office's picture tools like color adjustment and shadowing, as described earlier in this chapter. You can use this to turn, say, a drawing object into a picture and thus avail yourself of the picture tools.

On the other hand, the Add button takes the selected text, picture, table, or whatever, and transfers it to the Scrapbook. There are four options:

- **Add Selection**. An alternative to the Copy command, this option instantly adds your current selection to the Scrapbook. This is handy if you've highlighted a piece of text—a clever email joke, for example—that you wish to paste into other Office programs.

- **Add File**. Adds the current file to the Scrapbook. It can be any Office document.

- **Add From Clipboard**. Pastes whatever is in your clipboard to the Scrapbook.

- **Always Add Copy**. A good one for the time-challenged or compulsive hoarders among us. After you click this, *anything* you copy or cut is pasted directly into the Scrapbook.

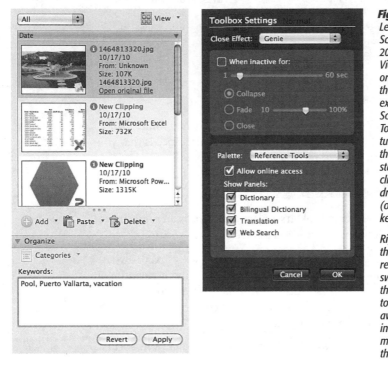

Figure 21-16:
*Left: You can open the
Scrapbook in any Office
2011 program by selecting
View→Toolbox→Scrapbook
or clicking the Toolbox icon on
the Standard toolbar (Outlook
excepted), and then clicking the
Scrapbook icon at the top of the
Toolbox. Drag or paste text, pictures, or Excel spreadsheets into
the Scrapbook—and there they'll
stay until you need them. Copy a
clipping from the Scrapbook by
dragging it onto your document
(or by using any of the usual
keyboard shortcuts).*

*Right: Click the arrow button in
the upper-right-hand corner to
reach the Toolbox Settings, which
swivel into view (right). Turn on
the "When inactive for" checkbox
to cause the toolbox to stash itself
away after a certain period of
inactivity. The bottom panel determines what you see when you use
the various toolbox palettes.*

If you have a scrap you no longer need, you can delete it with the delete key or by
pressing the Delete button. Three delete options exist on the Delete pop-up menu:

- **Delete**. This choice is the plain, garden-variety delete. It deletes the currently
  selected clipping.

- **Delete Visible**. Deletes the clipping in the preview window.

- **Delete All**. Deletes all clippings.

Note: When you delete a clipping, it's gone—a part of history. There's no way to get it back. Kind of like
your first kiss.

Object Linking and Embedding (OLE)

Linked and *embedded* objects are both chunks of data, like drawings or spreadsheets,
nestled within a document in one Office program, but actually created by another.

You edit them in whatever program created them, but behind the scenes, there's a big difference in where their data is stored. A *linked* object's data is stored in a separate file (what Microsoft calls the *source* file). An *embedded* object, on the other hand, is an integral part of the file in which it appears. All its data is stored right there in the document. That's why an embedded object bloats the file size of the document containing it. However, embedding an object means that you'll never have to endure that sickening jolt when you realize you're missing an important speech that you copied to your laptop (as you might if you had only used linking).

The whole process is called Object Linking and Embedding, or OLE for short. You can't get very far on a Microsoft newsgroup or discussion board without seeing that acronym. At user group meetings, the preferred pronunciation is "olé".

Creating Linked Objects

To add a linked object to your Office document, you first have to create that object in a program that offers OLE features. On the Mac, that includes Word, Excel, and PowerPoint 2011. For example, you can use linking to incorporate a drawing, spreadsheet, or chart into a Word document; weirdly enough, even another Word document can be incorporated into a Word document.

When you've created the source document, save the file, open the destination Word document, and choose Insert→Object. Besides the usual Office suspects—Excel charts and sheets, and Word documents—the Object window lets you choose from two other object types:

- **Microsoft Equation**. The place to come to create mathematical formulas. You can use its 19 pop-up menus for operators, radicals, Greek letters, and other doodads to create anything from simple fractions to complex equations. When you're done, close the window and the equation appears in your document. Since these typographically impressive equations are graphic objects instead of text, you can resize or manipulate them like any object. If you discover an error in your equation, double-click it to return to the Equation Editor

- **Microsoft Graph Chart**. Office's aged, proto-Excel graphing tool. Very basic, but it does work.

In the Object window, highlight the Object type you're after, and click From File to open the Insert as Object dialog box (Figure 21-17), where you can navigate to the source document.

When you've located the source document, select it, turn on Link to File, and click Insert. The entire contents of the source file appear in the destination document inside a resizable border. You can format this object using Word's picture-formatting tools—but to edit the *content* of the linked object, you have to open the actual source file.

Editing Linked Objects

To edit a linked object, simply double-click it. (If you have many linked objects in one document, choose Edit→Links, and then click the link you want to edit in the list box. Links can be identified by the name of the source file.)

If it isn't already running, the source program launches, and the source document opens. Now you can edit the story, rotate the drawing, or revise the numbers in the spreadsheet. When you close the source document, the linked object is automatically updated.

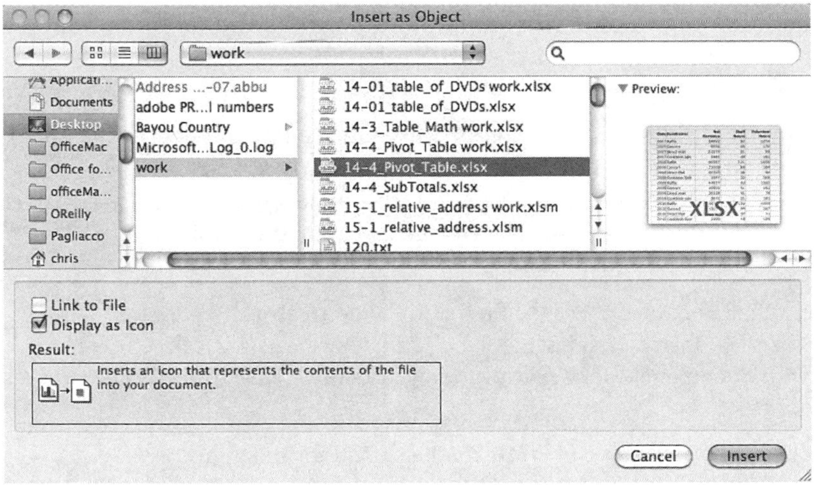

Figure 21-17:
Checking the "Display as icon" box in the Object dialog box creates an icon that links to the source document. Both linked and embedded objects can be displayed as icons.

It's easy to see the limitation of linked objects: Without the source file and the destination file on the same Mac, you can't edit the linked object. If you copy a document containing a linked object to a USB flash drive, email it, or transfer it to your MacBook Air, you'll be able to see, but not edit, the linked object. The bottom line: If you have to edit it on the road, be sure to copy the source file onto the same disk or laptop.

Repairing a Broken Link

If Office can't find the source file for a linked object—perhaps because you've moved or renamed it—there's a way to remind Office of its location. Choose Edit→Links and select the link in question; click Change Source. An Open dialog box appears where you can choose the source file; this is what tells Office to reconnect it to that link. Navigate to the file and double-click it.

You can use the same technique to change a linked object to a new source file altogether—such as a different graphic or a new fiscal year's ledger. Bear in mind that the new source file has to be in the same program as the original one.

Tip: This is also the technique to use if you want to create a link to only a certain part of a source file—for example, a range of cells in an Excel spreadsheet or an excerpt of a Word document that you've marked with a bookmark. (See page 213 for details on bookmarks.) Type the name of the range or bookmark in the Range/Bookmark box.

Overriding Automatic Updating

Office automatically updates linked objects every time you edit the source document. If, however, you want the linked object to remain unchanged (permanently or temporarily), there are a number of ways to go about it. Begin by choosing Edit→Links to open the Links dialog box (Figure 21-18).

- **Break Link**. This button uncouples the connection between source document and object. (Because this choice is irrevocable, Office asks if you're sure.) From now on, editing the source document does nothing at all to the destination document.

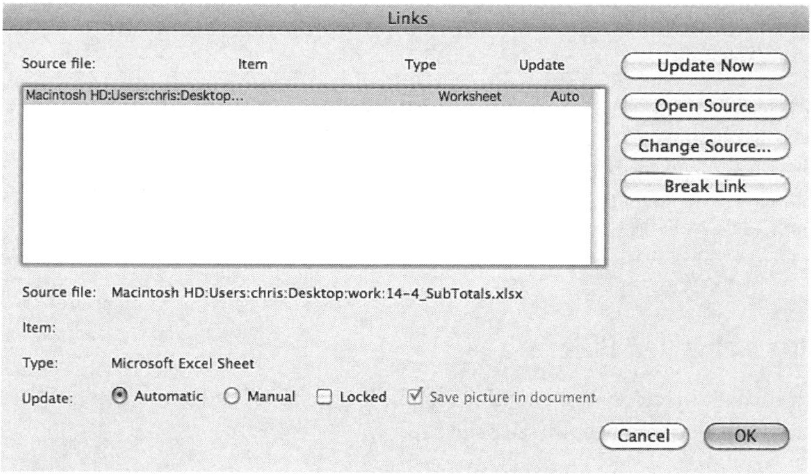

Figure 21-18:
When you click a link in the "Source file" box, the full file name and location appear just under the box.

You can't even repair the link, since the object no longer *is* a link. It becomes a picture, however, and still can be formatted as such (see page 613).

Tip: If you act quickly, you can reinstate a broken link by choosing Edit→Undo Links or pressing ⌘-Z.

- **Locked**. This box prevents changes to the source document from affecting the destination object. You can still double-click the link to open the source document, but any editing you perform there won't have any effect until you turn off the Locked box again *and* click the Update Now button in the Links dialog box.

- **Manual Updating**. Automatic is Office's default way of updating linked documents. When you choose the Manual radio button at the bottom of the Links dialog box, Word updates the linked object only when you click Update Now.

Creating Embedded Objects

Creating an embedded object from an existing file is the same as creating a linked object, except you do *not* turn on "Link to File".

To bring in an external file using this technique, choose Insert→Object. In the dialog box, proceed like this:

- **If the file you want to embed already exists**: Choose the type of file and then click From File. Navigate to and open the source document to embed a copy of it in your Office document.

- **To create a new file (for embedding) on the spot**: In the list box, double-click the kind of object you want to create: Chart, Worksheet, Picture, or whatever. A new window opens, complete with menus and toolbars, where you can begin creating the object. When you're done, close the window; the object appears in your document.

Tip: When creating an embedded picture, you can use any of Word's drawing tools, as described earlier in this chapter. However, when you close the window, the result is a *picture*, not a drawing—you can no longer edit it as you would a drawing.

If, on the other hand, you simply want to insert a drawing object in a Word, Excel, or PowerPoint document, just head over to the Insert menu!

Editing Embedded Objects

Like a linked object, an embedded object has a surrounding frame. You can format it using Office's picture tools (see page 613).

To edit it, though, you have to double-click it. (Or click it and choose Edit→Object→ Edit. The Edit menu changes to specify the type of object you've selected—Document Object, Worksheet Object, and so on.) The object opens in a separate document window, where you can edit it using the appropriate menus and toolbars.

You can edit an embedded object in any compatible program on your Mac. Just click the object and then choose Edit→Object→Convert. Choose a program in the list that appears, and then click OK. (Most of the time, the Microsoft Office programs will be the only ones available.)

CHAPTER 22

Customizing Office

L ots of people use Office: graphic artists, school teachers, screenplay writers, legal secretaries and even rocket scientists. Everyone can think of ways to make Office work better. In an effort to capture market share and keep all its users happy, Microsoft has made Office extremely customizable.

Very few elements of the way you work in Office are set in stone. Word, Excel, and PowerPoint each let you redesign the toolbars and even rework the menus. In Word and Excel, you can also choose different keyboard equivalents for commands. (Outlook is closest to off-the-rack software. You can customize its toolbar, but that's about it.)

Even if you're a novice, customization is worth exploring. There will almost certainly come a day when you wish you could choose an easier function keystroke than the one Microsoft chose, or find yourself repeatedly digging for a submenu command. With this chapter as your guide, you can be your own software tailor.

Customizing the Ribbon

The ribbon wasn't designed to be customized—in fact, just the opposite. Microsoft wanted to group the most commonly used commands on a toolbar-like panel; but, unlike the highly customizable toolbars, the ribbon widgets were meant to stay in one place. Why? If you're responsible for training and troubleshooting Office issues at your company, you already know the answer. It's hard to help colleagues who have completely rearranged their menus and toolbars. Customizable toolbars are great for power-users, but average mortals usually only "customize" their toolbars by accident. So, the tools on a given tab on the ribbon stay put.

That said, there are a few things you can do to show and hide elements of the ribbon, and you can rearrange the order of the tabs. In most cases, the process is similar in Word, Excel, and PowerPoint—this chapter lets you know where and when. Outlook doesn't let you customize ribbon features at all. The ribbon settings are specific for each application, so, for example, if you want to hide the ribbon entirely, you need to do that for each application.

- **Collapse and expand the ribbon**. The ribbon takes up a bit of screen real estate, but it's easy to hide the tools so that only the tab tops show. Click the currently selected tab, and the tools disappear. The next time you click any tab, the tools come back.

- **Hide ribbon completely**. You'll have to work a lot harder if you want to hide the ribbon entirely. But if you absolutely hate the ribbon, you can remove it from your application. In Word, go to Word→Preferences→Personal Settings→Ribbon. Then in the ribbon preferences pane, deselect the first option "Turn on the ribbon".

Note: If you're looking for an uncluttered working environment, you may want to work in one of the full screen views, which provide the most commonly used tools while making the most of your screen. For Word and Excel, choose View→Full Screen.

- **Show and hide group titles**. In Word, Excel, and PowerPoint, the tools on the ribbon are grouped under titles. These are particularly helpful when you're first learning how to use a program, but may not be necessary later. For example, to turn off group titles in Excel, go to Excel→Preferences→ Ribbon. In the General group at the top, select "Hide group titles".

- **Change the ribbon color scheme**. While it's not an earth-shaking difference, you can choose the color scheme for the ribbon. Photographers and graphics artists, who work with color images, may prefer the Graphite scheme to more colorful options. Go to PowerPoint→Preferences→Ribbon and set the appearance menu to Graphite.

- **Show and hide individual tabs**. You can choose which tabs appear on your ribbon. Perhaps you never collaborate and don't need the Review tab in Word. Or maybe you despise SmartArt. Go to Word→Preferences→Personal Settings→Ribbon to open the preferences pane. In the middle there's a scrolling list of tabs. Select the ones that you want to show and deselect the others. The only one you can't change is the Home tab. Note that in Word, there are separate tab settings for the different views: Print Layout View, Publishing Layout View, and Notebook Layout View. That's not the case with Excel and PowerPoint.

Tip: If you're interested in recording macros, you'll want to display the Developer tab in your applications. See page 446 for the details.

- **Rearrange tab order on the ribbon**. If you'd like to have the tabs you use the most on the left side of the ribbon, you can do that. The only one that's unmovable is the Home tab. To reorder your tabs go to the right end of the ribbon and open the menu shown in Figure 22-1, then choose "Customize Ribbon Tab Order". Each tab displays a little three line grip, and you can drag them to a new location or click the X button to hide the tab.

Figure 22-1:
On the right side of the ribbon, you'll find tools to that help you customize. On the menu shown here, choose Customize Ribbon Tab Order and you can drag tabs to different locations.

Customizing Your Toolbars

With Office 2011, you get the distinct feeling that toolbars are on their way out and the ribbon is coming in as the replacement. Office still has toolbars and you can still create your own toolbars, but there are far fewer in Office 2011 than there were in previous versions. The Standard toolbar is still attached to the top of the document window, as it was in Office 2008, and it still offers several valuable, basic tools. You can turn it on and off via the View menu, but you can't drag it to another location. To move any other Toolbar, just drag it, using its skinny title bar (next to the close button) as a handle.

You'll soon discover that toolbars are "magnetic." That is, they like to snap against the sides of the menu, and other toolbars.

Tip: This snappiness is designed to help you keep your screen tidy, but if you want to stifle your toolbars' law of attraction, press Shift as you drag them.

You can also reshape your toolbar by resizing it as if it were a window: Just drag the diagonally striped area in the lower-right corner, as shown in Figure 22-2.

Figure 22-2:
Top: If you right-click any empty gray space in a toolbar, you get a pop-up menu leading to a submenu listing all toolbars. Checkmarks indicate currently visible toolbars. Choose a toolbar name to make it appear or disappear. The Standard toolbar gives you the additional option of whether or not to display the text label next to your toolbar buttons.

Bottom: The toolbar turns into an outline as you drag its resizing corner. As you drag diagonally, it goes from a vertical toolbar to various incarnations of a rectangle, and finally to a horizontal toolbar—or the other way around.

Showing Other Toolbars

All the Office programs display the Standard toolbar at the top of document windows. The buttons displayed in those toolbars vary, but always show the most common file saving, opening, printing, and editing chores. Each application includes a Formatting toolbar that duplicates the tools on the ribbon. You may also have custom toolbars that you or a colleague created, as described in the next section. You can summon or dismiss any of these toolbars as needed.

You can open and close toolbars in any of three ways:

- Right-click (Control-click) the More Buttons toolbar icon (usually at the far right or bottom edge of a non-docked toolbar), or right-click an empty area on any open toolbar or palette. As shown in Figure 22-2, you get a pop-up menu of what Microsoft considers to be the most useful toolbars. Choose the name of the one you'd like to open or close.

- Choose from the View→Toolbars submenu. Here again, you see the same list of toolbars.

- Choose View→"Customize Toolbars and Menus", or right-click a gray area of a toolbar and choose "Customize Toolbars and Menus" from the pop-up menu. Now you see a list of *all* of the toolbars, even the obscure ones. Turn on a checkbox to make the corresponding toolbar appear or disappear instantly. (Because you don't even have to close the dialog box between experiments, this is the fastest way to have a quick look at all the available toolbars.) Click OK to close the dialog box.

Creating Custom Toolbars

The likelihood of Microsoft *perfectly* predicting which buttons you'd like on which toolbars is about the same as finding the exact wrench you want the first time you reach into your pile of tools, while laying on your back under the '59 TR3 with oil dribbling on your chin. Fortunately, it's very easy to delete or add buttons on Excel, PowerPoint, or Word toolbars—much easier than crawling out from under that Triumph. In fact, you can, and should, create entirely new toolbars that contain nothing but your own favorite buttons. If you use Word's styles, as described on page 119, for example, it's a no-brainer to create a palette of your favorite styles, so that you can apply them with a single click.

To move a button or delete it from a toolbar

To move a button, open the "Customize Toolbars and Menus" dialog box by choosing View→"Customize Toolbars and Menus", and then just drag the button to a new spot on the toolbar—or even to another toolbar. (You can ignore the Customize dialog box itself for the moment, but the Customize dialog box needs to be open for this dragging to work.) The button assumes its new place, and the other buttons rearrange themselves to make room.

To get rid of a button on a non-docked toolbar, Control-click the button you wish to remove, and then choose Hide Command from the shortcut menu that appears. For docked toolbars, or if you already have the Customize dialog box open, you can delete a button by dragging it off the toolbar to the desktop or anywhere else in the document window. (Either way, you can get the button back later if you like; read on.)

To add a button to a toolbar

Every now and then, you'll wish you had a one-shot button that triggers some useful command—for inserting the current date into your document, for example.

To add a button to an existing toolbar, choose View→"Customize Toolbars and Menus" and then click the Commands tab. A list of command categories appears, grouped by menu. Click a category in the left box, and a list of associated commands appears on the right, along with an icon for each command, if one exists. It's a staggeringly long list that includes almost every command in the program.

If you click the All Commands category, you'll notice that the names of Office's commands in the All Commands list are a tad user-hostile: No spaces are allowed, and the command's name often runs together with the name of the menu that contains it (such as ToolsSpelling). You'll also notice that each of your Office programs has *hundreds* of commands that don't appear in the regular menus. Furthermore, the names of some commands don't quite correspond to their menu-bar equivalents. For example, the command for Insert→Comment is Insert→Annotation in the All Commands list. So check the menu categories before you resort to the All Commands list.

Tip: Trying to move around quickly in the All Commands category? You can type a letter (or letters) to move to the part of the list beginning with that letter. For instance, type *v* to scroll to commands for viewing or *ins* to jump to commands for inserting.

You can drag *any* of the command icons (and hence the command) in the Customize dialog box onto a toolbar, as shown in Figure 22-3. Some of them, such as Font Color, even take the form of pop-up menus which then become part of your toolbar. In fact, if you drag the command at the bottom of the Categories list called New Menu onto a toolbar, it turns into a pop-up menu that you can fill with any commands you like. You might decide to set up several custom pop-up menus filled with small lists of related styles—one just for headings, for example. The more logical the arrangement, the quicker the access. You can rename your homemade pop-up menu as described in the Tip on the next page.

Weirder yet, look at the top of your screen—there's a *duplicate menu bar* there, floating on its own toolbar! Click one of these phony menus to open it. Now you can drag any menu command *right off the menu* onto your new toolbar, where it will be available for quicker access. Once buttons are on the toolbar, you can drag them around, or even drag them off the toolbar to get rid of them, as long as you don't close the Customize dialog box.

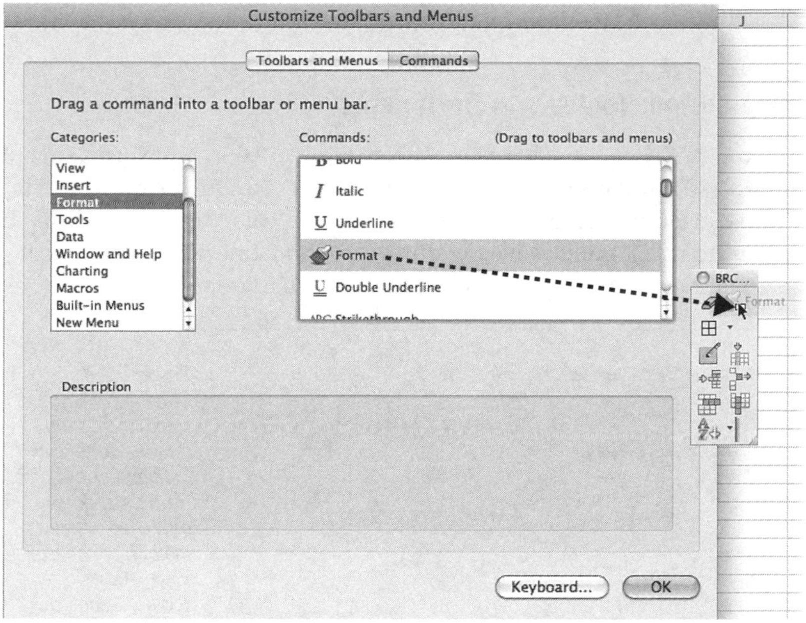

Figure 22-3:
You can easily add commands to a custom toolbar: just drag them one by one from the Commands section of the Customize window to the toolbar. Once you let go, feel free to drag them or their toolbar-mates around into a more pleasing arrangement, or drag the lower-right corner of the toolbar to reshape it.

Tip: If you double-click a toolbar button or pop-up menu while the Customize dialog box is open, you summon the Command Properties dialog box. Here's where you get to specify how you want the command to look in the toolbar: as a little icon, as a plain English word, or both (see the box below). You can also add a separator line before the button (above it or to its left) by turning on "Begin a group".

You can even perform this kind of button editing on non-docked toolbars when the Customize window *isn't* open—in the middle of your everyday work. The trick is to Control-click the button and choose Properties from the shortcut menu.

To design a new toolbar from scratch

Designing a completely new toolbar works much the same way as adding buttons. Choose View→"Customize Toolbars and Menus", select the Toolbars and Menus tab, and then click the New button. You'll be asked to name your new toolbar, which then appears as an empty square floating oddly above the Customize dialog box—an embryonic toolbar just waiting for you to provide commands. Now click the Commands tab and begin filling your new toolbar with commands and buttons, just as described earlier. Click OK when you're finished.

Note: As shown in Figure 22-4, your options for customizing Outlook are more limited than those for other Office Programs.

Attaching Custom Toolbars to Documents

In Word, you can store a toolbar you've created or edited in the Normal template (see page 68), so it will be available for use in any new documents you create if you choose "Save in Normal.dotm" in the "Customize Toolbars and Menus" dialog box. But after spending 20 minutes handcrafting the world's most brilliant toolbar, the last thing you want is to confine it forever to your own Mac.

Figure 22-4:
Outlook limits your command customization efforts to its toolbar. Control-click (or right-click) a gray area of the toolbar, or choose View→Customize Toolbar to unfurl this sheet of button possibilities. Drag buttons onto or off of the toolbar, and use the controls at the bottom to determine how you want your buttons to appear. If you later decide that Microsoft's stock arrangement of buttons speaks to you on so many levels, just drag the original set back to the toolbar.

Fortunately, you can share your brilliance with other people just by attaching the custom toolbar to an Excel workbook or Word document (PowerPoint lacks this feature).

- **In Excel**. Choose View→Toolbars→"Customize Toolbars and Menus", and then click the "Toolbars and Menus" tab. Click a toolbar's name in the pane on the left side of the Customize window, and then click Attach.

  The Attach Toolbars window appears. It works exactly like the Organizer, described on page 85. Use it to select the destination document and copy the toolbar into it.

- **In Word**. Choose Tools→"Templates and Add-Ins". Click the Organizer button. Use the Organizer as described on page 68 to copy any toolbar into any document *or* template.

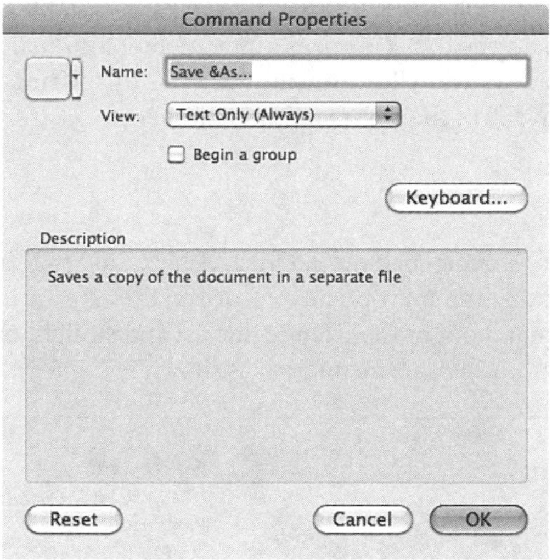

Figure 22-5:
Control-click a toolbar button and choose Properties to open the Command Properties window. The button pop-up menu lets you choose a different button image from this collection of icons, circa 1987. Or, copy the cutting-edge icon you designed in Photoshop and choose Paste Button Image to give the toolbar your distinct imprint.

OBSESSIVE USERS' CLINIC

Drawing Your Own Buttons

Not all commands that you drag onto your toolbars come with associated picture buttons (Save As is a good example). Most of the time, all you get is a text button. If you'd prefer an icon, though, you can add one.

The trick is to Control-click the new button on a non-docked toolbar and choose the Properties command. You get the Command Properties dialog box where you see a little blank button icon in the upper-left corner. Click the pop-up menu attached to find 42 alternative button icons vying for your affection (see Figure 22-5). If one of Microsoft's ready-made buttons will do, choose it from this pop-up menu.

If you don't care for any of Microsoft's microscopic masterpieces, you can design your own button in some other program (Photoshop, for example). Copy it, switch to the Office program you're editing, and then paste the graphic onto a button by choosing Paste Button Image from the menu. Microsoft recommends a 20 x 20 pixel image for maximum good looks. To restore the button's original icon (or lack of icon), choose Reset Button Image at the bottom of the menu.

Redesigning Your Menus

Not only can you build your own toolbars in Excel, PowerPoint, and Word, you can also twist and shape the *menus* of these programs to suit your schemes. You can add and remove items from the various menus, and you can even move the menus themselves so that they appear in different places on the menu bar.

More than one Excel owner, for example, has found happiness by stripping out the commands he never used. Conversely, you're missing out in Word if you don't *add* commands to the menus that you usually need to trigger by burrowing through nested dialog boxes.

As noted earlier, choosing View→Toolbars→"Customize Toolbars and Menus" doesn't just open the Customize dialog box. It also opens a strange-looking *duplicate* menu bar just beneath the real one. If you click a menu name on this Menu Bar "toolbar," the menu opens, revealing all of the commands in that menu.

Adding a Command

To add a command to a menu, choose, and click the Commands tab. Find the command that you want to add (by clicking the appropriate category on the left side first, for example). Then drag the command out of the Commands list and straight onto the *name* of the desired menu (on the *duplicate* menu bar), as shown in Figure 22-6.

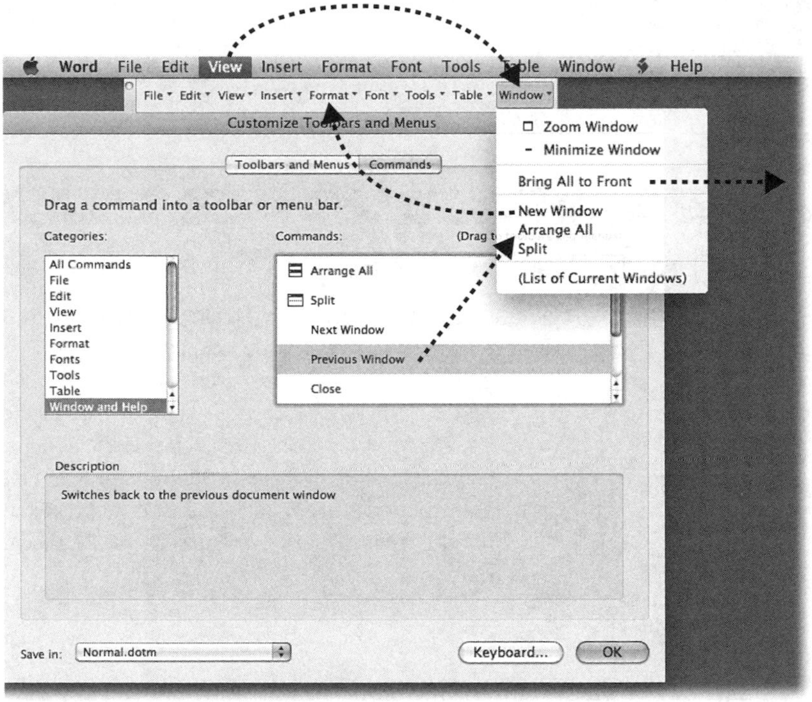

Figure 22-6:
Once you've chosen View→Toolbars→ "Customize Toolbars and Menus", you see the duplicate, editable menu bar. By dragging menus and commands as shown here, you show Office how you want to modify your real menu bar.

Note: Excel has *two* menu bars—a Worksheet Menu Bar and a Chart Menu Bar. They're listed individually in the Customize dialog box's Toolbars tab. That's because Excel's Data menu changes into a Chart menu when you select a chart. These two menu bars are independent, so if you make changes to the Insert menu item on the Chart Menu Bar toolbar, those changes *won't* be reflected in the Insert menu item on the Worksheet Menu Bar.

As you drag your command over the duplicate menu, the menu opens automatically. As you drag down the menu, a line shows you where the new command will appear when you release the mouse.

Tip: You can even rename your newly installed menu command. Open the duplicate menu bar, then double-click your command to open the Command Properties dialog box. Type the new name and press Return.

Removing a Menu Command

Suppose that you never use the Dictionary command in Excel's Tools menu; the only word *you* need to know is "Profit."

Getting rid of a menu command—whether *you* put it on the menu or not—is easy. Choose View→"Customize Toolbars and Menus" to summon the strange duplicate menu bar shown in Figure 22-6. Now click the menu title (in the duplicate menu bar) containing the command. Finally, drag the command itself off the menu.

Removing commands from menus doesn't delete them from the program, of course. To restore a command you've removed from a menu, reinstall it as described in the previous section.

Adding a Menu

You can do more than just add commands to existing menus. You can also create completely *new* menus, name them whatever you please, and fill them with any commands you like, in any order you like. This feature opens up staggering possibilities of customization: You can create a stripped-down "just the commands you really need" menu for an absolute novice, for example.

To do so, choose View→Toolbars→"Customize Toolbars and Menus", click the Commands tab, scroll to the bottom of the Categories list, and click New Menu. Drag the New Menu command from the Commands list (right side of the window) to the Menu Bar toolbar. Put it anywhere you want—between the File and Edit menus, for example, or to the right of the Help menu.

With the new menu still selected, Control-click your new menu and choose Properties from the shortcut menu. Type a name for your new menu into the Name field. Finally, press Return. (The Command Properties box also has a "Begin a group" checkbox, which inserts a separator line into your menu-under-construction.)

Your new menu is installed. Now you can add to it any commands you want, using the same technique described in "Adding a command," on page 640.

Removing a Menu

You don't have to stare at the complex Microsoft menus that you rarely use. If you're one of the 99.9% of people who never, ever use the Tables in Word, for example, you can ditch it.

Doing so couldn't be easier. Choose View→Toolbars→"Customize Toolbars and Menus" to make the phantom double menu bar appear. Point to the name of the menu you no longer need and drag it directly downward and off the menu bar. Once it's gone, the other menus tighten up and fill its space. (Never fear: You can always bring it back, as described below.)

Moving Whole Menus, or Specific Commands

Even the order of menus on the menu bar isn't sacrosanct in Office 2011. If it occurs to you that perhaps the Fonts menu should come *before* the Edit menu, choose View→Toolbars→"Customize Toolbars and Menus". Now you can start dragging around the menu titles themselves (on the duplicate menu bar) until you've created an arrangement that you like.

While you're at it, you can also drag individual commands from menu to menu. As shown in Figure 22-6, start by choosing View→Toolbars→ "Customize Toolbars and Menus". Then bring the menu command to the screen by opening its current menu in the duplicate menu bar. Now drag the command to the *name* of a new menu, which opens automatically; without releasing the mouse, drag downward until the command is positioned where you want it. Finally, release the mouse button.

Resetting Everything Back to Normal

When you delete a command, it's not gone from Office. You've merely removed it from its menu or toolbar, and it's easy enough to put it back—a handy fact to remember the morning after a late night with some geek buddies that featured a pitcher of Red Bull daiquiris and some overzealous menu modifications.

Open the Customize window (by choosing View→ Toolbars→"Customize Toolbars and Menus"). Click the Toolbars tab. In the list at left, click Menu Bar, and then click Reset. You've just restored your menus and commands to their original, factory-fresh condition.

Tip: You can use this technique to restore any of the factory toolbars, too. On the "Customize Toolbars and Menus" Toolbars tab, just turn on the checkbox next to the toolbar you want restored, and then click Reset.

Reassigning Key Combinations

Pressing a staggering number of keyboard shortcuts can trigger an equally stagger-ing number of Office commands. The only problem arises when you discover that Microsoft has chosen something bizarre (like Option-⌘-R for Thesaurus) instead of something more natural (like ⌘-T).

The good news is that you can reassign key combinations for any menu command—in Word and Excel, anyway. (You can't fiddle with the keyboard commands in Power-Point or Outlook from within the programs. Instead you have to go to ⌘→System Preferences→Keyboard and Mouse→Keyboard Shortcuts and do it there.)

To begin, choose Tools→Customize Keyboard to conjure up the Customize Key-board window (see Figure 22-7). It works much like the toolbar-editing dialog box described earlier in this chapter. At left, click a command category; at right, click the name of the command you want to reassign. (After clicking or tabbing into one of these lists, you can jump to a particular category or command by typing the first couple of letters of its name.)

After highlighting the command for which you'd like to change or add a key com-bination, click in the box beneath the "Press new shortcut key" field. Now press the keys you'd like to use as the new key combo, using any combination of the Shift, Command, Option, and Control keys, along with a letter, F-key, or number key.

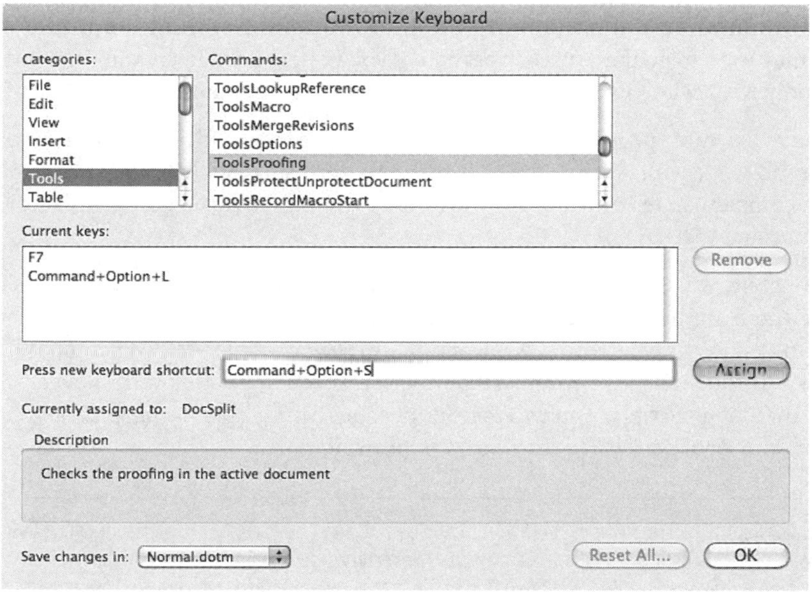

Figure 22-7:
Here, the "Spell-ing and Grammar" option is being given another keyboard shortcut—Option-⌘-S. Word warns that Option-⌘-S is already in use by another command ("Doc-Split," which splits the document window into two panes); if you don't care, just click Assign.

If that keystroke already "belongs" to another command in the Office 2011 program you're using, the Customize dialog box shows you which command has it (Figure 22-7). To reassign that keystroke to the new command and remove it from the original one, click the Assign button. To keep the current setting, press Delete, and then try another keystroke.

Obviously, you can't have two commands linked to a single keystroke. However, you *can* create more than one keyboard shortcut for a single command. For instance, in Word 2011, both ⌘-B and Shift-⌘-B are assigned to Bold.

Tip: If you find yourself frequently triggering a command *accidentally*, you may want to *remove* its assigned keystroke. To do so, click the command name in the list, highlight the keystroke in the "Current keys" list, and then click the Remove button. Click OK to save the changes.

If you don't like the key combinations that you've edited, you can always reset them by clicking the Reset All button in the lower-right portion of the dialog box.

AppleScripting Office

If you want to customize Office with custom scripts and programming code, you can choose between Microsoft's Visual Basic for Applications (VBA) or your Mac's native scripting language: AppleScript. If you work in an office full of Windows types, you may have access to VBA code or experts. In that case, you may want to go the Visual Basic route. You can find an introductory chapter on the subject on page 441. You may want to go the AppleScript route if you're interested in creating scripts that not only work with Office applications but other Mac programs, like FileMaker Pro.

If you're like most people, you probably didn't upgrade to Office 2011 because of its ability to work with AppleScript. But if you're not using AppleScript to streamline your complex or repetitive tasks, you're not tapping Office's true potential for efficiency and speed.

Fortunately, you don't have to actually be a scripter to reap AppleScript's benefits, since there are hundreds of ready-made scripts you can download and use (turn first to that nexus of all things AppleScript, *http://macscripter.net*). What follows is a quick introduction to the world of AppleScript. If you do want to learn how to write your own AppleScripts, Apple's AppleScript pages (*http://developer.apple.com/applescript*) and *AppleScript: The Missing Manual* await.

Note: For information on switching from VBA to AppleScript, and AppleScript user guides for Office, visit Microsoft's Office scripting headquarters at *www.microsoft.com/mac/developers/*. In addition, MacTech Magazine has published a 150-page VBA-to-AppleScript transition guide, filled with detailed examples of converting VBA scripts to AppleScript. You can find it at *www.mactech.com/vba-transition-guide/index-toc.html*.

What is AppleScript?

AppleScript is the Mac's built-in *scripting*—that is, programming—language. (It's been around since 1993, with System 7.1.) Even without learning to write your own scripts, you can use scripts to control any program (Apple's or otherwise) whose developers have made it *scriptable*, meaning that they've built the necessary code into their program and provided an AppleScript dictionary. In other words, although the AppleScript language is built into Mac OS X, you can use it to control *programs* like Outlook, Word, iCal, iTunes, Adobe InDesign, and Photoshop.

Why Use AppleScript?

The vast majority of Office fans never dip a toe into AppleScript. But if you use Office to run a business or manage a department, you'll probably find a use for it. The advantage of AppleScript is that you only need to learn one programming language to communicate with *every* scriptable program on your Mac. For example, you can create a workflow that takes data from the Outlook Address Book and puts it into both Excel and FileMaker Pro, then prepares a Mail Merge in Word using the same information to type personalized form letters and envelopes, and then sends an email message from Outlook.

- **Automate**. Perform repetitive tasks automatically in a few seconds, instead of spending minutes or even hours plowing through them yourself. For example, you can run a script in Outlook to set the default address to the Home address, rather than Outlook's default of the Work address. If you have 1,000 contacts, this script will take about a minute to run, as opposed to multiple hours opening and changing each contact manually. Now you can print address labels for your Wear-Your-Bathrobe-to-Work Day cards without skipping the folks whose work addresses you don't know.

- **Customize**. Devise your own routines, sometimes even doing things that are impossible to do yourself onscreen in the first place. The world is your oyster: You can write scripts to duplicate calendar events (Outlook can't do that on its own), add a BCC to your boss on all email messages you send out, add a contact to a particular group without messing with finding or opening the group, remove all single carriage returns pasted into a Word document in one fell swoop without affecting double-returns at ends of paragraphs, and much, much more.

- **Interact**. Control several different programs in one workflow. You can take a letterhead document you've created in Word and have it open as a new letter addressed to a selected Outlook contact, complete with date, address, salutation, and signature already in place. Or you can export full contact information (street, city, state, phone numbers, email addresses, and so on) for every member of a group or category to an Excel worksheet or FileMaker Pro database—or both.

Installing and Running Office Scripts

Whether you choose to write your own scripts or not, you can always run scripts that others have written. Scripts come in two basic forms—*applets* (script programs, also called *droplets*), or *scripts* (script documents). Developers create their scripts in either of these two forms when they save them.

Installing Applets and Droplets

If the icon is an applet, you can store it, and its folder, anywhere at all on your computer. You can move it to your Applications folder, or to a subfolder for scripts within it; or to your Microsoft User Data folder (even though it's not data), or to a subfolder you create within it for Office script applets. You can also drag the applet icon to your Dock, as with any program, so you can launch it from there. If it's a script you'll be using often, dock it.

Run the applet by double-clicking it, like any program, or by clicking it in the Dock (if it's there). Or if it's a droplet (with the down-arrow icon), drag one or more files of the appropriate type—usually a Word, Excel, or PowerPoint document—onto it. You can even store droplets in the Dock and drop files onto it there.

If the icon is a *script document* (it may or may not bear an .scpt extension), then you have to put it in a specific place depending on whether it's a script for Outlook or for one of the other Office programs. Read on.

Installing Script Menu Scripts

When you're in any Office 2011 program, you'll notice a dark, scroll-shaped icon just to the right of the Help menu in the menu bar. That's the Office Script menu, and Outlook's comes preloaded with a few AppleScripts that automate multistep Outlook processes, like turning the selected email message into an Outlook note. Word, Excel, and PowerPoint don't come with any AppleScripts.

Note: All four Office programs come with a handful of Automator workflows, listed in the Script menu. With Mac OS X Tiger (10.4), Apple introduced Automator, a simple way to automate repetitive tasks with a basic drag-and-drop *workflow* creation. Automator comes with its own library of actions (such as file renaming, folder copying, creating a new mail message, and so on) that you can put together one after the other to create a workflow. You can also add AppleScripts to an Automator workflow, as you would any other action.

To learn more about Automator, check the Mac Help, Sal Soghoian's Automator site (*www.automator.us*), or *Mac OS X Snow Leopard: The Missing Manual*.

Here's how to add to this menu any AppleScripts you've downloaded from the Web or written yourself:

1. **If the script is a script document for Outlook, drag the icon into your Home→ Documents→Microsoft User Data→Outlook Script Menu Items folder. (You'll find similar folders for the three other Office programs in the Microsoft User Data folder.)**

   You now see a menu item with the name of the script in Outlook's Script menu.

2. **Select the menu item to run the script.**

   You can also set up an Outlook rule to run the script when messages are downloaded or sent, or an Outlook schedule to run the script automatically at startup, when you quit, or on a repeating regular schedule (see page 285).

3. **If you wish, you can create a keyboard shortcut for the script if it doesn't already have one. In Word and Excel, go to Tools→Customize Keyboard.**

Running the Scripts

Once you've installed a script, it's ready to run. Here's a quick review of the many ways you can run an AppleScript script:

- To run an applet, just double-click its icon in the Finder or click it once in the Dock

- To run a droplet, drag and drop files onto it.

- To run a Script menu script, just select it in the menu.

- To run an Outlook script automatically, set up a Rule (page 336) or Schedule (page 285) to *Run AppleScript*.

Part Six: Appendixes

6

Appendix A: Installation and Troubleshooting

Appendix A: The Office Help System

Appendix A: Office 2011, Menu by Menu

Appendix A: SkyDrive and Office Web Apps

Installation and Troubleshooting

Installing Office

If you've installed a previous version of Office, you may have used Microsoft's super-simple drag-and-drop installation—which is no more. Office 2011 now uses Apple's Installer technology.

Using the Installer

The Installer walks you gently through the installation process as it checks to see if your computer is up to snuff, looks for other copies of Office, and asks you if you'd like to install the entire package or just individual programs.

Figuring Out the Formatting

Microsoft recommends that you install Office on a hard drive that's been formatted using Mac OS Extended (HFS +), the default format for Mac OS X. If your Mac came with OS X preinstalled, chances are excellent that your disk is already formatted in this way.

If you inherited this Mac from your cousin and aren't sure how Mac OS X made its way onto your hard disk, check your disk's format by running Apple System Profiler. Choose →About This Mac and click the More Info button to summon the Apple System Profiler. Choose ATA in the Hardware section of the Contents pane on the left, and look for your hard drive on the right. Highlight the hard

drive model name—it may be something like ST3320620A— and look in the bottom pane for the more familiar hard drive name you're used to seeing on your computer. Finally, beneath that, you'll find an indication of the File System—which should say something similar to *Journaled HFS+*.

If it turns out that your disk uses the wrong format, but you're not sure how to proceed, be aware that you are treading firmly on power-user territory. See *Mac OS X Snow Leopard: The Missing Manual* for more information about disk formatting— or call in your cousin.

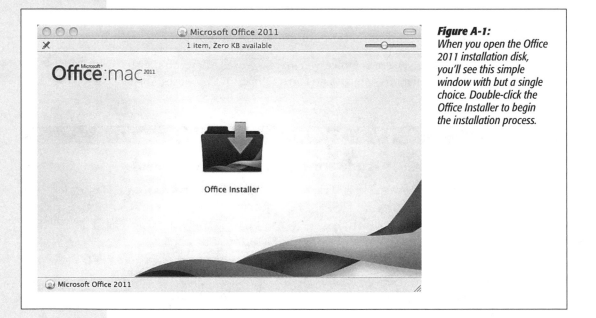

Figure A-1:
When you open the Office 2011 installation disk, you'll see this simple window with but a single choice. Double-click the Office Installer to begin the installation process.

1. **Start by quitting all of your running programs—especially Office programs.**

   The Office installer makes changes to your font collection, which could confuse other running programs.

2. **Insert the Microsoft Office 2011 DVD in your computer and, if necessary, double-click the Microsoft Office 2011 disk icon.**

3. **When the Office: Mac 2011 installer window appears (Figure A-1), double-click the Office Installer icon to get this show on the road.**

   When the installer launches, you see a Welcome screen (Figure A-2). This screen says, "The installer will guide you through the steps to install this software. To get started, click Continue."

Note: In Mac OS X, only people with Administrator accounts can do important stuff like install new software. If you're not sure, you can check in →System Preferences→Accounts. If you don't have "Admin" listed under your user name, ask someone who does for help. (You can learn more about all this account business in *Mac OS X Snow Leopard: The Missing Manual*.)

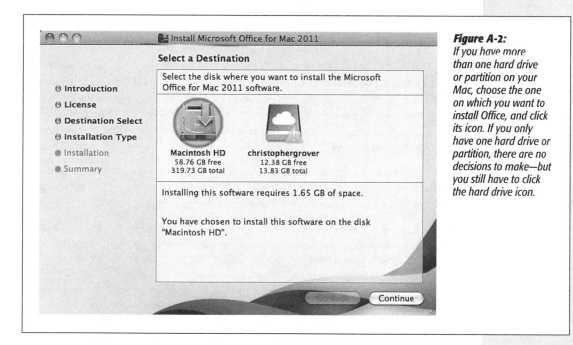

Figure A-2:
If you have more than one hard drive or partition on your Mac, choose the one on which you want to install Office, and click its icon. If you only have one hard drive or partition, there are no decisions to make—but you still have to click the hard drive icon.

4. **Click Continue.**

   The Software License Agreement appears, which you may read in any of 13 languages. Don't worry, you're not signing your life away. (Well, probably not… no one's ever read all the way through to find out.)

5. **Click Continue again, and a software license agreement dialog box appears. Click Agree to move on.**

6. **Click Continue.**

   The Standard Install window appears. To install the entire Office package, just click Install.

7. **If you'd like some say about exactly what is about to be installed, click Customize.**

   The Custom Install window appears, bearing checkboxes for the various Office components (Figure A-3). Click the flippy triangle next to Microsoft Office 2011 in order to turn off any individual programs.

   The Standard installation gives you a full installation of all four Office programs described in this book, plus Microsoft Messenger, Microsoft Communicator (used with Exchange), Remote Desktop Connection, Microsoft Document Connection (used with SharePoint and Windows Live SkyDrive), and Proofing Tools. This set of options is what Microsoft thinks most people want, without littering your hard drive with extras...sort of. If you click the flippy triangle next to Proofing Tools, you'll see that you're getting all kinds of foreign language spelling dictionaries. Click the checkboxes to turn off any languages you don't plan on writing in. You'll save about a megabyte of hard drive space for each language you eliminate.

   Click the flippy triangles to see everything that's available. If you'll never in a million years create a PowerPoint presentation, for example, you can turn it off now and save a ton of space. You can always pop the DVD in and install it later if you change your mind. If you're stuck on iChat, you may as well turn off Microsoft Messenger.

   If you have a change of heart while you're picking and choosing, click Standard Install to revert to installing the whole shebang. This puts everything you paid for on your Mac—it also eats up one and a half gigabytes of space.

Tip: The Dock Icons checkbox gives you an easy way to remember what you just installed and then launch those programs. Leave it turned on and drag any icons you *don't* want off the dock when the installation is complete.

---

8. **When you're happy with what you've decided to install, click Install.**

   The installer gets to work. (It may ask you to type your password *again*. Just do it.)

   Office copies the files it needs from the DVD to your hard drive and keeps you updated on the progress and how long it is expected to take. When it's finished, a "Installation completed successfully" message appears.

   The next message alerts you to how many versions of Office it moved to the Trash.

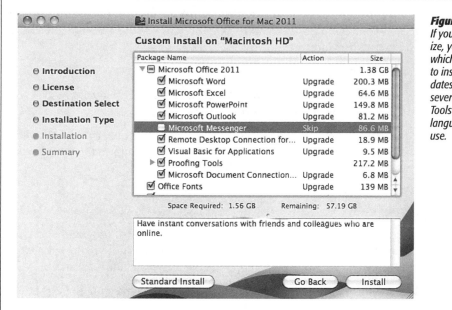

Figure A-3:
If you click Customize, you can choose which pieces of Office to install. Good candidates for exclusion are several of the Proofing Tools dictionaries in languages you don't use.

9. **Click Continue one last time.**

   The "Welcome to Office:mac 2011" window appears where you can enter your product key—that is your license code that permits you to use Office. If you don't have one, there's a link to Microsoft's web where you can purchase a product key. If you prefer, you can try Office for 30 days without buying a license.

10. **Click "Enter your product key" and in the text box that appears, type in the product key.**

    The product key for Office is inside or on the back of the disc sleeve that came with the software. If you purchased a license online, you received the product key at that time. If you make a mistake entering the key, just hit delete and re-type it.

11. **Click Activate.**

    Over the Internet, the installer checks back with the Microsoft powers that be and if all goes well, you see a message that says your copy is activated. If you aren't connected to the Internet, your product won't be activated. If you're not successful activating Office, a message appears and you're given the opportunity to activate by telephone.

12. **Click Continue and choose "Use existing settings" or "Create new Settings".**

    Use the first option "Use existing settings" if you have a previous version of Office on your computer and you'd like Office 2011 to use the same preferences and user information.

13. **Click Continue.**

    Office personalizes your software. When it's done, a screen congratulates you and lets you know that Office is ready to use.

After the Setup Assistant vanishes, you find yourself staring once again at the Microsoft Office 2011 DVD installer window. Eject the DVD, and head to your Dock or Applications folder and start using Office 2011.

Removing Office

Unlike earlier versions of Office for Mac, there's no uninstall program with Office 2011. This may change in the future, but for now, if you want to remove the largest Office files scattered around your computer's hard drive, follow these steps:

1. **Go to your *Applications* folder and then drag the *Microsoft Office 2011* folder to Trash.**

2. **Go to your Macintosh:Library and then drag the following folders to the trash: *Automator*, *Fonts/Microsoft* and *Application Support/Microsoft*. (Skip this step if you're planning on continuing to use a previous version of Office.)**

3. **In your *Documents/Microsoft User Data* folder drag the Office 2011 Auto-Recover and Office 2011 Identities folders to the trash.**

If you're on a serious search and destroy mission, you can find a complete list of the files installed by Office 2011 at *http://www.officeformachelp.com/office/install/installed-files-list-for-office-2011/*.

Troubleshooting

Once you've installed Office, you're supposed to leave its thousands of software pieces where they lie. If you drag Word out of the Microsoft Office 2011 folder, for example, it won't work; double-clicking it does absolutely nothing.

Nevertheless, it's possible that, while experimenting with your Mac or innocently trying to tidy up your hard drive, you'll end up trashing or moving a file that Office needs to operate. Even when you use Office programs the usual way, your software creates settings and preference files that keep track of how you use and customize the software. Occasionally, a settings file or a bit of software becomes *corrupted*, causing all manner of strange behavior, odd crashes, and chaos. If you're experiencing strange crashes, investigate the possibility that a settings file or a bit of Microsoft software has gone bad.

Check for a Bad Settings or Preference File

To test for a corrupt file, quit all Office programs, and dig into Home→Library→ Preferences→Microsoft→Office 2011, then drag onto your desktop *Microsoft Office 2011 Settings.plist* and any Preference (or Settings) files that relate to your problem program. When you next start the program, it creates fresh, clean copies of these preference files. If your problem goes away, move the old, corrupt files from your desktop to the Trash. (If the corrupt files contain a lot of customization work, you can try further testing to see which specific file causes the problem, or—if you have backups—try restoring a slightly older version of the file.) Here's where you can find these preference and settings files:

- You can find most of them in your Home folder→Library→Preferences→ Microsoft→Office 2011.

- Word stores custom style settings in a template called Normal, and this template may be the cause of your woe. You can most likely locate Normal.dotm in your Home→Library→ Application Support→Microsoft→Office→User Templates folder.

- Outlook stores custom information (and email) for its main user in Home→ Documents→Microsoft User Data→Office 2011 Identities→Main Identity. This folder (and all identity folders) are well worth backing up; if a file in Main Identity (or any identity folder) becomes corrupt, you'll have no recourse but to start again if you don't have backups.

Uninstall and Reinstall Office

With previous versions of the Mac OS, it was fairly easy to remove Microsoft shared libraries and such from the System Folder as a quick test to see if they were corrupted. Under Mac OS X, this picky procedure takes the skills and patience of a brain surgeon, as you're well aware from reading the previous section.

If only, say, Outlook is crashing or behaving badly, it may be worthwhile to isolate and remove only its preferences and support files to see if that solves the problem. But if you have no idea where the problem is coming from, and don't have the patience to figure it out, you may want to take the faster—but more drastic—step of removing *all* of Office's preference files, or removing all Office folders, programs, and their accoutrements from your Mac. You'll have to spend extra time resetting your preferences later, but in return, you get the chance to truly start fresh.

For pernicious problems you can uninstall and then reinstall Office. To remove Office 2011 from your Mac move these folders to the trash:

- /Applications/Microsoft Office 2011/
- /Applications/Remote Desktop Connection
- /Applications/Microsoft Communicator

- /Applications/Microsoft Messenger
- /Users/username/Library/Preferences/Microsoft/Office 2011/
- /Users/username/Library/Logs/<Communicator logs>
- /Users/username/Library/Application Support/Microsoft/
- /Users/username/Documents/Microsoft User Data/
- /Library/Automator
- /Library/Application Support/Microsoft/MAU2.0/
- /Library/Application Support/Microsoft/MERP2.0/
- /Library/Fonts/Microsoft
- /Library/Preferences/com.microsoft.office.licensing.plist
- /Library/LaunchDaemons/com.microsoft.office.licensing.helper.plist
- /Library/PrivilegedHelperTools/com.microsoft.office.licensing.helper
- /Library/Internet Plug-Ins/<all SharePoint files>
- /Library/Receipts/<all Office 2011 files> on Mac OS X v10.5 (Leopard)
- /var/db/receipts/com.microsoft.office.* on Mac OS X v10.6 (Snow Leopard)

Research Your Problem Online

If you want to hunt online for information, you can always try Microsoft's Knowledge Base at *http://support.microsoft.com*. Or, try *www.microsoft.com/mac/help.mspx*, the Mactopia Help Center, with links to top support issues and information for IT professionals. Here you'll find the Office Resource Kit, Microsoft's reference guide aimed at network administrators and consultants.

Your best bet may be turning to your fellow Office 2011 fans and asking them for help. Visit Microsoft's online forum at *www.officeformac.com*. Here you can search for questions similar to yours and see if someone's already answered them. Chances are good someone has, but if not, you can post your question and see if you get an answer. (While you're at it, you might see if you can answer a question or two for someone else.)

Microsoft MVPs—Most Valuable Professionals—maintain several help websites where they volunteer their Office expertise for the greater good:

- **List of MVP websites:** *www.mvps.org*.
- **Word:mac**. *http://word.mvps.org/Mac/WordMacHome.html*
- **The PowerPoint FAQ List**. *http://pptfaq.com*

The Office Help System

Given enough time and determination, it's possible that you *could* figure out Microsoft Office 2011 all by yourself. But the fact that you're reading this book indicates you have better things to do with your time. When you need help, there are various resources available, starting with Office's built-in Help system. Of course, the help system can't substitute for a good book, but it can get you out of a jam, show you different—and often faster—ways of doing things, and reveal Office features you never knew existed.

Part of Office 2011's help system is always with you, like a friend tapping your shoulder with the occasional unsolicited hint. Tooltips often pop up to reveal, say, the names of toolbar buttons or AutoText suggestions. The often-ignored Description panels of dialog boxes clarify what you're looking at. (Open Word→Preferences, click any of the preference buttons, and watch what happens at the bottom of the box when you pass the cursor over the various options.)

But if you're really having trouble figuring out how to make an Office program do what you want, you can turn to Office's help screens.

Office Help

You don't have to learn to use a new help system with you use Office 2011. It uses the same help system as the other applications on your Mac. No annoying little cartoon dogs, no multiple windows. When you open Help using one of the options listed below, you see the Mac's familiar Help window as shown in Figure B-1.

The Office for Mac Help window—which is supposed to take the place of a hard-copy manual in Office 2011—appears when you use one of these methods:

- Choose Help→[Program Name] Help (or press ⌘-?).

- Click the purple Help button on the Standard toolbar.

- Click the "More help on this function" link at the bottom of Excel's Formula Builder.

The Help window opens, as shown in Figure B-1, titled Word Help, PowerPoint Help, and so on. Each program has its own separate set of help files, meaning you can't look up your Excel questions in the Word Help window. However, you can use the menu at the top of the help window to open another set of documents. The adornments on this window offer a variety of aids to finding information in the Help system:

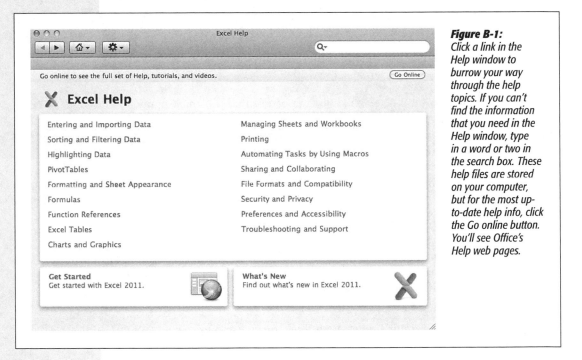

Figure B-1:
Click a link in the Help window to burrow your way through the help topics. If you can't find the information that you need in the Help window, type in a word or two in the search box. These help files are stored on your computer, but for the most up-to-date help info, click the Go online button. You'll see Office's Help web pages.

- **To return to the first help page,** click the Home button, which looks like a house.

- **To move to the last or previous help page,** click one of the arrow buttons in the right hand corner.

- **To find the help files for a different application,** click and hold the Home menu and choose from the list of apps installed on your computer.

- **To make help text bigger or smaller,** click the gear button and choose an option.

- **To find a word in the help page text,** click the gear button and choose Find (⌘-F). A new search box appears below the Spotlight search box as shown in Figure B-2. Type your search term in the box, and Help highlights the word in the text. You see how many times your word appears in the help text, and you can use the arrow buttons to navigate between the occurrences. When you're finished, click Done to hide the page search tools.

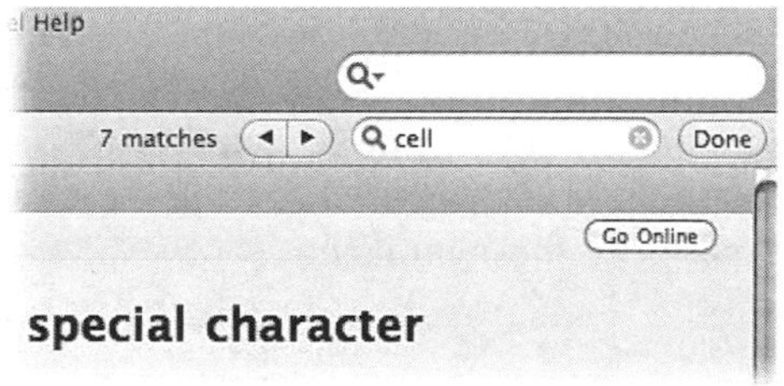

Figure B-2:
To search for words or phrases on a specific help page, press ⌘-F to open this search box. Use the arrow keys to navigate between occurrences of the matching words.

- **To search through the entire help document,** use the Spotlight search box. Type in a word or two and press Return. The help window shows topics that match.

- **To search through all the Office help files,** click the magnifying glass menu in the Spotlight search box and choose Search All Books.

- **To backtrack through the help path,** click on the path topics in the upper-left corner as shown in Figure B-3.

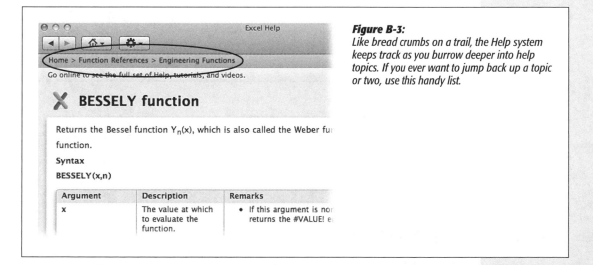

Figure B-3:
Like bread crumbs on a trail, the Help system keeps track as you burrow deeper into help topics. If you ever want to jump back up a topic or two, use this handy list.

Help from Mac OS X

Mac OS X 10.5 and later versions feature a search field right in the Help menu. It searches the *Mac's* Help system for the installed applications. This menu search capability works great with Office programs. This feature's a lifesaver when you're having one of those menu moments—you know there's a command in a menu somewhere that lets you insert a row in a Word table, for example, but you're not sure exactly where. In Word, choose Help (or press ⌘-?) and type *insert row* into the Search field. OS X immediately responds with a menu item titled Insert > Rows Above and Insert > Rows Below listed below the search field. Hold your mouse over an item in the search results, and the Word menu and submenu unfurls before your eyes with a big blue arrow pointing to the command in question (see Figure B-4). Without moving your mouse, click that item, and Word performs the command.

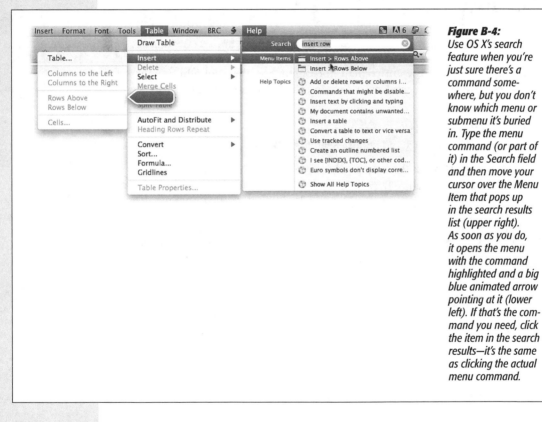

Figure B-4:
Use OS X's search feature when you're just sure there's a command somewhere, but you don't know which menu or submenu it's buried in. Type the menu command (or part of it) in the Search field and then move your cursor over the Menu Item that pops up in the search results list (upper right). As soon as you do, it opens the menu with the command highlighted and a big blue animated arrow pointing at it (lower left). If that's the command you need, click the item in the search results—it's the same as clicking the actual menu command.

Web-Based Help

Microsoft does a fine job of keeping you updated about what's happening in the world of Office for the Mac. The Microsoft Office for the Mac website (called Mactopia) contains online tutorials, instructional articles, software updates and bug fixes, and, when all else fails, a gateway to Microsoft's technical support department.

To go directly to Microsoft's Mac website, choose Help→Visit the Product Website. Office launches your Web browser and displays the Office 2011 for Mac product page where all kinds of goodies await, like an online tour and email newsletter sign-up.

The links at the top of the Office 2011 page are the important ones for folks looking to learn more about the program.

- The **Products** link takes you to a page giving an Office 2011 overview with links to the individual programs. It's a great place to start if you're updating from an earlier version of Office.

- **Downloads** is a page listing the newest and most popular Mac downloads for Microsoft products. Come here for Office software updates if you're not using AutoUpdate (see the box on page 11). You'll also find a link to find out more about AutoUpdate.

- **Help and How-to** opens a gem of a page that includes how-to articles, top support issues, popular discussions in the forums—and a link to the forums page where you can interact with other Office fans and Office experts. You'll also find links to the IT Professionals pages and, at the bottom, a Get Technical Support link where you can search Microsoft's Office for Mac Knowledge Base and find links to contacting a Microsoft support person by email, online, or phone. (You're free to browse or post to a newsgroup; individual assistance by email or phone can cost you.) This page also has unexpected pleasures like a link to Office-related news releases and press coverage, and a link to sign up to participate in a Usability Study (that is, potentially get to test new software and get a "free gift" for your efforts).

- The **Blog** link opens Office for Mac blog where the engineers who actually created Office hang out and post on various Office issues. You can leave comments on their postings and feel relatively confident that someone in the know is reading—and perhaps responding to them.

Office 2011, Menu by Menu

Because Microsoft Office 2011 is four big programs that work together, there are a lot of menus to cover—one set for each program. Although you can get to the commands you use most often on the ribbon, some in-depth commands only appear on the menus. These menus also change depending on what's selected in your currently open document. Consider this appendix your cheat sheet for those times when you know something's possible in Office, but you just can't seem to find the command for it.

This appendix takes the menus program by program, so you can look up what you need easily. Here's the first page for each program's Application Menu (all programs): page 665; Excel: page 667; Outlook: page 668; PowerPoint: page 709; Word: page 721.

Application Menu

Like Mac OS X programs everywhere, each Office program has a menu bearing its name, just to the right of the menu. It contains the Quit command, access to Preferences, and other commands that pertain to the program as a whole. It also has a few Finder commands, potentially saving you a trip to the desktop.

About [Program Name]

Opens a window displaying some legalese and, more importantly, the product ID for your copy of Office. A Microsoft representative may ask you for this number when you call a technical support phone number (which you can find by clicking the Support button).

The Reference Tools button doesn't actually help with looking anything up; it just offers more legalese about any foreign language dictionaries you've installed.

Online Registration

In case you clicked Register Later when you first installed Office (see Appendix A), choose this command when you have the time to go through the registration process.

Application Menu Preferences

This command opens up the Preference window, which contains different panels for various types of settings (these are discussed throughout this book). *Keyboard shortcut*: ⌘-comma (,).

Work Offline (Outlook only)

Disconnects Outlook from the Internet or network, so that you can you write email messages, reply to news messages, or work with tasks, calendar items, or contacts without being interrupted by Outlook's automatic mail-getting schedule (which would otherwise remind you every 10 minutes, "Mail could not be received at this time"). Great for use on planes and in waiting rooms.

Turn Off (or On) Office Reminders (Outlook only)

Tells the Office Reminders program to stop reminding you about events, tasks, and documents that you've set for follow-up; or if it's already off, tells it you'd like to see your reminders.

Services

This is a standard Mac OS X menu, listing useful inter-program commands that mostly do nothing in Office. (That's because Services generally work only in Cocoa programs—programs that were written from scratch for Mac OS X rather than adapted from earlier software, as Office was.) For the full story on Services, see *Mac OS X: The Missing Manual*.

Hide [Program Name]

Hides the current program's windows from view without minimizing the program to the Dock. *Keyboard shortcut*: ⌘-H.

Hide Others

Hides the windows of all other windows, including Finder windows, leaving only windows from the frontmost Office program visible. *Keyboard shortcut*: Option-⌘-H.

Show All

Brings back all hidden windows of the program you're using.

Quit [Program Name]

Quits the frontmost program, but before doing so, gives you a chance to save any changes you've made. *Keyboard shortcut*: ⌘-Q.

Excel Menus

These menus help you manage your workbooks and worksheets and all the data they contain. Unlike some of the other applications, notably Outlook, these menus don't change very much. The exception is when you've selected a Chart.

File Menu

The commands in the File menu operate on Excel workbooks, whether you're opening them, saving them, or printing them.

New Workbook

Creates a new Excel workbook. *Keyboard shortcut*: ⌘-N.

New from Template

Opens the Excel Workbook Gallery window full of templates for different types of spreadsheet projects. *Keyboard shortcut*: Shift-⌘-P.

Open

Opens Excel's Open dialog box, which you can use to navigate to a file for Excel to open. *Keyboard shortcut*: ⌘-O.

Open URL

Opens a spreadsheet that's stored on network server, this could be local or off on some distant web server.

Open Recent

Lets you choose from a list of recently opened Excel documents.

Close

Closes the frontmost Excel workbook window. If the workbook has unsaved changes, Excel will ask you if you want to save those changes. *Keyboard shortcut*: ⌘-W.

Save

Saves any changes to the frontmost window. If the file is a new, unsaved workbook, Excel prompts you to name it and choose a location for it. *Keyboard shortcut*: ⌘-S.

Save As

Saves the frontmost window as another file. This command essentially makes a copy of the file and closes the original file, allowing you to choose a new name and location for the file, if you want. *Keyboard shortcut*: Shift-⌘-S

Save as Web Page

Saves the frontmost Excel workbook as a web page, converting graphics and graphs to the right kind of graphic formats, and saving all of the data in HTML tables (page 391).

Save Layout

Memorizes the positions and sizes of any open workbook windows into a separate file. Later, when you open that file, all of the workbooks will be opened to the same size and position.

Web Page Preview

Shows you, in your web browser, what your workbook will look like as a web page.

Page Setup

Opens the Page Setup dialog box, where you can set up your Excel printouts. The options depend on the kind of printer you have selected as your default printer.

Print Area

Offers three commands:

- **Set Print Area**. Lets you drag to select the cells you want to print.
- **Clear Print Area**. Undoes the Set Print Area command, so that nothing is selected for printing.
- **Add to Print Area**. Add your selection to the current print area.

Print

Prints the frontmost document on the printer selected in the Chooser. It opens the Print dialog box, where you can specify how many copies you want printed and make other printing-related settings. *Keyboard shortcut*: ⌘-P.

Properties

Opens the Workbook Properties window, where you can view and type in keywords and other information about the frontmost workbook, for later use by the Finder's Spotlight search feature (which appears when you choose File→Open).

Edit Menu

The Edit menu gathers together all of Excel's editing tools in one handy place. Many of these commands are similar to, but not identical to, those in other Office programs.

Undo

As in other programs, this command restores the last change you made; in Excel, you can undo (or redo) many steps, taking your spreadsheet all the way back to the way you found it. *Keyboard shortcut*: ⌘-Z.

Repeat/Redo

When you've done something that Excel can do over and over again, you can do so just by selecting the Repeat command. If you've just used the Undo command, the Repeat menu item turns into Redo, which undoes the undo you just did. *Keyboard shortcut*: ⌘-Y.

Note: Undo and Repeat may appear as grayed out commands Can't Undo and Can't Repeat if your most recent action is something that can't be undone or repeated.

Cut, Copy, Copy to Scrapbook

Cuts or copies to the clipboard, or copies to the Office Scrapbook, the selected cell, cells, or object. *Keyboard shortcut*: ⌘-X, ⌘-C, and Shift-⌘-C.

Paste, Paste from Scrapbook, Paste Special

Pastes what you've just copied to the clipboard or to the Office Scrapbook. Paste Special lets you exercise some control when pasting, by pulling up the Paste Special window where you can apply formatting. It also lets you link or embed the clipboard contents. *Keyboard shortcut*: ⌘-V, Shift-⌘-V.

Paste Special

Give you options before you paste something into your workbook. For example, pastes the clipboard contents into Excel as a hyperlink, either to a website or to a Word document. (This requires that you've first copied an Internet address or some text out of a Word document.)

Fill

Fills the selected range of cells in the manner you specify in the Fill submenu. There are several different kinds of fills:

- **Down, Right, Up, Left**. Fills the selected range of cells with the contents and formatting the first select cell, in the specified direction (see page 359 for a more patient discussion).

- **Across Sheets**. If you have multiple sheets selected, this copies the selected range of cells across all of the selected worksheets in the same place as the original selection.

- **Series**. Intelligently fills the selected range of cells using the contents of the first cell in the selected row or column as a pattern—useful for filling in a series of dates, for example.

- **Justify**. Spreads the text in the leftmost cell across the selected row of cells.

Clear

The Clear menu empties out a cell or cells; although you might not know it, there are several ways to clear cells. Here are your choices:

- **All**. Clears everything in the cell, including formatting, the cell's contents, and any comments.

- **Formats**. Clears just the cell's formatting, leaving contents and comments alone.

- **Contents**. Clears just the cell's contents, leaving formatting and comments alone.

- **Comments**. Clears any comments, leaving formatting and contents alone.

- **Hyperlinks**. Clears links from the selection.

Delete

Deletes the selected cells or object from the sheet. If you're deleting cells, Excel will ask you whether you want to shift cells up or to the left, or remove entire rows or columns.

Delete Sheet

Deletes the currently active sheet from the workbook. Be sure about it; you can't undo this action.

Move or Copy Sheet

Moves the selected sheet or sheets to a different location in the same workbook or another workbook. It opens the Move or Copy window, in which you can specify where you want to move the sheet and whether or not a copy is made.

Find

Opens the Find panel, which you can use to search for a string in formulas, values, or comments. *Keyboard shortcut*: ⌘-F.

Replace

Looks for a string of text and replaces it with another.

Go To

Opens the Go To window, which you can use to go to a specific cell. By clicking the resulting Special button, you can also use it to select a specific type of cells, such as those containing formulas or constants.

Links

Pulls up a window showing information about every link in the currently active document. If the document doesn't have any links to other documents, this option is dimmed.

Object

Lets you edit an embedded object, such as a Microsoft Graph object or an Office document. This menu's name changes to reflect the kind of object that's embedded here, and it lets you either edit an embedded object or convert one OLE object to a different type.

View Menu

The View menu's commands govern what view mode the windows are in, what toolbars are shown, and so on.

Normal

This is the standard Excel spreadsheet view.

Page Layout

Switches to Page Layout view. See the box on page 24.

Ribbon

Collapses and expands the Ribbon. When it's collapsed, the tops of the ribbon tabs remain visible. To hide the ribbon entirely, go to Excel→Preferences→Ribbon.

Toolbars

Using this command's submenu, you can hide or show Excel's toolbars: Standard, Formatting, Border Drawing, Chart, Drawing, External Data, Forms, Formula Auditing, List, Movie, PivotTable, and Reviewing. If you want to change toolbars or create your own, choose Customize Toolbars and Menus.

Formula Bar

Hides or shows the formula bar. This is one that you should probably leave on, as you'll be using the formula bar quite a bit.

Status Bar

Hides or shows the status bar at the bottom of an open workbook.

Media Browser

Opens the floating palette that holds pictures, clip art, audio and video clips.

Toolbox

All the various palettes below are part of the Toolbox—you can't click this menu item directly.

Formula Builder

Hides or shows the Formula Builder.

Scrapbook

Hides or shows the Scrapbook.

Reference Tools

Hides or shows the Reference Tools.

Compatibility Report

Hides or shows the Compatibility Report.

Header and Footer

Lets you edit the headers and footers that appear at the top and bottom of every page.

Comments

Shows all comments in the document if they're hidden, and opens the Reviewing toolbar. If comments are already visible, choosing this hides them.

Ruler

(Page Layout view only.) Displays a ruler along the top of the Excel page.

Custom Views

Opens the Custom Views window, which you can use to add, delete, or show custom views that you've saved.

Full Screen

Turns Full Screen mode on and off. In Full Screen mode, your workbook enlarges to take over the entire screen, and Excel hides other elements (such as toolbars and the Formatting Palette).

Zoom

Opens the Zoom window, where you can choose one of seven zoom levels (25, 50, 75, 100, 125, 150, or 200 percent) for magnifying or shrinking the onscreen representation of your spreadsheet, or you can zoom in or out to fit a selection. You can also enter a custom zoom level (from 10 to 400 percent).

Sized with Window

If you have a chart embedded in its own chart sheet, this command ties the size of the chart to the size of the window in which it's embedded. If this command isn't checked, resizing the window has no effect on the size of the chart.

Chart Window

If you have a chart selected, this appears at the bottom of the View menu. It makes Excel open the existing chart in a new chart window.

Insert Menu

If you want to insert something into your Excel documents, then this menu is your best friend. If not, there's no need to go to its parties.

Cells

Inserts a number of blank cells equivalent to the number you've first selected, and opens the Insert window, which lets you set how those cells are placed.

Rows

Inserts a number of blank rows equivalent to the number you've first selected, moving the selected rows down. If you have only one cell selected, Excel inserts only one row.

Columns

Inserts a number of blank columns equivalent to the number you've first selected, moving the selected columns to the right. If you only have one cell selected, Excel inserts only one column.

Chart

Opens the Charts Gallery, which walks you through the creation of a chart. Then it inserts your newly minted chart either into the currently active worksheet or into a whole new sheet reserved for the chart alone.

Sparklines

Sparklines are mini graphs that appear in cells. They're good for examining micro trends within your data. Opens the Insert Sparklines box where you can choose a range that you want to graph and the cells where you place the graph. After the sparklines are in place, the special, purple Sparklines tab appears where you can choose formatting options for the mini graphs.

Table

Inserts a data table in the selected cells. Data tables include drop-down menus that open a window with tools for sorting and filtering the data within the table.

Sheet

Lets you choose from its submenu a Blank Sheet, Chart Sheet, Macro Sheet, Dialog Sheet, or a List Sheet to insert into your current workbook.

Page Break

Inserts a page break above the currently selected cell. If the cell is adjacent to a manually placed page break, this command changes to Remove Page Break, which (as you might guess) removes the break.

Function

Opens the Formula Builder, from which you can select one of Excel's functions to insert into the currently active cell.

Name

The Name menu has four submenu choices that let you deal with names in Excel worksheets. Names are plain-English ways of referring to a cell or selection of cells (see page 383).

- **Define**. Opens the Define Name window, where you can add or delete names for a cell or group of cells.

- **Paste**. Opens the Paste Name window, which you can use to paste a named group of cells into a formula. You can also paste a list of your defined names, including the cells to which those names refer.

- **Create**. Opens the Create Names window, which lets you create names based on labels in selected cells.

- **Apply**. Opens the Apply Names window, where you can choose a name range to replace a cell range inside a formula. That cell range has to match an existing named cell range; otherwise, the function doesn't work.

New Comment

Inserts a comment attached to the selected cell or cells.

Photo

From the submenu choose Photo Browser to open the Media browser to the Photos panel. Choose Picture from File to search through folders on your computer.

Audio

From the submenu, choose Audio Browser to open the Media browser to the sound clips panel. Choose Audio from File to search through folders on your computer.

Movie

From the submenu, choose Movie Browser to open the Media browser to the movie clips panel. Choose Movie from File to search through folders on your computer.

Clip Art

From the submenu, choose Clip Art Browser to open the Media browser to the clip art panel where you'll find the photos and clip art added to your computer when you installed Office. The Clip Art Gallery option leads to a larger collection of clip art and links to Microsoft's online clip art offerings.

Symbol

Opens the Media Browser to the Symbols panel. Symbols are grouped into categories like Currency, Fractions, Math, Shapes, Arrows, Check Marks and more.

Shape

Opens the Object Palette; you can start drawing in your worksheet using the Auto-Shapes tools.

Text Box

Lets you draw a text box onto your spreadsheet.

SmartArt Graphic

Opens the SmartArt tab on the ribbon where you can choose from a variety of highly-adaptable charts in categories like: Process, Cycle, and Hierarchy. These charts are easily customizable and it's easy to examine your data in different configurations.

WordArt

Opens the WordArt Gallery, where you can create text art for insertion into the currently active sheet.

Object

Opens the Insert Object window where you can choose from a number of Microsoft OLE objects like Word documents, or Microsoft Graph Charts. OLE stands for object linking and embedding, and that's exactly your choice when you insert an object. You can choose whether you want to embed the object (making it part of the Excel document) or link the external file. When you link files, you need to specify how and when the data in your Excel document gets updated if the external file changes.

Hyperlink

Opens the Insert Hyperlink window, where you can insert a new hyperlink to a web page, a document, or an email address. If there's already a link in the selected cell, this command opens the link for editing. *Keyboard shortcut*: ⌘-K.

Format Menu

The Format menu gathers together all of the commands that you're likely to use while altering the formatting of your sheets and workbooks.

Cells

Opens the Format Cells window, where you can choose all kinds of formatting options for the selected cells. This menu item changes to reflect the type of object selected—Photo, Object, WordArt, or AutoShape—and then opens the appropriate Format window. *Keyboard shortcut*: ⌘-1.

Row

This menu has four options that govern the appearance of the selected row or rows:

- **Height**. Opens the Row Height window, where you can set the height of the selected row or rows in pixels. If a worksheet is protected, this option is unavailable.

- **AutoFit**. Makes the selected row precisely as high as it needs to be to accommodate the tallest text in the row. Measured in pixels.

- **Hide**. Hides the selected row or rows from view (it doesn't delete them).

- **Unhide**. Reveals any hidden rows.

Column

Like its sibling menu item, Format→Row, this menu has five options that let you edit the appearance of the selected column or columns:

- **Width**. Opens the column width window, where you can set the width of the selected column or columns (measured in characters).

- **AutoFit Selection**. Makes the selected column precisely as wide as it needs to be to accommodate the longest text in the column. Measured in characters.

- **Hide**. Hides the selected column or columns from view.

- **Unhide**. Reveals any hidden columns.

- **Standard Width**. Resets the selected column or columns to the original setting.

Selected Chart Area

If you have a chart selected, the Select Data Series menu item appears; it lets you format the selected chart's area. This menu item changes to reflect the various items selected in the chart, including data series, plot areas, labels, and legends. All of these open in the appropriate Format window.

Sheet

This menu item has four submenus, each of which deals with a formatting aspect for the active worksheet.

- **Rename**. Lets you rename the currently active sheet.

- **Hide**. Hides the selected sheet or sheets.

- **Unhide**. Reveals any hidden sheets in the workbook by presenting you with a list of hidden sheets and letting you choose those you want shown.

- **Background**. Lets you select a graphics file to use as a background for the frontmost sheet.

- **Tab Color**. Lets you color code the tabs that appear at the bottom of the workbook, identifying the individual sheets.

Conditional Formatting

Opens the Conditional Formatting window, where you can change the selected cells' formatting based on conditions that you define—such as changing a cell's text color to red when its value is negative.

Style

Opens the Style window, where you can add, edit, or remove styles. Styles are a saved set of formatting commands that you can apply to a cell or range of cells with ease.

Tools Menu

Although all menu items are tools, in a sense, most are grouped together because they have some commonality (such as the Insert and Format menus). The Tools menu, on the other hand, is more general in nature. It includes a mix of text tools, sharing tools, and other miscellaneous functions that are powerful but don't necessarily have a common thread.

Spelling

Runs a spell check on the frontmost spreadsheet.

Thesaurus

Opens the Reference Tools and looks up the selected word.

Dictionary

Opens the Reference Tools, and looks up the selected word.

Language

Lets you choose your language for spell checking.

AutoCorrect

Opens the AutoCorrect window, where you can edit what Excel tries to correct while you type, such as changing "abbout" to "about." You can add your own items for Excel to AutoCorrect here.

Error Checking

Checks the sheet for invalid equations and operations. Provides summary.

Share Workbook

Opens the Share Workbook window, where you can change an ordinary workbook into one that can be shared by many Excel fans at once on a network. In this window, you can turn workbook sharing on and off, and you can adjust how changes to the shared workbook are treated.

Track Changes

The Track Changes controls how Excel keeps tabs of changes to worksheets and workbooks made by your collaborators. This menu has two submenu options:

- **Highlight Changes**. Opens the Highlight Changes window, where you can turn change tracking on and control which changes are highlighted.

- **Accept or Reject Changes**. Walks you through the changes that have been made to a workbook, giving you a chance to accept or reject each.

Merge Workbooks

Merges all of the changes from a series of shared workbooks into one single workbook.

Protection

The Protection menu has three submenu choices that let you choose a level of protection for the currently open worksheet or workbook.

- **Protect Sheet**. Protects the frontmost sheet from changes to cells, charts, graphics, or Visual Basic code.

- **Protect Workbook**. Protects a workbook's structure from changes such as deleting, adding, hiding, or showing sheets; also keeps windows from being resized.

- **Protect and Share Workbook**. Protects the workbook's change tracking and sharing status. If the workbook isn't yet shared, Excel will ask you if you want to do so when this item is selected. If it's already shared, this command changes to Unprotect Shared Workbook.

Flag for Follow Up

Opens the "Flag for Follow Up" window, where you can set a reminder attached to the currently open workbook. That reminder will pop up at the time you specify, to remind you to do something with the workbook in question.

Goal Seek

Changes the value in a cell until a formula using that cell reaches a value you specify (page 429).

Scenarios

Opens the Scenarios Manager window, where you can add, edit, merge, and delete a series of scenarios, which are a way of playing "what if" with an Excel worksheet (page 430).

Auditing

The Auditing menu controls how formulas in a worksheet or workbook interrelate. It has five submenu choices, all of which involve colorful arrows that appear on your spreadsheet, pointing to cells that refer to each other.

- **Trace Precedents**. Makes arrows point to a cell or cells that provide values for the formula in the selected cell. Useful if you're looking for where data comes from.

- **Trace Dependents**. Points to a cell or cells where the value in the selected cell is being used.

- **Trace Error**. If the selected cell contains an error caused by a bad value in a cell that its formula references, an arrow identifies the offending cell.

- **Remove All Arrows**. Removes all of the arrows drawn by auditing commands.

Macros

Provides tools for recording, managing and editing macros that you record in Excel. There are three submenu options:

- **Macros** opens the Macro dialog box which is command central for working with macros. From the box, you can create, run, debug and edit your macros.

- **Record New Macro** turns on the macro recorder, which translates your actions in Excel into Visual Basic for Applications (VBA) code.

- **Visual Basic Editor** opens the VBA programming environment, where you can dig deep into the code created by the macro recorder. If the programming spirit moves you, you can even write your own macros from scratch.

Add-Ins

Opens the Add-Ins window, where you can turn on or turn off various Add-Ins for Excel. Add-Ins are conceptually similar to Photoshop plug-ins in that they add new functions to Excel.

Customize Keyboard

Opens the Customize Keyboard window, where you can add or modify keyboard commands.

Data Menu

This menu's commands all process the numbers and characters in your worksheet.

Sort

Sorts the selected rows alphabetically, by date, or numerically.

Filter

The Filter option lets you hide rows of a list or selection according to criteria that you specify.

Clear Filters

Removes the filters that have been previously applied to a range in your spreadsheet, making all the data visible again.

Advanced Filter

Opens the Advanced Filter window, which lets you create your own filters for a selected range of cells.

Form

Opens a data form window, which you can use to view, edit, add, and delete data in a list object (page 406).

Subtotals

Figures out a subtotal and grand total for the selected labeled column; automatically inserts the appropriate cells, moving the selected cells to the right, and puts the spreadsheet in outline mode.

Validation

Opens the Data Validation menu, which lets you control what kind of data is entered in a cell or cell. It also lets you choose a message to display when a cell is selected.

Data Table

Creates a data table based on a selected row and column input cell. Data tables are useful to show how changing formula values affect a sheet's data (see page 426).

Text to Columns

Opens the "Convert Text to Columns" wizard, which walks you through the process of converting a chunk of text in a cell (either separated by spaces or by commas) into a series of columns.

Consolidate

Grabs data from one of several sources and consolidates it into a table for easy viewing. This command opens the Consolidate window, where you can choose your consolidation function and add data sources.

Group and Outline

The commands in this menu let you group data together and create outlines from your groupings. By using grouping and outlining, you can hide and show detailed data, grouping it in ways that help make sense of it (see page 436). For your grouping pleasure, the Group and Outline menu has seven submenu items.

- **Hide Detail**. If you have a summary row or column, this command hides the detail rows or columns. For PivotTables, this command hides detail data in an outer row or column field item.

- **Show Detail**. If you have hidden detail rows or columns, this command shows them. For PivotTables, this command reveals detail data in an outer row or column field item.

- **Group**. Groups data (either cells or items in a PivotTable) together for easy analysis and printing. Grouping cells automatically creates an outline in the frontmost sheet.

- **Ungroup**. Ungroups formerly grouped data, separating group members into individual items.

- **Auto Outline**. Tells Excel to automatically create an outline, which it happily does from the formulas and cell references in the given spreadsheet.

- **Clear Outline**. Removes outlining, of course. If you have selected a set of cells that are in groups, then this command removes the outline in that area. If the selected cells aren't in a group, the outline is removed from the worksheet.

- **Settings**. Opens the Settings window, where you can set some options for outlining and summarizing data in a worksheet.

PivotTable Report

Opens the PivotTable Wizard, which walks you through creating a PivotTable or editing an existing PivotTable (see page 422).

Get External Data

This menu has a collection of commands that link Excel to other data sources (such as databases or web-based data sources). There are eight commands in this submenu.

- **Run Saved Query**. Pops up the "Choose a Query" dialog box, where you can select a saved data query to run. Excel ships with four presaved web-based queries ready for you to use.

- **New Database Query**. Opens the Query Wizard, where you can create your own database query, you mad scientist, you. (This requires an ODBC driver.)

- **Import Text File**. Imports an entire text file into the currently open worksheet. This command opens the Text Import Wizard, which walks you through how Excel will parse and place the data from the text file.

- **Import from FileMaker Pro**. Pops up the "Choose a Database" dialog box, where you can choose a FileMaker Pro database document to import data from (see page 418).

- **Import from FileMaker Server**. Does the same thing as above, but for FileMaker databases stored on a network.

- **Edit Query**. Edits a query that you created using Microsoft Query to get at data in an external database. If you have used the Import Text File command to bring in a text file, this menu item changes to Edit Text Import, and performs accordingly.

- **Data Range Properties**. Opens the External Data Range Properties window, which lets you change some of the settings for an imported bit of external data (such as whether the query definition is saved, how data is refreshed, and how data is laid out).

- **Parameters**. Lets you set options for a parameter query, a special kind of query that asks you for some information that it will use to retrieve data from the database's tables.

Refresh Data

Refreshes the data in a PivotTable if the table's source data has changed.

Chart Menu

The Chart menu appears only when a chart is selected in Excel; it replaces the Data menu on the menu bar. Many of these options duplicate settings in the chart wizard, giving you a chance to revisit some of those choices.

Chart Type

Opens the Chart Type window, where you can choose a new chart type for the selected chart (see page 477).

Save as Template

Use this option to save your chart as a template in the chart document format (.crtx).

Move Chart

Opens the Chart Location window, where you set where the chart is placed: as a new sheet or as an object in an existing sheet.

Source Data

Opens the Source Data window, where you can choose a different range of cells from which the chart draws its data.

Add Data

Opens the Add Data window, which lets you add additional cells to the chart.

Add Trendline

Opens the Add Trendline window, where you can add a trendline to your chart, or change one that's already there (see page 494).

3-D Rotation

Summons the 3-D format window, which lets you manipulate your 3D chart as if it were a real-world, solid item by rotating it, scaling it, or changing its elevation. If the selected chart isn't a 3-D chart, this menu item isn't available.

Window Menu

These commands help you manage your spreadsheet windows. If you have a chart selected, you won't see all the options listed here.

Minimize

Sends the frontmost Excel window to the Dock. *Keyboard shortcut*: ⌘-M.

Zoom Window

Does the same thing as the green zoom button in the upper-right corner of the window: resizes it to its full size, so that it fills up most of the screen.

Bring All to Front

Makes all the open, windows non-minimized Excel windows visible, pulling them out from behind other windows.

New Window

Opens a new window on the same file that's currently open—a duplicate view of the same spreadsheet. This arrangement lets you view two (or more) places in the same file at the same time, scrolled to different spots and zoomed independently.

Arrange

Arranges all open windows so that at least a portion of each is visible—which makes switching or dragging data between open files much easier. An Arrange Windows dialog box opens, where you can set how those windows are arranged (Tiled, Horizontal, Vertical, or Cascade).

Hide

Hides the frontmost workbook window without closing it.

Unhide

Displays a list of windows that have been hidden with the Hide command, which you can then Unhide.

Split

Splits the active window horizontally and vertically into four, independently scrolling panes. If the currently active window has been split, this menu command changes to Remove Split.

Freeze Panes

If your sheet has been split into two or four panes, this command freezes the top pane, the left pane, or both. That way, those panes stay in place while you scroll the lower-right panes—it keeps column and row titles visible while you scroll through your worksheet. (None of this affects how the sheet prints.) This command changes to Unfreeze Panes if you have already frozen the panes on the sheet.

Window List

The last item on the Window menu is a list of currently open workbook windows. You can switch between them by selecting their names from this menu.

Help Menu

The Help menu gives you access to resources for learning about and troubleshooting Office. Some are stored in the Help system that Office installed on your computer; others arc on Microsoft's website.

Search

Search Outlook help. Among other things, this search box is great for finding commands on Outlook's many menus.

Excel Help

Opens up Excel's online help, as described in Appendix B.

Welcome to Excel

Goes to a website with introductory information about Excel.

Get Started with Excel

Goes to a website that provides a brief tutorial on Excel basics.

Check for Updates

Launches the Microsoft AutoUpdate program (see the box on page 11).

Visit the Product Web Site

Opens your web browser to Microsoft's home page for its Macintosh products.

Send Feedback about Excel

Opens your web browser to a Microsoft web page containing a simple feedback web form.

Scripts Menu

Outlook works well with AppleScript and Automator—so well that it reserves an entire menu for scripts and workflows. You can use one of the included scripts, and you can add your own scripts to this menu.

About this Menu

Opens a dialog box containing a short description of the Scripts Menu and a button that opens the Word Script Menu Items folder.

Sample Automator Workflows

Displays a submenu with a collection of Automator workflows from which to choose.

Outlook Menus

Outlook's menus change depending on whether you're working on your email, calendar, contacts, tasks, or notes. When you change your view to one of these topics, menus change to accommodate your current activity.

File Menu

Like any other good Macintosh program, Outlook comes equipped with the File menu, which is mainly used for working with files on your hard drive—whether that's creating new files, saving them, or printing them.

New

Creates a new Outlook file. Since Outlook can create a variety of files, the New command has its own submenu, filled with commands that create a new Outlook document or element.

- **New**. This top item changes, depending on your Outlook view. If you're in E-mail view (⌘-1) the New command creates a new email message. If you're in Contact view (⌘-3) the command opens a new contact form. *Keyboard shortcut*: ⌘-N. For good measure, the file menu always lists options where you can create new items no matter what view you're in.

- **E-mail Message**. Creates a blank email message. *Keyboard shortcut*: Option-⌘-N.

- **Meeting**. Creates a calendar meeting event.

- **Appointment**. Creates a calendar appointment event.

- **Contact**. Creates a blank Address Book entry.

- **Contact Group**. Creates a blank group where you can gather together contacts.

- **Task**. Creates a blank task.

- **Note**. Creates a blank note.

- **Folder**. Creates a new folder in the folder list. *Keyboard shortcut*: Shift-⌘-N.

- **Open New Main Window**. Creates a brand-new main Outlook window so you can have, for example, your email and your calendar open at the same time.

Open

Opens the selected item, whether it's an item in the Folder List (such as a mail folder or the Address Book) or an item inside the list pane (such as an email, contact or task). The command even tells you what you're about to open ("Open Message" for example). *Keyboard shortcut*: ⌘-O.

Open Another User's Folder

Opens another Exchange account's shared mail folder, calendar, or contacts list. (This command is only available if Outlook has an Exchange account configured.)

Close

Closes the frontmost open window, even if it's the Progress window. If Outlook's main window is the only one open, this command closes it. *Keyboard shortcut*: ⌘-W.

Save

Saves any changes made to the frontmost window, whether that window is an email message (which then gets placed in the Drafts folder) or a contact. If the document in the frontmost window hasn't been changed, then the Save command is disabled. *Keyboard shortcut*: ⌘-S.

Save As

Saves the frontmost window as another file. This command essentially makes a copy of the file and closes the original, allowing you to choose a new name and location for the file. *Keyboard shortcut*: Shift-⌘-S.

Folder

Used with Exchange accounts, the Folder submenu command lets you set permissions and properties for shared folders.

Import

Opens Outlook's Import window, which lets you bring in information from various email, personal information manager, and text-based mail and contact files (page 295).

Export

Saves Outlook's data (email, calendar, contacts, tasks and notes) in a variety of standard formats so that it can be used in other programs, including non-Microsoft applications.

Page Setup

Opens the Page Setup dialog box, where you can control how Outlook prints your pages (on which kind of paper, and so on). The options here depend on the kind of printer you have selected.

Print

Opens the Print dialog box, where you can specify the number copies you want printed, among a multitude of other settings. *Keyboard shortcut*: ⌘-P.

Edit Menu

The Edit menu commands focus on editing tools, whether that means moving text around in an email message or memo, looking for a text string inside Outlook's files, managing message threads, or changing an item's category.

Undo

Takes back the last thing that you did, like deleting that vital chunk of text by accident. *Keyboard shortcut*: ⌘-Z.

Redo

Once you've undone something, then the Redo command becomes available, in case you change your mind. *Keyboard shortcut*: ⌘-Y.

Cut

Cuts the selected text or object out of the document and puts it on the Clipboard, ready for pasting into a different window or program. *Keyboard shortcut*: ⌘-X.

Copy

Copies the selected text or object and puts it on the Clipboard, ready for pasting into a different window or program. *Keyboard shortcut*: ⌘-C.

Copy to Scrapbook

Copies to the Scrapbook. You can store clips on the Scrapbook—and subsequently paste them—from any Office program. *Keyboard shortcut*: Control-Option-C.

Paste

Pastes the contents of the Clipboard into a document at the location of the insertion point. *Keyboard shortcut*: ⌘-V.

Paste From Scrapbook

Pastes a clip from the Scrapbook. *Keyboard shortcut*: Control-Option-V.

Paste and Match Style

Pastes text from the clipboard into an item (email, note, and so forth) and automatically changes the text to match the format of item that it is being pasted into.

Clear

Deletes the selected text (or object) from the document without putting it on the clipboard.

Select All

Selects everything (whether that's text, pictures or other objects) in the frontmost window. *Keyboard shortcut*: ⌘-A.

Duplicate

Duplicates the currently selected item, whether it's a message or a calendar event. This command's wording changes to reflect the kind of object that's selected; it may say Duplicate Message or Duplicate Task, for example. (It can't duplicate items on a remote server, such as an online email account or a news server.) *Keyboard shortcut*: ⌘-D.

Delete

Deletes the selected item (such as a mail message, contact, or folder in the Folder list). Like Duplicate, the Delete command's wording changes to reflect the item being deleted, and it can't be used to delete messages on a news server. *Keyboard shortcut*: ⌘-Delete.

Find

Leads to a submenu full of different search options, from a simple search for Outlook items to advanced find tools where you can build a complex search based on multiple criteria, as explained on page 302.

Spelling and Grammar

Options on the submenu let you initiate spelling and grammar checking or set options so that checking occurs as you work.

Substitutions

Office programs automatically convert characters like plain quotes to typographically correct open and close quotes. Different types of computers (Macs, Windows, Linux) display some of these characters differently, so you may not want to use these automatic conversions in your emails which are likely to be viewed on alien computer systems. Use this menu to choose your settings and turn on and off substitutions for: quotes, dashes and links.

Transformations

Options on the transformations menu let you convert text to all upper case, all lower case or initial caps (first letter capitalized).

Speech

Want your Mac to read your email messages out loud? Select text and choose Speech→Start Speaking. To stop the audio, choose Speech→Stop Speaking.

Special Characters

Opens the Mac OS X Characters Palette, giving you access to every possible special character on your system.

View Menu

The View menu could also be called the show, hide, sort and filter menu. You choice changes some of the options displayed on this menu and changes one of the option on the main menu bar. For example, if you choose Contact view, Outlook displays the Contact menu.

Previous

Moves to the previous item in the currently selected folder. If a message is open, the contents of the open window changes to the previous message. *Keyboard shortcut*: Control-[.

Next

Moves to the next item in the currently selected folder. If a message is open, the contents of the open window changes to the next message. *Keyboard shortcut*: Control-].

Go To

Choosing one of the items from the submenu does the same thing as clicking the Mail, Calendar, Contact, Tasks, and Notes buttons.

Columns

This option is activated when you close the reading pane and Outlook displays additional columns of data in the list pane. Use the submenu to choose which data fields are shown in the columns. This option is only available in Calendar view if you use the View→List option (Control-⌘-0).

Arrange By

Use this option to sort the items in the list by one of the fields. For example, you can sort emails by the date you received them or you could sort tasks by their priority.

View specific Menus:

When you select one of the five main views in Outlook, the items between the Go to menu and the Reading Pane option change to match the view. Here's what you find in the view specific menus:

- In **E-Mail view,** you can choose to Filter the list by the criteria: Unread, Flagged, Has Attachment, Date Sent, Date Received, Overdue, High Priority, Any Recipient is Me, and Category. The Clear All Filters command removes filters showing all the email in a particular folder or mailbox.

- The **Calender view** options let choose to view your schedule by: Day, Work Week, Week, and Month. The list view shows your meetings and appoints as a simple list rather than a calendar-style grid.

- The **Contact view** has only one special option: Me Contact. Use this to see the contact card for yourself: the current identity for the Outlook account. This in formation is used in replies and return address blocks.

- In **Tasks view,** you see menu options to filter the tasks list. Flagged Items, Overdue, and Completed appear following the Go To menu. The Filters option includes: Due Date, Start Date, Overdue, Completed, High Priority, Unread, and a Clear All Filters command.

Reading Pane

Select an email, contact, task or note in the list and the contents appears in the reading pane. Use these commands to display the reading pane right, bottom or hidden. When the reading pane is at the bottom or hidden, you'll see additional field columns in the list. If the reading pane is hidden, double-click items to open them in a separate window for reading and editing.

Media Browser

Opens the Office media browser, giving you easy access to photos and audiovisual clips that you can include in email and notes.

Toolbox – Scrapbook

Opens your Scrapbook where you can store snippets of text and media. Keep content that you frequently insert in to emails in your scrapbook to make it easy to find and paste.

Toolbox – Reference Tools

Stored in the same floating palette as the scrapbook, your reference tools include: Thesaurus, Dictionary (with definitions), Bilingual Dictionary, Translation, and Web Search tools.

Navigation Pane

Initially, the navigation pane is on the left side of Outlook's main window, but you don't have to have it displayed all the time. For example, if you choose your email inbox, you can close the navigation pane and see a list of the items currently in your Inbox.

Ribbon

This option collapses and expands the ribbon. When the ribbon is collapsed, the only part that is visible are the tops of the tabs. You can also collapse the ribbon by clicking the currently displayed tab. *Keyboard shortcut*: Option-⌘-R.

Hide/Show Toolbar

Hides or shows the toolbar in Outlook's main window (a space-saving gesture).

Customize Toolbar

Opens Outlook's toolbar customization pane so you can add or remove buttons to the Toolbar (page 633).

Message Menu

The Message Menu and the options listed below are only available when you're in E-mail view (⌘-1).

Reply

Creates an outgoing reply message for the selected message, with subject and address already filled in. If the message comes from a mailing list, the reply will be addressed to the mailing list. *Keyboard shortcut*: ⌘-R.

Reply to All

Creates a reply to the selected message, preaddressed to every recipient of the original message. *Keyboard shortcut*: Shift-⌘-R.

Forward

Forwards the message to a third party, first permitting you to add your own comments to it before you send it along to someone else. *Keyboard shortcut*: ⌘-J.

Forward Special

You can forward a message as an attachment to a new message or you can forward a message as a meeting.

Forward as Attachment

Forwards the message to a third party as a file attachment, which is useful when you want to preserve the formatting of forwarded HTML messages. *Keyboard shortcut*: Control-⌘-J.

Mark as Read

Marks the currently selected message so that it looks like you've already read it (it stops being bold). *Keyboard shortcut*: ⌘-T.

Mark as Unread

Marks the currently selected message as unread (it turns bold)—useful if you've already read it but want to pretend you haven't. *Keyboard shortcut*: Shift-⌘-T.

Mark All as Read

Marks all messages in a folder as having been read. *Keyboard shortcut*: Option-⌘-T.

Attachments

The submenu for attachments includes options to Save, Preview, or Remove Attachments from your email. For emails with more than one attachment, you can use the Save All, Preview All, and Remove All commands.

Sender

The Sender options give you a quick way to add or find names and email addresses to your Contacts address book.

Junk Mail

In your Junk Mail options, you can mark and automatically consign a message to the ignominy of the junk mail folder. If you use Block Sender, you will no longer see that person's mail in your inbox.

Priority

Outlook has three priority settings: High, Normal, and Low. You can use these when you create email messages, and you can mark or change the status of emails that you receive. If you mark an email priority and send it to someone who doesn't use Outlook, the priority may not be visible in the alien email program.

Follow Up

Use the follow-up options to tag messages that require attention later. The options on the submenu cover a range from Today to Two Weeks. You can use the Custom option to set whatever time period you wish.

Categorize

Apply categories to your messages and they receive a word label and color coding. Outlook uses these categories in several different ways to filter and search for messages. Using the Add New and Edit Categories, you can create your own category labels.

Rules

You can create rules that determine how Outlook handles your email. For example, you can choose to have all the email sent from you boss categorized as High Priority and placed in a special My Boss folder. Use the Rules→Edit Rules option to build your rules. Many rules run automatically, but you can force them to run using the Rules→Apply All command.

Move

Select an email, click Move, and then choose one of your folders from the submenu. Outlook removes your message from the current folder or inbox and stores it in the designated folder. If the folder you want isn't on the list, use the Choose Folder command where you can type in the name of your folder. If you want to retain a copy in the current folder, use the "Copy to Folder" command.

Draft

The Draft menu appears on the main menu bar when you are composing an email message and disappears once the email is sent.

Send

Sends the currently open email message. *Keyboard shortcut*: ⌘-Return.

HTML Format

When the HTML format is used, emails can use a wide variety of text formatting and they may include pictures. Check this option to send HTML formatted emails. Deselect this option to use plain text. *Keyboard shortcut*: Shift-⌘-T.

Check Names.

Verifies that email addresses are correctly formatted. *Keyboard shortcut*: Control-⌘-C.

Attachments

Save, Add (⌘-E), or Remove attached files to the currently open email.

Signatures

Lets you select the signature for your outgoing message. (See page 277).

Security

This submenu, available when you're composing a new message, lets you apply two encryption features that help prevent evildoers from reading your email during its electronic journey. Because you and your recipients need to share each other's digital *certificates* (files that identify you as the sender and decode the encrypted messages), you'll usually use this feature when a corporate administrator has gotten everyone set up for it.

- **Digitally Sign Message**. Adds the file that digitally identifies you as you. Usually your administrator purchases these certificates for everyone using the network.

- **Encrypt Message**. Scrambles the message so that only you and others with the right certificates can read it.

Priority

Outlook has three priority settings: High, Normal, and Low. You can use these when you create emails, and you can mark or change the status of emails that you receive. If you mark an email priority and send it to someone who doesn't use Outlook, the priority may not be visible in the alien email program.

Follow Up

Use the follow-up options to tag messages that require attention later. The options on the submenu cover a range from Today to Two Weeks. You can use the Custom option to set whatever time period you wish.

Categorize

Apply categories to your messages and they receive a word label and color coding. Outlook uses these categories in several different ways to filter and search for messages. Using the Add New and Edit Categories, you can create your own category labels.

Meeting

The Meeting menu and the options listed below are only available when you're in Calendar view (⌘-2).

Invite Attendees

Use this option to choose the attendees for a meeting. Outlook provides the tools to keep track of the messages and responses you send to attendees. See page 311.

Recurrence

Meetings and Appointments can be set to recur. For example, if you have a club that meets on the third Thursday of each month you can automatically add those dates to your calendar. If the options on the submenu don't meet your needs, use the Custom option.

Time Zone

Outlook automatically uses your local time zone. However, if you're traveling, you may want to use this option to establish the time zone for meetings and appointments.

Signatures

Use the Signatures option to automatically add signatures to emails sent with meeting invitations and messages.

Show As

The Show As options let you block off periods of time as: Free, Tentative, Busy, or Out of Office. If your calendar is shared, others will be able to use this information to schedule meetings involving you.

Private

If you're sharing your calendar with colleagues, you can use the private option to conceal appointments and meetings from visitors to your calendar.

Categorize

Apply categories to your messages and they receive a word label and color coding. Outlook uses these categories in several different ways to filter and search for messages. Using the Add New and Edit Categories, you can create your own category labels.

Contact

The Contact Menu and the options listed below are only available when you're in Contacts view (⌘-3).

New E-Mail Message To

Select a contact and then choose this option to open a new email message with the contact's name and address.

New Meeting With

Create a meeting and automatically add the selected contacts as Invitees.

New IM Contact

Send an instant message (IM) to a selected contact.

Forward as vCard

Create an email and attach the selected contacts details as a vCard. (vCards are a standard format for importing and exporting contact information. They can be used by many different programs.)

Map Address

Find a contact's address on a Microsoft Bing map. You can also use this option to create driving directions.

Update from Directory

If your office keeps contacts information in a shared network directory, you can use this option to make sure you have the most up-to-date contact information.

This Contact is Me

You use this option to let Outlook know your personal contact details. This information is used when you create meetings and send messages.

Follow Up

Use the follow-up options to tag contacts that require attention later. The options on the submenu cover a range from Today to Two Weeks. You can use the Custom option to set whatever time period you wish.

Categorize

Apply categories to your contacts and they receive a word label and color coding. Outlook uses these categories in several different ways to filter and search for contacts. Using the Add New and Edit Categories, you can create your own category labels.

Move

Select a contact, click Move, and then choose one of your folders from the submenu. Outlook removes your contact from the current folder and stores it in the designated folder. If the folder you want isn't on the list, use the Choose Folder command where you can type in the name of your folder. If you want to retain a copy in the current folder, use the Copy to Folder command.

Task

The Task Menu and the options listed below are only available when you're in Tasks view (⌘-4).

Mark as Complete

As you finish the tasks on your list, you can mark them complete. The "complete" flag can be used when you filter your view. For example, if you want to impress someone you share the chores with, just show them all the tasks you've completed. If you want to focus on what to do next, filter out the completed tasks.

Reply

Email that you've marked for follow-up will appear in your task list. Use this option to reply to the sender of that email.

Reply All

Use this option to reply to the sender and everyone else listed on an email that's in your task list.

Forward

Email that's marked for follow-up appears in your task list. Use this option to forward that email to someone else—ideally, send it to a subordinate who will handle the job.

Recurrence

Tasks, such as take out the recycling, can be set to recur. Outlook tries to guess the recurrence based on the Task's date, but if the options on the submenu don't meet your needs, use the Custom option.

Priority

Outlook has three priority settings: High, Normal, and Low. You can use these when you create tasks and you can mark or change the status. The priority status can be used when you filter or search for tasks.

Follow Up

Use the follow-up options to tag tasks that require attention later. The options on the submenu cover a range from Today to Two Weeks. You can use the Custom option to set whatever time period you wish.

Categorize

Apply categories to your tasks and they receive a word label and color coding. Outlook uses these categories in several different ways to filter and search for tasks. Using the Add New and Edit Categories, you can create your own category labels.

Move

Select a task, click Move, and then choose one of your folders from the submenu. Outlook removes your task from the current folder and stores it in the designated folder. If the folder you want isn't on the list, use the Choose Folder command where you can type in the name of your folder. If you want to retain a copy in the current folder, use the "Copy to Folder" command.

Note

The Note Menu and the options listed below are only available when you're in Notes view (⌘-4). Notes are the simplest of all the Outlook items, and their short menu reflects that.

Forward as Email

Send the body of a note as an email message. Notes can be made up of text and pictures.

Forward as Attachment

Send the note as an email attachment in the HTML format. On the other, the recipient can open the note in their web browser.

Categorize

Apply categories to your notes and they receive a word label and color coding. Outlook uses these categories in several different ways to filter and search for notes. Using the Add New and Edit Categories, you can create your own category labels.

Move

Select a note, click Move, and then choose one of your folders from the submenu. Outlook removes your note from the current folder and stores it in the designated folder. If the folder you want isn't on the list, use the Choose Folder command where you can type in the name of your folder. If you want to retain a copy in the current folder, use the "Copy to Folder" command.

Format Menu

Even though email and news messages both trace their origins to plain text (which doesn't contain much in the way of formatting), the advent of HTML email lets you use a variety of formatting in your missives. Those commands are thoughtfully grouped in the Format menu.

Font

Lists all of the fonts installed on your Mac. Choose one to use in your message.

Style

Lets you choose from five different styles for your text, detailed below:

- **Regular**. You guessed it—plain vanilla text.

- **Bold**. Makes the selected text bold. *Keyboard shortcut*: ⌘-B.

- **Italic**. Makes the selected text italic. *Keyboard shortcut*: ⌘-I.

- **Underline**. Underlines the selected text (and makes it look like a hyperlink—great for practical jokes). *Keyboard shortcut*: ⌘-U.

- **Strikethrough**. Puts a horizontal line through the text, a common marking for text that is to be deleted. *Keyboard shortcut*: Shift-⌘-X.

- **Fixed Width Font**. Uses a fixed-width font, such as Monaco. A fixed-width font is one in which each character takes up the same amount of horizontal space (for example, an "i" takes up as much space as an "m," making it easier for you to line up text in columns).

Size

Lets you choose a specific point size for your text, just as you would when formatting text in Word (page 271).

Color

Lets you choose a color for your HTML-based email fonts. It lists 13 colors and gives you the option to choose your own via the color picker (page 271).

Highlight

Choose a background highlight for your text.

Text Encoding

Lets you choose a language character set for your mail: Western European, Central European, Chinese, Cyrillic, Greek, Japanese, Korean, Turkish, or Unicode. This submenu comes factory set to Automatic, meaning that Outlook can detect the languages used in incoming messages. If you get a message loaded with nonsense characters, try choosing the correct language manually.

Increase Font Size

Increases the size of the selected text. *Keyboard shortcut*: ⌘- +.

Decrease Font Size

Decreases the size of the selected text. *Keyboard shortcut*: ⌘- –.

Alignment

Chooses alignment for the selected paragraphs: Left, Center, or Right.

Numbered List

Turns the selected text into an HTML numbered list.

Bulleted List

Turns the selected text into an HTML bulleted list.

Increase Indent

Indents the selected paragraphs (when creating a quotation, for example). *Keyboard shortcut*: ⌘-].

Decrease Indent

Decreases the indent level. *Keyboard shortcut*: ⌘-[.

Hyperlink

Insert a hyperlink address in your email. Hyperlinks usually lead to web pages, but if you're on a network with shared folders, your hyperlink can also lead to a specific file.

Tools Menu

Where would a Microsoft program be without a Tools menu? Here you'll find commands that deal with Entourage's general utility operations.

Run Schedule

Here's a look at each item in the submenu (see page 285 for more on schedules):

- **Empty Deleted Items Folder**. Empties the Deleted Items folder of its contents.
- **Send & Receive All**. Sends all queued messages and gets mail from all accounts.
- **Send All**. Sends all waiting messages.
- **Edit Schedules**. Opens the Schedules window, where you can create, edit, and delete schedules.

Send & Receive

This command's submenu lets you send your waiting outgoing mail and download any email waiting for you.

- **Send & Receive All**. Sends all waiting messages and gets mail from all accounts. *Keyboard shortcut*: ⌘-K.

- **Send All**. Sends all waiting messages (but doesn't download incoming mail). *Keyboard shortcut*: Shift-⌘-K.

- **Sync this folder**. Depending on the type of email account you use, your email is stored on your computer or on a network mail server. Use this command to make sure that the selected Outlook folder is up-to-date.

IMAP Folders

If you have an IMAP email account, your messages are stored on a network mail server. Click this option to open a window that lists all of your email folders on the network mail server. You can browse through your folders, examine their properties and create new folders. Folders that you Subscribe to appear in Outlook. Click Unsubscribe if you don't need to view a folder in Outlook.

Out of Office (used with Exchange)

If you have a corporate, educational, or hosted Exchange Server account, then this command lets you set a rule to automatically respond to messages while you're away on vacation or out of the office. Your correspondents will know not to expect an answer from you until you return. This rule runs from the server, which means you don't need to keep Entourage running on your computer.

Public Folders (used with Exchange)

If you use Exchange, you can share your email folder with colleagues. Perhaps you have an assistant that handles your email when you're on the road.

Rules

Opens the Rules window, where you can create, edit, or delete message rules (see page 336).

Junk E-Mail Protection

Opens the Junk E-Mail Protection window, where you can set the filter's options (see the box on page 287).

Accounts

Opens the Account window, where you can create, edit, or delete mail accounts (see page 263).

Window Menu

The Window menu corrals all of the window-related Outlook commands in one place.

Minimize

Sends the frontmost Entourage window to the Dock. *Keyboard shortcut:* ⌘-M.

Zoom Window

Does the same thing as the green zoom button in the upper-right corner of the window: resizes it to its full size, so that it fills up most of the screen.

Progress

Opens the Progress window, which shows how network operations are progressing. *Keyboard shortcut:* ⌘-7.

Error Log

Open Outlook's Error Log, which tells you about any problems the program had in sending or receiving your messages. *Keyboard shortcut:* ⌘-8.

My Day

Opens the My Day program (page 340). *Keyboard shortcut:* ⌘-9.

Contact Search

Opens the Contact Search pane of the My Day program. *Keyboard shortcut:* ⌘-0.

Window List

All of the open windows are listed at the bottom of the Window menu. To switch to an open window, select it from this list.

Help Menu

The Help menu gives you access to resources for learning about and troubleshooting Office. Some are stored in the Help system that Office installed on your computer; others are on Microsoft's website.

Search

Search Outlook help. Among other things, this search box is great for finding commands on Outlook's many menus.

Outlook Help

Opens up Entourage's online help, as described in Appendix B.

Welcome to Outlook

Goes to a website with introductory information about Outlook.

Get Started with Outlook

Goes to a website that provides a brief tutorial on Outlook basics.

Check for Updates

Launches the Microsoft AutoUpdate program (see the box on page 11).

Visit the Product Web Site

Opens your web browser to Microsoft's home page for its Macintosh products.

Send Feedback about Outlook

Opens your web browser to a Microsoft web page containing a simple feedback web form.

Scripts Menu

Outlook works well with AppleScript and Automator—so well that it reserves an entire menu for scripts and workflows. You can use one of the included scripts, and you can add your own scripts to this menu.

About this Menu

Opens a dialog box containing a short description of the Scripts Menu and a button that opens the Outlook Script Menu Items folder.

PowerPoint Menus

PowerPoint has many commands in common with the other Office programs. What unique menus it has are dedicated to manipulating slides, text, and images, which is what PowerPoint does so well.

File Menu

PowerPoint's File menu, of course, is for working with files on your hard drive—whether that's creating new files, saving them, or printing them.

New, New from Template, Open, Open URL, Open Recent, Close, Save, Save As

These commands work exactly as they do in Excel; the only distinction here is the wording of the New command (New Presentation).

Save as Pictures

Saves each slide as a graphics file.

Save as Movie

Creates a QuickTime movie from the frontmost open presentation (see page 586).

Share

The Share submenu gives you several ways to distribute your PowerPoint presentation:

- **Save to SkyDrive.** Uploads your presentation to Microsoft's SkyDrive, which is similar to Mac's MobileMe. You need to have registered for an account to use this service.

- **Save to SharePoint.** If your office uses SharePoint as a way to collaborate, you can share your presentation over the SharePoint server with your colleagues.

- **E-mail (as Attachment).** Creates an email and attaches your PowerPoint presentation. Recipients will need to have a program that can view PowerPoint's .pptx file format.

- **E-mail (as Link).** Creates a link to your PowerPoint presentation and places the link in a blank email that you can address. The presentation must be in a network folder that's accessible to the recipient.

- **Send to iPhoto.** Sends the slides in your presentation to iPhoto where they can be stored in JPEG or PNG format. You can send the entire presentation or you can preselect individual slides before choosing this option.

- **Broadcast Slide Show.** You can run your presentation on the Internet using Microsoft's PowerPoint Broadcast service. This option helps you upload your presentation and run your presentation. There are a few caveats, as explained on page 588.

Reduce File Size

Opens a window where you can choose the resolution and other options for the slides in your slideshow that help minimize the file size.

Restrict Permissions

Using certificates (described on page 279), you can control whether someone can open, view and change your presentation.

Page Setup, Print

These commands work just as they do in Excel.

Properties

This command works just as it does in Excel (page 669).

Edit Menu

The Edit Menu gathers together all of PowerPoint's Edit tools into one handy place. Many of these commands are similar to those in other Office programs, but they aren't all the same.

Undo, Repeat/Redo, Cut, Copy, Copy to Scrapbook

These commands work just as they do in Excel.

Paste, Paste from Scrapbook

These commands work just as they do in Excel (page 669).

Paste Special

Opens the Paste Special window, which you can use to paste the contents of the clipboard into the presentation as a linked or embedded file. It also gives you some formatting options when pasting such a file. *Keyboard shortcut*: Control-⌘-V.

Clear

Clears the selected item from the frontmost presentation document.

Select All

Selects all objects on the screen. If the cursor is currently in an active text object, selects all of the text inside that object. *Keyboard shortcut*: ⌘-A.

Duplicate

Duplicates the selected object, placing the copy slightly below and to the right of the original. Duplicating an item doesn't put it on the clipboard. *Keyboard shortcut*: ⌘-D.

Delete Slide

Deletes the current slide (Normal or Notes view) or the selected slides (in Slide Sorter view).

Find

Use the submenu under this option for various find and replace operations:

- **Find.** Type in the text you want to find. *Keyboard shortcut*: ⌘-F.
- **Find Next.** Moves to the next matching occurrence. *Keyboard shortcut*: ⌘-G.
- **Find Previous.** Moves to the previous matching occurrence. *Keyboard shortcut*: Shift-⌘-G.
- **Replace.** Opens the find and replace dialog box. Shift-⌘-H.
- **Advanced Find.** Opens the Advanced Find dialog box where you can choose options like Match Case or Find Whole Words Only.

Special Characters

Opens the Mac OS X Characters Palette, giving you access to every possible special character on your system.

Object

If you've been editing the text inside a text box or table, it's a darned nuisance to have to switch to the arrow tool just to adjust, say, the placement, formatting, or size of that text box or table. This command neatly toggles back and forth between (a) placing the insertion point inside the selected text box or table and (b) selecting the text box or table itself. It saves you a couple of mouse clicks when doing frantic alternation between editing and tweaking.

View Menu

The View menu is home to the commands that govern what you see when you're working with PowerPoint: its view mode, whether the presentation is in color or grayscale, and what toolbars and palettes are showing.

Normal, Slide Sorter, Notes Page, Presenter View, Slide Show

Switches to the corresponding view; see page 546 for details on these views.

Master

The Master menu takes you to the various master elements in a presentation. It has three submenu choices:

- **Slide Master**. Takes you to the Slide Master for the currently active presentation, where you can add elements, or make formatting changes, that will show up on every slide.

- **Handout Master**. Takes you to the Handout Master, which lets you tweak settings that will appear on every handout page in the presentation.

- **Notes Master**. Takes you to the Notes Master, which lets you change settings for every notes page in the presentation.

Ribbon

Expands and collapses the ribbon. When the ribbon is collapsed, the tab and labels are visible but the tools are hidden. *Keyboard shortcut*: Option-⌘-R.

Toolbars

Shows or hides any of the PowerPoint toolbars: Standard, Formatting, and Outlining. Use the Customize Toolbars and Menus options to make changes as described on page 633.

Message Bar

Opens and closes the Message Bar that appears below the ribbon. This area is used to display security warnings, for example, to let you know that you're opening a document that has macros.

Media Browser

Opens the media browser window which stores photos, audio, movies, clip art, symbols and shapes.

Toolbox

All the various palettes below are part of the Toolbox—you can't click this menu item directly.

Custom Animation

Opens and closes the Custom Animation tab in the Toolbox.

Scrapbook

Hides or shows the Scrapbook.

Reference Tools

Hides or shows the Reference Tools.

Compatibility Report

Hides or shows the Compatibility Report.

Header and Footer

Opens the "Header and Footer" window, where you can create text that repeats on the top or bottom of every slide.

Comments

Shows or hides any comments ("sticky notes") that you or your coworkers have placed in PowerPoint slides.

Ruler

Hides or shows PowerPoint's rulers (for aligning objects on the page).

Guides

Turns the horizontal and vertical Dynamic and Static Guides on or off (useful T-square-like lines that help you align objects on your slide with each other). Also lets you turn on or off Snap to Grid or Snap to Shape. *Static Guides keyboard shortcut*: ⌘-G.

Zoom

Opens the Zoom window, where you can choose from one of six preset values for magnifying or reducing the onscreen representation of your slides, or enter your own zoom percentage.

Insert Menu

Use the commands in this menu to add things to your PowerPoint presentations or to individual slides.

New Slide

Creates a new slide after the selected slide. *Keyboard shortcut*: Shift-⌘-N.

Duplicate Slide

Duplicates the active slide; places the duplicate after that slide. *Keyboard shortcut*: Shift-⌘-D.

Slides From

- **Other Presentation**. Lets you pull slides out of another PowerPoint file to insert into the currently active presentation.

- **Outline File**. Imports a Word outline and creates slides (and slide text) from it. Each first-level item is given its own new slide (see page 540).

Section

Divides your presentation into separate sections, letting you use different formatting and features in each section. For example, you can have separate header and footer options for different sections.

Text Box

Inserts an empty text box on the active slide.

WordArt

Opens the WordArt tab on the ribbon and places a text box in the current slide, so you can click a WordArt style to insert in your slide.

Header and Footer

Opens the Header and Footer dialog box, where you can choose the text to be displayed at the top and bottom of slides, notes and handouts.

Date and Time

Opens the "Header and Footer" window, which you can use to add the current date and time in one of several formats to the current slide. If you want to add the date and time to every slide, again, use a header or footer.

Slide Number

Adds the slide number to a text box on the active slide (not every slide—you'll have to use a header or footer for that purpose).

Table

Opens the Insert Table window, where you can specify the size of the table that gets inserted when you select this command.

Chart

Opens the Charts tab on the ribbon so you can click a chart type to insert in your slide.

SmartArt Graphic

Opens the Elements Gallery's SmartArt Graphics tab so you can click a SmartArt layout to insert into your slide.

Photo, Audio, Movie, Clip Art, Symbol, Shape, Object, and Hyperlink

These Insert options work the same in Excel, PowerPoint, and Word. For details, see the Excel options described on page 676.

Format Menu

This menu contains all of PowerPoint's formatting commands, which let you manipulate fonts, text alignment and spacing, and colors. When you're working with text, they work exactly the same as text formatting in Word.

Font

Opens the Font tab of the Format Text dialog box, where you can set all kinds of font options for the currently selected text: the font, size, style, color, and effects. *Keyboard shortcut*: ⌘-T.

Paragraph

Opens the Paragraph tab of the Format Text dialog box, giving you control over things like indentation, line spacing, and alignment. *Keyboard shortcut*: Option-⌘-M.

Bullets and Numbering

Opens the "Bullets and Numbering" tab of the Format Text dialog box, where you can select a style for your bulleted or numbered items. You can also use this window to insert a picture or character of your own choosing to use as a bullet.

Columns

Opens the Columns tab of the Format Text dialog box, where you can choose the number of columns and the spacing between them.

Alignment

Aligns the selected text in one of five ways: left, center, right, justified, or distributed.

Text Direction

Opens the Text Box tab of the Format Text dialog box, where you can set vertical alignment, text direction, autofit, and internal margins.

Change Case

Opens the Change Case window, where you can change the capitalization of the selected text: sentence case, lowercase, uppercase, title case, and toggle case.

Replace Fonts

Lets you replace one specified font in your presentation with a different font, globally, wherever it may appear—a great tactic when you move your file to a different machine that doesn't have the fonts you used originally.

Theme Colors

Pops open the Create Theme Colors window, where you can choose from a set of standard color schemes or create a custom one.

Slide Background

Opens the Format Background window, where you can choose a background fill color for the current slide (or for all of the slides in the presentation).

Shape

Opens the Format Shape box, where you can tweak every single detail of the selected shape.

Arrange

PowerPoint slides are built from many elements. Some are in the background, others in front. Often you want to align objects with each other or in relation to the edges of the slide. The Arrange menu gives you the power.

Reorder Objects

Changes your view of the slide to a 3D angle view where it's easy to see the top-to-bottom hierarchy of visual elements. You can drag layers to move them to a different level.

Reorder Overlapping Objects

Same as the Reorder objects view but focuses on the object that overlap each other.

Bring to Front

Move the selected object to the front of the stack.

Send to Back

Move the selected object to the back of the stack.

Bring Forward

Move the selected object forward one position in the stack.

Send Backward

Move the selected object back one position in the stack.

Group

When you group objects, they work as if they were a single element. This is great for graphics where you want the elements to maintain the same relative position. Grouped objects can be moved, cut, copied, and pasted as a single element.

Ungroup

Breaks apart a group of elements so they can be treated as individual elements.

Regroup

Recreates a group that has been broken apart with Ungroup. Unlike the Group command, you only have to select a single element of the group to use Regroup.

Rotate or Flip

Rotate objects in 90 degree increments or flip objects horizontally and vertically. Choose Rotation Options for more granular rotation effects.

Align or Distribute

Align selected objects or distribute them evenly within the slide.

Tools Menu

Most of these commands work just as they do in the other Office programs.

Spelling, Thesaurus, Dictionary, Language, AutoCorrect, Flag for Follow Up

These commands work just as they do in Excel.

Macros

Provides tools for managing and editing macros in PowerPoint. Unlike Excel and Word, there's no option for recording macros based on your actions. That means you have to roll your own:

- **Macros** opens the Macro dialog box which is command central for working with macros. From the box you can create, run, debug, and edit your macros.

- **Visual Basic Editor** opens the VBA programming environment where you can dig deep into the macro or VBA code.

Add-Ins

Opens the Add-Ins window, where you can turn on or turn off various Add-Ins for PowerPoint. Add-Ins are conceptually similar to PowerPoint plug-ins in that they add new functions to PowerPoint.

Slide Show Menu

This menu contains all of the slideshow-related menu commands, used for preparing and running a slideshow.

Play from Start

Plays your presentation starting with the first slide. *Keyboard shortcut*: Shift-⌘-Return.

Play from Current Slide

Starts the slideshow from the current slide. *Keyboard shortcut*: ⌘-Return.

Broadcast Slide Show

Starts a slideshow using Microsoft's PowerPoint Broadcast Service. For details, see page 588.

Custom Shows

Opens the Custom Shows window, where you can add, edit, or remove custom slideshow variations on the currently open presentation.

Presenter View

Starts the slideshow using the Presenter Tools display (page 584).

Rehearse

Runs through your slideshow, keeping track of the amount of time that it takes to show each slide. Those times can be saved with the presentation so that it runs just as long as it did during rehearsal.

Record Slide Show

Runs through your slideshow, keeping track of the amount of time that it takes to show each slide. You can record narration as you run through the slideshow. The audio plays back as a series of audio clips to the timings that you set while recording your narration. At the end, PowerPoint prompts you to save the timings to create an automated slideshow.

Action Buttons

Lets you add action buttons to your slides. You can choose the kind of action button (mostly used for navigating, playing media clips, or opening files) from the submenu: custom, home, help, information, previous slide, next slide, first slide, last slide, last slide viewed, document, sound, and movie.

Action Settings

If you have an Action Button selected, this command opens the Action Settings window, where you can decide what the selected Action Button does.

Custom Animation

Opens the Custom Animation palette in the Toolbox (page 569).

Transitions

Opens the PowerPoint Presentation Gallery's Transitions tab, where you can select a transition for the current slide (page 563).

Hide Slide

Hides the current slide so that it's not displayed during a slideshow.

Set Up Show

Opens the Set Up Show window, where you can set options for the currently open presentation.

Window Menu

The Window menu commands let you shuffle and manipulate multiple PowerPoint windows.

Minimize Window, Zoom Window, New Window, Arrange All, Bring All to Front

These commands work exactly the same as in Excel (page 686).

Cascade

Resizes and rearranges all open windows so that one is on top of the next, and you can see the title bar and a small portion of each window.

Next Pane

Rotates clockwise to the next window pane, making it active.

Window List

The last item on the Window menu is a list of currently open PowerPoint windows. You can switch between them by selecting their names from this menu.

Help Menu

See "Help Menu" on page 687.

AppleScript Menu

See "Script Menus" on page 688.

Word Menus

Word's menus, once again, have many functions described earlier in this appendix, but there are significant differences.

File Menu

Word comes equipped with a File menu (like almost all other Mac programs), which is mainly used for working with files on your hard drive—whether that's creating new files, saving them, or printing them.

New Blank Document, New from Template, Open, Open URL, Open Recent, Close, Save, Save As

These commands work just as they do in Excel.

Save as Web Page

Converts the frontmost Word document into a web page, converting graphics into the appropriate graphic formats (page 34).

Share

These options work as they do for Excel, described on page 34.

Web Page Preview

Shows you what your document would look like as a web page. It opens a temporary web page conversion of your file in your browser of choice.

Restrict Permissions

Using certificates (described on page 33), you can control whether someone can open, view, and change your presentation.

Reduce File Size

Opens the Reduce File Size dialog box where you can reduce the size of the Word document file by choosing options like: "Best for Printing", "Best for viewing on Screen", or "Best for Sending an Email".

Page Setup, Print

These commands work just as they do in Excel.

Properties

Opens the document Properties window.

Edit Menu

The Edit menu gathers together all of Word's Edit tools into one handy place. Many of these commands are similar to those in other Office programs.

Undo, Repeat/Redo, Cut, Copy, Copy to Scrapbook

These commands work just as they do in Excel.

Paste, Paste Special

Again, these commands do the same things as in Excel (page 669)…but in Word.

Paste and Match Formatting

The pasted content conforms to the formatting of the document it's being pasted into.

Clear

Word's Clear command has a submenu giving you a choice of how much to clear away:

- **Clear Formatting**. Like the Clear Formatting option on the Formatting Palette's Style menu, this option removes formatting while leaving text intact.

- **Contents**. This is the new name of the true Clear command, which deletes selected text without copying it to the Clipboard.

Select All

Selects all text and objects in the document, ready for (for example) copying or deleting. *Keyboard shortcut*: ⌘-A.

Use the submenu under this option for various find and replace operations:

- **Find**. Type in the text you want to find. *Keyboard shortcut*: ⌘-F.

- **Find Next**. Moves to the next matching occurrence. *Keyboard shortcut*: ⌘-G.

- **Find Previous**. Moves to the previous matching occurrence. *Keyboard shortcut*: Shift-⌘-G.

- **Replace**. Opens the find and replace dialog box. Shift-⌘-H.

- **Go To**. Opens the Go to portion of the Find panel where you can choose to go to a specific page or bookmark.

- **Advanced Find**. Opens the Advanced Find dialog box where you can choose options like Match Case or Find Whole Words Only. *Keyboard shortcut*: Option-⌘-G.

Links

Pulls up a window showing information about every link in the currently active document. If the document doesn't have any links to other documents, this option is dimmed.

Object

Lets you edit an embedded object, such as a Microsoft Graph object or a Microsoft Organization Chart object.

View Menu

This menu's commands govern what view mode the windows are in, what toolbars are shown, and so on.

Draft, Web Layout, Outline, Print Layout, Notebook Layout, Publishing Layout, Full Screen

Switches among Word's various document views; see page 24 for descriptions.

Ribbon

Expands and collapses the ribbon. When the ribbon is collapsed, the tab and labels are visible but the tools are hidden. *Keyboard shortcut*: Option-⌘-R.

Toolbars

Shows or hides any of Word toolbars: Standard, Formatting, and Database. Use the Customize Toolbars and Menus options to make changes as described on page 633.

Sidebar

Opens the sidebar on the left side of the document window to display one of the following: Document Map Pane, Thumbnail Pane, Reviewing Pane, or Search Pane.

Message Bar

Opens and closes the Message Bar that appears below the ribbon. This area displays security warnings, for example, to let you know that you're opening a document that has macros.

Toolbox

All the various palettes below are part of the Toolbox—you can't click this menu item directly.

Styles

Hides or shows the Styles panel, where you can choose styles to apply to your text and create new styles.

Citations

Hides or shows the Citations panel in the toolbox. For help with citations, see page 221.

Scrapbook

Hides or shows the Scrapbook.

Reference Tools

Hides or shows the Reference Tools.

Compatibility Report

Hides or shows the Compatibility Report.

Ruler

Hides or shows the ruler in the currently active document (see page 106).

Header and Footer

Switches the currently active Word document to "Header and Footer" mode (and shows the purple "Header and Footer" tab on the ribbon), where you can enter headers or footers that will show up at the top or bottom of every page (see page 111).

Footnotes

Shows footnotes, which also makes them available for editing (see page 218).

Master Document

Opens the Master Document toolbar, where you can combine several separate document files to create a single master document.

Markup

Shows or hides comments or additions and deletions if Track Changes is turned on.

Reveal Formatting

Hides or shows the Reveal Formatting mode, which pops up a balloon with all kinds of details about the formatting where you click.

Zoom

Lets you magnify or reduce the onscreen display of your document.

Insert Menu

This collection of Word commands lets you insert specialized text, entire documents or other pictures and objects into your Word documents.

Break

Inserts one of six kinds of breaks into the Word document that interrupt your text at the insertion point: page breaks, section breaks, column breaks, and so on (see page 47).

Page Numbers

Opens the Page Numbers window, which lets you choose a place for page numbers that update automatically.

Date and Time

Opens the "Date and Time" window, from which you can insert the current date and time in a variety of formats. The date and time appear at the insertion point, and it can be made to update automatically to the current date and time whenever the document is printed.

AutoText

The AutoText menu (see page) contains several premade commands that let you automatically enter canned bits of text (such as letter salutations) at the insertion point.

Field

Opens the Field window, where you can insert a Word field (self-updating text code) at the insertion point (see page 115).

New Comment

Inserts a comment into the currently active document (see page 241).

Caption

Opens the Caption window, which you can use to insert a picture caption at the insertion point (see page 215).

Cross-reference

Opens the Cross-reference window, which lets you insert cross-references to items in the document (see page 214).

Index and Tables

Opens the "Index and Tables" window, where you can create various indexes, table of contents entries, and authority citations (see page 203).

Watermark

Lets you choose an image or text to place as a watermark (faint background) on each page of your document.

Tables

Opens the Tables tab on the ribbon with tools to create and format tables.

Chart

Opens the Charts tab on the ribbon with the tools you need to create and format charts.

SmartArt Graphic

Opens the SmartArt Graphics tab on the ribbon with the tools you need to insert SmartArt into your document.

Photo, Audio, Movie, Clip Art, Symbol, Shape,

These Insert options work the same in Excel, PowerPoint and Word. For details, see the Excel options described on page 676.

Text Box

Adds a text box to your document and opens the Format tab so you can modify the text box's appearance. Text boxes are a sort of hybrid made of text and graphics. You can always edit the text in the box but there are many more artistic opportunities because the text is treated as a graphic.

WordArt

Places text in a Text Box (see above) and opens the Format tab where you can apply effects to your text.

Equation

Creates an equation box in your document and opens the special, purple Equation Tools menu with all the mathematical symbols and structures you ever dreamt of. Anyone for pi?

File

Lets you insert one Word file into another—at the insertion point—just as though you'd copied and pasted it.

Object

Opens the Object window, where you can select one of several Office object types for insertion (see page 626).

HTML Object

This menu is meant to help build web pages. It has nine submenus:

- **Background Sound**. Inserts a sound of your choice that will be played back when the page is viewed in a browser.

- **Scrolling Text**. Adds text that scrolls annoyingly when your page is viewed in a web browser.

- **Checkbox**. Inserts an HTML checkbox (complete with name and value) at the insertion point.

- **Option Button**. Inserts an HTML option button (or radio button) at the insertion point.

- **List Box**. Inserts an HTML list box at the insertion point.

- **Textbox**. Inserts an HTML text box at the insertion point.

- **Submit**. Inserts an HTML button (automatically titled Submit) at the insertion point.

- **Reset**. Inserts an HTML Reset button at the insertion point (for resetting a form).

- **Hidden**. Inserts a hidden HTML field at the insertion point.

Bookmark

Inserts a bookmark in the currently open document. The bookmark can be used to mark text, pictures or tables (see page 213).

Hyperlink

Opens the Insert Hyperlink window, where you can insert a new hyperlink to a web page, a document, or an email address (see page 210). *Keyboard shortcut*: ⌘-K.

Format Menu

This menu contains all of Word's formatting commands, which let you work with text controls, alignment, and spacing.

Font

Opens the Font window, where you can make all kinds of marvelous tweaks to the type choices of the selected (or about-to-be-typed) text. *Keyboard shortcut*: ⌘-D.

Paragraph

Opens the Paragraph window, where you can change paragraph-level formatting options (such as line spacing and indents). *Keyboard shortcut*: Option-⌘-M.

Document

Opens the Document window, where you can change document-level formatting options (such as margins and how sections begin).

Bullets and Numbering

Opens the "Bullets and Numbering" window, where you can control how bulleted and numbered lists look (see page 44).

Borders and Shading

Opens the "Borders and Shading" window, where you can add and change borders and shaded areas in your Word document (see page 74).

Columns

Opens the Columns window, where you can set the number of columns used in the current document (see page 47). You can also control the column width and spacing in this window.

Tabs

Opens the Tabs window, where you can add, edit, and remove tab stops in the currently open Word document (see page 130).

Drop Cap

Lets you add a drop cap to the currently open Word document. You can choose from one of three styles in the window that pops up.

Text Direction

Lets you choose from three text direction orientations: left to right, top to bottom, or bottom to top. For use primarily in table cells (see page 69).

Change Case

Opens the Change Case window, where you can change the capitalization of the selected text: sentence case, lowercase, uppercase, title case, and toggle case.

AutoFormat

Automatically adds formatting according to the AutoFormat rules that you set to the currently open Word document (see page 54).

Style

Lets you add, edit, and remove styles in the currently open Word document (see page 119).

[Object]

This menu's wording reflects whatever's selected in the document window (Picture, AutoShape, and so on). It opens the corresponding Format window.

Font Menu

This menu lists every font you have installed. To select a font, choose its name. Word renders the font names in the actual font, so that you can see what you're selecting.

Tools Menu

The Tools menu includes a mix of text tools, sharing tools, and other miscellaneous functions.

Spelling and Grammar

Checks the document for spelling and grammar errors; if Word finds any questionable items, pops open the "Spelling and Grammar" window to give you the opportunity to correct them. *Keyboard shortcut*: Option-⌘-L.

Thesaurus

Opens the Reference Tools palette, which lets you find synonyms or antonyms for the selected word. *Keyboard shortcut*: Control-Option-⌘-R.

Hyphenation

Hyphenates the currently active Word document, which gives better spacing between words in individual lines.

Dictionary

Opens the Reference Tools palette, where you can view the selected word's definition.

Language

Flags selected text as being in a given language. The advantage of doing this is that Word will thereafter apply the appropriate language dictionary for spelling checks and AutoCorrect entries.

Word Count

Counts up the statistics for the currently open Word document: the number of words, lines, characters, and paragraphs.

AutoCorrect

Opens the AutoCorrect window, where you can determine what Word tries to automatically correct when it thinks it sees an error in your typing (see page 57). It also lets you enter AutoText items that will fill in automatically as you type, and it lets you set the automatic formatting that's applied to your Word documents both as you type and if you select the AutoFormat command.

Track Changes

The Track Changes menu controls how word keeps tabs of changes to documents. This menu has two submenu options: Highlight Changes and Compare Documents.

- **Highlight Changes**. Opens the Highlight Changes window, where you can turn change tracking on. Plus, you can control which changes are highlighted.

- **Compare Documents**. Compares the open document with the original saved version of that same document, and shows any changes that you've made.

Merge Documents

Merges changes that have been tracked in the currently open Word document into another document of your choice.

Protect Document

Keeps people from making the kinds of changes that you specify to a document. You can optionally enter a password to protect the currently open document from those changes.

Block Authors

When you share documents over SkyDrive or SharePoint, you can block authors from changing specific sections of the document.

Unblock All My Blocked Areas

Removes blocks from the document, provided you have sufficient permission.

Protect Documents

Set different protection levels to keep others from making changes to your document.

Flag for Follow Up

Opens the "Flag for Follow Up" window, where you can set a reminder attached to the currently open Word document. That reminder will pop up at the time you specify to remind you to do something with that document.

Mail Merge Manager

Opens the Mail Merge Manager palette, which you can use to take control over your mail merge operations (such as mail merges for mass mailings).

Envelopes

Helps you create an envelope, including things such as the delivery address and return address. It also has an option to do a data merge, so that you can draw addresses for your envelopes from a data file.

Labels

Lets you use Word to create mailing labels of all kinds. This command takes advantage of Word's plethora of mailing label templates, and it lets you format those labels for either dot-matrix or laser printing.

Letter Wizard

Opens the Letter Wizard, which walks you through the process of creating a letter suitable for mailing to businesses, friends, or even writing crank letters to the government.

Contacts

Opens the Office Address Book window (which looks suspiciously like the Outlook Address Book), where you can quickly look up contact information.

Macros

Provides tools for recording, managing and editing macros that you record in Word. There are three submenu options:

- **Macros** opens the Macro dialog box which is command central for working with macros. From the box you can create, run, debug, and edit your macros.
- **Record New Macro** turns on the macro recorder, which translates your actions in Word into Visual Basic for Applications (VBA) code.
- **Visual Basic Editor** opens the VBA programming environment where you can dig deep into the code created by the macro recorder. If the programming spirit moves you, you can even write your own macros from scratch.

Templates and Add-Ins

Opens the "Templates and Add-ins" window, where you can attach a different template to the currently open Word document. Plus, you can use this window to turn on or off various Add-Ins for Word.

Customize Keyboard

Opens the Customize Keyboard window, where you can add or modify keyboard commands.

Table Menu

Word's Table menu contains a variety of commands to help you draw the perfect table to hold your precious data.

Draw Table

Turns the cursor into a pencil, which you can use to draw a table and divide it into individual cells. When you begin to draw, the ribbon displays the purple Table Layout tab.

Insert

This menu has several options that let you take a little more conservative approach to table creation. It has six options:

- **Table**. Opens the Insert Table window, where you can specify the size and characteristics of your new table.
- **Columns to the Left**. Adds a column to the left of the insertion point in the currently active table. If you have more than one column selected, this command will insert the same number of columns to the left of the insertion point.
- **Columns to the Right**. Adds a column to the right of the insertion point in the currently active table. If you have more than one column selected, this command will insert the same number of columns to the right of the insertion point.
- **Rows Above**. Inserts a row above the insertion point in the currently active table. If you have more than one row selected, this command will insert the same number of rows above the insertion point.
- **Rows Below**. Inserts a row below the insertion point in the currently active table. If you have more than one row selected, this command will insert the same number of rows below the insertion point.
- **Cells**. Inserts the number of cells that you have selected into the currently active table. It also opens the Insert Cells window, where you can specify how things move around to make room for those cells.

Delete

Sometimes you want to remove a table from a document, and this menu (with its four submenu choices) has you covered.

- **Table**. Deletes the currently selected table.
- **Columns**. Deletes the currently selected columns.
- **Rows**. Deletes the currently selected rows.
- **Cells**. Deletes the currently selected cells, and it gives you the option of how you want to shift the remaining cells to take up the room left vacant by the now missing cells.

Select

That's right—there's a special Select menu item for use with tables, and it has four submenu options to help you select just the portions of the table with which you want to work.

- **Table**. Selects the entire table. If the insertion point isn't in a table, this option is left blank.

- **Column**. Selects the column in which the insertion point is located.

- **Row**. Selects the row in which the insertion point is located.

- **Cell**. Selects the cell in which the insertion point is located.

Merge Cells

Merges two or more adjacent selected cells (including the data contained in those cells) into one large cell.

Split Cells

Splits a cell into the number of rows and columns that you set.

Split Table

Plays King Solomon and splits a table at the insertion point, placing a paragraph mark between the two new tables.

AutoFit and Distribute

The AutoFit menu item lets you automatically resize a table to fit a variety of factors. This menu item has five submenu selections.

- **AutoFit to Contents**. Makes the table's columns resize themselves to fit the text or numbers that you type in.

- **AutoFit to Window**. Makes the table resize itself to fit a web browser window. Useful for creating tables meant for the web.

- **Fixed Column Width**. Makes the width of the selected columns a fixed value. That way, they won't vary in size.

- **Distribute Rows Evenly**. Makes the selected rows the same height.

- **Distribute Columns Evenly**. Makes the selected columns the same width.

Heading Rows Repeat

Makes the selected row a heading row, which means that it will repeat at the top of every page if the table that it's in spans more than one page.

Convert

The two commands in the Convert submenu let you move text into tables and back out again.

- **Convert Text to Table**. Converts the selected text into a table, placing the text in one or more of the table's cells.
- **Convert Table to Text**. Converts the selected table cells into regular text.

Sort

Opens the Sort Text window, where you can sort your table's contents alphabetically, numerically, and so on.

Formula

Sort of a mini-Excel. This command lets you insert a formula into the currently active cell to do basic calculations.

Gridlines

Hides or shows the table's dotted gridlines. These gridlines help you see what you're doing in your current table.

Table Properties

Opens the Table Properties window, where you can set all kinds of options for the currently selected table.

Window Menu

The Window menu provides a home for all menu commands that are window-related.

Zoom Window, Minimize Window, Bring All to Front

These commands work exactly as they do in Excel.

New Window

Opens a new window on the same file that's currently open. That way, you can view two (or more) places in the same file at the same time.

Arrange All

Arranges all open windows so that you can see each one. They're stacked vertically. This makes it easy to drag items between them.

Split

Splits the currently active Word window into two independently scrolling panes. If the window is already split, this menu command changes to say Remove Split, which removes the split screen effect.

Window List

The last item on the Window menu is a list of currently open Word documents. You can switch between them by selecting names from this menu.

AppleScript Menu

See "Script Menus" on page 688.

Help Menu

Contains the same commands for Office's Help system, as described on page 687.

SkyDrive and Office Web Apps

B ack in prehistoric days, there were no *personal* computers. Computers looked like the big monolith in Stanley Kubrick's *2001* and people used *terminals*—keyboards and screens—to access information and run programs that lived on those monstrous machines. Then the Apple II arrived on the scene, freeing the world from the giant mainframe computer. You could keep your own documents and programs right on your own desktop machine. These days, with the advent of *cloud computing*, you're no longer even tied down to your desktop. You can keep your information on a big network of computers (the Internet) and you can work with it anywhere in the world using programs that also live on the Internet. All you need is a screen and a keyboard—like the one on your MacBook, iPhone, or iPad.

The big guns in today's computer business provide storage and applications over the Internet. For its part, Apple integrates an online iDisk into your Mac—you can see it right there in Finder. Apple also offers iWork.com, a website where you can use an online version of its productivity suite. Google started out with Gmail and then enticed you with Google Calendar and Google Documents. Microsoft joins the party with SkyDrive, 25 GB of free online storage, and Office Web Apps—lite versions of Word, Excel, PowerPoint, and OneNote.

Why Compute in the Cloud?

Computing over the Internet gives you the freedom to work anywhere. For example, you may start a budget in Excel from your office computer. When you're on the road visiting clients, you can keep working on that file from your laptop. Finally, the weekend before the big board meeting, you want to use those figures in your PowerPoint presentation. No problem if those files are on SkyDrive. Even if you find yourself at a computer that doesn't have Office installed, you can still tweak the files a bit using Office Web Apps.

If you work with a team that shares files, SkyDrive offers even more benefits. You can save your files to SkyDrive and use the reviewing tools to track the changes each person makes, as described on page 245 for Word and page 510 for Excel. For example, in Excel, two or more people can work on a spreadsheet at the same time. If there are attempts to change the same cells at the same time, you get to decide whose changes to use.

Signing Up for SkyDrive and Office Web Apps

SkyDrive and Office Web Apps are free—everyone's favorite price. You don't even have to own a copy of Office to use SkyDrive or the Office Web Apps. All you need is access to the Internet and a free Windows Live account. Windows Live is the new brand name for a number of Microsoft web offerings; it's sort of an umbrella for several new and old web services. If you've ever signed up for Windows Live, Hotmail, MSN (Microsoft Network), or Xbox LIVE, you can use one of those IDs to access SkyDrive and Office Web Apps. If you haven't already ventured into Microsoft's online offerings, you can sign up at *http://skydrive.live.com* (Figure D-1). You must provide your email address, name, country, state/region, Zip code, gender, and date of birth. Unlike some other online signups, *all* of the fields shown in the form are required.

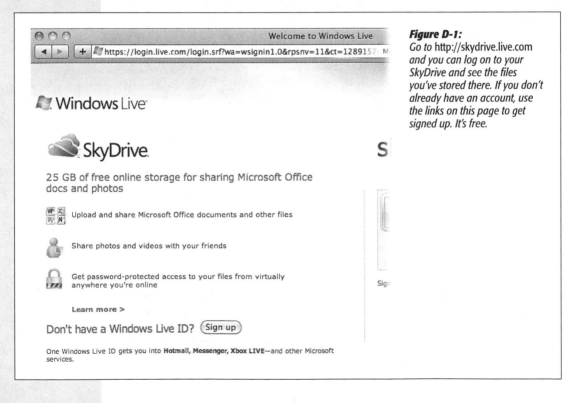

Figure D-1:
Go to http://skydrive.live.com *and you can log on to your SkyDrive and see the files you've stored there. If you don't already have an account, use the links on this page to get signed up. It's free.*

Finding Your Way in Microsoft's Cloud

When you're starting out with SkyDrive, it seems like the Windows Live site shows different views of your folders and files every time you access them. There's one view when you first get to SkyDrive, and another view if you go to Office→Recent Documents. There's yet another view when you close an Office Web App.

You're not imagining things. Confusingly, Windows Live has different web pages that give you access to stored files and folders. The solution is to approach your stored files from the same direction until you become more familiar with this Microsoft madness. For example, if you use the menu under the Windows Live logo to go to SkyDrive, you'll start off with the same, familiar view of your folders and files. Point to the Windows Live logo, and a menu appears. Choose SkyDrive from the menu, and you see a

page divided into three groups: Documents, Favorites, and Photos. The Documents group includes your private My Documents folder and your shared-with-everyone Public folder. To make it easy to find this exact page again, add the page to your browser bookmarks. In Safari, you do that by clicking the + button next to the page address. (You can show or hide the Bookmarks bar by pressing Shift-⌘-B.)

The Windows Live menu and its companions appear on most pages, but you don't see them when you're working in one of the Office Web Apps—Word, Excel, PowerPoint, or OneNote. However, once you close the app or document (File→Close), you'll see the familiar menus at the top of the page.

Once you log into your account, you're in the Microsoft's Windows Live website. (Don't worry, your Mac friends need not know that you ventured to the dark side.) Like most things Microsoft, the pages appear to be designed by engineers, not artists. Often, so many things are crammed on each page that you aren't sure what to do next. Read on for tips to help you get around.

At the top of most pages you'll see the following items, each of which reveal related menus:

- **Windows Live**. This is the main navigation menu for the Windows Live website. On the menu you'll find links to Devices, SkyDrive, Mobile, Downloads, and All Services. For your work with Office, the SkyDrive is the one you'll use most often, as explained in the box above. The Downloads link leads to downloadable Windows programs.

- **Hotmail**. Microsoft's Hotmail email service has been around for ages. Perhaps you've used it. If not, you've received spam from someone who has. Like Google's offerings, the Hotmail service includes an address book and calendar.

- **Messenger**. Microsoft's instant messaging service is called Microsoft Messenger or Live Messenger. It works like Apple's iChat, letting you send text, audio or video messages in real time.

- **Office**. Click this link to create new documents using the Office Web Apps: Word, Excel, PowerPoint, and OneNote.

- **Photos**. This link leads to online photo albums. You can upload your pictures and share them with your friends and colleagues.

- **MSN**. The Microsoft Network is a web portal that combines web-based services for shopping, searching, and other activities.

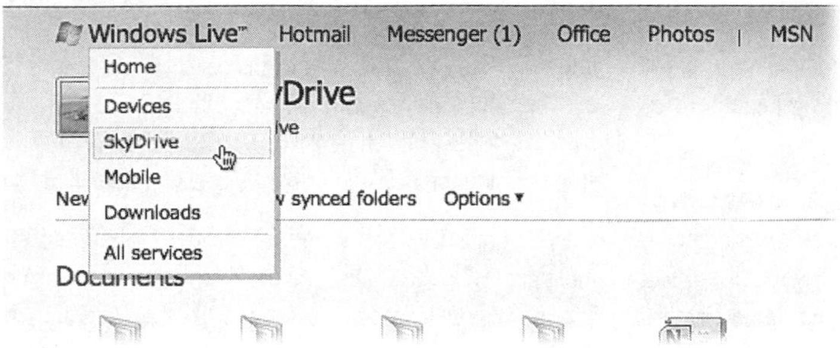

Figure D-2:
At the top of most of the Windows Live web pages, you'll see these menus. They look more like links than menus, but when you mouse over them, they sprout pop-up menus like the one shown here under the Windows Live logo.

When you choose the SkyDrive link under the Windows Live logo, you see a page with three groups: Documents, Favorites, and Photos. Off on the right, you see some advertising. Windows Live may be free, but advertising is the price you pay. Just grit your teeth and remember the 25 GB of free storage space Microsoft is giving you. For more details on the ads, see the box on page 743.

- The **Documents** group holds the files that you share or save to SkyDrive when you're working in Office 2011 or when you work with the web apps.

- The **Favorites** group is a place where you can save links to websites and share those links with your contacts.

- The **Photos** group is your online photo album. You can create personal albums that no one else sees, or you can create shared albums.

Tip: To keep your personal files truly personal, you *must* protect your user name and password. If someone logs on to Windows Live under your name and password, Microsoft just assumes it's you. A strong password is your best protection, so create one with ten or more characters, and a tricky combination of letters, numbers, and punctuation.

Storing Files on SkyDrive

When you're working in Word, Excel, or PowerPoint, you can save your file to your SkyDrive instead of saving it to a folder on your computer. Use the menu command, File→Share→Save to SkyDrive. You might think that means you must share the file if it's on SkyDrive, but that's not the case. At first, there are two folders on Sky-Drive—My Documents and Public. Save files that you don't want to share in your My Documents folder. As shown in Figure D-3, you can create additional folders in SkyDrive and dictate who has access to those folders.

OFFICE 2011 FOR MACINTOSH: THE MISSING MANUAL

Living with Live.com Ads

Microsoft provides gigabytes of free storage and web apps, but there's still a price to be paid. On Live.com, that price is advertising (over there on the right side of the SkyDrive pages). You can try to ignore the ads or, if you're inclined, you can manage them a bit using the three links that surround each ad:

- **To remove an ad**, click the X button in the lower-right corner. That ad will disappear, but the relief is temporary. When you move to another page, or refresh the current page, a new ad takes its place. They've got millions of 'em.

- **To send Microsoft a message about a particular ad,** click the Ad Feedback link, also in the lower-right corner. They're interested to find out whether you find

a particular ad offensive, or you don't trust the advertiser, or the ad feed doesn't seem to be working.

- **To personalize the ads displayed for you,** click the Ad Choices link in the upper-right corner. As with most websites, particularly those that include search tools, Microsoft collects information about you as you search and surf the web. It uses that information to serve up ads likely to interest you. If you find that just a bit creepy, under "Ad choices", you can "opt out" of personalized ads. You'll still get ads, but they won't be tailored specifically for you. If you want to go the other direction, you can give Microsoft more information about your interests, and get even more tempting advertising.

Once you get used to it, saving an Office document to SkyDrive isn't much different from saving it to a folder on your computer. When you press ⌘-S to save a file that you opened in SkyDrive, the new, edited version replaces the existing SkyDrive file. After you close a file, its name appears in the File→Open Recent list in your Office application. In the list, the location for the file always starts with *https://*—the HTML code for a secure website (see Figure D-4).

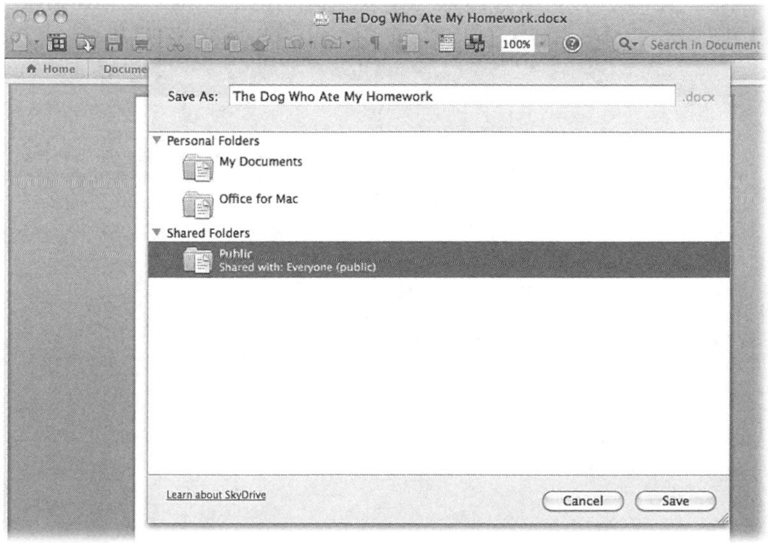

Figure D-3:
After you create your account, there are two folders on your SkyDrive. Use the My Documents folder for files you don't want to share. Use Public for files you want to share with everyone. When you want to share a file with a limited number of people, create a new folder and change the "Share with" attributes, as described on page 746. The Office for Mac folder shown here was user-created.

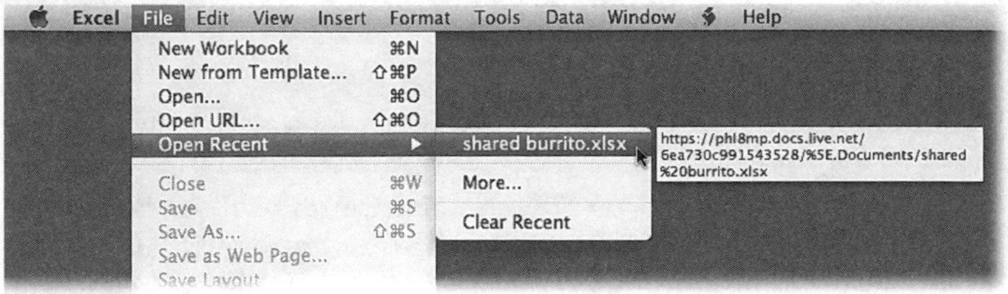

Figure D-4:
In Excel, if you hold the cursor over a file name in the File→Open Recent list, a tool tip displays the file's location. SkyDrive files always start with https://

If the file doesn't appear on your File→Open Recent list, you can open it from the SkyDrive website, or you can open it using Microsoft Document Connection as described in the next section:

Here's how to open a file on SkyDrive:

1. **Go to *skydrive.live.com* and log in.**

2. **Click the folder that holds the file.**

3. **Point to the file name and then choose Open in Word, Excel, or PowerPoint, as shown in Figure D-5.**

A copy of the file is downloaded to your computer. Depending on the file size and your Internet connection, it may take a few moments. If it's not already running, the program that created the file launches. Once the file is loaded in the program, you can edit it just as you would any Office document. When you're finished, close and save your file; any changes are stored on SkyDrive.

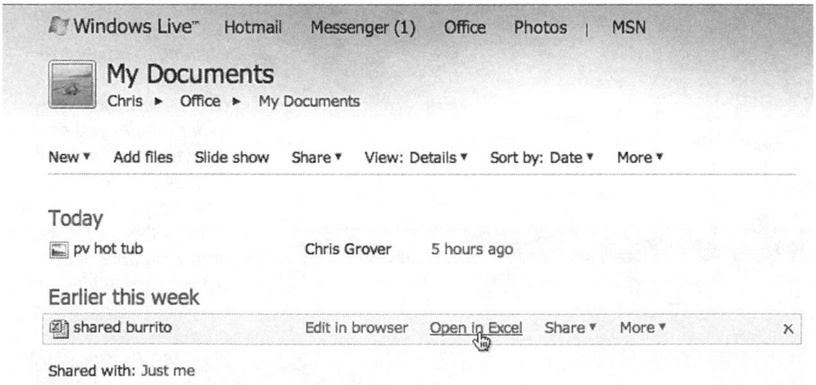

Figure D-5:
When you point to a file in SkyDrive, a menu of options appear, including one to open the file in the Office program that created it.

Using the Document Connection to SkyDrive

When you first install Office for Mac 2011, a number of apps are added to your dock; one of those is Microsoft Document Connection. It's there to help you work with documents stored on SharePoint servers or SkyDrive. Think of it as a portal to files that are stored somewhere other than your computer. In fact, many of the techniques work with SharePoint, too.

The first thing you have to do with Document Connection is sign into your Windows Live account. That lets Document Connection and SkyDrive know who you are and where your files are stored. Using the Document Connection menus, choose Location→Sign In to SkyDrive. Provide your ID and password, and you're all set.

Tip: If you save your ID and password in your Mac keychain, you won't need to enter the details each time you use Document Connection.

Once you're logged in, you see a window like the one in Figure D-6. In the Navigation pane, under SkyDrive, click *live.docs.net* to see your SkyDrive folders. Click to open folders and see their contents. You can open files in their native program by double-clicking. For more options, right-click (Control-click) the file name. From the shortcut menu, you open the file as Read-Only or open the file with another compatible program. Choose the "Add to Favorites" command to list the file in the Navigation pane.

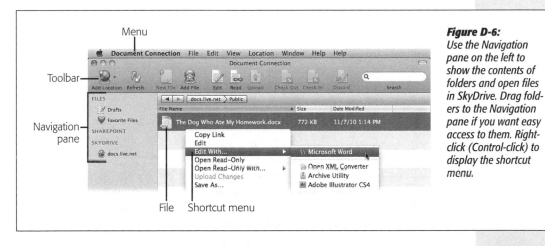

Figure D-6:
Use the Navigation pane on the left to show the contents of folders and open files in SkyDrive. Drag folders to the Navigation pane if you want easy access to them. Right-click (Control-click) to display the shortcut menu.

Tip: Document Connection doesn't like working with more than one SkyDrive account at a time. If you need to sign in to SkyDrive with a different ID, you have to delete the current account details in the navigation pane and start over. To delete the current account, right-click (Control-click) the locations listed in the pane on the left and then choose Remove Location. This doesn't erase your files—you can still access them through a browser. Deleting an account simply removes the account details from Document Connection.

Creating SkyDrive and Sharing Folders

Files that you create in Office for Mac 2011 programs are always stored in folders on SkyDrive. (As you'll see later, files created in the Office Web Apps are not stored in folders.) You control who can see, read and edit your files by adjusting the "Share with" attributes of a folder. As explained earlier, you start off with the My Documents folder, which only you can use, and the Public folder, which is available to everyone. If you want to share files with a limited number of people, you can create new folders and choose who gets to peek inside.

1. **Go to** *skydrive.live.com* **and, if necessary, sign in with your account ID and password.**

    Your SkyDrive page shows your documents and folders.

2. **Right above the Document group, click New→Folder.**

    A new page opens where you can name your folder and change the "Share with" attributes, which are initially set to "Just me."

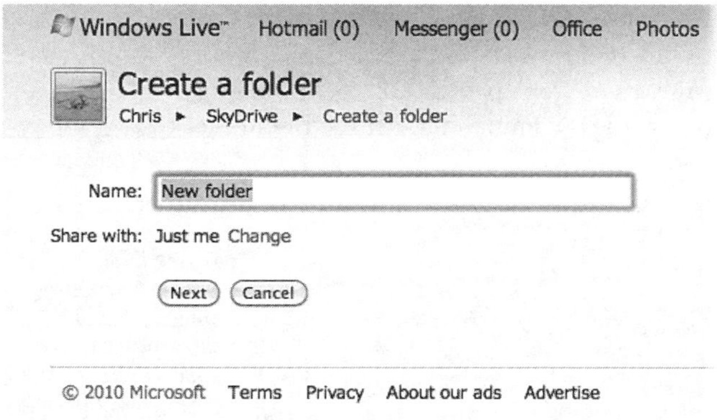

<table>
<tr><td>

 Windows Live™   Hotmail (0)   Messenger (0)   Office   Photos

Create a folder

Chris ▸ SkyDrive ▸ Create a folder

Name: New folder

Share with: Just me Change

(Next) (Cancel)

© 2010 Microsoft   Terms   Privacy   About our ads   Advertise

</td><td>

Figure D-7:
After you choose New→Folder, SkyDrive displays this page where you can enter a name for your folder. Click the Change link to adjust the "Share with" permissions.

</td></tr>
</table>

3. **In the text box, type a name for your folder.**

    Folder names can include letters, numbers and some punctuation marks like commas, periods, underscores, parentheses, and plus, minus, and equal signs. Periods can't appear at the beginning or end of folder names. If you use a character that's not accepted, you get a warning and a chance to change the name.

    If you want to create a personal folder, click the Next button now. If you want to share your folder, continue with the next step.

4. **Next to "Just me", click the Change link.**

The page shown in Figure D-8 appears with tools for adjusting the sharing options. Use the slider to create general rules for who can see and use your folders and files. For example, you can choose to let friends or friends of friends see your folder, à la social networking. At the bottom of the page is a text box labeled "Add additional people", where you can strictly limit the people who access the files in this folder.

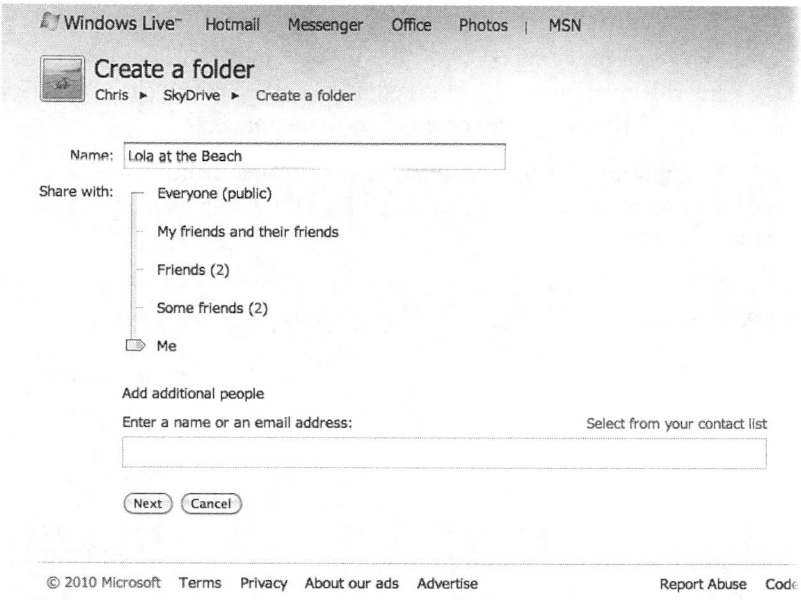

Figure D-8:
Use this page to set the "Share with" permissions for a folder. Using the slider, you can set general sharing options, like friends or friends of friends. If you want to be more specific, add email addresses using the text box at the bottom.

5. **In the text box, type an email address and press Return.**

When you press Return, the email address appears under the text box.

6. **Use the menu to the right of the name to set the level of access.**

There are two options: "Can view files" and "Can add, edit details and delete files".

7. **Continue to add people and set their access options.**

If you have contacts stored in your Hotmail contact list, you can easily add them. Just click the "Select from your contact list" link above the text box. If you want to remove contacts from the list, click the X next to their email address.

8. **Click Next when you've completed your people list.**

SkyDrive churns a bit, and then displays a new page with a message letting you know that it's time to start uploading documents.

9. Click the "Select new documents from your computer" link.

A Finder window opens where you can browse the folders and files on your computer.

10. ⌘-click to select more than one file, or Shift-click to select adjacent files. Click Open.

The files you selected appear in the box on the web page. The number of files and their size is listed at the top of the box.

11. Click Continue.

A new web page shows the contents of your new folder. Below the file names, the "Share with" attributes are set to "People I selected". If you click those words, you see a list of the people who have access to the folder.

Your new folder appears with the other folders when you log into SkyDrive. Because it's shared with a limited number of people, you see the two-person icon next to the folder, as shown in Figure D-9.

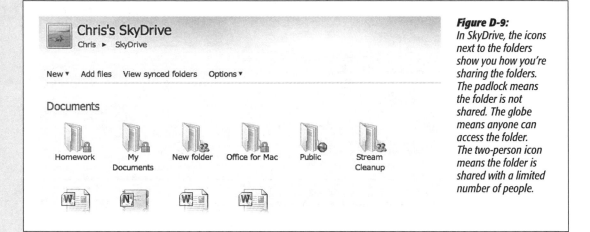

Figure D-9:
In SkyDrive, the icons next to the folders show you how you're sharing the folders. The padlock means the folder is not shared. The globe means anyone can access the folder. The two-person icon means the folder is shared with a limited number of people.

Managing Your SkyDrive Folders

You can rename, remove, and change the sharing options of any folders that you create. The first step for each of these operations is to open the folder by clicking on it. The new page that opens shows the folder's contents and displays a menu of commands for making changes to the folder. Here are some of the things you can do:

- **Rename a folder.** Choose More→Rename. Type a new name in the text box.

- **Delete a folder**. Choose More→Delete. (If the folder is empty, the command is simply Delete.) Click OK to confirm the removal of the folder and all the files it holds from SkyDrive. Anyone you've shared this folder with can no longer access it.

- **Change a folder's sharing permissions.** Choose Share→Edit permissions. This option opens a page like the one in Figure D-8, where you can determine how to share the folder.

- **Add files to a folder.** Choose Add Files. A new page appears where you can choose files from your computer to upload to SkyDrive.

Note: You're not limited to storing Office files on SkyDrive. You can upload other types of files, too, like PDFs and graphics.

- **Download a file to your computer.** Point to the filename and then choose More→Download. The file downloads courtesy of your web browser. For example, in Safari, the Downloads window appears, showing the file transfer progress. You can right-click (Control-click) the file's listing in the window to display a shortcut menu that lets you open the file or display it in Finder.

- **Download *all* the files in a folder.** Choose "Download as .zip file". The entire contents of the folder are compressed in a single zip file and automatically downloaded to your computer.

Working with the Office Web Apps

Office Web Apps are stripped-down versions of the Office programs that you installed on your Mac. If your needs are simple, the web app versions of Word, Excel, PowerPoint, and OneNote are perfectly capable tools. They look a bit different from their computer-based cousins, and they're missing the most advanced features. For example, with the Word web app, you can insert pictures and tables into your documents, but you can't create tables of contents or indexes. With the Excel Web app, you use formulas to massage your numbers and create charts and data tables; however, there's no way to create pivot tables. Likewise, PowerPoint and OneNote have some but not all of the features of the related programs.

Note: OneNote is part of Microsoft Office for Windows as a standalone program. Like the other Office Web Apps, the OneNote web app is a simplified version of the program—see the bottom of Figure D-10. It works much like Word's Notebook view, described on page 183.

Web apps don't have the traditional Mac menus at the top of the screen. Because the apps live inside of your browser, all you see are the browser's menus. Instead, web apps put all commands on ribbons, so if you've gotten used to working with the ribbon in Word, Excel, and PowerPoint, so much the better. As shown in Figure D-10, the web app ribbons have similar tabs: File, Home, Insert, and View. Naturally, the specific commands on the ribbon differ depending on the app:

- **File**. This tab provides access to the usual suspects. Use it to save, print, share, and close your web app documents. The "Open in" command lets you switch between the web app and the full version on your computer. For more details on moving files between web apps and computer-based programs, see page 752.

- **Home**. When you want to format characters, paragraphs, or spreadsheet cells, turn to the Home tab. It gives you access to Font, Paragraph, and Number Style tools. In general, the Home tab has the commands that you use most frequently.

- **Insert**. Want to add a picture, charts, tables, or links to your document? The Insert tab has the buttons to do the job. If you insert a picture in your document, you can format it by clicking on the picture and then using the command in the special Picture Tools Format tab.

- **View**. The View tab differs depending on the program. In Word and OneNote, you can switch between Editing View and Reading View. In PowerPoint, you can see your presentation as a slideshow and read the slide notes, and Excel doesn't have a view tab at all.

As you work with the web apps, you'll notice quite a few differences. Whether these differences are deal breakers depends on your working habits and adaptability. For example, web apps don't have shortcut menus. You can right-click (Control-click) on any number of objects in your Word page, Excel workbook, or PowerPoint presentation, but you won't see one of those handy pop-up menus. If a command is available in the web app, it's on the ribbon, period. The standard shortcut keys—⌘-X (Cut), ⌘-C (Copy), ⌘-V (Paste), and ⌘-Z (Undo)—work, as always. However, if you're used to editing by dragging words from one place to another, you'll have to retrain yourself. No drag-and-drop editing; you have to cut and paste instead.

If you're familiar with their computer-based cousins, the Office Web Apps are easy to use because they're simplified versions of Word (top), Excel (second from top), PowerPoint (third from top), and OneNote (bottom).

Moving Documents Between Web Apps and Office 2011 Programs

Web apps don't have nearly as many features as their Mac-based cousins. So, if you create a document in a web app, you can easily open it in the computer-based program later. It's not as easy when you try to go the other direction. For example, suppose you create a Word app on your Mac and turn on Track Changes so you and your colleagues can add comments and review changes. If you try to open that document in the Word web app, you'll see a message like the one in Figure D-11. In some cases, you'll have the option to convert the file so the web app can open it. In other cases, you'll get the option to open the file in its computer-based counterpart instead.

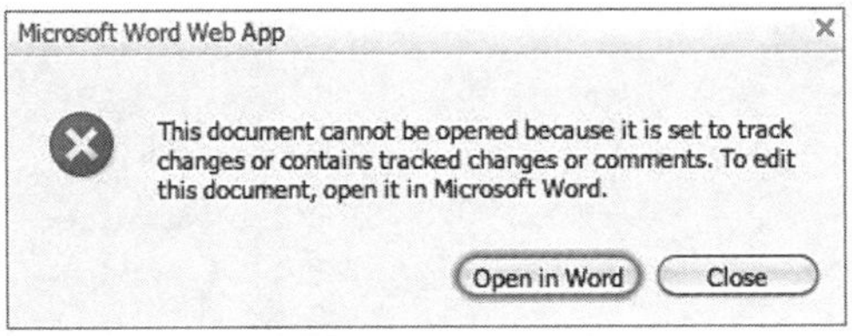

Figure D-11:
Sometimes web apps can't open a document you created with the Office program on your Mac. This happens when the web app doesn't have features to handle the document. This warning message explains that the web app can't work with tracked changes.

Microsoft Word Web App

This document cannot be opened because it is set to track changes or contains tracked changes or comments. To edit this document, open it in Microsoft Word.

Open in Word   Close

Index

Colophon

Kristen Borg and Adam Witwer provided quality control for *Office 2011 for Macintosh: The Missing Manual*. The book was composed in Adobe InDesign CS4 by Nate McDermott.

The cover of this book is based on a series design originally created by David Freedman and modified by Mike Kohnke, Karen Montgomery, and Fitch (*www.fitch.com*). Back cover design, dog illustration, and color selection by Fitch.

David Futato designed the interior layout, based on a series design by Phil Simpson. The text font is Adobe Minion; the heading font is Adobe Formata Condensed; and the code font is LucasFont's TheSansMonoCondensed. The illustrations that appear in the book were produced by Robert Romano using Adobe Photoshop and Illustrator CS.

Office 2011
for Macintosh

THE MISSING CD

There's no CD with this book; you just saved $5.00.

Instead, every single Web address, practice file, and piece of downloadable software mentioned in this book is available at *missingmanuals.com* (click the Missing CD icon). There you'll find a tidy list of links, organized by chapter.

Don't miss a thing!
Sign up for the free Missing Manual email announcement list at missingmanuals.com. We'll let you know when we release new titles, make free sample chapters available, and update the features and articles on the Missing Manual website.